THE USBORNE
SCIENCE
ENCYCLOPEDIA

This revised edition first published in 2015 by Usborne Publishing Ltd, Usborne House, 83-85 Saffron Hill, London EC1N 8RT, England.

www.usborne.com

THE USBORNE SCIENCE ENCYCLOPEDIA

Kirsteen Robson, Phillip Clarke, Laura Howell,
Alastair Smith and Corinne Henderson

Designed by Ruth Russell, Karen Tomlins,
Chloë Rafferty, Candice Whatmore and Jane Rigby

Digital illustrations by Verinder Bhachu
Digital imagery by Joanne Kirkby

Cover design: Tom Lalonde

Consultants: Dr Margaret Rostron, Dr John Rostron, Dr Tom Petersen,
Elaine Wilson, Dr Roger Trend, Stuart Atkinson, Mark Beard

Internet researcher: Jacqueline Clark
Editorial assistant: Valerie Modd

Senior designer: Ruth Russell
Managing editor: Judy Tatchell

INTERNET LINKS

Throughout this book you'll see QR codes, like the one below. These are links that take you straight to websites with video clips or other multimedia content that you can watch on a smartphone or tablet.

Internet links

- Scan the code to tour a plane's cockpit and see the controls.

- For links to more websites where you can explore the four forces of flight, find out more about how planes are controlled and fly a plane online, go to **www.usborne.com/quicklinks**

Don't worry if you don't have a smartphone or tablet – all the recommended websites can also be viewed on a computer via the Usborne Quicklinks website.

USBORNE QUICKLINKS

At Usborne Quicklinks you'll find links to click on to visit over 1,000 recommended websites, plus downloadable pictures from this book. All the pictures marked with a ★ in this book can be downloaded for home or school use, but not for commercial purposes.

To visit the Quicklinks website go to **www.usborne.com/quicklinks** and type the keyword "science" in the search box.

WHAT YOU CAN DO

Here are some of the things you can do at the recommended websites:
- Design a rollercoaster online and find out more about forces
- Explore the surface of Mars with a robot rover
- Discover unusual creatures that live at the bottom of the ocean
- Investigate the greenhouse effect and climate change with video clips and activities
- Watch a video clip about the discovery of the smallest particle, called a "boson", at CERN's Large Hadron Collider

VISITING THE QR LINKS

To visit the QR links you need a smartphone or tablet with a free app called a "QR reader" that you can download from your device's app store. Just point the device's camera at a QR code and follow your QR reader's instructions to scan the code and visit the recommended website. Many of the recommended websites include video clips and multimedia, so we recommend that you access them via a WiFi connection.

LINKS TO EXTERNAL WEBSITES

Usborne internet links go to websites that have been carefully selected by Usborne editors to enhance the information in Usborne books. Usborne Publishing is not responsible or liable for the content or availability of external websites. We regularly review the recommended sites and update our links, so you'll always find a selection of the best sites on the internet at Usborne Quicklinks.

INTERNET SAFETY

When using the internet, please make sure you follow our three basic rules:
- Always ask an adult's permission before using the internet.
- Never give out personal information, such as your name, address, the name of your school or telephone number.
- If a website asks you to type in your name or email address, check with an adult first.

HELP AND ADVICE

For more advice on using the internet and scanning QR codes, see the "Help and advice" area at the Usborne Quicklinks website.

You don't need a smartphone or tablet to use this book. All the recommended websites are also available at the Usborne Quicklinks website. Just go to **www.usborne.com/quicklinks** and enter the keyword "science".

CONTENTS

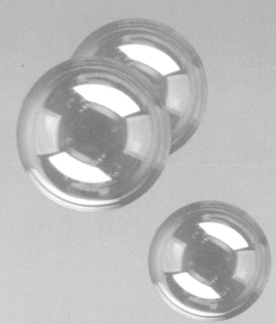

MATERIALS

ATOMIC STRUCTURE

Atoms are the tiny particles of which everything is made. It is impossible to imagine how small an atom is. A hundred million atoms side by side would measure only 1cm, and a sheet of paper, like the ones that make up this book, is probably a million atoms thick.

This diagram uses coloured balls to represent the parts of an atom and illustrate the relationships between them.

SUBATOMIC PARTICLES

Atoms are made of smaller particles called **subatomic particles**. In the middle of every atom is its **nucleus**. The nucleus contains two types of subatomic particles, called **protons** and **neutrons**.

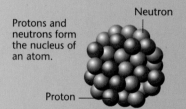

Protons and neutrons form the nucleus of an atom.

Neutron

Proton

Subatomic particles of a third type, called **electrons**, move around the nucleus. The electrons exist at different energy levels, called **shells**, around the nucleus. Each shell can have up to a certain number of electrons. When it is full, a new shell is started.

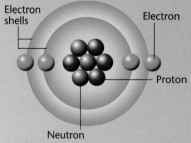

Electron shells

Electron

Proton

Neutron

Scientists now think that protons and neutrons are made of even smaller subatomic particles, called **quarks**.

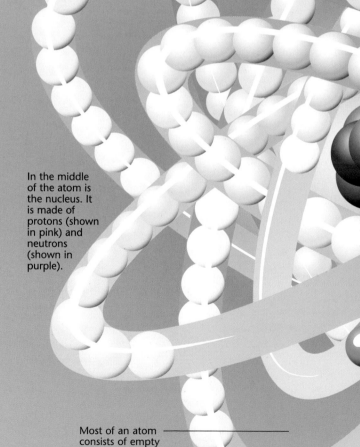

In the middle of the atom is the nucleus. It is made of protons (shown in pink) and neutrons (shown in purple).

Most of an atom consists of empty space between the particles.

Electrons are trapped by their attraction to protons, which are in the nucleus. They whizz around the nucleus at different levels, called shells.

The two electrons shown in green exist in the first shell of this atom. Those in blue are in the second shell.

*

Electron

ELECTRICAL CHARGES

The subatomic particles that make up an atom are held together by electrical charges. Particles with opposite electrical charges are attracted to one another.

The protons have a positive electrical charge and the electrons have a negative charge. Neutrons have no electrical charge, so they are neutral.

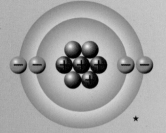

★

Proton: positive electrical charge.

Electron: negative electrical charge.

Neutron: no electrical charge.

An atom usually has an equal number of positively charged protons and negatively charged electrons. This makes the atom itself electrically neutral.

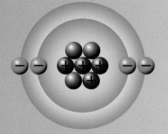

This atom is electrically neutral.

It has four protons.

It has four electrons.

Its three neutrons have no effect on its electrical charge.

REPRESENTING ATOMS

Although atoms are often represented by diagrams like the main picture, scientists now believe that the electrons are held in cloud-like regions around the nucleus, as in the **electron cloud model** below.

Electron cloud model

Electrons can be anywhere within their cloud, at any time. Sometimes they even move outside it.

ELECTRON DENSITY

In the picture below, different colours show different levels of density of electrons in a group of atoms. The turquoise areas show where the electrons are most dense.

This is a picture of what you might see through an extremely powerful microscope.

Internet links

• Scan the code to discover how small atoms are and what's inside them.

• For links to more websites about atoms and particles, go to www.usborne.com/quicklinks

11

ATOMIC NUMBER

Atoms of different substances have different numbers of protons in their nucleus. The number of protons in the nucleus is called the **atomic number**.

The atomic number of an atom indicates what substance it is.

An atom usually has an equal number of protons and electrons, so the atomic number also shows how many electrons it has.

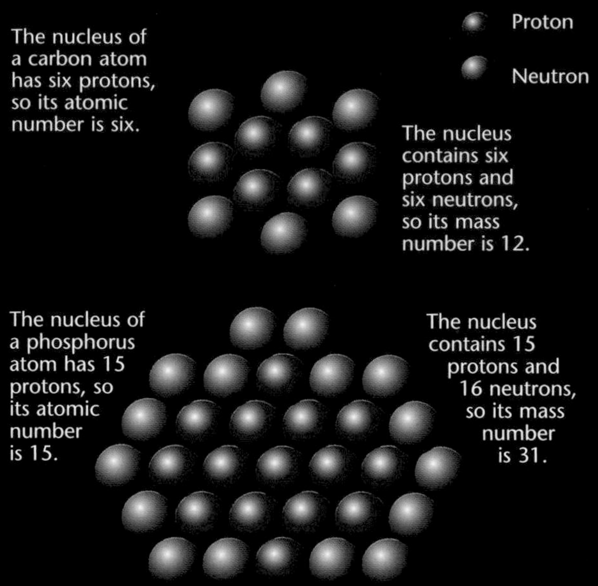

The nucleus of a carbon atom has six protons, so its atomic number is six.

Proton

Neutron

The nucleus contains six protons and six neutrons, so its mass number is 12.

The nucleus of a phosphorus atom has 15 protons, so its atomic number is 15.

The nucleus contains 15 protons and 16 neutrons, so its mass number is 31.

MASS NUMBER

The more protons and neutrons an atom has, the greater its mass (the measurement of the amount of matter in the atom). The total number of protons and neutrons in an atom is called its **mass number**.

Electrons are left out of the mass calculation as they add so little to the mass of an atom.

A machine called a **mass spectrometer** can be used to help identify atoms by sorting them by mass.

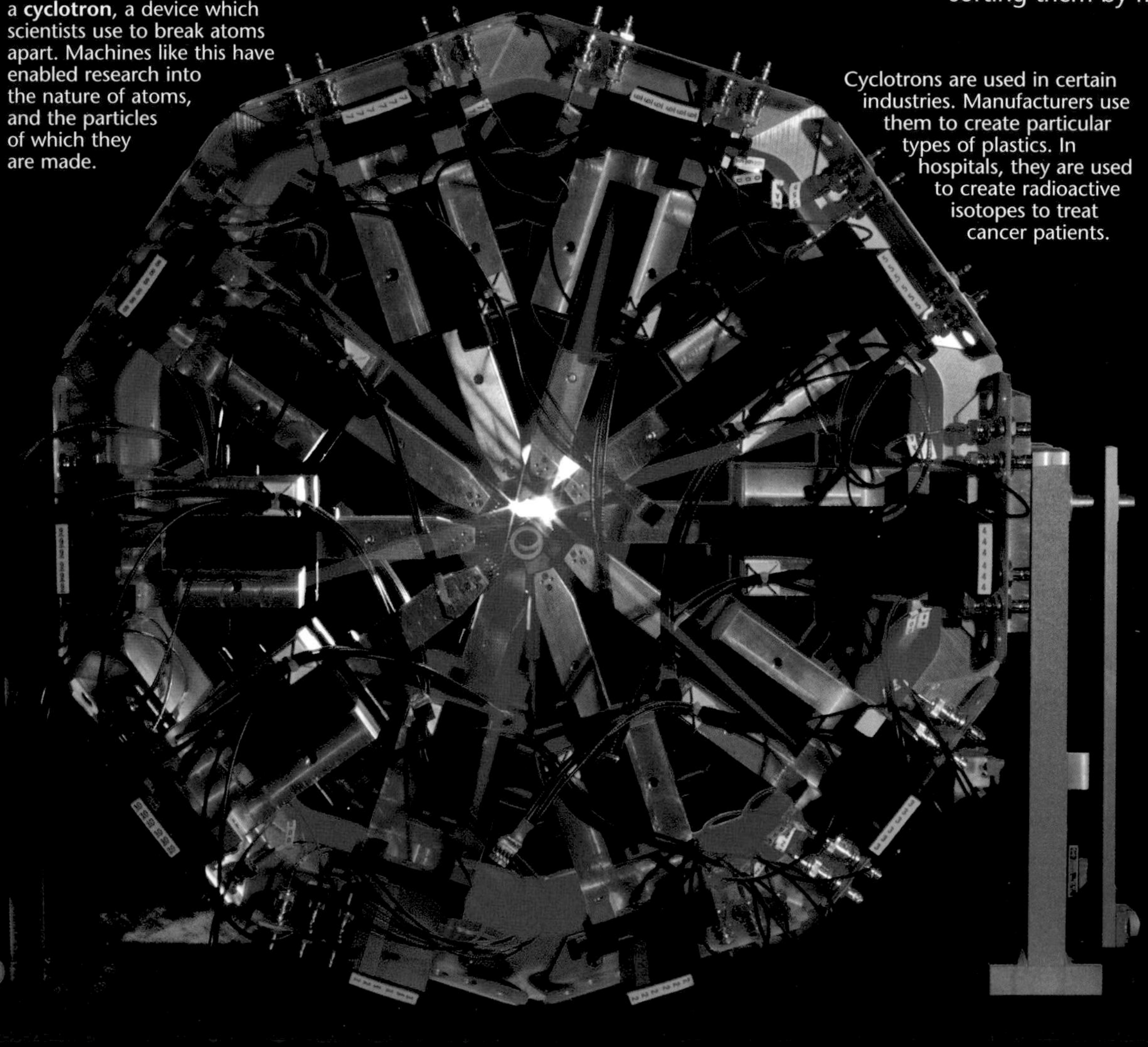

This type of machine is called a **cyclotron**, a device which scientists use to break atoms apart. Machines like this have enabled research into the nature of atoms, and the particles of which they are made.

Cyclotrons are used in certain industries. Manufacturers use them to create particular types of plastics. In hospitals, they are used to create radioactive isotopes to treat cancer patients.

ISOTOPES

Most atoms exist in a number of different forms, called **isotopes**. Each form has the same number of protons and electrons, but a different number of neutrons. So all the isotopes of an atom have the same atomic number, but they have different mass numbers.

The mass number of the isotope of an atom is written beside its name. For instance, carbon-12 has six protons and six neutrons.

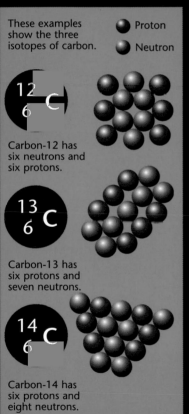

These examples show the three isotopes of carbon.

● Proton
● Neutron

$^{12}_{6}$ **C**

Carbon-12 has six neutrons and six protons.

$^{13}_{6}$ **C**

Carbon-13 has six protons and seven neutrons.

$^{14}_{6}$ **C**

Carbon-14 has six protons and eight neutrons.

Isotopes have different physical properties but their chemical properties are the same. Most of the atoms in an **element** (a substance made up of only one type of atom) are a single isotope, with small amounts of other isotopes.

ANCIENT IDEAS

The idea that everything in the universe is made up of atoms is not a new one. Philosophers in Ancient Greece, 2,500 years ago, believed that matter was made up of particles that could not be cut any smaller. The word "atom" comes from the Greek word atomos, which means "uncuttable".

The theories of Aristotle, an Ancient Greek philosopher, influenced atomic science for centuries.

Aristotle
(384-322BC)

ATOMIC THEORY

The term "atom" was first used by the British chemist, John Dalton, when he put forward his **atomic theory** in 1807.

Dalton suggested that all chemical elements were made of very small particles, called atoms, that did not break up when chemicals reacted. He thought that every chemical reaction was the result of atoms joining or separating. Dalton's atomic theory provided the basis for modern science.

John Dalton
(1766-1844)

Dalton used symbols to represent one atom of each element or substance.

Examples of Dalton's symbols

Zinc   Mercury   Sulphur

EARLY MODELS

Early in the twentieth century, scientists began to make models of atoms.

Ernest Rutherford (1871-1937) showed electrons with a negative electric charge circling a positively charged nucleus.

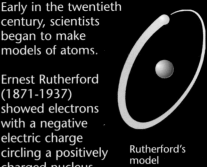

Rutherford's model

Niels Bohr (1885-1962) showed a model with electrons following specific orbits. In 1932, James Chadwick (1891-1974) showed the nucleus made of particles called neutrons and protons.

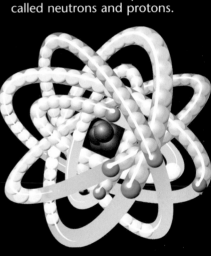

This model of an atom, which is also shown larger on pages 10-11, is based on models by Rutherford, Bohr and Chadwick.

Internet links

• Scan the code to find out about the world's largest cyclotron.

MOLECULES

Atoms are rarely found on their own. They usually cling, or bond, together to form molecules or large lattice structures. A **molecule** is a group of atoms that are bonded together to form the smallest piece of a substance that normally exists on its own. Molecules are much too small to be seen with the naked eye.

SHELLS AND BONDING

Most atoms have several shells of electrons*. The first shell of an atom can hold two electrons. The second and third shells can hold eight, although some atoms can hold up to 18 electrons in their third shells. When a shell is full, the electrons start a new shell. An atom is particularly stable when it has a full outer shell of electrons.

An argon atom has three full shells of electrons. It is a stable atom.

A sodium atom is unstable. It has only one electron in its third shell.

Atoms bond together in order to become stable. They do this by sharing electrons, or by giving up or taking electrons from another atom in order to achieve a full, or fuller, outer shell. Two hydrogen atoms, for instance, bond together to make a hydrogen molecule. They share their electrons, giving each atom a full outer shell. (For more about bonding, see pages 68-71.)

Two hydrogen atoms

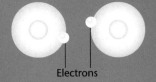

Electrons

Hydrogen molecule

Each atom has a full shell of two electrons, so it is stable.

* Electrons, 10.

This is a model of a molecule of DNA, a complicated chemical compound found in the cells of all living things.

CHEMICAL FORMULAE

An atom's name can be shown by a symbol (its **chemical symbol**). This is usually the first letter or two of its name in English, Latin or German.

O — The symbol for oxygen

Au — The symbol for gold, from the Latin word aurum

Fe — The symbol for iron, from the Latin word ferrum

K — The symbol for potassium, from the German word kalium

A **chemical formula** shows the atoms of which a substance is made and in what proportions. For example, each molecule of carbon dioxide is made up of one atom of carbon and two atoms of oxygen, so the formula for carbon dioxide is CO_2. The figure "2" shows the number of oxygen atoms in the molecule.

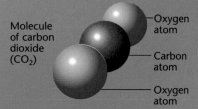

Molecule of carbon dioxide (CO_2) — Oxygen atom — Carbon atom — Oxygen atom

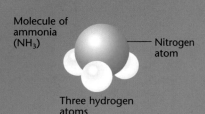

Molecule of ammonia (NH_3) — Nitrogen atom

Three hydrogen atoms

MODELS OF MOLECULES

When studying molecules, scientists often use models to represent them. There are two main types: ball-and-spoke models and space-filling models.

In **ball-and-spoke models**, the bonds that hold the atoms together are shown as sticks.

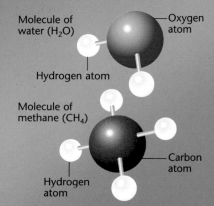

Molecule of water (H_2O) — Oxygen atom

Hydrogen atom

Molecule of methane (CH_4) — Carbon atom

Hydrogen atom

In **space-filling models**, atoms are shown clinging together.

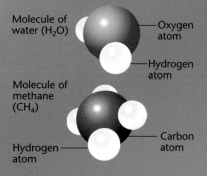

Molecule of water (H_2O) — Oxygen atom — Hydrogen atom

Molecule of methane (CH_4) — Carbon atom

Hydrogen atom

Neither model looks like an actual molecule, but they are simple ways of showing the atoms that form the molecule.

Internet links

• Scan the code to see a simulation of atoms and molecules.

WATER MOLECULE

A water molecule consists of two different elements: hydrogen and oxygen. The two hydrogen atoms share electrons with the oxygen atom, so each has a complete shell. The oxygen atom uses two electrons (one from each hydrogen atom) to complete its own outer shell. All the atoms become stable.

The oxygen atom contains six electrons in its outer shell. It needs two more electrons to complete its outer shell and become stable.

Each hydrogen atom contains one electron in its shell. They each seek one electron to complete their shells and become stable.

SOLIDS, LIQUIDS AND GASES

Most substances can exist in three different forms: as solids, liquids or gases. These are called the **states of matter**. A solid has a definite volume and shape. A liquid has a definite volume, but its shape changes according to the shape of its container. A gas has neither shape nor volume. It will move to fill the space available.

THE KINETIC THEORY

The theory that explains the properties of solids, liquids and gases is called the **kinetic theory**. It is based on the idea that all substances are made up of moving particles. It explains the properties of solids, liquids and gases in terms of the energy of these particles.

Heating a substance gives the particles more energy, enabling them to move around faster and change from one state to another. (See Changes of State, pages 18-19).

Like many scientific theories, the kinetic theory has never been proved. It provides an explanation, though, for how solids, liquids and gases are seen to behave, and why substances change from one state to another.

Movement of particles in solids, liquids and gases

The particles in a solid have the least energy and cannot overcome the attraction between one another. They vibrate, but stay where they are.

Heating a solid gives the particles more energy so they can escape from each other. The solid melts and becomes a liquid.

The particles in a gas have even more energy. They easily move far apart and spread out through the available space.

This is a geyser. Water heated to boiling point under the ground turns from a liquid to a gas (steam) and shoots out of a crack. You can find out more about what causes geysers over the page.

BROWNIAN MOTION

Random movement of particles in a liquid

The movement of particles in liquids and gases is known as **Brownian motion**, named after a British biologist, Robert Brown (1773-1858). In 1827, Brown observed how tiny grains of pollen moved around randomly in a liquid, but he could not explain what caused this movement.

The German-born scientist Albert Einstein (1879-1955) later explained that the movement of particles in a liquid or gas is caused by the particles being hit by the invisible molecules of the fluid in which the particles are floating.

MEASURING SUBSTANCES

Volume is the amount of space occupied by a solid or liquid. It is measured in cubic metres (m³).

You can calculate the volume of a rectangular solid using this formula:

> **Volume =
> Length x Breadth x Height**

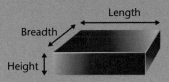

The volume of a liquid can be found by pouring the liquid into a measuring cylinder marked with a scale.

Measuring cylinder

The volume of an irregularly shaped solid is measured by finding how much liquid it displaces, using a Eureka can.

Eureka can

1. Eureka can is filled with water to base of spout.

2. Object is put into Eureka can.

3. Volume of displaced water is measured.

The **mass** of a solid, liquid or gas is the amount of matter it contains. This is measured in kilograms. Mass is different from **weight**, which is a measure of the strength of the pull of gravity* on an object. Mass is measured by weighing a substance and comparing its mass with a known mass.

Unknown mass

Known mass

Density is the mass of a substance compared with its volume. For example, the same volumes of cork and metal have different densities because the mass of the metal is much greater than that of the cork. Density is found by dividing the mass of an object by its volume, and it is measured in kilograms per cubic metre (kg/m³).

> $$\text{Density} = \frac{\text{Mass}}{\text{Volume}}$$

The density of a liquid is measured using a **hydrometer**. The hydrometer floats near the surface in a dense liquid, as only a small volume of liquid needs to be displaced to equal the weight of the hydrometer (see Why Things Float, page 138).

Scale marked on hydrometer

(see Why Things Float, page 138).

* Gravity, 130-131.

See for yourself

You can do an experiment to find the volumes of irregularly shaped solids without using a Eureka can.

You will need a measuring jug, a cake mixing bowl and a washing-up bowl.

First, put your mixing bowl inside the washing-up bowl. Then carefully fill the mixing bowl with water up to the brim.

Now take the object that you want to measure and hold it just on top of the water's surface. Let the object sink into the water. Water will slop over the side of the mixing bowl and be caught in the washing-up bowl.

Mixing bowl

Object to be measured

Washing-up bowl

Take the mixing bowl out of the washing-up bowl. Now pour the water from the washing-up bowl into the measuring jug. The volume of water is equal to the volume of the object.

Internet links

- Scan the code to watch a video about the states of matter.

- For links to more websites where you can find out how gases mix and try virtual experiments, go to **www.usborne.com/quicklinks**

CHANGES OF STATE

An ice cream melts and becomes a liquid in the heat of the Sun.

A substance changes from one **state of matter**, that is solid, liquid or gas, to another, depending on its temperature and pressure. When something changes state, heat is produced or lost as the energy of its particles is increased or decreased. Different substances change state at different temperatures.

The heat from a flame melts candle wax, but the wax sets as it drips away from the flame and cools.

MELTING AND BOILING

When a solid is heated, its temperature rises and its particles gain energy until it reaches its **melting point**. The particles now have enough energy to break away from their neighbours so the solid melts.

Further heat causes the temperature of the liquid to rise until it reaches its **boiling point** and the particles break free of each other completely. The liquid becomes a gas.

Some substances, for example carbon dioxide, change from gas to solid, or solid to gas, without passing through a liquid form. This is called **sublimation**.

The temperature at which a substance melts or boils changes if it contains traces of any other substances. For instance, ice (the solid form of water) melts at 0°C. Adding salt to the ice lowers its melting point.

This ice melts at a lower temperature than pure water ice because orange juice has been added to it.

When steam cools down, it turns back into water.

GEYSERS

Geysers are jets of boiling hot water and steam that shoot out from the Earth's crust.

They occur when water under the ground is heated by hot rocks and begins to boil.

As the water turns to steam, the pressure builds up in the channels between the rocks. The geyser then erupts, shooting a jet of steam and water high up into the air.

How geysers occur

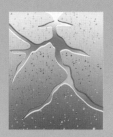

Water flows into cavities between the rocks under the ground.

Pressure builds as the water heats and expands. Eventually, it turns to steam.

The pressure builds until boiling water and steam shoot out of a crack in the ground.

CONDENSATION

When a gas cools down enough, it **condenses**, becoming a liquid. This is because as it cools down, its particles lose energy and are unable to stay as far away from each other.

Condensation

Water vapour in the air in a room condenses on a cold window. Droplets of water are formed on the inside of the window.

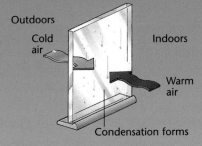

Outdoors

Cold air

Indoors

Warm air

Condensation forms

FREEZING

When a liquid cools enough, it sets or **freezes**, becoming a solid. Its particles lose further energy and are unable to overcome the attraction between each other.

When tiny droplets of water in the atmosphere freeze, they sometimes join together in beautiful patterns of crystals and form snowflakes like these.

PRESSURE

Air pressure has an effect on the melting or boiling point of a substance. The air naturally presses down on the Earth with a force called **atmospheric pressure**. At sea level, this is described as **one atmosphere**, or **standard pressure**.

At sea level, pure water boils at 100°C.

Higher up, the atmospheric pressure is less. It is easier for the particles in liquids to escape into the air, so their boiling points are lower.

At the top of Mount Everest (8,850m above sea level), where the pressure is less than one atmosphere, pure water boils at 71°C.

WATERLESS PLANET

The surface of Mars is dry. Scientists think that this is because the atmospheric pressure is very low, so any water immediately boils away.

Most of Mars is covered by a reddish dust.

SOLID LIQUID OR GAS?

Whether something is classified as a solid, liquid or gas depends on its state at room temperature (20°C).

Mercury melts at -40°C. It is a liquid at room temperature.

Chlorine boils at -35°C so is a gas at room temperature.

See for yourself

Fill a metal container with ice cubes. Stand it in a warm place and leave it for a few minutes. Then look at the container. You will see drops of water on the outside of it.

Water molecules in the warm air lose energy and slow down when they are cooled by the ice. They stick to each other, forming water droplets.

Droplets of water on the side of the can

Internet links

- Scan the code to watch a video about how snowflakes form.

- For links to more websites where you can watch substances change state, go to **www.usborne.com/quicklinks**

HOW LIQUIDS BEHAVE

A **liquid** has a definite volume but it flows and changes shape to fill its container. The particles in a liquid are fairly close together, but have more energy than the particles in a solid, so are free to move about (see *The Kinetic Theory*, page 16).

EVAPORATION

Some of the molecules on the surface of a liquid have more energy than others, and they escape, or **evaporate**, into the air. Liquids are evaporating all the time, even when they are not being heated.

The particles in water (like all liquids) are free to move about.

These particles have enough energy to escape, or evaporate, from the surface of the liquid to form a vapour.

RATE OF EVAPORATION

The **rate of evaporation** increases with any one or a combination of the following:

• an increase in temperature.

• a decrease in pressure. For instance, water evaporates more quickly at the top of Mount Everest, where the atmospheric pressure is less, than it does at sea level.

• the immediate removal of the vapour from above the liquid by a flow of air. This is why washing hung out to dry on a windy day dries more quickly than on a still day.

• an increase in surface area. For instance, a spilled drink will evaporate or dry up more quickly than the same drink in a glass.

COOLING DOWN

When a liquid is evaporating, its temperature falls because the average energy of the molecules that are left in the liquid has fallen.

SURFACE TENSION

The molecules in a liquid are attracted by all the other liquid molecules around them. The ones on the surface, though, are not pulled upwards because there are no liquid molecules above them. They are more attracted to the other liquid molecules than to the air.

This sideways and downwards attraction at the surface creates a force called **surface tension**. It makes a liquid seem to have a "skin".

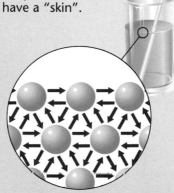

Molecules at the surface are attracted to each other, and to those below them. This creates surface tension.

Water forms into droplets because surface tension pulls inwards from all sides, keeping the molecules together.

The drips on these leaves form because surface tension pulls molecules of rainwater together.

STRETCHY SKIN

As a result of surface tension, a liquid's surface is like a stretchy skin, strong enough to support very light objects, such as dust or even insects.

Pond skaters can walk on the surface of water as they are not heavy enough to break the skin-like surface tension.

COHESION

Cohesion happens when molecules of one substance are more attracted to each other than to a substance they are touching. Surface tension is an example of this. Molecules at the water's surface try to stay together rather than move towards the air above.

ADHESION

When molecules of a liquid are more attracted to a substance they are touching than to each other, **adhesion** occurs. The liquid adheres (sticks) to the other substance. Water does this when it touches the sides of a glass.

See for yourself

To see how surface tension can support certain objects, try this quick activity.

Fill a container with water. Put a needle on a small piece of tissue paper and lay it gently on the water.

The tissue soon becomes waterlogged and sinks, but the needle stays afloat, supported by surface tension.

Look closely and you will see that the needle actually dents the water's surface.

Internet links

• Scan the code for an experiment about surface tension.

• For links to more websites, go to **www.usborne.com/quicklinks**

HOW GASES BEHAVE

A **gas** is a substance that has no definite volume or shape. Its particles have enough energy to spread far apart from each other and fill the space available.

Smells, such as the scent of flowers, are gases that travel through the air by diffusion.

DIFFUSION

The molecules in a gas have enough energy to break free of the forces between them (see *The Kinetic Theory*, page 16). They spread out to fill the available space. This is called **diffusion**.

During diffusion, molecules move from an area where they are in higher concentration to one where their concentration is lower. Diffusion stops when the molecules are evenly distributed.

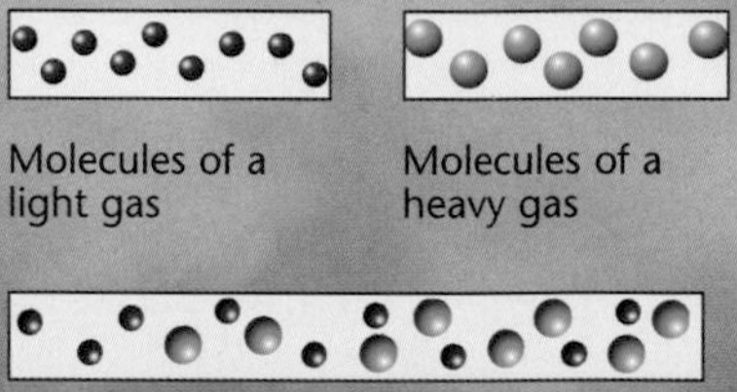

Molecules of a light gas

Molecules of a heavy gas

Molecules of these two gases diffuse together over time. Light gases diffuse faster than heavy ones. ★

This scientist is taking samples of gases emerging from holes in the side of a volcano. Some of the gases are harmful, so the scientist has to wear a breathing mask.

The set-up below shows how two gases mix by diffusion. A jar of air is turned upside down on top of a jar of bromine, which is heavier than air.

After fifteen minutes, the air and bromine in the jars become mixed by diffusion as their molecules spread through the two jars.

Air

Bromine gas

Gases mixed by diffusion ★

PRESSURE, TEMPERATURE AND VOLUME

Gases exert a push on things that they are contained in. This push, called **pressure**, is felt in all directions. It is the rate at which molecules in a gas hit the sides of its container.

Any change in pressure, temperature, or the container's volume will cause a change in the molecules' behaviour.

If the volume of a gas at a constant temperature is decreased, for example by reducing the size of its container, the pressure of the gas increases. This is because the gas molecules hit the walls of the container more frequently.

When heated, the molecules in a gas gain energy, move around faster and become even further apart – the gas expands and becomes less dense. This is why hot-air balloons float – the air inside them is less dense than the air around them.

If a gas is heated but is not allowed to expand, then its pressure increases. This is because the molecules in the gas gain energy, move around more quickly and hit the walls of the container more frequently.

Under the ground, volcanic gases become extremely hot. The pressure builds and builds until they shoot out of cracks and holes in the ground.

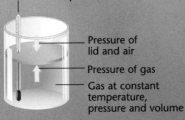

Thermometer, to measure temperature

Pressure of lid and air

Pressure of gas

Gas at constant temperature, pressure and volume

Temperature is the same as before.

Pressure increased to reduce size of container.

Volume decreases, pressure increases.

Temperature increased.

Pressure kept the same as before.

Volume increases until pressures are equal.

Temperature increased.

Pressure increased, to keep volume same as before.

Pressure increases.

★

Balloons stretch as air spreads out to fill them.

See for yourself

Next time you use a balloon pump, see how it uses pressure to fill the balloon with air.

1. When you pump the handle, the volume of the pump's chamber is decreased so the air pressure inside it is increased.

Chamber

2. Air shoots out of the nozzle, into the balloon.

3. A valve in the pump prevents air from being sucked back out of the balloon.

4. Pressure inside the balloon increases so it stretches and expands. Its volume increases.

Internet links

• Scan the code to see what happens when a balloon is plunged into liquid nitrogen.

• For links to more websites about how gases behave, go to www.usborne.com/quicklinks

THE ELEMENTS

An **element** is a substance that contains only one kind of atom – the tiny particles of which all substances are made. For example, sulphur, helium and iron are elements: they contain only sulphur, helium or iron atoms and they cannot be broken down into simpler substances.

GROUPING ELEMENTS

So far, 118 elements have been discovered, but only 90 occur naturally on Earth. Elements can be sorted into metals, non-metals and semi-metals and arranged in a table, called the periodic table, which is shown on pages 28-29.

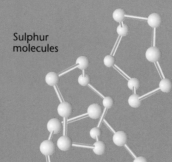

Sulphur molecules

Sulphur is one of the 90 elements that occur naturally on Earth. It is a non-metal. Its molecules, as shown in this diagram, form irregular ring shapes consisting of eight sulphur atoms.

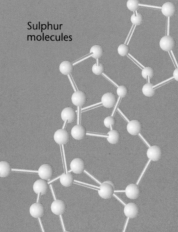

Sulphur atom

METAL ELEMENTS

Over three-quarters of all the elements are **metals**. Most of the metal elements are dense and shiny. They have many uses as they are strong, but can be easily shaped. They are also good conductors of heat and electricity. Metals are usually found combined with other elements in the Earth's crust (see pages 26-27).

The Space Shuttle relied on burning elements to blast it into space. It burned the non-metal hydrogen (stored in the red-brown coloured external fuel tank) and powdered aluminium metal (stored in the two white rockets).

These chocolate eggs are wrapped in thin aluminium foil to keep them fresh. Aluminium is the most common metal on Earth.

Here, aluminium is rolled into a long, thin sheet. It can be re-shaped easily without breaking because its atoms, which are closely packed, slide over each other.

NON-METALS

There are 16 naturally occurring **non-metal** elements. All (apart from graphite, a form of carbon) are insulators – poor conductors of heat and electricity.

At room temperature, four non-metals (phosphorus, carbon, sulphur and iodine) are solids, and bromine is a liquid. The other 11 non-metals are gases.

Non-metals

Hydrogen	Sulphur
Helium	Chlorine
Carbon	Argon
Nitrogen	Bromine
Oxygen	Krypton
Fluorine	Iodine
Neon	Xenon
Phosphorus	Radon

SEMI-METALS

Semi-metals, also called **metalloids**, can act as poor conductors, just like non-metals. They can also be made to conduct well, like metals. Because of this, semi-metal elements are called **semiconductors**. There are nine semi-metals (see list, right). They are all solids at room temperature.

Semi-metals

Boron	Antimony
Silicon	Tellurium
Germanium	Polonium
Arsenic	Astatine
Selenium	

The semi-metal germanium is used to make transistors* like this one. They are used in radios.

Silicon is used to make integrated circuits* such as this one. Microscopic pathways in the circuit conduct and block electrical pulses.

See for yourself

Finding out how well a substance conducts heat can help to identify whether it is a metal or a non-metal. Try the experiment below.

You will need several long objects such as a metal spoon, a wooden spoon and a plastic ruler. Put a smear of cold butter near the end of each object.

Place the objects in a mug filled with warm water.

Butter

As the heat travels up the object, it melts the butter. You should find that the butter melts on the metal things first, because metals are better conductors of heat than non-metals. Eventually, the warmth of the rising air melts the butter on all the objects.

Internet links

• Scan the code to find out about elements used in smartphones.

• For links to more websites about the elements, go to **www.usborne.com/quicklinks**

Integrated circuits, 239; Transistors, 237.

25

ELEMENTS IN THE EARTH

The outermost layer of the Earth is called the **crust**. Most of it is made of only five elements. It is rare for these elements to occur alone, though some, like gold, do. More often they are found together as combined substances called **compounds**. The pure and combined elements found in the crust are called **minerals**. Minerals that contain metals are called **ores**.

Some minerals, such as this chalcedony, can be polished to make beautiful decorative objects.

COMMON ELEMENTS

Oxygen is the most common element in the Earth's crust. It often occurs combined with silicon, the second most common element, and with aluminium and iron, the commonest metals.

This pie chart shows the proportions, by mass, of the five main elements in the Earth's crust.

- Oxygen 46.6%
- Silicon 27.7%
- Aluminium 8.1%
- Iron 5%
- Calcium 3.6%
- Others 9%

MINERAL FORMATION

Most minerals are formed when hot **magma** (molten rock that contains dissolved gases) pushes up from deep below the Earth's crust, cools and solidifies.

The conditions in the place where magma cools determine which type of mineral forms. Geometric shapes called **crystals** form when minerals cool slowly. The cooling process can be so quick, though, that the mineral has no time to crystallize. A kind of shiny black glass, called obsidian, forms in these conditions.

This picture shows huge clumps of shiny black obsidian jutting out of its surrounding rock.

Magma cools on surface

Cracks in Earth's crust

Magma

Molten magma is less dense than the surrounding crust. It rises up through cracks and cools to form minerals.

MINERAL GROUPS

Minerals are divided into groups according to the elements which make them up. Minerals made of a single element are called **native elements**.

Pure silver on a piece of rock

This rock contains specks of pure gold.

Diamonds are crystals of pure carbon. Most are found in a rock called kimberlite, which forms under great heat and pressure.

Silicates, which contain **silica** (silicon combined with oxygen), are the largest group, making up 92% of minerals in the crust.

Beryl is a silicate made up of the elements silicon, oxygen, aluminium and beryllium.

Carbonates are minerals that contain elements combined with carbon and oxygen. They are the most abundant minerals after the silicates.

Smithsonite is zinc carbonate.

Malachite is copper carbonate. It is often polished and used in jewellery.

Halides are a group of minerals which contain halogen* elements.

Rock salt (halite) is formed when salt water evaporates.

Sulphides are a group of minerals that contain elements combined with sulphur.

Sphalerite is made of zinc and sulphur. Most of the world's zinc is mined from this mineral.

Phosphates are minerals formed when phosphorus reacts with oxygen and other elements.

Turquoise is a semi-precious mineral which is a phosphate of aluminium and copper.

Many elements combine with oxygen in the crust to form the group of minerals called **oxides**.

Haematite is a red iron oxide used to produce iron. This type is called "kidney-stone" because of its shape.

There are a number of other mineral groups containing oxygen. These all have names ending in "ate". The first part of their names (see below) show the other elements involved.

Mineral group	Element
Arsenates	Arsenic
Borates	Boron
Chromates	Chromium
Molybdates	Molybdenum
Nitrates	Nitrogen
Sulphates	Sulphur
Tungstates	Tungsten
Vanadates	Vanadium

See for yourself

Rocks are made up of a mixture of minerals. If you look at a rock with a magnifying glass, you can sometimes see the different minerals in it.

Magnified piece of granite

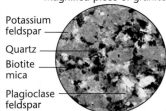

Potassium feldspar

Quartz

Biotite mica

Plagioclase feldspar

* Halogens, 48.

THE PERIODIC TABLE

The **periodic table** is an arrangement of the elements placed in order of increasing atomic number (the number of protons in the nucleus). Each element is represented by a box containing its chemical symbol, atomic number and relative atomic mass (see far right). Some versions, such as the one shown here, also give the elements' names. New elements are added when they are discovered.

Structure of an atom

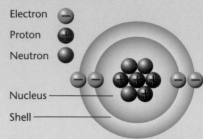

Electron
Proton
Neutron
Nucleus
Shell

READING THE TABLE

The table is arranged into rows and columns. Looking at the table you will see that it has numbered rows (called **periods**) and columns (**groups**).

PERIODS

Each period is numbered, from 1–7. The atoms of all the elements in one period have the same number of shells, which contain electrons. For example, elements in period 2 have two shells and those in period 3 have three.

Moving from left to right across a period, each successive element has one more electron in the outer shell of its atoms. This leads to a fairly regular pattern of change in the chemical behaviour of the elements across a period.

GROUPS

Each group has a Roman numeral, from I-VIII. Elements in the same group have the same number of electrons in their outer shell. This means that, chemically, they behave in similar ways.

Period number — **1**
Group number — **I**

Hydrogen is the lightest element. It has an atomic number of 1. It is not a metal so it is placed separately.

Key

Each element has a separate box in the periodic table containing the information below.

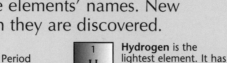

50	Atomic number
Sn	Chemical symbol
Tin	Name
118.7	Relative atomic mass

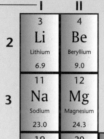

Group	I	II
1	1 H Hydrogen 1.0	
2	3 Li Lithium 6.9	4 Be Beryllium 9.0
3	11 Na Sodium 23.0	12 Mg Magnesium 24.3

	I	II							
4	19 K Potassium 39.1	20 Ca Calcium 40.1	21 Sc Scandium 45.0	22 Ti Titanium 47.9	23 V Vanadium 50.9	24 Cr Chromium 52.0	25 Mn Manganese 54.9	26 Fe Iron 55.8	27 Co Cobalt 58.9
5	37 Rb Rubidium 85.5	38 Sr Strontium 87.6	39 Y Yttrium 88.9	40 Zr Zirconium 91.2	41 Nb Niobium 92.9	42 Mo Molybdenum 96.0	43 Tc Technetium (98)	44 Ru Ruthenium 101.1	45 Rh Rhodium 102.9
6	55 Cs Caesium 132.9	56 Ba Barium 137.3	71 Lu Lutetium 175.0	72 Hf Hafnium 178.5	73 Ta Tantalum 180.9	74 W Tungsten 183.8	75 Re Rhenium 186.2	76 Os Osmium 190.2	77 Ir Iridium 192.2
7	87 Fr Francium (223)	88 Ra Radium (226)	103 Lr Lawrencium (262)	104 Rf Ruther-fordium (267)	105 Db Dubnium (268)	106 Sg Seaborgium (271)	107 Bh Bohrium (272)	108 Hs Hassium (277)	109 Mt Meitnerium (276)

The relative atomic masses for unstable, radioactive* elements are shown in brackets.

The elements with atomic numbers 57-70 belong to period 6.

57 La Lanthanum 138.9	58 Ce Cerium 140.1	59 Pr Praseo-dymium 140.9	60 Nd Neodymium 144.2	61 Pm Promethium (145)	62 Sm Samarium 150.4	63 Eu Europium 152.0
89 Ac Actinium (227)	90 Th Thorium 232.0	91 Pa Protactinium 231.0	92 U Uranium 238.0	93 Np Neptunium (237)	94 Pu Plutonium (244)	95 Am Americium (243)

The elements with atomic numbers 89-102 belong to period 7.

* Radioactivity, 114-115.

SIMILAR BEHAVIOUR

On this periodic table, all elements that behave more-or-less in similar ways have the same coloured background. The colour-coding is explained here.

Non-metals
Mostly solid or gas, and non-shiny. Melt and boil at low temperatures.

Semi-metals
Also called metalloids, these have a mixture of the properties of metals and non-metals.

Behaviour unknown

Metals
All are solid (except mercury, a liquid). Generally, they are shiny and have high melting points.

Transition metals are mostly hard and tough. Many are used in industry or jewellery.

Inner-transition metals are rare and tend to react easily with other elements, which makes them difficult to use in their natural state.

RELATIVE ATOMIC MASS

Relative atomic mass is the average mass number of the atoms in a sample of an element. (The mass number is the total number of protons and neutrons in a nucleus.) Moving through the periodic table, elements are progressively heavier. For example, hydrogen (relative atomic mass: 1) is the lightest element. Ruthenium (101.1) is over a hundred times heavier.

GROUPS WITH NAMES

Some of the groups in the periodic table have names. For example, the metals in group I are all alkali metals and group II are alkaline earth metals. The elements in group VII are halogens and group VIII (sometimes called group 0) are called noble gases.

DIFFERENT VERSION

An alternative version of the periodic table shows it split into 18 groups rather than eight. This is achieved by treating each column in the transition metals section of the table as a separate group, numbered from 3-12. In this version, all groups are referred to by ordinary numbers, not Roman numerals.

			III	IV	V	VI	VII	VIII
								2 He Helium 4
			5 B Boron 10.8	6 C Carbon 12.0	7 N Nitrogen 14.0	8 O Oxygen 16.0	9 F Fluorine 19.0	10 Ne Neon 20.2
			13 Al Aluminium 27.0	14 Si Silicon 28.1	15 P Phosphorus 31.0	16 S Sulphur 32.1	17 Cl Chlorine 35.5	18 Ar Argon 39.9

Transition metals

28 Ni Nickel 58.7	29 Cu Copper 63.5	30 Zn Zinc 65.4	31 Ga Gallium 69.7	32 Ge Germanium 72.6	33 As Arsenic 74.9	34 Se Selenium 79.0	35 Br Bromine 79.9	36 Kr Krypton 83.8
46 Pd Palladium 106.4	47 Ag Silver 107.9	48 Cd Cadmium 112.4	49 In Indium 114.8	50 Sn Tin 118.7	51 Sb Antimony 121.8	52 Te Tellurium 127.6	53 I Iodine 126.9	54 Xe Xenon 131.3
78 Pt Platinum 195.1	79 Au Gold 197.0	80 Hg Mercury 200.6	81 Tl Thallium 204.4	82 Pb Lead 207.2	83 Bi Bismuth 209.0	84 Po Polonium (209)	85 At Astatine (210)	86 Rn Radon (222)
110 Ds Darmstadtium (281)	111 Rg Roentgenium (280)	112 Cn Copernicium (285)	113 Uut Ununtrium (284)	114 Fl Flerovium (289)	115 Uup Ununpentium (288)	116 Lv Livermorium (293)	117 Uus Ununseptium (294)	118 Uuo Ununoctium (294)

Inner-transition metals

64 Gd Gadolinium 157.2	65 Tb Terbium 158.9	66 Dy Dysprosium 162.5	67 Ho Holmium 164.9	68 Er Erbium 167.3	69 Tm Thulium 168.9	70 Yb Ytterbium 173.1
96 Cm Curium (247)	97 Bk Berkelium (247)	98 Cf Californium (251)	99 Es Einsteinium (252)	100 Fm Fermium (257)	101 Md Mendelevium (258)	102 No Nobelium (259)

Elements 57-70 are called the **lanthanoids** or **rare earth elements**.

Elements 89-102 are called the **actinoids** or **radioactive rare earth elements**.

Internet links

• Scan the code for a link to a video about the periodic table of elements.

METALS

All the metal elements share certain properties. For example, they are shiny and they conduct electricity. They are classified according to the way they behave. For instance some, such as potassium and sodium, are very reactive and react violently with water and air, while others, such as gold, do not react at all.

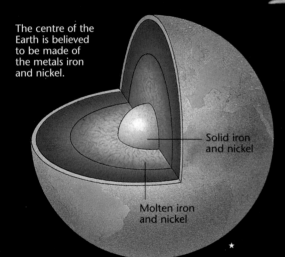

The centre of the Earth is believed to be made of the metals iron and nickel.

Solid iron and nickel

Molten iron and nickel

Fireworks contain metal compounds that burn with brilliant colours.

PROPERTIES OF METALS

All metals, except for mercury, are solid at room temperature (20°C) and they are good conductors of electricity and heat. They are shiny when cut, and some, such as iron and nickel, are magnetic.

Metals that can be pulled out to make wire are described as **ductile**. Those that can be beaten flat are described as **malleable**.

Flat panel of malleable metal

Metal wire

THE REACTIVITY SERIES

The **reactivity series** is a list of metals showing how reactive they are. The position of each metal is decided by observing how they behave during reactions involving other metals. For instance, more reactive metals pull oxygen from less reactive metals.

Reactive metals are difficult to separate from the minerals in which they are found, while the least reactive metals can be found as pure metals.

Sodium and potassium are stored in oil as they react violently with air and water.

Copper is the least reactive metal that can be produced at a reasonable cost. It is used for pipes, hot-water tanks and electrical wiring.

Reactivity series

Reactivity series
Most reactive
Potassium
Sodium
Calcium
Magnesium
Aluminium
Zinc
Iron
Tin
Lead
Copper
Silver
Gold
Platinum
Least reactive

Metals conduct electricity, so a simple way to test whether something is made of metal is to see if you can pass an electric current through it. You can see this for yourself, using a simple electrical circuit.

You need:
3 pieces of insulated copper wire, each 20cm long
4.5 volt battery
3.5 volt bulb and holder

Using one wire, twist one end around a battery terminal and the other around one of the bulb holder's terminals. With a second wire, twist one end around the remaining terminal of the bulb holder. Twist one end of the third wire around the remaining battery terminal. (You can use sticky tape to hold the wires in place.)

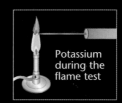

Carry the equipment around your home, touching the free wire ends to one object at a time. If the wires touch metal, electricity will flow through it and the light bulb will shine.

CAUTION
Never use mains electricity for this experiment. It will kill you.

FLAME TESTS

When some metals burn, they produce distinctive coloured flames. Burning a substance can be used as a way to test for the presence of a particular metal. The substance is held in a flame on a piece of unreactive platinum wire.

Potassium during the flame test

Sodium	Copper	Calcium	Barium	Potassium
	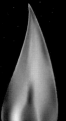			
Yellow flame	Blue-green flame	Red flame	Green flame	Lilac flame

Internet links

• Scan the code to see flames produced by burning metals.

• For links to more websites where you can find out about metals, go to www.usborne.com/quicklinks

GROUPS OF METALS

Metals can be grouped according to their chemical properties and the way they behave. There are five main groups of metals, called noble metals, alkali metals, alkaline earth metals, poor metals and transition metals. The noble metals are also transition metals.

The copper in this ore has not reacted with any other elements. Copper is a noble metal.

NOBLE METALS

Noble metals are those that can be found as pure metals, not as part of compounds, in the Earth's crust. These metals are copper, palladium, silver, platinum and gold.

The noble metals are all unreactive (see The Reactivity Series, page 30). They do not easily combine with other elements to form compounds.

Because they are unreactive, noble metals do not easily corrode and they are used for jewellery and coins. Gold is very unreactive and ancient gold objects are still shiny.

This ancient Greek gold mask was untarnished when it was found.

ALKALI METALS

The **alkali metals** are six very reactive metals, including sodium and potassium, that form group I of the periodic table. They have low melting points – potassium melts at 64°C – and they are soft and can be cut with a knife. They form alkaline* solutions when they react with water, which is why they are called alkali metals.

Potassium reacts violently with water, giving off hydrogen that bursts into lilac coloured flames.

ALKALINE EARTH METALS

The **alkaline earth metals** are six metals, including magnesium, calcium and barium, that form group II of the periodic table. These metals are found in many different minerals in the Earth's crust. For example, calcium is found in calcite, which forms veins in limestone and chalk.

Alkaline earth metals are not as reactive as the alkali metals and they are harder and have higher melting points.

This shell contains large amounts of calcium, in the form of calcium carbonate.

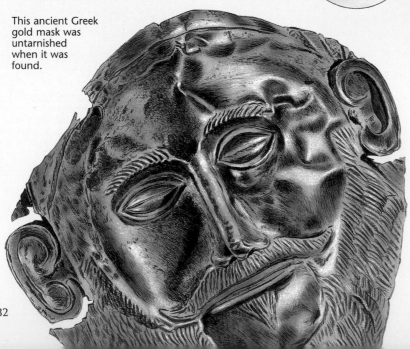

Magnesium is found in chlorophyll, the green pigment needed by plants for photosynthesis.

* Alkaline, 85.

TRANSITION METALS

The **transition metals** can be regarded as typical metals. They are strong, hard and shiny and have high melting points. They are less reactive than the alkali and alkaline earth metals.

Iron, gold, silver, chromium, nickel and copper are all transition metals. They are easy to shape and have many different industrial uses, both on their own and as alloys (see next page).

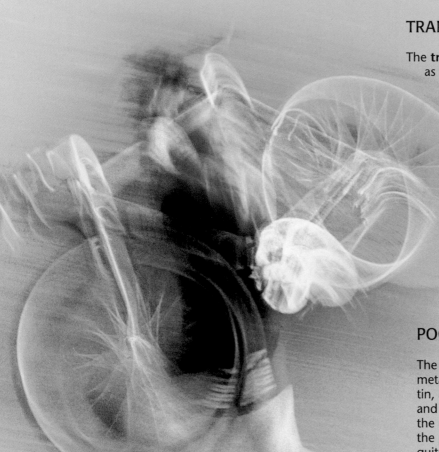

The frame of this bike is made mostly from titanium, a very light and extremely strong transition metal.

POOR METALS

The **poor metals** are a group of nine metals: aluminium, gallium, indium, tin, antimony, thallium, lead, bismuth and polonium. They are grouped to the right of the transition metals in the periodic table. In general they are quite soft, and are not much use on their own. Many are used to make more useful substances, though.

RARE EARTH ELEMENTS

Rare earth elements (or **rare earth metals**) are a group of 17 elements: the lanthanoids*, scandium, yttrium and lutetium. They are found in almost every car, gadget and household appliance and so have become some of the world's most valued resources. Most of the world's supply of rare earths is now mined in China.

See for yourself

Many tooth fillings are made using mercury, a transition metal. A mercury-based filling (called **dental amalgam**) is inexpensive, hard wearing and easy for dentists to press into shape. Fillings made with mercury are a dull, light grey colour.

You might also notice that some people have fillings or even an entire tooth made of a noble metal, particularly gold. Gold is used as a filling because it is harder wearing than a mercury filling, so it will last longer. Entire teeth are made of gold because it is practically unbreakable.

Internet links

• Scan the code to see how alkali metals react to water, some with explosive results!

• For links to websites where you can discover more about the different groups of metals, go to **www.usborne.com/quicklinks**

* Lanthanoids, 29.

ALLOYS

An **alloy** is any mixture of two or more metals, or a metal and another substance. Alloys are made because they combine the properties, such as lightness or strength, of the different metals which make them up.

Stainless steel, such as that used for cutlery, is an alloy of steel, nickel and chromium.

This ship's propeller is made of bronze, an alloy of copper and tin. The bronze has been strengthened further by adding manganese.

Bronze is often used in ship building, because it is highly resistant to corrosion by sea water.

ADDING STRENGTH

In pure metals, the atoms are arranged tightly in rows. The rows can slide over each other and this makes the metal soft. Sudden pressure, however, can cause cracks to form across the rows, making the pure metal brittle.

Arrangement of atoms in pure metal

Slide

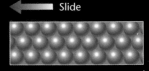

Slide

When another metal is added, its atoms help to strengthen the first metal. It does this by holding the parts of the metal together, so stopping its rows from sliding over each other.

Arrangement of atoms in an alloy

Atom of alloy

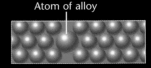

Atoms cannot slide

ALLOY PROPERTIES

An alloy's properties depend on exactly what it is made of. Steel, for example, which is an alloy of iron and carbon, combines strength with ease of use. It can easily be worked into different shapes in a forge. It can also be melted without releasing poisonous fumes.

Steel's hard-wearing properties are increased by adding manganese. Steel-manganese alloys are used for industrial cutting equipment.

Railway tracks are made of steel strengthened with manganese.

Some pure metals, such as gold and silver, are good at resisting corrosion, so they are ideal for use outside. But they are very expensive. Some alloys are just as good at resisting corrosion, yet are much cheaper to produce. Brass, an alloy of copper and zinc, is a good example.

Some alloys, such as bronze, a mixture of copper and tin, are easily shaped, even at room temperature. Because of this, bronze has been used for thousands of years to make decorative objects.

Ancient Greek bronze sculpture

STRONG, LIGHT ALLOYS

Like steel and brass, alloys of aluminium and magnesium, for example duralumin, are strong and corrosion resistant. But they are also much lighter. They are used for aircraft and bicycle frames.

Most modern jets are made from alloys of aluminium or super-strong titanium.

Metallurgists (scientists who study metals) have discovered that metals are often strongest if they are alloyed with only very tiny amounts of other substances. This has made it possible to create alloys that are very strong but still light.

This plane's engines are constructed from superalloys.

SUPERALLOYS

The elements nickel, iron and cobalt have all been used as the main ingredient in what are called **superalloys**. These alloys are not only extremely strong, but also retain their strength even when exposed to great temperatures for long periods. They are used in jet and rocket engines.

Since the 1950s, the mining of titanium, a metal as strong as steel but with half its weight, has become affordable. Titanium is widely used in alloys that form the bodies of planes.

See for yourself

Next time you come across these everyday things, notice the useful qualities of the alloys of which they are made.

• Cutlery made from **stainless steel**. It is tough and, unlike silver, doesn't tarnish.

• Door handles made from **brass**. This is shiny and decorative when polished.

• Bike frame made from **aluminium alloy**. This is strong but much lighter than a bike with a steel frame.

• Metal tools such as hammers, screwdrivers and spanners made from **toughened steel**. They are practically unbreakable because the steel contains added quantities of vanadium or chromium. If they were not toughened, the tools would splinter or shatter dangerously when used.

Internet links

• Scan the code to watch a video clip about alloys.

• For links to more websites with animations and online activities about alloys and their uses, go to www.usborne.com/quicklinks

IRON AND STEEL

Nearly all iron mined from the Earth is found as an **ore** (that is, combined with another substance). Most of it is made into steel, which is used to make many useful things, ranging from paper clips and tools to frames for giant buildings.

ELEMENT OR ALLOY?

Iron is an element which is extracted mostly from an ore called haematite, a compound of iron and oxygen. **Steel** is an alloy (that is, a mixture) of iron, carbon and traces of other metals.

Magnetite

Haematite

Magnetite and haematite are the two most common iron ores.

MAKING IRON

Iron is extracted from iron ore in a **blast furnace**. In the furnace, iron ore, limestone and **coke** (coal heated to burn off oils and leave carbon) are blasted with very hot air. This process is called **smelting**. The carbon combines with oxygen to form carbon monoxide. The carbon monoxide then becomes carbon dioxide by pulling the oxygen away from the iron ore. This is an example of a reduction* reaction.

The iron extracted from iron ore contains some left-over carbon (about 4%) from the smelting process, plus other impurities such as sulphur. Called **pig iron**, it is used to make cast iron, or refined further to make steel.

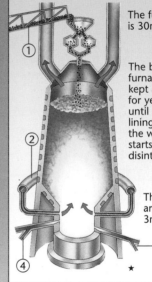

The furnace is 30m tall.

The blast furnace is kept alight for years until the lining of the walls starts to disintegrate.

The walls are over 3m thick.

The steel frame of this unfinished building will eventually be covered with concrete panels, to create a huge office block like those in the background.

* Reduction, 81.

MAKING STEEL

Steel is made of iron that has been through a blast furnace, with other elements added to make it stronger. To make steel, molten iron is blasted with oxygen, removing more carbon. The oxygen combines with carbon in the iron to form the gas carbon monoxide, which is collected and used as fuel. At the end, the steel may contain as little as 0.04% carbon, although different grades of steel contain different amounts.

To convert iron to steel, molten iron is poured into a furnace called a **converter**.

A high-pressure jet of almost pure oxygen is blasted into the converter. The oxygen combines with the carbon, forming carbon monoxide.

Steel is also made by melting down scrap steel in an **electric arc furnace**. The metal is melted by a powerful current of electricity.

See for yourself

Look out for iron and steel objects around your home. You can test to see if an object really is made of iron or steel (and not some other metal) by holding a magnet near it. If the object contains iron or steel, it will be attracted to the magnet.

Here are a few examples of things that you may have around your home, which you could test for their iron content.

Metal door handles
Hinges
Knives and forks
Garden gate
Washing machine
Bath
Bike parts
Food mixer
Spectacles
Belt buckles
Taps
Radiators

CAUTION
Do not put a magnet near to computers, television sets or watches. You could damage them.

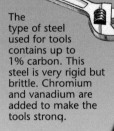

The type of steel used for tools contains up to 1% carbon. This steel is very rigid but brittle. Chromium and vanadium are added to make the tools strong.

Steel that is used in construction, like the frame shown here, is painted to protect it from rusting before it is covered over by the rest of the building. A rusting frame would be dangerously weak.

Steel paper clips contain about 0.08% carbon. This makes them bendy. Those shown here are plastic coated to make them eye-catching.

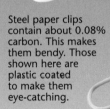

Internet links

• Scan the code to see how iron ore is turned into steel.

• For links to more websites where you can investigate how iron and steel are made, go to www.usborne.com/quicklinks

MAIN METALS AND ALLOYS

There are 65 metals that naturally exist on Earth. Of these, just 20 are used, on their own or as part of an alloy, to produce nearly all manufactured, metal-based things. You can find out about those metals here, plus the five most common alloys, and see examples of how some of them are used.

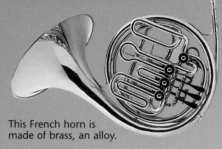

This French horn is made of brass, an alloy.

Aluminium
A very light, silvery-white metal that is resistant to corrosion. It is extracted from its ore, bauxite, by electrolysis*. Aluminium is used in overhead electric cables, aircraft, ships, cars, drinks cans and kitchen foil.

Brass
An alloy of copper and zinc. It is easy to shape and is used for decorative ornaments, musical instruments, screws and tacks.

Bronze
An alloy of copper and tin known since ancient times. It resists corrosion and is easy to shape. Coins made of bronze are used as low-value currency in many countries.

Calcium
A malleable, silvery-white metal found in limestone and chalk. It also occurs in animal bones and teeth. It is used to make cement and high-grade steel.

Chromium
A hard, grey metal used to make stainless steel and for plating other metals to protect them or give them a shiny, reflective finish.

Copper
A malleable, reddish metal used to make electrical wires, hot water tanks and the alloys brass, bronze and cupronickel.

Cupronickel
An alloy made from copper and nickel from which most silver-coloured coins are made.

Gold
A soft, unreactive, bright yellow element that is used for jewellery and in electronics.

Iron
A malleable, grey-white magnetic metal extracted mainly from the ore haematite by smelting in a blast furnace. It is used in building and engineering, and to make the alloy steel.

Lead
A heavy, malleable, poisonous blue-white metal extracted from the mineral galena and used in batteries, roofing and as a shield against radiation from X-rays.

Magnesium
A light, silvery-white metal that burns with a bright white flame. It is used in rescue flares and fireworks and in lightweight alloys.

Mercury
A heavy, silvery-white, poisonous liquid metal used in thermometers, dental amalgam for filling teeth, and in some explosives.

Platinum
A malleable, silvery-white unreactive metal used for making jewellery, in electronics and as a catalyst*.

Plutonium
A radioactive metal produced by bombarding uranium (see opposite) in nuclear reactors and used in nuclear weapons.

Potassium
A light, silvery, highly reactive metal. Potassium compounds are used in chemical fertilizers and to make glass.

Three million aluminium fasteners hold this jet's body together.

* Catalysts, 79; Electrolysis, 82.

Silver

A malleable, grey-white metal that is a very good conductor of heat and electricity. It is used for making jewellery, silverware and electronics.

Sodium

A very reactive, soft, silvery-white metal that occurs in common salt and is used in street lamps and in the chemical industry.

Solder

An alloy of tin and lead that has a low melting point and is used for joining wires in electronics.

Stanene

Stanene is a new material made mainly of a single layer of tin atoms. When fluorine atoms are added to it, stanene can conduct electricity perfectly up to 100°C (212°F). It could replace copper wires in computer chips, making them run even faster, but using less energy.

Steel

An alloy of iron and carbon that is one of the most important materials in industry. Stainless steel, an alloy of steel and chromium, resists corrosion and is used in aerospace industries.

Tin

Soft, malleable and silvery-white, tin is used for tin-plating steel to stop it corroding, and in the alloys bronze, pewter and solder.

Titanium

A strong, white, malleable metal. It is very resistant to corrosion and is used in alloys for spacecraft, aircraft and bicycle frames.

Tungsten

A hard, grey-white metal. It is used for lamp filaments, in electronics, and in steel alloys for making sharp-edged cutting tools.

Uranium

A silvery-white, radioactive metal used as a source of nuclear energy and also in nuclear weapons.

Vanadium

A hard, white, poisonous metal used to increase the strength and hardness of steel alloys. A vanadium compound is used as a catalyst* for making sulphuric acid.

Zinc

A blue-white metal used as a coating on iron to prevent rusting (called galvanizing), zinc is also used in certain electric batteries and in alloys such as brass.

This Boeing 747 is built using a high-strength alloy that contains mostly aluminium – a very light metal. The jet engines are made of titanium, which is also light, but can easily withstand the enormous temperatures generated in the engines.

Internet links

• Scan the code for a video about gold and its properties.

• For links to more websites about the production and uses of main metals and alloys, go to **www.usborne.com/quicklinks**

* Catalysts, 79; Chips, 239; Galvanizing, 41.

CORROSION

Corrosion is the chemical reaction that takes place when a metal is in contact with oxygen. The metal reacts with the oxygen to form a compound called an **oxide** on the surface of the metal. The metal becomes tarnished – that is, it loses its shine. Metals high in the reactivity series* corrode more quickly than less reactive metals.

Steel armour used to be rubbed with oil or beeswax to stop it from rusting.

USING METALS THAT CORRODE

Iron (from which steel is made) corrodes easily, but it is very strong and fairly easy to form into different shapes. It is ideal for building giant structures, such as bridges, but it has to be protected from corrosion, normally by painting it.

This bridge is protected from corrosion by painting it with phosphoric acid. The acid bonds to the metal and forms a protective coating, preventing rusting of the metal beneath. It is further protected by a layer of paint.

See for yourself

To remove the oxidized layer from a tarnished copper coin, leave it overnight in a glass containing a little vinegar. The acidic vinegar will react with the tarnish, removing it from the coin and exposing the copper alloy underneath. The coin will be left looking bright and shiny. Once it is back in the air though, it will corrode again, leaving a dull oxide layer on the surface.

* Reactivity series, 30.

EFFECTS OF CORROSION

When a metal corrodes, the surface becomes coated with a layer of oxide. On some, such as aluminium, this layer clings to the metal and protects it from further corrosion. On others this protective layer does not form. On iron and steel, for example, a flaky layer of **rust** (iron oxide) forms. This lifts away, allowing the metal beneath to corrode.

Aluminium immediately forms a layer of oxide on its surface. It is an ideal material for food trays, because it will not corrode further.

These steel drums were painted to protect them from rusting, but even a small scratch can let moisture under the paint, and rusting begins.

Moving parts, such as these gears, are coated with a layer of grease to stop them from rusting.

GALVANIZING

Galvanizing is a method of protecting steel by coating it with zinc. Zinc is more reactive than steel so oxygen reacts with it rather than the steel. Even if the layer of zinc is scratched, the oxygen in the air continues to react with the zinc rather than the steel.

Ships and oil rigs are protected by attaching a block of zinc or magnesium to them. This metal corrodes before the iron and is called **sacrificial metal**.

Most modern cars are made from steel that has been galvanized. This stops them from rusting.

Internet links

• Scan the code to watch steel being galvanized – coated with zinc.

• For links to more websites about the effects of corrosion on metals, go to **www.usborne.com/quicklinks**

THE DISCOVERY OF METALS

People probably discovered how to extract metals from their ores by accident, when rocks containing a metal were heated with charcoal in fireplaces. A chemical reaction called reduction would have taken place which freed the metal from its ore. The same reaction is still used in blast furnaces (see page 36) to extract iron.

This decorated cauldron was made from bronze (a mixture of copper and tin) by the ancient Chinese, in around 1500BC.

THE FIRST METALS

The first metals worked by people were copper, gold and silver, probably because these are found as pure metals (see Noble Metals, page 32).

Later, in about 3500BC, the Sumerians learned how to make bronze by combining copper and tin. Bronze is stronger than the pure metals.

Iron was not used until about 1350BC, probably because it needs much higher temperatures to separate it from its compounds.

This golden cup was made in Northern Europe in about 3000BC.

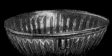

Sumerian bronze bowl, made around 3000BC

Bronze axe-head made in 500BC

Here, molten iron is being poured into a furnace which will produce steel.

Sumerian people in the Middle East made this golden dagger and sheath in about 4000BC.

NEW METALS

Until 1735, the only known metals were copper, silver, gold, iron, mercury, tin, zinc, bismuth, antimony and lead. Aluminium was discovered in 1825.

Nowadays scientists can create new metal elements, such as mendelevium, by bombarding atoms with electrons in a type of nuclear reactor called a **particle accelerator**. The atoms break apart under the bombardment, enabling scientists to get a glimpse of their structure.

This is part of a huge particle accelerator. It can be used to create new metals. These metals are unstable and break down in a very short time.

In this furnace, oxygen is blasted through the molten iron. The oxygen removes carbon from the iron, leaving steel. This photograph was taken in 1958, but the steel-making process has changed little since then.

Internet links

• Scan the code for a video about the recent discovery of a new metal element.

• For links to more sites about how metals were first used, go to **www.usborne.com/quicklinks**

RECYCLING METALS

Mining and extracting metals from ores is an expensive process. Fortunately, though, metals can be used again. The process of making them re-usable is called **recycling**, and it is much cheaper than extracting metals from ores. Recycling is done by melting down used metal, to produce a metal that is almost as good as new. It can be done over and over again.

THE RECYCLING PROCESS

Before a metal can be recycled it needs to be collected and separated from any other types of metal. This ensures that the recycled metal is as pure as possible. It is then melted down and poured into moulds. The metal cools into a solid block, ready to be made into a new, finished product.

WHICH METALS?

The most commonly recycled metals are steel and aluminium. However, other metals, such as copper, tin and lead and even precious metals, including gold, silver and platinum, are recycled too. Mobile phones contain around 65 different elements including metals. They are recycled by smashing, shredding and grinding them into powder which can then be separated.

This giant electromagnet* is picking up vast quantities of junk iron and steel. The metal will be dumped in a blast furnace to be melted down.

STEEL

Most steel for recycling comes from scrapped vehicles, such as cars and ships. Old industrial machinery is a good source too. Factories that use steel save offcuts and return them to steelworks to be melted and re-used.

Some of the things that people throw out from their homes, such as old washing machines, also contain steel. Much of this can be recycled.

Here, red-hot recycled steel is being poured into a mould.

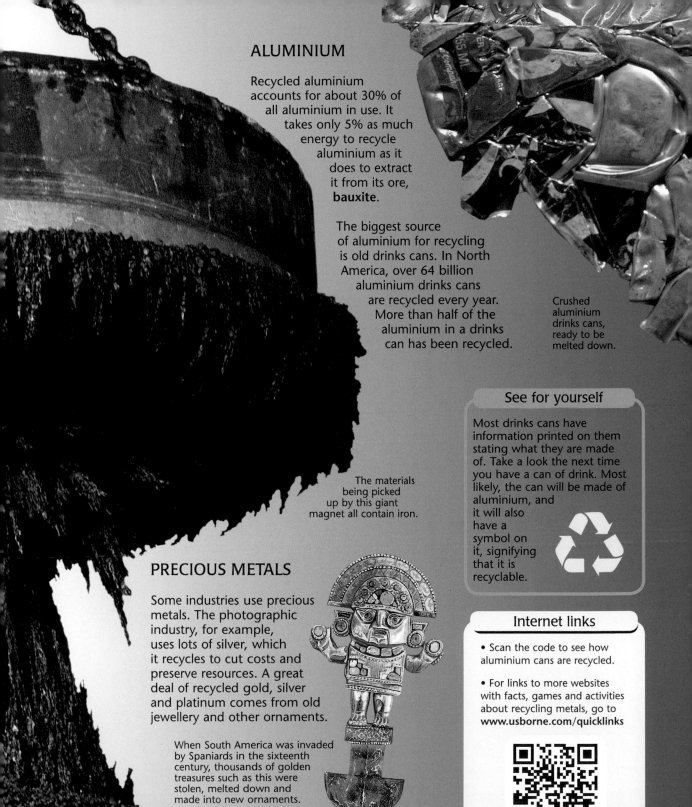

ALUMINIUM

Recycled aluminium accounts for about 30% of all aluminium in use. It takes only 5% as much energy to recycle aluminium as it does to extract it from its ore, **bauxite**.

The biggest source of aluminium for recycling is old drinks cans. In North America, over 64 billion aluminium drinks cans are recycled every year. More than half of the aluminium in a drinks can has been recycled.

Crushed aluminium drinks cans, ready to be melted down.

The materials being picked up by this giant magnet all contain iron.

See for yourself

Most drinks cans have information printed on them stating what they are made of. Take a look the next time you have a can of drink. Most likely, the can will be made of aluminium, and it will also have a symbol on it, signifying that it is recyclable.

PRECIOUS METALS

Some industries use precious metals. The photographic industry, for example, uses lots of silver, which it recycles to cut costs and preserve resources. A great deal of recycled gold, silver and platinum comes from old jewellery and other ornaments.

When South America was invaded by Spaniards in the sixteenth century, thousands of golden treasures such as this were stolen, melted down and made into new ornaments.

Internet links

• Scan the code to see how aluminium cans are recycled.

• For links to more websites with facts, games and activities about recycling metals, go to **www.usborne.com/quicklinks**

HYDROGEN

Hydrogen is the lightest and most abundant element in the entire universe. The Sun and the stars are made of hydrogen gas, but on Earth, hydrogen is found only in compounds and does not occur naturally as a free element (that is, on its own).

Stars are globes of extremely hot hydrogen and other gases.

REACTIVE HYDROGEN

Hydrogen is very reactive. It burns easily and combines with many other elements. For example, water, the most plentiful compound on Earth, is made of hydrogen and oxygen. Fossil fuels, such as coal and oil, are compounds of hydrogen and carbon, and sugars and starch also contain hydrogen.

Sucrose ($C_{12}H_{22}O_{11}$) the sugar in sweets, is a compound of carbon, hydrogen and oxygen.

See for yourself

If you pour yourself a glass of water, try to imagine what it is made of. Water (H_2O) is a compound of hydrogen (H) and oxygen (O). It contains twice as many hydrogen atoms as oxygen atoms. However, although there are more of them, the hydrogen atoms have such a small mass that they make up only 12.5% of the water's total mass.

Hydrogen

Oxygen

The Sun is a massive ball of constantly exploding gases. It consists mostly of hydrogen and helium.

Occasionally, vast streams of burning hydrogen flare out from the Sun. These are **solar prominences**.

MAKING HYDROGEN

Hydrogen (H_2) can be made by reacting methane gas (CH_4) with steam (H_2O) as shown by the following chemical equation:

$$CH_4 + 2H_2O \longrightarrow 4H_2 + CO_2$$

Most hydrogen made in this way is used to make ammonia (NH_3) for fertilizers. To make ammonia, hydrogen is combined with nitrogen using the **Haber process**, discovered by Fritz Haber in 1909.

THE HABER PROCESS

In the Haber process, nitrogen gas from the air and hydrogen extracted from methane (CH_4) are passed over a catalyst* of iron. Under very high pressure and at a high temperature, the gases react to produce ammonia gas (NH_3). This is cooled to form liquid ammonia.

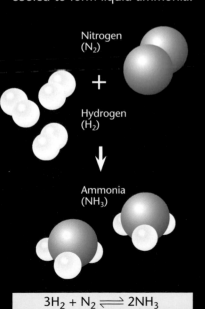

Nitrogen
(N_2)

+

Hydrogen
(H_2)

↓

Ammonia
(NH_3)

$$3H_2 + N_2 \rightleftharpoons 2NH_3$$

⇌ This symbol signifies that the reaction is reversible.

BURNING HYDROGEN

If hydrogen is mixed with air and then lit, it explodes. This can be used in the laboratory as a test for small amounts of gas. If the gas is hydrogen, it makes a little pop.

Hydrogen gas makes a small pop when tested with a burning splint.

If pure hydrogen (H_2) is burned in air or oxygen (O_2), it burns quietly with a blue flame and forms steam, as shown in this equation:

$$2H_2 + O_2 \longrightarrow 2H_2O$$

In theory, hydrogen is an ideal fuel as it produces a lot of energy when it burns and the only product is water, which is not a pollutant. But at present it is not suitable as an everyday fuel because it is difficult to store and transport safely.

In 1937, the Hindenburg airship caught fire. It was filled with hydrogen, which exploded, killing 36 people.

ROCKET FUEL

Liquid hydrogen is used as a fuel for rockets. In order for the fuel to burn in space, where there is no oxygen, rockets also carry separate tanks of oxygen. The liquid hydrogen and oxygen are fed into a combustion chamber where they burn safely.

The fuel tanks have to be extremely strong to prevent the pressurized liquids from escaping.

Oxygen tank ———

Liquid hydrogen fuel tank ———

Internet links

• Scan the code to see how hydrogen is used as rocket fuel.

• For links to more websites with fascinating facts and experiments about hydrogen, go to **www.usborne.com/quicklinks**

THE HALOGENS

The **halogens** are a group of elements that includes fluorine, chlorine, bromine, iodine and astatine. They are all very reactive and poisonous and together form group VII of the periodic table.

Halogen lamps contain compounds of bromine that make them shine really brightly.

FLUORINE

Fluorine is a poisonous gas. It is extracted from the mineral fluorite. **Fluorides** (non-poisonous compounds of fluorine) are added to toothpaste and drinking water to reduce tooth decay.

Toothpaste and water containing fluoride

Fluorine is also combined with carbon to make useful compounds called **fluorocarbons**. An example is PTFE (polytetrafluoroethene), which is used as a non-stick coating on frying pans and skis.

These skis have a coating of PTFE on their undersides. This non-stick layer helps them to slide freely over snow and ice.

This huge salt flat in South America contains sodium iodate. This is collected and used to produce the halogen iodine.

CHLORINE

On its own, **chlorine** is a poisonous gas. It is very reactive and only occurs naturally in compounds, such as sodium chloride (common salt). Chlorine is used as a disinfectant and to make hydrochloric acid and PVC (polyvinylchloride) plastic.

Compounds of chlorine have many uses. **Sodium hypochlorite**, for example, is used to make household bleach, and to bleach paper pulp so that it turns white.

This juggling equipment is made from PVC.

Writing paper is bleached using sodium hypochlorite, a compound of chlorine.

BROMINE

Bromine is a foul-smelling brown liquid. Traces of bromine are found in sea water and mineral springs. Compounds of bromine and one other element are called **bromides**. Silver bromide is used in photographic film.

When light hits silver bromide on photographic film, a reaction takes place in different layers of the film, creating various-coloured patches.

Bromine compounds are used to make rat poisons and products that treat wood for termite infestation.

IODINE

Iodine is a purple-black solid. It is used in medicine, photography and dyes, and is produced in large quantities from sodium iodate.

Traces of iodine are found in foods, and without it the cells in our bodies would not be able to convert food into energy. However, large quantities of iodine are harmful.

Iodine is found in seaweed, and in vegetables and fruit.

ASTATINE

Astatine is an unstable, radioactive element. It is the heaviest of all halogens, but hardly any of it is found in nature. Scientists estimate that only about 30g of astatine exists in the entire Earth's crust. They have been able to create more than 20 different astatine isotopes* during experiments, though.

See for yourself

You can buy iodine solution from a pharmacy and use it to test for the presence of starch. Drip some drops onto slices of food, such as raw potato, apple and a piece of bread. If starch is present, the food will turn blue-black very quickly.

This type of dropper is called a pipette.

Iodine tastes unpleasant, so make sure that you don't get any in your mouth.

Internet links

• Scan the code to compare four of the halogen elements.

• For links to more websites with facts and test-yourself quizzes about the halogens, go to **www.usborne.com/quicklinks**

CARBON

Carbon is a solid non-metallic element found in all living things. It occurs as a **free element** (on its own) mainly in the forms of hard, colourless diamond and crumbly black graphite.

FORMS OF CARBON

Carbon atoms can bond* together in different ways. These different forms are called **allotropes**. Carbon has three main allotropes – diamond, graphite and buckminsterfullerene.

DIAMOND

In **diamond**, each carbon atom is bonded to four other atoms. This makes diamond very hard – it is the hardest substance found in nature. Diamond forms naturally as tetrahedral (four-sided) crystals.

Rough diamonds, like these, are cut into shape using a fast-spinning bronze saw, a laser, or other diamonds.

Cut diamonds sparkle with an intensity that is unmatched in the natural world. They can be several different colours, and are used to make expensive jewellery. The purest ones are transparent.

Carbon atom in diamond

Diamonds are cut in such a way that their surfaces split up light into the colours of the rainbow.

* Bonding, 68-69.

DIAMOND VARIETIES

Impure varieties of diamond, such as **carbonado** (also called **black diamond**) are valued in industry for their hardness. They are used in cutting and drilling equipment, as well as in some very accurate watches.

Naturally occuring varieties of diamonds are mined from the Earth, but diamonds can also be manufactured. These synthetic diamonds are created by mixing graphite with a catalyst* and subjecting it to great heat and pressure.

GRAPHITE

In **graphite** (sometimes called **plumbago**), each atom of carbon is bonded to three other atoms, arranged in a honeycomb-like network of plates that easily slide over each other. This makes graphite soft and flaky. The plate network is held together by weak forces.

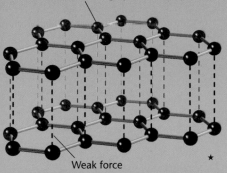

Carbon atom in graphite

Weak force *

The weak forces between the plates give graphite a very slippery structure. This makes graphite a very good lubricant, and it is used to reduce friction between the moving parts of machines. The weak forces also mean it is a good conductor of electricity so it is often used to make electrodes*.

BUCKMINSTERFULLERENE

Buckminsterfullerene is an allotrope of carbon discovered in 1985. Each molecule contains 60 carbon atoms linked in the shape of a hollow ball. It is formed by heating graphite in helium until it vaporizes, and then letting it cool and condense.

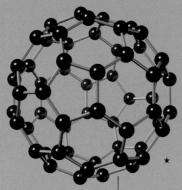

A buckminsterfullerene molecule

Buckminsterfullerene molecules are sometimes called **buckyballs**. Their atoms are arranged in a pattern of hexagons and pentagons similar to that on footballs.

Due to their robust spherical structure, buckyballs are really strong – a hundred times stronger than steel, but only a sixth of its weight.

Using a method similar to that for making buckyballs, scientists can also make tiny **nanotubes**. They hope to use them to build super-strong materials.

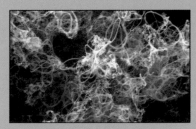

Nanotubes – made by vaporizing graphite with a laser and adding a metal catalyst*.

GRAPHENE

In 2004, scientists made another allotrope called **graphene**. This form of carbon is a very thin honeycomb-like sheet only one atom thick. The transparent sheets are incredibly strong and flexible, repel water and are also excellent conductors of heat and electricity.

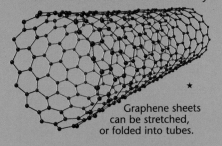

*

Graphene sheets can be stretched, or folded into tubes.

See for yourself

Pencil "leads" are made from powdered graphite mixed with clay. Take a look at your pencils, and compare the darkness of the lines that they make. A pencil containing more graphite than clay gives a darker, more smudgy line than one that has more clay than graphite.

Letters and numbers printed on the side of a pencil indicate its graphite/clay content. A number followed by a B (for black) means that it has more graphite than clay. A number followed by an H (for hard) means it has more clay than graphite. A medium pencil, one that gives lines that are neither dark nor light, has HB written on it.

This 4B pencil gives a soft, dark line. 9B is the darkest.

This 2H pencil gives a light, grey line. 9H is the lightest.

* Catalysts, 79; Electrodes, 82.

THE CARBON CYCLE

Most carbon atoms have existed since the world began. They circulate through animals, plants and the air in a process called the **carbon cycle**.

Plants use carbon dioxide to make carbon compounds by photosynthesis*. Animals eat plants (or other animals) and use the carbon compounds in their bodies. Carbon dioxide returns to the air when fuels burn and living things decay, and as a result of internal respiration, which is the way plants and animals break down sugars to release energy.

The carbon cycle

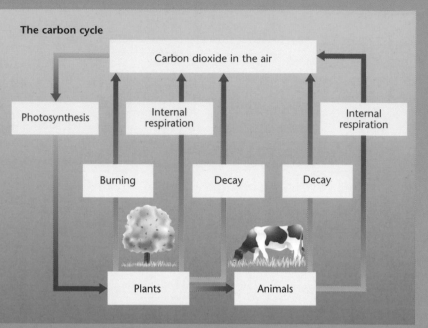

Carbon dioxide in the air

Photosynthesis — Internal respiration — Internal respiration

Burning — Decay — Decay

Plants — Animals

CARBON COMPOUNDS

Carbon atoms can bond with up to four other atoms, including other carbon atoms. This allows carbon to combine to form a vast number of different compounds. There are many more compounds of carbon than of any other element. All those compounds of carbon that are found in living things are called **organic compounds**.

Like all living things, both this kingfisher and the branch it is sitting on are made from compounds of carbon.

CARBON FIBRES

Silky threads of pure carbon, called **carbon fibres**, are used to reinforce plastics. This material is used to make lightweight boats and tennis racquets. A racing bike made of carbon fibre is eight times stronger than a steel one, but many times lighter.

This bike's frame is made from carbon fibre.

CARBON MIXTURES

Carbon can be found mixed with other elements and compounds. **Coal**, for example, is mainly carbon, but contains hydrogen, oxygen, nitrogen and sulphur. It is a **fossil fuel**, that is, a fuel formed over millions of years from the remains of plants.

There are three types of coal, containing varying amounts of carbon. **Lignite**, also called brown coal, only has 60-70% carbon. **Bituminous coal**, which is shiny and black, has more than 80%. **Anthracite** has more than 90% carbon.

Charcoal is another impure form of carbon. To make it, wood is heated in an airtight space. This removes the chemicals that produce wood smoke, leaving flaky black chunks of charcoal, which burn cleanly when ignited.

Unlike diamond and graphite, neither coal nor charcoal have a regular structure.

USING COAL AND CHARCOAL

Coal is an important fuel. Over a third of the world's electricity is produced by power stations that burn coal. Lignite is cheap and plentiful, but produces a lot of pollution. Bituminous coal and anthracite are better since they cause less air pollution.

A form of charcoal called **activated charcoal** is used in filters and gas masks to remove poisonous fumes. It has countless tiny holes in its surface, which are ideal for trapping fumes. It is made by allowing charcoal to burn briefly in oxygen at the end of the charcoal-making process.

Charcoal is often used as a fuel on barbecues, and can be shaped into sticks to be used as an artists' drawing material.

See for yourself

The next time you see coal burning, try to imagine what is happening to the molecules that it is made of.

The heat gives the molecules enough energy to break apart. This gives off heat energy. As the bonds break, atoms, such as hydrogen, are freed from the molecules. These liberated atoms burn too, giving off additional heat.

Power stations fuelled by coal can produce an average of 600 megawatts of electrical energy in an hour.

Charcoal burns without smoke. This makes it an ideal heat source for barbecues, because it cooks things without coating them in soot.

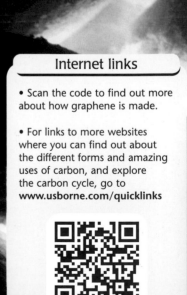

Internet links

• Scan the code to find out more about how graphene is made.

• For links to more websites where you can find out about the different forms and amazing uses of carbon, and explore the carbon cycle, go to **www.usborne.com/quicklinks**

SULPHUR

The element **sulphur** is a bright yellow, crumbly solid. It is found in underground deposits in volcanic areas. It is also found in minerals such as iron pyrites and copper pyrites.

Pure sulphur

Iron pyrites, a compound of iron and sulphur

FORMS OF SULPHUR

Sulphur molecules form in crooked rings of eight atoms, sometimes referred to as crowns. The rings can combine together in different ways to make two distinct crystal forms, known as allotropes.

Most sulphur is found in the form of **rhombic sulphur**.

Rhombic sulphur crystal

The molecules fit together closely in rhombic sulphur.

Above 96°C, **monoclinic sulphur** forms. Monoclinic sulphur crystals are long, thin and angular. They look a little like needles.

Monoclinic sulphur crystal

The molecules are less closely packed than in rhombic sulphur, so it is less dense.

Sulphur becomes a gas at 444°C. The molecules split apart and float freely, as shown here.

PRODUCING SULPHUR

Most sulphur is obtained from fossil fuels*. It is also extracted from underground deposits by melting it with pressurized steam. This is called the **Frasch process**.

USES OF SULPHUR

One of the most important uses of sulphur is in the manufacture of **sulphuric acid**, which is used to make fertilizers, plastics and batteries. It is also used to **vulcanize** rubber (harden it), in black gunpowder and in medicines.

SULPHUR DIOXIDE

Sulphur burns with a blue flame to form **sulphur dioxide**, a poisonous gas made of sulphur and oxygen. This gas is used to kill insects and fungi, and as a preservative for fruit.

Sulphur dioxide can be used to preserve the colour of dried apricots.

Internet links

• Scan the code to find out more about where sulphur is found in nature.

*Fossil fuels, 108.

PHOSPHORUS

Phosphorus is a non-metallic element. It occurs naturally in bones, teeth and the chemicals in the body that store energy. It is also found in the Earth, for example in the mineral apatite. Its most reactive form, white phosphorus, glows in the dark.

The minerals apatite (left) and turquoise (right) contain phosphorus.

FORMS OF PHOSPHORUS

Phosphorus occurs in three crystal forms, or allotropes.

White phosphorus is a poisonous, waxy, white solid that ignites easily when it is exposed to air.

Red phosphorus is a non-poisonous, dark red powder. It is made by heating white phosphorus without air. It is less reactive than white phosphorus.

Black phosphorus is made by heating white phosphorus under pressure using mercury as a catalyst*. Its name comes from its appearance, which is much like graphite. It is the least reactive form of phosphorus.

USES OF PHOSPHORUS

One of the main uses of phosphorus is in the production of **phosphoric acid** (H_3PO_4). This is used to make iron and steel rust-proof, and also in the manufacture of fizzy drinks.

Phosphoric acid is used to add fizz and flavour to cola drinks.

Red phosphorus is used in matches, pesticides, alloys and distress flares.

White phosphorus is used in rat poison.

When a match is struck, the red phosphorus becomes white phosphorus, burning fiercely in the air.

Compounds of phosphorus and oxygen are called **phosphates**. Phosphates are important in animal and plant growth. They are added to animal feed and used to make fertilizers.

Farm crops, like this cabbage, are fed with large amounts of phosphate-rich fertilizers.

See for yourself

Take a look at the list of ingredients on a tube of toothpaste.

The list will probably include certain phosphates, such as sodium phosphate and trisodium phosphate. These are compounds that contain phosphorus.

These phosphates are used in toothpastes because they help to loosen stain-forming chemicals from your teeth, helping to keep them white.

Internet links

• Scan the code to watch phosphorus catch fire on contact with air.

* Catalysts, 79.

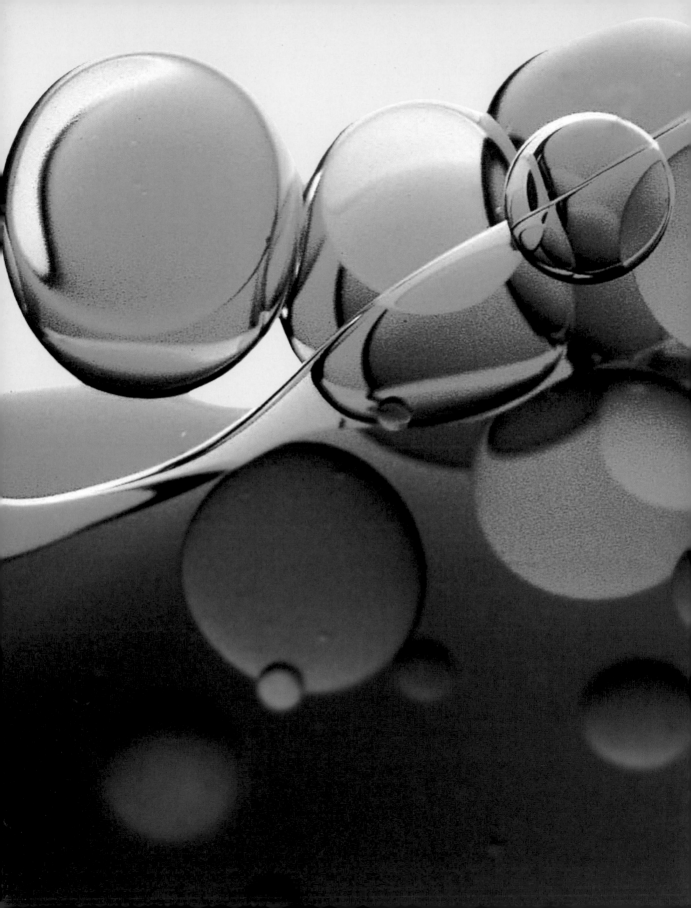

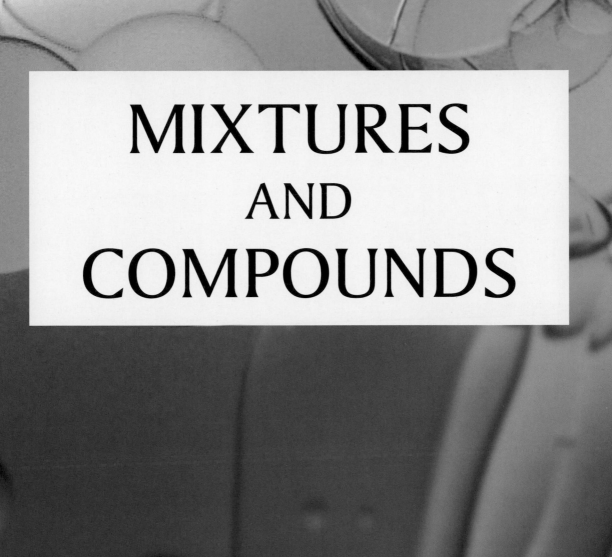

MIXTURES
AND
COMPOUNDS

MIXTURES

Most of the natural substances around us, such as sea water and the air, are mixtures. A **mixture** is a combination of different substances that can be separated because they have different physical properties – such as different boiling points.

Ice cream is a mixture of ice, milk fat, flavourings and air.

WHAT IS A MIXTURE?

The ingredients in a mixture are not chemically bonded*, so they can usually be separated easily. For example, iron can be removed from a mixture of iron filings and sulphur using a magnet. Other methods of separating mixtures are shown on pages 60-61.

This magnet is covered with iron filings. When held in a mixture of sulphur and iron filings, the filings cling to the magnet, leaving sulphur behind.

A mixture may contain any proportion of the substances of which it is made.

The substances keep their own properties, and the mixture has all the properties of the substances, except, for example, in a solution. In this case, the boiling and freezing points may change depending on the mixture.

* Bonding, 68-71.

WHAT'S IN A MIXTURE?

Some mixtures contain two or more elements (substances made up of only one type of atom), as shown in the diagram below.

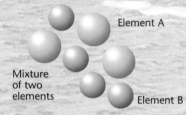

Mixture of two elements

Element A

Element B

Some mixtures contain two or more different compounds (substances made up of different atoms bonded together).

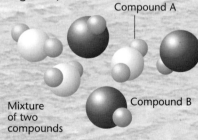

Compound A

Mixture of two compounds

Compound B

Other mixtures contain elements and compounds. Air is a mixture of elements such as oxygen, and compounds such as carbon dioxide and soot.

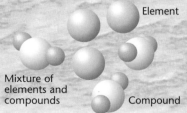

Element

Mixture of elements and compounds

Compound

TYPES OF MIXTURE

A mixture can be any combination of solids, liquids and gases. For example, air is a mixture of gases, and sea water is a mixture of salt (a solid) and water (a liquid).

These metal tacks are made of brass, a mixture of copper and zinc. Mixtures of metals are called **alloys**.

A mixture of a solid dissolved in a liquid, such as salt in water, is called a **solution**. The liquid is called the **solvent** and the solid is called the **solute**. A solid that dissolves easily is said to be **soluble**, while a solid that won't dissolve is **insoluble**.

A mixture of solid particles floating in a liquid or a gas is called a **suspension**. Blood, milk and smoke are suspensions.

Milk is a suspension of fat particles in water.

A beach is a mixture of sand, seashells and pebbles.

MIXING LIQUIDS

Liquids that mix easily, such as ink and water, are called **miscible** liquids. Liquids that don't mix easily, such as oil and water, are said to be **immiscible**.

They can be made to mix by adding an emulsifier. An **emulsifier** makes one liquid, such as oil, break up into minute droplets in another, such as water. The resulting liquid is called an **emulsion**.

Sea water is mainly a solution of salt (sodium chloride) and water.

Blobs of oil in water. If an emulsifier is added to this mixture, the oil breaks down into tiny beads, forming an emulsion with the water.

Emulsion paint is made from water, droplets of oil, coloured pigment and chemical emulsifiers.

Fizzy drinks are a mixture of two liquids (water and flavouring) and a gas (carbon dioxide). The gas makes the fizzy bubbles.

Mayonnaise is an emulsion of oil and vinegar. The emulsifier is egg yolk.

See for yourself

You can compare a solution with a mixture that contains insoluble substances. Stir some sand into a jar of water. Then stir a spoonful of salt into a different jar of water.

The sand won't dissolve, no matter how hard you stir it. You are left with a simple mixture of water and sand.

As you stir the salt into the water, it dissolves and forms a solution. It breaks down into tiny parts and can't be seen. Both jars, though, contain mixtures.

Salt

Sand

Water

Salt dissolves in water

Internet links

• Scan the code to watch a video about what's in a mixture.

• For links to more websites where you can investigate different types of mixtures with experiments, animations and quizzes, go to **www.usborne.com/quicklinks**

59

SEPARATING MIXTURES

There are a number of different ways to separate the substances in a mixture. The method that you choose depends on the physical properties of the substances that the mixture contains.

In this coffee pot, the wire mesh separates the ground coffee from the hot drink.

DECANTATION

Decantation is a simple method of separating solid, insoluble particles from a liquid by leaving the particles to settle and pouring off the liquid.

Sand, soil and other matter settle in layers in a jar of muddy water.

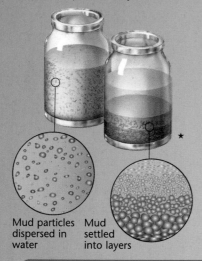

★

Mud particles dispersed in water

Mud settled into layers

FILTRATION

Filtration is another method of separating insoluble, solid particles from a liquid. The mixture is poured through a filter which traps the particles and only allows the molecules of liquid to pass through. This method is used in waterworks* as part of the process of producing clean drinking water.

The liquid that passes through the filter is called the **filtrate**. The solid that remains behind is the **residue**.

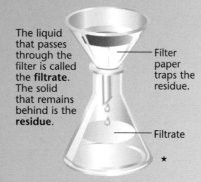

Filter paper traps the residue.

Filtrate

★

CHROMATOGRAPHY

Chromatography is used to analyse the substances in a mixture. The mixture is dissolved and some of the solution is put on a piece of filter paper. The substances in the solution which dissolve most easily travel farthest, and form bands of colour called a **chromatogram**.

Scientists can identify the substances in a solution by comparing their chromatograms with those of known substances. This method can be used, for example, to identify the colourings used in foods.

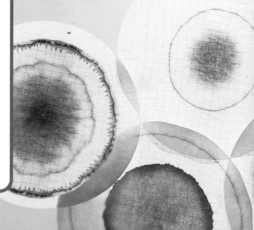

This chemist is studying paper chromatograms to identify the chemicals used in various clothes dyes.

See for yourself

You can use chromatography (see above right) to separate the different coloured chemicals that make up inks. You need a piece of filter paper or kitchen towel, a bowl of water and some felt-tip pens.

1. Put some spots of ink about 3cm from the bottom of the paper.

2. Hang the paper over a bowl of water so that the water touches the paper but not the ink spots.

3. The paper absorbs the water. As the water reaches the blobs of ink, the dyes in the inks dissolve and are carried upwards. The dyes that dissolve most easily travel farthest.

* Waterworks, 74.

EVAPORATION

Evaporation is a method of separating a soluble solid from the solvent* in which it is dissolved. The solution is heated until all the liquid turns to vapour (evaporates), leaving the solid behind.

Lemon juice, which is a solution of citric acid in water, separates by evaporation.

Water evaporates from boiling lemon juice. Eventually, only solid crystals of citric acid are left behind.

DISTILLATION

Distillation is a way of obtaining pure solvent, such as water, from a solution. First, the liquid is boiled. As it boils, the water evaporates into steam. This is cooled and condenses into pure water. The pure water is collected in another vessel. The other part of the solution is left behind.

Water boils and becomes steam.

Steam cools and becomes droplets of pure water, which collect in test tube.

Solution

Spirit burner

★

CENTRIFUGING

Centrifuging separates solid particles from a suspension*. The liquid is spun around very quickly in a machine called a **centrifuge**.

This forces the solid particles to the sides of the container and the liquid can be poured or filtered off.

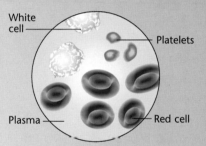

This is a centrifuge being used in a hospital to separate the components of human blood.

White cell — — Platelets

Plasma — — Red cell

Blood can be separated in a centrifuge because it is a suspension of cells and platelets in a clear fluid called plasma.

Internet links

• Scan the code for an experiment about separating mixtures.

• For links to more websites where you can see how different mixtures are separated, go to **www.usborne.com/quicklinks**

* Solvent, Suspension, 58.

THE AIR

The **air** is a mixture of gases that form a protective layer called the **atmosphere** around the Earth. Air is essential for life on Earth – for animals to breathe and for plants to make their food – and it also helps to protect the Earth from the Sun's dangerous ultraviolet rays*. The main gases in air are nitrogen and oxygen. There are also traces of the noble gases and of carbon dioxide, plus solid particles such as soot and pollen.

About 21% of air is oxygen. A molecule of oxygen (O_2) consists of two oxygen atoms bonded together.

GASES IN THE AIR

The amounts of the different gases in the air vary slightly from place to place, season to season and day to night. The pie chart below shows the average volumes of the gases as percentages.

Composition of the air

Nitrogen and oxygen are the main gases. The remaining 1% is noble gases, carbon dioxide, water vapour and pollutants such as nitrogen dioxide.

Nitrogen 78%

Oxygen 21%

Other gases 1%

This diver is carrying a cylinder of compressed air on his back, which contains oxygen, to breathe under water.

SEPARATING GASES

The gases in air can be separated by a process called **fractional distillation**. The air is cooled and compressed until the gases become liquids. This mixture is heated. Each liquid boils at a different temperature and is collected separately as it boils.

Oxygen, nitrogen and carbon dioxide are continually removed and returned to the air by living things as part of natural cycles.

OXYGEN

Oxygen (O_2) is vital for life. Animals take oxygen into their bodies and use it to break down food and release energy. Plants also use oxygen to release energy from their food.

Oxygen is essential for **combustion** (burning). If there is lots of oxygen, things will burn very quickly. If there is no oxygen, nothing can burn.

All animals need oxygen. They take in oxygen when they breathe in, and release carbon dioxide when they breathe out.

Gills are under here.

When water is gulped in by a fish, it passes over its gills. The gills take oxygen that is dissolved in the water so that it can be used in the body.

* Ultraviolet rays, 213.

CARBON DIOXIDE

Carbon dioxide (CO_2) is a compound made of the elements carbon and oxygen. The air contains about 0.03% carbon dioxide.

A carbon dioxide (CO_2) molecule has a carbon atom and two oxygen atoms.

Carbon dioxide is slightly soluble in water, dissolving to form a weak solution of carbonic acid. Carbon dioxide is part of the carbon cycle*. Animals breathe it out. Plants release it, and use it in photosynthesis*.

Most substances cannot burn in carbon dioxide. That is why it is used in fire extinguishers.

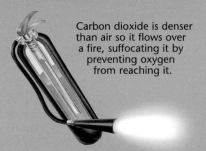

Carbon dioxide is denser than air so it flows over a fire, suffocating it by preventing oxygen from reaching it.

Fuels containing carbon, such as wood, coal and petrol, produce carbon dioxide when they burn. Because we now burn so much fuel, the amount of carbon dioxide in the air is increasing. This has led to problems of global warming (see *Greenhouse Effect*, page 65).

See for yourself

Try this test to see how carbon dioxide gas puts out fire. Light a small candle. Put five tablespoons of vinegar into a bottle. Add half a tablespoon of bicarbonate of soda. As the mixture fizzes, hold the mouth of the bottle near the candle, making sure no liquid escapes.

Small candle

The candle goes out as carbon dioxide from the reaction stops oxygen reaching the flame.

AIR QUALITY

Many polluting substances are released into the air from industrial chimneys. Many chimneys contain filters and neutralizing substances to make waste gases safer. Samples of the gases released are frequently taken and levels of pollution checked.

The Daily Air Quality Index (DAQI) indicates levels of air pollution and provides recommended actions and health advice. The index is split into four bands: low (1–3), moderate (4–6) and high (7–10).

This cooling tower releases harmless water vapour into the air. Waste gases from the tall chimney need to be filtered or neutralized before they are released, to reduce pollution.

THE NOBLE GASES

The six **noble gases** found in the air are the only elements that exist as single atoms. They are all very unreactive and they rarely form molecules.

Argon (Ar) is often used to fill the space inside household light bulbs. It is so unreactive that the glowing filament does not react with it and burn out. **Krypton (Kr)** is used inside fluorescent tubes. **Neon (Ne)** glows orange-red when electricity passes through it, so it is used in neon lights and, with sodium, in street lamps.

Xenon (Xe) is used in flash photography. **Radon (Rn)** is radioactive and occurs as a result of the radioactive decay* of radium, a metal element. **Helium (He)** is not known to form any compounds and it is thought to be completely unreactive. It is seven times less dense than air, so it is used in airships.

A helium-filled balloon carries these scientific instruments into the upper atmosphere.

Internet links

- Scan the code to discover the properties of the noble gases.

- For links to more websites about gases in the air including oxygen and the noble gases, go to **www.usborne.com/quicklinks**

---

* Carbon cycle, 52; Photosynthesis, 81; Radioactive decay, 115.

NITROGEN

Most of the air (about 78%) is **nitrogen (N₂)**. Nitrogen is continually being recycled between the air and living things. This is called the **nitrogen cycle**.

Nitrogen molecules in the air are split up by lightning, and the freed atoms bond with oxygen to form nitrogen oxide gases. Pollution from power stations also contains these gases.

The gases react with water to become nitric acid in rainwater. This forms nitrogen salts* called **nitrates** in the soil.

Fertilizers* also have a high nitrate content, so they add to the nitrates in the soil. Certain bacteria, in the roots of some plants, also add to the nitrates by taking nitrogen directly from the air and converting it into nitrates.

Plants absorb the nitrates and use them to make proteins. Animals eat plants and use the proteins in their own bodies. Ammonia and other nitrogen compounds are returned to the soil in animal waste, and when animals and plants decay after death.

The compounds are turned back into nitrates by the action of one type of bacteria in the soil. Another type takes in nitrates, breaks them down, and releases nitrogen back into the air.

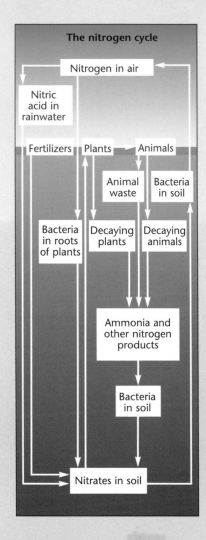

The nitrogen cycle

Nitrogen in air

Nitric acid in rainwater

Fertilizers — Plants — Animals

Animal waste | Bacteria in soil

Bacteria in roots of plants | Decaying plants | Decaying animals

Ammonia and other nitrogen products

Bacteria in soil

Nitrates in soil

USES OF NITROGEN

The main use of nitrogen is in the production of ammonia for making fertilizers*. To do this, nitrogen is combined with hydrogen. Nitrogen is also used in packaging food such as bacon and crisps, because ordinary air would cause the food to oxidize* and go bad.

Liquid nitrogen is so cold and unreactive that it is used to preserve human organs for transplants.

GASES THAT POLLUTE

Carbon monoxide (CO) is formed when fuels burn in a limited air supply, such as in a car's engine. Most fuels burn so quickly it is difficult for them to get enough oxygen, and carbon monoxide is produced instead of carbon dioxide. Carbon monoxide is a very toxic gas that stops the red cells in animals' blood from carrying oxygen.

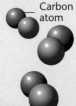

Carbon atom

Oxygen atom

Carbon monoxide molecules have only one atom of oxygen.

Sulphur dioxide (SO₂) is produced by burning fossil fuels*, especially coal. Sulphur dioxide is poisonous and causes breathing problems. It reacts with rainwater to produce acid rain (see opposite page).

Sulphur dioxide molecules

Sulphur atom

Oxygen atom

Particles of soot, dust and lead compounds produced by industry are other forms of pollution that can be breathed in and which settle on plants. Lead compounds are poisons that build up in the body and can cause brain damage in young children.

The pollution shrouding this city is made up of **smog**, a mixture of fog, smoke particles and sulphur dioxide. It can be very harmful to living things.

THE OZONE LAYER

In the upper atmosphere, oxygen atoms combine in threes, forming molecules of **ozone (O_3)**. This is an allotrope* (an alternative form) of oxygen. It is a poisonous gas, but it forms a layer in the upper atmosphere that absorbs most of the Sun's harmful ultraviolet rays* and protects the Earth.

Without the protective ozone layer around it, the Earth could not sustain life.

Carbon dioxide in the air prevents heat escaping from the Earth in the same way that glass prevents heat escaping from a greenhouse.

GLOBAL WARMING

Global warming is the rise in temperature of Earth's atmosphere. It is said that by the time a baby born today is 80 years old, the world will be between 2°C and 4°C warmer than it is now.

GREENHOUSE EFFECT

This term is used to describe the way that increasing levels of carbon dioxide in the air are causing global warming.

As the level of carbon dioxide increases, more heat is trapped in the Earth's atmosphere (see picture above). Even a slight rise in temperature causes the sea level to rise as the water expands, affecting winds and weather and causing some of the ice at the polar ice caps to melt.

ACID RAIN

Rain is always slightly acidic from dissolved carbon dioxide, but pollutants such as sulphur dioxide and nitrogen dioxide make it more acidic. Rain containing dangerous levels of acid is called **acid rain**. It corrodes metals and damages stone buildings, and also makes the water in rivers and lakes more acidic.

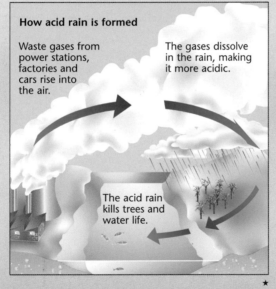

How acid rain is formed

Waste gases from power stations, factories and cars rise into the air.

The gases dissolve in the rain, making it more acidic.

The acid rain kills trees and water life.

Internet links

- Scan the code to learn amazing facts about liquid nitrogen.

- For links to more websites about global warming, the ozone layer and acid rain, go to **www.usborne.com/quicklinks**

See for yourself

Try this test to see how acids affect building materials.

Put a small lump of dried cement into a glass and pour in enough vinegar to cover it. Leave the experiment for two to three days.

Ethanoic acid in the vinegar reacts with the cement, which is gradually dissolved by the acid.

* *Allotropes, 71, Ultraviolet rays, 205.*

COMPOUNDS

There are just over a hundred different chemical elements, but they combine together in many different ways to make at least two million different compound substances. A **compound** contains atoms from two or more elements chemically bonded to form a new and different substance.

Quartz is a compound of silicon and oxygen that occurs naturally in the ground. There are several types of quartz. This type is called milky quartz.

CHEMICAL FORMULAE

Every sample of a compound contains the same proportions of the elements that make it up. These can be written as a **chemical formula**, which shows the proportions of the elements in the compound.

For example, the formula for water (hydrogen oxide) is H_2O, because every two atoms of hydrogen are bonded with one atom of oxygen.

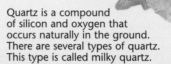

Hydrogen atom

Oxygen atom

Hydrogen atom

GROUPS OF COMPOUNDS

Compounds can be organized into separate groups, such as acids and bases, according to their chemical properties.

Compounds can also be classified according to the atoms they contain. For example, chloride compounds all contain chlorine, and oxides contain oxygen.

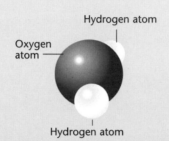

Oxygen

Carbon

Molecules of carbon dioxide gas. Carbon dioxide is an oxide (it contains oxygen). Each carbon atom is bonded to two oxygen atoms.

CHARACTERISTICS OF COMPOUNDS

Compounds have two main characteristics:
• they cannot be separated by physical means, such as filtration or evaporation, because they are chemically bonded.
• they have different properties from the elements of which they are made.

Sodium chloride (NaCl), or **common salt**, for example, is a compound made from chlorine, a poisonous gas, and sodium, a very reactive metal. When they join together, they lose their dangerous properties.

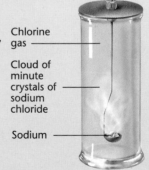

Chlorine gas

Cloud of minute crystals of sodium chloride

Sodium

When iron and sulphur are heated together, the compound formed (iron sulphide) has different properties from the original elements.

Iron and sulphur

Unlike iron, iron sulphide is not magnetic and unlike powdered sulphur, it sinks in water, as shown in the picture on the right.

After the reaction, the iron and sulphur can no longer be separated.

Water

Iron sulphide

EVERYDAY COMPOUNDS

Many common substances are compounds. Bicarbonate of soda, used in cakes, combines sodium, hydrogen, carbon and oxygen. Its chemical name is **sodium hydrogencarbonate (NaHCO3)**.

Glass contains compounds of silicon, oxygen, sodium and calcium.

Eggshells are made of a compound called calcium carbonate, which is also found in nature as limestone and chalk.

Butter is a mixture of compounds of carbon, hydrogen and oxygen.

Lemon juice contains citric acid, a compound of carbon, hydrogen and oxygen, mixed with water.

Eggs contain compounds of carbon, nitrogen, phosphorus, hydrogen, oxygen and sulphur.

See for yourself

Before a cake is cooked, its ingredients are a gooey mixture of different elements, compounds and other mixtures.

When the cake mixture is cooked, however, the heat causes chemical reactions* to occur, bonding the different substances into new compounds.

ORGANIC COMPOUNDS

Organic compounds all contain the element carbon. All living things are made of organic compounds. They are also used in the manufacture of plastics, detergents, paints and medicines. For more about organic compounds, see pages 92-95.

Many cosmetics contain organic compounds such as oils to give them their texture. Many of the compounds which give them colour, called pigments, are inorganic.

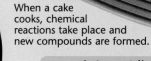

When a cake cooks, chemical reactions take place and new compounds are formed.

Internet links

• Scan the code to see sodium and chlorine react to form the compound sodium chloride – common table salt.

• For links to more websites, go to **www.usborne.com/quicklinks**

*Chemical reactions, 76-79.

67

BONDING

The beautiful, symmetrical shapes of ice crystals and the hard, glittery surfaces of a diamond result from the way their atoms are joined together, or **bonded**. The properties of a substance, and the way it reacts with other substances, depend on those bonds.

Crystals of ice

ELECTRON SHELLS

A **stable atom** does not need to lose or gain electrons* from the outer electron shell around its nucleus (see *Atomic Structure*, pages 10-11). **Unstable atoms** attempt to bond with other atoms to become stable.

Neon has a full outer shell of electrons. It is stable and is not known to bond with any other atoms.

Electron

Most atoms have several shells of electrons. The first shell can hold up to two electrons and the second and third shells up to eight, although some atoms in compounds can have up to 18 electrons in their third shells. When a shell is full, the electrons begin a new shell.

The arrangement of electrons around the nucleus is called the **electron configuration**. This can be written as numbers after an atom's name.

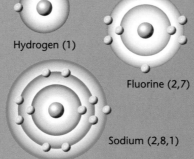

Hydrogen (1)

Fluorine (2,7)

Sodium (2,8,1)

To achieve a stable outer shell, an atom may share electrons with other atoms or give or take electrons from another atom (see *Covalent*, *Ionic* and *Metallic Bonding* on pages 69-70).

See for yourself

The atomic number of an atom shows how many protons* it has. An atom has the same number of protons as electrons. Try calculating the electron configurations of the atoms below. Remember that they can have two electrons in the first shell, and up to eight in the second shell.

Magnesium (atomic number 12)
Argon (atomic number 18)
Nitrogen (atomic number 7)
Potassium (atomic number 19)
Silicon (atomic number 14)

(Answers on page 447.)

SHELL MODELS

Shell models, like the one on the left, are useful for understanding the make-up of an atom, but atoms don't actually look like this and the positions of electrons cannot be pinpointed with accuracy.

This is a shell model of an atom. There are two electrons in the first shell and eight in the second. The third shell can have up to 18 electrons.

The gaps in the third shell show where extra electrons could go if this atom were to bond with another.

First shell

Second shell

Third shell

* Electrons, Protons, 10.

COVALENT BONDING

A **covalent bond** is formed when atoms share electrons. In most covalent elements and compounds, the atoms bond to form molecules. For example, hydrogen atoms have one electron, and a molecule of hydrogen is formed when two atoms share their electrons. This gives both atoms a full outer shell.

The atoms in carbon dioxide are also held together by covalent bonds. In this case, each of the atoms shares two electrons with its partner. This is called a **double bond**. For more about covalent bonds, see pages 92-93.

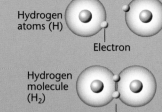

Hydrogen atoms (H)

Electron

Hydrogen molecule (H_2)

Covalent bond

Carbon dioxide molecule (CO_2)

Double covalent bonds

Oxygen atom (O)   Carbon atom (C)   Oxygen atom (O)

COVALENT SUBSTANCES

Non-metal elements, and compounds made only of non-metals, tend to form covalent bonds.

Covalent bonds between atoms in a molecule are strong, but the attraction between two molecules is not very strong. The molecules tend to break apart from each other when heated, so these substances have quite low melting and boiling points. Many are liquids or gases at room temperature.

Water, for example, is liquid at room temperature and evaporates easily. This is because the attraction between water molecules is not very strong.

Many covalent substances, such as oil, don't dissolve in water and don't conduct electricity.

Water molecules (H_2O)

The atoms in a molecule of water are held together by covalent bonds.

Oxygen atom

Hydrogen atom

Heat weakens the attraction between the water molecules in ice, and makes the ice melt.

GIANT MOLECULES

Some covalent elements, such as carbon, and many covalent compounds form giant molecules. Each atom is covalently bonded to the next atom, forming a huge, single covalent molecule that is very strong. These substances have very high melting and boiling points.

In this giant molecule of silicon dioxide, each atom of silicon (red) is bonded to three oxygen atoms behind it and one on top.

Oxygen

Silicon

Internet links

• Scan the code to watch a video clip about how snowflakes form.

• For links to more websites about bonding, go to **www.usborne.com/quicklinks**

IONIC BONDING

An atom that has gained or lost electrons becomes an **ion**. Ions have electrical charges as they do not have an equal number of positively charged protons* and negatively charged electrons.

An atom that has lost electrons becomes a **cation**. It has a positive charge. An atom that has gained electrons becomes an **anion**. An anion has a negative charge as it has more electrons than protons.

Ionic bonds are created by ions that combine in order to share electrons and therefore become electrically stable. Compounds made of a metal and a non-metal bond in this way. Electrons from the outer shell of the metal ions become part of the outer shell of the non-metal ions. The compound is an **ionic compound**.

Here, an electron from a sodium atom is shared by a chlorine atom. Effectively, sodium becomes a cation with 11 protons and only 10 electrons.

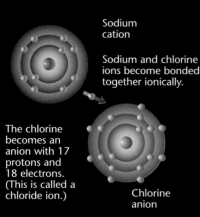

Sodium
cation

Sodium and chlorine ions become bonded together ionically.

The chlorine becomes an anion with 17 protons and 18 electrons. (This is called a chloride ion.)

Chlorine
anion

The type and strength of the charge is written after the ion's name. For example, Na^+ shows that sodium has lost one electron and Cl^- shows that chlorine has gained one electron. O^{2-} shows oxygen has gained two electrons.

LATTICES

Ions with opposite charges are attracted to each other. This creates the ionic bond that holds them together. Ionic compounds are not made of separate molecules. Instead, the ions gather in a regular arrangement called an **ionic lattice**. The bonds are strong. It takes a lot of heat to break them, so ionic compounds have high melting and boiling points.

Molecular lattices are a different type of lattice. They are made of molecules that are held together by weak forces, which tend to break apart when heated. Crystals with low melting and boiling points tend to have molecules formed in this way.

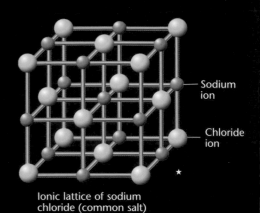

Sodium
ion

Chloride
ion

Ionic lattice of sodium chloride (common salt)

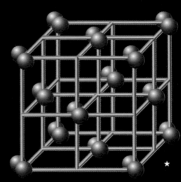

Molecular lattice of solid iodine. The molecules come apart easily.

METALLIC BONDING

Metallic bonding is the type of bonding found in metal elements. The atoms cling together to form a **metallic lattice** which is a regular arrangement of metal cations with free electrons travelling between them. Free electrons allow the atoms to cling together.

The forces between the electrons and the cations are strong. Most metals have high melting and boiling points, and because the electrons can move, metals can conduct heat and electricity. (See *Conduction*, page 113 and *Electric Current*, page 230.)

Free-moving electrons

A giant metallic lattice of zinc

Zinc
cation

* Protons, 10.

VALENCY

The number of electrons an atom needs to gain or lose to form a stable outer shell of electrons is called its **valency**, or **combining power**.

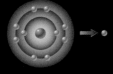

A sodium atom needs to lose one electron. Its valency is 1.

A sulphur atom needs to gain two electrons. Its valency is 2.

An atom with a stable outer shell of electrons has a valency of 0. If an atom needs to gain or lose just one electron it has a valency of 1. Valencies of 2, 3 or 4 indicate that atoms have two, three or four electrons more or less than a stable structure.

Fluorine has seven electrons in its outer shell. It needs to gain one electron to have a full shell so its valency is 1.

Fluorine

Extra electron

Phosphorus has five electrons in its outer shell and needs to gain three to form a full shell, so its valency is 3.

Phosphorus

Extra electrons

The valency of an ion is the same as the size of its charge. For instance, the oxide ion (O^{2-}) has a negative charge of 2 and its valency is 2. Some elements can form different ions so can have more than one valency. Iron, for example, forms Fe^{2+} and Fe^{3+} ions. Roman numerals after the name, for example iron(II) and iron(III), indicate the valency.

ALLOTROPES

Some elements can exist in different physical forms because their atoms can bond together in different ways. The different forms are called **allotropes**. Diamond and graphite are both allotropes of the element carbon.

In **diamond**, each carbon atom is linked to four other carbon atoms and the atoms are packed tightly together. Because of this, diamond is very strong.

Diamond molecule

In **graphite**, each carbon atom bonds to just three other carbon atoms. The atoms form layers and the forces between the layers are quite weak, making graphite flaky.

Graphite molecule

Carbon has a third allotrope, **buckminsterfullerene**, in which 60 carbon atoms are bonded together to make a hollow sphere. In 2004, scientists made a fourth allotrope, **graphene** – a sheet only one atom thick. Many other elements, such as phosphorus, tin and sulphur, also have allotropes.

A model of a buckminsterfullerene molecule. These are usually hollow, but one in a million, like this one, traps an atom of helium during its formation.

Internet links

• Scan the code to watch a video about graphene, an allotrope of carbon.

WATER

Water is one of the most common compounds on Earth. As well as the water in rivers and seas, all living things contain water and cannot survive without it. Blood and plant sap are mainly water. Water is a very good solvent – other substances dissolve easily in it.

About 70% of the surface of the Earth is covered with water.

WHAT IS WATER?

Water is a compound. Each molecule of water contains two atoms of hydrogen bonded to an atom of oxygen. The chemical formula for water is H_2O. The chemical name for water is **hydrogen oxide**. Water is formed when hydrogen burns in air.

Pure water, that is, water that does not contain any dissolved substances, boils at 100°C and freezes at 0°C. If water contains any dissolved substances, the boiling point is raised and the freezing point is lowered. This fact can be used to test whether a liquid is pure water.

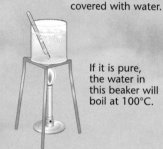

If it is pure, the water in this beaker will boil at 100°C.

Model of a molecule of water

Oxygen atom

Hydrogen atom

Ice is the solid form of water. Icebergs float because ice is less dense than water. This huge iceberg in Antarctica rises 100m above the sea.

When water evaporates*, it forms a gas called **water vapour**. When it freezes, it forms a solid called **ice**. Unlike most other substances, water expands when it freezes, so ice is less dense* than water and it floats on water. Because of this, fish and other creatures can live in the water under the ice at the Poles.

* Density, 17, 138; Evaporation, 20.

WATER AS A SOLVENT

Water is a very good **solvent**, that is, many substances dissolve easily in water to form a solution*. This is why water is rarely found in a pure state.

Many substances, like these paints, dissolve easily in water.

Water molecules have a slight electrical charge because their hydrogen atoms are grouped on one side. Because of this, ionic compounds* dissolve easily in water. Their ions* have an electrical charge and they are attracted to the charges on the water molecules.

The electrons (yellow) give this side of the molecule a slight negative charge.

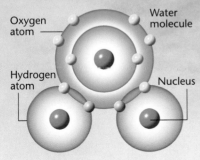

Oxygen atom

Water molecule

Hydrogen atom

Nucleus

Protons in the hydrogen nuclei give this side a slight positive charge.

A solvent, such as water, will only accept a certain amount of a substance dissolved in it. When no more will dissolve, the solution is **saturated**. The amount of solid that will dissolve usually increases if the liquid is heated.

It is easier to dissolve sugar in a hot drink than in a cold one.

FIZZY DRINKS

The fizz in fizzy drinks is made by dissolving carbon dioxide gas in water, under pressure. The amount of gas that can be dissolved in a solution decreases when the pressure of the solution is decreased. This is why carbon dioxide bubbles out when you open a fizzy drink and release (lower) the pressure.

HARD WATER

Hard water contains dissolved minerals from rocks it has flowed over. Soap does not lather well in hard water – the minerals react with the soap to form scum. There are two types of hard water, depending on which minerals it contains.

Temporary hard water is caused by a chemical reaction between limestone and rainwater. Limestone is made of calcium carbonate, which is insoluble, and rainwater is a weak solution of carbonic acid. The acid reacts with the calcium carbonate to form calcium hydrogencarbonate which then dissolves in the water, making it hard.

Cutaway view of kettle

When temporary hard water boils in a kettle, some of the minerals are left behind and can be seen as a chalky deposit.

Chalky deposit

Permanent hard water contains calcium and magnesium compounds from rocks such as gypsum. These cannot be removed by boiling.

Water contains dissolved oxygen. This is why plants and animals can live in it.

SOFTENING WATER

The minerals that make water hard can be removed by adding washing soda, or by ion exchange.

Ion exchange tank

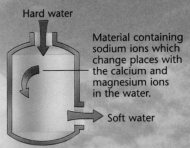

Hard water

Material containing sodium ions which change places with the calcium and magnesium ions in the water.

Soft water

In an **ion exchange tank**, hard water containing calcium and magnesium compounds is passed through a material such as zeolite (sodium aluminium silicate). The calcium and magnesium ions are swapped for sodium ions which do not make the water hard.

Washing soda is sodium carbonate. When added to hard water, it reacts with the calcium and magnesium compounds and changes them into insoluble compounds that do not make scum.

Internet links

• Scan the code for a video clip about why ice floats in water.

---

* Ionic compounds, Ions, 70; Solution, 58.

THE WATER CYCLE

All the Earth's water is continually being recycled between the Earth, the atmosphere and living things. This is called the **water cycle**.

The water in rivers, lakes and seas is continually evaporating* and becoming tiny droplets of water vapour in the air. The droplets form clouds and fall again as rain, hail or snow.

CLEANING WATER

Water that has flowed over land and through rocks contains impurities. These impurities can be removed at a **waterworks**. The water is stored in reservoirs to allow solid matter to settle and then, in the waterworks, the water is filtered to remove smaller particles of mud and solids.

A waterworks

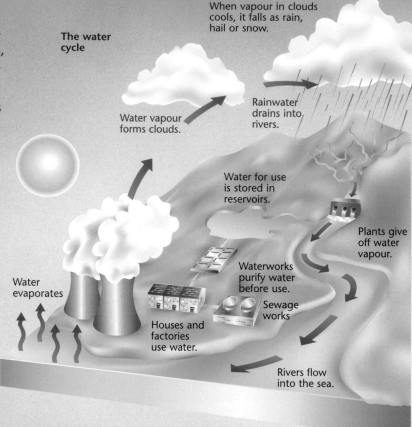

The water cycle

When vapour in clouds cools, it falls as rain, hail or snow.

Water vapour forms clouds.

Rainwater drains into rivers.

Water for use is stored in reservoirs.

Plants give off water vapour.

Water evaporates

Waterworks purify water before use.

Sewage works

Houses and factories use water.

Rivers flow into the sea.

Filter bed

Water trickles through beds of clean gravel and sand, or carbon, to remove particles of mud and other solids. After filtering, the water is treated with chlorine to kill harmful bacteria and then pumped to storage tanks and piped to houses and factories.

SEWAGE TREATMENT

Sewage (waste water) should be cleaned before it is pumped into the sea. In a **sewage works**, the water is filtered to remove rubbish, and then left in **sedimentation tanks** for the solid particles to settle. Bacteria decompose any remaining organic matter and break it down into harmless substances.

Here you can see part of the water cycle in action. Water vapour is rising from a rainforest and forming clouds.

*Evaporation, 20.

PURIFYING WATER

Water is a good solvent*, so it usually contains dissolved substances. Pure water can be obtained by distillation*, but a more efficient method is by **deionization**. Ions are atoms or molecules that have lost or gained an electron and so have a positive or negative electrical charge (see also page 70).

Deionization

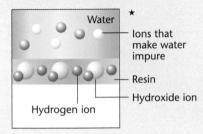

Ion exchange resin has hydrogen ions (H+) and hydroxide ions (OH-) clinging to it. The water contains different ions which make it impure. The water is passed through the ion exchange resin.

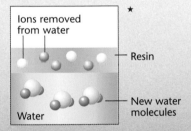

As the water goes through the resin, the ions in the water are more strongly attracted to the resin than to the water. The ions from the resin are displaced. They pass into the water, and combine to create extra molecules of water (H_2O).

WATER POLLUTION

Water pollution is caused by untreated water from houses and factories flowing into rivers and the sea. 90% of dirty wastewater in developing countries flows straight into rivers, lakes and the sea. This untreated water pollutes drinking water and is very harmful to people's health.

When water contains a lot of waste, bacteria that break down organic matter become very numerous and use up most of the oxygen. The water becomes lifeless, except for other, harmful bacteria that can survive in water without oxygen.

Oxygen in water can also be used up by too much plant growth caused when fertilizers from farmland, and detergents that contain phosphates, drain into rivers. The oxygen in the water is used up by the plants and by bacteria that feed on the plants when they die.

POISONOUS POLLUTION

Pollution is also caused by litter, pesticides and by poisonous substances such as lead and mercury. Poisonous substances build up in the bodies of fish and may be passed on to other animals and to people. Pesticides kill tiny creatures and larger animals and disturb the balance between living things.

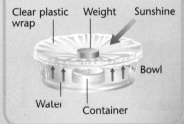

Untreated factory waste like this can harm the environment.

See for yourself

You can make a miniature water cycle by copying the set-up below. Leave the bowl in a sunny window, with some water in it. The heat evaporates the water, which rises and then condenses on the cool plastic, to fall into the container.

Internet links

• Scan the code to watch a video about sewage treatment.

• For links to more websites where you can explore the water cycle and find out about water purificaton and pollution, go to **www.usborne.com/quicklinks**

CHEMICAL REACTIONS

Chemical reactions are happening around us all the time – in our digestive system when we eat, in a baking cake or in a car's engine when it's being driven. During a chemical reaction, the atoms in the substances, called the **reactants**, are rearranged to form new substances, called the **products**.

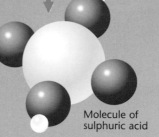
Striking a match activates the chemical reaction that takes place when the match burns.

WHAT HAPPENS IN A REACTION

During a chemical reaction, the bonds between the atoms of substances are broken. The atoms rearrange themselves and form bonds with new partners. The diagrams on the right show what happens when water and sulphur trioxide react together to form sulphuric acid.

During a chemical reaction energy is always either taken in or given out. Breaking bonds requires energy and creating new bonds releases energy. This is usually heat energy, although some reactions give off or take in light. A reaction that produces heat is called an **exothermic reaction**. If heat is taken in, it is an **endothermic reaction**. For more about these, see page 78.

Most chemical reactions also need a certain amount of energy, usually in the form of heat, to start them off. This makes the molecules in the substances move around so they collide and can react together. The minimum amount of energy needed to start off a reaction is called the **activation energy**.

Each molecule of water (H_2O) is made of two atoms of hydrogen and one atom of oxygen. Sulphur trioxide (SO_3) is made of three atoms of oxygen bonded to one atom of sulphur.

Molecule of sulphur trioxide

Water molecule

The atoms in the substances separate and combine with each other to form a molecule of sulphuric acid (H_2SO_4).

Molecule of sulphuric acid

These unusual formations at Mono Lake in California, USA, are called tufa towers. They are formed when a chemical reaction takes place between carbonates in the lake water and calcium from spring water (the reactants). The product is calcium carbonate, or limestone.

LAW OF CONSERVATION OF MASS

Matter cannot be created or destroyed during a chemical reaction. This is the **law of conservation of mass**. (Mass is the amount of matter a substance contains.)

During a reaction between iron and sulphur, the atoms in the substances rearrange themselves.

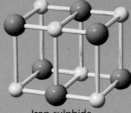

After the reaction there is the same number of atoms and there is therefore the same amount of matter.

Iron sulphide

CHEMICAL EQUATIONS

Chemical reactions can be written as **equations** using the chemical formulae of the substances. In an equation, the reactants are written on the left and the products are written on the right. They are separated by an arrow. Because of the law of conservation of mass, both sides of an equation balance: the reactants and the products contain the same number of atoms.

This equation shows how hydrogen and oxygen react to form water. Both sides of the equation have the same number of atoms.

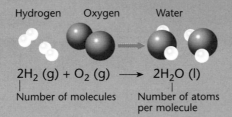

Hydrogen   Oxygen   Water

$$2H_2\,(g) + O_2\,(g) \longrightarrow 2H_2O\,(l)$$

Number of molecules

Number of atoms per molecule

Equations may also show the physical states of the substances involved in the reaction (**g** for gas, **l** for liquid, **s** for solid and **aq** for aqueous, that is, dissolved in water). If a catalyst* is used, it is shown above the arrow.

MOLES

Chemists measure chemical substances in **moles**. One mole is 602,300 billion, billion molecules or atoms. This can be written as 6.023×10^{23} and is called the **Avogadro number**. It is the number of atoms found in a mass of 12g of carbon-12. A mole of a different element will have a different mass, but the same number of particles. A mole of magnesium has a mass of 24g because magnesium atoms weigh twice as much as carbon atoms.

A mole of magnesium has a mass of 24g.

A mole of carbon has a mass of 12g.

* Catalysts, 79; Hydration, 91.

TYPES OF REACTION

All chemical reactions either give off or take in energy. In **endothermic reactions**, energy is absorbed in the form of heat. For instance, when sherbet reacts with moisture on your tongue, heat is taken from your tongue, making it feel cool.

Any reactions that give off heat energy are **exothermic reactions**. (Combustion, also called burning, is one example of an exothermic reaction.) Your body feels warm because of exothermic reactions which are happening inside you all the time.

Some reactions take in or give off energy in the form of light rather than heat. These are called **photochemical reactions**. Plants take in light energy from sunlight. This enables them to make food, as part of a process called photosynthesis*.

These plants are taking energy from sunlight and making food in a photochemical reaction.

Synthesis reactions (also called **combination reactions**) involve substances combining to make a single new substance. For example, when magnesium is heated, it combines with oxygen in the air to produce a white ash called magnesium oxide.

Neutralization reactions take place when one substance reacts with another and each cancels out the other's properties. This is what happens when acids and alkalis are mixed. (See *Bases and Alkalis*, page 85.)

Reactions where a single substance breaks down into simpler substances are called **decomposition reactions**. When food rots, many of these reactions take place.

When heat is needed to break down a compound, the reaction is called a **thermal decomposition reaction**. For example, when limestone (calcium carbonate) is heated, it breaks down to form quicklime (calcium oxide) and carbon dioxide.

Heating limestone causes it to break down into different substances.

Reversible reactions are reactions in which the products, given the right conditions, react together to form the original reactants once again. Reactions of this type can be written as an equation. A symbol indicates that the reaction is reversible:

$$2NO_2 \rightleftharpoons 2NO + O_2$$

Nitrogen dioxide (NO_2) splits to produce nitrogen monoxide (NO) and oxygen (O_2). As they cool, they recombine to give nitrogen dioxide.

The first part of the reaction is called the **forward reaction**. The second part is called the **backward reaction**.

Displacement reactions occur when a more reactive substance displaces a less reactive one. For example, when an iron nail is placed in copper(II) sulphate solution, the iron "pulls" the copper out of the solution and takes its place in the solution. The copper collects around the nail. The more reactive element (iron) displaces the less reactive copper.

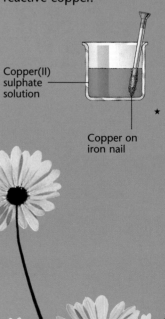

Copper(II) sulphate solution

★

Copper on iron nail

* Photosynthesis, 81

RATES OF REACTION

Some chemical reactions, such as rusting, take place slowly over a long period of time. Others, such as the chemical reaction that takes place when gunpowder explodes, are almost instantaneous.

The rate of a reaction is affected by the **reactivity** of the substances. Very reactive elements react more quickly than less reactive elements.

During a chemical reaction, the atoms of the different substances must come into contact with each other in order to form new bonds. This happens more easily in gases and liquids, in which molecules are free to move around, so they tend to be more reactive than solid substances.

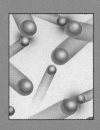

Heating substances increases the rate of a reaction. The heat makes more of the particles move fast enough to collide and react.

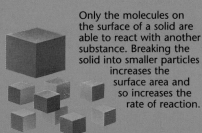

Only the molecules on the surface of a solid are able to react with another substance. Breaking the solid into smaller particles increases the surface area and so increases the rate of reaction.

When rainwater hits limestone, a chemical reaction occurs. The rainwater slowly dissolves the limestone to form carbonic acid. This eats away the limestone further.

CATALYSTS

Catalysts are substances that can change the rate of a chemical reaction, but are themselves left unchanged. Some catalysts speed up reactions while others, called **inhibitors**, slow them down.

Catalysts work by lowering the activation energy* of a reaction. They make it easier for the reaction to take place.

Metals are often used as catalysts. For example, **catalytic converters**, which remove toxic gases from car exhaust fumes, use metal catalysts, as shown below.

How a catalytic converter works

Exhaust fumes containing carbon monoxide and hydrocarbons.

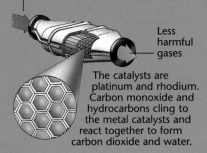

Less harmful gases

The catalysts are platinum and rhodium. Carbon monoxide and hydrocarbons cling to the metal catalysts and react together to form carbon dioxide and water.

See for yourself

Here you can see how to make use of an exothermic reaction to reveal something written in invisible ink.

Dip a fine paintbrush in lemon juice and write a message on a piece of paper. Leave it to dry until it is invisible. To reveal the message, place the paper face down on a shelf in the oven and leave it there for ten minutes at 175°C.

The heat of the oven causes the lemon juice to burn – an exothermic reaction which makes the writing go brown. The heat is not enough, though, to burn the paper.

ENZYMES

Many chemical reactions that take place in living things are speeded up by catalysts called **enzymes**.

Enzymes, and many other catalysts, are **action specific**, that is, each speeds up only one type of reaction. Many different enzymes in the digestive systems of animals, including humans, help speed up the chemical reactions that break complex foods into simpler substances.

The picture shows the three main areas of your digestive system where enzymes work on your food.

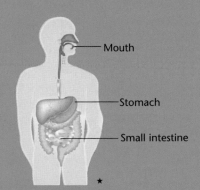

Mouth

Stomach

Small intestine

★

Internet links

• Scan the code to watch dramatic chemical reactions.

• For links to more websites where you can find quizzes and animations about different types of reactions, go to **www.usborne.com/quicklinks**

* Activation energy, 76.

OXIDATION AND REDUCTION

Oxidation and reduction are terms which describe two types of chemical reaction. Unless specific conditions prevent it, these two reactions always occur together, that are described as **redox reactions**. In a redox reaction, when one substance is oxidized, the other is reduced. For example, when wood burns, it is oxidized, while the air around it is reduced.

OXIDATION

The term **oxidation** describes reactions in which a substance combines with oxygen. This comes from another substance, called the **oxidizing agent** (which itself is reduced). For example, when iron is exposed to damp air, it slowly combines with oxygen in the air, forming hydrated iron oxide (rust).

Rusting (the corrosion of iron) is an oxidation reaction.

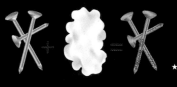

| Iron | Damp air | Rust |

Oxidation also describes reactions in which a substance loses hydrogen or electrons to another substance (the oxidizing agent). For example, when magnesium and chlorine combine to form magnesium chloride, magnesium loses two electrons (see Ionic Bonding, page 70). It is oxidized.

The magnesium atom loses two electrons to the chlorine atoms, and is oxidized.

Magnesium atom

Two chlorine atoms

INTERNAL RESPIRATION

Internal respiration, the process by which animals and plants break down glucose to release energy, is an oxidation reaction. In fact, it is a slow form of combustion (see below). This is the equation for internal respiration:

$$C_6H_{12}O_6 + 6O_2 \longrightarrow 6CO_2 + 6H_2O$$

Glucose + Oxygen ⟶ Carbon dioxide + Water

COMBUSTION

Combustion (burning) is an oxidation reaction that gives off energy in the form of heat. When a substance burns, it combines with oxygen to form an oxide. Most fuels, for example, wood, gas and petrol, contain hydrogen and carbon. Both these substances oxidize to produce water and carbon dioxide when they burn.

We now burn so much fuel for energy that the level of carbon dioxide in the air is increasing. Scientists think that the amount of combustion may be causing changes in the weather (see *Greenhouse Effect*, page 65).

The colours in fireworks come from the combustion of different elements. For example, strontium burns to give red sparks, copper gives blue and magnesium brilliant white.

Petrol burning inside a motorbike's engine is an example of combustion.

REDUCTION

During **reduction**, a substance loses oxygen to, or gains hydrogen or electrons from, another substance (the **reducing agent**, which is oxidized). For example, when copper oxide reacts with carbon, the copper oxide loses oxygen to the carbon, as shown below.

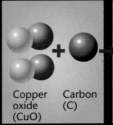

| Copper oxide (CuO) | Carbon (C) | Copper (Cu) | Carbon dioxide (CO_2) |

In this reaction, the copper oxide is reduced to pure copper by carbon, and the carbon is oxidized to form carbon dioxide.

$$2CuO + C \rightarrow CO_2 + 2Cu$$

Copper oxide + Carbon $\longrightarrow$ Carbon dioxide + Copper

IRON SMELTING

The iron production process, called **smelting**, produces pure iron from iron ore. It is an example of a useful redox reaction.

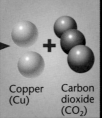

Iron ore

Inside a blast furnace, carbon is used to reduce iron ore (iron oxide) to pure iron. The carbon pulls oxygen away from (reduces) the ore. The carbon itself oxidizes to become carbon dioxide.

See for yourself

When a chunk of apple is left for a few minutes, it begins to turn brown. This is because chemicals on the apple's flesh take part in an oxidation reaction, using oxygen from the surrounding air. If you cover the apple with plastic food wrap, you stop the air from reacting with the apple, so it doesn't go brown.

PHOTOSYNTHESIS

Photosynthesis, the process by which plants make their food, is a reduction reaction. In photosynthesis, plants build glucose ($C_6H_{12}O_6$) from carbon dioxide and water, using energy from sunlight. Photosynthesis is the opposite of internal respiration (see opposite page). This is the equation for photosynthesis:

$$6CO_2 + 6H_2O \longrightarrow C_6H_{12}O_6 + 6O_2$$

Carbon dioxide + Water $\longrightarrow$ Glucose + Oxygen

This tulip plant feeds itself with the glucose it makes during photosynthesis.

Plants produce oxygen when they are photosynthesizing. They use some of it for internal respiration and the rest goes back into the air.

Internet links

• Scan the code to discover the chemistry behind fireworks.

• For links to more websites about combustion, redox reactions and fireworks, go to **www.usborne.com/quicklinks**

ELECTROLYSIS

Electrolysis is a method of separating the elements in a compound by passing an electric current through the compound when it is molten or in a solution. The process is used to separate very reactive metals from their ores and to purify metals. It is also used to coat objects with a thin layer of metal in a process called electroplating.

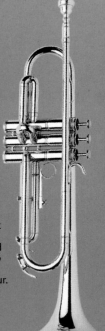

The nib of this pen has been plated with a thin layer of gold by electrolysis.

HOW ELECTROLYSIS WORKS

Only ionic compounds* can conduct electricity during electrolysis. This is because the particles that make up an ionic compound, called ions, have an electrical charge. Some of the particles (called **anions**) are negatively charged. Others (called **cations**) are positively charged.

During electrolysis, the ionic compound is called the **electrolyte**. An electric current is carried to it by two **electrodes**. One electrode (the **anode**) carries a positive charge. The other (the **cathode**) carries a negative charge.

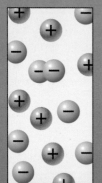
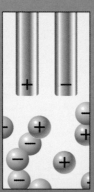
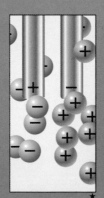

Copper(II) chloride solution can be used as an electrolyte. It is made up of positively charged copper cations and negatively charged chloride anions.

To carry the current, two electrodes, attached to an electric source, are placed in the compound. Nothing happens until the electric current flows.

As the electric current flows, the cations flow to the negative electrode where they gain electrons. The anions rush to the positive electrode and lose electrons.

ELECTROPLATING

Electroplating uses electrolysis to cover objects with a thin layer of metal. The object that is to be plated is used as a cathode and during electrolysis it becomes coated with metal from the electrolyte.

In industry, electroplating is used to protect cheap but reactive metals with a layer of less reactive metal. For example, steel is plated with tin or chromium to stop it rusting.

These steel food cans have been plated with a very fine layer of tin to prevent rust.

This trumpet has been electroplated with brass to give a rich golden colour.

* Ionic compounds, 70.

ELECTROREFINING

Electrorefining purifies metals by electrolysis. To purify copper, impure copper is used as an anode and pure copper as a cathode. A solution of copper(II) sulphate is used as an electrolyte.

Copper ions in the solution are attracted to the cathode. They are replaced in the solution by copper ions which split off from the anode, leaving the impurities behind.

Electrorefining copper

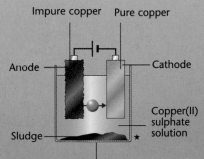

The anode disintegrates as the copper ions split off. Its impurities fall off, forming a sludge.

ANODIZING

Electrolysis can be used to coat some metals, such as aluminium, with a thin layer of their oxide (the compound it forms when it reacts with oxygen). This is called **anodizing**. The oxide forms a protective layer that prevents corrosion of the metal.

When anodizing aluminium, the object is used as the anode and placed in a solution of sulphuric acid, which is the electrolyte.

Oxide ions from the electrolyte collect at the anode and they react with the aluminium to form a layer of aluminium oxide.

METAL EXTRACTION

Very reactive metals, such as aluminium, are extracted from impure forms by electrolysis.

Aluminium is mined as **bauxite**, which is mainly aluminium oxide. For electrolysis, aluminium oxide is dissolved in cryolite to allow the ions to move. A graphite-lined tank forms the cathode. Aluminium ions are attracted to the cathode and become atoms of molten aluminium.

Extracting aluminium

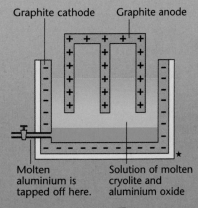

Molten aluminium is tapped off here.

Solution of molten cryolite and aluminium oxide

Anodized aluminium water flasks

The handlebars on this mountain bike are made of anodized aluminium that has been dyed blue.

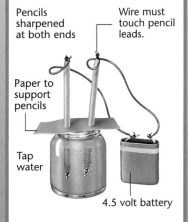

ACIDS AND BASES

The word acid comes from the Latin word *acer*, which means "sour". Acids contained in some foods make the food taste sour. For example, citrus fruits such as lemons, limes, oranges and grapefruits contain citric acid and ascorbic acid. The chemical opposite of an acid is a base. (A substance that is neither an acid nor a base is neutral.)

A bee's sting contains an acid. It can be neutralized with soap, which is an alkali.

ACIDS

Acids are compounds that contain hydrogen and which dissolve in water to produce hydrogen ions (H^+). Ions are particles that have an electrical charge. The hydrogen ions give acids their special properties, but they only exist in solution, so an acid only displays its properties when it is dissolved.

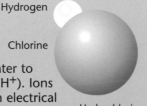

Hydrogen

Chlorine

Hydrochloric acid (HCl) is made from hydrogen and chlorine.

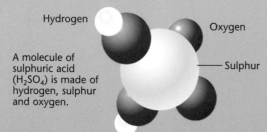

Hydrogen

Oxygen

Sulphur

A molecule of sulphuric acid (H_2SO_4) is made of hydrogen, sulphur and oxygen.

A **strong acid** is one in which most of the molecules separate to form a large number of hydrogen ions when it is in solution. Hydrochloric, sulphuric and nitric acid are all strong acids.

Strong acids are very **corrosive**. This means that they will burn your skin or the surface of an object.

The containers of strong acids are marked with the international warning symbols shown below, which mean corrosive (left) and harmful (right).

Corrosive

Harmful

ORGANIC ACIDS

Acids that are produced by living things, such as citric acid and ethanoic acid, are called **organic acids**. These are examples of **weak acids** (they contain few hydrogen ions). There is more about organic acids on page 94.

The colourful markings on the skin of sea slugs contain acids that taste horrible. This discourages predators from eating them.

Vinegar, which can be made from grapes, contains a weak acid called ethanoic acid.

Ants that can sting contain an acid called methanoic (or formic) acid.

Tomatoes contain an organic acid called salicylic acid.

HOW ACIDS BEHAVE

Acids react in certain ways with other substances. For example, they react with most metals to form salts and hydrogen gas. They also react with carbonates to give a salt, carbon dioxide gas and water.

BASES AND ALKALIS

A **base** is the chemical opposite of an acid. A base that can dissolve in water is called an **alkali**. When a base is mixed with an acid, it **neutralizes** (cancels out) the properties of the acid and the reaction produces a salt plus water.

Toothpaste is a base that neutralizes the acids made in your mouth.

Indigestion tablets contain alkalis that neutralize the acids produced by the stomach.

When this wasp stings, it injects an alkali into its victim. If you get stung, you can neutralize the sting with vinegar (an acid).

Bases neutralize acids because they contain negative ions, which cancel out the positive hydrogen ions. The oxide ion (O^{2-}) and the hydroxide ion (OH^-) are both negative, so metal oxides, such as magnesium oxide, and metal hydroxides, such as sodium hydroxide (caustic soda), are bases.

Sodium ion (positive charge)

Hydroxide ion (negative charge) cancels out sodium's positive charge, producing a base.

Magnesium ion (positive charge)

Hydroxide ions (negative charge) cancel out magnesium's positive charge, producing a base.

USING BASES

Many bases and alkalis can be very dangerous as they are **caustic** (dissolve the flesh). Liquid floor cleaners contain alkalis, such as ammonium hydroxide, that dissolve dirt. Sodium hydroxide is used in paper-making to dissolve the resin in wood, leaving the natural fibres of cellulose that are used to make paper.

Sodium hydroxide is also used to make oven cleaners, and mixed with potassium hydroxide to make soap.

See for yourself

To see how an acid and a base react together, pour some vinegar into a glass and add some bicarbonate of soda.

Bicarbonate of soda is a base. It reacts with ethanoic acid in the vinegar to produce sodium ethanoate (a salt), water and carbon dioxide.

As the substances mix, carbon dioxide bubbles out.

Internet links

• Scan the code to watch a video about acids and bases.

• For links to more websites where you can experiment with acids and bases, go to www.usborne.com/quicklinks

pH NUMBERS

The strength of an acid or base can be expressed as a **pH number**. pH stands for "power of hydrogen" and is a measure of the concentration of hydrogen ions in a solution. pH values generally range between 0 and 14. The lower the pH number, the greater the concentration of hydrogen ions. A solution with a pH value of less than 7 is an acid. Substances with a pH value of 7 are neutral and those with pH values higher than 7 are bases or alkalis.

Orange juice has a pH value of 4, so it is a weak acid.

INDICATORS

An **indicator** can show whether something is an acid or an alkali. An indicator is a substance that changes colour when it is placed in an acid or an alkali. One indicator, called **litmus**, turns red in an acid and blue in an alkali.

This wasp's sting is a weak alkali with a pH of 9.

Blue litmus paper

Red litmus paper

Alkali

Acid

Acids turn blue litmus paper red.
Alkalis turn red litmus paper blue.

Litmus is an extract from plant-like organisms called lichens. Some plants, for example hydrangeas and red cabbage, are also natural indicators. Another indicator, called **universal indicator**, is a mixture of several dyes that change colour according to the pH scale, as shown in the picture below.

Paper strips containing universal indicator change colour when they touch an acid or alkali. The numbers beside each colour show the pH value.

1
2
3
4
5
6
7
8
9
10
11
12
13
14

ACIDS IN THE SOIL

The acidity of the soil depends on the type of rocks from which it is formed and the plants that grow in it. In chalk or limestone areas, the soil is usually alkaline, but in moorlands, sandstone and forested areas, it is more acidic. Acid rain* also adds to the acidity of the soil. Neutral or slightly acid soils with pH values of 6.5 to 7 are the best for farming.

In areas where the soil is too acidic, it can be improved by adding limestone (calcium carbonate) or slaked lime (calcium hydroxide). These are bases that neutralize the acidity.

Some plants, such as azaleas and rhododendrons, grow well in acid soil. Plants such as hydrangeas have blue flowers in acid soils and pink ones in alkaline soils.

Pure water is neutral. It has a pH of 7.

Sodium hydroxide, used in household cleaners, is a strong alkali with a pH of 13.

Hydrangeas are natural indicators, producing different coloured flowers in acid and alkaline soils.

When leaves die and decompose, they form an acid called humic acid, which adds to the acidity of the soil.

* Acid rain, 65.

SULPHURIC ACID

Sulphuric acid (H_2SO_4) is a chemical used in many different industries. Its main use is in the production of superphosphates and ammonium sulphate for fertilizers. Sulphuric acid is also used in car batteries, and in the manufacture of some synthetic fibres (such as rayon), dyes, plastics, drugs, explosives and detergents.

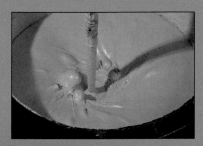

Sulphuric acid is used in the production of titanium oxide, a pigment used to make coloured paint such as this.

Sulphuric acid is a type of **mineral acid**. Mineral acids are made from elements (in this case, sulphur) found as minerals in the Earth's crust.

Here you can see yellow crystals of sulphur produced by a volcano. Sulphur can be collected from volcanic areas and used in the manufacture of sulphuric acid.

Concentrated sulphuric acid is very reactive and highly corrosive. It produces lots of heat when dissolved in water and must always be added to the water, not the other way around. That way, the acid is rapidly diluted and the heat is absorbed by the water.

Concentrated sulphuric acid is a powerful oxidizing agent (it gives oxygen to other substances during oxidation*). It is also a **dehydrating agent** (it removes water that is chemically combined in another substance).

Sugar

Sulphuric acid

Carbon   Water

When sugar is warmed with concentrated sulphuric acid, the acid removes water from the sugar, leaving a foamy mass of black carbon and water.

See for yourself

You can do your own tests to see whether something is acidic or alkaline.

First, make an indicator from red cabbage. Chop three large cabbage leaves and boil them in half a litre of water for ten minutes. Cool, strain and pour a little of this indicator into three jars. Add half a teaspoon of bicarbonate of soda to one jar, some vinegar to the second jar and some rainwater to the third jar.

Bicarbonate, an alkali, turns the indicator blue-green.

Vinegar, an acid, turns the indicator pink.

Compare the colour of the rainwater jar to the other two jars.

If the rainwater is acidic, the cabbage water will turn pink when it is added.

Internet links

• Scan the code to watch an experiment about indicators.

• For links to more websites where you can test substances and learn about the pH scale, go to **www.usborne.com/quicklinks**

* Oxidation, 80.

SALTS

In chemical terms, compounds made of a metal and a non-metal bonded together are **salts**. Many salts occur naturally in the Earth's crust and under the right conditions they form beautiful crystals. Salts have many different uses. For example, anhydrous calcium sulphate, also called **plaster of Paris**, is a salt used in decorative mouldings, model-making and to make protective casts for broken limbs.

Here, plaster of Paris, a salt that sets hard when it is mixed with water, is being used to make a cast of an animal track.

WHAT IS A SALT?

Salts are ionic compounds*, that is, they are made up of ions (particles with an electric charge). Most salts form into regular crystal structures.

Salts are made when the hydrogen ions in an acid are replaced by a metal. For example, when hydrochloric acid and sodium hydroxide (an alkali) react together, sodium replaces the acid's hydrogen ions, creating sodium chloride (a salt) and water. (See picture, above right.)

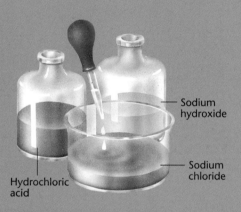

Sodium hydroxide

Sodium chloride

Hydrochloric acid

In the picture above, each ingredient of the experiment has had litmus added to it to show whether it is an acid or a base.

SALT FAMILIES

There are several families of salts made with different acids. **Sulphates** are made with sulphuric acid, **chlorides** are made with hydrochloric acid, **nitrates** are made with nitric acid and **carbonates** with carbonic acid.

Bath salts and washing soda are sodium carbonate. They react with magnesium and calcium salts in hard water* to form insoluble particles of calcium carbonate.

Soluble salts are those, such as washing soda, that dissolve in water to form a solution. **Insoluble salts** are ones that do not dissolve in water. Limestone and chalk are made of calcium carbonate, which is an insoluble salt.

Vermilion red

Malachite green

Cadmium yellow

The salts vermilion, cadmium sulphide and malachite are used to make artists' paints.

* Hard water, 73; Ionic compounds, 70.

SODIUM CHLORIDE

Sodium chloride (NaCl) is the chemical name for common salt. It is a soluble salt. A concentrated solution of sodium chloride in water is called **brine**.

Sodium chloride can be extracted from sea water by evaporation, and it is also found in solid form as **rock salt**, or **halite**. It is used to flavour and preserve food and is essential to animal life.

Sodium chloride is an important raw material and it is used in the manufacture of hydrochloric acid, chlorine, sodium hydroxide (caustic soda) and sodium carbonate (washing soda). It is sprinkled on roads in winter because it lowers the freezing point of water and stops ice from forming.

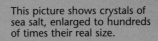

This picture shows crystals of sea salt, enlarged to hundreds of times their real size.

MAKING SALTS

There are several ways to make salts in the laboratory. Soluble salts can be made by reacting an acid and a metal, or metal oxide (a base).

Copper(II) sulphate is made by adding copper oxide to dilute sulphuric acid.

Copper oxide

The mixture is then filtered. The filtrate is a solution of copper(II) sulphate. Unused copper oxide is left in the filter paper.

Filtrate

The solution is heated to remove water, then left to form crystals of copper(II) sulphate.

★

Insoluble salts are made from two soluble salts that react together to form a **precipitate** (insoluble solid particles) of salt in a solution. The solution is then filtered to remove the precipitate. Salts can also be made by combining two elements. For example, iron sulphide is made by heating iron with sulphur (see page 66).

FERTILIZERS

Fertilizers are nutrients that help plants to grow. Many fertilizers contain salts, such as nitrates, phosphates and potash, that are soluble in water and can be absorbed by plants' roots. Nitrates contain nitrogen, phosphates contain phosphorus, and potash contains potassium salts. All of these are needed for healthy plant growth.

The smaller plant shown here was grown in poor soil. The larger one was grown in fertilized soil.

See for yourself

Crystals of common salt contain water (see Hydration, page 91), but you can turn them powdery just by leaving them on a plate for a few days.

When you leave the crystals in the air the water escapes, leaving a dry powder. Similarly, if you leave the lid off a bottle of bath crystals, these also lose their shape and turn powdery.

Internet links

• Scan the code to find out how other useful chemicals can be made from salt.

• For links to more websites, go to **www.usborne.com/quicklinks**

CRYSTALS

When allowed to form slowly, salts and many other substances form crystals. A **crystal** is a solid that has a definite geometrical shape with straight edges and flat surfaces. Most solids, even metals, are made up of crystals but they are so small that you cannot see them. Some of the minerals in the Earth's crust form beautiful crystals, such as diamonds and emeralds.

Pyrite (also called iron pyrites or fools' gold) is a common mineral made of iron and sulphur. Its crystals are often cubic in shape.

HOW CRYSTALS FORM

Some substances form crystals as they cool and solidify. Others crystallize when the water in which they were dissolved evaporates. The shape of the crystals depends on the regular arrangement and bonding of the particles in the substance. Different substances form different shaped crystals. The main crystal shapes are shown in the picture below.

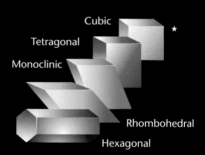

Cubic
Tetragonal
Monoclinic ★
Rhombohedral
Hexagonal

Calcite crystals can be ground up to make cement.

SPLITTING CRYSTALS

The boundaries between the particles in a crystal are called **cleavage planes**. Crystals split along these planes, leaving the flat surfaces of the crystal exposed. If a crystal is not split along a cleavage plane, it will shatter.

Natural emerald embedded in limestone

The emerald set in this ring has been split along its cleavage planes to make a beautiful gem.

Amethyst crystals form from the mineral quartz.

LIQUID CRYSTALS

Liquid crystals behave like both solid crystals and liquids. Their molecules* line up (like solid crystals) but, unlike solid crystals, the molecules line up in only one dimension, not three. In other dimensions they can move freely, as they would in a liquid.

When light shines through liquid crystals, it follows the direction of their molecules. If an electric current is passed through the crystals, the molecules twist around, blocking the light. This effect is used to create images on **liquid crystal displays (LCDs)**, as on digital watches, or flat TV or computer screens.

In a liquid crystal, the molecules are able to move around, but only in a single dimension.

Crystals of apatite. This substance is also found in teeth.

HYDRATION

Hydration occurs when a substance combines with water. The substance is said to be **hydrated**. Many salts combine and chemically bond with water to form crystals. The water is then known as **water of crystallization**.

Hydrated copper(II) sulphate crystals ($CuSO_4.5H_2O$) form when copper(II) sulphate ($CuSO_4$) bonds with water (H_2O).

In a crystal, the water is chemically bonded with the atoms of the substance, unlike in a solution where the atoms of the substance are mixed but not bonded with the molecules of water. Water can be made to separate from a hydrated solid by heating the solid. This is called **dehydration**.

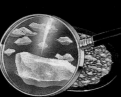

If you heat washing soda ($Na_2CO_3.10H_2O$) crystals, the water of crystallization separates off, and a solution of washing soda is formed.

Dehydration can also be carried out using a **dehydrating agent**, such as sulphuric acid.

The dry solid which results from dehydration is said to be **anhydrous**.

White, anhydrous copper(II) sulphate powder goes blue when water is added. It can be used to test for the presence of water.

This crystal is halite. It was formed by the evaporation of sea water thousands of years ago.

See for yourself

You can grow a crystal using **alum** (a sulphate of potassium and aluminium). It will take about three weeks to grow. You can buy alum from a pharmacist. Alum can be harmful if eaten, so remember to wash your hands after touching it.

1. Gently warm 100g of alum in 500ml of water over a low heat until it dissolves, then add more alum until no more will dissolve.

2. Pour a little of this saturated solution into a saucer and leave it for three days. Keep the rest of the solution in a clean, covered jar.

3. When crystals appear on the saucer, tie a thread around one and suspend it in the solution in the jar. This crystal is called the **seed crystal**. The solution will slowly crystallize around it.

Seed crystal on saucer

QUARTZ CRYSTALS

Quartz crystals are crystals of the mineral quartz that form in the Earth's crust. When a current of electricity is passed through a quartz crystal, it vibrates 32,768 times a second. This is called the **piezoelectric effect**. The vibrations can be used to measure time in clocks and watches.

Quartz crystals inside a watch are often shaped into two prongs. The current from the watch battery makes them vibrate.

Internet links

• Scan the code to discover how liquid crystals behave.

• For links to more websites where you can zoom in on photographs of crystals, watch crystals grow and find out more about liquid crystals, go to **www.usborne.com/quicklinks**

ORGANIC CHEMISTRY

Organic chemistry is the study of compounds of carbon, called **organic compounds**. All living things contain organic compounds, and many can be made artificially. They are used to create fabrics, medicines, plastics, paints, cosmetics and many other products.

Paints contain organic compounds.

ORGANIC COMPOUNDS

Organic compounds are made up of carbon atoms bonded to atoms of other elements such as hydrogen and oxygen. The atoms are held together by strong covalent bonds (see right). Compounds that contain only carbon and hydrogen atoms are called **hydrocarbons**.

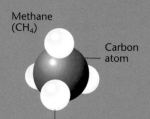

Methane
(CH_4)

Carbon atom

Hydrogen atom

Organic compounds are grouped in families called **homologous series**. For example, alkanes and alkenes (see pages 96-97) are two homologous series. Each series contains hundreds of compounds, with increasing numbers of carbon and hydrogen atoms in their molecules.

Ethane
(C_2H_6)

Here are models of molecules of the first three compounds in the alkane series. **Methane** has one carbon atom, **ethane** has two and **propane** has three.

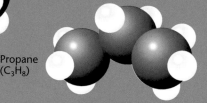

Propane
(C_3H_8)

The names of compounds with molecules containing one carbon atom start with "meth". Those with molecules containing two carbon atoms start with "eth" and those with three carbon atoms begin with "prop". The compounds in each homologous series have the same chemical properties, but their physical properties change from gas to liquid to solid as the molecules increase in size.

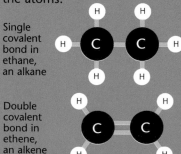

The dyes used on these ballet shoes are made from an organic compound called **aniline**, which is found in coal tar.

COVALENT BONDS

Covalent bonds (see page 69) are the strong links between atoms that share electrons in their outer shells.

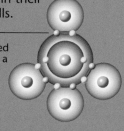

Pair of shared electrons in a molecule of methane

Each carbon atom can form single bonds with four other atoms, or it can form double, or even triple bonds. In **single bonds**, each pair of atoms shares one pair of electrons, in **double bonds** they share two and in **triple bonds** they share three pairs of electrons. In diagrams of organic molecules, the bonds are usually shown as sticks between the atoms.

Single covalent bond in ethane, an alkane

Double covalent bond in ethene, an alkene

Carbon atoms can join together to form long chains or rings which makes a huge number of organic compounds possible.

UNSATURATED

Organic compounds with double or triple bonds are described as **unsaturated**. They have bonds that can open up and join with other atoms without the original molecules breaking up. When this happens, the type of reaction that takes place is called an **addition reaction**.

Unsaturated compounds are more reactive than saturated compounds (see right).

An addition reaction

When ethene reacts with bromine, its double bonds open up, making space for bromine atoms.

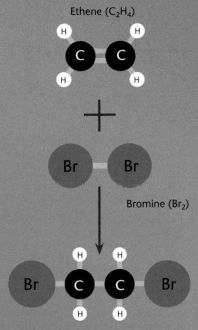

Ethene (C_2H_4)

+

Bromine (Br_2)

1,2-dibromoethane (CH_2BrCH_2Br)

$$C_2H_4 + Br_2 \longrightarrow CH_2BrCH_2Br$$

Ethene and bromine react to form 1,2-dibromoethane, which is used in insecticides and rat poisons.

Tablet containers like these are called blister packs. They are made from artificial organic compounds such as PVC (polyvinylchloride).

SATURATED

Organic compounds with single bonds are said to be **saturated**, or "full up", as they have no free bonds to join with other atoms.

When saturated organic compounds react with other compounds, the bonds in their molecules break open and some of their atoms are replaced by different atoms. This is called a **substitution reaction**. For example, dichlorodifluoromethane (CCl_2F_2) is made by replacing the hydrogen atoms in methane (CH_4) with chlorine (Cl) and fluorine (F).

$$CH_4 + 2Cl_2 + 2F_2 \longrightarrow CCl_2F_2 + 2HF + 2HCl$$

Aerosol propellants used to be made of dichlorodifluoromethane, but this is a chlorofluorocarbon (a chlorine-fluorine-carbon compound) and damages the atmosphere. Other propellants are now used in aerosols.

SYNTHETIC COMPOUNDS

By studying the way different organic compounds react, chemists have been able to synthesize (copy) substances that occur naturally, and make them in laboratories. Chemists have also created completely new, artificial organic compounds.

Chemists make vitamin tablets by synthesizing (copying) the structure of vitamins, which are naturally occurring organic compounds.

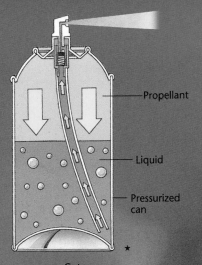

Propellant

Liquid

Pressurized can

★

Cutaway drawing of an aerosol spray-can.

Internet links

• Scan the code to see how cars of the future may be made entirely of plastic.

• For links to more websites about organic chemistry, go to **www.usborne.com/quicklinks**

ALCOHOLS

Alcohols are organic compounds that contain carbon, oxygen and hydrogen. They are a **homologous series**, that is, a group of compounds with the same chemical properties.

The oxygen and hydrogen atoms in an alcohol molecule form a **hydroxyl group** that gives the alcohols their special properties.

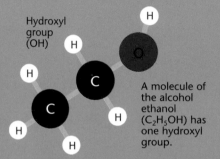

Hydroxyl group (OH)

A molecule of the alcohol ethanol (C_2H_5OH) has one hydroxyl group.

In industry, an alcohol called **ethanol** (C_2H_5OH) is made by fermentation (see below), or by reacting ethene (C_2H_4) with steam:

$$C_2H_4 + H_2O \longrightarrow C_2H_5OH$$

Ethanol is used as a solvent* for paints, varnishes and perfumes. Drinks such as wine and beer contain ethanol.

FERMENTATION

Fermentation is a chemical reaction that has been used for thousands of years to produce alcoholic drinks. It is now an important industrial process for producing the alcohol ethanol.

Yeast, a fungus, causes fermentation. It produces **enzymes** – catalysts that speed up chemical reactions in living things. These convert the sugars in fruit or grain into ethanol and carbon dioxide.

ORGANIC ACIDS

Organic compounds that are acidic are called **organic acids**. They behave like typical acids, turning litmus paper red and forming salts when they react with bases.

Organic acids can be made by oxidizing (adding oxygen to) alcohols. Vinegar has been made for thousands of years by allowing wine, which contains the alcohol ethanol, to oxidize and form ethanoic acid.

TYPES OF ORGANIC ACID

Ethanoic acid, which gives vinegar its sour taste, and **methanoic acid**, the poison in the sting of some ants, are organic acids. They belong to a group called **carboxylic acids**.

Carboxylic acids contained in natural oils and fats are called **fatty acids**.

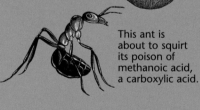

Coconut oil contains a fatty acid called lauric acid or dodecanoic acid.

This ant is about to squirt its poison of methanoic acid, a carboxylic acid.

Ethanoic acid is used in the manufacture of polyester. This can be spun very fine and dyed to make sewing threads.

DETERGENT

A **detergent** is a substance that enables water to remove dirt. Detergents reduce the attraction between the water molecules so the water spreads easily over the washing. It is this loss of attraction between the molecules that allows stretchy bubbles to form on the water.

Without detergent, water molecules will not stretch apart very well. Any bubbles that form will pop within seconds.

Soap is a type of detergent made from vegetable oils, which contain fatty acids. When the oils are boiled with sodium hydroxide, an alkali, the acids react with the alkali to produce a salt, which is soap.

How detergents work

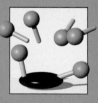

Detergents are made of ions* that have a charge at one end. This end is attracted to water. The other end (the tail) is attracted to grease.

The tails attach themselves to grease and form a bridge between the water and the grease. Their attraction to water pulls the grease away ★ from the washing.

Soapless detergents work in the same way as soap. However, they are unaffected by the minerals in hard water*, which react with the soap to form a scum.

To see a detergent at work, sprinkle some talcum powder over the surface of a bowl of water. The talc will settle on the water's surface.

Now drip a drop of washing-up liquid (a detergent) into the middle of the bowl and watch.

The detergent reduces the water's pulling power near where it lands, but not further away. As a result, the talc is pulled outwards by the water with the greater pulling power.

ESTERS

When carboxylic acids react with alcohols, they produce compounds called **esters**, and water. Esters give fruit and flowers their flavours and smells. **Fats** and **oils** are esters made from propan-1,2,3-triol (an alcohol known as **glycerol**) combined with fatty acids.

This picture shows how esters from a rose are dispersed into the air. The metal devices are used to measure the strength of the scent. The areas containing most esters are shown in pink.

Internet links

• Scan the code to find out about esters and how they are used in perfumes.

• For links to more sites about organic compounds, go to **www.usborne.com/quicklinks**

Hard water, 73; Ions, 70.

ALKANES AND ALKENES

Alkanes are found in the Earth's crust in crude oil and natural gas, and many are used as fuels. Alkenes are not found naturally in great quantities and are obtained by breaking up large alkane molecules. They are both homologous series of hydrocarbons (see *Organic Compounds*, page 92).

Propane fuel (an alkane) is kept in these cylinders.

The alkane propane is used as a fuel to heat the air in hot-air balloons.

ALKANES

Alkanes are a homologous series of saturated compounds. This means that their carbon atoms are held together by single covalent bonds*.

All alkane names end in "ane". Those with small molecules, such as methane, are gases, but those with larger ones are liquids. Alkanes with more than 16 carbon atoms are solids.

USES OF ALKANES

Alkanes burn easily and many are used as fuels. Petrol is a mixture of alkanes, and propane and butane are used in caravans and camping stoves, stored under pressure as liquids in portable cylinders.

Alkanes are used to make many other organic chemicals. For example, the hydrogen atoms in methane can be replaced with chlorine and fluorine to make compounds called **chlorofluorocarbons** (**CFCs**). Many chlorofluorocarbons are no longer used, though, as they are thought to harm the atmosphere.

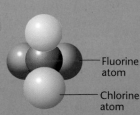

Fluorine atom

Chlorine atom

The molecule above is dichlorodifluoromethane, a CFC. It was once widely used as a coolant in refrigerators and in car air conditioning systems.

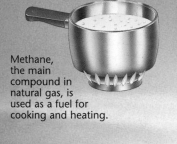

Methane, the main compound in natural gas, is used as a fuel for cooking and heating.

Aircraft use kerosene, a mixture of alkanes, for fuel. It is produced by the purification of petroleum.

Enormous amounts of fuel are used by jet planes. A Boeing 747 can carry over 215,000 litres. It uses the fuel at a rate of about 11 litres per kilometre.

Kerosene is an ideal fuel for a jet engine because, unlike some other fuels, it burns well in the freezing temperatures of high altitudes.

* Covalent bonds, 92.

ALKENES

Alkenes are a homologous series of hydrocarbons whose molecules contain some double covalent bonds (see page 93). The names of the compounds in this series end in "ene". Ethene (C_2H_4) is the first alkene. There is no alkene beginning with "meth" (see page 92) as all alkenes must have at least two carbon atoms to form a double bond.

The diagrams below show molecules of the first two compounds in the alkene series.

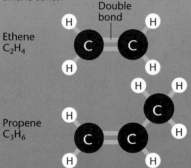

Ethene
C_2H_4

Double bond

Propene
C_3H_6

Alkenes are unsaturated* compounds and are more reactive than alkanes. Each carbon atom can give up one of its double bonds to other atoms in an addition reaction* without the molecules breaking open. Alkenes are used in industry to make plastics, such as polythene, by joining many molecules together.

Plastic clothes pegs. Plastics are manufactured by addition reactions, using molecules of compounds such as ethene.

Racing cars are made of a very strong, rigid material called Kevlar®, which is plastic reinforced with synthetic fibres. It is much lighter than metal.

HYDROGENATION

Hydrogenation is an addition reaction* in which atoms of hydrogen are added to unsaturated* molecules, such as those of alkenes, to fill up the double covalent bonds. The new compounds are saturated* as they contain only single covalent bonds.

Ethene and hydrogen react together to form ethane. The hydrogen fills up the spare bonds in the double covalent bond.

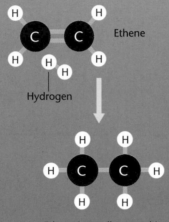

Ethene

Hydrogen

Ethane is an alkane and it is a saturated compound.

See for yourself

Watch out for advertisements for margarines. There is a strong chance that the manufacturers will claim that their product is the "healthy" alternative to butter.

This is because margarines contain more unsaturated compounds than butter (which consists mostly of saturated compounds).

Scientists think that saturated compounds are bad for you, since your body converts them into a type of cholesterol that can clog up your blood vessels. The unsaturated compounds in many margarines don't do this.

Food scientists use hydrogenation to make margarines from certain vegetable oils, such as olive oil. These oils contain alkenes.

To create the margarine, hydrogen is forced through the oil while it is hot and pressurized. Some bonds break open and the hydrogen atoms attach to the newly available bonds. This causes the runny oil to become more solid.

Peanut oils consist of alkanes. They are used to make margarines.

The more hydrogenated vegetable oil becomes, the harder it is to spread.

Internet links

• Scan the code to find out more about the compounds in butter and margarine.

• For links to more websites about alkanes, alkenes and hydrogenation, go to **www.usborne.com/quicklinks**

* Addition reactions, Saturated, Unsaturated, 93.

CRUDE OIL

Crude oil is the raw material from which fuels such as heating oil, petrol and gas are obtained, as well as many different chemicals for industry. It is a mixture of hydrocarbons, which are organic compounds made only of carbon and hydrogen. The different compounds in the mixture are separated in oil refineries by a process called fractional distillation.

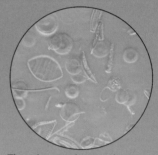

The microscopic organisms from which oil formed were similar to these plankton that live in the sea today.

Oil platforms like this one are used to drill for deposits under the seabed.

HOW OIL AND GAS FORMED

Crude oil and natural gas are **fossil fuels**. They formed from the bodies of microscopic organisms that lived in the sea millions of years ago. When the organisms died, their bodies sank to the bottom of the sea and became buried in sand and mud. As the layers of sand and mud built up and became rock, the minute organisms rotted and formed oil and gas.

OIL FROM UNDER THE SEA

Nearly a third of all oil supplies are found under the seabed. The oil and gas are contained in pockets, called **reservoirs**, which are found in porous layers of rock. These reservoirs can be hundreds of metres below the seabed.

To extract the oil, giant oil platforms, like the one on the left, are built out at sea. Wells are drilled down from the seabed into the reservoirs. Oil is piped up to the platform from the reservoirs.

Drill pipes

Oil platform

This picture shows four separate wells which have been drilled down from one platform.

Layers of rock

Sea

Seabed

Well

Oil reservoir

FRACTIONAL DISTILLATION

Fractional distillation is a process by which substances in a mixture can be separated by boiling. In an oil refinery, crude oil is heated until the compounds become gases at about 340°C. The gases are piped into a tower called a **fractionating column**. As they rise up the tower, they cool, condense (become liquids again) and are collected.

Fractionating columns at an oil refinery

The compounds with the largest, heaviest molecules condense first and are collected near the bottom of the tower. Compounds with smaller, lighter molecules have lower boiling points, so they rise higher up the tower before they condense. The mixture of compounds that condense at each level is called a **fraction**.

Furnace where crude oil is heated until it boils and the compounds become gases.

Fractionating column

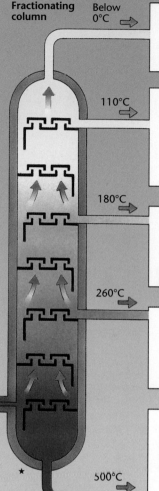

Below 0°C
110°C
180°C
260°C
500°C
★

Refinery gases
1-4 carbon atoms per molecule. Used as fuels for heating and cooking.

Gasoline compounds
5-12 carbon atoms per molecule. Used for petrol and for making medicines, plastics, paints and chemicals.

Kerosene compounds
9-15 carbon atoms per molecule. Used for heating, lighting and jet fuels.

Diesel oils
12-25 carbon atoms per molecule. Used as fuels for trucks and trains.

Residue compounds
20-40 carbon atoms per molecule. Used for heating oil, candle waxes, polishes, lubricants and bitumen for surfacing roads.

CRACKING

Cracking is a method by which compounds with large molecules, such as decane, an alkane*, are converted to compounds with smaller molecules that are more useful and can be used as fuels or in the chemicals industry.

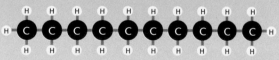
Decane ($C_{10}H_{22}$)

When heated and mixed with steam and a catalyst*, the large molecules break up to make smaller, lighter molecules.

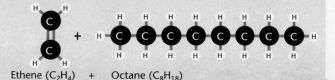
Ethene (C_2H_4)   +   Octane (C_8H_{18})

Internet links

• Scan the code for a video about how crude oil is refined.

• For links to more websites where you can see where oil comes from and how it's refined, go to **www.usborne.com/quicklinks**

* Alkanes, 96; Catalyst, 79.

99

POLYMERS AND PLASTICS

Polymers are substances made of many small molecules joined together to make long chains. Plastics and synthetic fibres, such as **nylon**, are polymers made from chemicals found in crude oil. As well as these synthetic polymers, there are natural polymers, such as rubber, starch, wool and silk – and the hair on your head.

Plastic balls are made by pouring molten polymers into a mould. As they cool, the shape solidifies.

MAKING PLASTICS

Plastics are easily-moulded synthetic polymers made from the organic compounds found in crude oil. Many plastics, such as polythene, PVC and polystyrene, are made using ethene, which belongs to the group of organic compounds called alkenes*.

PVC drinks bottles are light and shatterproof.

Polythene can be made into thin sheets for wrapping food.

Polythene and polystyrene can be moulded to make things such as cups.

See for yourself

To make your own polymer, put a tablespoon of water in a cup with a teaspoon of egg white and a teaspoon of baking soda, and mix well. Then sprinkle a teaspoon of citric acid into the mixture and swirl it around.

The baking soda reacts with the citric acid, producing bubbles of carbon dioxide gas, turning the mixture into a foam. As this happens, monomers in the egg white bond together to form a polymer.

Don't eat the polymer – it may upset your stomach.

POLYMERIZATION

Joining molecules together to make polymers is called **polymerization**. The small molecules that make up polymers are called **monomers**.

For example, using heat, pressure and catalysts*, monomers of ethene are made to react together. Ethene has double bonds which open up and the carbon atoms join together to form long chains that are giant molecules of **polythene**.

Different plastics can be made by changing some of the atoms in the monomers. For example, by replacing a hydrogen atom in ethene with an atom of chlorine, chloroethene monomers are made. Long chains of these form **PVC** (polyvinylchloride).

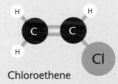

Chloroethene

Making polythene

Each monomer of ethene (C_2H_4) contains two atoms of carbon joined by a double bond.

The double bond opens up to form bonds with other monomers to build the polymer.

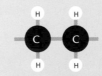

A giant molecule of polythene contains up to 20,000 atoms of carbon.

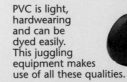

PVC is light, hardwearing and can be dyed easily. This juggling equipment makes use of all these qualities.

* Alkenes, 97; Catalysts, 79.

TYPES OF PLASTIC

Plastics can be divided into two groups. **Thermoplastics** can be melted and used again, while **thermosetting plastics** can be moulded only once.

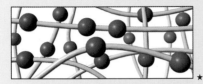

In thermoplastics, the polymer chains are not linked together.

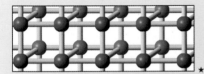

In thermosetting plastics the polymers are linked firmly together.

Thermoplastics are flexible but they are not heat resistant. Polythene, polystyrene, nylon and polyester fabrics are thermoplastics. These types of plastic are widely recycled.

Fibres for clothing can be made from recycled thermoplastics.

Thermosetting plastics have a rigid structure and are hard and heat resistant. Melamine, from which mugs, plates and kitchen work surfaces are made, is a thermosetting plastic.

Protective cases for electrical equipment, such as this drill, are often made from thermoplastics reinforced with glass fibre. They are strong, light and do not conduct electricity.

SYNTHETIC FIBRES

Some plastics can be drawn out to make fibres. Nylon, polyester and acrylic are three different types of plastic used to make fibres. They can be spun and woven, often together with natural fibres such as wool and cotton, to make clothes, carpets, ropes and strong fabrics for sails and parachutes.

This swimmer's costume is made from a strong, lightweight, flexible synthetic fibre. The material doesn't hold water, so it won't become heavy when wet.

Synthetic fibres are stronger and lighter than natural fibres such as wool and cotton. They can also be drawn out to make very long threads, unlike most natural fibres that have to be spun to make long lengths.

This picture shows a microscopic view of nylon fibres in a stocking. Nylon is a plastic made by reacting carboxylic acids and amine.

NATURAL POLYMERS

Not all polymers are synthetic. Before the invention of plastics, natural polymers such as wool and plant fibres (such as cotton and jute) were used for weaving. Like plastics, natural polymers are chains of simple molecules. The proteins in your body are also natural polymers.

Rubber is made from a natural polymer called **latex**, a milky fluid that seeps out of the bark of rubber trees. Rubber is strengthened by heating it with sulphur. This is called **vulcanized rubber** and is used mainly for making tyres.

Latex is a natural polymer produced by rubber trees. It is collected in pots that are nailed to the sides of the trees. It is used to make tough, waterproof items such as wellington boots.

Internet links

- Scan the code for facts about natural and synthetic polymers.

- For links to more websites with experiments, activities and video clips about polymers and plastics, go to **www.usborne.com/quicklinks**

USING PLASTICS

Plastics are extremely versatile. They have been developed to the point where they are now used to make all sorts of different appliances, toys, tools and gadgets. Here are some examples of common plastics, along with examples of how they are used.

Plastics don't conduct electricity, so they are used as a protective covering for things that do, such as computer cables.

THE FIRST PLASTICS

The first plastics were made over 150 years ago. After early experiments, celluloid and then Bakelite were developed. Early in the twentieth century, Bakelite was used to make equipment such as radios and telephones.

Bakelite is heavy, so lighter plastics were developed to take its place.

This mobile phone has a lightweight case made from polycarbonate.

A 1930s telephone made from Bakelite

POLYTHENE

Polythene was first made in the 1930s. It can be made into thick, chunky shapes, or drawn out into very thin sheets.

Polythene is used to make many different things, from tough buckets to lightweight carrier bags.

Polythene is a good material for everyday products because it is easily moulded and doesn't break if you drop it.

Polythene is waterproof so it is good for moulding into bath toys such as these ducks.

These polythene ducks are safe for children. Some plastics, though, are never used for toys because they can give off poisonous chemicals if chewed.

See for yourself

Most products have some plastic parts, or plastic in the packaging. Look around you now. You will probably see many different types of plastics.

POLYSTYRENE

Polystyrene is a plastic which sets firm. It can be made into lightweight foam which is a very good insulator. It is used for packaging food and fragile equipment.

Polystyrene cup

Polystyrene packaging keeps food warm.

PLASTICS IN SPACE

Since space exploration began in the 1950s, lots of research has been done into finding new, lightweight, tough fabrics to protect astronauts. This has resulted in the invention of new plastics, such as those mentioned below.

Space suits contain eight or nine layers of plastic fabrics that can resist extremes of cold and heat.

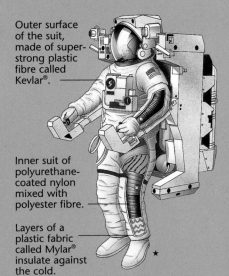

Outer surface of the suit, made of super-strong plastic fibre called Kevlar®.

Inner suit of polyurethane-coated nylon mixed with polyester fibre.

Layers of a plastic fabric called Mylar® insulate against the cold.

COMPOSITES

Many modern plastics can be combined to make even stronger materials called **composites**. These are used in spacecraft, aircraft, car components and sports goods as they are much stronger and lighter than more traditional materials.

Windsurfing boards are made of plastics reinforced with carbon or synthetic fibres.

Sails made of plastic fibre called Mylar® are extremely strong and light.

This remotely operated vehicle is used for underwater filming and gathering samples. It is made from plastics, which do not corrode.

Transparent, shatterproof PVC covering for video camera.

PLASTIC PROTECTION

Plastics can be both strong enough to resist impact and light enough to wear, making them ideal for protective headgear.

American Football helmets are made of polycarbonate. The steel face mask is coated with polyvinyl.

Scientists have developed a plastic that can repair itself. It first rapidly forms a gel framework over the hole, and this is then sealed by another polymer, restoring most of the material's strength. This could have many uses, from self-mending electronic computer chips to self-healing water pipes and satellites.

Internet links

• Scan the code to explore a timeline of the history of plastics.

ENERGY, FORCES
AND
MOTION

ENERGY

Without energy, nothing could live or grow, and there would be no movement, light, heat or noise. Energy can take many different forms: heat, light and sound are all different forms of energy. For anything to happen, energy is needed, and whenever anything happens, energy is converted from one form to another.

The energy from the Sun is about equal to that supplied by one million million million large power stations.

FORMS OF ENERGY

Energy can exist in many forms and the different forms make different things happen. As well as heat, light and sound, there are other forms such as chemical energy, kinetic energy and potential energy.

Chemical energy is energy that is released during chemical reactions. Batteries, food, and fuels such as coal, oil and petrol, are stores of chemical energy.

The energy used to move this hammer comes from food eaten and stored in the body of the person using the hammer. Chemical energy is released from the food by reactions in the body cells.

Potential energy (PE) is the energy an object has bcause it is in a position where it is affected by a force, such as magnetism* or gravity*. Objects that can be stretched or squashed, such as elastic bands and springs, have **elastic potential energy** or **strain energy**.

The higher the hammer, the greater its gravitational potential energy (GPE).

Moving objects have **kinetic energy (KE)**, the energy of movement. The faster something moves, the more kinetic energy it has. As it slows down, it loses kinetic energy.

The moving hammer transfers kinetic energy to the nail, which moves into the wood.

Gravity, 130; Magnetism, 232.

ENERGY CONVERSION

The **law of conservation of energy** states that energy can never be created or destroyed. Whenever anything happens, energy is converted into a different form. This is what happens, for example, when plants use energy from sunlight to make food, and when animals eat them in turn.

Example of energy conversion

1. Plant uses energy from sunlight to make food.

2. Plant stores food as chemical energy.

3. Hummingbird feeds on plant. Chemical energy is converted to kinetic energy and some heat energy when bird moves.

★ Chemical energy in batteries is changed to electrical energy in a flashlight.

Electrical energy is changed to light and heat energy in the bulb.

ENERGY CHAINS

An **energy chain** is a way of showing how energy is converted from one form to another. The pictures on the right show the energy changes that take place in a power station, where the chemical energy in coal is converted into electrical energy.

A coal-fired power station

The final form in all energy chains is heat. Even this energy is not lost, but it spreads out into the environment and is very difficult to harness for any useful purpose.

Energy conversion in a power station

Coal is the fossilized remains of plants that grew long ago. It is a chemical store of energy that came originally from the Sun.

When the coal is burned, the chemical energy is converted to heat energy, which is used to heat water to make steam.

The steam turns turbines*. This produces kinetic energy – the energy of movement.

The kinetic energy is converted to electrical energy in a device called a **generator**.

Appliances such as lamps, televisions, heaters and audio equipment convert electrical energy into light, heat and sound.

* Turbines, 147.

See for yourself

In this matchbox paddle-boat, the elastic potential energy stored by a twisted elastic band is changed into kinetic energy that moves the boat forwards.

Empty matchbox

1. Place a piece of cardboard in the elastic band and twist it to wind up the band.

Used match

Elastic band

2. Float the boat in water.

Internet links

- Scan the code to watch a video clip about energy.

- For links to more websites about forms of energy and how energy is converted, go to **www.usborne.com/quicklinks**

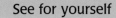

107

ENERGY RESOURCES

Energy is used to heat and light houses, to cook food and provide the power for factories and cars. This energy can be obtained by burning fuels, or by harnessing the power of, say, the wind, the Sun, or moving water.

This wind turbine uses the power of the wind to provide energy. The turning motion of the massive blades is transformed into electricity in a generator, which is in a box just behind the blades.

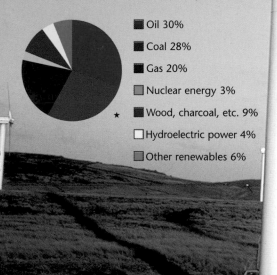

About half the people of the world burn wood, dung or charcoal to provide the energy that they need for cooking and heating.

Oil, coal, natural gas and nuclear fuel are called **non-renewable fuels** because their supply is limited. Other sources of energy, such as wood, wind, water, and the Sun, are called **renewable energy resources** because they regrow, or generate power without being used up.

ENERGY USAGE

The pie chart below shows the percentages of the different energy resources that are used to provide energy for homes and industry.

- Oil 30%
- Coal 28%
- Gas 20%
- Nuclear energy 3%
- ★ Wood, charcoal, etc. 9%
- Hydroelectric power 4%
- Other renewables 6%

FOSSIL FUELS

Coal, oil and natural gas are called **fossil fuels** because they formed from the fossilized remains of plants or animals. Over 25% of the world's energy comes from coal.

Here you can see the fossilized remains of a prehistoric plant in a lump of coal.

When fossil fuels burn, they release carbon dioxide and other gases into the air and they are partly to blame for problems such as the greenhouse effect*.

RENEWABLE ENERGY

Only about 19% of the world's energy comes from renewable resources, so the world's oil supplies are running out. Most renewable resources also produce far less carbon dioxide than fossil fuels.

Hydroelectric power

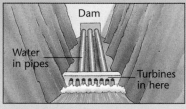

Dam

Water in pipes

Turbines in here

Water stored behind a dam as gravitational potential energy is released. As it gushes through pipes, it turns turbines, generating electricity. This is hydroelectric power.

Biofuel

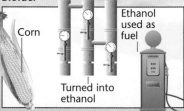

Corn

Ethanol used as fuel

Turned into ethanol

Biofuel is fuel that can be made from fermented* corn or sugar cane. But the process of land clearing, farming and transporting produces carbon dioxide.

* Greenhouse effect, 65; Nuclear energy, 116, Fermentation, 94.

SOLAR ENERGY

Energy from the Sun is called **solar energy**. It consists of heat and light energy, both of which move in the form of electromagnetic waves*. It can be used to produce electricity with a device called a **solar cell**, or to heat water using **solar collectors**.

In a solar collector, heat from the Sun is absorbed by the black absorber panel, which heats the water in the pipes.

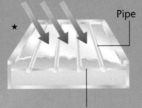

Sun's rays

Pipe

★

Absorber panel

Cutaway diagram of a roof with a solar heating system. The hot water is for domestic use, such as washing, and also for the central heating system.

★

Cold water goes to solar collectors

Solar collectors absorb heat from the Sun's rays.

Water heated by Sun

Chemical storage unit. This absorbs surplus heat which is stored and released when needed.

Mains water supply

ENERGY EFFICIENCY

Machines take one form of energy, for example, electricity, and change it into another form of energy. Machines are described as efficient if they change most of the energy that is used to power them into the useful form of energy that is needed.

Energy-saving compact fluorescent lamps (CFLs)* are much more efficient than the older filament light bulbs because they turn more electrical energy into light and waste less as heat.

MEASURING ENERGY

Energy is measured using units called **joules (J)**. One thousand joules is a **kilojoule (kJ)**. The foods that you eat give you varying amounts of energy.

An ordinary sized apple (100g) contains 150kJ of chemical energy. The same mass of chocolate contains 2,335kJ.

Power is the energy used in a certain time and it is measured in units called **watts (W)**. One watt is equal to one joule per second. The more energy a machine produces in a certain period of time, the more powerful it is.

An 11 watt light bulb uses 11 joules of energy each second. An 18 watt bulb uses 18 joules per second and produces more heat and light energy.

11 watt light bulb

18 watt light bulb

See for yourself

On a hot day you can see how the Sun's energy heats things up. Coil a garden hose so that as much of it as possible is in sunlight. Attach it to a water supply and turn it on so that water comes out. Then turn off the water and block up the end of the pipe using, say, a cork. Leave it in the sun for an hour.

When you go back to the hose, unblock the pipe and feel the warmth of the water that runs out. The hose will have soaked up the Sun's energy, heating up the water inside.

Internet links

• Scan the code to see how a wind turbine works.

• For links to more websites where you can find out about renewable energy and fossil fuels, and see how they produce electricity, go to **www.usborne.com/quicklinks**

HEAT

Heat is a form of energy that flows from one place to another because of a difference in temperature. **Temperature** is a measure of how hot something is.

HEAT ENERGY

When a substance absorbs heat, its **internal energy** increases. Internal energy is made up of two types of energy. Firstly, there is the kinetic energy* of the particles as they move about in the substance. Secondly, there is the potential energy* of the particles, ready to be used.

This red-hot river of liquid rock was formed when rocks inside the Earth absorbed so much heat that they melted.

*
Ice in water

Heat energy flows from hot objects to cooler ones and continues to flow until they reach the same temperature. For example, water that has ice in it loses heat energy to the ice, which gains heat energy. Eventually, all the water molecules (from the water and the ice) reach the same temperature.

MEASURING HEAT ENERGY

Like all forms of energy, heat is measured in **joules (J)**, named after the English scientist James Joule (1818-89). He was the first to recognize that heat is a form of energy. Using a contraption like the one below, Joule showed how gravitational potential energy lost by the falling weights was gained by the water in the form of heat energy, as its temperature rose.

Joule's experiment

Thermometer

Pulley

Weight

Falling weights made the paddles in the container turn, causing the water to swirl about and heat up.

Water

It takes 4,200J to raise the temperature of 1kg of pure water by just 1°C.

Kinetic energy, Potential energy, 106.

HEAT AND EXPANSION

Most substances expand when they are heated because, as their particles vibrate more vigorously, they push each other further apart. Gases and most liquids expand more than solids because their molecules have more energy to break free of the forces that hold them together (see *The Kinetic Theory*, page 16).

Different solids expand at different rates. This can be seen in a **bimetallic strip**, a strip of copper and iron fixed firmly together. When heated, the copper expands more than the iron, so the strip bends.

Bimetallic strips are used in **thermostats** – devices that switch an electrical circuit on and off in response to a change in temperature.

Bimetallic strip in a thermostat

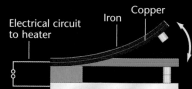

Electrical circuit to heater

Iron   Copper

*

See for yourself

Take a jar of dried peas or beans and shake it gently. The contents vibrate but stay in roughly the same places. This is what happens to the particles in a solid when they are heated a little.

THERMAL CAPACITY

If you put the same amount of heat into two different objects and their temperatures change by different amounts, the objects are said to have different **thermal (or heat) capacities**. If these objects have the same mass, then the substances of which the objects are made, are said to have different **specific thermal (or specific heat) capacities**. (Specific means "for 1 kg".)

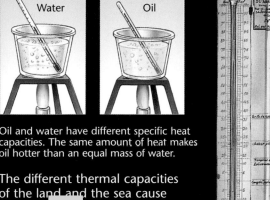

Water   Oil

Oil and water have different specific heat capacities. The same amount of heat makes oil hotter than an equal mass of water.

The different thermal capacities of the land and the sea cause sea breezes. In the day, the land heats up faster than the sea. Warm air over the land rises and cooler air blows in from the sea.

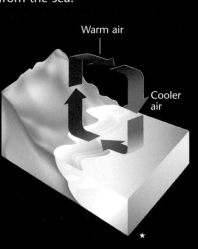

Warm air

Cooler air

Coastal wind patterns like this one develop mostly during spells of warm weather.

THERMOMETERS continued

Temperature can be measured in degrees Celsius (°C) or Fahrenheit (°F), or on the absolute temperature scale.

The **Celsius scale** has two fixed points: ice point (0°C) and steam point (100°C). Each Celsius degree is one hundredth of the difference between these two points.

An early Celsius thermometer

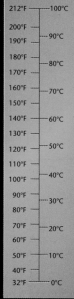

The Celsius and Fahrenheit scales

In the **Fahrenheit scale**, the values 32°F and 212°F are given to the ice and steam points. There are 180 degrees between them.

The **absolute temperature scale** is measured in units called **kelvins (K)**, which are the same size as degrees Celsius. The scale starts at a point called **absolute zero** (zero K) which is the same as -273°C. This is the temperature at which no more energy can be removed from a substance.

THERMOMETERS

A **thermometer** is an instrument for measuring temperature. It may, for example, contain a liquid that expands when heated, or a wire whose resistance* to electric current changes if the temperature changes.

Liquid in glass thermometers contain mercury or, for measuring very low temperatures, alcohol.

In a clinical thermometer, a constriction stops liquid returning to the bulb before a reading is taken.

Maximum and **minimum thermometers** contain pointers that record the highest or lowest temperature reached.

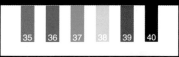

35 36 37 38 39 40

Liquid crystal thermometers contain liquid crystals that change colour when heated.

Digital thermometers contain an electronic component that is sensitive to heat. It shows the temperature on a digital display.

Internet links

• Scan the code for a link to a website where you can find out more about heat.

* Resistance, 236.

HEAT TRANSFER

Heat can be transferred from one place to another by convection, conduction or radiation.

CONVECTION

Convection is the main way in which heat energy is transferred in liquids and gases. When a liquid or gas is heated, the part nearest the heat source expands and becomes less dense*, so it rises. The cooler, denser liquid sinks. Movements like this in liquids or gases are called **convection currents**.

The pattern of winds around the Earth are caused by convection currents. These occur because more of the Sun's energy hits the surface near the equator. As the air is heated, it expands and rises and colder, denser air rushes in, creating a wind.

— Warm air rises.

— Air cools and sinks.

Fridges are kept cold by convection currents. Cool air near the top of the fridge sinks, while warmer air rises to be cooled.

Glider plane takes spiral path upwards.

★ Convection currents in the atmosphere lift the glider.

Convection currents are carrying clouds of ash from this volcano into the upper atmosphere.

See for yourself

Gently drop a small feather or piece of tissue paper above a warm radiator. See which way the feather or paper floats.

The radiator heats the air above it, causing the air to rise and form a convection current. If it is light enough, the feather or paper will be carried upwards on the convection current.

* Density, 138.

CONDUCTION

Conduction is the main way in which heat energy in a solid is transferred. The energy of the particles nearest to the heat source increases. These particles vibrate and pass on some of their energy, spreading heat through the substance.

A desert fox has large ears which help it to keep cool. Excess heat is transferred from its ears to the air by conduction and spreads away by convection.

Metals are good **conductors** because, as well as their vibrating particles, they contain freely moving electrons*. These carry heat energy around more quickly than the vibrations alone. Substances that conduct heat slowly, such as wood and water, are called **insulators**. Air is a good insulator and so are materials that trap air, such as wool, fur and feathers.

Metal heats up quickly as it is a very good conductor of heat.

Heat spreads quickly through metal particles.

Fat and feathers insulate birds such as penguins, helping to keep them warm.

RADIATION

Heat transfer by **radiation** refers to energy that moves in the form of electromagnetic waves*.

The Sun's radiation travels at 300 million metres per second. It takes about eight minutes to reach the Earth.

Radiation does not involve particles, and is the only form of energy that can cross a **vacuum** (a space completely empty of matter). All types of radiation, for instance light rays, cause things to heat up, but **infrared radiation** is the type which causes the greatest temperature rise.

The Sun sends out infrared radiation, as do hot objects, such as fires and light bulbs. Dark-coloured objects absorb the radiation, while light ones reflect it, and stay cool.

In Antarctica, the snow reflects over 90% of the radiation from the Sun back into the atmosphere. The surface absorbs very little heat, so the air remains cold.

Radiation

Snow reflects the Sun's radiation.

Electromagnetic waves, 212; Electrons, 10.

Sun's heat

VACUUM FLASKS

A **vacuum flask** is a container for keeping liquids at a constant temperature. It is made up of two glass containers, one inside the other, with a vacuum between them. The vacuum prevents the transfer of heat by conduction or convection (see left). Very shiny surfaces reduce the amount of heat transferred by radiation.

Vacuum flask

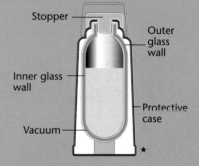

Stopper

Outer glass wall

Inner glass wall

Protective case

Vacuum

Internet links

- Scan the code to watch a video about convection currents.

- For links to more websites about convection, conduction and radiation, go to **www.usborne.com/quicklinks**

RADIOACTIVITY

All matter is made of particles called **atoms**. Every atom contains a **nucleus** which is made up of **protons** and neutrons. Nuclei hold vast amounts of energy, called **nuclear energy**. Some substances are **radioactive**. This means that their atoms release some of this energy as radiation*. This can be dangerous to living things, but can be used in many ways.

Nucleus—

Beta particles are very high-energy electrons emitted when a neutron in the nucleus decays.

Alpha particles are clusters containing two protons and two neutrons.

TYPES OF RADIATION

When a substance is radioactive, it is said to be **unstable**. The atoms become stable by losing some of their nuclear energy as radiation.

The type of radiation that the atoms give out is either **alpha**, **beta** or **gamma radiation**. The first two are streams of particles. The last takes the form of **gamma rays**, which are an extremely powerful form of electromagnetic waves*.

The Greek letters below are used to describe the different types of radiation.

Alpha   Beta   Gamma

A nucleus first throws off either alpha or beta particles, and then, if it has extra energy, gamma radiation.

The three nuclei shown on this page are all unstable. Each nucleus is emitting a different type of radiation.

Alpha particles move slowly and are stopped by any substance thicker than paper. They are identical to the nuclei of helium atoms and are given off by naturally radioactive substances in the Earth. Beta particles are more penetrating than alpha particles and many move almost at the speed of light. Gamma rays are the most penetrating.

Range of radioactive particles

Symbol for radioactive substances

Alpha particles travel less than 10cm in air and are absorbed by thick paper.

Beta particles have a range of 1m in air and are absorbed by 1mm of copper.

The intensity of gamma rays is halved by 13mm of lead or by about 120m of air.

★

Gamma rays are very high-energy electromagnetic waves that move at the speed of light.

* Electromagnetic waves, 212; Radiation, 113.

USES OF RADIATION

In industry, radiation is used to check the thickness of sheets of paper and plastic. Tiny irregularities can be detected by measuring the amount of beta radiation that passes through the sheets. Food, such as fruit and meat, can be irradiated with gamma rays, and this keeps it fresh.

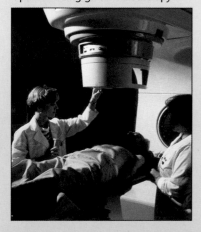

After two weeks, these irradiated strawberries are still fresh.

In hospitals, doctors use **radioactive tracing** to follow a substance through a patient's body. For example, to see how a patient's body deals with sugar, they can attach some radioactive carbon-14 to molecules of sugar and track the radiation given off by the carbon-14.

Radiotherapy uses carefully controlled doses of radiation to kill cancer cells, which are living cells that are growing in a disorderly way.

A patient being given radiotherapy

RADIOACTIVE DECAY

After ejecting particles, a nucleus becomes the nucleus of a different element. This is called **radioactive decay**. If the new element is also unstable, the process of decay will continue until there are atoms with stable nuclei.

For example, when the unstable radioactive substance plutonium-242 gives off an alpha particle (which consists of two protons and two neutrons), it becomes uranium-238. The diagram below shows how plutonium decays to become uranium and then thorium.

The numbers written in front of the symbol for the substance are the mass number (top) and atomic number (bottom). The **mass number** is the number of neutrons and protons in a nucleus. The **atomic number** is just the number of protons.

Radioactive decay of plutonium

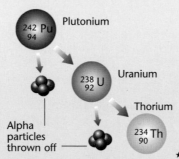

242 Pu 94 — Plutonium

238 U 92 — Uranium

234 Th 90 — Thorium

Alpha particles thrown off

The length of time it takes for the nuclei of an element to decay is measured by its **half-life**. This is the time taken for half of the nuclei in a sample to decay. Every element has a different half-life. Radium-221 has a half-life of 30 seconds. Uranium-238 has a half-life of 4,500,000,000 years.

CARBON DATING

Carbon dating is a method of calculating the time that has passed since living matter died. All living things contain a small amount of carbon-14, which has a half-life of 5,700 years. When living things die, they no longer breathe in air containing radioactive carbon-14. The age of the remains can be calculated by measuring how much radiation is still being given off.

Carbon dating showed that this insect was trapped in amber resin five thousand years ago.

DANGER!

Radioactive substances are transported in thick lead containers to prevent radiation from escaping. Exposure to radiation can cause burns, cataracts and cancer.

Robots are used to handle dangerous radioactive substances.

Internet links

• Scan the code to watch a video about how carbon dating works.

• For links to more websites about radiation and its uses, go to **www.usborne.com/quicklinks**

NUCLEAR POWER

Nuclear energy can be harnessed, using controlled nuclear reactions, to produce power for industrial and home use. It can also be released, in an extremely violent way, when nuclear weapons explode.

NUCLEAR REACTIONS

There are two types of nuclear reactions: **nuclear fusion** and **nuclear fission**. Fusion means "joining" and during nuclear fusion, two small nuclei combine to form a larger one. Nuclear fusion only takes place at extremely high temperatures and pressures, and releases huge amounts of energy.

The dust created by this nuclear explosion is highly radioactive*. It contaminates everything on which it falls.

Nuclear fusion

Two nuclei join to form one large one.

Fission means "splitting apart" and nuclear fission occurs when the nucleus of an atom is bombarded with neutrons*. The nucleus splits open, releasing neutrons and large amounts of energy. This process takes place inside nuclear reactors (see opposite page).

Nuclear fission

A nucleus splits open, forming two new nuclei and releasing two or more neutrons.

NUCLEAR WEAPONS

Nuclear weapons produce uncontrolled nuclear reactions. The energy is released in massive explosions. **Atomic bombs** use nuclear fission reactions. **Hydrogen bombs** use nuclear fusion. In World War II, the USA dropped atomic bombs on the cities of Hiroshima and Nagasaki in Japan, killing many thousands of people.

World War II atomic bomb

Radioactive*
plutonium
in here

* Neutrons, Radioactivity, 114.

NUCLEAR REACTORS

The energy released by controlled fission reactions can be used to generate electricity, and to power submarines and aircraft carriers.

Such reactions take place in **nuclear reactors**, such as the pressurized water reactor shown in the diagram at the bottom of the page.

Inside a nuclear reactor, rods made of a radioactive substance such as uranium are bombarded with neutrons*. The nuclei split up, releasing radiation and more neutrons, which set up a chain reaction.

Nuclear power stations generate lots of electricity. However, the used fuel rods remain dangerously radioactive for thousands of years. Disposing of them safely is very difficult.

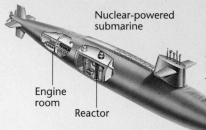

Nuclear-powered submarine

Engine room

Reactor

Nuclear power station

PRESSURIZED WATER REACTOR

A **pressurized water reactor** is one type of nuclear reactor found in power stations. The energy released in the core of the reactor is used to heat water to make steam. The steam turns turbines* that generate electricity.

Nuclear fission reactions take place in the core of the nuclear reactor (1).

The energy released heats pressurized water in the primary water circuit (2).

Heat from the primary water circuit heats the water in the secondary circuit to make steam (3).

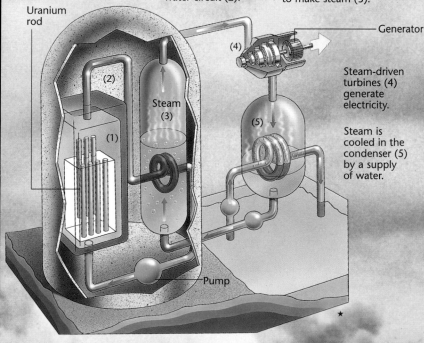

Uranium rod

(2)

Steam (3)

(1)

(4)

Generator

Steam-driven turbines (4) generate electricity.

(5)

Steam is cooled in the condenser (5) by a supply of water.

Pump

SAFETY FIRST

Nuclear reactions are dangerous to living things. To prevent accidents which would pollute land and air with radiation, the workings in power stations are monitored closely.

Dangerous processes inside a nuclear power station are carefully monitored.

Internet links

• Scan the code to see inside a nuclear reactor.

• For links to more websites where you can investigate nuclear power, go to **www.usborne.com/quicklinks**

---

* Neutrons, 114; Turbines, 147.

FORCES

A **force** is any push or pull on an object. When you pick up an object, you are exerting a force on it. If you leave it sitting where it is, there are still forces acting on it, but they cancel each other out. Forces can make things move faster or slower, stop, change direction, or change size or shape.

The force of gravity makes these dice fall downwards.

TYPES OF FORCES

Forces affect objects in many different ways. There are forces you can see, such as a foot kicking a ball, and invisible forces, such as magnetism* and gravity*.

The magnetic force which pulls these tacks to the magnet is an invisible force.

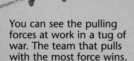

You can see the pulling forces at work in a tug of war. The team that pulls with the most force wins.

A single force acting on an object will make it start to move, or move faster or slower. Two equal forces acting on the same object but in opposite directions try to change the object's size or shape.

Forces that need two or more objects to be touching each other are called **contact forces**. You are using contact forces when you move an object with your hands.

See for yourself

Try rolling one ball into another on a smooth surface. Your push will set the ball sliding and rolling. This moving ball will exert a force on the stationary one, causing it to move too.

The surface will exert a force (friction*) on both balls causing them both to slow down, and eventually stop. Air resistance (friction in air) also helps to slow them down.

Some forces don't need objects to be touching. The forces that act at a distance include electric force*, magnetism and the force of gravity.

Compasses work because of the Earth's magnetism*.

The contact force of friction* enables pencils to make marks on paper.

When you kick a football, the single force of your kick makes the football start to move.

As you catch a ball, the pushing force of your hands makes the ball slow down and stop.

If you step on a ball, the equal forces of your foot pushing down and the ground pushing up squash it.

* Electric force, 228; Friction, 124; Gravity, 130; Magnetism, 232.

A rollercoaster makes use of lots of different forces to gain speed, twist, turn upside down and race along without flying off the track.

When you are on a rollercoaster, you can feel the different forces acting on your body as you are thrown around.

MEASURING FORCES

The strength of a force is measured in **newtons (N)**, named after the English scientist, Isaac Newton (1642-1727). One newton of force causes a mass of 1kg to accelerate* by one metre per second per second ($1m/s^2$). This is about the force you would need to lift an empty glass.

A **spring balance** (see right) measures how many newtons a force is exerting. The spring, fixed at one end, is extended (stretched) by the force. **Hooke's law** states that the extension of a material is proportional to the force stretching it, as long as it is not stretched beyond its elastic limit*. The more the spring stretches, the more newtons the force is applying.

Spring balance

Downward force of weight stretches spring.

The scale gives the strength of the force in newtons.

5

VECTOR AND SCALAR QUANTITIES

Forces have magnitude (size) and direction. In physics, things that have both these quantities are called **vector quantities**. Acceleration* and velocity* are also vector quantities. A quantity that has magnitude but no direction is called a **scalar quantity**. Temperature, time and mass are examples of scalar quantities. These quantities can be low or high, but they don't have a direction.

Temperature has only magnitude, so it is a scalar quantity.

Internet links

• Scan the code to find out about the forces used in sports.

• For links to more websites where you can experiment with forces online, go to **www.usborne.com/quicklinks**

* Acceleration, 127; Elastic limit, 121; Velocity, 127.

119

COMBINING FORCES

There is usually more than one force acting on an object. For example, a sailboard can experience the forces of gravity, the wind, upthrust and waves. The combined effect is a single force called the **resultant force**. If the strength and direction of all forces is known, you can calculate the resultant force and predict what will happen to the object.

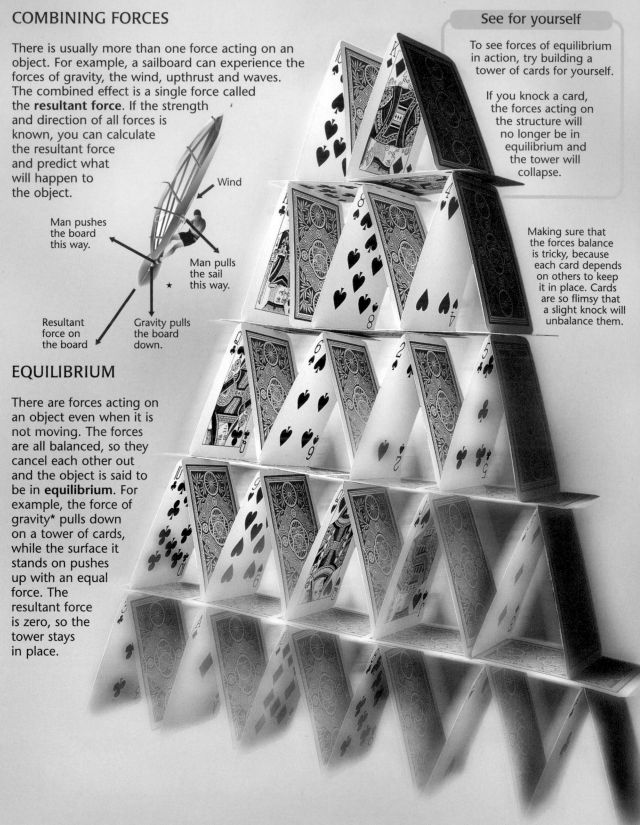

Wind

Man pushes the board this way.

Man pulls the sail this way.

Resultant force on the board

Gravity pulls the board down.

See for yourself

To see forces of equilibrium in action, try building a tower of cards for yourself.

If you knock a card, the forces acting on the structure will no longer be in equilibrium and the tower will collapse.

Making sure that the forces balance is tricky, because each card depends on others to keep it in place. Cards are so flimsy that a slight knock will unbalance them.

EQUILIBRIUM

There are forces acting on an object even when it is not moving. The forces are all balanced, so they cancel each other out and the object is said to be in **equilibrium**. For example, the force of gravity* pulls down on a tower of cards, while the surface it stands on pushes up with an equal force. The resultant force is zero, so the tower stays in place.

* Gravity, 130; Upthrust, 138.

TURNING FORCES

To turn something around a fixed point, for example a door around its hinges, a force with a turning effect is needed. The fixed point is known as a **fulcrum** or **pivot**. It is much easier to turn something around a fulcrum if the force is applied at a distance. This is why a long spanner is more efficient than a shorter one.

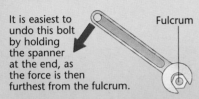

It is easiest to undo this bolt by holding the spanner at the end, as the force is then furthest from the fulcrum.

Fulcrum

The turning effect of a force is called a **moment**. The moment around a fulcrum is found by multiplying the strength of the force by its perpendicular distance from the fulcrum. Moment is measured in **newton metres (Nm)** and can be either clockwise or anticlockwise in direction.

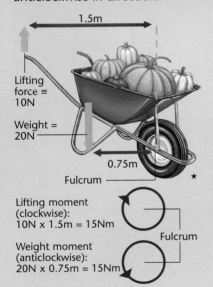

1.5m

Lifting force = 10N

Weight = 20N

0.75m

Fulcrum ⎯ ★

Lifting moment (clockwise): 10N x 1.5m = 15Nm

Weight moment (anticlockwise): 20N x 0.75m = 15Nm

Fulcrum

The picture of the wheelbarrow above shows how turning forces can be in equilibrium just like any other forces. The clockwise moment can cancel out the anticlockwise moment.

ELASTICITY

When forces act on an object that cannot move, they may change its size or shape. Some substances, like rubber, return to their original form when the force is removed. These are called **elastic** substances.

A trampoline is elastic. When the forces stretching it are removed, it goes back to its original shape.

The amount that an elastic substance will stretch obeys Hooke's law*, which states that if the force increases in equal steps, so does the stretch.

If something is stretched beyond its elastic limit, though, Hooke's law no longer works. The **elastic limit** is the point at which a substance alters permanently when it is stretched.

A rubber band is elastic, but will snap if you stretch it too far (that is, beyond its elastic limit).

Some materials do not return to their original form after being stretched and they can hold a new shape. This is called **plastic** behaviour.

Modelling clay behaves in a plastic way.

After it has been modelled, the clay keeps the shape that it has been given. This is an example of plastic behaviour.

Internet links

• Scan the code to see examples of equilibrium – in bridges made of pennies.

• For links to more websites where you can find out about forces acting on objects, turning forces and elasticity, go to **www.usborne.com/quicklinks**

* Hooke's law, 119.

DYNAMICS

The study of how forces affect movement is called **dynamics**. The terms inertia and momentum are used to describe how easily objects both start and stop moving. There are three laws of motion which explain the principles governing the movement of all objects. These laws were formulated by the English scientist, Isaac Newton, in 1687.

Isaac Newton, English scientist (1642-1727)

NEWTON'S LAWS OF MOTION

Isaac Newton made important discoveries about many subjects, including motion, gravity and light. His three **laws of motion** have had a major influence on scientific thinking.

Newton's first law states that if an object is not being acted on by a resultant force, it will either stay still or continue moving at a constant speed in a straight line. This is the principle of inertia (see right).

To start this truck moving, it will take a force to overcome its inertia. (See Newton's first law.)

Newton's second law states that any resultant force acting on an object will change its motion. How much change there is depends on the object's mass and the size of the force.

The same force of wind will move a pine cone less than a leaf because the cone's mass is greater. (See Newton's second law.)

Newton's third law states that for forces to act, there must be two objects. When one object exerts a force on a second object, then this object exerts an equal force in the opposite direction on the first object. The first force is called the **action** and the second is the **reaction**. They do not cancel out as they are acting on different objects.

The ball exerts a force on a bat, felt as the slowing down of the bat, that is equal and opposite to the force the bat exerts on the ball causing it to change direction and speed up. (See Newton's third law.)

INERTIA

Objects resist change in their movement. This tendency, called **inertia**, applies to stationary and moving objects. The inertia of a stationary object makes it hard to get moving. If moving, inertia makes the object want to continue moving in a straight line. It takes a force to overcome inertia.

Without the restraining force of a seatbelt or airbag, the inertia of this crash test dummy would send it through the windscreen.

The larger an object's mass, the more inertia it has. A big animal has to exert more force to change its movement than a small one. Twice the mass means twice the inertia.

This adult elephant has five times as much mass as the baby. Its inertia is five times as great.

* Resultant force, 120.

MOMENTUM

Momentum is a measure of an object's tendency to carry on moving. It is found by multiplying the object's mass by its velocity. The greater the mass and/or the velocity, the greater the momentum. Like velocity, momentum is a vector quantity, which means it has both size and direction.

Buzzard

Seagull

If a buzzard and seagull are flying at the same speed, the bird with the greater mass (the buzzard) has greater momentum.

This full trolley's mass is 10kg and its velocity is 1m/s east. Its momentum is 10kg m/s east.

This almost empty trolley has a mass of 2kg and a velocity of 5m/s east. Its momentum is also 10kg m/s east.

An object with a small mass can have the same momentum as an object with a large mass, providing it is moving faster.

See for yourself

Contraptions called Newton's cradles are sometimes sold as interesting, grown-up "toys" which show conservation of momentum. See if you can find one. As the first ball hits the other balls, its momentum is transferred through to the last ball, making it move.

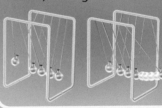

CONSERVATION OF MOMENTUM

When two objects collide, such as the pink ball and the blue ball shown here, their total momentum stays the same as it was just before the collision. This is called the **law of conservation of momentum**. So when one object loses momentum in a collision, the other gains the same amount.

The pink ball rolls towards the blue ball.

As the pink ball hits the blue ball, it transfers momentum through the blue ball to the red ball.

As their masses are the same, the pink ball stops and the red ball accelerates to the speed that the pink ball had before the collision.

Internet links

• Scan the code for a video about Newton's three laws of motion.

• For links to more websites about Newton and his laws of motion, go to **www.usborne.com/quicklinks**

FRICTION

When a moving object is touching another object, like a coin sliding across a table, the moving object slows down. The force that causes this is called **friction**. The rougher the surfaces are, and the harder they press together, the more friction there will be. Friction occurs in liquids and gases as well as between solids. Anything that experiences friction warms up.

New shoe

Old shoe

Constant friction with the floor means a ballet dancer's shoes wear out after a few weeks.

USING FRICTION

Friction is useful in some situations and a nuisance in others. If there were no friction between surfaces, it would be impossible to grip anything.

Many kinds of machines make use of friction. With too little friction between tyres and the surface of a road, for example, drivers wouldn't be able to stop their vehicles from sliding around.

The skis' smooth undersides minimize friction with the snow, allowing them to slide very easily. However, their sharp edges create friction when the skier turns, enabling him to control his speed and direction.

Some devices need friction to be able to work at all. For example, friction between a match and a matchbox generates enough heat for chemicals in the match head to burn. All brakes work by using friction to slow down a vehicle's wheels.

Water and mud on the road reduce friction because they act as lubricants (see opposite page). The grooves on a tyre channel water or mud through them, so that the raised rubber pieces (the **tread**) can grip the surface of the road.

Disc brake

Brake pad

Brake pads press against this steel wheel, causing enough friction to slow it down. ★

The soles of sports shoes are made from materials, such as rubber, which provide a lot of friction.

REDUCING FRICTION

Lots of friction between machine parts is damaging. It causes wear and tear, and some of the energy needed to run the machine is wasted on heat instead of movement. Oil is used to reduce friction because it is smoother than any solid surface, so it allows objects to slide across each other more easily. A liquid used like this is called a **lubricant**.

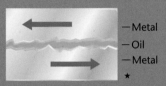

—Metal
—Oil
—Metal

Magnification shows how a smooth-seeming metal surface is actually fairly rough. A layer of oil between moving metal surfaces reduces friction.

A layer of **ball bearings** between two surfaces in a machine reduces wear by using friction. The ball bearings rotate because of friction, making the two surfaces slide more easily as if friction has been reduced.

Ball bearings lie around the axle of this wheel. They rotate as the wheel turns.

FRICTION IN AIR AND SPACE

Drag, or **air resistance**, is the friction that occurs between air and any object moving through it (see also page 142). In space, there is no air, so there is no friction. The Space Shuttle, for instance, experienced no friction as it moved through space, until it re-entered the Earth's atmosphere.

Drag slowed down the Shuttle as it entered Earth's atmosphere. The friction between the Shuttle and the air made it glow red hot.

See for yourself

You can see how ball bearings act as if friction is reduced, by using some marbles and a big book. First, push the book along on its own. Notice the friction. Now put marbles under the book and push again. The marbles roll between the book and the surface because of friction, and so make the book slide more easily as if friction has been reduced.

Marble

STREAMLINING

To reduce drag, vehicles are designed so that they are **streamlined**. Streamlining lets the air flow over a vehicle in smooth lines, so that it can move forwards with less effort.

Car manufacturers use jets of smoke to test the streamlining of new cars. Here, the Ford Ka is being tested.

FRICTION IN WATER

Water is denser* than air, so more friction acts on objects moving through water. Fish, and sea mammals such as whales, have naturally streamlined bodies that reduce the friction between themselves and the water.

Water flows easily over a whale's streamlined body.

Internet links

• Scan the code to watch a video about how friction works.

• For links to more websites where you can discover how friction affects your everyday life and watch video clips about friction and other forces, go to **www.usborne.com/quicklinks**

MOTION

In physics, **motion** is the study of how something moves, whether it is a planet moving around the Sun or a snowboarder flying through the air. An object's motion is usually described in terms of its velocity and acceleration, and its motion only changes if a force, or several forces, act on it.

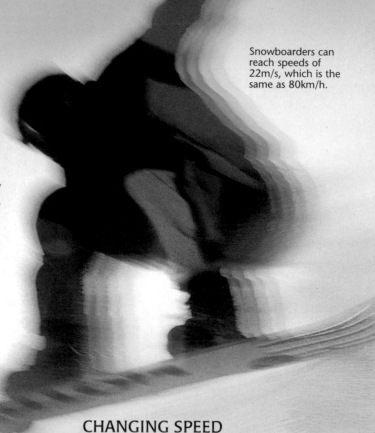

Snowboarders can reach speeds of 22m/s, which is the same as 80km/h.

SPEED

Speed is a measure of how fast an object is moving. The average speed of a moving object can be calculated by dividing the distance it has travelled by the time it has taken to do so.

Speed calculation

This cyclist has gone 500m in 40 seconds. The calculation below gives her average speed.

$$\text{Average speed} = \frac{\text{Distance (metres)}}{\text{Time (seconds)}}$$

$$= \frac{500}{40} = 12.5\text{m/s}$$

Speed is a scalar quantity. This means that it measures the amount of speed a moving object has, but not the direction in which it is moving. In physics, the unit of measurement most often used is metres per second (m/s). However, you will often see kilometres per hour (km/h) as well. This measures how far something will go in an hour.

CHANGING SPEED

The speed of a moving object can change from moment to moment. A sprinter, for instance, runs slowest when setting off at the start of a race. He is likely to be running fastest as he approaches the finishing line. The speed of something at any particular moment is called its **instantaneous speed**.

For example, the men's world record for the 100m race, set in 2009, was 9.58 seconds. This is an average speed of 10.44m/s. After running 1m of the race, though, the winner's instantaneous speed might have been 3m/s. After a few more metres, it could have been as high as 11m/s.

A 100m sprinter doesn't reach top speed until 60m.

VELOCITY

Velocity measures the direction in which an object is travelling as well as its speed. This makes velocity a vector quantity. The velocity of a moving object can change even if its speed remains exactly the same because a change in direction changes the velocity.

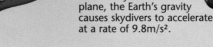

When they first leave the plane, the Earth's gravity causes skydivers to accelerate at a rate of 9.8m/s².

Although this car is travelling at a steady speed of 10km/h, (6mph) its velocity is changing all the time because it is constantly changing direction.

Path of car

Velocity is measured in metres per second (m/s) in a particular direction. For instance, someone walking north at 1.5m/s has a velocity of 1.5m/s north. **Relative velocity** is the velocity a moving object appears to have when viewed from another moving object.

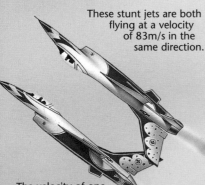

These stunt jets are both flying at a velocity of 83m/s in the same direction.

The velocity of one jet relative to the other (from the point of view of either) is zero.

ACCELERATION

Acceleration is a change in the velocity of an object, that is, a change in its speed or direction, in a given time. In physics, acceleration is measured in metres per second per second, or m/s². This is not as confusing as it looks. If something accelerates at 1m/s² (1 metre per second per second), it gets faster by one metre a second, every second.

A decrease in velocity is called **negative acceleration**, or **deceleration**. Any change in speed or direction means that an object accelerates, or decelerates, as both affect velocity. Car manufacturers usually consider acceleration in kilometres (or miles) per hour per second. This is simply using different units to measure the same thing.

If a car is travelling at a steady 50km/h (30 mph) in one direction, its acceleration is zero. This is because neither its speed nor its direction are changing.

This Porsche 911 Turbo accelerates from 0-100km/h (0-60mph) in 4.5 seconds. This works out at an average acceleration of 6.2m/s².

When skydivers open their parachutes, they suddenly decelerate.

See for yourself

Make three small balls using modelling clay. Drop each one from a different height. The greater the drop, the bigger the dent in the ball when it hits the floor. This is because the further things fall, the faster they go.

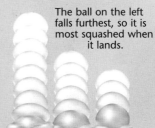

The ball on the left falls furthest, so it is most squashed when it lands.

Internet links

• Scan the code to see how snowboarders use speed, velocity and acceleration.

• For links to more websites, go to www.usborne.com/quicklinks

TERMINAL VELOCITY

When something falls through a gas or liquid it accelerates, at a decreasing rate, until it reaches its maximum constant velocity. This is called its **terminal velocity**.

As an example, imagine skydivers jumping from a plane. They start to accelerate the moment they jump from the plane.

They continue accelerating, but at a slower and slower rate, until they reach a speed of about 200km/h. At this point they stop accelerating.

When the acceleration has dropped to zero, they have reached their terminal velocity.

When something begins to fall, it accelerates quickly.

The longer it falls, the less quickly it accelerates.

When it stops accelerating. It has reached its terminal velocity.

RESISTANCE

The pull of **gravity** is the force that makes an object accelerate downwards. But as the object starts to move, it experiences **resistance**, an upward force, from the gas or liquid it is falling through. The faster the object falls, the stronger the resistance becomes, until it equals the downward force of the weight of the object. The object stops accelerating at this point and has reached its terminal velocity.

The terminal velocity of an object is slower in a liquid than it is in a gas. This is because a liquid provides more resistance than a gas. As a result, the forces become balanced earlier and the object stops accelerating sooner.

A falling coin takes longer to reach its terminal velocity in air than in water.

MOTION IN A CIRCLE

All moving objects try to continue to travel in a straight line (see Newton's first law, page 122). The force which makes something turn in a circle instead is called a **centripetal** force. This is any force that constantly pulls towards the centre of a circle.

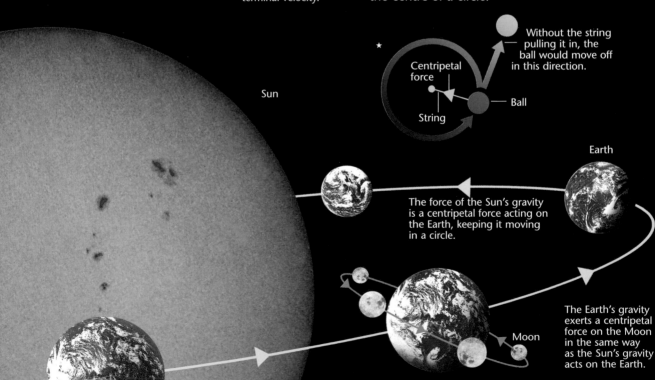

Without the string pulling it in, the ball would move off in this direction.

Centripetal force

String

Ball

Sun

The force of the Sun's gravity is a centripetal force acting on the Earth, keeping it moving in a circle.

Earth

The Earth's gravity exerts a centripetal force on the Moon in the same way as the Sun's gravity acts on the Earth.

Moon

CENTRIPETAL FORCE – AN EXAMPLE

If you tie a small object to a piece of string and whirl it around your head, the pull of the string on the object is a centripetal force. As long as you whirl fast enough, the object will not fall in on you. If you let go of the string, you remove the centripetal force and the object will fly off at a tangent, as when an athlete throws the "hammer".

1. The athlete pulls on the wire to make the hammer move.

2. His pull is a centripetal force on the hammer as it moves.

3. The faster the hammer moves, the more centripetal force is needed.

4. The hammer flies off when the centripetal force is removed.

GYROSCOPES

Gyroscopes are wheels that can spin very fast within a frame. The centripetal force created means that the frame can resist the force of gravity. It can even tilt steeply without toppling over. However, when the wheel slows, the gyroscope will fall. (You can buy gyroscopes in some toy shops.)

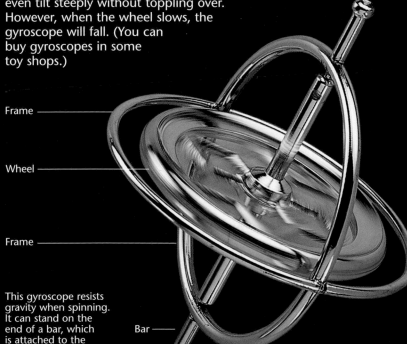

Frame

Wheel

Frame

Bar

This gyroscope resists gravity when spinning. It can stand on the end of a bar, which is attached to the frame directly beneath the middle of the spinning wheel.

See for yourself

You can see the effect of centripetal force for yourself.

Put a marble in a plastic bowl and move the bowl so that the marble moves in a circle. You have created a centripetal force on the marble.

However, the marble will fly out of the bowl when it reaches a certain speed. The centripetal force is not strong enough to keep it moving in such a tight circle.

Notice that the marble flies off in a straight line.

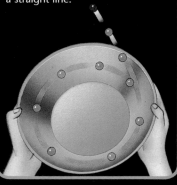

Internet links

• Scan the code to watch skydivers reach terminal velocity.

• For links to more websites where you can find out about terminal velocity, watch experiments about centripetal force and see how gyroscopes work, go to **www.usborne.com/quicklinks**

GRAVITY

The force of **gravity** attracts objects to
each other. This attraction is not noticeable unless
one of the objects has a very large mass (that is, it contains
lots of matter), such as a planet. The area within which
gravity has an effect is called a **gravitational field**. The Earth
and Moon both have gravitational fields, although the Earth's
is a lot stronger than the Moon's because it has more mass.

The force of the
Sun's gravity keeps
a belt of rocks,
called asteroids,
orbiting around it.

GRAVITY AND MASS

The strength of the pull of gravity
between two objects depends on
how far apart they are and their
masses. **Mass** is the amount of
matter that an object contains
and this never varies. Any two
objects, such as two tomatoes,
are attracted to each other, but as
their masses are small, the force
of gravity between them is tiny
and there is no visible effect.

The attraction
between these small
objects is so tiny that
it cannot be felt.

EARTH'S GRAVITY

The force of gravity
between the Earth
and anything on it is
extremely noticeable
because the mass of
the Earth is so large.

The pull of the Earth's gravity
makes any object, such as this
conker, fall to the ground.

GRAVITY AND WEIGHT

Weight is a measure of the
pull of gravity on an object's
mass. The further away an
object is from the centre of
the Earth, the less the pull of
gravity on it. Because of this,
you weigh slightly less at a
high altitude (for example,
at the top of a high
mountain) than at
the bottom, even
though your mass
stays the same.

When they are space walking,
astronauts weigh far less than
they do on Earth. They are so
far from the Earth's centre
that the planet's gravity
has little effect on them.

CENTRE OF GRAVITY

Gravity affects every part of an object, but there is one point where the object's whole weight seems to act. This is its **centre of gravity** An object can often be balanced at its centre of gravity.

X = centre of gravity

Regularly shaped and symmetrical objects, like this handweight, have their centre of gravity exactly in the middle.

A **stable object** returns to its original position when tilted. Centre of gravity is the key to stability If an object tilts, but its centre of gravity remains above its base, it won't fall over.

A racing car is very stable Its centre of gravity is low and its base is wide.

An **unstable object** has its centre of gravity high up, and has a relatively narrow base. If an unstable object is tilted, its centre of gravity soon stops being above its base.

A stationary motorbike is a good example of an unstable object. It will soon fall over when it is tilted.

Tall, narrow things aren't necessarily unstable. For example a double-decker bus is built so that its centre of gravity is low, making it stable.

The bottom part of the bus is heavy, containing the engine, wheels and chassis. The top part of the bus is light. As a result, the centre of gravity is low.

See for yourself

Follow these steps to find the centre of gravity of a piece of paper.

1. Hold up the paper and let it dangle.

2. Hold it against a wall and draw a line straight down the paper from where you are holding it.

3. Hold the paper at a different point and repeat step 2. The centre of gravity will be where the lines cross. If you carry on repeating this, the lines should cross in the same place.

Stable object   **X** = centre of gravity

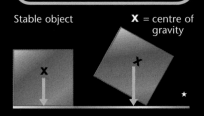

Unless a stable object is tilted a very long way, its centre of gravity stays above its base. As a result, it tends to fall back onto its base.

Unstable object   **X** = centre of gravity

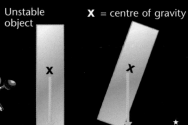

When an unstable object is tilted, its centre of gravity quickly stops being above its base. This causes the object to topple over.

Tall, stable object   **X** = centre of gravity

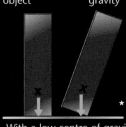

With a low centre of gravity, the tall object must tilt a long way before it topples.

EARTH AND MOON

As the Moon goes around the Earth, its gravity pulls at the planet. This has an effect on the seas of the Earth, which rise and fall. Areas where the water has risen are having a **high tide**. Areas that are not having a high tide are having a **low tide**.

The Moon's effect on the tides

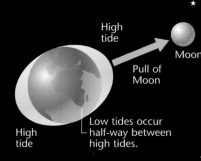

High tide

Moon

Pull of Moon

High tide

Low tides occur half-way between high tides.

Similarly, the Earth's gravity also pulls at the Moon. It is providing the force, called centripetal force, which is needed to keep the Moon locked in orbit around the Earth itself.

For more information on centripetal force, see *Motion in a Circle*, on page 128.

Internet links

• Scan the code to find out more about centre of gravity.

• For links to more websites about the force of gravity on Earth and in space, go to **www.usborne.com/quicklinks**

PRESSURE

A needle will go through a piece of cloth, but with the same amount of force, a pencil will not. The differently shaped points of the needle and pencil exert different amounts of pressure. Pressure is everywhere. It operates many machines and affects our weather. Solids, liquids and gases all apply pressure to the surfaces they touch.

Sharp scissors cut well because the blades exert pressure over a tiny area.

WHAT IS PRESSURE?

When a force acts on an object it exerts **pressure**. The pressure acts at a right-angle to the object itself, and its strength depends on the amount of force and the area over which it is applied. For example, someone walking on soft snow will sink into it in normal shoes but not if they wear snowshoes. The person's weight is the same but snowshoes spread the weight over a larger area. This reduces the pressure.

The bottom of a snowshoe is about six times bigger than the sole of a foot.

ATMOSPHERIC PRESSURE

Atmospheric pressure is due to the weight of air pressing down on the Earth's surface. Over one square metre, the weight of air pressing down is heavier than a large elephant. Air pressure is greatest near the ground, and reduces with height. At 10,000m above the ground, where jets fly, air pressure is very low as there is less air pressing down on anything up there. Less air means less oxygen, and aircraft have pressurized cabins so that people can breathe. The air pressure inside the plane is kept roughly the same as it would be at ground level.

Pressure is measured in **pascals (Pa)**, which are named after the French scientist Blaise Pascal (1623-1662), who made many discoveries about air pressure.

CHANGING WEATHER

Atmospheric pressure is measured in **millibars (mb)**. Weather changes as the pressure changes, with low pressure signalling bad weather and high pressure bringing a settled, fine spell. For example, usual atmospheric pressure at sea level is 1,013mb. However, this can fall to 910mb in a hurricane.

Heavy rains and strong winds are brought by low atmospheric pressure.

PRESSURE IN FLUIDS

Fluids (liquids and gases) change shape according to the container that they are in. The pressure inside them acts outwards in all directions.

Air inside a beach ball pushes out in all directions, keeping it blown up.

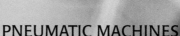

Liquid in a glass exerts pressure against the sides as well as the bottom.

HYDRAULIC MACHINES

Hydraulic machines are machines powered by liquid pressure. A liquid cannot be squashed, so if you press one part of the liquid, pressure increases throughout and the liquid has to move somewhere.

This robot arm works using hydraulic pressure.

Car brakes are hydraulic. Brake fluid is pushed through the brake system, forcing the wheels to slow down.

How a car's footbrake works

Driver presses pedal, pushing piston (1) which forces fluid through cylinder (2). Fluid goes down pipe into two more cylinders (red arrows). These press brake pads (3) against disc in wheel. Friction* slows down wheel (4).

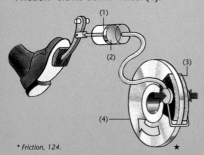

PNEUMATIC MACHINES

Pneumatic machines are driven by the pressure of gases, usually air. Unlike liquid, air can be compressed into a smaller space, and this increases its pressure.

A pneumatic drill, for example, is powered by a piston which squashes air inside the drill to a very high pressure. The compressed air pushes out with enough force to power the drill to crack rock.

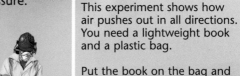

Pneumatic drill

A foam and water fire extinguisher is a pneumatic machine which uses compressed carbon dioxide gas.

How a fire extinguisher works

Squeezing handle (1) releases carbon dioxide gas from canister (2). Gas pushes down on a mixture of water and detergent (3), forcing it up a tube (4) and through a hose (5). It shoots out as a jet of foam and water.

See for yourself

This experiment shows how air pushes out in all directions. You need a lightweight book and a plastic bag.

Put the book on the bag and blow into the bag.

Air pressure increases inside the bag and lifts the book.

Internet links

• Scan the code to see the force of air pressure.

• For links to more websites with video clips and experiments about pressure, go to **www.usborne.com/quicklinks**

SIMPLE MACHINES

All machines make physical work easier to do by taking the effort needed to operate them and using it in a more efficient way. Simple machines are devices such as levers and screws. Complex machines, such as drills and cranes, are made up of combinations of simple machines.

The wheel, one of the most important devices ever invented, forms the basis of many machines.

OVERCOMING LOAD

To move any object, you need to overcome a force called the **load**, which is often the weight of the object. A simple machine helps you to do this by taking the force of your **effort** and applying it more efficiently.

The effort is the force that turns the handle.

The effort applied at the handle creates a greater force here, enabling the screwdriver to overcome the load applied by the screw.

It is possible to find out how much more force a simple machine provides compared with the amount of effort that is put in. This is done by dividing the load by the amount of effort used, and is called the **force ratio**.

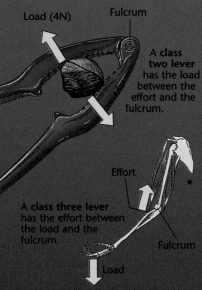

Load (4N)

Fulcrum

A **class two lever** has the load between the effort and the fulcrum.

Effort (1N)

The load exerted by the nutshell is 4N. But squeezing the nutcracker handles to crack it only takes 1N. So the force ratio is 4:1.

If a force ratio is 4:1, the load which the machine overcomes is four times greater than the effort used. Machines like this are called **force magnifiers**.

LEVERS

A **lever** is a rod that turns at a fixed point, called a **fulcrum**, making it easier to perform a task. There are three classes of lever, each with a different arrangement of the fulcrum, effort and load.

A **class one lever** has the fulcrum between the effort and the load.

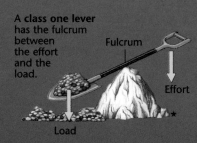

Fulcrum

Effort

Load

A **class three lever** has the effort between the load and the fulcrum.

Effort

Fulcrum

Load

The further the effort is from the fulcrum, the easier a lever is to use, so longer levers are generally more useful. (See *Turning Forces* on page 121.)

WHEELS

When a **wheel** turns a rod (such as a steering wheel turning a steering column in a car) the force applied on the wheel is turned into a bigger force by the rod. The bigger the wheel is, the more easily the rod turns.

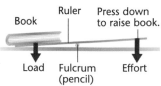

Turning the steering wheel exerts a big enough force at the steering column to turn a car's front wheels.

Steering column

When an axle is turned, a wheel connected to it will convert the axle's circular motion into a straight line motion that can move loads across the ground. A car's wheels are an example of this. The wheel turns further than the axle because it is bigger.

See for yourself

To see how a class one lever works, put a pencil under the middle of a rigid ruler. Put a lightweight book on one end.

Ruler

Press down to raise book.

Book

Load   Fulcrum   Effort
        (pencil)

Try changing the position of the pencil under the ruler. The further the effort is from the fulcrum, the easier it is to lift the load.

PULLEYS

Pulleys help to lift heavy loads and are often used in lifts and cranes. The load is attached to a rope which passes around one or more grooved wheels. When the other end of the rope is pulled, the load is lifted.

Pulley

Pulleys let you pull down instead of up, so you can use your weight to help.

★

The more wheels a pulley has, the easier it is to lift a load, as the weight of the load is spread out over several sections of rope.

This crane works like a giant pulley. The rope is made of strong steel cable. The pulling strength is provided by the crane's engine.

The strong steel cable passes over grooved wheels.

The cable can lift very heavy objects, such as steel and concrete building materials.

SCREWS

A **screw** has an axle and a thread which work together like an inclined plane (see below) wrapped around a cylinder. The axle is the cylinder and the thread the inclined plane.

The turning screw converts the force applied into a much greater straight line force. As a result, the axle easily drives straight into the object.

A corkscrew converts a turning motion into a straight line force.

GEARS

Gears are used to change speed in many different kinds of complex machines, from cars to clocks. They do this by changing the size of a turning force.

Gears consist of two or more toothed wheels, or **cogs**, that fit into each other, so that turning one cog turns the other. A large cog makes a smaller one turn faster.

This gear changes the size and direction of the turning force.

★

This clock works using a complicated system of geared wheels.

The crane's engine is housed here.

Internet links

• Scan the code to watch a demonstration of a lever.

• For links to more websites about levers, wheels, pulleys, screws and gears, go to **www.usborne.com/quicklinks**

INCLINED PLANES

An **inclined plane** is just a slope, like a ramp. It is easier to move an object up an inclined plane than vertically upwards, because you travel further, so less force is needed for the same amount of work.

80m slope

10m vertical

★

If you push an object eight times as far up an inclined plane as lifting it straight up, you only need one eighth of the force.

USING SIMPLE MACHINES

Simple machines can be used to make up more complex machines. Here are some examples. Even animals, such as the lobster on the right, can have body parts which work in the same way as a machine.

Big gear wheel

Small gear wheel

Handle

Blades

Gears on a whisk increase the size of the turning force needed to move the handle, so that the blades can be turned very fast.

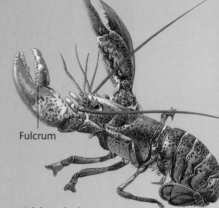

Fulcrum

A lobster's claws, or pincers, are third class levers.

Propellers are a simple form of screw. They are used to push ships through water – and to pull aircraft through the air.

Drill bit

Gears   Drive shaft

An electric drill combines gears and a screw at the tip, called a **bit**. The gears change the speed at which the bit rotates, so that it can drill a hole quickly or slowly.

An axe turns a downward force into a sideways cutting force. The blade is a **wedge** that pushes apart as it cuts down.

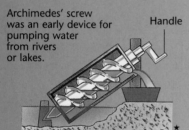

Archimedes' screw was an early device for pumping water from rivers or lakes.

Handle

Water was drawn up on the inclined planes of a turning screw.

A motor provides power to a system of gears and wheels which move the stairs and handrails on an escalator.

Your front teeth, called incisors, are wedges. They work like axes, pushing food apart as they cut down.

Downward force

Sideways force

Scissors are class one levers. The blades are sharp wedges that force surfaces apart.

Fulcrum

A fan is a third class lever. When you wave it, your wrist acts as the fulcrum.

The Ancient Egyptians, who built the pyramids, may have used inclined planes, in the form of spiral slopes, to push enormous blocks of stone up into place. The tallest pyramids were about 146m high.

WORK AND POWER

In science, the word "work" has a particular meaning. **Work** is done when a force makes an object move. Work is only done when the object moves.

MEASURING WORK

Work transfers energy from one object to another and, like energy, is measured in **joules (J)**. One joule equals the work done (and energy transferred) when a force of 1 newton (N) moves an object 1 metre in the direction of the force.

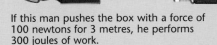

If this man pushes the box with a force of 100 newtons for 3 metres, he performs 300 joules of work.

POWER

Power is the rate at which work is done, or energy is transferred. It is measured in **watts (W)**, named after James Watt, and is worked out by dividing the work done by the time taken to do it.

It takes twice as much power to move the box 3 metres in one minute as to move it 3 metres in two minutes.

* Potential energy, 106.

AN EXAMPLE OF WORK

In the picture, the male dancer's lifting force is overcoming the force of gravity, and work is being done as he raises the ballerina in the air.

The male dancer is using his energy to lift the ballerina. Most of this energy is being converted to potential energy* in the dancer in the air. Also, some heat energy is being released by the male dancer's body.

The ballerina has to do work as she moves her body into the correct pose.

See for yourself

You can measure how much work you do (in joules) when you go upstairs by measuring the height of the stairs and multiplying it by your weight in newtons (your weight in kilograms x 10). Divide the work you do by the time it takes to do it to find out how much power you exert (in watts). The quicker you go, the more power you exert.

Height of stairs

Internet links

• Scan the code to watch a video about work and power.

• For links to more websites where you can investigate work and the forces that make objects move, go to **www.usborne.com/quicklinks**

137

FLOATING

Why do some substances float in water, but not others? And why are there so few substances that are able to float in air? By understanding the principles of floating (and sinking), engineers can build ships out of metals that are heavier than the water they float in, and design airships and hot-air balloons that can float in the air.

Hot-air balloons are filled with air that is lighter than the cool air outside them. They rise up because hot air floats.

WHY THINGS FLOAT

When an object is put into water, it pushes aside, or **displaces**, some of the water. It takes up the space where the water was, and the level of the water rises.

According to legend, the Ancient Greek scientist Archimedes (287-212BC) first realized how objects displace water when he got into his bath.

This is a medieval picture of Archimedes making his discovery.

Water pushes back against an object placed in it with a force called **upthrust**. If this is the same as the weight of the object, the object floats. The weight of the object and the weight of the water it displaces are equal.

ARCHIMEDES' PRINCIPLE

Archimedes' principle states that the upthrust acting on an object is equal to the weight of the fluid that the object displaces. An object will sink into a fluid, such as water, and keep on sinking unless the upthrust from the fluid becomes equal to the weight of the object.

Water is displaced (yellow arrows) as boat is lowered. Upthrust (red arrow) pushes back on boat.

When upthrust of water equals weight of boat, boat settles on water and floats steadily.

DENSITY

One object may float while another of the same size may sink. Same-sized objects have different weights if their density is different. **Density** is a measure of the amount of matter in an object (its **mass**) compared to its volume (size).

A steel ball is heavier than an apple of the same size because it is denser. Its matter is packed more tightly together. The apple floats (just) in water but the steel ball sinks.

FLOATING IN THE AIR

Air, like water, pushes back at an object with a force called upthrust. This equals the weight of air pushed aside by the object. If the upthrust equals the weight of the object, the object floats. But air is so light that few things float in it. Hot-air balloons and helium-filled airships can both float in air, though, because hot air and helium are both lighter than cold air.

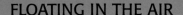

Airships are built so that the helium is held in a series of separate cells. If one cell bursts, only the helium in that section will be lost.

This cutaway drawing shows an airship filled with helium gas, which is lighter than air.

Metal frames give the airship a stable shape.

Helium gas cell

HOW SHIPS FLOAT

Modern ships are made of steel, which is eight times denser than water. But they don't sink because their overall density is lower than water. This is because ships are hollow. All the space inside them makes them less dense than water. Their huge volume pushes aside (or displaces) a large amount of water and so creates a lot of upthrust on the ship.

When fully laden, a container ship sinks lower into the water to displace more water. This increases the upthrust until it is equal to the new, heavier weight of the ship, which continues to float.

RELATIVE DENSITIES

For an object to float in water, its density needs to be less than, or the same as, the density of water. If not, the water cannot provide enough upthrust to support it.

The **relative density** of an object is its density when compared to the density of water. The relative density of water is 1, so an object will sink if its relative density is more than 1, but float if it is 1 or less.

Water 1   Cork 0.2   Air 0.0012

Aluminium 2.7   Steel 8   Copper 9

This picture shows the relative densities of different substances. Nearly all metals are denser than water.

See for yourself

You can use a ball of modelling clay to show how a ship floats. If you drop the ball into water it will sink. This is because the ball is denser than the water. If you shape the same piece of clay into a hollow bowl, though, it should float.

Although it is the same weight as the ball, the bowl floats because it pushes aside more water. The upthrust is equal to its weight.

Bowl-shaped clay floats.

Ball of clay sinks.

Internet links

• Scan the code for a video about Archimedes' principle.

• For links to more websites about how things float in water and in the air, go to www.usborne.com/quicklinks

SHIPS AND BOATS

Ships and boats once relied on the wind or human strength for their power. The invention of engines meant that propellers* could be used to drive ships through the water. More recent boat designs include hydrofoils and hovercraft.

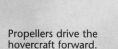

Viking ship

In the ninth century, the Vikings used ships like this. For power, they used sails as well as oars.

Tankers

Tankers carry oil or other liquid cargo in tanks. Big tankers, called supertankers, are the largest ships in the world.

Helicopter landing pad

Control deck

Hovercraft

A hovercraft (also called an Air-Cushion Vehicle, or ACV) skims over the water on a cushion of air inside a rubber skirt.

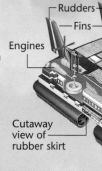

Rudders

Fins

Engines

Propellers drive the hovercraft forward.

Control cabin

Cutaway view of rubber skirt

Cruise ships

Large, luxurious cruise ships are designed to carry hundreds of people on holidays.

Hydrofoils

Hydrofoils have stilts attached to underwater "wings" called foils. When a hydrofoil speeds up, its hull lifts out of the water, reducing water resistance. Two designs of foil are surface-piercing foils and ladder foils.

Hull

Surface-piercing foil

Hydrofoil with surface-piercing foils

Hydrofoil with ladder foils

Container ships

Container ships carry goods in large metal boxes. These can be unloaded or loaded quickly by cranes. One ship can carry hundreds of containers.

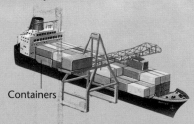

Containers

Racing yacht

This racing yacht was built using heavy wood, and has weighty canvas sails. Modern versions use more lightweight materials, so they are faster and easier to steer.

* Propellers, 136.

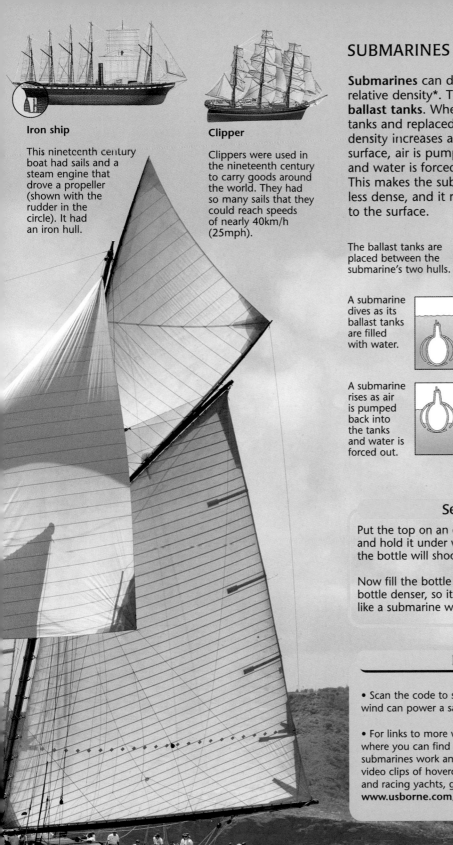

Iron ship

This nineteenth century boat had sails and a steam engine that drove a propeller (shown with the rudder in the circle). It had an iron hull.

Clipper

Clippers were used in the nineteenth century to carry goods around the world. They had so many sails that they could reach speeds of nearly 40km/h (25mph).

SUBMARINES

Submarines can dive and surface by altering their relative density*. They carry large containers called **ballast tanks**. When air is expelled from these tanks and replaced with water, the submarine's density increases and it dives. When it needs to surface, air is pumped back into the tanks and water is forced back out. This makes the submarine less dense, and it rises to the surface.

Periscope

The ballast tanks are placed between the submarine's two hulls.

A submarine dives as its ballast tanks are filled with water.

A submarine rises as air is pumped back into the tanks and water is forced out.

Outer hull

Inner hull

Submarines have powerful propellers to drive them through the water. Some have engines driven by nuclear power.

Propeller

See for yourself

Put the top on an empty plastic bottle and hold it under water. Let it go and the bottle will shoot up to the surface.

Now fill the bottle with water. You are making the bottle denser, so it will now remain underwater, just like a submarine with water in its ballast tanks.

Internet links

• Scan the code to see how wind can power a sailboat.

• For links to more websites where you can find out how submarines work and watch video clips of hovercraft, ships and racing yachts, go to **www.usborne.com/quicklinks**

*Relative density, 139.

FLIGHT

The first powered flight took place a century ago and lasted only twelve seconds. Now planes can travel faster than the speed of sound, and helicopters can hover in the air without moving. The wings of planes and the blades of helicopters have a special shape which helps them to fly.

Kites were the first things that people managed to fly.

HOW PLANES FLY

Planes stay up in the air because of the shape of their wings. The wings are curved on top and flatter underneath. A bird's wings have the same shape. It is called an **aerofoil**.

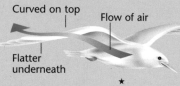

Cross section of an aerofoil shape

Curved on top

Flow of air

Flatter underneath

★

The air above an aerofoil wing has further to travel than the air under it. When the flow of a gas such as air gets faster, its pressure is reduced. This is called **Bernoulli's principle**. Because of this, the slower air flowing under the wing has a higher pressure and pushes up on it. This force is called **lift**, and it causes the wing to rise up into the air.

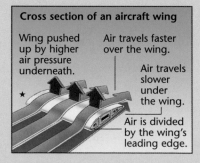

Cross section of an aircraft wing

Wing pushed up by higher air pressure underneath.

Air travels faster over the wing.

Air travels slower under the wing.

★

Air is divided by the wing's leading edge.

Gliders are very light and the lift from their wings is strong enough to overcome the downward pull of gravity. Heavier aircraft need a force called **thrust** to stay in the air. Thrust, the force that moves a plane forwards, is provided by a plane's engines.

The more thrust an engine provides, the faster the plane goes. This greater speed improves the lift on the aircraft. The faster the wings are moving through the air, the greater the difference in air pressure above and below them.

The four forces of flight

The arrows on this picture show the four forces of flight: lift, gravity, drag and thrust.

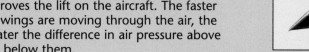

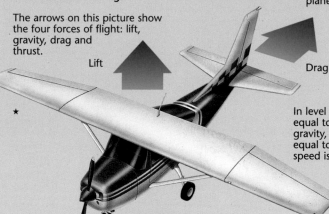

Lift

★

Drag

Thrust

Gravity

In level flight, lift is equal to the pull of gravity, and thrust is equal to drag if the speed is constant.

Drag, or **air resistance**, is another force acting on a plane. It is the force of friction* that occurs when something moves in air.

Drag increases as speed increases, so very fast aircraft are streamlined to reduce drag. A streamlined plane is designed so that air moves around it more smoothly.

Propellers provide thrust by pulling a plane through the air.

Jet engines provide thrust by pushing a plane through the air.

* Friction, 124.

HOW PLANES ARE CONTROLLED

A plane needs to be able to move up and down, and to turn and bank (tip) to each side. To do this, the wings and tail are fitted with hinged flaps. These are known as **control surfaces**. They are made up of **ailerons** on the wings, and **elevators** and a **rudder** on the tail. By using a particular control surface, a pilot increases the drag on that part of the plane. This pushes it into a new position, as shown in the diagrams below.

How control surfaces work

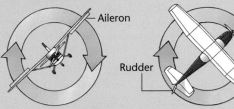 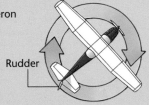 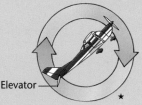

Aileron

Rudder

Elevator

When turning, a plane also banks. This is called **rolling**. It is controlled by the ailerons on the wings.

Turning to the left or right is called **yawing**, and is controlled by the rudder on the tail fin.

Moving up and down is called **pitching**. Elevators on the tailplane control this.

Aileron. The next time you fly, look out for these moving on the backs of the wings.

The wings also have high-lift flaps on their back edge and adjustable slats on their leading edge that can add lift for take-off and landing, but reduce drag during cruising flight.

Nose

Its nose is shaped to reduce drag, allow the pilot to see, and reduce noise heard in the cabin.

Big jets like this tuck their wheels, or undercarriage, away during flights to reduce the drag on the plane.

The Airbus has four engines.

This Airbus A380 is flying past at an air show. During flight, the pilot controls the jet's ailerons, elevators and rudders to adjust the plane's height and direction.

Internet links

• Scan the code to tour a plane's cockpit and see the controls.

• For links to more websites where you can explore the four forces of flight, find out more about how planes are controlled and fly a plane online, go to **www.usborne.com/quicklinks**

AIRCRAFT DESIGN

The design of an aircraft depends on its function. Some planes need to be able to land on water, and some helicopters are used to lift huge weights. Here you can see some examples of different aircraft designs.

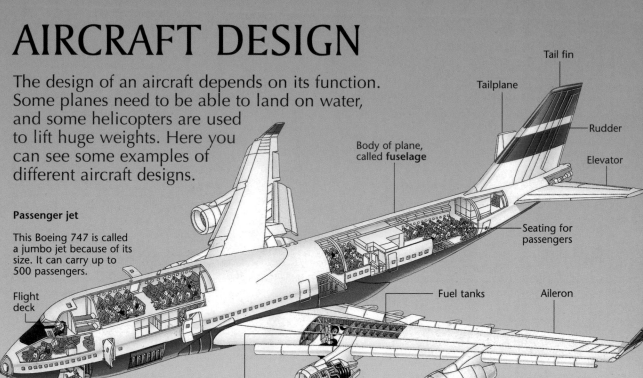

Tail fin

Tailplane

Rudder

Body of plane, called **fuselage**

Elevator

Passenger jet

This Boeing 747 is called a jumbo jet because of its size. It can carry up to 500 passengers.

Seating for passengers

Flight deck

Fuel tanks

Aileron

Radar equipment

Undercarriage (main landing gear)

Jet engines

★

Swing-wing plane

This Panavia Tornado is a swing-wing jet fighter. Its moveable wings can be straight (better for flying at slow speeds and landing) or swept-back (better for high-speed flying).

Wings sweep through this angle.

Sea plane

This Canadair CL-415 is a sea plane. It can take off and land on water. It floats because its body is shaped like a boat.

This plane also has wheels so it can move on land. Planes like this are called amphibians.

Supersonic passenger plane

Supersonic planes fly faster than the speed of sound*. The Concorde was the only supersonic passenger plane.

Concorde's delta-shaped wings (see page 145) helped it to fly at speeds of up to 2,333km/h (1,450mph).

"Invisible" plane

The Northrop B2 Stealth bomber's strange "flying wing" shape helps it to avoid radar detection. It has a wingspan of over 52m.

The Stealth bomber is made of radar-absorbent materials.

Load-carrying helicopter

The Sikorsky Skycrane carries heavy loads to hard-to-reach places.

The Skycrane can carry the weight of over 150 people. Here, it is unloading a ready-made cabin to a building site.

*Speed of sound. 207.

FIRST FLIGHT

The first successful powered flight was made in 1903 by Flyer I. It was designed and built by the Wright brothers in the USA. The plane flew for about twelve seconds and lifted only a little way off the ground.

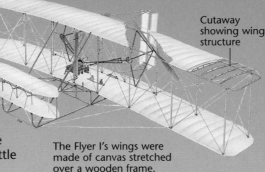

Cutaway showing wing structure

The Flyer I's wings were made of canvas stretched over a wooden frame.

HELICOPTERS

Helicopters can travel in any direction, or just hover in the air without moving. Their rotor blades are aerofoils*, which provide lift as they spin around rapidly. To provide thrust*, the blades are tilted forwards. They push the air behind them and this moves the helicopter forwards.

This Robinson R22 has two main rotor blades. Some helicopters have three or four.

The tail blades keep the helicopter stable. Without them, it would spin around. The tail blades are also used for turning.

This helicopter does not have wheels, but rests on the ground on flat blades called **skids**.

JUMP JETS

A **Vertical Take Off and Landing (VTOL)** plane, or **jump jet** does not need a runway to take off. Harriers were VTOL planes.

A VTOL plane has thrusters which direct the power from its jet engines. In normal flight, the thrusters point to the back. This pushes the plane forwards.

Thruster

This Harrier is taking off. Its thrusters point down at the ground, pushing the plane upwards.

WING SHAPE

How fast a plane can go depends on the shape of its wings, as well as the size of its engines.

Straight wings give enough lift* for low-speed flying, with not much drag*.

Swept-back wings reduce drag at greater speeds, and are needed for larger-sized planes, such as passenger jets.

Delta-shaped wings enable an aircraft to fly at supersonic speeds. The fastest planes use this wing shape.

See for yourself

The wings on a model plane work in the same way as on a real plane.

You can make a paper plane of your own that can do turns and stunts. For a template, plus a step-by-step guide and flying tips, go to the website **www.usborne.com/quicklinks** and follow the instructions.

Internet links

• Scan the code to learn about the design of a passenger jet.

• For links to more websites about the Wright brothers and different types of aircraft, go to **www.usborne.com/quicklinks**

* Aerofoil, Drag, Lift, Thrust, 142.

ENGINES

Engines are machines that convert the energy stored in fuel into movement. They release the energy in fuel by **combustion**, that is, by burning it. This can take place outside the engine (**external combustion**) or inside the engine (**internal combustion**).

STEAM ENGINES

The first engines were **steam engines**. They were invented about 300 years ago, and used external combustion.

In a chamber outside the engine called the **furnace**, wood or coal was burned to boil water. This produced steam. Because steam expands to take up to 2,000 times more space than water, it could be used to move a piston.

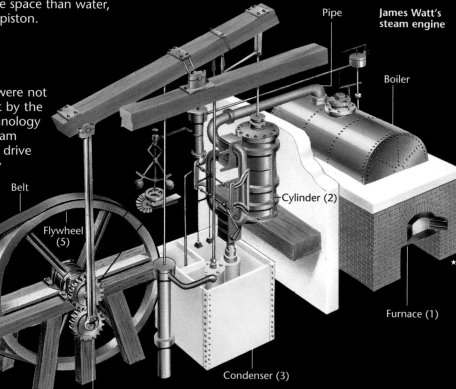

Piston

Cylinder

Early steam engine, built by Thomas Newcomen (1663-1729)

BETTER ENGINES

The earliest steam engines were not very reliable or efficient, but by the nineteenth century the technology had been improved and steam engines were being used to drive trains and power machinery in factories. James Watt (1736-1819) designed the widely-used steam engine shown here.

Pipe

James Watt's steam engine

Boiler

Belt

Flywheel (5)

Cylinder (2)

Sun-and-planet gear (4)

Condenser (3)

Furnace (1)

See for yourself

You can see the power of steam when a covered pan of water boils on a stove.

As the water boils, notice that the lid starts to bounce up and down. This is the expanding steam pushing against the lid.

Steam engines make use of this power to make things move.

1. To make this steam engine work, coal was burned in a furnace to heat water in the boiler.

2. A pipe carried steam from the boiler to the cylinder. The steam pushed a piston up inside the cylinder.

3. The condenser took used steam from the cylinder and the piston went down. The steam turned back into water.

4. A gear called a sun-and-planet gear converted the up-and-down movement of the piston into a rotating motion.

5. The flywheel rotated to power industrial machinery, to which it was connected by a belt.

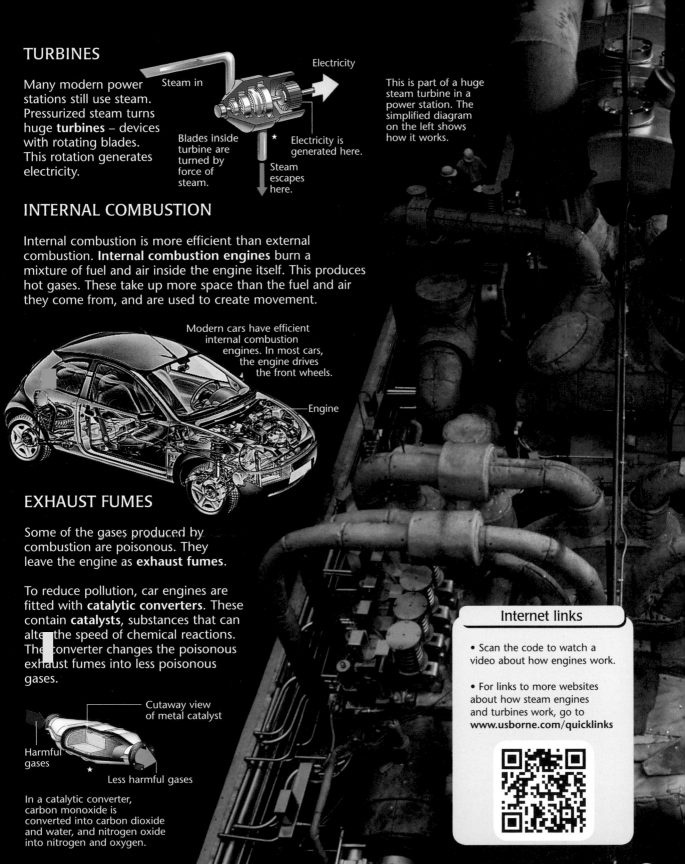

TURBINES

Many modern power stations still use steam. Pressurized steam turns huge **turbines** – devices with rotating blades. This rotation generates electricity.

Steam in

Electricity

Blades inside turbine are turned by force of steam.

★ Electricity is generated here.

Steam escapes here.

This is part of a huge steam turbine in a power station. The simplified diagram on the left shows how it works.

INTERNAL COMBUSTION

Internal combustion is more efficient than external combustion. **Internal combustion engines** burn a mixture of fuel and air inside the engine itself. This produces hot gases. These take up more space than the fuel and air they come from, and are used to create movement.

Modern cars have efficient internal combustion engines. In most cars, the engine drives the front wheels.

Engine

EXHAUST FUMES

Some of the gases produced by combustion are poisonous. They leave the engine as **exhaust fumes**.

To reduce pollution, car engines are fitted with **catalytic converters**. These contain **catalysts**, substances that can alter the speed of chemical reactions. The converter changes the poisonous exhaust fumes into less poisonous gases.

Cutaway view of metal catalyst

Harmful gases

★ Less harmful gases

In a catalytic converter, carbon monoxide is converted into carbon dioxide and water, and nitrogen oxide into nitrogen and oxygen.

Internet links

• Scan the code to watch a video about how engines work.

• For links to more websites about how steam engines and turbines work, go to **www.usborne.com/quicklinks**

147

PETROL ENGINES

Most car engines burn petrol. **Petrol engines** use internal combustion* to drive pistons up and down in hollow cylinders.

Each piston works in four stages called a **four-stroke combustion cycle**, as shown in the pictures on the right.

How a four-stroke engine works

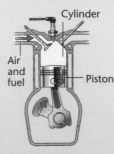

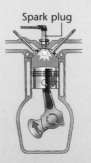
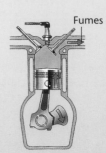

1. Piston goes down, sucking a mixture of air and fuel into cylinder.

2. Piston goes up, compressing fuel and air mixture. This heats mixture.

3. Spark from spark plug ignites mixture. Gases expand and force piston down.

4. Piston rises again, pushing out remains of burned gases as exhaust fumes.

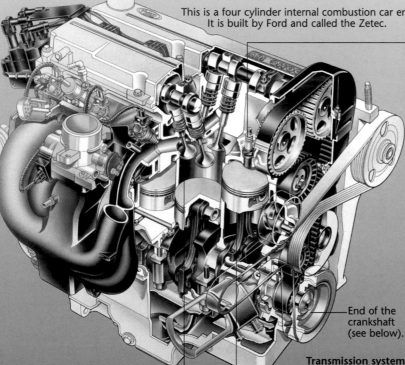

This is a four cylinder internal combustion car engine. It is built by Ford and called the Zetec.

A small spark is set off at this end of the plug.

Spark plug

One of the cylinders

One of the pistons

End of the crankshaft (see below).

DIESEL ENGINES

Diesel engines are fuelled by diesel. They work in a similar way to petrol engines, but at stroke one, only air is taken into the cylinder. This is compressed and heated to a very high temperature at stroke two. Fuel is forced into the cylinder at stroke three, where it is so hot that the fuel burns without a spark. Some cars and many large vehicles have diesel engines, which use fuel more efficiently than petrol engines and so use less fuel.

TRANSMISSION

The four-stroke combustion cycle takes place in each of a car's cylinders. A series of shafts and gears, called the transmission, converts the up-and-down motion of the pistons into a rotating motion used to turn the wheels of the car. The system works in a similar way whether it drives the front or rear wheels of the car. (See also *Transmission* on page 151.)

Transmission system of a rear-wheel drive car

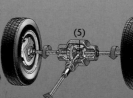

Up-and-down movement of pistons (1) turns crankshaft (2).

Gears (3) connect crankshaft to drive shaft (4).

Drive shaft turns wheels through more gears, called the differential* (5).

JET ENGINES

Jet engines are very powerful internal combustion engines* used by aircraft. The hot gases they produce are forced out of the back of the engine at high speed. This pushes the plane through the air.

Jet engines are also known as **gas turbine engines** because the hot gases turn blades called turbines in the engine. The turbines suck air into the engine and compress it before it is mixed with fuel and burned.

TURBOJET ENGINES

The **turbojet engine** below is the simplest and fastest type of jet engine. It is noisy and less efficient with fuel than a turbofan engine (see right). Turbojet engines are only used for high-speed jet planes.

Cutaway of a turbojet engine

Air enters front of engine (1). Turbines in compression chamber (2) compress air. Compressed air is channelled into combustion chamber (3) and mixed with kerosene fuel. Mixture burns and produces hot, expanding gases.

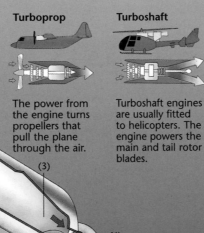

Hot gases turn another turbine (4) as they pass through back of engine. This helps to drive compression turbines near front. Gases are forced out of exhaust tailpipe (5), pushing plane forwards.

TURBOFAN ENGINES

Turbofan engines are not as fast as turbojets, but they are quieter and use less fuel. They are fitted to passenger jets.

Cutaway of a turbofan engine

Extra large fan at front (1) sucks in huge amounts of air. Some air goes through compression and combustion chambers (2), as in turbojet, producing hot expanding gases which are forced out of back (3).

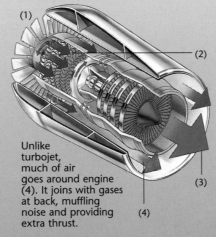

Unlike turbojet, much of air goes around engine (4). It joins with gases at back, muffling noise and providing extra thrust.

There are two other kinds of gas turbine engine:

Turboprop

Turboshaft

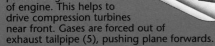

The power from the engine turns propellers that pull the plane through the air.

Turboshaft engines are usually fitted to helicopters. The engine powers the main and tail rotor blades.

ROCKET ENGINES

Like jet engines, **rocket engines** produce hot gases which are forced out at speed. Instead of sucking in air for combustion, rocket engines carry liquid oxygen. This means that they can travel in space where there is no air.

Space rockets were developed from rocket missiles, such as this V-2 made in 1942.

Rocket fuel

Liquid oxygen tank

Rocket fuel and oxygen burn in the combustion chamber.

Hot gases shoot out of the exhaust.

See for yourself

Try this to give you an idea of how jet engines work. Thread some string through a straw and tie it tightly between two pieces of furniture. Blow up a balloon and hold the end so that it doesn't deflate. Ask a friend to tape the balloon to the straw.

Now let go of the balloon. The air rushes out and the balloon shoots forwards.

Balloon

Straw   String

Internet links

• Scan the code to watch the launch of a space rocket.

* Internal combustion engines, 147.

CARS AND MOTORBIKES

Cars, motorbikes and other road vehicles have transformed the way we live. They allow us to move from one place to another quickly and whenever we want to. But their popularity has led to problems of pollution and traffic jams. Car makers are constantly trying to develop cars that are less damaging to the environment.

This is one of the very first cars. It was built in Germany in 1885.

CAR TECHNOLOGY

The first cars were invented about 120 years ago. At first, they were slow, noisy, unreliable and dangerous. Since then, engineers and designers have refined all aspects of how cars work. These include making improvements to vital parts such as the engine, brakes, transmission and suspension. The vehicle below shows a good example of modern car design.

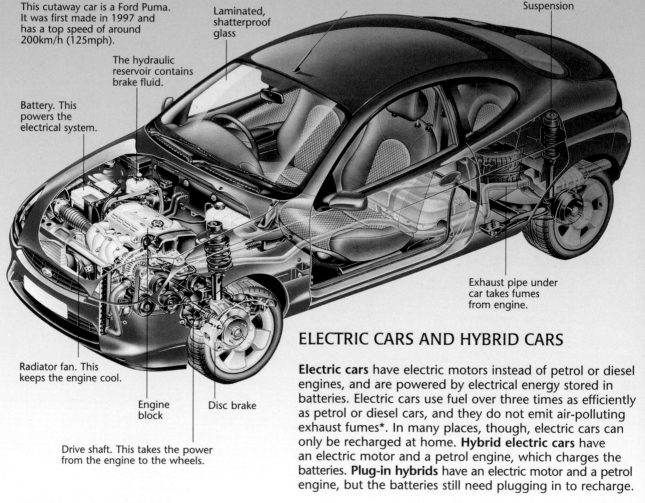

This cutaway car is a Ford Puma. It was first made in 1997 and has a top speed of around 200km/h (125mph).

The hydraulic reservoir contains brake fluid.

Battery. This powers the electrical system.

Laminated, shatterproof glass

Suspension

Exhaust pipe under car takes fumes from engine.

Radiator fan. This keeps the engine cool.

Engine block

Disc brake

Drive shaft. This takes the power from the engine to the wheels.

ELECTRIC CARS AND HYBRID CARS

Electric cars have electric motors instead of petrol or diesel engines, and are powered by electrical energy stored in batteries. Electric cars use fuel over three times as efficiently as petrol or diesel cars, and they do not emit air-polluting exhaust fumes*. In many places, though, electric cars can only be recharged at home. **Hybrid electric cars** have an electric motor and a petrol engine, which charges the batteries. **Plug-in hybrids** have an electric motor and a petrol engine, but the batteries still need plugging in to recharge.

*Exhaust fumes, Internal combustion engines, 147.

MOTORBIKES

Motorbikes and cars share many features, although motorbikes don't need a differential (see below). Because they are relatively light, motorbikes can have engines with small cylinder capacities, down to about 50cm³ (50 cubic centimetres) in total. Bikes with large engines are powerful, and can accelerate faster than cars.

Rear indicator

Pillion seat

Low seat for low centre of gravity*

Petrol tank

Fairing (covering) reduces drag*.

Suspension

Exhaust

Disc brake

This Honda FireBlade has a 900cm³ engine.

Steel frame

TRANSMISSION

The **transmission** (see also page 148) is a system of **gears** that transmits an engine's power to the wheels. Gears are made of cogs (metal wheels with serrated edges called teeth). Engine power turns a rod called the input shaft, which is attached to one set of cogs. These turn another set of cogs which are attached to another rod – the output shaft. The output shaft turns drive shafts, which are attached to the wheels. (Electric cars have no transmission as their motors fit directly to the wheels.)

DIFFERENTIAL

The **differential** is a vital part of a car's transmission. It is a system of gears on the axles which allows the wheels to spin at different speeds. This is necessary for corners, when the outer wheels turn further and faster than the inner ones.

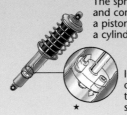

The inner wheel travels a shorter distance than the outer one.

★

SUSPENSION

Suspension is made up of two parts, a spring and a damper. The spring compresses and expands as the wheel goes over a bump. The damper delays the spring's action, so that the ride is not too bouncy.

The spring expands and contracts, moving a piston up and down a cylinder.

★

In the damper, oil is forced through valves, slowing down the piston.

BRAKES

Cars and motorbikes use **disc brakes**. When the brake pedal or lever is pressed, brake fluid is pushed down tubes, forcing brake pads to press against a disc in the wheel. The friction* causes the wheel to slow down.

Brake fluid is forced down pipes.

Fluid pushes brake pads against the disc.

★

Brake disc

* Centre of gravity, 131; Drag, 142; Friction, 124.

EARTH
AND
SPACE

THE UNIVERSE

The **universe** or **cosmos** is the name used to describe the collection of all matter, energy and space that exists. How the universe was created is not fully understood. Most scientists believe that it began about 14 billion years ago with an unimaginably violent explosion known as the **Big Bang**. This idea is called the **Big Bang theory**.

After the Big Bang, the fireball spread out and the universe started to expand.

SIZE AND DISTANCE

The universe is so enormous, it is impossible to imagine. Distances across it are colossal and are usually measured in **light years**. One light year is the distance light travels in one year – that is about 9.46 trillion kilometres. Light travels 300,000 kilometres in a second.

The nearest star to the Earth is the Sun. It is about 150 million kilometres away.

A ray of light takes eight minutes to travel from the Sun to the Earth.

The universe contains billions of stars gathered together in huge collections called **galaxies**. So far, astronomers have spotted galaxies that are up to 30 billion light years away, which gives an idea of just how vast the universe must be.

This cluster of galaxies, called Abell 2218, is about 2 billion light years away from the Earth.

THE BIG BANG THEORY

The Big Bang created a huge fireball, which cooled and formed into tiny particles. Everything in the universe is made up of these tiny particles, called **matter**.

The particles spread out and the universe began to expand. Over time, thick clouds of hydrogen and helium gases formed. These clouds then gathered together in dense clumps.

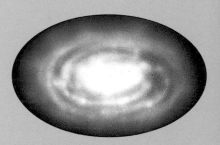

Thick clouds of gases collected into vast clumps of dense matter.

To begin with, the universe was so dense that light could not travel far within it, so it was very dark. After a few thousand years, the temperature fell to a few thousand degrees.

Very gradually, the fog cleared. This meant that light could travel further, and the universe became as transparent as it is today. The first galaxies began to form from the dense clumps of gases.

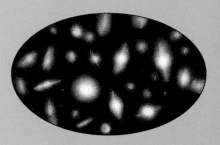

Stars and galaxies began to form. The universe became transparent as light was now able to travel through it.

About 9 billion years after the Big Bang, the Sun and planets of our Solar System formed near the edge of a galaxy that would later be named the Milky Way.

The modern universe contains countless millions of stars and planets, and huge clouds of dust and gas, separated by vast areas of empty space. Even today, parts of the universe are still forming.

About 9 billion years after the Big Bang, the Solar System formed.

When you look at the night sky, you are looking out upon millions and millions of stars.

BIG BANG EVIDENCE

The strongest evidence for the Big Bang theory is that powerful radio telescopes have detected faint levels of microwave* radiation across the whole night sky. These waves are known as the **Cosmic Microwave Background (CMB)**.

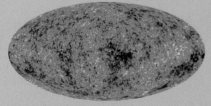

This computer map of the night sky shows slight variations in the CMB.

The CMB is thought to be an afterglow from the time when the universe first became transparent enough for light to travel. As the universe expanded, this early radiation was stretched out into longer wavelength microwaves.

The CMB's pattern gives scientists clues to the way that the universe expanded. The **Inflation theory** is the idea that it didn't expand steadily but, in the first split second of the Big Bang, inflated from much tinier than an atom to the size of a golfball. A second later, it was a trillion kilometres wide. The universe then carried on expanding, at a slower rate.

THE FUTURE

There are three main theories about the future of the universe.

The **Big Freeze theory** states that the universe could go on expanding continuously, and everything would gradually fade away. Eventually the whole universe would become just a mist of cold particles.

The universe could slow down and then simply fade away.

The force of gravity* may one day slow down the universe's expansion, pulling everything back until the galaxies crash. There could then be a Big Crunch, like the Big Bang in reverse. This idea, called the **Big Crunch theory**, now looks less likely because a mysterious force called **dark energy** seems to be making the universe expand faster and faster.

The galaxies could collide in a Big Crunch.

Some scientists think that the universe works like a heart, beating in rhythm. They believe that it expands, then shrinks, then expands again, and so on. So a Big Bang is followed by a Big Crunch, in a repeating cycle. This idea is called the **Big Bounce theory**.

Big Bang   Big Crunch   Big Bang

Internet links

• Scan the code to watch a video about the size of the universe.

• For links to other amazing websites about the universe and the Big Bang, go to www.usborne.com/quicklinks

* Gravity, 130; Microwaves, 213.

GALAXIES

Stars are grouped together in vast collections called **galaxies**. Each galaxy contains billions of stars. Galaxies are themselves generally grouped together. Our Solar System forms a tiny part of a galaxy called the **Milky Way** in a group called the **Local Group**. This contains about 60 galaxies and stretches across ten million light years*.

The Cartwheel galaxy is 500 million light years away.

STAR CLUSTERS

Inside galaxies, stars often group together in clusters. Stars within a cluster move at the same speed and in the same direction. There are two types of star clusters.

Open clusters are found in areas of space that are rich in gas and dust. They contain from a few dozen to a thousand bright young stars which are scattered loosely in the cluster.

This is an open cluster of stars called the Pleiades.

Globular clusters are much larger than open clusters. They contain up to a million stars, densely packed together in sphere-shaped clumps.

Globular clusters like this one appear like very faint stars to the naked eye.

TYPES OF GALAXIES

Galaxies form in different shapes. The four most common shapes are spiral, barred spiral, elliptical and irregular.

A **spiral galaxy** has a bright middle and two or more curved arms of stars.

A **barred spiral galaxy** has a central bar of stars with an arm at each end.

Elliptical galaxies vary in shape from round to oval. They contain many old, red stars.

An **irregular galaxy** is a cloud of stars with no definite shape.

One third of all known galaxies are spiral shaped. Using sophisticated telescopes, astronomers have recently found new galaxies which are bigger and less tightly packed with stars than any they have seen before. These galaxies do not give off much light, so they are known as **low surface brightness galaxies**.

CARTWHEEL GALAXY

The Cartwheel galaxy (shown above) is an enormous galaxy, 150,000 light years across. Its rare shape was formed when a smaller galaxy smashed into it.

The outer ring is a vast circle of billions of new stars. These formed from the gas and dust which expanded from the core after the collision. It is now starting to re-form its original spiral shape.

NEAREST GALAXIES

Apart from some "dwarf" galaxies that orbit the Milky Way, our closest neighbours are two small, irregular galaxies called the Large and Small Magellanic Clouds. The nearest large galaxy is the spiral Andromeda galaxy. It is over 2.5 million light years away, and is the most distant object that can be seen with the eye on its own.

In this UV* image of Andromeda, only its hottest, youngest stars are visible.

Light years, 154; UV (Ultraviolet), 213.

THE MILKY WAY

Compared with other galaxies, the Milky Way is relatively large, measuring about 100,000 light years across. The Earth and the rest of our Solar System lie about 32,000 light years from the middle of the Milky Way.

Most astronomers believe that the Milky Way is a spiral galaxy, although some describe it as a barred spiral galaxy. It gets its name because in ancient times, people thought that it looked like a trail of spilled milk in the night sky.

The Earth and the Solar System are here in the Milky Way.

The Milky Way

This is one of at least 150 huge globular star clusters that hover above or below the middle of our galaxy.

Areas of glowing pink gas are nebulae, the regions where new stars form. For more about nebulae, see page 158.

See for yourself

On a clear night you could look for the Milky Way. In the northern hemisphere, the best time to see it is between July and September, although it also looks impressive on dark midwinter nights.

In the southern hemisphere, the Milky Way is at its most spectacular between October and December. It looks like a band of glowing light.

Like all spiral galaxies, the Milky Way rotates slowly. Closer to the middle it spins faster than at its edges. Our Solar System is thought to revolve around the middle of the galaxy about once every 225 million years. According to this theory, the Milky Way has rotated only once since the dinosaurs were living on the Earth.

This side view of the Milky Way shows that it has a bulge in the middle, like two fried eggs placed back to back.

Internet links

• Scan the code to see images of galaxies taken by the Hubble Space Telescope.

• For links to sites about the Milky Way and other galaxies, go to www.usborne.com/quicklinks

STARS

Every galaxy in the universe contains millions and millions of stars. A **star** is a ball of tremendously hot gas, which produces heat and light from nuclear reactions within its core. The nearest star to the Earth is the Sun, which is 150 million kilometres away. The second closest star is Proxima Centauri, 4.5 light years* away.

NEBULAE

Stars are formed in huge clouds of dust and gas called **nebulae**. Some nebulae are bright and some are dark. **Dark nebulae** look like dark patches in the sky. They are made mostly of dust, which blots out the light of stars behind them. The gases in **bright nebulae** are so hot that they glow in beautiful colours.

The Horse's Head Nebula is a dark nebula. It is silhouetted against a bright nebula.

The colours in a bright nebula depend on the types of gases it contains. For example, hydrogen glows pink, while oxygen glows green-blue.

The Trifid Nebula is a bright nebula. Its colours are caused by hot, glowing gases.

These columns of gas and dust, known as the Pillars of Creation, are part of the Eagle Nebula. The taller column measures about a light year from base to tip.

THE BIRTH OF A STAR

The clouds of gases and dust in some nebulae swirl around and form into clumps which grow larger and larger. Eventually, something causes these new clouds to collapse. Astronomers think this might happen when they pass through the arms of a spiral galaxy, or that the collapse is caused by a shock wave from an exploding star.

As each cloud collapses, the temperature inside it rises. After tens of thousands of years of collapse, a hot core forms. The core gets hotter and hotter until nuclear reactions begin inside, making the cloud of gases, now a star, start to shine.

Gases and dust in the nebula swirl around.

The clouds collapse.

A hot core forms.

A new star is born.

VARIABLE STARS

Some stars appear to change occasionally in brilliance. These are called **variable stars** and they fall into three main types – pulsating, eclipsing and cataclysmic variables.

Pulsating variables are usually larger than the Sun. They change in size and temperature, giving off more light when large and less light when small. Some variable stars shrink and grow in a regular cycle, but others are more erratic. The series of pictures below shows Mira, a pulsating variable star with a regular cycle.

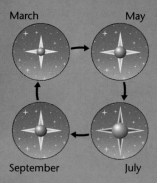

March   May

September   July

An **eclipsing variable (EcV)** is a type of **binary star**. A binary is actually two stars which orbit around each other, held in place by gravity. In an EcV, one star passes behind the other, as seen from Earth, so the brightness changes. The diagram below shows an EcV with a small, bright star and a larger, dimmer one.

An eclipsing variable

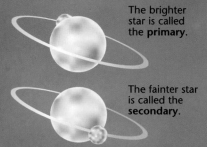

The brighter star is called the **primary**.

The fainter star is called the **secondary**.

Cataclysmic variables are binary stars that are very close together. When the gravity of one of them (usually a white dwarf*) pulls material away from the other (usually a red giant*), a huge and sudden increase in brightness occurs between and around them. This is caused by violent nuclear reactions.

One type of cataclysmic variable, called a **nova**, flares suddenly, then fades back to its original brightness. It does this over several months or even years.

THE LIFE OF A STAR

At first, most new stars burn very brightly, appearing either blue or white. They exist in this state for millions of years. As a star gets older, it shines less brightly but more steadily.

The lifespan of a star varies. Stars such as our Sun have a lifespan of about 10 billion years. Stars smaller than the Sun, called **dwarf stars**, live longer. Stars that are larger than our Sun are **giant stars**. The biggest stars of all are **supergiant stars**. They have short lives of only a few million years.

Four bright stars

Here is a comparison of the sizes and colours of some stars. You can find out more about star colours over the page.

Arcturus is an orange giant star.

Rigel is a blue supergiant star.

See for yourself

If you look up at the sky on a clear night, you will notice that some stars seem to twinkle.

This happens because starlight passing through the Earth's atmosphere is bent and broken up. The angle at which it bends depends on the temperature of the air. The light passes through both warm and cold air, so the starlight shines at you from different directions at once, making it appear to flicker.

Starlight bending on its way through the Earth's atmosphere.

Barnard's Star is a red dwarf star, cooler than our Sun.

The Sun is a yellow star.

Internet links

• Scan the code to find out more about the life of a star.

• For links to more websites with fascinating facts and images of stars and nebulae, go to www.usborne.com/quicklinks

* Red giant, White dwarf, 161.

DESCRIBING STARS

Stars burn with different amounts of brightness. Star brightness is measured [on] a scale called **magnitude**. The actual brilliance of [a star] in space is its **absolute magnitude**. A star's brightness [seen] from the Earth is its **apparent magnitude**. The brightest stars are classed as 0 or even minus magnitude.

Magnitude scale

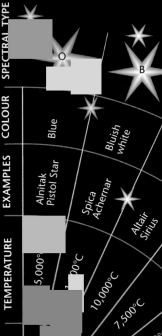

| -1 | 0 | 1 | 2 | 3 | 4 | 5 | 6 | 7 | 8 | 9 |

Brightest stars   Dimmest stars

Stars are classified by their colour. The youngest, hottest stars are usu[ally blue o]r white, and the old[er, cooles]t ones are red. A class [of star is] called a **spectral type**. [The] main spectral types are shown in the chart below.

SPECTRAL TYPE

O   B   A   F   G   K   M

COLOUR

Blue   Bluish white   White   Yellowish white   Yellow   Orange   Red

EXAMPLES

Alnitak / Pistol Star   Spica / Achernar   Altair / Sirius   Canopus / Procyon   Sun / Capella   Aldebaran / Pollux   Arcturus / Antares

TEMPERATURE

5,000°   [1]0,000°C   10,000°C   7,500°C   6,[0]00°C   4,7[00°C]   [3],300°C

CONSTELLATIONS

Since earliest times, people have noticed patterns of bright stars in the sky. These patterns are called constellations. There are 88 **constellations** visible from the Earth. Many of them are named after characters or objects taken from ancient Greek myths.

Within constellations, there are smaller patterns called **asterisms**. The Plough, or Big Dipper, is a famous asterism. It is part of the constellation Ursa Major.

The constellation of Ursa Major, or the Great Bear. Here, the imaginary shape of a bear is drawn around it.

The seven stars of the tail and hips make the asterism called the Plough.

The constellations are made up of the most prominent stars in the sky. From the Earth, the stars in a constellation may look quite close to one another. In reality, they are extremely far apart. The stars in the constellation Orion, for example, vary between less than 500 light years* and over 2,000 light years away. Viewed from the Earth, the stars look like a connected group, as they lie in the same direction.

The stars in Orion look close together and the same distance from the Earth.

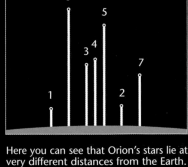

Here you can see that Orion's stars lie at very different distances from the Earth.

See for yourself

All constellations and asterisms can be seen with the naked eye, though what you can see depends on the time of year and your geographical position. Next time you are outside on a clear, starry night, se[e if yo]u can spot the P[lough] in t[he nor]thern hemisphere, or the four stars that make the Southern Cross in the southern hemisphere.

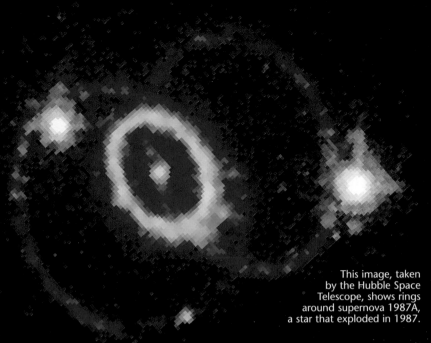

This image, taken by the Hubble Space Telescope, shows rings around supernova 1987A, a star that exploded in 1987.

BLACK HOLES

When the very biggest stars die, they form red supergiants, then explode into a supernova. However, when they collapse, they shrink so much that they virtually vanish from the universe. They may become what are called **black holes** – bottomless pits from which nothing escapes.

A black hole is so heavy and dense that its gravity sucks everything inside it, even light. This makes it invisible. Anything falling into a black hole will be crushed. Scientists think that an enormous black hole, known as **Sagittarius A*** (said "A-star"), lies in the middle of our galaxy. It has the pull of 4 million Suns, and is surrounded by ancient red stars.

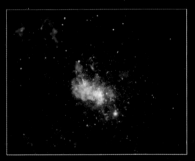

This photo shows the heart of the Milky Way. The bright, cloudy part is dust heated to amazing temperatures by the intense pull of the huge black hole inside.

THE DEATH OF A STAR

Eventually a star's supply of gas runs out and it dies. As it dies, a star the size of the Sun swells up and turns red. At this stage it is called a **red giant**.

Slowly it puffs its outer layers of gas into space, leaving behind a small, almost dead star called a **white dwarf**. This is about the size of a planet and is extremely dense and heavy for its size. (Imagine a golf ball that weighs as much as a truck.) The white dwarf gradually cools and fades.

This Hubble Space Telescope* image shows six white dwarf stars (shown in circles) surrounded by yellow, Sun-like stars and cooler, red dwarf stars*.

SUPERNOVAS

Giant stars* have a really spectacular death. First they swell into vast red stars, called **red supergiants**. Then they blow up with a colossal explosion, called a **supernova**.

The supernova leaves a rapidly expanding layer of gases and dust with a small, spinning star in the middle. This is a **neutron star**. It is even denser and heavier than a white dwarf (see left). (Imagine a golf ball that weighs as much as a skyscraper.)

Some neutron stars send out beams of radiation that swing around as the star spins. These stars are called **pulsars**.

When a star dies in a huge supernova explosion, only its dense core may survive.

Pulsars are neutron stars that spin rapidly and flash like lighthouses.

Internet links

• Scan the code to hear stories about how stars were named.

• For links to more websites where you can explore constellations and black holes, go to **www.usborne.com/quicklinks**

* Dwarf stars, Giant stars, 159; Hubble Space Telescope, 175.

THE SUN

Like all stars, the **Sun** is a massive ball of exploding gas. Although it is only a medium-sized star, life on Earth could not exist without the heat and light it provides. It also applies a pulling force called **gravity** to everything within billions of kilometres. This is why planets, moons and other objects travel around or **orbit** the Sun.

Although the Sun is larger than everything else in the Solar System put together, it is only a medium-sized star.

INSIDE THE SUN

Within the Sun, atoms of hydrogen are continually split apart. The pieces fuse together in a different structure to make a light gas called helium. This process, called a **nuclear fusion reaction**, gives out massive amounts of energy.

Structure of the Sun

1. The Sun's **core** is 27 times wider than the Earth, and has a temperature of over 15 million degrees Celsius.

2. The **radiative zone** surrounds the core. Heat produced in the core spreads through this part in waves.

3. The **convective zone** carries the Sun's energy up to the surface. The red arrows on the diagram show its churning motion.

4. The **photosphere** is the Sun's "surface". It is made of churning gases.

SURFACE OF THE SUN

Sunspots are small, dark patches on the Sun's surface which are slightly cooler than their surroundings. Clouds of glowing gas called **faculae** often surround sunspots. Huge loops of gas, called **prominences**, leap from the surface at up to 600 kilometres per second. Explosions called **solar flares** are even more violent and spectacular.

ECLIPSES

The Moon occasionally passes between the Earth and the Sun, blocking its light. This is called a **total solar eclipse**. The Moon can cover the Sun because although it is much smaller, it is also closer to us. If you close one eye and hold up a coin between your face and a ceiling light, you can see how this works.

During a total solar eclipse, a thin layer of gas around the Sun, called the **corona**, can be seen.

AURORAS

The Sun blows a constant stream of invisible particles out into space, in all directions. This is called the **solar wind**. When particles become trapped near the Earth's Poles, they create a dazzling light display called an **aurora**. In the north, this is called the **aurora borealis**, or **northern lights**. In the south, it is called the **aurora australis**, or **southern lights**.

See for yourself

You should never look directly at the Sun, as even glimpsing it could blind you. But there is a simple way in which you can see it indirectly.

Point a pair of binoculars at the Sun with a piece of white cardboard behind them. Move the binoculars around until a white circle appears on the cardboard, then focus them until the image is sharp. You may see dark smudges on the image. These are sunspots.

Keep cover on this lens.

Sun's image

Light enters here.

THE SOLAR SYSTEM

Together, the Sun and everything that orbits it is called the Solar System. It includes planets, moons, chunks of rock, metal and icy debris, and huge amounts of dust.

After the Sun, the most important members of the Solar System are its planets – Mercury, Venus, Earth, Mars, Jupiter, Saturn, Uranus and Neptune. They all orbit the Sun at different distances and speeds, spinning as they do so.

A planet's **day** is the length of time it takes to make a complete 360° turn. An Earth day, for example, lasts 24 hours. A planet's **year** is the length of time it takes to orbit the Sun. The Earth's year is 365.3 days long.

Many of the planets in the Solar System have smaller companions, called **moons**, orbiting them. Moons vary greatly in size, shape and number. For instance, Earth has only one, but Saturn has at least 60. You can find out more about Earth's moon on page 167.

Earth's moon is a rocky, dusty ball.

The Solar System

Below are the planets of the Solar System, and Pluto. The distances between them are not shown to scale because they are too vast.

Dwarf planets are round, like a planet, but aren't large enough to have cleared their orbit of other objects. There's more about dwarf planets on page 171. Large lumps of rock and metal called **asteroids**, and chunks of frozen gas and dirt called **comets**, also orbit the Sun. Most asteroids are found between Mars and Jupiter, but a comet's orbit may be in any part of the Solar System. Find out about asteroids and comets on pages 172-173.

Pluto (dwarf planet)

Neptune

Uranus

Sun

Mercury

Venus

Mars

Earth

Most asteroids are found in this area, called the **Asteroid Belt**.

Jupiter

Saturn

Internet links

• Scan the code for a video about the Sun and auroras.

• For links to more websites about the Sun, eclipses, auroras and the Solar System, go to **www.usborne.com/quicklinks**

THE INNER PLANETS

Mercury, Venus, Earth and Mars are known as the **inner planets**. This is because they are the closest planets to the Sun. Although they all have a similar small size and rocky structure, only Earth is the right distance from the Sun for life to exist on its surface. You can find out more about Earth on pages 166-167.

Venus   Sun   Mercury

Earth   Mars

The diagram above shows the four inner planets and their orbits around the Sun.

MERCURY

Mercury is a very small planet, with a diameter of only 4,880km. It is the nearest planet to the Sun, orbiting it at a distance of about 58 million kilometres. This closeness means that Mercury is blasted by the Sun's rays. Its daytime temperature can reach 427°C, which is over four times hotter than boiling water.

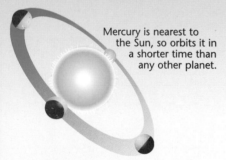

Mercury is nearest to the Sun, so orbits it in a shorter time than any other planet.

It takes Mercury 88 Earth days to orbit the Sun. As it travels, it spins slowly. In fact, each day on Mercury is equal to 58.7 Earth days. This means that there are fewer than two days in one Mercury year. So during its long night, when half of the planet faces away from the Sun, the temperature can plummet as low as -183°C.

VENUS

Venus, the second planet from the Sun, is a similar size to the Earth. It orbits the Sun at a distance of about 108 million kilometres. The planet's surface is mainly flat, but it has raised areas which look like Earth's continents.

Venus has an atmosphere that is mostly made up of carbon dioxide gas. It presses down on the planet's surface like a great weight. Dense clouds of sulphuric acid reflect the Sun's rays, making Venus shine like a very bright star. Any rays which are not reflected become trapped around the planet, raising its temperature to around 480°C.

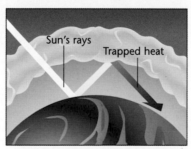

Sun's rays

Trapped heat

Venus's thick atmosphere acts like the glass in a greenhouse. Any rays that travel through it become trapped.

This computer-coloured image shows dense clouds swirling around Venus.

See for yourself

You can try spotting the inner planets yourself. Mercury and Venus can sometimes be seen just before sunrise and just after sunset. After the Sun and Moon, Venus is the brightest object in the sky. It is often called the **Morning Star** or the **Evening Star**, depending on what time of day it appears. Mercury looks like a bright star close to the horizon.

CAUTION
When you are planet spotting, always make sure that the Sun has not begun to rise in the morning or has fully set in the evening. Glimpsing the Sun's rays might damage your eyes.

STUDYING VENUS

Nobody knew what the surface of Venus looked like until 1975, when two space probes named Venera were sent by the Soviet Union. Smaller probes were dropped from them. Their cameras revealed a surface covered with sharp rocks that looked like a gloomy, orange-brown desert.

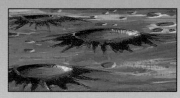

Venus's surface has shallow craters. Objects cannot strike with enough force to make deep craters because the atmosphere slows them down.

In 1990, a space probe named Magellan started using radar to map the planet's surface in greater detail. It was found to be covered mostly by areas of solidified lava, which had flowed out of Venus's many volcanoes. In 2006, a probe called Venus Express arrived to study its atmosphere. It discovered lightning, and signs that Venus's volcanoes may not all be dead.

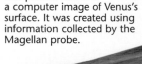

Magellan space probe

The picture below is a computer image of Venus's surface. It was created using information collected by the Magellan probe.

MARS

Mars is the fourth planet from the Sun. It is just half the size of the Earth and orbits the Sun at a distance of about 228 million kilometres, taking just under 687 days to do so.

Mars is sometimes called the **Red Planet**, because of the reddish dust covering its surface.

Mars has two moons, called **Phobos** and **Deimos**, which are dark and dusty. Many scientists think that these odd-shaped moons are really asteroids that became trapped in orbit around Mars millions of years ago.

Deimos, Mars's smaller moon, is about 15km across at its widest.

Phobos is 28km across at its widest. It has a large crater named Stickney on its surface which is about 5km across.

STUDYING THE SURFACE

In the 1960s and 1970s, the Mariner and Viking space probes sent back detailed pictures of the surface of Mars. It was shown to be covered in reddish-orange dust, with many rocky canyons and craters. Huge dust storms, which may last for weeks, often rage across the landscape.

In 2004, twin robot rovers, Spirit and Opportunity, started exploring Mars from opposite sides. Among their discoveries have been signs of water in Mars's past. Curiosity, a car-sized rover, landed in 2012 to find out if Mars can ever have supported life. It has many scientific tools, including a robotic arm and a laser to vaporize rock samples so it can test their chemical make-up.

Curiosity has confirmed that Mars once had flowing water, and other conditions that long ago may have let simple living things such as bacteria survive there.

Internet links

• Scan the code for a video about the Mars rover Curiosity.

• For links to more sites about the inner planets Mars, Mercury and Venus, go to **www.usborne.com/quicklinks**

THE EARTH AND MOON

The **Earth** orbits the Sun at a distance of 149.6 million kilometres. This distance makes it just the right temperature for water to exist as a liquid, rather than just ice or vapour. The Earth also has a breathable atmosphere. All these things create the right conditions for life to exist.

The Earth as seen from space. Early astronauts described it as a beautiful blue jewel.

EARTH'S ATMOSPHERE

From space, the Earth's atmosphere looks like a very thin blue layer surrounding the planet. It is a mixture of nitrogen and oxygen, with traces of other gases. It contains more oxygen than the atmosphere of any other planet. This gas is vital to life.

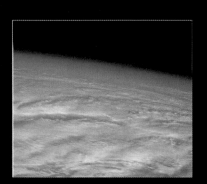

From space, the Earth's atmosphere looks like a thin haze. It appears blue because of the way sunlight is filtered through atmospheric gases.

EARTH'S SURFACE

Beneath the atmosphere is the planet's surface, called the **crust**. This is split into a number of enormous slabs called plates*, which have pushed and pulled against each other for millions of years, creating mountains, valleys and other features.

Mountain ranges like the Himalayas formed when the Earth's vast plates crushed together.

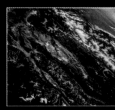

Two-thirds of the Earth's surface is covered in vast oceans of water. These are believed to be the birthplace of Earth's first life-forms, around 3,500 million years ago. Scientists study other planets and moons for signs of water or ice on their surface. This could show that they are or were once home to primitive life.

THE EARTH FROM SPACE

Today, people are learning more and more about the Earth, from information sent back by satellites and space stations. For instance, weather forecasters use data collected by satellites to predict weather patterns. They can use this information to warn people of severe weather anywhere in the world.

Information from satellites is also used to find out more about the Earth's surface. Even areas that are normally hard to see, such as the ocean floor, can now be seen in detail using sophisticated satellites.

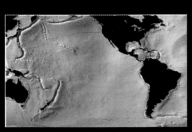

This map of the ocean floor was produced by a satellite named Seasat. The dark shapes are continents.

The Earth is the only planet in the Solar System which is definitely known to support life. This is because it is mostly covered in water, which has yet to be found on any other planet's surface.

* Plates, 181.

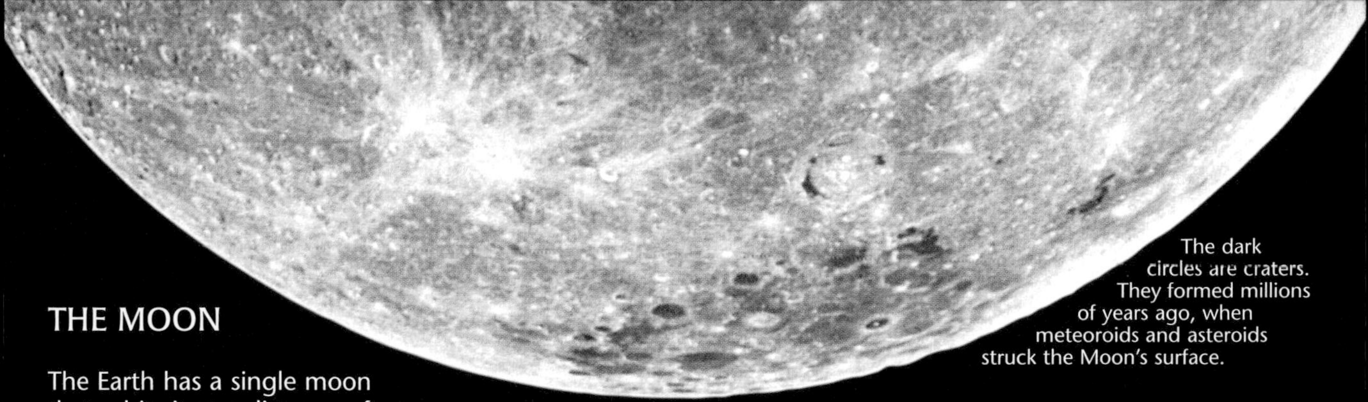

The dark circles are craters. They formed millions of years ago, when meteoroids and asteroids struck the Moon's surface.

THE MOON

The Earth has a single moon that orbits it at a distance of about 384,400km. Most moons are tiny compared to the objects they orbit, but our **Moon** is a quarter of the Earth's size.

The Moon is kept in orbit by the pull of the Earth's gravity.

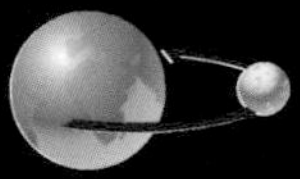

Because of the Earth's gravity, the same side of the Moon always faces Earth as it orbits. The other side of the Moon, known as the **far** or **dark side**, has only ever been seen by space probes and astronauts.

Unlike the Earth, the Moon has no atmosphere to prevent it from becoming too hot or too cold. This means that the Sun's rays can make its temperature rise to 123°C. When the Sun is not shining on the Moon, the temperature can fall to -163°C.

See for yourself

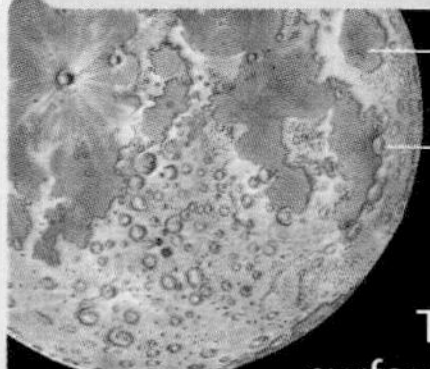

— Sea

— Crater

The Moon's surface is marked with many craters. You can see some of them with the naked eye, but binoculars will give a much better view. The dark patches you can see on the Moon's surface are known as seas. They formed millions of years ago from solidified lava.

PHASES OF THE MOON

The Moon does not make its own light, but it reflects the Sun's rays. This can make it look very bright in the night sky. Different amounts of the Moon's sunlit side can be seen as it orbits the Earth. This makes the Moon appear to change shape each night. The different shapes are called the **phases** of the Moon.

It takes 28 days for the Moon to orbit the Earth once. The diagram below shows the Moon's phases during this time.

The phases of the Moon

Direction of sunlight

Moon

Earth

The pictures below show what the Moon looks like from the northern hemisphere* when it is in each of the numbered positions shown above.

1. New moon
2. Waxing (growing) crescent
3. First quarter
4. Waxing gibbous
5. Full moon
6. Waning (shrinking) gibbous
7. Last quarter
8. Waning crescent

THE MOON'S FORMATION

Scientists are still not completely sure where the Moon came from. They used to think it was formed at the same time as the Earth, but studies of Moon rocks seem to show that this is not the case.

Most astronomers now think that the Moon was formed when a massive object, the size of a small planet, collided with the Earth. This threw out an enormous amount of rocky debris, which joined together in a single mass to form the Moon.

Large object

Earth

The Moon may have formed from rocky debris thrown out after a huge object smashed into the Earth.

Moon

Internet links

• Scan the code to watch a video clip about the Moon.

THE OUTER PLANETS

Jupiter, Saturn, Uranus and Neptune are known as the outer planets. They lie in the outer regions of the Solar System. Being huge balls made almost entirely of gas, they are also called the gas giants. Beyond Neptune lie many icy objects such as the dwarf planet Pluto.

The New Horizons space probe studied Jupiter in 2007, on its way to Pluto.

JUPITER

Jupiter is the largest planet in the Solar System, measuring 142,984km at its equator. It takes about 11.9 Earth years to orbit the Sun once. Despite its distance from the Sun, Jupiter is not a frozen planet. Pressurized hydrogen at its heart breaks down to create huge amounts of heat.

Several space probes have been sent to Jupiter. In 1979 the Voyager probes discovered that Jupiter has faint rings, which cannot be seen from the Earth.

In 1995, the Galileo space probe took a new series of photos, and sent a mini-probe down into Jupiter's atmosphere. The probe discovered Jupiter's winds blew harder than any on Earth, and Galileo gathered information on the planet's rings and moons.

JUPITER'S MOONS

So far, astronomers have discovered at least 67 moons around Jupiter. The four largest are called the **Galilean Moons**, after the Italian scientist Galileo, who discovered them in 1610. Jupiter's other moons are much smaller. Some may be just asteroids, captured by the planet's gravity.

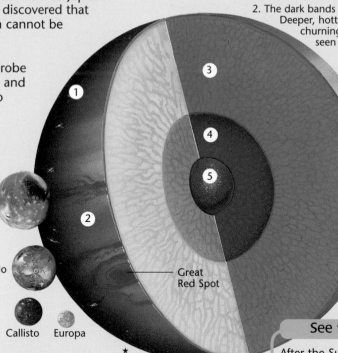

Ganymede

Io

Callisto   Europa

Great Red Spot

★

Structure of Jupiter

Scientists base this idea of Jupiter's structure on information from space probes.

1. The atmosphere's top layer is broken into vast clouds by high winds. Violent storms rage around the planet.

2. The dark bands are gaps in the clouds. Deeper, hotter layers of the planet's churning atmosphere can be seen beneath.

3. This layer is 17,000km thick. It is made of hydrogen gas which is so compressed that it acts like a liquid.

4. This layer is also made of hydrogen, but it is so compressed that it behaves like a solid.

5. The core, which is slightly larger than the Earth, is thought to be solid and rocky.

The Galilean Moons (not shown to scale above)

Ganymede is the largest moon in the Solar System. It is even bigger than the planet Mercury.

Io is covered with volcanoes that pour sulphur onto its surface.

Callisto is a ball of dusty ice. Its surface is scarred with hundreds of craters.

Europa may have a deep ocean beneath its fractured, icy crust. Some scientists believe that this ocean may contain simple life.

See for yourself

After the Sun, Moon and Venus, Jupiter is the brightest object in the sky. With the naked eye it looks like a very bright star. If you have a telescope, you may be able to see its tinted cloud bands and the **Great Red Spot**, a vast storm which rages through the planet's atmosphere.

SATURN

Saturn is the second largest planet in the Solar System. It measures about 120,536km around its equator – nine times wider than the Earth. Saturn orbits the Sun once every 29.5 Earth years, at a distance of about 1,429 million kilometres.

The planet is made up mostly of hydrogen and helium, which are very light gases. This makes Saturn very light compared to the other planets. Astronomers believe that Saturn may be similar to Jupiter on the inside, because it also generates its own fierce heat.

Saturn's rings are made of dust and rocks.

SATURN'S RINGS

Saturn is often called the **Ringed Planet**, because it is surrounded by rings of rock and dust. These were identified in the seventeenth century by Galileo. Space probes such as the Voyagers and Cassini have sent back thousands of incredible pictures of Saturn's rings, and astronomers have discovered rings around other planets too.

Saturn's rings are about one kilometre thick and are made up of dust, rocks and icy boulders. The rings that can be seen from the Earth are actually made up of thousands of smaller **ringlets**. The outer ring particles are kept in place by the gravity of a small moon, Prometheus, known as the **Shepherd Moon**.

SATURN'S MOONS

Saturn has at least 62 moons, some of which are shown on the right. Scientists think that Saturn's and Jupiter's moons are among the places in the Solar System where evidence of simple life is most likely to be found.

Saturn is the second largest planet in the Solar System. It is about nine times the size of the Earth.

Saturn's biggest moon, **Titan**, is surrounded by dense orange clouds. Dark lakes of methane and ethane have been found on its surface.

Mimas is 398km wide and covered in craters. The impact that created its largest crater almost destroyed it completely.

Enceladus is slightly larger than Mimas. Giant jets of water vapour erupt through its smooth, icy surface. A salty sea is thought to lie below, where some think life could survive.

Tethys has huge craters and long valleys. The longest valley, Ithaca, is 2,000km. The largest crater, Odysseus, is 400km wide.

Saturn spins so fast that it appears to bulge slightly in the middle and to be squashed at the poles.

Internet links

• Scan the code to discover more about Saturn's rings.

• For links to more websites about Jupiter and Saturn and their many moons, go to **www.usborne.com/quicklinks**

URANUS

Uranus was discovered by British astronomer William Herschel in 1781. It takes just over 84 Earth years to orbit the Sun, at a distance of around 2,870 million kilometres. It travels slowly, moving at about 7 kilometres per second. By comparison, the Earth moves at nearly 30 kilometres per second.

Most planets spin around like tops, but Uranus rolls around the Sun on its side, like a barrel. It may have been tipped onto its side millions of years ago by a collision with a planet-sized comet. Uranus spins quickly, making one turn in 17.9 hours.

Like Saturn, Uranus has a system of rings, which were discovered in 1977. In 1986, the Voyager 2 space probe photographed and measured them. The rings were found to be made up mostly of dark dust.

MOONS OF URANUS

For many years, Uranus was thought to have 15 moons. By 2003, astronomers had officially identified 27, and there may be more awaiting discovery.

The five largest moons are shown below. **Ariel** and **Umbriel** are both dark and cratered, while **Titania** has deep, long valleys. **Oberon** is heavily cratered, but little else is known about it. **Miranda** is a small ball of ice, about 472km across. It is thought that it may once have been broken apart by a comet.

Ariel

Umbriel

Titania

Oberon

Miranda

This picture of Uranus and its rings was created using information taken with the HST's* Near Infrared Camera. The red patches are high clouds.

A photo of Neptune, taken by the Voyager 2 space probe in 1989.

NEPTUNE

Neptune was first discovered by astronomers John Couch Adams and Urbain Jean LeVerrier. It is slightly smaller than Uranus, and spins once every 19.2 hours. Neptune is about 4,504 million kilometres from the Sun. It takes about 165 Earth years to complete a single orbit.

You cannot see Neptune with the naked eye, and even through a telescope it only looks like a small, bluish circle.

NEPTUNE'S ATMOSPHERE

Methane gas in the atmosphere gives Neptune its blue appearance. Neptune's atmosphere also contains ammonia and helium. Beneath its dense blanket of gases, the planet is thought to have an outer layer of liquid hydrogen.

Voyager 2 observed long, wispy clouds swirling around Neptune, blown by winds of up to 2,000 kilometres per hour. It also saw dark spots. The largest, named the **Great Dark Spot**, was a vast storm the size of the Earth.

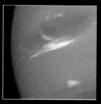

Neptune's Great Dark Spot. Voyager 2 scientists named the little cloud below it the Scooter, because it raced around the planet every 16 hours.

* HST (Hubble Space Telescope).

PLUTO

Pluto was first discovered in 1930 by American astronomer Clyde Tombaugh. For a long time it was known as the Solar System's smallest planet (measuring just 2,274km across), but the discovery of many other nearby objects of a similar size led to scientists reclassifying Pluto as a dwarf planet*. It was believed to be the largest dwarf planet in the Solar System until the discovery, in 2005, of **Eris**, which may be bigger. It is thought that at least 200 of the 1,500 or more objects that orbit beyond Neptune may be dwarf planets.

Pluto has an oval orbit, so its distance from the Sun varies a great deal. For 20 years of its 248-year orbit, Pluto is actually closer to the Sun than Neptune. Pluto has at least five moons. The largest is called **Charon**, which was discovered in 1978. It is nearly half Pluto's size, making it unusually large for a moon.

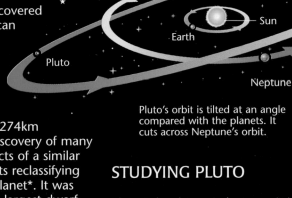

Pluto's orbit is tilted at an angle compared with the planets. It cuts across Neptune's orbit.

STUDYING PLUTO

Pluto is hard to see, because it is so far away. Even powerful telescopes on Earth show Pluto as just a tiny circle with no surface markings. But images from the Hubble Space Telescope* suggest a dark orange ball of ice and rock with black and white patches, and an atmosphere of frozen nitrogen and methane.

NASA's New Horizons space probe was launched in 2006 to study Pluto in more detail. When it flies past the dwarf planet in 2015 it will provide astronomers with their first detailed pictures of its surface, and will assess the atmosphere to confirm what it's made from. The probe will also examine Charon, and will then continue on into the outer regions of the Solar System, where it will explore small objects that orbit the Sun even further out.

NEPTUNE'S MOONS

Neptune has at least 14 moons. The largest of them are **Triton** and **Nereid**. Triton is bigger than the dwarf planet Pluto. Most moons orbit their planet in the same direction as the planet spins. Triton, however, travels in the opposite direction.

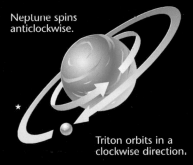

Neptune spins anticlockwise.

Triton orbits in a clockwise direction.

Most of Triton's surface is bright and smooth. It has some dark streaks over it and pink ice around its south pole. Triton has a thin atmosphere of nitrogen and methane.

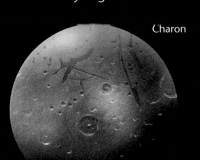

Charon

An artist's impression of Pluto and its largest moon, Charon. They're very close to each other, only about 20,000km apart.

Pluto

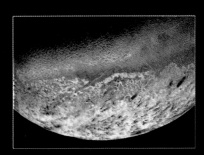

This photograph of Triton shows the polar cap. Its pink tinge may be due to the evaporation of frozen nitrogen gas.

Internet links

• Scan the code for more about NASA's mission to study Pluto.

• For links to more websites with picture galleries of Uranus, Neptune and Pluto, go to **www.usborne.com/quicklinks**

* Dwarf planet, 163; Hubble Space Telescope, 175; NASA (National Aeronautics Space Administration), 175.

SPACE DEBRIS

As well as many planets and moons, the Solar System also contains millions of smaller objects, called asteroids, comets and meteoroids. They are believed to be pieces of debris left over from the birth of the universe.

This photograph of Comet Lovejoy was taken by an astronaut on the International Space Station.

ASTEROIDS

Asteroids are large pieces of rock, or rock and metal. The first was spotted in 1801, by an Italian astronomer named Piazzi. He found an object in space which he believed was a tiny planet. Piazzi named his discovery **Ceres**.

Soon, other astronomers noticed similar objects, which they called asteroids. This means "like stars". Most orbit the Sun between Mars and Jupiter, in an area called the **Asteroid Belt**. Ceres is still by far the largest object there, but it is now classed as a dwarf planet.

The first close-up pictures of an asteroid, named **Gaspra**, were taken in 1991, by the space probe Galileo. The images showed it to be about 19km across with an irregular shape. Its surface is grooved and pitted with craters.

Gaspra is one of the largest asteroids in the Asteroid Belt. It is dark reddish-brown, with patches of grey and blue.

NUMBERS AND TYPES

Several hundred thousand asteroids have already been discovered and many more are discovered every year. Most asteroids fall into one of three main groups, depending on what they are made of. These groups are carbonaceous (like Ceres), silicaceous (like Gaspra) and metallic.

Carbonaceous (or **C-type**) asteroids are the most common. They are stony and darker than coal.

Silicaceous (or **S-type**) asteroids are bright and shiny. They contain metal.

Metallic (or **M-type**) asteroids may be the exposed, metal cores of originally much larger objects.

Asteroids are often scarred with craters, made by smaller pieces of space debris colliding with them.

TROJANS AND APOLLOS

There are several other groups of asteroids besides the ones in the main Asteroid Belt. For instance, Jupiter holds clusters of asteroids in its gravity. These asteroids are called the **Trojans**. Some orbit in front of Jupiter, and others orbit behind it.

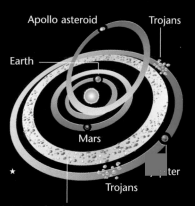

Apollo asteroid — Trojans — Earth — Mars — Jupiter — Trojans — Asteroid Belt

Other asteroids, known as the **Apollo asteroids**, sometimes cross the Earth's path. Their usual orbit, however, is further away from the Sun.

Although they are shown close together here, the distances between these asteroids are so huge that spacecraft can pass through without hitting any of them.

ASTEROIDS AND PROBES

Asteroids that closely approach the Earth are called **near-Earth asteroids**. The space probe NEAR, short for **Near Earth Asteroid Rendezvous**, orbited the asteroid Eros in 2000–2001. NEAR ended its mission by becoming the first probe to land on an asteroid.

In 2005, the Hayabusa space probe landed on the asteroid Itokawa and took a dust sample. It then took off again and safely returned with it to Earth.

In 2011, the probe Dawn reached Vesta, the second-largest object in the Asteroid Belt, studying it for over a year before flying on towards the dwarf planet Ceres.

The NEAR spacecraft. Pictures from it have revealed lots of new information about near-Earth asteroids.

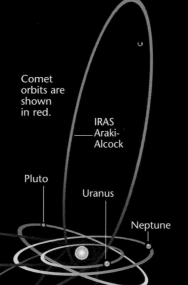

COMETS

Comets are balls of dirty ice. They travel around the Sun in huge, oval orbits. This means that they spend most of their time far away from the Sun. Some comets have such wide orbits that they may travel far above or below the Solar System for thousands of years. The diagram on the right shows some comets' orbits.

Kohoutek

Halley

Comet orbits are shown in red.

IRAS Araki-Alcock

Pluto

Uranus

Neptune

Ikeya Seki

A COMET'S TAIL

The central, solid part of a comet is called the **nucleus**. This is made up of frozen gases, ice, grit and rock. When a comet is near to the Sun, its nucleus becomes warmer. As the comet begins to melt, a tail is formed. Some comets have more than one tail.

How a comet tail forms

This is a comet flying through space, far from the Sun. At this stage it has no tail.

As the comet approaches the Sun, it melts. Gas and dust stream out into space, forming a cloud called a **coma**.

A constant stream of particles from the Sun, called the **solar wind**, blows the coma out behind. This creates the comet's tail.

★

METEOROIDS

Meteoroids are very small pieces of space debris. They may be grains of dust from comets, chunks of rock, or even bits of shattered asteroids.

Occasionally, the Earth crosses the path of these meteoroids. As they plummet through the atmosphere, they burn up in a streak of light. At this stage, they are called **meteors**, or **shooting stars**. Meteoroids that survive their fiery passage through the atmosphere to land on the Earth are called **meteorites**.

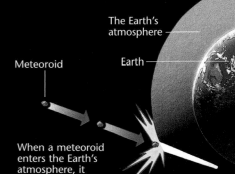

The Earth's atmosphere

Meteoroid

Earth

When a meteoroid enters the Earth's atmosphere, it becomes a meteor.

See for yourself

A **meteor storm** is a short but spectacular display of meteors caused by the Earth crossing a comet's path. Astronomy magazines and the internet can tell you the best dates to look for storms in your hemisphere.

Internet links

• Scan the code for a video about meteoroids, or for more sites about asteroids and comets, go to **www.usborne.com/quicklinks**

173

SPACE EXPLORATION

Studying space in detail only became possible after the invention of the telescope in the seventeenth century. Since then, astronomers have used many more sophisticated devices to look further and further into space. In the twentieth century, scientists worked out how to send man-made satellites, and then people, into space to study it in even greater detail.

The first true astronomical telescope was built by Galileo in 1610. It could magnify up to nine times, but his later ones could magnify up to 30 times.

OPTICAL TELESCOPES

Optical telescopes create images using light. Some optical telescopes, called **refractors**, collect light through lenses. **Reflectors** use mirrors to collect light and reflect it back to the observer. Astronomers use vast reflector telescopes, housed in buildings called **observatories**, to look far into space.

The Keck observatories in Hawaii house the world's most powerful optical telescopes. Like many observatories, they are built on mountaintops, which are above most of the haze and pollution in the atmosphere.

This reflector telescope, Keck 1, is over 10m wide. Its mirror is made up of 36 segments which act like a single, giant mirror.

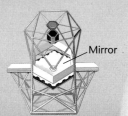

Mirror

RADIO TELESCOPES

Radio telescopes have very large dishes with moveable antennas, that collect the faint signals given out by objects in space. They allow astronomers to detect things that are too dark or too far away to see, even through the most powerful optical telescope.

The largest radio telescope is the Arecibo dish in Puerto Rico. Its 305m wide dish is built into a natural valley. It has been used to make many discoveries, from the existence of neutron stars in 1968 to planets orbiting a pulsar* in 1992 – the first planets discovered outside the Solar System.

A radio telescope. It can be steered to face a particular target in space.

SPACE TELESCOPES

Telescopes placed out in space can see much further than those on Earth, because the planet's atmosphere does not distort their view. The largest space telescope so far is the Hubble Space Telescope (HST), an optical telescope launched by NASA (the USA's National Aeronautics and Space Administration) in 1990.

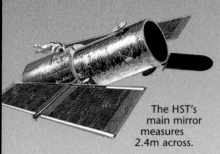

The HST's main mirror measures 2.4m across.

Since its launch, the HST has sent back many astonishing space images, including a comet crashing into Jupiter in 1994, and the farthest and oldest stars yet seen. Its discoveries include evidence that black holes* are common in the hearts of galaxies, and that the expansion of the universe* is speeding up.

This image, taken by the HST in 2009 using infrared light, peers deep into the universe to show galaxies over 13 billion years old.

SATELLITES

There are many man-made devices orbiting the Earth. These are known as **satellites** – the same word that is used for any object, such as a moon, which orbits a planet or star. Some man-made satellites gather and transmit information about space directly to scientists on Earth. Others pick up radio, TV or telephone signals, and send them back down to other places on Earth.

The first man-made object ever to go into space was a satellite named Sputnik 1, launched in 1957 by the Soviet Union. It could not take pictures or record information, but it proved that man-made structures could be launched successfully into space.

PLANET HUNTING

In 2009, NASA launched the Kepler spacecraft. Using highly sensitive light detectors, it scans space for planets outside our Solar System. It has found over 900 new planets so far.

An artist's idea of Kepler 186f: a rocky, Earth-sized planet orbiting a red dwarf star. It is the right distance from its sun to have liquid water, and perhaps life.

This satellite orbits at the same speed as the Earth spins. This is known as **a geostationary** orbit.

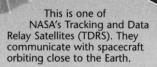

This is one of NASA's Tracking and Data Relay Satellites (TDRS). They communicate with spacecraft orbiting close to the Earth.

See for yourself

If you want to spot satellites yourself, information about when they will be passing overhead in your area can be found on the internet, or using one of the many satellite-tracking smartphone apps that are available. Satellites appear as lights that move quickly in a straight line across dark skies. They shine with reflected sunlight, so they often blink as they turn, or disappear as they pass into Earth's shadow.

Internet links

- Scan the code to find out how astronomers explore space.

- For links to more websites about telescopes, satellites and planet hunting, go to **www.usborne.com/quicklinks**

* Black holes, 161; Expansion of the universe, 154; Pulsars, 161.

175

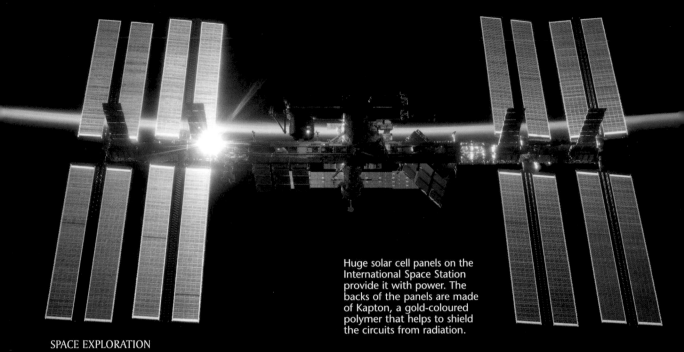

Huge solar cell panels on the International Space Station provide it with power. The backs of the panels are made of Kapton, a gold-coloured polymer that helps to shield the circuits from radiation.

SPACE PROBES

Since the 1960s, unmanned spacecraft called **space probes** have been sent out to explore the Solar System. Many carry cameras, which take detailed photographs of distant planets. They beam the pictures back to Earth, where they are studied by space scientists.

One such project was NASA's Cassini mission to Saturn, launched in 1997. It entered into orbit around Saturn in 2004, and began sending back detailed images of the planet's surface, its famous rings, and its moons. Cassini also carried a small probe called Huygens, which split from its mother ship and landed on Saturn's largest moon, Titan.

So far, Voyager 1 (which studied Jupiter and Saturn) and Pioneer 10 (which studied Jupiter) have journeyed further than any other probes. Only Voyager is still sending signals. Both probes will one day escape the Sun's gravity and leave the Solar System.

FIRST MAN IN SPACE

For many years, space travel was thought to be too dangerous for humans. But advances in technology throughout the 1950s led to Russian astronaut Yuri Gagarin becoming the first man in space, in 1961. His flight lasted for one and a half hours.

MEN ON THE MOON

In 1959, a Soviet space probe, Luna 9, was the first man-made object to land on the Moon. Ten years later, American astronauts Neil Armstrong and Edwin "Buzz" Aldrin travelled to the Moon in the Apollo 11 spacecraft and became the first people to walk on its surface.

During the 1960s and 1970s there were six Moon landings. Each crew collected information and rock samples. Scientists are still studying these rocks in order to understand more about how the Moon formed and evolved billions of years ago. This may also offer clues about the Earth's formation.

As long as a football field, the International Space Station is the largest man-made structure ever to be built in space.

The most recent manned Moon mission was Apollo 17, in 1972.

SPACE STATIONS

Space stations are orbiting laboratories where astronauts can carry out experiments and work in space that cannot be done on Earth. They may remain on a space station for over a year. Astronauts' reactions to life in space help scientists on Earth to understand more about the effects of low gravity on the human body.

The first space station was Russia's Salyut 1, in 1971. The USA launched their first space station, Skylab, in 1973. It fell to Earth in 1979, by which time Russia's more modern station, Mir, was in orbit. Mir was made of modules that are connected together in space. This allows space stations to develop over time and to house larger crews. Mir was retired in 2001.

An astronaut in the ISS's low gravity

In 1998, the first module of the **International Space Station** **(ISS)** was launched into orbit. A joint project between over 20 nations, the ISS has been permanently manned since 2000. It currently contains five laboratories used for space science and to test equipment that could be used in future missions to the Moon and Mars.

THE SPACE SHUTTLE

From 1981, a fleet of US **Space Shuttles** carried astronauts and supplies into orbit. They were launched into space by two huge booster rockets with an external fuel tank. The tank could not be reused, but unlike older rockets, the boosters could be parachuted into the sea, to be retrieved. A Shuttle glided back to Earth on its return, landing on a runway like a plane.

COMMERCIAL CRAFT

Since the last Shuttle was retired in 2011, astronauts and supplies have mainly been ferried to the ISS on single-use Russian Soyuz rockets and spacecraft. In 2012, a private firm, SpaceX, flew their partly reusable spacecraft, Dragon, to the ISS, and now resupply it. Future Dragons, and the rockets that lift them, are planned to be fully reusable, and to carry crew.

A SpaceX Dragon spacecraft

See for yourself

There are video cameras on the ISS that send back live views of the Earth. For a link to a site that gives you an astronaut's-eye-view of our planet, go to **www.usborne.com/quicklinks**, type in the keyword "science" then go to pages 176-177.

Internet links

• Scan the code to take a virtual tour of the International Space Station.

• For links to more websites about space exploration, go to **www.usborne.com/quicklinks**

THE EARLY EARTH

The Earth is a tiny planet in a vast universe, which contains billions of stars, planets and moons, as well as huge areas of space containing other, smaller particles. There is no definite proof of how ancient events such as the Earth's formation took place. Most scientists, however, think that patterns of radiation in space show that the universe was created in a huge explosion about 14 billion years ago. This idea is called the **Big Bang theory**.

About 4 billion years ago, huge asteroids and comets bombarded the early Earth, the Moon, and Mars.

BIRTH OF THE EARTH

The Earth is thought to have formed 4.6 billion years ago, and it has been constantly changing and developing ever since. It probably started as a huge, swirling cloud of dust and gases. Over time, this cloud began to shrink and become solid. Heavy minerals collected at the middle of the growing planet, eventually creating a core of iron and nickel.

As the Earth formed, gases such as methane, hydrogen and ammonia rose from volcanoes on its surface. Over time, ultraviolet radiation from the Sun broke down these poisonous gases, leaving a thick blanket of nitrogen and carbon dioxide. At the same time, early oceans are thought to have been formed, either by volcanic steam combining with ice from asteroids and comets that rained down from space, or by water seeping up from inside the Earth.

This cluster of stars formed many billions of years before the Earth and Sun. Scientists study these ancient stars to try to learn more about the early universe.

EARLY LIFE

Around 3.5 billion years ago, simple life-forms developed from the churning chemical soup of the Earth's early oceans. Like modern green plants, they made food using water, carbon dioxide and energy from sunlight. This released oxygen into the early atmosphere.

For many millions of years, these tiny organisms continued to make oxygen from the carbon dioxide surrounding the Earth. This formed a barrier, preventing most of the Sun's harmful ultraviolet rays from reaching the planet. Eventually, conditions were right for complex life-forms to begin their development. For more about life on Earth, see pages 186-187.

ANCIENT HISTORY

The amount of time it has taken the Earth to develop is so vast that it can barely be imagined. For some idea of how ancient the Earth is, try to picture its entire history taking place in one hour. On this scale, each minute would equal about 77 million years. Because the history of the Earth goes back so far, scientists must measure its development in periods of millions and billions of years. They use the terms **deep time** or **geological time** to refer to such a vast timescale.

CHANGING CLIMATE

Ever since the Earth began to form, its climate has been changing. For instance, at certain times it was much warmer than it is now. At other times, huge areas were covered with ice.

A glacier forms as snow builds up over many years and becomes a mass of ice. Its huge weight causes it to move slowly downhill.

Ice ages are periods of time lasting thousands of years, when some continents and oceans are covered by huge **ice sheets** and many valleys are filled by slowly moving rivers of ice called **valley glaciers**. Scientists think that past ice ages were caused by the Earth's orbit around the Sun changing shape. This would have reduced the amount of sunlight the planet received, leading to an ice age as its climate cooled.

Diagram showing change in Earth's orbit

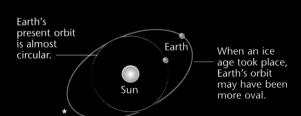

Earth's present orbit is almost circular.

Earth

When an ice age took place, Earth's orbit may have been more oval.

Sun

During an ice age, glaciers travel slowly across the land. In the past, these have helped to shape the landscape in many parts of the world, by carving vast valleys out of rock as they moved. Most of the ice of Greenland and Antarctica may also have been formed during the last ice age.

THE SHAPE OF THE LAND

Soon after the Earth was formed, the first landmasses appeared. They moved around, joined together and split up again many times. About 250 million years ago there was just one giant landmass, called **Pangaea**. It began to split up about 225 million years ago, and the continents which exist today were slowly formed.

Development of modern continents

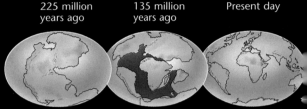

225 million years ago	135 million years ago	Present day

Pangaea

The spreading sea floor (pink area) caused the land to break up.

STUDYING THE PAST

Most of the information scientists have about the Earth's past comes from rocks. Most rocks form in layers over many thousands and millions of years. By studying these layers, scientists called **geologists** can work out what conditions may have been like as each one was formed.

Rocks formed in warm climates contain more fossils than those formed in cooler climates.

Rocks which were on the Earth's surface during ice ages show signs of being worn away by glaciers.

Internet links

• Scan the code to watch a video clip about the formation of the Earth.

• For links to more websites where you can find out about the history of the Earth, go to **www.usborne.com/quicklinks**

EARTH'S STRUCTURE

The Earth has a solid surface, but is not solid all the way through. Inside, it is made up of layers, some of which are partly **molten**. This means that they are partly made up of hot liquid. The Earth's middle is an incredibly hot ball of iron and nickel. All the layers are pulled together by the enormous force of gravity from the centre.

Diamonds are formed by the tremendous heat and pressure within the Earth's crust.

Cutaway showing the Earth's layers

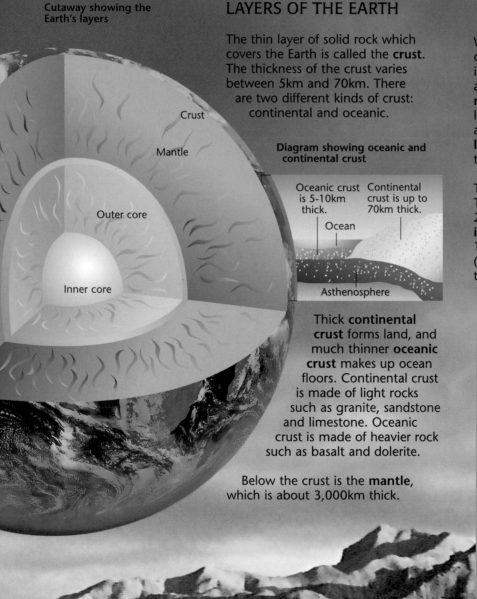

Crust

Mantle

Outer core

Inner core

LAYERS OF THE EARTH

The thin layer of solid rock which covers the Earth is called the **crust**. The thickness of the crust varies between 5km and 70km. There are two different kinds of crust: continental and oceanic.

Diagram showing oceanic and continental crust

Oceanic crust is 5-10km thick.

Continental crust is up to 70km thick.

Ocean

Asthenosphere

Thick **continental crust** forms land, and much thinner **oceanic crust** makes up ocean floors. Continental crust is made of light rocks such as granite, sandstone and limestone. Oceanic crust is made of heavier rock such as basalt and dolerite.

Below the crust is the **mantle**, which is about 3,000km thick.

Within the mantle is a thin layer called the **asthenosphere**. This is mostly solid rock, but a small amount is molten rock, called **magma**. This makes the whole layer weak. The upper mantle and crust, together called the **lithosphere**, move about on this weak layer.

The Earth's **core** has two parts. The **outer core**, which is about 2,200km thick, is molten. The **inner core** is solid. It is about 1,250km thick, extremely hot (about 5,000°C), and is about the same size as the Moon.

See for yourself

The movement of the liquid outer core is believed to create the Earth's magnetic field. This field creates two poles, called magnetic north and magnetic south. You can see their effects using an ordinary compass. Whichever way you hold the compass, its needle always points to magnetic north.

Magnetic north

Earth's magnetic field is just like that of a giant bar magnet.

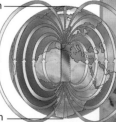

Magnetic south

PLATES

The lithosphere is divided into large areas called **plates**, which are constantly moving. There are about seven main plates and many smaller ones. Each one is made of continental or oceanic lithosphere, or both. The areas where the plates' edges meet are called **plate boundaries**.

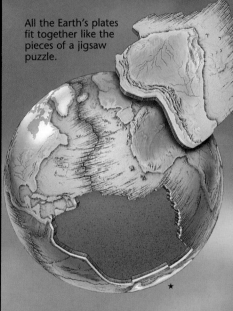

All the Earth's plates fit together like the pieces of a jigsaw puzzle.

The plates move very slowly over the asthenosphere, typically at about 3cm per year. They can move towards each other, move apart or shift sideways.

Because all the plates fit together, movement of one plate affects the others around it. The study of plate movement and its effects is called **plate tectonics**.

NEW FEATURES

Plate movement is constantly causing the formation of new features on the Earth's surface. For example, where plates move apart, magma from the mantle wells up all along the boundary. It cools and hardens to form a mountain range, or **ridge**, of new crust on the ocean floor, or sometimes on land. As the movement continues and more magma wells up along the centre, the ridge spreads out sideways, becoming a **spreading ridge**. Boundaries where new crust is formed are called **constructive boundaries**.

A **destructive boundary**, or **subduction zone**, occurs where an oceanic and continental plate move together. The heavier oceanic plate moves beneath the lighter continental plate, forming a **trench** where they meet. As the plate sinks, some of it becomes molten, forming new magma.

Formation of ridges and trenches

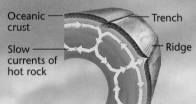

Oceanic crust — Trench

Slow currents of hot rock — Ridge

Where two plates push together above ground, the crust buckles and folds upwards to form high mountain ranges, called **fold mountains**. The Earth's crust is thickest at these points.

This mountain range was formed by two plates crushing together.

TYPES OF ROCK

The rock that makes up the Earth's surface is constantly being added to. It can be divided into three basic types: igneous, sedimentary and metamorphic.

Igneous rock is formed when molten rock cools and becomes solid. **Sedimentary rock** is formed when sediments, such as rock particles, are deposited by water or weather, buried and then squashed into layers called **strata**. When any type of rock is changed by intense heat or pressure, **metamorphic rock** is formed.

Granite is a type of igneous rock.

Limestone is a type of sedimentary rock.

Marble is a type of metamorphic rock.

Internet links

- Scan the code for amazing facts about the Earth's structure.

- For links to more websites about the layers of the Earth, go to **www.usborne.com/quicklinks**

FAULTS

As plates move, the strain sometimes causes brittle rock to crack. These cracks, called **faults**, are often weak zones where more movement or cracking may occur. For example, **rift valleys** may form when land containing faults is forced in opposite directions. All plate boundaries are major faults which began as minor ones.

Formation of a rift valley

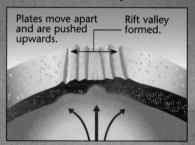

Plates move apart and are pushed upwards.

Rift valley formed.

Rock is pushed upwards from underneath and pulled apart at faults.

EARTHQUAKES

The constant movement of plates causes pressure to build up at faults, and at the plate boundaries themselves. If there is a sudden slippage of rock, this pressure is released quickly, and an **earthquake** occurs. Most earthquakes are too weak to be felt by people, but some cause huge damage, as the ground shakes and buildings collapse.

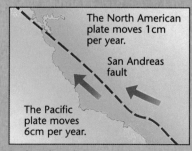

The North American plate moves 1cm per year.

San Andreas fault

The Pacific plate moves 6cm per year.

Earthquakes often occur on the San Andreas fault, on America's west coast. This is because the two plates on either side of the fault slide in the same direction at different speeds.

FOCUS

The point where energy is suddenly released and an earthquake starts is called the **focus**. It is usually 5–15km under the ground. The point on the surface directly above the focus is called the **epicentre**. Vibrations called **seismic waves** travel from the focus in all directions.

An earthquake is caused when rock gives way at a fault, releasing vast amounts of built-up energy.

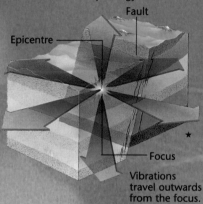

Fault

Epicentre

Focus

Vibrations travel outwards from the focus.

PREDICTION

Scientists who study earthquakes, called **seismologists**, use plate movement to predict when major earthquakes are going to happen. Horizontal movement along plates can be measured by bouncing a laser beam off a series of reflectors on the ground. A computer records the time it takes to travel between them. If this changes, it shows that ground movement has taken place. Animal behaviour may also be used to predict an earthquake.

Snakes came out of hibernation early before an earthquake in China in 1975. This may have been because they were disturbed by very slight vibrations in the ground.

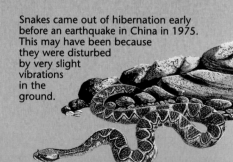

VOLCANOES

The magma within the largely solid mantle sometimes rises and collects in certain places. **Volcanoes** are formed when it rises to the Earth's surface and bursts out. At this stage magma becomes known as **lava**. This explosive effect is known as an **eruption**. Most volcanoes form along plate boundaries, either on land or under the sea.

Inside an erupting volcano*

The volcano below, called a **composite volcano**, is made up of alternating layers of lava and ash. These have built up over long periods of time to form a steep-sided cone.

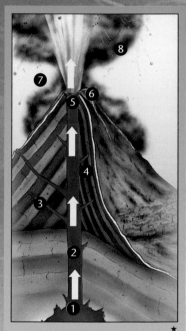

1. **Magma chamber** – magma gathers here beneath the crust
2. **Pipe** – the main channel up the middle of a volcano
3. **Dyke** – a sheet of igneous rock which cuts across existing rocks
4. Layers of ash and lava
5. **Vent** – the point where the magma comes out of the pipe
6. **Crater** – bowl-shaped opening around the vent
7. Dust, ash and gases
8. **Volcanic bombs** – lumps of lava

* Note: diagram is stretched vertically to show detail

VOLCANO FORMATION

A row of volcanoes may form where plates are moving apart, particularly at spreading ridges*.

Spreading ridges form when plates move apart.

Volcanoes may also form above subduction zones*, where one plate is forced beneath the other.

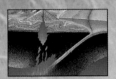

At subduction zones, one plate is forced below the other plate, where it starts to melt.

Some volcanoes form away from plate boundaries, near the middle of plates. Extremely hot currents of magma known as **plumes** rise from deep within the mantle, punching through the crust to form a volcano. These places are called **hot spots**.

DEAD OR ALIVE?

Volcanoes that erupt regularly are known as **active** volcanoes. If it is thought that a volcano will never erupt again, it is said to be **extinct**. Sometimes, people think a volcano has become extinct, but it is actually just inactive, or **dormant**.

SUPERVOLCANOES

Supervolcanoes are formed from huge collapsed craters, called **calderas**, with a magma chamber beneath. Only a few supervolcanoes exist, but they are so powerful and destructive that a single eruption could alter all life on Earth. This is because enormous pressure builds up in the magma chamber over thousands of years, then bursts in a devastating explosion.

Scientists think that the last supervolcano eruption was in Sumatra, 74,000 years ago. It is believed that this eruption blew out enough ash to block the Sun's light for around six months, causing the Earth to cool down. This would have caused environmental changes all over the world, killing huge numbers of living things.

Here, fountains of lava are shooting out of an erupting volcano. They may travel up to 600m into the air.

See for yourself

You can do a simple test to show how seismic waves travel from an earthquake focus. Place a handful of sand or grit on a table, then tap the table gently with a hammer. This point is the "focus", and the waves which travel outwards will make the sand jump. Try striking the table further from the sand, and see what happens. The waves lose strength as they travel further away from the focus.

Internet links

• Scan the code to watch a video clip about volcanoes.

• For links to more websites with amazing video clips and picture galleries of volcanoes and earthquakes, go to **www.usborne.com/quicklinks**

THE ATMOSPHERE

The Earth is surrounded by a blanket of different gases called the **atmosphere**. It is the presence of this atmosphere that allows life on Earth to exist, as it contains oxygen and other gases needed by living things. The atmosphere also acts as a shield against harmful ultraviolet rays from the Sun.

The atmosphere protects our planet from the Sun's powerful rays.

EARLY FORMATION

When the Earth was forming, it was first surrounded by hydrogen and helium. However, as the Sun heated these light gases, they escaped into space.

An atmosphere which could be held in place by the Earth's gravity was eventually formed from gases such as methane, ammonia and water vapour. These poured out of volcanoes on the surface, in a process known as **outgassing**. Over billions of years, these gases reacted to form an atmosphere of nitrogen and carbon dioxide.

Earth's early atmosphere would have been poisonous to living things. It took millions of years to become the way it is today.

The atmosphere as we know it did not start to form until plant-like organisms appeared in Earth's oceans, around 3,500 million years ago. These very simple living things used the Sun's light to make food from water and carbon dioxide, releasing oxygen as a by-product. This process continued for many millions of years, until there was enough oxygen in the atmosphere to support other forms of life.

These single-celled cyanobacteria were among the first organisms on Earth.

OUR ATMOSPHERE

The atmosphere is a mixture of gases – around four-fifths nitrogen and one-fifth oxygen, with traces of others. Water also exists in the atmosphere as vapour, droplets in clouds, and as ice crystals.

Snowflakes are formed from ice crystals.

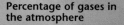

Percentage of gases in the atmosphere

Nitrogen	78%
Oxygen	21%
Argon	0.9%
Carbon dioxide	0.03%
Other gases (such as xenon, neon, krypton)	0.07%

ATMOSPHERIC LAYERS

The atmosphere is around 500km thick and is made up of several layers. These are densest near the Earth's surface where its gravity* is strongest, and fade into space. All the Earth's weather happens in the layer nearest the surface. Most of the higher atmosphere is a thin mix of calm, unchanging gases.

Atmospheric layers, showing height

Exosphere (over 500km)

The atmosphere merges into space. This layer contains almost no gases.

Thermosphere (up to 500km)

Temperature in this layer is very high, because of a gas called atomic oxygen. This helps to absorb some radiation from the Sun.

The International Space Station orbits in the thermosphere.

Mesosphere (up to 80km)

This layer has no ozone and no clouds, so the temperature is low.

Meteors burn up here.

Stratosphere (up to 50km)

This layer contains about 19% of all the atmosphere's gases. Temperature is higher, because it contains the ozone layer (see right).

Jet planes fly in the stratosphere.

Troposphere (up to 10km)

Contains 80% of all gases in the atmosphere, as well as all weather. Temperature in this layer decreases with height.

CHANGING ATMOSPHERE

Some gases, such as carbon dioxide, trap heat around the Earth rather like a greenhouse, keeping it warm enough for life to exist. This **greenhouse effect** is strengthened as fuel and forest burning add more of these greenhouse gases. This leads to **global warming**, a rise in world temperatures.

Smoke from burning fuels adds carbon dioxide to the atmosphere.

The Sun's rays, absorbed and given back out by the Earth, are trapped by the carbon dioxide and sent back down.

Governments and businesses are being urged to cut the amount of carbon dioxide released into the atmosphere as scientists predict this will reduce the effects of global warming. Energy sources such as wind or solar power release much less carbon dioxide.

This mountaineer has to carry a supply of oxygen, because the air in the troposphere contains less oxygen as he climbs higher.

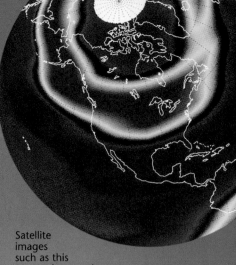

Satellite images such as this are used to monitor the ozone layer. Orange areas show where ozone levels are highest.

THE OZONE LAYER

Within the stratosphere is a layer of **ozone*** gas. This absorbs most of the Sun's harmful ultraviolet radiation, preventing it from reaching the Earth.

The ozone layer is being damaged by man-made gases called **chlorofluorocarbons (CFCs)**. These are released by some refrigerators and aerosols, and react with sunlight in the stratosphere. The products of this reaction break down the ozone. As the layer becomes thinner, more ultraviolet rays reach the Earth's surface.

Internet links

• Scan the code for a video about the Earth's atmosphere.

• For links to more websites about the atmosphere and global warming, go to www.usborne.com/quicklinks

* Gravity, 130; Ozone, 65.

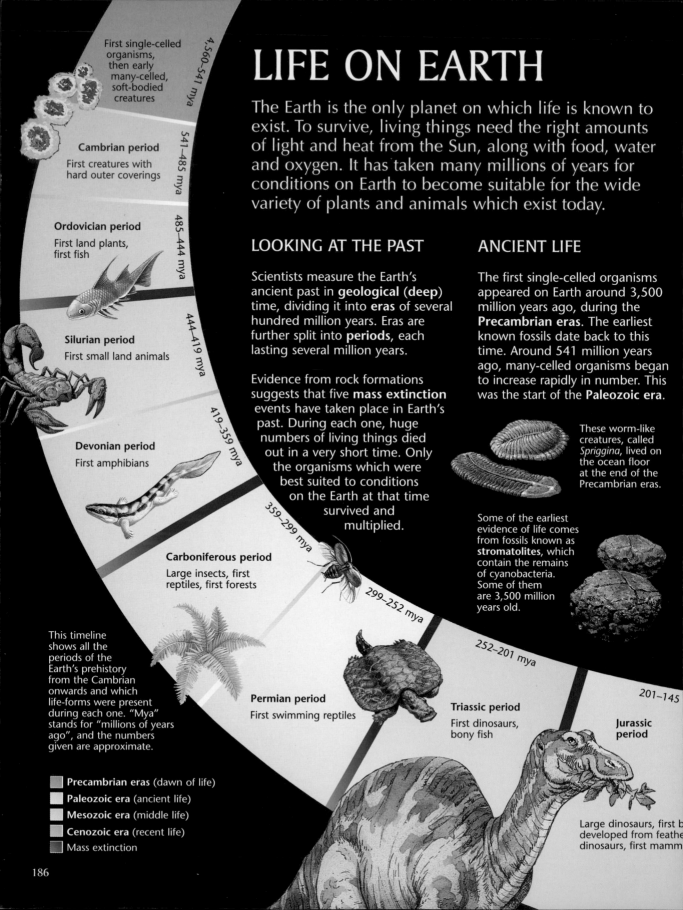

LIFE ON EARTH

The Earth is the only planet on which life is known to exist. To survive, living things need the right amounts of light and heat from the Sun, along with food, water and oxygen. It has taken many millions of years for conditions on Earth to become suitable for the wide variety of plants and animals which exist today.

LOOKING AT THE PAST

Scientists measure the Earth's ancient past in **geological (deep)** time, dividing it into **eras** of several hundred million years. Eras are further split into **periods**, each lasting several million years.

Evidence from rock formations suggests that five **mass extinction** events have taken place in Earth's past. During each one, huge numbers of living things died out in a very short time. Only the organisms which were best suited to conditions on the Earth at that time survived and multiplied.

ANCIENT LIFE

The first single-celled organisms appeared on Earth around 3,500 million years ago, during the **Precambrian eras**. The earliest known fossils date back to this time. Around 541 million years ago, many-celled organisms began to increase rapidly in number. This was the start of the **Paleozoic era**.

These worm-like creatures, called *Spriggina*, lived on the ocean floor at the end of the Precambrian eras.

Some of the earliest evidence of life comes from fossils known as **stromatolites**, which contain the remains of cyanobacteria. Some of them are 3,500 million years old.

First single-celled organisms, then early many-celled, soft-bodied creatures

4,560–541 mya

Cambrian period
First creatures with hard outer coverings

541–485 mya

Ordovician period
First land plants, first fish

485–444 mya

Silurian period
First small land animals

444–419 mya

Devonian period
First amphibians

419–359 mya

Carboniferous period
Large insects, first reptiles, first forests

359–299 mya

299–252 mya

Permian period
First swimming reptiles

252–201 mya

Triassic period
First dinosaurs, bony fish

201–145

Jurassic period

Large dinosaurs, first b[...]
developed from feathe[...]
dinosaurs, first mamm[...]

This timeline shows all the periods of the Earth's prehistory from the Cambrian onwards and which life-forms were present during each one. "Mya" stands for "millions of years ago", and the numbers given are approximate.

- Precambrian eras (dawn of life)
- Paleozoic era (ancient life)
- Mesozoic era (middle life)
- Cenozoic era (recent life)
- Mass extinction

DEVELOPING LIFE

Fossil records suggest that in a part of the Paleozoic era called the **Cambrian period**, there was a huge increase in the number of different creatures on the Earth. Sea creatures began to develop hard body parts. These protective coverings would have made the creatures tougher, increasing their chances of living long enough to reproduce.

Many creatures with hard body coverings, like this trilobite, began to appear in seas during the Cambrian period.

Some small arthropods (creatures with jointed bodies), such as millipedes and insects, were able to move onto the land. This was because the Earth's temperature had cooled enough for land plants to grow in large numbers, providing food. The earliest vertebrates (animals with backbones) also appeared.

During the **Devonian period** (around 419–359 million years ago), the climate in many areas was hot and dry, and water levels dropped in rivers and lakes. One group of fish became able to breathe both in and out of water. These were the earliest amphibians.

This fossil shows that seed-carrying plants existed in the Devonian period.

Around 359 million years ago, during the **Carboniferous period**, many parts of the world became hot and humid. This allowed huge numbers of plants to grow, forming vast, steamy swamps. These became home to many types of bugs and amphibians.

Meganeura, a giant dragonfly, had wings that measured 60cm across.

THE AGE OF REPTILES

During the **Permian period**, amphibians evolved into early reptiles. They were able to spread all over the world because all the land became joined together as one huge continent. At the same time, huge numbers of sea creatures died because the shallow seas around the continents disappeared.

Hylonomus was one of the earliest known reptiles.

The **Mesozoic era** began 252 million years ago, with numbers of reptiles increasing rapidly. During this era, the dinosaurs appeared. They became the dominant vertebrate life-forms on the Earth until 66 million years ago, when they suddenly died out, probably as a result of climate change and an asteroid striking the Earth.

THE AGE OF MAMMALS

The current age of mammals, called the **Cenozoic era**, began after the dinosaurs died out. It is thought that mammals (and birds) survived the changes that killed the dinosaurs because, being smaller, they needed less food to survive and were able to find shelter more easily.

MODERN EXTINCTION

Extinction has always happened naturally over time. However, the current extinction rate is thought to be about 10,000 times greater than it would be if humans did not exist. Modern extinctions are almost always caused by pollution or loss of habitats (natural living spaces), brought about by the growing human race, and its need for land, food and water.

The white rhino is one of many species threatened by habitat loss or hunting.

Unless we can make better use of the Earth's resources, it is possible that humans may be responsible for the next major extinction event.

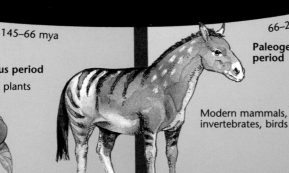

Cretaceous period 145–66 mya
Flowering plants

Paleogene period 66–23 mya
Modern mammals, invertebrates, birds

Neogene period 23–2.6 mya
Appearance of humans

Quaternary period 2.6 mya to present day
Ice ages, spread of modern humans

Internet links

- Scan the code for a video to help you understand the age of the Earth.

SEAS AND OCEANS

Around 71% of the Earth's surface is covered in salty water, which makes up five vast oceans and several smaller seas. Oceans are very important to life on Earth, and are home to huge numbers of living things. The oceans also influence weather and climate conditions all over the world.

Pacific Ocean

The largest of Earth's vast oceans, called the Pacific, covers around 30% of the planet's surface.

OCEAN CURRENTS

Ocean water constantly moves in huge, flowing bands called **currents**. These carry vast amounts of water around the Earth. There are two main types of ocean currents: surface and deep. **Surface currents** affect the top 350m or so of oceans. They are pushed along by **prevailing winds** (the most common types of wind in an area).

Deep currents are made up of very cold water coming from the North and South Poles. Cold water is heavier, so it sinks beneath the warmer surface currents that constantly arrive at the Poles. It then drifts towards the equator, where it warms up and rises to become a surface current itself. It then changes direction and starts to drift back towards the Poles.

See for yourself

You can do a simple activity to show that cold water is heavier than warmer water. Half fill a large, clear bowl with warm water. Fill a jug with ice-cold water containing a little food colouring. Gently pour the water into the bowl. You should notice that it sinks, just as cold water does at the Poles.

Ice-cold water sinks to the bottom of the bowl.

How currents circulate

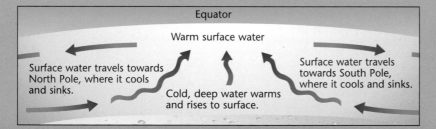

Equator

Warm surface water

Surface water travels towards North Pole, where it cools and sinks.

Cold, deep water warms and rises to surface.

Surface water travels towards South Pole, where it cools and sinks.

Waves such as this are created by strong winds sweeping across the surface of the water.

CLIMATE CONTROL

Oceans and seas play an important role in controlling the world's climate. Their waters absorb heat from the Sun, especially in tropical regions, and spread it around the Earth in surface currents.

Warm ocean currents may cause **tropical cyclones** (called **hurricanes** in America and **typhoons** in the Far East). These are fierce storms, with strong winds which form waves up to 25m high.

How a tropical cyclone forms

Moist, warm air above the ocean rises and cools, forming clouds.

Air from the surrounding ocean surface rushes into the space and begins to spiral upwards.

Wind speeds increase, and land in the cyclone's path is hit by a fierce storm.

TIDAL MOVEMENT

Seas and oceans are constantly moved by the tides. Tidal movement is caused mainly by the Moon. As it travels around the Earth, the force of its gravity makes the water on either side of the Earth bulge out. In a 24-hour period, this causes two **high tides**, when sea levels are at their highest, and two **low tides**, when they are at their lowest.

Tides are also influenced by the Earth, Moon and Sun lining up in certain ways. At full moon and new moon, there are very high **spring tides**. At quarters, when the Moon and Sun are at right angles to each other, there are very low **neap tides**.

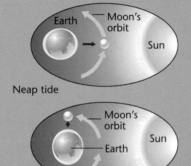

Spring tide

Neap tide

Earth — Moon's orbit — Sun

Moon's orbit — Sun — Earth

LIFE IN THE OCEANS

Seas and oceans contain a huge variety of plant and animal life, from the surface all the way down to the deepest trenches. Billions of microscopic plants called **phytoplankton** drift near the surface of the water. These are the main source of food for many creatures which live and feed at different ocean levels, called **zones**.

Ocean feeding zones

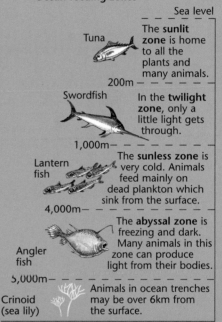

Sea level

Tuna — The **sunlit zone** is home to all the plants and many animals.

200m

Swordfish — In the **twilight zone**, only a little light gets through.

1,000m

Lantern fish — The **sunless zone** is very cold. Animals feed mainly on dead plankton which sink from the surface.

4,000m

Angler fish — The **abyssal zone** is freezing and dark. Many animals in this zone can produce light from their bodies.

5,000m

Crinoid (sea lily) — Animals in ocean trenches may be over 6km from the surface.

RIVERS

Rivers are formed when small streams join together and flow across the land, eventually flowing into a sea or lake. Rivers shape the Earth's surface by wearing away the rock they flow over and depositing rocks, pebbles, sand and silt as they do so.

A RIVER'S SOURCE

The beginning of a river is called its **source**. Many rivers have their source in mountain regions where water has run across the surface from various places and flowed into one channel. A river may also begin as a spring or a flow from a glacier*.

How springs are formed

Rain or snow falls on **permeable** rock, which lets in water.

Water soaks into rock, building up from the lowest permeable level.

Springs begin to flow where the water-filled rock meets the surface.

STAGES OF A RIVER

A river's course can be divided into three stages. In its **upper** stage, the valley tends to be V-shaped with steep sides, formed as the turbulent water cuts down into the rock. The slope or **gradient** of the river's rocky bed is steep.

In the **middle** stage, the river's speed increases because the bed is smoother. The gradient is more gentle, and the valley becomes wider as the water wears away its sides. The river flows from side to side in wide loops. This is called **meandering**.

In the **lower** stage, the river's muddy or sandy bed is even smoother, so it flows faster. The river is large, because it has been joined by others, called **tributaries**. At its end it flows into the sea or a lake.

A waterfall forms when a river flows from hard to soft rock. The water wears away the soft rock more quickly and forms a ledge.

V-shaped valley

Upper stage

Each wide loop is called a **meander**.

The wide, flat valley floor is called the **flood plain**.

Middle stage

The river has split into several channels. This area is called a delta.

Lower stage

EROSION

Running water wears away or **erodes** rock by the constant movement of the pebbles and sand grains it carries. This is how a river bed forms. The amount of erosion depends on the speed and amount of water, how much material it carries and the rock it flows over. Softer rock, such as sandstone, is eroded faster than harder rock, such as granite.

The diagram below shows four types of erosion which take place at different stages of a river's course. The length of the river is not shown to scale.

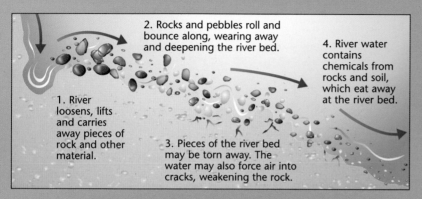

2. Rocks and pebbles roll and bounce along, wearing away and deepening the river bed.

4. River water contains chemicals from rocks and soil, which eat away at the river bed.

1. River loosens, lifts and carries away pieces of rock and other material.

3. Pieces of the river bed may be torn away. The water may also force air into cracks, weakening the rock.

TRANSPORTATION

All the material **transported**, or carried along, by a river is called its **load**. Finer particles of clay and silt are carried along with heavier ones, such as pebbles and boulders. Wherever a river slows down, some of this material is deposited. The heaviest material is deposited first, followed by the smaller particles, creating a layering effect.

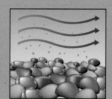

Large particles sink to the river bed before smaller ones.

DELTAS

As a river flows into the sea, any material it is still carrying is deposited. If this is deposited faster than it is washed away by the sea's currents and tides, it builds up in an area of flat land called a **delta**. The river splits into narrower channels as it crosses the delta and travels to the sea, creating a number of **sediment islands**. As the fresh river water and the salty sea water meet, chemical reactions take place and minerals that have been carried down, dissolved in the fresh water, come out of solution and are added to the sediment.

This is a delta in the Tenakee Inlet, Alaska. You can see how the sediment has built up in islands.

The mineral-rich sediment in delta areas makes the land fertile and ideal for farming. In Bangladesh, for example, millions of people live on islands formed in the delta of the River Ganges, despite the threat of flooding.

See for yourself

You can show how water deposits materials in layers. First, cut two 2cm slits in the bottom of a 2 litre plastic bottle. Cover each slit with sticky tape.

Tape over slits.

Next, use a funnel to half fill the bottle with soil. Then almost fill the bottle with water. Screw on the lid, shake vigorously, and leave for 24 hours.

Plastic tubing

Remove the lid and place one end of some plastic tubing in the water. Suck the water up, making sure not to swallow any, then put your thumb over the end. Bend the tube downwards into the sink or a container. Move your thumb, and the water will drain out.

Finally, pull the tape off the slits in the base, and leave to drain for 24 hours. You should see the soil has settled in layers.

Bottle cut away

Internet links

• Scan the code to travel along a river and over a waterfall.

• For links to more websites where you can see how rivers shape the Earth's surface, go to **www.usborne.com/quicklinks**

WEATHER

The conditions in the atmosphere near the Earth's surface are called the **weather**. These conditions include the temperature of the air, wind speed, air pressure, and the amount of water in the air, called **humidity**. Other factors include the amount of cloud and how much rain or snow falls, called **precipitation**.

THE SUN'S EFFECT

The Sun plays the most important part in causing the weather. Its heat and light, known as **solar radiation**, is absorbed by the Earth, which warms up as a result. In turn, the heat passes out from the Earth to the air above, which also becomes warmer.

The Sun's rays have the strongest effect where they hit the Earth's surface straight on, that is, around the middle of the Earth (the **equator**). Further away from the equator, the rays do not strike directly, so the heat is spread over a larger area. Its effect is therefore weaker.

How the Sun's rays strike the Earth

AIR PRESSURE

Because of gravity*, the atmosphere presses down on the Earth's surface, creating **atmospheric pressure**. When air is heated from below, it expands and begins to rise. As it does so it stops pressing down so hard on the surface. This creates an area of **low pressure**. At the surface, air flows in from surrounding areas to even up the pressure.

Low pressure

As warm air rises from the surface, more air moves in from higher pressure areas.

High pressure

As cooler air pushes down, the surface air moves away to lower pressure areas.

Around the Earth there are areas of high and low pressure. These areas are called **belts**. Strong winds blow from high pressure belts to low pressure belts. However, the winds do not just blow straight from one belt to the other. They are deflected sideways (made to swerve) by the Earth's rotation. This is known as the **Coriolis effect**.

Red arrows show how winds are deflected around the Earth. Yellow arrow shows which way the Earth rotates.

HOT AND COLD AIR

As warm air rises, it cools and sinks back to Earth. There, it may be heated again if the surface is still warmer than the air above. The circulation of warm and cold currents of air is called **convection** and the currents are **convection currents**.

Rising current of warm air

Warm air eventually cools and sinks.

Surrounding cooler air moves in to replace warm air.

Regions around the middle of the Earth (the equator) receive the strongest solar radiation because the rays hit them almost straight on all the time.

Areas where the rays have spread out receive less heat.

* Gravity, 130.

These dark clouds are full of water droplets, which may fall as rain, snow or hail.

CLOUDS

The Sun's heat causes water to evaporate from the seas. The invisible water vapour rises and cools, condensing as it does so, to form tiny water droplets. These mass together as **clouds**. When clouds form slowly and steadily, they spread out across the sky in sheets. On hot days, they grow faster and puff up into heaps.

Common types of cloud

Cirrus clouds are high and wispy.

Cumulus clouds often form high in the sky in warm, sunny weather.

Stratus clouds form low, flat layers.

THE SEASONS

Weather conditions change throughout the year. These changes are called the **seasons**, and they occur because the Earth is tilted at an angle in relation to the Sun. As the planet makes its year-long journey around the Sun, the most direct sunlight falls on different areas.

Diagram showing how seasons change

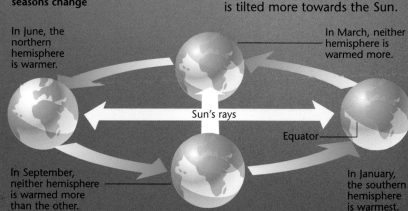

In June, the northern hemisphere is warmer.

In March, neither hemisphere is warmed more.

Sun's rays

Equator

In September, neither hemisphere is warmed more than the other.

In January, the southern hemisphere is warmest.

In January, at the start of each orbit, the **southern hemisphere** (the half of the Earth below the equator), is tilted towards the Sun, causing temperatures to rise there. In June, the **northern hemisphere** is tilted towards the Sun. Temperatures rise in the north and fall in the south. In spring and autumn, neither hemisphere is tilted more towards the Sun.

See for yourself

You can do this simple activity to create a miniature cloud. First, fill a large, clear plastic container about a third full with hot water. Next, place some ice cubes on a baking tray and put this on top of the container. As the air inside the container rises and is cooled by the ice, the water vapour it contains forms droplets, making a small "cloud".

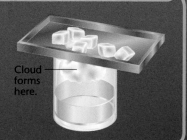

Cloud forms here.

Internet links

• Scan the code to watch a video clip about clouds.

CLIMATE

An area's **climate** is its typical pattern of weather conditions and temperature over a long period of time. One type of climate may affect a large region, or a small, local area, where it is called a **microclimate**. Climates depend on latitude, distance from the sea, and height above sea level.

Banana trees such as this grow in equatorial areas.

CLIMATIC REGIONS

A **climatic region** is a large area on the Earth within which the climate is generally the same. The world's major climatic regions are described on this page.

Polar climates are harsh and change very little throughout the year. The temperature is extremely low and there is little rain or snowfall. Hardly any plant life can grow in these conditions.

Many polar animals, such as this polar bear, are kept warm by a thick layer of fur or fat.

Tundra regions have harsh winds and low winter temperatures, averaging from -30°C to -20°C. The temperature rises to around 17°C during the summer.

Tough, low-growing land plants such as lichens are examples of tundra vegetation.

In **temperate** regions, rain falls throughout the year, and the temperature varies with the seasons. It is generally between -6°C and 25°C. Day-to-day weather changes are a feature of temperate regions.

Deciduous trees, which lose their leaves in autumn, are found in temperate areas.

Tropical regions have a warm climate all year round. There are two seasons, dry and wet. Temperatures tend to be between 21°C and 30°C.

Grasslands in tropical regions are mostly made up of scattered trees and tall grasses, which die off in the dry season.

Mediterranean areas are warm and wet in winter but dry in summer. Their climate is heavily influenced by currents of air which move between the land and sea.

Citrus fruits grow well in Mediterranean climates. Their thick skins prevent them from drying up during the hot summer months.

Continental areas, such as the central parts of Asia and North America, have hot summers and cold winters.

North American prairies have very hot summers.

Equatorial regions have a constantly hot and wet climate, which supports rainforests in many areas. The temperature never drops below around 17°C, creating ideal growing conditions for huge numbers of plants.

Desert climates are generally very dry, with less than 250mm of rainfall per year. Daytime temperatures in the hottest deserts may be over 38°C, although some become much cooler in winter. Many living things in the desert can store water.

Cacti and many other desert plants store large amounts of water in their thick, fleshy leaves.

MOUNTAIN CLIMATES

In mountain areas, temperatures drop as height above sea level (**altitude**) increases, producing different climates and vegetation at different altitudes. Trees can't survive on high mountain slopes because there is little soil, and the ground may be frozen and blasted by harsh, icy winds.

The direction which a mountainside faces (called its **aspect**) also affects its climate. If one side of a mountain receives more sunlight than the other, more vegetation may grow there.

Plant life in a mountain climate

Small, low-growing plants such as moss and lichens grow on the high mountainside.

Above a certain level, called the **treeline**, it is too cold for trees to grow.

Trees

COASTAL CLIMATES

In coastal areas, the land and sea gain and lose heat at different rates during the day and night. The air above them constantly circulates, creating a mild, wet climate. This is known as a **coastal** or **maritime** climate.

During the day

Land warms up more quickly. This heats up the air above it, which rises.

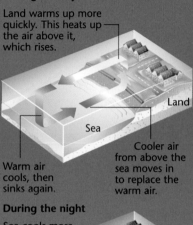

Land

Sea

Warm air cools, then sinks again.

Cooler air from above the sea moves in to replace the warm air.

During the night

Sea cools more slowly.

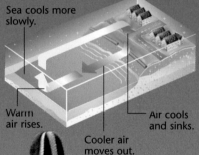

Warm air rises.

Cooler air moves out.

Air cools and sinks.

CITY CLIMATES

Cities tend to be warmer than the areas surrounding them. This is because concrete absorbs more heat than vegetation. It also holds on to heat for longer, making nights warmer in cities than in the countryside.

The ground beneath a city also tends to be drier, as roads and pavements prevent water from draining into the soil beneath.

CLIMATE CHANGE

Most climate scientists think that **global warming** is causing more extreme weather in many parts of the world. For example, areas in Africa that already get little rain are getting still less, making it even more difficult for people to grow crops to eat.

Many places, such as Bangladesh, London and New York, are at increased risk of flooding. Ocean water expands as it warms, and this, together with the melting of ice sheets and glaciers, means that sea levels are rising.

Large areas of China and India may suffer drought, because major rivers could dry up entirely for parts of the year, as the glaciers supplying them with water disappear.

Internet links

- Scan the code for more about climates and global warming.

WORLD POPULATION

All the people living in a particular place are called its **population**. Today, the world's population is greater than ever before, and it is increasing all the time. People's need for food, shelter and fuel creates demands on the Earth and its resources. As a result, people have altered the natural environment to suit their needs.

In some places, where the land is crowded, some people live in houseboats on rivers or lakes.

SPREADING OUT

If all the Earth's surface were suitable to live on, there would be plenty of room for everyone. However, few people live where the climate is very hot or cold, or where the soil is unsuitable for farming. This means that the world's population is spread unevenly over the continents.

There are now over 7 billion people in the world, compared to around 4 billion in 1980. In countries with fast-growing populations, more people are being forced to live in overcrowded conditions or unsuitable places.

This satellite image shows Washington DC, USA. Over half of the world's population lives in cities, like this.

Graph showing world population since the year 1000

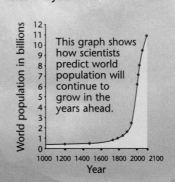

This graph shows how scientists predict world population will continue to grow in the years ahead.

World population in billions / Year

CITY PROBLEMS

All over the world, people move from the country into towns and cities, to find work. This is called **urban migration**. As city populations grow, some areas become crowded, and pollution increases.

In some countries, **shanty towns**, made up of makeshift buildings, build up on the edges of cities to house the extra people. Houses in shanty towns are usually built from waste materials and scrap. There is often no clean water supply, electricity or sewage system.

This is a shanty town on the outskirts of Cape Town, South Africa. People may be forced to build these when they can't afford housing in the city, or when there isn't enough available.

POPULATION CONTROL

Many countries are trying to prevent their population from growing too quickly. For example, in China, couples are discouraged from having more than one child. Health education projects also teach people **birth control** – how to avoid having too many children. However, many people object to birth control because of their religious or cultural beliefs.

PEOPLE AND THE LAND

Since early times, people's lives have been influenced by the natural features of their surroundings. People looked for areas where they could find water, food and safety from attack. When they discovered a suitable place, they formed permanent groups called **communities**.

Many communities began near rivers, springs or wells, or in areas that were not likely to flood. Fertile soils for farming and natural resources, such as coal, also encouraged people to settle in particular places.

EFFECTS ON THE LAND

People often change their surroundings to suit their needs. Over the centuries, more and more land has been cleared for building, transport systems and growing crops. Huge areas of forest have been destroyed and natural wetlands drained. Dry areas have been watered artificially or **irrigated**.

Here, a wooded area is being cleared to make way for a building site.

These methods help to provide more food, housing, and transport routes. But the natural world suffers as a result. In many areas of cleared land, fertile topsoil has been washed or blown away. This is called **soil erosion**. It leaves infertile soil, which cannot be used to grow crops. In some countries, soil erosion combined with drought has led to famine.

FARMING

As the world's population increases, so does the demand for food. Many international charities are helping to improve farming techniques in developing countries. They set up projects to teach farmers how to produce more crops from the same amount of land. This removes the need to clear more land.

Some new farmland has been created in desert border land. These areas once had trees and shrubs, but have been turned to desert through soil erosion. This is caused by overgrazing, tree felling and dry winds. But with the help of irrigation, this land may be used to grow crops.

In areas with very little water, drip irrigators deliver water drop by drop to each plant. Sometimes fertilizers are added to the water. This is known as **fertigation**.

Internet links

• Scan the code for a video about world population growth.

• For links to more websites with population maps, facts, graphs and activities, go to **www.usborne.com/quicklinks**

EARTH'S RESOURCES

Beneath the Earth's surface are many resources which are used by people all over the world. Some of these are precious stones, which can be sold or traded; others are metals, which are used for building and other purposes. Almost all the fuel currently used also comes from within the Earth.

This drinks can contains aluminium, one of several metals that can be melted down and reused.

FOSSIL FUELS

Oil, coal and gas are known as **fossil fuels**. They are formed from the remains of plants and animals which have built up in rock for millions of years. The chemical energy trapped in these organisms is released when fossil fuels are burned.

Coal is formed from the remains of ancient plants.

People need fuel for cooking, heating, lighting, running motor vehicles, generating electricity, and many other things. But demand is great and supplies are limited, so all of the Earth's oil and gas may be used up within a few decades. This means that people need to find other fuel sources to meet their needs.

RENEWABLE ENERGY

Sources of energy which don't run out are called **renewable**. These include the Sun's rays, which are captured by solar panels*; the wind, which turns wind turbines*; and moving water, used in hydroelectric power stations. **Geothermal energy** (heat energy from underground rocks) is used in volcanic areas. **Biofuel**, made from fermented corn or sugar cane, can also be used as fuel.

Only about 19% of the Earth's total energy and 22% of its electricity currently come from renewable sources. Many experts think that fossil fuels, which cause global warming*, could be largely replaced with renewable sources if governments spent enough money on them.

NUCLEAR POWER

Nuclear energy is produced from radioactive substances, such as uranium, when their tiny particles, called atoms, are broken apart. Many people believe it could be the most convenient energy source for the future, but it creates dangerous radioactive waste, which is difficult to dispose of safely.

Waste from nuclear power plants may remain dangerous for thousands of years. Radioactive material carries a warning symbol.

These rows of huge, reflective solar panels capture the Sun's rays and use the energy to generate electricity.

Solar power provides a clean, safe form of energy.

* Global warming, 185; Solar panels, 109; Wind turbines, 108.

MINERALS

For centuries, people have dug rocks out of the Earth because of the useful **minerals** they contain. Minerals are usually made up of a mixture of elements, for instance carbon, silicon and metals such as iron.

Gemstones, such as these garnets, are minerals which are mined for their beauty. They are usually cut and polished before being sold.

Rocks which contain a high level of valuable or useful minerals, particularly metals, are called **ores**. Metal ores taken from the Earth have to be processed to extract the pure metal. There are various ways of doing this, including smelting*, which involves heat, and electrolysis*, which uses electricity.

Iron is extracted from an ore called **haematite**.

MINING

Rocks which contain useful minerals are **mined**, or taken from the ground. The mining technique used depends on the depth, value and amount of the ore. If it is found in large amounts underground, tunnels are dug beneath the Earth's surface to reach it. Ore near the surface can be dug out from an open pit.

Here, coal is being extracted from a mine at the surface of the ground. This is called an **open cast** mine.

Although people rely heavily on mining to supply many substances that they need, it can be bad for the environment. Mining for a single tonne of ore may produce thousands of tonnes of waste rock, which may be spread over a wide area. Plant and animal life in the areas around a mine may be badly affected.

MANAGING RESOURCES

People have always depended on metals, fuels and the Earth's other natural resources. But mining and extracting different fuels and ores is an expensive and difficult process. Some substances, such as oil, are also becoming harder to find, as the best sources have already been used up.

At some time in the future, there will no longer be enough non-renewable resources to meet everyone's needs. Reusing and recycling materials, and using renewable fuel sources wherever possible, are the best ways to make the Earth's existing resources last as long as possible.

See for yourself

There are many materials which can be recycled. These include paper, glass, aluminium cans and steel. You could find out if there are any recycling points near to where you live. Your school might also organize recycling activities.

You can help to save energy by remembering to switch off lights when leaving a room, or by asking your parents to use energy-efficient light bulbs, like this one.

Internet links

• Scan the code to watch a video about biofuels, or to discover more about the Earth's resources, go to **www.usborne.com/quicklinks**

* Electrolysis, 82-83; Smelting, 36.

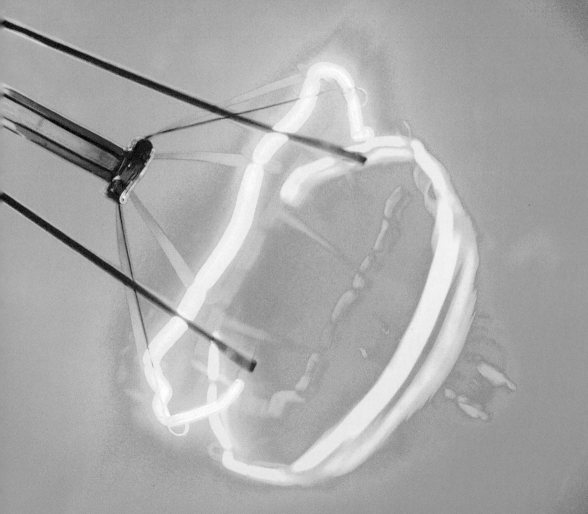

LIGHT, SOUND
AND
ELECTRICITY

WAVES

All **waves** carry energy. There are two main types of wave – mechanical and electromagnetic. **Mechanical waves**, including water waves and sound waves, are vibrations in a solid, liquid or gas. Electromagnetic waves, such as light waves and radio waves, are vibrations of a different kind. For more about these waves see pages 212-213.

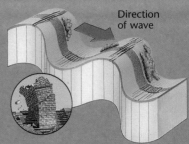

Direction of wave

Earthquakes are waves that travel through rock. The vibrations can be strong enough to destroy buildings.

TRANSFERRING ENERGY

Any substance through which waves travel is called a **medium**. Water, glass and air are different types of medium. A mechanical wave carries energy through a medium by making its particles vibrate. Each vibrating particle makes its neighbour vibrate, so passing the energy through the substance.

As these droplets fall into the water, waves spread out in a circle, carrying energy away from the disturbed area.

Waves such as those shown in the pictures below are caused by the water's particles vibrating up and down. The particles don't travel onwards with the wave.

Like the water particles themselves, the bird isn't moved forwards by the passing wave (yellow arrow).

A wave does not permanently disturb the medium it travels through. Each particle gradually stops vibrating and settles in its original position.

The particles in a wave vibrate less as they lose energy, and the water becomes still.

The ripples on this pond are water waves. As they move away from the source of the disturbance they lose energy, and so become smaller.

TYPES OF WAVE

All waves can be described as either transverse or longitudinal, depending on the direction of their vibrations.

Transverse waves are waves in which the vibrations that make up the wave are at right angles to the direction the wave is travelling. Water waves are transverse waves.

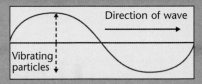

Particles in a transverse wave vibrate at right angles to the direction of the wave.

In **longitudinal waves**, the particles vibrate in the same direction as the wave is travelling. The particles of the medium vibrate forwards and backwards, acting like the coils in a spring as they are squeezed together and then spread out. Sound waves are longitudinal waves.

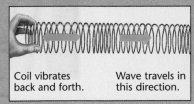

The coils in this moving spring show how longitudinal waves travel.

MEASURING WAVES

Transverse waves create a regular pattern of high points, called **peaks**, and low points, called **troughs**. A complete wave is known as a **cycle**. It has one peak and one trough.

The number of complete waves that pass a point in one second is called the **frequency**. This is measured in **hertz (Hz)**, named after the German scientist, Heinrich Hertz (1857-1894), who was the first person to discover and use radio waves.

The distance between a point on one wave and the same point on the next, for example, between two troughs, is called the **wavelength**.

The height from a particle's rest position to a peak is called **amplitude**. This becomes less as a wave moves away from its source and loses energy.

A wave is measured by its frequency, wavelength and amplitude.

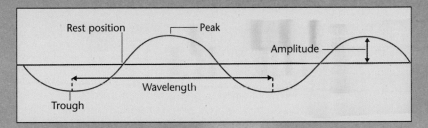

See for yourself

You can use this experiment to see the form of a transverse wave. Tie one end of a piece of string to a fixed point, such as a door knob, hold the other end and give it a sharp shake. You will see the form of the wave moving along the string. The string vibrates at right angles to the direction of the wave.

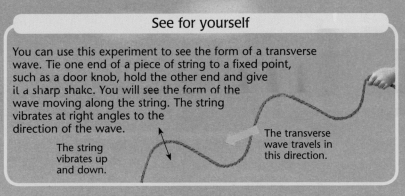

The string vibrates up and down.

The transverse wave travels in this direction.

Internet links

• Scan the code to find out more about how waves move.

• For links to more websites where you can watch animations and try quizzes about waves, amplitude, wavelength and frequency, go to **www.usborne.com/quicklinks**

WAVE BEHAVIOUR

When a wave hits an obstacle, or passes from one substance (medium) to another, it can change in speed, direction or shape. Before the change, the wave is called the **incident wave**. The examples on these pages show water waves, but all waves behave in the same way.

Tsunamis are giant waves that slow down and rapidly increase in height as they enter shallow water.

REFLECTION

When an incident wave hits an obstacle, for example when a water wave hits a sea wall, it bounces back. This is called **reflection**. The wave is reflected back at an angle equal to its angle of approach. It is then called a **reflected wave**.

The angle of reflection of a wave is the same as the angle of approach of the incident wave.

The shape of a reflected wave depends both on the shape of the incident wave and the shape of the obstacle it hits. The diagrams below show what happens when straight and curved incident waves hit differently shaped obstacles.

Straight waves hitting a straight barrier produce straight reflected waves.

Circular waves hitting a straight barrier produce circular reflected waves.

Circular waves hitting an inward-curving barrier producing straight reflected waves

Waves at sea are relatively straight. As they approach the shallow waters of a beach, they bend until they match the curves of its shoreline. This is an example of refraction.

REFRACTION

When an incident wave enters a new medium it changes speed. Its wavelength* changes, but its frequency* doesn't. In the diagram below, the waves slow down in the new medium. Their wavelength gets shorter, but the number of peaks passing in a second (the frequency) stays the same.

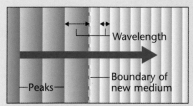

Waves change speed as they enter a new medium.

If a wave enters a new medium at an angle, it changes both speed and direction. This is called **refraction**. A wave that has undergone refraction is called a **refracted wave**.

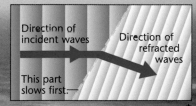

Waves change speed and direction as they enter a new medium at an angle.

Deep and shallow water act as different substances. The first part of the wave to enter the shallows slows down before the rest of the wave. This changes the wave's direction.

INTERFERENCE

If two or more waves meet, they have an effect on each other. This effect is called **interference**. The kind of interference depends on which parts of the waves coincide.

If two peaks of the same amplitude* arrive in the same place at the same time, they combine to form a peak twice as large. This is an example of **constructive interference**.

If a peak meets a trough of the same size, they cancel each other out and the wave disappears. This is an example of **destructive interference**.

See for yourself

To see wave interference, hold a small pebble in each hand and drop them, at the same time, into a bath filled with water. The ripples made by the pebbles will move out in circles. Where they cross each other you might see, very briefly, both constructive and destructive interference.

Constructive interference

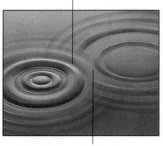

Destructive interference

DIFFRACTION

When an incident wave passes through a gap, it spreads out and bends. This is an example of **diffraction**. The smaller the gap compared to the wavelength of the wave, the more it is diffracted.

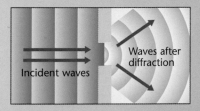

A wave passing through a gap smaller than its wavelength is diffracted a lot.

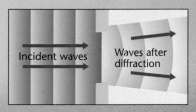

A wave passing through a gap larger than its wavelength is hardly diffracted at all.

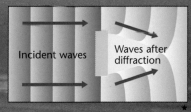

Waves can also be diffracted when striking the edge of an obstacle.

Internet links

• Scan the code to see how tsunamis occur, or for more links to websites about waves, go to **www.usborne.com/quicklinks**

* Amplitude, Frequency, Wavelength, 203.

SOUND

Sound is a form of energy carried by waves of vibrating particles. These waves, called **sound waves**, can travel through solids, liquids and gases, but they cannot travel through a vacuum as there are no particles of any sort to vibrate. For this reason, sound cannot travel out in space.

The sound of falling leaves measures 10dB.

SOUND WAVES

Sound waves are longitudinal waves. This means that the particles vibrate in the same direction as the wave travels.

For instance, inside a loudspeaker a paper cone vibrates forwards and backwards, sending sound energy into the air. As the cone moves forwards, it presses together air particles in front of it. As it moves backwards, it leaves an area where the particles are more spaced out.

Cone of loudspeaker (not moving)

Air particles

Cone moves forwards.

Particles pressed together

Cone moves backwards.

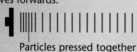
Particles spread out

See for yourself

You can feel sound vibrations with a balloon and a radio. Turn on a radio and hold a balloon about 10cm away from the speaker. The vibrations of the sounds make the air in the balloon vibrate.

Sound waves can be shown as a wavy line. The peaks show where particles have been squashed. The troughs show where particles are spread out. Wave diagrams show the number of waves per second (frequency) and their strength (amplitude).

Diagram showing sound waves

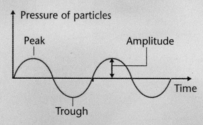

Wave frequency is measured in hertz (Hz). Sound waves with frequencies between about 20 and 20,000 hertz can be heard by the human ear and are commonly described as sound. Sound waves below this range are known as **infrasound**, and above it are **ultrasound**.

High sounds, such as birdsong, have high-frequency waves.

Low sounds, such as the rumble made by the engine of a heavy truck, have low-frequency waves.

LOUDNESS

Loud sounds are waves with a large amplitude. Soft sounds are waves with a small amplitude. As a sound travels further away from its source, the amplitude becomes smaller and so the sound becomes quieter.

The loudness of sound is measured in **decibels (dB)**. The blue whale is the loudest animal in the world. It makes sounds of up to 188dB.

Aircraft make such loud sounds that ground crew wear ear protectors to avoid hearing damage.

SPEED OF SOUND

Sound waves travel at different speeds in different substances. They travel more quickly in solids than in liquids, and more quickly in liquids than in gases.

The speed of sound waves as they travel through dry air at 0°C is 331 metres per second. This speed increases if the air temperature goes up, and decreases if the temperature of the air goes down.

A speed that is faster than the speed of sound in the same conditions is known as a **supersonic speed**. One that is slower is a **subsonic speed**.

As it reaches supersonic speed, an aircraft makes a deafening bang called a **sonic boom**. In this photo, the sound waves can be seen as they disturb the misty air.

The sound of an aircraft landing measures about 120dB.

ECHOES

Echoes are sound waves that have reflected (bounced) off a surface and are heard shortly after the original sound. Echoes can be used to find the position of objects. This is done by timing how long the echoes take to return to their source.

Ultrasonic sound waves are most often used because waves of high frequency bend less around obstacles in their path. The waves spread out less than ordinary sound waves and give more accurate information about the surface reflecting them.

When animals such as bats and dolphins use echoes, it is called **echo location**. They use it to find their way around or to locate prey.

Sonar (which stands for **so**und **n**avigation **a**nd **r**anging) is the name given to the method used by equipment on board ships to measure the depth of sea water, or to detect underwater objects, such as shipwrecks or shoals of fish.

Ultrasound waves sent from the ship bounce off the wreck. A computer times the echoes to find the wreck's depth and position.

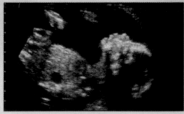

Dolphins send out streams of over 700 ultrasonic clicks in a second. The time the echoes take to return can tell them how far away they are from shoals of fish.

Echoes are also used in **ultrasound scanning** to see inside the body – for example to check on the growth of an unborn baby inside its mother. Bone, muscle and fat all reflect ultrasonic waves differently. A computer uses this information to make a picture.

Ultrasound scan of an unborn baby

Internet links

• Scan the code for a video about sound, or for links to more websites, go to **www.usborne.com/quicklinks**

MUSICAL INSTRUMENTS

Musical instruments work by making sound waves. The shape and size of the instrument and the material of which it is made affect the sound. Some instruments have a soundbox that **resonates**. This means that it vibrates at the same frequency as the air vibrations created by the original sound, making the sound fuller and richer.

A French horn is a wind instrument. Air vibrates inside it making sound.

TYPES OF INSTRUMENTS

Musical instruments can be divided into groups depending on the way they make sounds. **Stringed instruments**, such as harps and violins, have stretched strings that vibrate when you pluck or slide a bow across them. The strings inside a piano vibrate when they are hit by felt-covered hammers controlled by the keys. The more the strings vibrate, the louder the sound.

The bridge of this violin carries vibrations from the strings into the body of the instrument (its soundbox).

The bow strings are made of horsehairs. They slide across the strings, making them vibrate.

The soundbox resonates, making the sound fuller and louder.

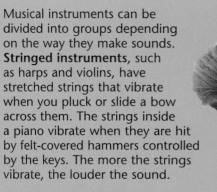

Wind instruments work by making a column of air vibrate inside them. The vibrations are produced in different ways. For example in a trumpet, the player's lips vibrate in a cup-shaped mouthpiece. This sound is then made louder, or **amplified**, by the tube and the flared end of the instrument.

Early trumpets had long, straight tubes. In modern trumpets like this one, the tube is coiled, making it easier to hold.

Clarinets and oboes have a mouthpiece that contains one or two pieces of reed. These vibrate as air is blown past them.

Percussion instruments produce sound when they are beaten, scraped or shaken. A drum, for example, has a tight skin which you beat with your hand or a stick. The vibrations make the air inside the drum vibrate, and the hollow shape of the drum amplifies the sound.

The vibrations of a drum skin resonate inside the drum and are amplified.

ELECTRIC INSTRUMENTS

In **electric instruments**, such as an electric guitar, small sound vibrations produced by the strings are amplified by an electronic amplifier instead of a soundbox. Special effects, such as echoes, can also be added electronically to the sound.

Vibrations from the strings of this electric guitar are changed into electrical signals. These are amplified and then changed back into sound.

SYNTHESIZED SOUND

A **sound synthesizer** is an instrument that stores sound waves as binary code* in its electronic memory. The synthesizer can reproduce a sound by converting the code for the sound into an electric current and sending it to a loudspeaker.

The sounds of musical instruments, as well as other noises, such as dogs barking, can be stored as binary code and reproduced by a synthesizer.

This keyboard synthesizer contains binary code for the sound waves of many different instruments.

PITCH

The highness or lowness of a sound is known as its **pitch**. Sound waves with a high frequency produce sounds of a high pitch, those with a low frequency, a low pitch. Musical sounds of a specific pitch are called **notes**. For example, the note known as **Middle C**, which is the C nearest to the middle of a piano keyboard, has a frequency of about 262 hertz*. The next C above it has a higher frequency – about 523 hertz.

The size of an instrument affects the pitch of the notes that can be played on it. For example, in a stringed instrument, the longer the string, the lower the pitch. This is why a double bass makes lower notes than a violin.

A harp has strings that vibrate as they are plucked. Strings of different lengths make notes of different pitches.

Players can change the pitch of the sounds an instrument makes. For example, a guitar or violin player presses down on the strings. This shortens the length of string that can vibrate, and so it makes higher notes. On a flute or recorder, the player covers and uncovers holes. This alters the length of the column of air that can vibrate inside it, and so changes the notes produced.

Pressing the keys on this flute covers the holes. This lengthens the air column, and so lowers the pitch of the note.

HARMONICS

Most instruments produce complex sound waves that have higher, quieter sounds mixed in. These sounds are called **harmonics**. They give an instrument its individual sound quality, or **timbre**.

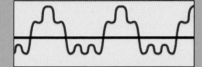

On a sound wave diagram, harmonics look like extra little waves. This diagram shows the waves made by an instrument.

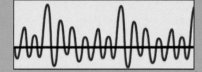

These are the sound waves of the same note played by a different instrument.

See for yourself

Try blowing across the top of an open, empty bottle. If you get it right, you will make the air column inside the bottle vibrate, producing a musical note. Now pour some water into the bottle and blow again. The water will have reduced the size of the air column, so the note that you produce will be higher.

Internet links

• Scan the code to see how instruments make sounds, or for more links to websites about instruments, go to **www.usborne.com/quicklinks**

* Binary code, 238; Hertz 203.

SOUND REPRODUCTION

By changing sound energy into electrical energy, sounds can be recorded and stored, to be played back at another time. In this form, sounds can also be sent over long distances, for example, over the internet.

An early gramophone, made in the 1890s. Grooves on a disc made a needle vibrate, creating sound waves that were amplified (made louder) by the horn.

Horn

MICROPHONES

Sounds can be converted into an electric current by a device called a **microphone**. This contains a thin metal disc called a **diaphragm**, which is attached to an electromagnet*, that is, a coil of wire and a ring-shaped magnet.

When sound waves hit the diaphragm, it vibrates at the same frequency* as the waves. The diaphragm makes the wire coil vibrate. When the coil moves near the magnet, it creates an electric current which flows along the wire. The current produced varies according to the size and frequency of the sound waves.

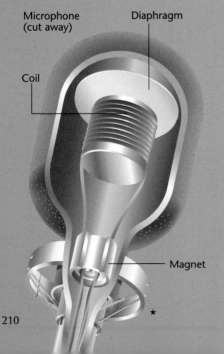

Microphone (cut away)

Diaphragm

Coil

Magnet

LOUDSPEAKERS

A **loudspeaker** turns an electric current from a source such as a microphone back into sound waves. Inside the loudspeaker there is an electromagnet. When an electric current flows through the coil in the electromagnet, it becomes magnetic. The coil is attached to a cone-shaped paper diaphragm.

The parts that make up a loudspeaker

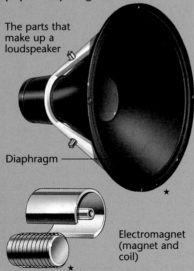

Diaphragm

Electromagnet (magnet and coil)

When a varying current produced from a sound wave flows through the coil, the force between the coil's magnetic field and that of the magnet makes both the coil and the diaphragm vibrate.

The air in front of the diaphragm vibrates to create sound waves of the same frequency as the original sound.

ANALOGUE RECORDING

In **analogue recording**, a continuous record of a sound wave is made. For example, the varying current from a microphone was once mostly recorded as grooves of varying depth on a vinyl disc, or as a varying pattern of magnetic particles on a cassette tape (see *Cassette recorders*, opposite).

Original sound wave

Recorded analogue sound wave

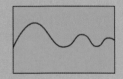

One problem with analogue recordings is that they can be changed by repeated use. For example, the playback heads on a cassette recorder gradually wear away the magnetic particles on the tape. This means that the sound heard become less like the original sound that was recorded.

Analogue sound wave distorted by frequent playing

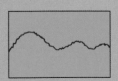

Another issue with tape recording is "tape hiss", a high-pitched background noise caused by the size of the magnetic particles.

* Electromagnet, 233; Frequency, 203.

CASSETTE RECORDERS

In a **cassette recorder**, sounds are recorded as a pattern of magnetized particles of iron or chromium oxide on plastic tape.

Cassette

The plastic tape in a cassette is covered with particles of iron or chromium oxide. ★

This is done by a part called the **recording head**, which is an electromagnet. A varying current produced from a sound wave passes from a microphone through a metal coil in the recording head. This causes variations in the head's magnetic field which arranges the metal particles on the tape into different patterns.

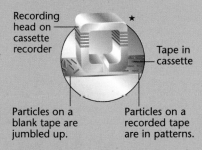

Recording head on cassette recorder ★

Tape in cassette

Particles on a blank tape are jumbled up.

Particles on a recorded tape are in patterns.

The patterns of particles on the tape are read by a part called the **playback head**. It produces a varying current which is converted back into sound by a loudspeaker.

DIGITAL RECORDING

In **digital recording**, an electric current representing a sound is described by a code made up of the numbers 0 and 1 (binary code*). This is done by measuring the current at different points, a process called **sampling**.

The more points that are sampled, the closer to the original sound the recording is when played back. For example, in CD recording, 44,100 samples are taken every second. This produces a **high-fidelity recording** – one that sounds very similar to the original.

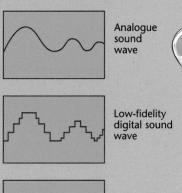

Analogue sound wave

Low-fidelity digital sound wave

High-fidelity digital sound wave

With a digital recording, the same series of numbers is used to make up the sound each time it is played back. This means that it always sounds the same as when it was first recorded and is known as **perfect sound reproduction**.

DIGITAL SOUND

Digital sound samples can be stored as files on a computer, phone or MP3 player, be recorded onto a CD, or sent across the internet. They can then be easily manipulated with a computer, or smartphone app*. **Audio mixing** is combining any number of samples, or **tracks**, into a playable recording made up of a number of **audio channels**. These usually equal the number of speakers. For example, **stereo** recordings have two channels.

COMPACT DISCS

A **compact disc**, or **CD**, uses digital methods to store sound or other information. The binary code is represented by tiny **bumps**, and flat areas called **land**, on the surface of the disc.

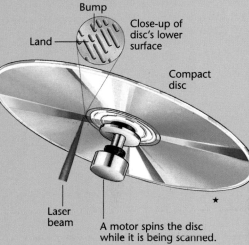

Bump

Close-up of disc's lower surface

Land

Compact disc

Laser beam

A motor spins the disc while it is being scanned. ★

Inside a CD player, a laser beam scans the disc's shiny underside. As light hits the edge of each bump, a light detector reads an electric pulse as a binary 1. As light hits the flat areas on and between the bumps, this is read as a 0. The stream of pulses is turned into sound by a loudspeaker.

Internet links

• Scan the code to watch a video about the invention of CDs.

• For links to more websites with experiments and activities about sound reproduction, go to **www.usborne.com/quicklinks**

ELECTROMAGNETIC WAVES

Electromagnetic waves are transverse waves* made up of continually changing electric and magnetic fields. Like mechanical waves, electromagnetic waves can travel through most solids, liquids and gases. They can also travel through a **vacuum** – an empty space where there are no particles of air or any other matter. All electromagnetic waves are invisible, except for those that make up light.

ELECTROMAGNETIC SPECTRUM

The complete range of electromagnetic waves, arranged in order of their wavelength* and frequency*, is known as the **electromagnetic spectrum**. At the high-energy end the waves have a short wavelength and high frequency, while waves at the low-energy end have a long wavelength and low frequency. They all travel at the same speed – approximately 300,000 kilometres per second. This is known as the **speed of light**.

GAMMA RAYS

Gamma rays are short, high-frequency waves. They can kill living cells and are used to sterilize medical equipment by destroying any germs on them.

Gamma rays are used to keep these forceps free of germs.

X-RAYS

X-rays can travel through most soft substances but not hard, dense ones. X-rays are used in hospitals to make shadow pictures of parts of the body. They travel through soft tissue, such as skin and muscle, but not through hard bone. X-rays are also used for security at airports to check what may be hidden in people's luggage.

X-rays were used to create this image of a woman's foot in a shoe. The bones and metal shoe parts show up most clearly because the X-rays could not pass through them.

The electromagnetic spectrum

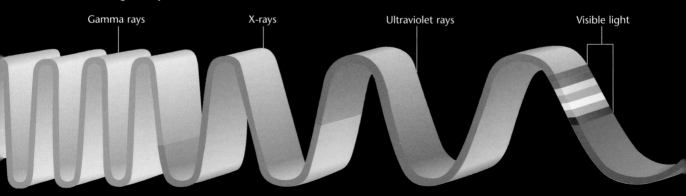

| Gamma rays | X-rays | Ultraviolet rays | Visible light |

Short wavelength
High frequency

UV RAYS

Ultraviolet (UV) rays have more energy than visible light (see below) and can cause chemical reactions to take place.

Suncreams protect skin by blocking out harmful UV rays.

For example, UV rays from the Sun cause the skin to increase its production of a brown chemical called **melanin**. This makes the skin tanned. Too much exposure to UV rays can result in high levels of melanin, and may lead to skin cancer.

VISIBLE LIGHT

There is a narrow section of the electromagnetic spectrum that humans can see. This is called the **visible light spectrum**. You can find out more about visible light and the way it behaves on pages 214-217.

INFRARED RAYS

Infrared rays are given out by anything hot. For example, heat from the Sun travels to the Earth as infrared rays.

RADIO WAVES

Radio waves are those with the longest wavelength and lowest frequency. You can read more about them on page 226.

Microwaves are radio waves with a relatively short wavelength. They are easy to control and direct, and have many different uses.

In an ordinary oven, heat is passed from molecules at the edge of the food to ones in the middle. Microwave ovens work by making all the molecules in a food substance vibrate at the same time. This heats and cooks the food more quickly.

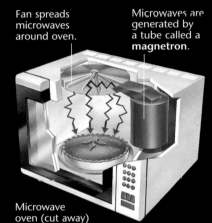

Fan spreads microwaves around oven.

Microwaves are generated by a tube called a **magnetron**.

Microwave oven (cut away)

RADAR

Radar (which stands for **ra**dio **d**etection **an**d **r**anging) uses microwaves to find the position of distant objects, such as ships and aircraft. A transmitter sends out a beam of microwaves that is reflected off a solid object and picked up again by a receiver. This information is transformed into a screen image that shows the distance (range) and direction of the object.

Radio telescope dishes like this one can pick up microwaves that travel from distant stars and planets. They can detect things that are too dark or too far away to be seen with normal telescopes.

Internet links

• Scan the code for more about visible and invisible waves.

• For links to more websites where you can explore the electromagnetic spectrum, go to **www.usborne.com/quicklinks**

Infrared rays

Radio waves

Microwaves

Waves used for standard radio and television broadcasting

Radio waves have the lowest frequency and longest wavelength. Gamma rays have the highest frequency and shortest wavelength.

Long wavelength

Low frequency

LIGHT AND SHADOW

Light is a form of energy. It is made up of electromagnetic waves which are part of the electromagnetic spectrum*. This part is known as **visible light** because it can be seen.

The beacon in this lighthouse rotates, flashing with intense bright light that can reach ships many kilometres out at sea.

LIGHT

Light waves are a type of transverse wave*. Like other waves, they transport energy from a source to its surroundings.

Any object that gives off light, for example the Sun or a light bulb, is said to be luminous. Most objects are non-luminous and can be seen only because they are reflecting the light from something luminous. For example, the Moon can only be seen when light from the Sun bounces off it.

Light from the Sun reflects off the surface of the Moon.

SHADOWS

Different types of substance allow different amounts of light to pass through them. Substances through which light can pass fully, such as clear glass, are said to be **transparent**. Substances which only let some light through are translucent. Frosted glass is translucent.

When light shines on an **opaque** object, the waves cannot pass through, so a dark area, called a **shadow**, forms on the other side.

Light

Light cannot pass through this ball, so a shadow is formed.

Some luminous objects give off more light than others. The level of brightness is called **intensity**. The further you are from a source of light, the less intense the light is. This is because light waves spread out as they travel away from the source.

The bright torch gives more intense light than the small candle.

Opaque objects cast two types of shadow. If no light reaches an area, a dark shadow, called an **umbra**, is formed. If some light reaches an area, grey shadow is formed. This is called a **penumbra**, and it forms around the edge of the umbra. The smaller the light source, the more umbra and less penumbra it creates.

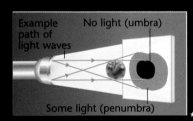

Example path of light waves

No light (umbra)

Some light (penumbra)

See for yourself

To see the two different kinds of shadow, hold a book over a piece of white paper under the light of a lamp. Notice the types of shadow it casts. If you move the book closer to the paper, you will see more umbra and less penumbra.

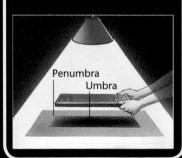

Penumbra
Umbra

* *Electromagnetic spectrum, 212-213; Transverse waves, 203.*

LASERS

Visible light is made up of several colours of different wavelengths* and frequencies*. Machines called **lasers** create beams of intense, pure colour of one wavelength and frequency.

In a simple laser, a ruby rod absorbs light energy from a bright lamp. Atoms in the ruby gain the energy and give off bursts of light of a certain wavelength and frequency. Each burst of light causes other atoms in the ruby to give off light waves of the exact same type. Together they form a **laser beam**.

In this laser, a rod of ruby absorbs light from a coiled flash lamp.

Ruby rod

The ruby re-emits the light as a concentrated red laser beam.

Coiled flash lamp

Laser beam

The waves in a laser beam are **coherent**. This means that they travel in step with each other as everything about them is exactly the same. They stay together in a narrow, concentrated beam, making them intense and easy to direct.

Some powerful lasers produce extremely hot beams of infrared light*. These are used in industry for melting through metals, diamonds and other tough materials. Less powerful lasers using short wavelength UV* light are used in certain types of eye surgery, such as correcting short and long sight* by making small, precise cuts to change the shape of the cornea.

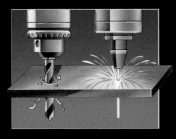

The drill (far left) makes a rough hole in the metal and produces waste shavings.

The powerful laser beam, by contrast, melts a clean hole.

FLUORESCENCE

Some substances can absorb energy, such as ultraviolet (UV) rays*, and give it out as light. They are described as **fluorescent** substances or **phosphors**. They are widely used in advertising and paints as they make colours seem to glow.

This T-shirt has been washed with a washing powder containing fluorescent substances that absorb UV rays from the Sun and make white clothes look whiter.

Fluorescent lights consist of a tube filled with a gas such as neon. Electricity passing through the tube gives energy to particles in the gas, which they give off as UV* rays. A phosphor coating inside the tube absorbs the UV rays, then gives out this energy as light of a certain colour, depending on the phosphor used.

The colours in these neon lights come from rare earth* phosphors such as europium.

Internet links

• Scan the code to discover some fun facts about light.

• For links to more websites where you can investigate light, shadows and lasers, go to **www.usborne.com/quicklinks**

COLOUR

Visible light appears colourless. It is also known as **white light**. In fact, it is made up of seven different colours: red, orange, yellow, green, blue, indigo and violet. Each colour has a different wavelength* and frequency*. Together they make up the **visible light spectrum**. Colours of the spectrum are called **chromatic colours**.

Rainbows, like this one, form when light hits tiny drops of water in the air and splits up into separate colours.

DISPERSION

In 1666, scientist Isaac Newton discovered that white light could be divided into separate colours. This process is called **dispersion**. He dispersed light using a **prism** – a transparent solid with two flat surfaces at an angle to each other.

The picture below shows a prism. As light hits the first surface, the colours in it are bent (refracted*) by various amounts. This splits up the light into its separate colours. This dispersed light is refracted further when it hits the second surface. Colours with the shortest wavelengths, namely blue and violet, are refracted the most.

A rainbow is a result of dispersion that happens naturally. Water particles in the air act like prisms, separating sunlight into colours.

Rays of white light are separated into seven colours as they shine through this glass prism.

COLOUR OF THE SKY

The colour of the sky is a result of sunlight being scattered by small particles in the atmosphere. They reflect and diffract* sunlight, scattering high-frequency light waves, such as blue, most of all. When you look up at the sky, it appears blue because some of this scattered blue light reaches your eyes.

The different colours of this evening sky are caused by light scattering.

At sunrise and sunset, the light has to travel through more of the atmosphere before reaching your eyes. This means that the blue is scattered out before you can see it, leaving the sky with an orange or red glow. These are the colours of light with the lowest frequencies.

MIXING LIGHT

Almost any colour of light can be made by **additive mixing**, that is, by using different combinations of red, green and blue light. For this reason red, green and blue are known as the **primary colours** of light.

Red, blue and green are the primary colours of light.

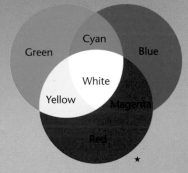

Cyan, magenta and yellow are the secondary colours of light.

When two primary colours are added together, the colour they make is called a **secondary colour**. Any two colours that can be added together to make white light, for example, red and cyan (opposite each other in the diagram above) are called **complementary colours**.

SEEING IN COLOUR

You can see colours when light reflecting off objects is detected by colour-sensitive cells in your eyes.

All coloured objects and paints contain **pigments**. These are substances that absorb certain colours and reflect others. You can see the colour of an object because it reflects only light of that colour. For example, a red flower reflects red light and absorbs all the other colours of the spectrum.

This bottle looks blue because it reflects only blue light and absorbs all the other colours.

White objects appear white because they reflect all the colours of light equally. Black objects absorb all the colours, so hardly any light is reflected, making the object look black. Black and white are known as **achromatic colours**.

The white feathers on this penguin reflect all the light that hits them.

The black feathers absorb all the light that hits them.

MIXING PIGMENTS

Pigments mix by a process called **subtractive mixing**. For example, the pigment in yellow paint absorbs blue light and the pigment in cyan paint absorbs red light. So when you mix yellow and cyan paints, the mixture can only reflect green light, making it look green. The primary colours of pigments are cyan, yellow and magenta. Red, blue and green are the secondary colours.

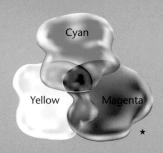

Cyan

Yellow   Magenta

★

Yellow and cyan pigments mix to make green because they absorb blue and red light.

See for yourself

You can see the colours of the spectrum form white light by making a colour spinner. Draw around the bottom of a jar on some stiff cardboard. Cut out the circle, divide it into seven sections and paint them with the colours of the rainbow. Push a pencil through the middle and spin it on a table. As it spins, the coloured light reflecting off it merges to make white.

COLOUR PRINTING

Colour printing in books and magazines uses dots of magenta, yellow and cyan ink, along with black ink to make the pictures look sharper. This process is called **four-colour printing**.

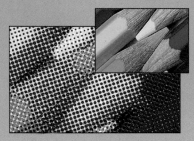

This magnified picture shows how all the colours are made up of tiny dots of magenta, yellow, cyan and black.

If you look through a magnifying glass at any picture in this book, you will see the dots which make up the image.

Colours used in four-colour printing

Cyan   Magenta   Yellow   Black

Internet links

- Scan the code to watch a video clip about light and colour.

- For links to more websites about light, color and pigments, go to **www.usborne.com/quicklinks**

LIGHT BEHAVIOUR

Like all electromagnetic waves, light travels incredibly quickly –
about 300,000 kilometres per second when measured in a
vacuum. The direction in which light waves travel is shown in
diagrams by arrows. These are called **light rays**. Light waves
usually travel in a straight path but may change direction when
they meet an obstacle, or move from one substance into another.

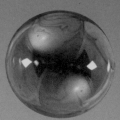

The colours on
the surface of soap
bubbles are caused
by light interference.

REFLECTION OF LIGHT

Light rays travelling towards an
object are known as **incident
rays**. If they hit the object and
bounce off it, they are then called
reflected rays. Each ray is
reflected at the same angle
as it hits the object.

When parallel light rays hit a
smooth, shiny surface, they are
reflected so that the reflected
rays are also parallel. This is called
regular reflection.

When parallel light rays hit a rough
surface, the reflected rays are
scattered in different directions.
This is **diffuse reflection**. It is
the most common type of
reflection as most surfaces are
rough (though they may not seem
so unless seen with a microscope).

**Regular reflection
of light rays**

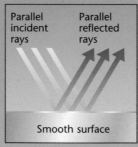

Parallel
incident
rays

Parallel
reflected
rays

Smooth surface

★

**Diffuse reflection
of light rays**

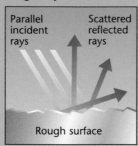

Parallel
incident
rays

Scattered
reflected
rays

Rough surface

★

When you look at an object, the light that reflects off it goes
directly into your eyes, so you see the object where it really
is. If you look at an object in a mirror, the rays bounce off the
object and then bounce off the mirror before entering your
eyes. What you are looking at is the **image** of the object. In
this case the image appears to be behind the mirror.

REFRACTION OF LIGHT

If light rays pass from one substance to
another of a different density, their speed
will change. If they are also bent, they are
known as **refracted rays**. The amount of
speed change and refraction depends on
the change in density. Light rays speed up
on moving into a less dense substance, and
slow down on moving into a denser one.

For instance, light rays bouncing off
objects in water can make the objects
look distorted. This is because the rays
are refracted as they pass out of the water
into the less dense air. You can find out
more about refraction on page 205.

See for yourself

To see light refraction, look at a
straw in a glass of water from all
sides. It seems to be bent in
different ways. The unbroken
lines in the diagram show the
real path of the
light rays looking
from above. But
the brain assumes
they travel straight,
so it sees the end
of the straw at X.

★

The rays of sunlight
breaking through these
clouds show that light
travels in straight lines.

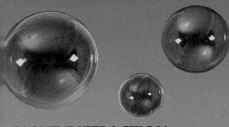

LIGHT DIFFRACTION

When light rays pass through tiny gaps, or meet the edge of an opaque object, they are diffracted, or spread out. For more about diffraction, see page 205.

LIGHT INTERFERENCE

When light rays are reflected or diffracted, their paths may cross, causing interference. See page 205 for more about interference.

As light rays interfere with each other, some wavelengths of light are strengthened and some are weakened, so certain colours become visible. The colours on a compact disc and on the surface of soap bubbles, for example, are caused by interference.

The metallic sheen on the wings of this butterfly is caused by light interference.

The shiny side of a compact disc has tiny bumps on it. When light enters the gaps between them, the waves are diffracted and interfere, so certain colours are seen at different angles.

Compact discs diffract white light, making its colours visible.

The rainbow colours on a soap bubble appear when light reflected off the outer surface of the bubble interferes with light reflected off the inner surface.

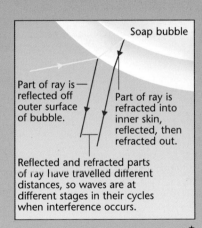

Soap bubble

Part of ray is reflected off outer surface of bubble.

Part of ray is refracted into inner skin, reflected, then refracted out.

Reflected and refracted parts of ray have travelled different distances, so waves are at different stages in their cycles when interference occurs.

The colours are constantly changing, giving a shimmering effect called **iridescence**. This is also seen on the wings of some insects and birds.

POLARIZATION

Light waves are made up of vibrations in electric and magnetic fields. The vibrations change direction many millions of times per second, but are always at right angles to the direction the wave is travelling.

Imagine a normal light wave travelling directly into your eye. Its vibrations are in many directions, as shown here.

When light is **polarized**, the vibrations only occur in one direction, such as up and down.

A polarized light wave is filtered so that its vibrations are in just one direction, as shown here.

Polarizing sunglasses work by filtering out all light wave vibrations that are not in a certain direction. This shields the eyes from excessive glare.

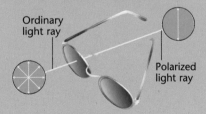

Ordinary light ray

Polarized light ray

Polarizing sunglasses only allow light vibrations through in one direction.

Internet links

• Scan the code to zoom into the wing of a butterfly, or for more websites about how light behaves, go to www.usborne.com/quicklinks

LENSES AND MIRRORS

A lens is a piece of transparent substance with curved surfaces, that makes light passing through it bend in a particular way. A **mirror** is a shiny surface that reflects nearly all of the light that hits it. Lenses and mirrors have many uses, for example in cameras and telescopes.

LENSES

Lenses are shaped so that light passing through them is refracted* (bent) in a certain way. There are two main lens shapes: **convex**, which is fatter in the middle, and **concave**, which is thinner in the middle.

This photograph of New York City was taken through a fish-eye lens. This curved lens creates a distorted, circular image, covering an angle of 180°.

Types of convex lenses

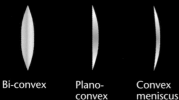

Bi-convex   Plano-convex   Convex meniscus

Types of concave lenses

Bi-concave   Plano-concave   Concave meniscus

Lenses are described as converging or diverging lenses, depending how the light rays are refracted. For example, a glass convex lens in air acts as a converging lens and a glass concave lens in air acts as a diverging lens.

Any point where parallel light rays come together or appear to come from is called a **focus**. A **converging lens** causes parallel rays of light passing through it to come together at a focus.

Converging lens

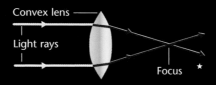

Convex lens

Light rays

Focus ★

A **diverging lens** makes parallel rays of light spread out.

Diverging lens

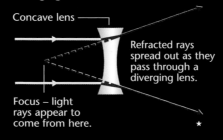

Concave lens

Refracted rays spread out as they pass through a diverging lens.

Focus – light rays appear to come from here. ★

The size and position of an image seen through a converging lens depends how far the object is from the lens. If the object is very close to a converging lens, the image is upright and enlarged.

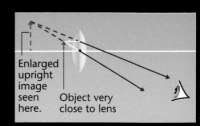

Enlarged upright image seen here.   Object very close to lens ★

If the object is further away from a converging lens, the image is upside down.

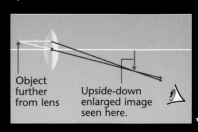

Object further from lens   Upside-down enlarged image seen here. ★

*Refraction, 205.

EYES AND EYESIGHT

Your eye turns light reflected from an object into an image that can be recognized by your brain. The front part of the eye is a convex converging lens. It focuses the light rays so that they form an image on a layer called the **retina**, at the back of the eye. The image formed is upside down, but your brain then corrects this so you see things the right way up.

Human eye

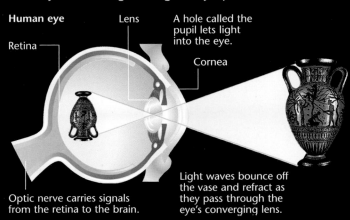

Lens

A hole called the pupil lets light into the eye.

Retina

Cornea

Optic nerve carries signals from the retina to the brain.

Light waves bounce off the vase and refract as they pass through the eye's converging lens.

Distant objects are blurred for people with short sight. This is because the eyeball is too long, or the lens is too thick, and the image forms in front of the retina.

Short sight

Rays from a distant object focus in front of the retina.

Diverging lens

A diverging lens corrects this, focusing rays on the retina.

Long-sighted people can't see nearby objects well. This is because the eyeball is too short, or the lens is too thin, so the rays focus behind the retina.

Long sight

Rays from a near object focus beyond the retina.

Converging lens

A converging lens corrects this, focusing rays on the retina.

See for yourself

Look at your reflection in the bowl of a shiny metal spoon. If you hold the spoon very close to your face, the reflection will be enlarged. If you hold it a little further away, the reflection will be upside down. Look at the two diagrams at the bottom of the column on the right to see why this happens.

MIRRORS

The image seen in a flat mirror is the same size and same way up as the object but the left and right sides are swapped around. The image is the same distance behind the mirror as the object is in front of the mirror.

Curved mirrors bounce light off at an angle, producing different kinds of images. A **convex mirror** curves outwards. The image formed is upright and reduced in size.

Car wing mirrors are convex.

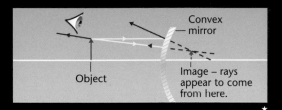

Convex mirror

Object

Image – rays appear to come from here.

★

Concave mirrors curve inwards. If an object is very close to the mirror, an enlarged image is produced. If the object is further away, the image is upside down. The bowl of a shiny metal spoon acts like a concave mirror.

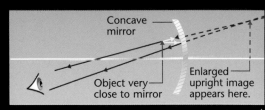

Concave mirror

Object very close to mirror

Enlarged upright image appears here.

★

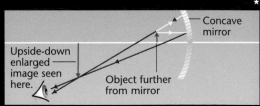

Concave mirror

Upside-down enlarged image seen here.

Object further from mirror

★

Internet links

• Scan the code to see how light bends when it travels through a lens, or for more about lenses and mirrors, go to **www.usborne.com/quicklinks**

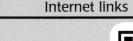

OPTICAL INSTRUMENTS

Optical instruments use combinations of lenses and mirrors to produce a particular type of image, for example, an image that appears larger than when viewed with the eye alone. These pages show some of the many kinds of optical instruments.

Binoculars use lenses to magnify distant objects.

OPTICAL MICROSCOPES

Optical microscopes use lenses to make small objects look bigger. Simple ones, such as magnifying glasses, have just one lens. More complex ones use two or more.

Inside an **optical microscope**, the object is first magnified by the **objective lens**, then further by the **eyepiece**, which produces the final image. Some optical microscopes can magnify over 2,000 times. In **digital microscopes**, the image can be viewed on a computer screen.

A stereo microscope

1. **Eyepieces**. These refract (bend) light from the objective lens, turn the image the right way up, and make it look much bigger. Two eyepieces let you observe objects in 3D.

2. **Focusing knob**. This controls the sharpness and clarity of the image.

3. **Zoom controls**. These allow ease of use when viewing details at different scales.

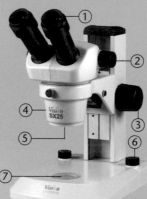

4. **Objective lens**. This refracts light from the object to form a larger, upside-down image. The eyepiece then further magnifies this image.

5. **LED* ringlight**. An extra light source can be attached when daylight is not enough.

6. **Ringlight controls** To adjust brightness

7. **Stage**. The object to be magnified goes on here.

Using magnifying lenses, scientists can learn about the structure of tiny living things, such as this ladybird.

On its own, the eye can only see small objects separately if they are at least a quarter of a millimetre apart. A microscope can show you objects separately that are up to 1,000 times closer together than this.

The tiny hairs on the ladybird's mouthparts are too small to be seen with the eye alone, but are easy to make out under a microscope's magnifying lens.

PERISCOPES

A **periscope** is an upright tube with prisms at each end. Prisms are glass shapes with two flat surfaces at an angle to each other. In a periscope they are used to reflect light around corners, which allows you to see something when you are far below it. For instance, periscopes are used in submarines to look above the surface of the water.

Diagram of a periscope

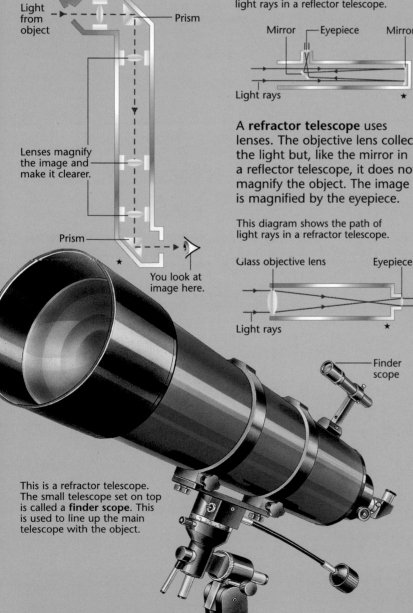

Light from object

Prism

Lenses magnify the image and make it clearer.

Prism

★

You look at image here.

TELESCOPES

Telescopes are used to make distant objects appear closer and therefore larger. They are often used for looking at the stars. There are two main types: reflector and refractor telescopes.

A **reflector telescope** uses a curved mirror to collect light. The light then reflects off a second mirror and an image is focused in front of the eyepiece, which magnifies it.

This diagram shows the path of light rays in a reflector telescope.

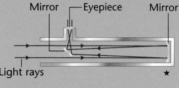

Mirror — Eyepiece — Mirror

Light rays ★

A **refractor telescope** uses lenses. The objective lens collects the light but, like the mirror in a reflector telescope, it does not magnify the object. The image is magnified by the eyepiece.

This diagram shows the path of light rays in a refractor telescope.

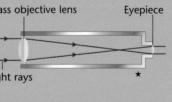

Glass objective lens — Eyepiece

Light rays ★

Finder scope

This is a refractor telescope. The small telescope set on top is called a **finder scope**. This is used to line up the main telescope with the object.

See for yourself

You could use a pair of binoculars to look at the stars.

Binoculars are made in various sizes and powers, shown by a pair of numbers, such as 7 x 35 or 10 x 50. The first number is the magnifying power. The second is the diameter, in mm, of the front, objective lenses. The larger the lenses, the more light they can collect, so the fainter the starlight they can pick out.

Stars seen with the eye alone are tiny pinpoints.

Seen through binoculars, more details are visible.

It is a good idea to rest your binoculars on a steady surface, such as a wall or fence. This will stop them shaking in your hand and give you a clearer view of the stars.

A good telescope can show the stars in even greater detail.

Many more distant stars can be seen through a good telescope.

Internet links

• Scan the code to discover how telescopes have helped scientists see deep into space.

• For links to more websites about microscopes and telescopes, go to **www.usborne.com/quicklinks**

*Light-emitting diode (LED), 237.

CAMERAS

Cameras are optical instruments that record pictures. They use lenses to focus light onto film or some other device that saves the picture so that you can look at it again later. Early cameras stored pictures on sheets of glass or metal coated with light-sensitive substances. From the 1880s glass and metal were replaced with light-sensitive film. Digital cameras, invented in the 1990s, store pictures electronically.

This is an early Polaroid camera. Polaroid film develops rapidly, so you see the picture just after you take it.

CAMERA PRINCIPLES

Light enters a camera through a lens. The amount of light that is let in is called the **exposure**. This is controlled by two things. First, an adjustable hole called an **aperture** determines how much light gets into the camera. Second, a flap called a **shutter** controls how long light is allowed to fall on the film or electronic image sensor.

Digital single-lens reflex (DSLR) camera

In this type of camera, light entering the lens is reflected off a mirror and refracted through a prism to a little window called the **viewfinder**. This lets the photographer see exactly what the lens sees.

The digital images are recorded on a memory card that slots into the side of the camera.

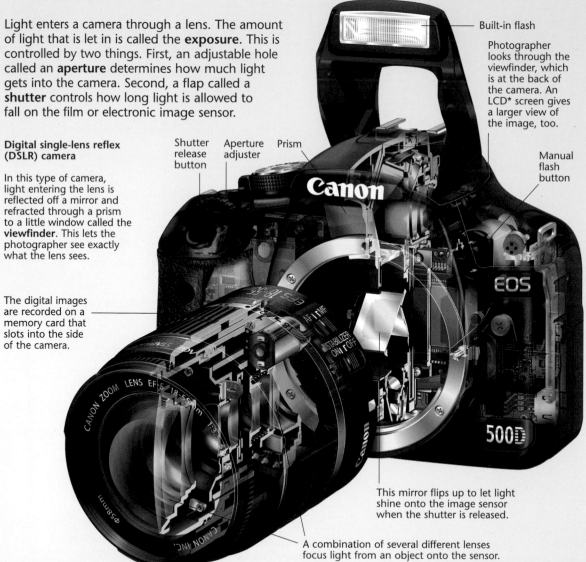

Built-in flash

Photographer looks through the viewfinder, which is at the back of the camera. An LCD* screen gives a larger view of the image, too.

Shutter release button

Aperture adjuster

Prism

Manual flash button

This mirror flips up to let light shine onto the image sensor when the shutter is released.

A combination of several different lenses focus light from an object onto the sensor.

PHOTOGRAPHIC FILM

Photographic film is coated with silver nitrate, a light-sensitive chemical. How the film reacts depends on the amount of light that reaches it. The exposed film is dipped into chemicals to produce the images and stop the film being sensitive to any more light. This process is called **developing**. In instant cameras, the chemicals to develop the film are inside.

Positive film, also called **transparency** or **slide film**, shows images with the correct colours.

Negative film. The light parts of the keyboard in the picture appear dark and the dark parts appear light.

Developed negative film is projected onto light-sensitive paper to make the final print.

MOVING PICTURES

Movie cameras take 24 separate pictures, called **frames**, every second, recording them either onto very long strips of film or digitally. To watch the film, it is converted to a digital format then played back through a digital projector at a rate of 24 **frames per second (fps)**.

This Red One digital movie camera can be carried in one hand.

The frames move so fast that you see the next frame before the last one fades in your brain. This is called **persistent vision**. Digital projectors usually run at 24fps but can screen movies at 48fps or higher for a clearer picture.

See for yourself

You can demonstrate persistent vision by making your own "movie" flick book.

On the back page of a small pad of paper draw a simple character. Turn over the page and trace this image, making slight changes to show the character moving. Draw at least 20 more images, changing each one a little.

When you flick the pad, the images appear as one moving picture.

TELEVISION CAMERAS

Television cameras do not use film, but turn the light that enters them into a series of electrical signals. These signals are sent down a cable and are either transmitted as a live broadcast, or recorded onto a computer to be transmitted at another tlme.

A television studio camera is heavy and is supported by a stand.

CAMCORDERS

A **video camcorder** is a combined TV camera and video recorder. Lenses direct an image onto a tiny electronic image sensor, such as a **charge-coupled device (CCD)** or a CMOS (see right). The sensor produces electrical signals which are recorded onto a memory card or hard disk.

Palmcorders are very small and light.

DIGITAL CAMERAS

Digital cameras record images onto a CCD or CMOS (see mobile photography, below). The images are broken down into tiny coloured squares called **pixels**. Information about the pixels is stored in the camera's memory as binary code*. To print the picture or see it on a computer screen, the pixels recombine, forming a complete picture.

The degree of detail in a picture is called its **resolution**. The more pixels a camera creates in an image, the higher the image's resolution.

Low-resolution image

High-resolution image

MOBILE PHOTOGRAPHY

Most mobile phones now include simple digital cameras. Their electronic image sensor is usually a **CMOS (complementary metal-oxide semiconductor)** which can be made smaller than a CCD and uses less power. Many smartphones* also have apps* that allow you to share and alter photos, for example, to add artistic effects, or to remove the "red eye" caused when a flash lights up the inside of someone's retina*.

* App, 240, Binary code, 238; LCDs, 90; Retina, 370; Smartphone, 240.

TV AND RADIO

The first radio transmissions were made about 100 years ago. Television was invented in 1926. The first signals could only be sent over very short distances, but today satellites can instantly broadcast clear signals around the world.

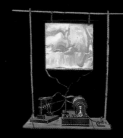

This early radio was invented by Marconi. It was called a marconiphone.

BROADCASTING

Most radio and television shows are broadcast as **radio waves**. These are a band of waves in the electromagnetic spectrum* with a range of different frequencies* and wavelengths*.

Radio waves

Radio waves are the longest waves in the electromagnetic spectrum.

Before broadcasting, sounds and images first have to be converted into electrical signals. Sounds are made into electrical signals by microphones. Cameras create electrical signals from images.

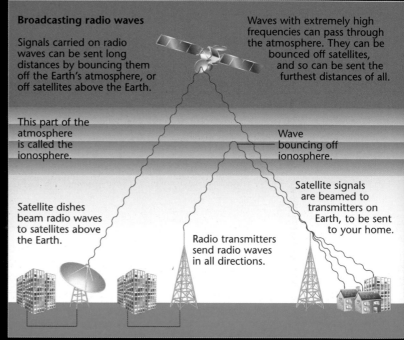

Broadcasting radio waves

Signals carried on radio waves can be sent long distances by bouncing them off the Earth's atmosphere, or off satellites above the Earth.

Waves with extremely high frequencies can pass through the atmosphere. They can be bounced off satellites, and so can be sent the furthest distances of all.

This part of the atmosphere is called the ionosphere.

Wave bouncing off ionosphere.

Satellite dishes beam radio waves to satellites above the Earth.

Radio transmitters send radio waves in all directions.

Satellite signals are beamed to transmitters on Earth, to be sent to your home.

MODULATION

To enable them to be broadcast, electrical signals have to be altered, using a method called **modulation**. This is done by mixing the electrical sound and picture signals with radio waves, called **carrier waves**.

As a result of modulation, the shape of the carrier wave varies depending on the electrical sound and picture signals. The picture on the right shows an example of this.

With **frequency modulation (FM)** the frequency of the carrier wave is altered to match the signal to be broadcasted. With **amplitude modulation (AM)** the amplitude* (strength) of the carrier wave is altered to match the signal.

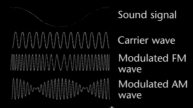

Sound signal

Carrier wave

Modulated FM wave

Modulated AM wave

HOW A RADIO WORKS

A radio works by receiving modulated radio waves through its aerial, and then converting them back into very weak electrical signals.

This is a digital radio. Digital modulation allows a perfect signal and many more channels.

The signal is strengthened (amplified) and a loudspeaker turns it into a sound that can be heard.

* Amplitude, 203; Electromagnetic spectrum, 212-213; Frequency, Wavelength, 203.

HOW TV WORKS

Television signals are carried by radio waves. As well as the sound signals, the waves carry picture signals. A TV converts the signals into sound and pictures. The sound is converted in the same way as in a radio. The picture signals are converted into pictures on an LCD*. The pictures are built up from many thousands of tiny shapes called **pixels**, each made up of three **sub-pixels** in the primary colours* of light.

An LCD TV

1. LED* back-lights
2. Rear filter: polarizes* light vertically
3. Rear electrode*
4. Liquid crystals
5. Front electrode
6. Colour filter
7. Pixel
8. Front filter: only lets horizontally polarized light reach display
9. Display

The picture signal is made up of a varying voltage* between the electrodes. The liquid crystals twist the polarized light and so allow some light through the front filter to reach the display. The voltage is varied from moment to moment, precisely controlling how the crystals twist, and so altering the pixels' brightness and colour. The pixels combine to form the picture on the display.

CABLE BROADCASTING

TV and radio signals can be carried along cables, too. Cable signals are less affected by weather conditions than satellite signals, so picture and sound quality is less variable. A vast network of underground cables exists. These can also be used to carry phone signals.

Fibre-optic cables are used for carrying television and radio signals.

DIGITAL BROADCASTING

In most countries, radio and television are broadcast **digitally**. Digital signals are electrical signals which carry information as a code made up of millions and millions of just two components: either "on" (1) or "off" (0). The digital code is mixed onto – and then carried by – radio waves. Digital information can be compressed (see *Transmission Speed*, page 245, for an example) so far more can be sent. As a result, broadcasters can offer hundreds of channels.

INTERACTIVE AND SMART TV

Digital broadcasting makes it possible to send information back through your TV, to order programmes to watch whenever you want, to buy things, or even to take part in competitions. This is called **interactive TV**. Some digital TVs, known as **smart TVs**, also allow you to use apps* and access parts of the internet*.

This smart TV allows viewers to download movies over the internet, or use messaging apps online.

SATELLITE TV

Satellite TV companies bounce signals off space satellites, to be received directly by a small dish that is fixed to the side of your home.

The dish focuses the TV signal onto a receiver. The signals travel along a cable to a television set.

Receiver
Satellite TV dish
Cable

See for yourself

Put a magnifying glass up close to your TV set while it is on. Look carefully and you'll be able to see the pixels that make up the picture.

Internet links

• Scan the code to find out about frequency and how radio stations work.

• For links to more websites about tv and radio, go to **www.usborne.com/quicklinks**

ELECTRICITY

Lightning is a form of electricity.

Electricity is a useful form of energy. It can easily be converted to other forms of energy, such as heat or light, and it can flow along cables, which makes it easy to transport. Electricity is used to power many devices, from kettles to computers, and to provide heat and light in homes, offices and factories.

ELECTRIC CHARGE

All matter is made up of tiny units called **atoms**. In the middle of each atom is a **nucleus**. This contains particles called **protons** which have a positive charge and neutrons which have no charge. Negatively charged particles called **electrons** whizz around the nucleus. Normally, the number of protons and electrons is equal. Their charges cancel each other out so the atom is electrically neutral.

Proton (positive charge)

Neutron (no charge)

Electron (negative charge)

An atom can gain or lose electrons, becoming a charged particle called an ion*. If it gains electrons, it becomes negatively charged (–). If it loses electrons, it becomes positively charged (+).

This atom has lost an electron so is a positively charged ion.

This atom has gained an electron so is a negatively charged ion.

If charged particles are near enough to each other, they have an effect on each other known as an **electric force**. The area in which this force has an effect is called an **electric field**.

Particles with opposite charges (positive and negative charges) attract each other. Particles with the same type of charge, for example two positively charged particles, push each other away.

Atoms with opposite charges attract each other.

Atoms with the same charge push each other away.

Electricity is the effect caused by the presence or movement of charged particles.

ELECTRIC CURRENT

The charged particles in some substances are able to flow. In metals, for example, electrons can move between atoms, and ions can flow in solutions of salts*. Any flow of charge is called an **electric current**. Substances through which current can pass are called **conductors**. Substances, such as plastic, which cannot conduct current, are called **insulators**.

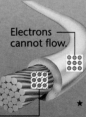

Wood and plastic are insulators.

Aluminium foil is a conductor.

Insulated wires are electrical wires, usually made of copper, covered with plastic to insulate them.

Electrons cannot flow.

Electrons can flow and make a current.

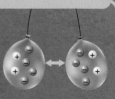

★

See for yourself

To see how charges affect each other, tape two equal lengths of nylon thread to the top of a door frame, spaced about 2.5cm apart. Tie a balloon to each thread, so that they touch and hang at the same height. Rub the balloons with a woollen scarf or sweater. The balloons become negatively charged and move away from each other. If you put your hand in between the balloons, they move towards your hand, which has a positive charge.

Matching charges repel each other.

STATIC ELECTRICITY

Some insulating materials become charged when rubbed. This happens because electrons from one material are transferred to the other. The charge cannot flow away because there is no conductor, so it builds up on the surface of the material. Electrical charge that is held by a material is called **static electricity**.

The diagrams below show how static electricity builds up if you rub a balloon on a wool sweater.

Before they are rubbed, the balloon and the sweater are electrically neutral.

As they are rubbed, some electrons from the sweater move to the balloon. This becomes negatively charged, and the sweater becomes positively charged. They cling together because their opposite charges attract each other. ★

Equipment such as laser printers and photocopiers use static electricity as part of their printing process.

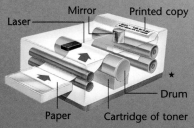

In a laser printer, a laser beam reflected by a mirror makes dots of static electricity on a drum. Toner clings to the dots of static and is pressed onto the paper.

LIGHTNING

Lightning is caused by static electricity that builds up when falling water droplets and rising ice crystals rub against each other in storm clouds.

Water droplets and ice crystals become charged as they rub against each other and the air.

Positive charges gather at the top of the cloud and negative charges in the base. As this happens, positive charges collect together on the ground beneath the cloud.

A giant spark, called a **leader stroke**, flashes out from the cloud, seeking a point with the opposite charge on the ground. When it finds it, it makes a path which is followed by a powerful stroke of lightning from the ground to the cloud. This is called the **return stroke**.

Lightning contains a vast amount of electrical energy, which is changed into light, heat and sound (thunder).

A build-up of negative charge at the base of a storm cloud causes a build-up of positive charge in the ground below.

When lightning strikes, an electric current flows between the cloud and the ground, leaving them both electrically neutral.

The air heated by the flashes of lightning expands very rapidly. This makes the noise that we hear as **thunder**. Light travels faster than sound, so unless the storm cloud is directly overhead, you see the lightning before you hear the thunder.

A stroke of lightning branches out in many directions as it seeks its way to the ground.

Internet links

• Scan the code to see a hair-raising experiment that demonstrates static electricity.

• For links to more websites about conductors, insulators, static electricity and lightning, go to **www.usborne.com/quicklinks**

* Ions, 70; Salts, 88–89.

CIRCUITS

An electric current flows from one place to another as a result of something called **potential difference**. This is similar to the pressure difference that causes water to flow through pipes. Potential difference is measured in **volts (V)** and is also called **voltage**. Current is measured in units called **amperes (amps)**.

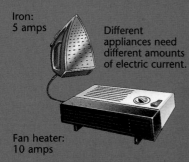

Iron:
5 amps

Different appliances need different amounts of electric current.

Fan heater:
10 amps

For an electric current to keep flowing there must be a power source, such as a battery (see opposite page), joined to an unbroken conducting pathway, such as a loop of copper wire. This pathway is called an **electric circuit**. The power source has two ends with opposite charges, called **poles** or **terminals**. These are where the circuit starts and finishes.

Terminals

A potential difference exists between the terminals of a battery. When they are joined, a circuit is formed and a current flows.

Components, such as bulbs, can be added to a circuit. These convert the electrical energy carried by the current into other forms of energy such as light and heat. The components in a circuit can be arranged in two ways: in series or in parallel.

In a **series circuit**, the current passes through the components one after the other. If one component is not working, it breaks the circuit and no current flows. Christmas tree lights are often in series circuits.

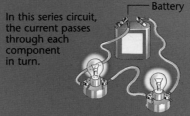

In this series circuit, the current passes through each component in turn.

Battery

A **parallel circuit** has more than one path for the current. If a component in one path does not work, current continues to flow through the other path.

In this parallel circuit, the current passes through the components by different paths at the same time.

ELECTRICITY AT HOME

Household or **mains** electricity is 240V in some countries, 110V in others. The large voltages and current the mains can provide can give you a deadly electric shock. Appliances are protected by **fuses** containing very thin pieces of wire. These melt, and cut off the current if it is too large.

Fuse with part of cover removed

Fuse wire

Electricity is carried to different parts of a house by parallel circuits. These circuits contain two wires called the **live** and **neutral wires**, which carry the current. In some countries there is also an **earth wire**. This is a safety device. It provides a path to the ground through which electric current can escape if the plug develops a fault.

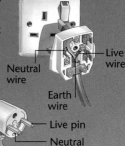

When a plug is put into a socket, the pins connect with the live and neutral points in the circuit.

Neutral wire

Live wire

Two-pin plugs

Earth wire

Live pin

Neutral pin

This electricity substation reduces to a lower level the massive voltage it receives from the main power station. The current travels along cables to homes and factories.

BATTERIES

A **battery** is a store of chemical energy that can be converted to electrical energy. The most common type of battery used at home is called a **dry cell**. It contains a paste called an **electrolyte** which contains charged particles that can move. Chemical reactions make the charges separate. Positive charges move to one terminal and negative ones move to the other.

Batteries produce an electric current that moves in a single direction. This is called **direct current (DC)**.

Cutaway view of a dry cell

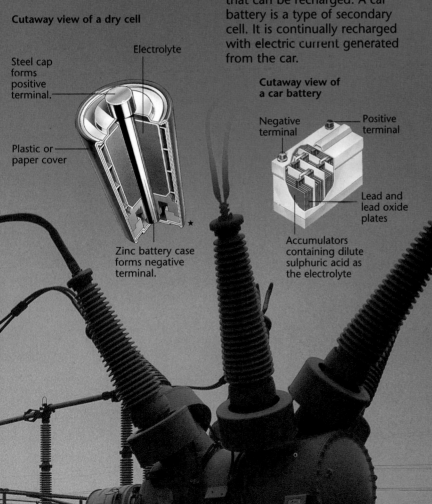

Steel cap forms positive terminal.

Electrolyte

Plastic or paper cover

Zinc battery case forms negative terminal.

A 1.5V battery, such as the type used in a personal stereo, is called a **single cell**. Larger batteries are made up of several single cells.

Single cell

9V battery contains six single cells.

Dry cells are **primary cells**. When the chemicals in the electrolyte run out, the battery is finished. **Secondary cells**, or **accumulators**, are batteries that can be recharged. A car battery is a type of secondary cell. It is continually recharged with electric current generated from the car.

Cutaway view of a car battery

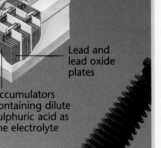

Negative terminal

Positive terminal

Lead and lead oxide plates

Accumulators containing dilute sulphuric acid as the electrolyte

A **solar cell** converts the Sun's energy into electricity. Sunlight falling on the layers of silicon makes the electrons move, creating a potential difference between the two layers.

Solar cells like this one are used in pocket calculators.

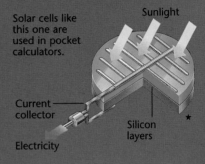

Sunlight

Current collector

Silicon layers

Electricity

See for yourself

To make a simple battery, draw around a coin to make twelve circles each on a sheet of foil and a paper towel, then cut them out. Dampen the paper circles in a cup of water with ten teaspoons of salt stirred in.

You need 12 copper coins. Pile the circles in groups of three (a cell), made up of one foil, one paper and one coin. Tape the bare end of a piece of insulated copper wire to the bottom of the pile, and another wire to the top. Touch the other two ends together. In a dark room you should see a spark.

Internet links

• Scan the code to watch a video clip about electric currents and circuits.

MAGNETISM

Magnetism is an invisible force that attracts some metals, especially iron and steel. Materials that create this force are said to be **magnetic** and are called **magnets**.

POLES

If you float a magnet in water or hang it from a thread tied around its middle, it will always point in a north-south direction. The part of the magnet that points north is the **north** or **north-seeking pole**. The other is the **south** or **south-seeking pole**.

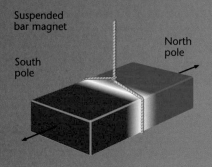

Suspended bar magnet

South pole

North pole

A north and a south pole of two magnets will pull toward or **attract** each other. Two north or two south poles will push each other away. This is called **repulsion**.

Like poles repel each other.

Unlike poles attract each other.

TYPES OF MAGNETS

Materials that can easily be magnetized (turned into magnets) are said to be **ferromagnetic**. They can be described as hard or soft.

Soft ferromagnetic materials such as iron quickly lose their magnetic properties. Magnets made from these materials are called **temporary magnets**. Hard ferromagnetic materials such as steel keep their magnetic properties for much longer. They are used to make **permanent magnets**.

Each paper clip in this chain has become magnetized by contact with the magnet. Each is a temporary magnet.

If the magnet is removed, the clips will lose their magnetism.

A compass needle is a permanent magnet. It points to the Earth's magnetic north pole.

Migrating terns like these may use the Earth's magnetic field to guide them.

DIPOLES AND DOMAINS

A ferromagnetic material has molecules which behave like tiny magnets. They are known as **dipoles** and are grouped in **domains**, in which they all point the same way. When the material is magnetized, all the domains become ordered and point the same way. The material loses its magnetism if its domains become jumbled up again.

When magnetic material is in a non-magnetized state, the domains are jumbled up.

When it is magnetized, the domains line up, with their poles all pointing the same way.

Ordered dipoles collectively form a magnet, but individually, each one is trying to flip round, as its poles are attracted to the opposite poles of the whole magnet. As they turn, the magnet loses its magnetism.

A metal **keeper** across a magnet's ends helps it to stay magnetic. The keeper becomes magnetized and attracts the magnet's dipoles to its poles.

Magnets

Keepers

MAGNETIC FIELDS

The region around a magnet in which objects are affected by its magnetic force is called a **magnetic field**. The strength and direction of the magnetic field are shown by **magnetic flux lines**. The arrows on the lines show the direction. The magnetic field is strongest where the lines are close together.

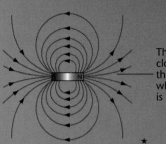

Magnetic flux lines showing the direction of the magnetic field around a bar magnet

The lines are closest near the poles, where the field is strongest.

The Earth itself has a magnetic field. It acts as though it has a giant bar magnet through its middle. The north pole of a compass points towards a point called **magnetic north**, its south pole points to **magnetic south**. These are slightly different from the geographical North and South Poles.

These magnetic flux lines show the direction of the magnetic field around the Earth.

ELECTROMAGNETISM

When an electric current flows through a wire, it produces a magnetic field around it. This effect is called **electromagnetism**.

The magnetic field of the wire can be made stronger if the wire is wound in a coil. When a current is passed through the coil, the coil behaves like a bar magnet and is called a **solenoid**. The region inside the coil is called the **core**.

If a solenoid has a rod of a soft ferromagnetic material such as iron placed inside it, the rod is quickly magnetized and adds its own magnetic field to that of the solenoid. Together the solenoid and the ferromagnetic core make an **electromagnet**. You can find out more about the uses of electromagnets over the page.

A simple electromagnet

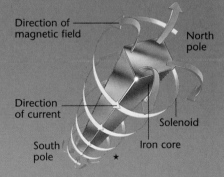

Direction of magnetic field

North pole

Direction of current

Solenoid

South pole

Iron core

The position of the north and south poles in an electromagnet depends on the direction of the current flowing through the wire.

Viewed end-on, current flowing anticlockwise gives a north pole.

Viewed end-on, current flowing clockwise gives a south pole.

See for yourself

To see magnetic flux lines, sprinkle some iron filings onto a sheet of clear plastic or a piece of white paper, then hold a magnet underneath. The iron filings will move to show the pattern of the magnetic field.

Clear plastic sheet

Internet links

• Scan the code to see how a simple electromagnet works, or for links to more websites about magnetism, go to www.usborne.com/quicklinks

233

USING ELECTROMAGNETS

Electromagnets often contain iron, a soft ferromagnetic material. The iron loses almost all of its magnetism when the current through the electromagnet is switched off. For this reason, electromagnets have many uses, such as in switches, bells and buzzers.

When you press the button of an electric bell, for example, current flows through the coils of an electromagnet and attracts a metal arm. As the arm moves nearer to the electromagnet, it loses touch with the contact through which the current is flowing, breaking the circuit. The arm is pulled back by a spring, making a hammer hit a bell. This completes the circuit and the cycle begins again.

Electric bell

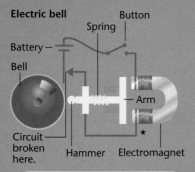

Battery

Bell

Button

Spring

Arm

Circuit broken here.

Hammer   Electromagnet

★

See for yourself

You can make an electromagnet using a 4.5V battery, a pencil, a large iron nail and some insulated copper wire. To make a solenoid*, wind the wire tightly around the pencil, and tape both ends to the battery. Your electromagnet should be strong enough to affect a compass needle, but too weak to pick anything up. If you replace the pencil with the nail, you will have an electromagnet that can pick up paper clips.

Home-made electromagnet

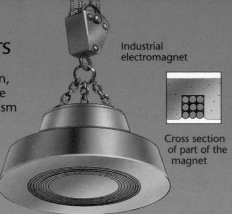

Industrial electromagnet

Cross section of part of the magnet

Very powerful electromagnets are used in steelworks to lift heavy loads. When current flows through the coil of wire, the iron becomes magnetized. It attracts steel, which can be moved from one place to another. When the current is switched off, the electromagnet releases its load.

Magnetic levitation (**maglev**) trains have electromagnets on the bottom. They run on tracks with electromagnets on them. The magnets repel each other, so the train hovers just above the track. This reduces the amount of friction between the train and the track, so the train needs less energy to make it move.

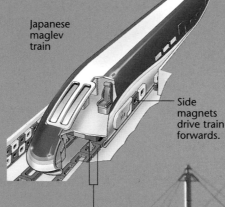

Japanese maglev train

Side magnets drive train forwards.

Electromagnets

ELECTRIC MOTORS

Electric motors change electrical energy into movement. A simple electric motor (see picture below) contains a flat coil of wire called an **armature** between two magnets.

When current flows through the armature, the combination of the electromagnetic field of the armature and the magnetic fields of the magnets pushes one side of the armature up and the other side down.

A simple electric motor

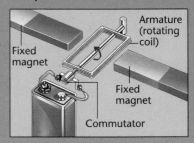

Armature (rotating coil)

Fixed magnet

Fixed magnet

Commutator

When the armature is in an upright position, a device called a **commutator** causes the direction of the electric current to be reversed, so the magnetic field of the armature is reversed. The side of the armature that was pushed up is now pulled down. The armature completes its circle and the cycle begins again.

* Solenoid, 233.

USES FOR MOTORS

Electric motors are used in all kinds of equipment, from washing machines and hairdryers to battery-driven toy cars and model trains. Tiny **micromotors** (see picture below) are used in microsurgery and space research.

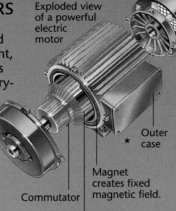

Exploded view of a powerful electric motor

Outer case

Commutator

Magnet creates fixed magnetic field.

Armature turns inside field.

This Toshiba micromotor is 0.8mm wide – about the same as the eye of the needle next to it.

GENERATING ELECTRICITY

A **dynamo** or **generator** is a machine for converting movement energy into electrical energy. It works rather like an electric motor in reverse. The diagrams below show how a generator produces electricity. As the armature turns between the two magnets, an electric current starts to flow. As the armature passes through its upright position, the direction of the current changes. This type of current is called **alternating current (AC)**.

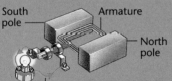

South pole

Armature

North pole

Direction of current for first half-turn

South pole

North pole

Direction of current for second half-turn

A **bicycle hub dynamo** is a type of generator. It uses the movement energy from a wheel to produce electric current to light a lamp.

A bicycle hub dynamo has an armature lined with magnets, which spins around a fixed coil.

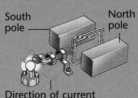

Copper coil inside fixed "stator"

Rotating armature ring

Permanent magnets

Electricity is generated on a larger scale in **power stations**. Many power stations use heat energy from burning coal to boil water and turn it to steam. The pressure of the steam is used to spin the shaft of a machine called a **turbine**. This then turns the shaft of a huge generator and produces alternating current.

Cutaway of steam turbine

Generator containing coils

Steam from water heated by furnaces

Turbines turned by force of steam

Electricity is produced.

Steam escapes here.

Generators can be powered by many different kinds of energy. Wind turbines, for example, use the energy of moving air (wind) to generate electricity.

The shafts of these wind turbines are made to spin by the wind. The movement energy is used to generate electricity.

Internet links

- Scan the code to watch a demonstration of magnetic levitation.

- For links to more websites about electromagnets, maglev trains and electric motors, go to **www.usborne.com/quicklinks**

ELECTRONICS

Electronics is the use of devices called **electronic components** to control the way electric current flows around a circuit, making it do particular tasks. A circuit controlled in this way is called an **electronic circuit**. All sorts of machines, such as TVs, robots and computers, use electronic circuits.

Copper tracks on the back of this Veroboard link electronic components to form a circuit.

BUILDING CIRCUITS

Electronic circuits can be made up using different components. The simple circuit below, for instance, contains a resistor (see right).

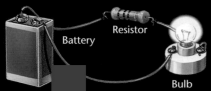

Battery

Resistor

Bulb

Circuits can be mapped out using diagrams like the one below. Each component is shown using a different circuit symbol*.

Circuit diagram of circuit above

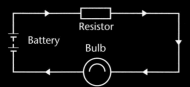

Battery

Resistor

Bulb

The arrows show the direction of **conventional current**. This is opposite to electron flow (see *Transistors*, 237).

You can make simple circuits using **Veroboard**. This has rows of holes and copper tracks on the back. Components are pushed through from the front, then their legs are soldered onto the tracks to form a circuit. **Printed circuit boards (PCBs)** are plastic boards which are imprinted with metal tracks. They are used, for example, in televisions. **Integrated circuits** are tiny circuits engraved onto small slices of silicon.

RESISTANCE

The ability of a substance to restrict the flow of electric current is known as **resistance**. All the parts in an electric circuit have a certain amount of resistance, and this reduces the amount of current that is able to flow around. When a substance resists an electric current, it converts some of the electrical energy into heat or heat and light.

A toaster's wire heating element is made of **Nichrome**, an alloy* of nickel and chromium. When a current passes through it, a lot of heat is produced.

Resistance is measured in units called **ohms**, named after Georg Ohm, a nineteenth-century physicist.

Ω The Greek letter omega is used as a symbol for ohms.

Resistors are electronic components which reduce the flow of current. Resistors have three or four colour-coded stripes on them which show how much resistance they give.

Resistor colour code chart	
1st to 3rd stripes	4th stripe
	Gold ±5%
	Silver ±10%
	No fourth
0 1 2 3 4 5 6 7 8 9	stripe ±20%

The first two stripes on a resistor stand for numbers. The third tells how many zeros to put on the end. The fourth stripe tells you the rating's range. The stripes on the resistor below, for example, are blue (6), red (2), black (0) and gold (±5%), so it has a resistance of 62 ohms, plus or minus 5%.

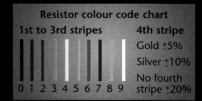

The stripes on this resistor show that it gives between 58.9 and 65.1Ω of resistance.

See for yourself

Using the colour code chart above, try to work out which of these two resistors has the highest ohm rating. (Answer on page 447.)

---

* Alloys, 34; Electrical and electronic circuit symbols, 409.

TYPES OF COMPONENTS

There are several types of electronic components. Each one is designed to do a different job in an electronic circuit. For example, different kinds of resistors are designed to resist current by greater or lesser amounts in different conditions.

A **variable resistor**, or **rheostat**, can be adjusted to give different amounts of resistance. The volume control on a radio uses a variable resistor to change the amount of current. This varies the amount of electrical energy that is converted to sound energy.

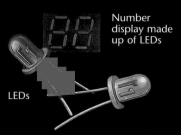

Variable resistor

A **thermistor** is a heat-sensitive resistor. Its resistance falls as the temperature rises, and rises as the temperature falls. They are used in some fire alarms to sense when a room is too hot.

Thermistor

Diodes allow the current to flow through them in only one direction. A **light-emitting diode (LED)** glows when current flows through it.

Number display made up of LEDs

LEDs

On this printed circuit board, the black oblong shapes contain integrated circuits. They are connected to each other and to other components by metal tracks.

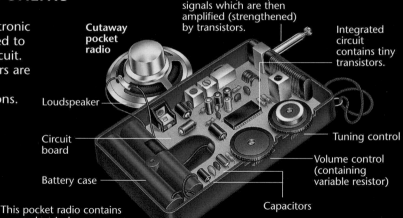

Cutaway pocket radio

Aerial. This picks up signals which are then amplified (strengthened) by transistors.

Integrated circuit contains tiny transistors.

Loudspeaker

Circuit board

Battery case

Tuning control

Volume control (containing variable resistor)

Capacitors

This pocket radio contains many electrical components arranged in a circuit called an amplifier circuit.

Transistor

Transistors are electronic switches that switch and amplify electronic signals. They contain three wires called the **gate**, **source** and **drain**. When a small voltage is applied to the gate it allows electrons to flow from the source to the drain. The transistor is then switched on. When no voltage is applied to the gate it is closed and the transistor is off.

This diagram shows the direction of **electron flow** (white arrows) through a transistor in a circuit.

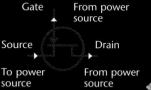

Gate

From power source

Source

Drain

To power source

From power source

Capacitors store up electrical energy and release it when it is needed. A television uses capacitors to build up and store energy at high voltage.

Capacitors

There are different kinds of capacitors.

Internet links

• Scan the code to find out about capacitors and how they work.

• For links to more websites where you can build circuits and find out about electronic components, go to www.usborne.com/quicklinks

DIGITAL ELECTRONICS

Digital electronics is a form of electronics that uses pulses of electricity instead of continuously flowing, or **analogue**, electricity. All sorts of electronic equipment, from digital watches and calculators to computers, use digital electronics.

Pocket calculators contain digital electronic circuits.

DIGITAL CIRCUITS

In a **digital circuit**, the electricity exists in pulses at either high voltage* or low voltage. Tiny electronic components* change and redirect these pulses as they flow around the circuits.

In an analogue circuit, electricity is continuous but varies in voltage.

In a digital circuit, the electricity is broken up into a series of pulses.

A digital watch is controlled by digital circuits.

Time display

Circuit

Battery

The pulses of electricity can be used to represent information in **binary code**. This expresses information using numbers made up of the digits 0 and 1. Words, sounds and pictures can be translated into binary, too. As there are only two options (0 and 1), devices that use digital electronics can process information very quickly.

Wave form of digital current

`1  0  1  0  0  1  0  1`

A pulse at high voltage represents a 1 and a pulse at low voltage represents a 0.

LOGIC GATES

A **logic gate** is an arrangement of transistors* used to carry out calculations in digital electronic circuits. Logic gates change or redirect the pulses that flow through them. Most logic gates have two **inputs**, which receive signals, and one **output**, which gives out a signal.

There are three main types of logic gate, and they are each represented by a different circuit symbol, as shown below.

AND gate   Input   Output

                  1
                  1   1

An AND gate gives out a 1 if it receives two 1s. Otherwise, it gives out a 0.

  0
  1   0

  0
  0   0

NOT gate   Input   Output

           1   0

A NOT gate has one input and one output. It changes a 1 to a 0 and a 0 to a 1.

      0   1

OR gate   Input   Output

      1
      0   1

An OR gate gives out a 1 if it receives a 1 in either of its inputs.

  1
  1   1

  0
  0   0   ★

Logic gates have many uses. For example, an AND gate might be used in a security system, such as that used in a bank, where two officials must turn keys at the same time to open a safe. Only when both keys are turned would two 1s pass through the AND gate, and so open the lock.

This security circuit uses an AND gate so that the lock only opens when keys X and Y are both turned.

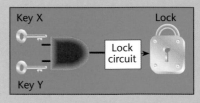
Key X   Lock

Lock circuit

Key Y

If the output is 1, current flows through the lock circuit and the lock opens.

FLIP-FLOPS

Logic gates are usually combined to make up more complex devices, such as **flip-flops**. Electric pulses circulate back and forth inside flip-flops in a process called **feedback**. This enables the flip-flops to "remember" pieces of binary information.

Integrated circuits in computers (see opposite) often contain many thousands of flip-flops. These are joined together to make the computer's memory.

INTEGRATED CIRCUITS

An **integrated circuit (IC)**, also known as a **silicon chip, microprocessor, microchip** or **chip**, is a complete electronic circuit containing billions of tiny components on a small piece of an element called silicon.

Large cylinders of silicon called **ingots** are sliced into thin sections called **wafers**, and the tiny circuits are printed onto them. The wafer is then cut up with a diamond saw to make the individual chips.

To make chips, silicon ingots are sliced into thin wafers.

Many circuits are printed onto each wafer. The wafer is then cut up into individual chips.

This is a **CPU** (**Central Processing Unit**) chip, the main chip in a computer. It contains over four billion tiny transistors arranged into logic gates, and connected by extremely fine copper threads. The transistors are so small that over six million could fit into the full stop at the end of this sentence.

The transistors are 3D, rather than flat, so that more can be fitted onto a chip, increasing its processing* power.

Silicon is used because it is a **semiconductor** – a type of material that acts as a conductor* or an insulator*, depending on its temperature. The components that make up the circuits are also semiconductors, made of silicon mixed with tiny amounts of elements such as phosphorus or boron.

When the chips are made, they are mounted in plastic fittings which have wire feet to attach them to other components on a circuit board.

Wire feet link chips to other components.

The main circuit board in a computer is called the **motherboard**. It is made up of a piece of plastic with chips fixed onto it. The chips are connected by metal tracks printed onto the motherboard. Other components on the board control the amount of electricity flowing through the chips.

Smaller board, called a **daughterboard**, slots into the motherboard.

Motherboard

Internet links

• Scan the code to watch a video clip about the Raspberry Pi™ computer.

• For links to more websites where you can investigate digital electronics, binary code and logic gates, and zoom in on integrated circuits, or chips, go to **www.usborne.com/quicklinks**

* *Conductor, Insulator, 228, Processing, 241.*

COMPUTERS

At their most basic, **computers** are machines that do calculations and sort information. When they were invented in the late 1940s, computers were so big they filled whole rooms. Since then, they have been continuously improved and made smaller. Today, a smartphone has more power than the early computers.

The Analytical Engine, a forerunner of the computer, built over a hundred years ago.

HARDWARE

The pieces that make up a computer are called **hardware**. Items of hardware that sit outside the case containing the computer's main electronic circuits are called **peripherals**. The screen, keyboard and mouse are all peripherals.

The type of computer shown below is an **all-in-one desktop personal computer (PC)**.

As technology improves, computers are growing less bulky and screens are getting thinner.

LCD* screen

Stand contains computer's main circuits.

Portable computers include **laptops**, which have a built-in keyboard and mouse pad; and smaller, handheld **tablets** and **smartphones**, which use a pop-up virtual keyboard, and a finger-sensitive touchscreen instead of a mouse.

A **touchscreen** is an LCD* with an extra layer containing capacitors* that store an electric charge. Touching the screen disrupts this charge. By measuring the disruptions, the computer can use finger movements to control the screen contents.

Many smartphones and tablets feature a touchscreen that can respond to multiple fingers, allowing such precise controls as pinching to zoom. New ways of using these "multi-touch" technologies are emerging all the time.

Wireless* keyboard. The **function keys** across the top are for special computer commands.

Wireless mouse. Used to control a pointer on the screen.

SOFTWARE

A computer won't work unless it has a set of instructions called a **program**, or **application** (**app**), or **software**, loaded into its memory. Software with overall control of how a computer works is called its **operating system**. For example, many PCs run on Microsoft® Windows® or Mac OS® from Apple®. Others include **open source** (free) systems such as Ubuntu.

This screen shows files containing Microsoft Windows 8 software and documents.

Further software is needed to let you use a computer for particular activities such as playing games or connecting to the internet.

See for yourself

When you start up a PC, watch out for lines of information which flash past your eyes. This is the computer checking through its own hardware and software, making sure that everything is working correctly.

* Capacitors, 236; LCD (Liquid Crystal Display), 227; Wireless network 243.

This stream of 0s and 1s gives an artist's impression of how digital information flows through a computer.

BITS AND BYTES

Computers do all their calculations using a code of only two numbers: 0 and 1. This is known as **binary code**. Each 0 or 1 is called a **bit** (short for **bi**nary dig**it**). Binary code is easy to express by pulses of high (1) or low (0) electrical voltage through the computer's circuits.

A group of eight bits, called a **byte**, is used to represent a small piece of data (information). Lots and lots of bytes together can represent complex data.

0 1 0 0 0 0 1 0

This byte stands for the keyboard letter B.

PROCESSING

Calculations in a computer are done by **microprocessors**. In a personal computer, the most important is called the **central processing unit**, or **CPU**. A computer can have more than one CPU. This is called **multiprocessing**.

A microprocessor

Since the CPUs (called **cores**) are very close to each other they can exchange data very quickly, performing billions of calculations per second. Most modern CPUs are dual (two cores) or quad core (four).

* Silicon chip, 239.

PROCESSING SPEED

How quickly a microprocessor can deal with information depends on two things:

- the number of bytes that it can process at once, called **bandwidth**

- the number of instructions it can deal with in one second, called **clock speed**. This is measured in gigahertz (GHz). A CPU that can process 3,000,000,000 calculations per second is said to have a clock speed of 3GHz.

A CPU microprocessor

Computer CDs look just like music CDs. All CDs store information in a similar way.

MEMORY

A computer stores information in its **memory**, on a set of magnetic disks called the **hard disk**. This information is retained when the computer is switched off. Information can also be stored on CDs, DVDs or USB devices, or by an internet **cloud storage** service that lets you access the same information from many devices.

A computer's **RAM (random access memory)** stores data on silicon chips* while other calculations are done by the CPU. RAM is emptied when the computer is shut down.

USB flash drives can hold more information than a CD, and are much smaller.

Internet links

- Scan the code to watch a video clip about binary code.

- For links to more websites where you can investigate how computers work, go to **www.usborne.com/quicklinks**

241

SOFTWARE PACKAGES

There are thousands of different types of software and apps available. These range from simple programs that let you type letters, through to super-sophisticated packages that are used to design modern jets.

This picture of an Airbus was made using design software only. When the image was created, no real versions had been built.

There is software available for almost every type of work. In advertising and publishing, for instance, graphics software is used to manipulate pictures to create special effects.

Scanning this photo converted it into a mass of tiny squares, called **pixels**. Using graphics software, the pixels were altered to give the result on the right.

Close-up of pixels

Software can come pre-loaded on a computer's hard disk, on a CD, or be be downloaded (copied) directly from the internet.

See for yourself

Windows® contains a simple graphics program called Paint®. Although it is not as powerful as the software used to create the images on these pages, you can use it to alter an image's colours and shapes.

A colour-selection panel from Paint®

HARDWARE CONTROL

How a piece of computer hardware, such as the screen, works is controlled by a set of microprocessors held on a small printed circuit board called a **card**.

A graphics card controls how pictures appear on the screen.

Each card slots into the computer's main circuit board. It is controlled in turn by software called a **driver**, which needs to be installed on the computer's hard disk.

You can often improve the performance of a computer by removing a card and installing a better one, and loading a new driver into the computer. This is called **upgrading**.

HOW THIS PICTURE WAS CREATED

This picture of a snowboarder was created using graphics software on a computer with a high-quality graphics card. First of all, the photo on the far left was scanned into the computer using a scanner (see opposite page).

Using the software, background colours were changed to make it more eye-catching. The snowboarder's left hand doesn't appear in the original photo, so the right hand was copied, reversed and added to the left arm. The picture was made to look blurred to give the impression of movement.

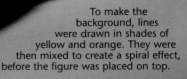

To make the background, lines were drawn in shades of yellow and orange. They were then mixed to create a spiral effect, before the figure was placed on top.

EXTRA HARDWARE

As well as basic hardware, other peripherals* can be attached to a computer, either directly, using wires, or wirelessly. These include printers, scanners, DVD recorders, external hard disks, speakers and USB hubs.

USB sockets allow many peripherals to be plugged into a computer. This **USB hub** lets you attach four at once.

This steering wheel and foot pedal attach to the computer and make computer driving games more realistic and exciting.

A scanner turns text and pictures into digital information which can be stored in the computer.

How a scanner works

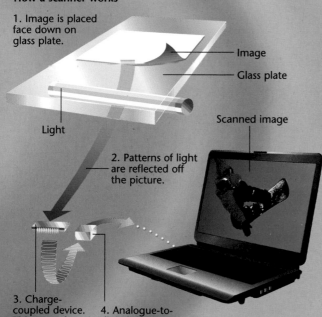

1. Image is placed face down on glass plate.

Image

Glass plate

Light

Scanned image

2. Patterns of light are reflected off the picture.

3. Charge-coupled device. This turns the light patterns into analogue* electrical signals.

4. Analogue-to-digital converter turns the information into digital* signals.

5. Digital signals are sent along a cable to the computer.

NETWORKS

Connecting computers directly with wires, or wirelessly using radio waves, to each other is called **networking**. It allows information to be shared easily. A network can consist of computers that are close to each other or thousands of miles apart.

A network of computers that are close together, for example all in the same room, is called a **local-area network**, or **LAN**. A wireless LAN is called a **WiFi network**. A network of computers that are far apart is called a **wide-area network (WAN)**.

The simplest LAN consists of just two computers in the same room.

A WAN can join computers anywhere in the world.

TYPES OF NETWORK

The simplest kind of network is called **peer-to-peer**. This means that the network is not controlled by any one computer. Peer-to-peer networks are fairly easy to set up.

A peer-to-peer network setup

In **client/server** networks, one computer, called the **server**, has control of the network. Important programs and data are held on the server. Other computers (the **clients**) collect these from the server to work on. If the server is not working, the clients can't use the data, so the network doesn't function.

A client/server network setup

Client/server networks can process more information than peer-to-peer networks.

Internet links

• Scan the code to learn more about computers.

• For links to more websites about what computers can do, go to **www.usborne.com/quicklinks**

* Analogue, Digital, 238; Peripherals, 240.

TELECOMS

Since the invention of the telephone in 1876, there have been continual improvements to telephone systems. Used with computers, there is now a whole range of ways that people can send and receive information. This branch of technology is called **telecommunications**, or **telecoms**.

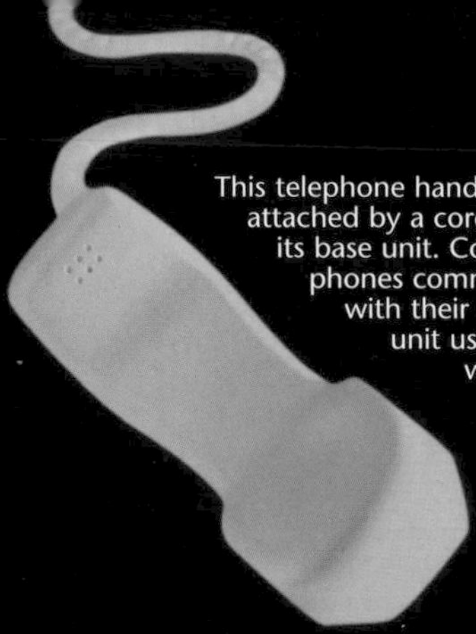

This telephone handset is attached by a cord to its base unit. Cordless phones communicate with their base unit using radio waves.

TELEPHONE LINES

Traditionally, telephone messages are carried by cables made of copper that are either buried underground or slung between poles.

Originally, these cables carried analogue* signals generated by the telephone. Most modern telephones send and receive digital information, which needs less power and takes up less room on the cable. As a result, more information can pass along the lines.

TELEPHONE SYSTEM

The **telephone system** consists of a complicated network of cables, switches and telephone exchanges.

If you make a long-distance call, your message may be bounced off a satellite in outer space, beamed between transmitter masts, or simply routed through huge lengths of cabling. Whichever route it takes, your call will reach its destination in a matter of seconds.

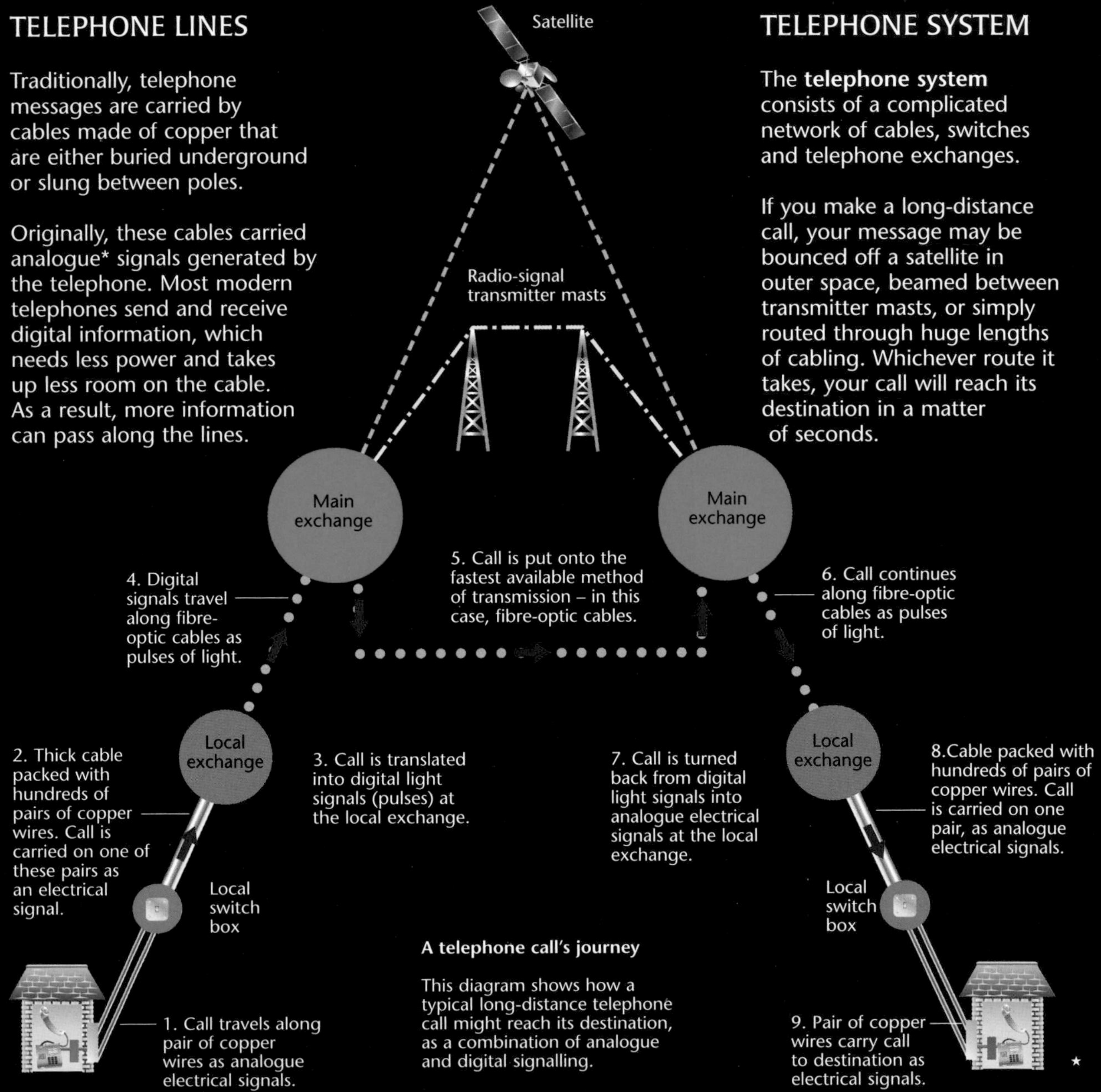

Satellite

Radio-signal transmitter masts

Main exchange

Main exchange

4. Digital signals travel along fibre-optic cables as pulses of light.

5. Call is put onto the fastest available method of transmission – in this case, fibre-optic cables.

6. Call continues along fibre-optic cables as pulses of light.

Local exchange

Local exchange

2. Thick cable packed with hundreds of pairs of copper wires. Call is carried on one of these pairs as an electrical signal.

3. Call is translated into digital light signals (pulses) at the local exchange.

7. Call is turned back from digital light signals into analogue electrical signals at the local exchange.

8. Cable packed with hundreds of pairs of copper wires. Call is carried on one pair, as analogue electrical signals.

Local switch box

Local switch box

1. Call travels along pair of copper wires as analogue electrical signals.

A telephone call's journey

This diagram shows how a typical long-distance telephone call might reach its destination, as a combination of analogue and digital signalling.

9. Pair of copper wires carry call to destination as electrical signals.

★

* Analogue, 238.

MODEMS

A **modem** allows a computer to send and receive information along telephone lines. "Modem" stands for **mo**dulator-**dem**odulator.

The modem modulates (converts) digital data from a computer into analogue radio waves. The modem receiving the information demodulates (turns back) the waves into digital code which is understood by another computer.

This wireless router* contains a modem.

TRANSMISSION SPEED

The amount of information that can be sent by a modem is limited by the speed at which it can process information. **Data compression** can speed this up by cutting out any information that is not vital.

For example, music can be compressed using **mp3** software. This removes parts of sound that your ears can't detect. A stripped-down version is left, which is quicker to send.

Amount of digital information on a music CD

Amount of digital information after mp3 compression

Mp3 software cuts out any very high or very low frequency soundwaves that are out of the range of sounds that you can hear. It also cuts out sounds that are masked by other sounds.

BANDWIDTH

The amount of information that can be processed each second by a telephone line is called its **bandwidth**. **Fibre-optic cables**, made of glass or plastic fibres, have a much greater bandwidth than older copper cables. Fibre-optics also lose less energy along long cables and aren't affected by electrical interference from power lines.

MOBILE PHONES

Mobile telephones don't use telephone lines. Instead, they send digital radio signals through the air to nearby transmitter masts, called **base stations**. These pass the signal on to the next station, and so on, until they reach the phone that you are calling.

How a mobile phone works

1. You find or dial a number and press the call button.

2. Your phone chooses an available radio channel and sends a digital radio signal of the phone number to the nearest base station.

— Radio signal

— Transmitter mast, or base station

3. The base station sends the signal around the network of base stations, until it finds the phone you are calling.

4. The phone you are calling sends a message back via the base stations, saying whether it is available. Only now do you hear a ringing tone.

Here you can see light shining out of the ends of a bundle of fibre-optic cables. Fibre-optic cables carry digital information as pulses of light.

MOBILE NAVIGATION

The **Global Positioning System (GPS)** is a network of 24 satellites orbiting the globe. **GPS receivers**, found in car **satellite navigation (satnav)** systems and smartphones*, receive signals from the satellites giving their position and an exact time. By comparing the positions of three or more satellites, the receiver can calculate its own exact position.

Satellite signals don't always reach indoors, so smartphones find their location in other ways, too. For example, by comparing the signals coming from nearby base stations or WiFi* hotspots.

Internet links

• Scan the code to watch a video clip about how smartphones work.

* Analogue, 238; Router, 246; Smartphones, 240; WiFi network, 243.

THE INTERNET

The **internet** is a vast computer network linking together millions of computers all over the world. It gives access to information put onto it by individuals, companies and organizations. The internet can also be used to exchange information, send messages and to buy things.

INTERNET BASICS

Most people connect, or **log on**, to the internet using software called a **browser**.

The basic structure of the internet is provided by telephone companies. Their phone lines carry the information that you send and receive when you use the internet.

Most home users use **internet service providers** (ISPs) to access the internet. When you are **online** (connected to the internet) messages go from your computer down the phone line to the ISP's powerful computers. The computers work like electronic post offices, automatically sorting and sending things on in a matter of seconds.

The World Wide Web is a huge network of websites that can be accessed from the internet.

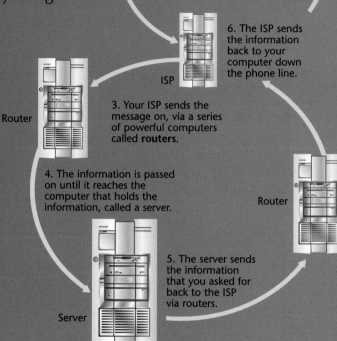

Using the internet

1. You log on to the internet via your phone line.

2. The message that you type into your computer's browser goes to your ISP.

6. The ISP sends the information back to your computer down the phone line.

ISP

3. Your ISP sends the message on, via a series of powerful computers called **routers**.

Router

4. The information is passed on until it reaches the computer that holds the information, called a server.

Router

5. The server sends the information that you asked for back to the ISP via routers.

Server

WORLD WIDE WEB

The **World Wide Web** (www) is a huge information resource, arena for social networking, and place to conduct ecommerce (see opposite page). It consists of thousands of individual websites. Each site is made up of individual documents, called web pages.

HTML

Web pages are written using a computer language called **HyperText Markup Language** (HTML). In many browsers, you can view a web page's HTML code by right-clicking with a mouse, then choosing "View Source" or "View Page Source".

HYPERLINKS

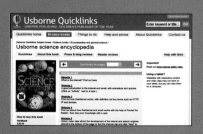

On web pages, some words or pictures are highlighted. Click on them and a new page with related information is shown, or **downloaded**. This is a **hyperlink**. These links enable you to jump really quickly from page to page all over the Web.

INTERNET NAMES

Each piece of information on the internet has an address, called a **URL (Uniform Resource Locator)**. A URL enables you to call up the exact piece of information you want. It also defines the format (called the **protocol**) in which the messages are sent.

A URL

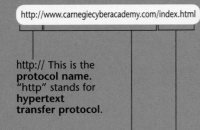

http:// This is the **protocol name**. "http" stands for **hypertext transfer protocol**.

www.carnegiecyberacademy.com/ is the **domain name**. This identifies the name of the site and the Web server it is held on.

index.html is the **file path**. This is the name of the file in which the page is stored. The *.html* part shows that the file is written in HTML code.

DOT COM

The final part of a domain name is called the top-level domain. Here are some examples and what they indicate:

.com - commercial organization
.edu - school or educational establishment
.gov - government agency
.org - non-profit organization (such as a charity)

Some domain names have an extra two letters to identify which country they are based in. For example:

.es - Spain
.th - Thailand
.uk - United Kingdom

EMAIL

Email stands for **electronic mail**. It is a way of using your computer to send messages to other internet users. You write and read emails using email software, such as Microsoft Outlook®, or Google's Gmail™.

Email is sent down the phone line to your ISP. It is sent on to the recipient's ISP via the internet, where it waits for delivery the next time the recipient logs on to the internet.

Email addresses have three parts. Here's a typical one:

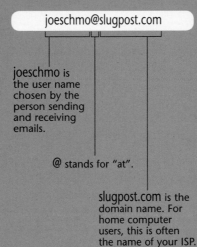

joeschmo is the user name chosen by the person sending and receiving emails.

@ stands for "at".

slugpost.com is the domain name. For home computer users, this is often the name of your ISP.

ECOMMERCE

Buying and selling things over the internet is called **ecommerce**. Goods and services offered for sale on a website can be ordered directly by filling in an order form which appears on the web page.

Ecommerce enables people to shop for just about anything, at any time, and from anywhere. In the UK, for example, at least one in ten purchases is now made online. Many supermarkets allow you to shop for groceries online, then deliver them to your door.

THE MOBILE WEB

Smartphones* can access the internet and be used to send email and other types of web messages. More and more people are surfing the internet wirelessly on phones and tablets, rather than on desktop computers.

Websites now need to work with the different screen sizes and technical limitations these devices have. Websites designed for the **mobile web** have to be simpler than regular internet pages because mobile phone lines can carry less digital information than a regular internet connection.

See for yourself

To see just how quickly email zips from place to place, try sending yourself an email. Write your own address in the "To:" window and then click "Send". (You don't need to add a subject name, even if the email software asks for one.)

The email should come back from your ISP (which could be in another country) in seconds. However, it may take longer, depending on how busy the internet is at the time.

Internet links

• Scan the code to find out about the World Wide Web.

• For links to more websites with videos, quizzes and activities about the internet, go to **www.usborne.com/quicklinks**

* Smartphones, 240.

PLANTS
AND
FUNGI

PLANT CELLS

Every living thing is made up of tiny structures called **cells**. A plant has a number of different types of cell, and each one plays an important part in keeping it alive, such as absorbing water and minerals or making food.

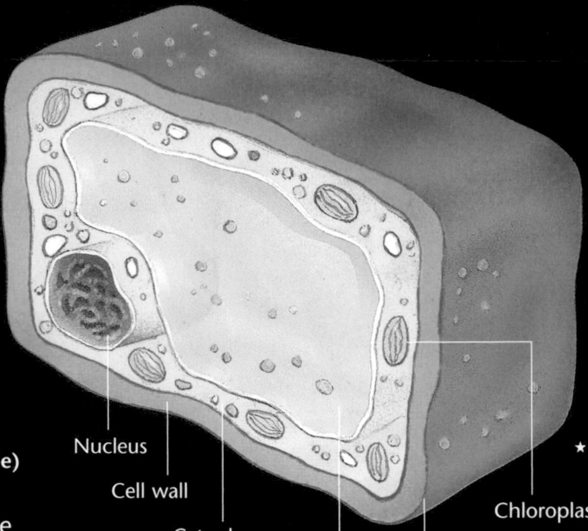

CELL STRUCTURE

Plant cells have many features in common with animal cells*, but are generally larger. Plant cells also have a number of unique structures, most of which help the plant to make its own food.

Around each plant cell is a **cell wall**. This is made of a tough substance called **cellulose**, and helps the cell to keep its shape. Directly beneath the cell wall is a thin layer called the **cell membrane**. Animal cells also have a cell membrane, but they do not have a cell wall.

Vacuoles are fluid-filled sacs. Most plant cells have one large, permanent vacuole filled with a sugary liquid called **cell sap**, which is made up of water and dissolved substances.

* Animal cells, 298-299.

Typical plant cell
(cutaway – not to scale)

Nucleus

Cell wall

Cytoplasm

Sap-filled vacuole

Cell membrane

Chloroplast

*

All plant cells, like animal cells, have a **nucleus**, which controls the activities inside the cell. The nucleus is surrounded by a gel-like fluid called **cytoplasm**, within which smaller structures, called **organelles**, are moved and arranged. These have different functions.

Chloroplasts, for example, are organelles which contain a green chemical called **chlorophyll**. These give plants their colour and help to make food.

Chloroplast

Chromoplasts have a similar function. They give some flowers, and vegetables such as carrots, their particular colour.

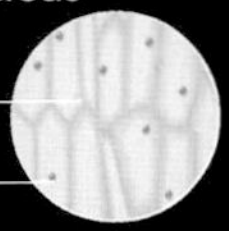

This is what leaf cells look like under a microscope. The dark spots inside the cells are the nuclei.

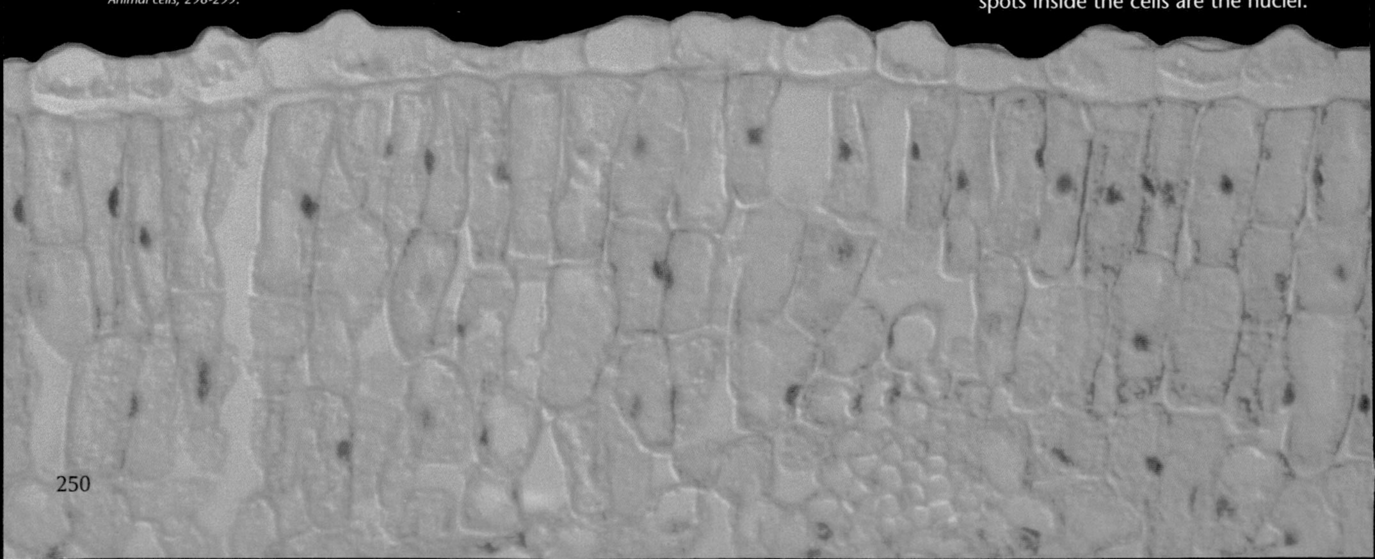

SPECIALIZED CELLS

Not all plant cells are exactly alike. Some have different shapes and structures, allowing them to do particular jobs. This is called **specialization**.

Palisade cells, for example, are found just beneath the upper surface of a leaf. They are column shaped, and contain a large number of chloroplasts.

Palisade cells

Spongy cells are found inside a leaf, beneath the layer of palisade cells. They have an irregular shape, which allows air spaces to form between them.

Spongy cells

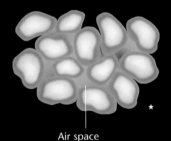

Air space

CELL DIVISION

Cells can divide to create new cells for growth or repair. Cell division happens in two stages. In the first stage, called **mitosis**, the nucleus divides into two parts, each becoming a new nucleus. Each of the two new nuclei, called **daughter nuclei**, are identical to the original.

This microscope image shows the contents of a nucleus dividing in two.

In the second stage of cell division, called **cytokinesis**, a dividing line called the **cell plate** forms. This runs down the middle of the cytoplasm. New cell walls build up along the cell plate, to separate the two new cells.

Cytokinesis in a plant cell

Plant cell after mitosis has taken place

Cell plate forming

New cell wall forming

PLANT TISSUE

Cells of the same kind join together to form types of **tissue**. Most stems and roots are made up of three types of tissue: dermal, ground and vascular.

Dermal tissue makes up the surface layer of most plants.

Dermal tissue

Ground tissue packs out most of the inside of younger plants.

Ground tissue

Vascular tissue is responsible for transporting food, water and other substances around the plant. For more about this, see page 254.

Vascular tissue

see page 254.

Internet links

• Scan the code to watch a video about the parts of a cell.

• For links to more websites with activities about plant cells, go to **www.usborne.com/quicklinks**

251

STEMS AND ROOTS

A plant is mainly supported by its stem and roots. In most plants, these also play an important part in carrying fluids. The stem and roots are made up of various parts, which change as the plant gets older. You can find out more about these changes on pages 256-257.

STEM STRUCTURE

The **stem** is the major above-ground or **aerial** part of a plant. It supports the plant, usually growing upwards. Stems contain a system of **vascular tissue**, which carries water and minerals throughout the plant.

A **shoot** is a new stem which grows out of a seed or off the main stem of a plant. A **bud** is a small growth on a stem, which develops into either a new shoot or a flower. There are two different kinds of buds, called **terminal** and **axillary buds**. Axillary buds are also known as **lateral** or **secondary buds**.

A **terminal bud** is a bud growing at the end of a stem or shoot.

A **node** is the place on a stem where a leaf has grown.

An **internode** is the area of a stem or shoot between two nodes.

An **axillary bud** is found between a shoot or leaf stalk and the stem. This spot is called an **axil**.

Main parts of a stem

GROWTH

A group of cells which divide to provide new growth is called a **meristem**. The main meristems are at the tip of the shoot and root. They are called **apical meristems**. A meristem formed in the main stem or a shoot is part of a terminal bud.

Meristems are found here.

This thick stem contains a system of tubes, which carry water and food through the plant.

PARTS OF A ROOT

The **root** of a plant usually grows down into the ground. Its main purpose is to take in water and minerals from the soil. These are absorbed through tiny, tube-shaped cells called **root hairs**. The root also acts as an anchor, holding the plant firmly in the soil.

A root grows when cells just behind its tip divide. This area is called the **growing point**. The area of new cells produced is called the **zone of elongation**. The new cells have soft cell walls, which allow them to stretch lengthways as water is taken into the root.

As the new cells lengthen, they push the tip of the root further into the soil. A layer of cells called the **root cap** protects the root tip as it is pushed down into the ground.

Parts of a root

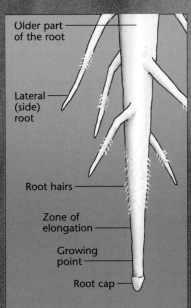

Older part of the root

Lateral (side) root

Root hairs

Zone of elongation

Growing point

Root cap

★

TYPES OF ROOTS

Roots can be many shapes and sizes, depending on the plant from which they grow. Some have particular tasks, such as allowing the plant to cling to other objects.

A **tap root**, or **primary root**, is a large root with smaller ones growing out of it. These small roots are called **lateral roots** or **secondary roots**. Many vegetables, such as carrots, are swollen tap roots and are known as **root vegetables**.

Tap root

Lateral root

★

Fibrous roots are a system of many equal-sized roots, all of which produce smaller lateral roots.

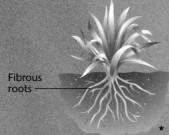

Fibrous roots

★

Adventitious roots grow directly from a stem. They are produced from gardeners' cuttings, or grow out of a special kind of stem called a bulb*.

Bulb

Adventitious roots

★

Aerial roots do not normally grow in the ground. Many can absorb moisture from the air. Some plants, such as ivy, also use them for climbing.

Aerial roots

Ivy

Prop roots are a particular kind of aerial root that grow outwards from a stem, then down into the ground. They support heavy plants, such as mangroves, which grow in ground which is often under water.

Mangrove

Prop roots

★

See for yourself

Look at a plant, and see how many parts of its stem you can identify. Notice what shapes and sizes they are. Be careful not to damage the plant.

Internet links

• Scan the code to see how roots and stems grow.

• For links to more websites about the structure of stems and roots, go to www.usborne.com/quicklinks

*Bulbs, 278.

PLANT TISSUE

All plants, except for algae, mosses and liverworts, are known as **vascular plants**. This means that they contain a complex system of **vascular tissue**, which gives support and carries food and water through the plant.

TISSUE TYPES

Vascular tissue is made up of two main kinds of tissue, called xylem and phloem.

Water is carried up from the roots by **xylem**. In flowering plants, this is made up of short tubes called **vessels** and long, narrow tubes called **tracheids**. Long, thin cells called **fibres** help to provide support between them. Vessels are made up of column-shaped cells that have lost their dividing walls. Non-flowering plants have only tracheids.

Food made in the leaves dissolves in water and is carried to all parts of the plant by **phloem**. This is made up of fluid-carrying cells called **sieve tubes**. These have other cells packed around them for support.

Sieve tubes are arranged in long columns. They have cell walls*, and though they do not have a nucleus*, they are living cells with a thin layer of cytoplasm*. The end walls between the cells, called **sieve plates**, have tiny holes which allow liquids to pass through.

The first tissue formed by a new plant is called **primary tissue**. The first xylem is called **primary xylem** and the first phloem is called **primary phloem**.

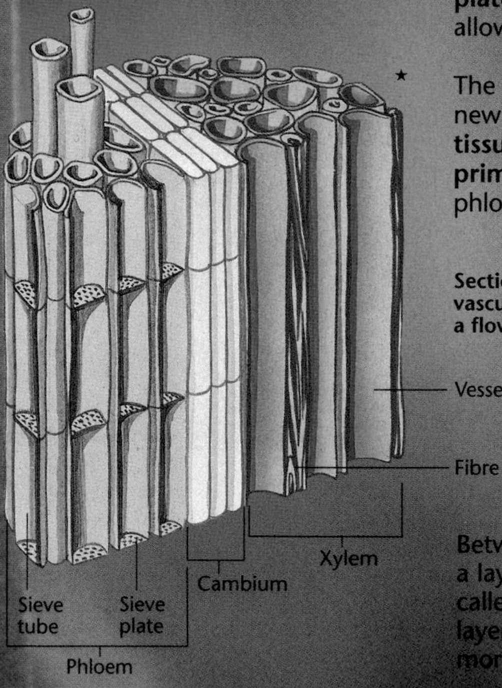

There is vascular tissue inside these tulip stems. It supports the plant and takes food and water around it.

Section of vascular tissue in a flowering plant

Vessel

Fibre

Xylem

Cambium

Sieve tube

Sieve plate

Phloem

Between the xylem and phloem is a layer of thin, narrow-walled cells called **cambium**. The cells in this layer are able to divide, making more xylem and phloem.

* Cell wall, Cytoplasm, Nucleus, 250.

INSIDE A STEM

In young stems, vascular tissue is usually arranged in groups called **vascular bundles**. These are surrounded by ground tissue* called cortex. In plants known as dicotyledons*, the bundles are arranged in a regular pattern, as shown below.

Cross section of a young dicotyledon stem

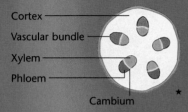

Cortex
Vascular bundle
Xylem
Phloem
Cambium

Cutaway of a young dicotyledon stem

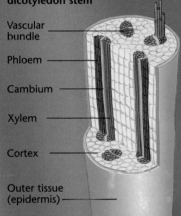

Vascular bundle
Phloem
Cambium
Xylem
Cortex
Outer tissue (epidermis)

In older dicotyledon stems, the bundles join up to form a central core called the **vascular cylinder**. You can read more about vascular tissue in older plants on page 256.

In plants known as monocotyledons*, such as the tulip on the left, the vascular bundles are not arranged regularly in the stem.

INSIDE A ROOT

In a young root, the tissue is arranged in a different way from a stem. A central core forms as the plant gets older.

Cross section of a young dicotyledon root

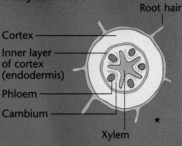

Root hair
Cortex
Inner layer of cortex (endodermis)
Phloem
Cambium
Xylem

Cutaway of a young dicotyledon root

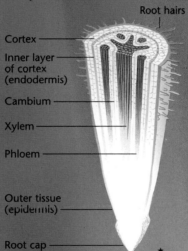

Root hairs
Cortex
Inner layer of cortex (endodermis)
Cambium
Xylem
Phloem
Outer tissue (epidermis)
Root cap

See for yourself

Try this experiment to see the xylem in a stick of celery. Fill a jar with about three centimetres of water, and add a few drops of ink or food colouring. Trim the end off a fresh celery stalk and stand it in the water. After a couple of hours, you can see the xylem as a pattern of coloured dots in the end of the stalk.

Xylem (seen as dots)

OTHER TISSUES

All parts of a young plant are surrounded by a thin layer of tissue called the **epidermis**. In older stems, the epidermis is replaced by bark. In older roots, it is replaced by a layer of hardened cells called the **exodermis**, then by bark. An outer tissue which encloses a plant, such as the epidermis, is known as **dermal tissue**.

The epidermis of stems and roots surrounds an area of **cortex**. In roots, this has an area called **endodermis** as its innermost layer. Cortex is made up mainly of **parenchyma**, a type of tissue with large cells and many air spaces. In some plants there is also some **collenchyma**, a type of supporting tissue with long, thick-walled cells. These are both types of ground tissue*.

The top layer of the epidermis is known as the **cuticle**. It is made of a waxy substance called **cutin**. The cuticle prevents a plant from losing or absorbing too much water.

Waxy cuticle gives these leaves their shiny appearance.

Internet links

- Scan the code to find out how water travels up inside a plant.

- For links to more websites about xylem and phloem, go to **www.usborne.com/quicklinks**

INSIDE OLDER PLANTS

Plants that live for many years, such as trees, form new tissue to support their original primary tissue. This process is known as **secondary thickening**. The new tissue is made up of more fluid-carrying tissue, formed between the vascular bundles*, and protective tissue, formed on the outside.

TISSUE GROWTH

The production of new tissue in young stems, called **secondary tissue**, happens in stages. The process is slightly different in roots, but the overall result is the same.

In a stem, secondary thickening starts when more cambium (growth tissue) forms between the vascular bundles*. This joins up to form a continuous cylinder of tissue.

The cambium starts to produce more xylem and phloem. These join up to form a **vascular cylinder**. Each year, new layers of xylem and phloem are produced.

Over time, the stem and roots thicken, and the plant becomes known as a **woody plant**. The new xylem is **secondary xylem**, and the new phloem is **secondary phloem**.

The core of vascular tissue, which is mostly xylem, gets bigger. By this stage, the xylem is also called **wood**. The phloem does not widen as much because the xylem pushes it outwards.

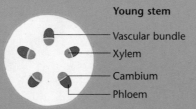

Young stem
- Vascular bundle
- Xylem
- Cambium
- Phloem

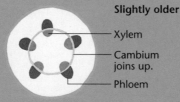

Slightly older
- Xylem
- Cambium joins up.
- Phloem

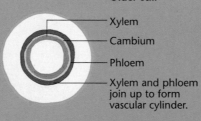

Older still
- Xylem
- Cambium
- Phloem
- Xylem and phloem join up to form vascular cylinder.

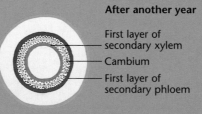

After another year
- First layer of secondary xylem
- Cambium
- First layer of secondary phloem

After a number of years

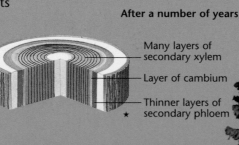

- Many layers of secondary xylem
- Layer of cambium
- Thinner layers of secondary phloem

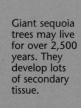

Giant sequoia trees may live for over 2,500 years. They develop lots of secondary tissue.

* Vascular bundles, 255.

TYPES OF WOOD

A single ring of xylem in a cross section of an older plant shows one year's growth and is called an **annual ring**. Each ring has two separate areas – **spring wood** and **summer wood**.

Soft spring wood (also called **early wood**) forms rapidly early in the growing season. It has large cells. Harder summer wood, or **late wood**, is produced later on. Its cells are smaller and more closely packed together.

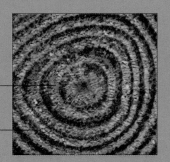

Annual rings in a tree stump

Light spring wood, with widely spaced cells, develops first.

Darker summer wood, with densely packed cells, develops later.

After a number of years, the annual rings themselves can also be divided into two separate areas. The area nearest the middle, where the rings are older, is called **heartwood**. Its vessels* have become solid and can no longer transport fluids, but they still provide the plant with support.

The outer area of rings is called **sapwood**. Its vessels are still able to carry fluid. Sapwood also helps to support the tree.

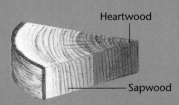

Heartwood

Sapwood

See for yourself

You can count the rings in a tree stump to discover the tree's age. For example, fifty rings show that the tree was fifty years old when it was cut down.

OUTER TISSUE

As well as new vascular tissue, an older plant also forms extra layers of protective tissue around its outside. These develop from a single layer of constantly dividing cells called **phellogen** or **cork cambium**.

As each new outer layer formed by the phellogen is pushed further out by new layers on its inside, it dies away to become waterproof **bark**. This contains tiny raised openings called **lenticels**, through which oxygen and carbon dioxide are exchanged. As a tree gets older, the layers of bark build up, making the trunk thicker and stronger.

Structure of bark in a mature tree

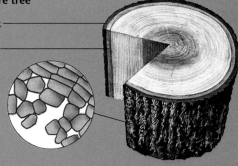

Outer bark

Inner bark

A lenticel. Loosely packed cells allow gases to move.

Bark stops the tree from drying out and helps to protect it from disease. It cannot grow or stretch, so it splits or peels as the trunk gets wider, and new layers of bark develop underneath.

Some types of bark

Silver birches have tough, papery bark.

English oak bark develops deep cracks.

Scots pine bark flakes off in small pieces.

Beech trees have very thin bark.

Internet links

• Scan the code to find out how scientists study tree rings.

• For links to more websites where you can find out how to read tree rings and see lots of different kinds of trees, go to **www.usborne.com/quicklinks**

* Vessels, 254.

LEAVES

The **leaves** of a green plant are its main food-making parts. They make food by a process called **photosynthesis**. A plant's leaves are collectively called its **foliage**. There are many different sizes and shapes of leaves, but only two main types: simple and compound leaves.

SIMPLE LEAVES

Simple leaves are made up of a single leaf blade, called a **lamina**. Lilies, elms and maples are examples of plants with simple leaves.

Maple leaf

This fern's pinnate leaves have pinnate leaflets.

COMPOUND LEAVES

Compound leaves are made up of small leaf blades called **leaflets**, which grow from a central leaf stalk. Clovers and ferns are examples of plants with compound leaves. The number and arrangement of leaflets on a compound leaf vary from plant to plant.

Palmate leaves have five or more leaflets growing from a single point.

Horse chestnut

Trifoliate leaves have three leaflets growing from a single point.

White clover

Ternate leaves are a type of trifoliate leaf. Each leaflet is made up of three lobes.

Columbine

In **pinnate leaves** the leaflets, called **pinnae**, are arranged in opposite pairs along the stalk.

Pinna

Pinnate leaf

A **bipinnate** or **tripinnate leaf** is a pinnate leaf with pinnate leaflets.

Bipinnate leaf

Tripinnate leaf

LEAF ARRANGEMENTS

Leaves can be arranged on a stem in several ways. **Opposite leaves**, for example, are leaf pairs whose members grow from opposite sides of the stem.

Decussate leaves are arranged in the form of a cross (+), that is, each opposite pair is at right angles to the next. In most plants with opposite leaves, the pairs are decussate.

This purple loosestrife has decussate leaves.

Perfoliate leaves are single or paired leaves. The bases of the leaves surround the stem.

The leaves of this yellow-wort are perfoliate.

A **rosette** or **whorl** describes a circle of leaves which grow from one point. An example of this is a **basal rosette**, which grows at the base of a stem.

A primrose has leaves which form a basal rosette.

Alternate leaves grow individually from the stem, rather than in groups or pairs. **Spiral leaves** are alternate leaves which grow out from separate points that form a spiral around the stem.

This orpine has spiral leaves.

SPECIALIZED LEAVES

Some leaves are adapted to do particular jobs. They are usually found on plants that grow in a particular place or climate.

A **bract** is a leaf at the base of a flower stalk. It often protects a bud.

— Bract

A pair of **stipules** may grow at the base of a leaf stalk. They protect a bud as it forms.

Stipules

A **tendril** is a special thread-like leaf or stem, which either twines around or sticks to a support.

Tendril

A **spine** is a modified leaf, which is thin and sharp. It has a much smaller surface area than most leaves, which prevents it from losing too much water.

This barrel cactus has many thin spines.

LEAF MARGINS

The edge of a leaf is known as the **leaf margin**. Some margins have a special shape, to help the plant's survival. For example, a leaf with a wavy margin allows more light to reach the leaves beneath. Some common leaf margins are described below.

An **entire** leaf margin has no indentation of any kind.

Lilac

A **serrate** leaf margin has tiny jagged teeth.

Lime

A **lobed** leaf margin forms sections, called **lobes**. It may also be serrate.

English oak

See for yourself

Collect some fresh leaves that have recently fallen from trees or other plants, and compare their shapes and arrangements. To preserve leaves, you can flatten them between sheets of tissue or blotting paper under some heavy books. Leave them for two weeks to dry out.

Internet links

- Scan the code for a quiz to test your knowledge about leaves.

LEAF STRUCTURE

Leaves are specially adapted to allow food production to take place. For example, most leaves have a broad, flat surface to collect sunlight, which is vital for making food. They also have areas which let out the waste substances created in the process.

INSIDE A LEAF

A leaf contains long strips of vascular tissue* called **veins**. These supply the leaf with water and minerals, and move the food made inside the leaf to other parts of the plant.

Some leaves, such as grasses, have long, parallel veins, but most contain one central vein called the **midrib**. This is an extension of the leaf stalk. The midrib branches into a number of smaller veins, called **side veins**. A leaf's whole vein system is called its **venation**.

Arrangement of leaf veins

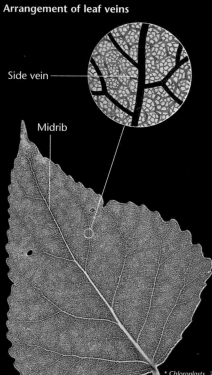

Side vein

Midrib

LEAF CELLS

A leaf is made up of layers of different types of cells. The **epidermis** is a layer of flat, waxy cells on the surface of the leaf. It prevents too much water from being gained or lost.

The **palisade layer** lies just beneath the epidermis, on the leaf's upper side. It is made up of column-shaped **palisade cells**, which contain many tiny green chloroplasts*. The contents of palisade cells are packed closely together, which helps them to absorb sunlight (see page 264).

Under the palisade layer is the **spongy layer**, made up of irregularly shaped **spongy cells** and air spaces. The spaces allow air to move around inside the leaf. The spongy layer and palisade layer together are called the **mesophyll**.

Cross section of a leaf

Upper epidermis

Lower epidermis

Spongy cells

Palisade cells

Vascular tissue

Air space

Veins

SURFACE OF A LEAF

On the underside of a leaf are tiny holes called **stomata**, each one called a **stoma**. These allow water and air to move in and out of the leaf.

On either side of each stoma is a crescent-shaped **guard cell**. These paired cells can change their shape to open and close the stoma, controlling how much air and water enters and leaves the leaf.

Close-up of stoma (cut in half)

Stoma (open)

Guard cell

Stoma (closed)

*Chloroplasts, 250, 264; Vascular tissue, 254.

LEAF STALKS

A **leaf stalk** or **petiole** is a thin structure which joins the main body of a leaf to the stem. It contains the **leaf trace**. This is an area of vascular tissue which branches off the vascular tissue of a stem and becomes the leaf's central vein. This vein allows minerals to be carried into the leaf.

Leaf stalk —
(petiole)

Before a leaf dies, a layer of cells called an **abscission layer** forms at the base of its stalk. The abscission layer separates the leaf from the rest of the plant. The leaf then falls off, creating a **leaf scar** on the stem.

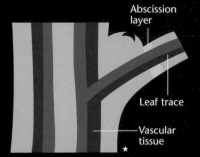

Abscission layer

Leaf trace

Vascular tissue

When leaves are dying, their green chlorophyll breaks down to reveal other colours.

COLOUR IN LEAVES

Leaves get their colour from chemicals called **pigments**. Most leaves are green because they contain a green pigment called chlorophyll. **Variegated leaves** are patterned because they only have pigments in certain places on their surface.

Other pigments include **xanthophylls**, which produce yellow shades, and **carotene**, which makes leaves look red or orange. These pigments are present in many plants, but are usually masked by chlorophyll. After summer has ended, the chlorophyll in most plants breaks down, revealing the other pigments.

See for yourself

Collect leaves that have fallen from different trees and compare their colours. See if you can find a plant with variegated leaves, or one whose leaves are a colour other than green all year round. These contain pigments in addition to green chlorophyll.

Internet links

• Scan the code for a video about why leaves change colour.

• For links to more websites about leaf structure, go to **www.usborne.com/quicklinks**

261

MOVEMENT OF FLUIDS

Fluids, such as water, need to reach all the parts of a plant for its cells to stay healthy. A plant's fluids are carried by its **vascular tissue**, made up of xylem and phloem. The **xylem** carries water from the roots to the leaves, and the **phloem** carries dissolved foods from the leaves to all other areas. The movement of fluids inside a plant is called **translocation**.

WATER MOVEMENT

Water is taken into a plant by its roots, and travels up in the xylem, through the stem to the leaves. There, some of it escapes as vapour through tiny holes called **stomata** on the underside of the leaves. This type of water loss is called **transpiration**.

As the outer leaf cells lose water by transpiration, the concentration of minerals and sugars inside them increases. So water from the cells further in passes into the outer cells, to replace the water that has been lost.

The inner cells in turn take water from cells further down, and so on. Water is "pulled" up through the plant from the roots, which take in more from the soil. This upward movement of water is called a **transpiration stream**.

At certain times, such as at night or on a damp, humid day, the rate of transpiration slows down. However, water from the soil continues to enter the roots. This is because it still has a weak attraction to the xylem walls, which drags it upwards. This is called **capillary action**.

As water is taken into the roots, **root pressure** begins to build up. This is strong enough to push the water up the stem and into the stream.

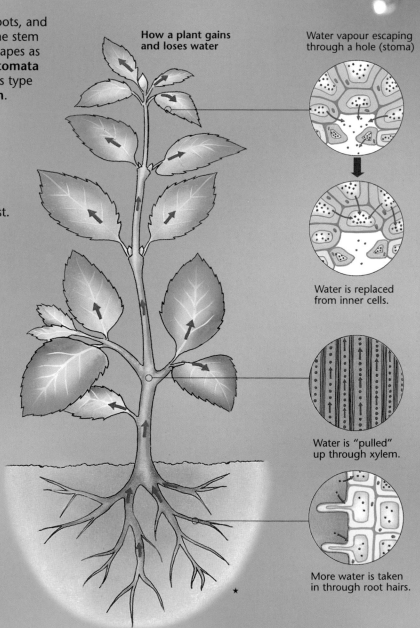

How a plant gains and loses water

Water vapour escaping through a hole (stoma)

Water is replaced from inner cells.

Water is "pulled" up through xylem.

More water is taken in through root hairs.

STANDING FIRM

Healthy plants usually stand firm and upright. This is because their vacuoles are full of cell sap, and push outwards against the cytoplasm and cell walls. Each cell is described as **turgid**, and the plant is in a state of **turgor**.

A healthy plant

WILTING

In hot or dry conditions, a plant may lose more water than it can take in. The pressure of water in its vacuoles drops to become less than that of the cell walls. This makes the cells limp. They cannot support the plant, so it droops. This state is known as **wilting**.

A wilting plant

In extreme cases, a plant may lose too much water through its leaves, and also through its roots into very dry or mineral-rich soil. Its cell vacuoles then shrink so much that the cytoplasm is pulled away from the cell walls. This state, called **plasmolysis**, may kill the plant unless it receives more water quickly.

A dying plant

Here you can see water droplets oozing out of tiny holes around the leaf's edge.

LOSING LIQUID

If a plant does not lose enough water vapour by transpiration, and root pressure is still pushing water up the stem, the plant may also lose water in liquid form. Droplets are forced out of the plant through tiny holes at the tips or along the edges of leaves. This type of water loss is called **guttation**.

Root cells of a healthy plant

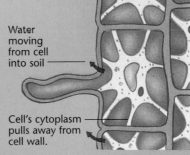

Cell sap in vacuole
Cell wall
Cytoplasm
Pressure of vacuole
No more water can enter.
Pressure of cell wall

Root cells of a wilting plant

Vacuole shrinks so its pressure is reduced.
Not enough water coming in

Root cells of a dying plant

Water moving from cell into soil
Cell's cytoplasm pulls away from cell wall.

See for yourself

To see how fluids move inside a plant, put some white flowers, such as carnations, into water containing blue ink. After a few days, their petals will have turned blue. This is because the inky water has been transported around the plants.

The lighter flowers in this picture have been in the dye for one day. The darker flowers have been in the dye for three days.

Water containing blue ink

Internet links

• Scan the code to try a quiz about the movement of fluids in plants.

PLANT FOOD

Unlike animals, most plants can make the food that they need. These plants are described as **autotrophic**. The process by which they make food is called **photosynthesis**. A small number of plants do not photosynthesize, but feed on living things. You can find out more about these over the page.

PHOTOSYNTHESIS

Photosynthesis uses water, sunlight, and carbon dioxide from the air. It takes place mainly in a plant's leaves, in the long, column-shaped **palisade cells**.

Palisade cells contain tiny structures called **chloroplasts**. These can move around inside the cell, according to how bright the light is and which direction it is coming from. Chloroplasts contain a green chemical called **chlorophyll** which absorbs the Sun's light energy. This is used to power photosynthesis.

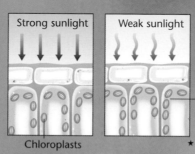

Strong sunlight | Weak sunlight

Chloroplasts

Chloroplasts cluster together

The pictures above show how chloroplasts change position to make the best use of available light.

All green plants can make their own food, using sunlight.

Carbon dioxide from the air is taken in through the surface of the leaves, and the roots take in water from the soil. The carbon dioxide and water are combined using energy taken in from sunlight by chloroplasts. This process produces chemicals called **carbohydrates** (the plant's food), and also oxygen.

Most of the food is used to produce energy for growth. The food that is not needed straight away is stored in the cells as a substance called **starch**.

The process of photosynthesis can be expressed in a word equation like this:

Carbon dioxide + Water + Energy (sunlight)
⬇
Carbohydrates + Oxygen

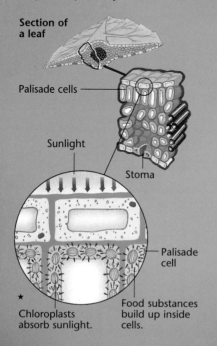

Section of a leaf

Palisade cells

Sunlight

Stoma

Palisade cell

Chloroplasts absorb sunlight.

Food substances build up inside cells.

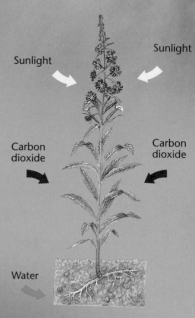

Photosynthesis in a green plant

Sunlight

Sunlight

Carbon dioxide

Carbon dioxide

Water

Nitrates and other minerals taken in by the roots are used to build new tissue.

INTERNAL RESPIRATION

Plants get energy from their food in a process called **internal respiration**. In most plants, carbohydrates are combined with oxygen to release energy, carbon dioxide and water.

The process of internal respiration can be expressed in a word equation like this:

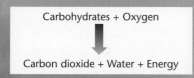

Carbohydrates + Oxygen

↓

Carbon dioxide + Water + Energy

WORKING TOGETHER

The processes of photosynthesis and internal respiration are closely linked. Photosynthesis produces oxygen and carbohydrates, which are both needed for respiration. Respiration produces carbon dioxide and water, which are needed for photosynthesis.

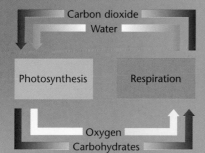

At most times of the day, one of the processes happens at a faster rate than the other. For example, in bright sunshine, photosynthesis happens faster. Overall, the plant produces more oxygen and carbohydrates by photosynthesis than it uses for respiration. The unused oxygen is given off into the air and the carbohydrates are stored in the plant as starch.

COMPENSATION POINTS

At two points in a 24 hour period, normally at dusk and dawn, the processes of photosynthesis and respiration are exactly balanced. This means that photosynthesis produces just the right amounts of carbohydrates and oxygen for respiration, which produces the right amounts of carbon dioxide and water for photosynthesis. These times are called **compensation points**.

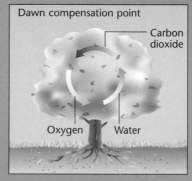

1. At dawn, rates of photosynthesis and respiration are equal.

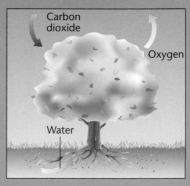

2. During the day the light is bright, so photosynthesis is faster.

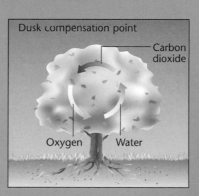

3. At dusk, rates of photosynthesis and respiration are equal.

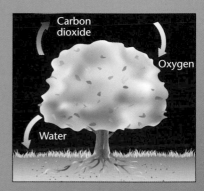

4. At night there is no sunlight, so no photosynthesis takes place.

See for yourself

You can do a simple test to show that sunlight is needed for photosynthesis. Take a houseplant with broad, light-green leaves and fold a piece of paper around one leaf. Secure it with a paper clip. Leave the plant in a sunny place for a few days, then remove the paper. The leaf will have a yellow strip, where it has been unable to photosynthesize.

Internet links

• Scan the code to watch a video clip about photosynthesis.

• For links to more websites with animations and fascinating facts about photosynthesis, go to **www.usborne.com/quicklinks**

PARASITES

A small number of plants are **parasites**. This means that they do not make their own food, but live and feed on other living things, called **hosts**. Some parasitic plants attack many different types of plants, and can be harmful to their host.

The dodder plant, for example, attaches itself firmly to its host plant by sinking thread-like ▭es called **haustoria** into it. Dodder stems then grow rapidly all over the host, which becomes completely covered and eventually dies.

Dodder stem —

Host plant

Dodder stems stretch from one plant to another in a hair-like mass.

Some parasites can only live on one host. A rafflesia plant, for example, can only grow on a particular type of vine. The rafflesia lives in its host's roots as a mass of tangled threads, causing it little harm.

When conditions are right, the rafflesia produces a huge, foul-smelling flower, which attracts the flies needed to spread its pollen.

Rafflesia flowers are the largest in the world. They can weigh up to 7kg.

HEMIPARASITES

Plants called **hemiparasites** steal water and minerals but, unlike true parasites, they have green leaves and can therefore also make their own food by photosynthesis*.

Some hemiparasites attach themselves to their host's roots underground. Others, such as common mistletoe, attack them above ground.

Common mistletoe is a hemiparasite found on trees. It grows on branches, and spreads by producing sticky, seed-filled berries that are carried away by birds.

Suckers, used to invade host

* Photosynthesis, 264.

SAPROTROPHS

Some organisms feed on dead matter instead of living on a host or making their own food. They are known as **saprotrophic plants** or **saprotrophs**. The main body of most saprotrophs is found underground. Fungi and some orchids are saprotrophic.

The main part of a fungus is a mass of threads. These grow and feed under the ground, where it is dark and damp.

EPIPHYTES

Plants called **epiphytes** make their own food, but grow high up on other plants to catch water and get a better share of the light. Most epiphytes do not harm their host, although some, such as strangler figs, kill their host when they are fully grown.

Development of a strangler fig

Small fig plant starts to grow on a branch. It sends roots down the tree.

Roots start to take water and nutrients from the soil, and fig plant grows rapidly.

Fig plant takes all of host's light, water and nutrients. Host dies and rots away.

MEAT EATERS

Some plants, called **carnivorous plants**, can kill and digest small creatures, such as insects. Carnivorous plants lure their victims into deadly traps using particular smells or colours. Once inside, the insect is dissolved by powerful chemicals called **enzymes**.

Plants that feed in this way usually grow in places which contain few minerals. They absorb what they need from the bodies of their prey by digesting them.

Pitcher plants, for example, catch animals in their jug-like leaves, called **pitchers**. Insects come to eat sweet nectar, which is made around the rim of the pitcher and under its lid. The insects fall down the pitcher's slippery walls, and die in a pool of liquid.

Lid (keeps rain out of pitcher)

Insects cannot climb back up the pitcher's slippery sides.

Sundews are carnivorous plants. Their leaves have hairs with sticky, gleaming drops at the end. These attract insects, which become trapped. As the insect struggles, the hairs start to curl over, wrapping up their prey tightly. The insect's body is then dissolved into a liquid and digested.

Fly trapped on a sundew leaf

The carnivorous Venus flytrap has folded leaves which snap shut like jaws to trap insects or other small animals. The leaves close when sensitive hairs on their surface are disturbed. Once trapped, the prey is slowly dissolved and digested by the plant.

This Venus flytrap will snap shut as soon as the fly settles. It will take about ten days for the plant to digest its prey. A trap wears out after four to six catches. It then withers and drops off, and other traps on the plant take over.

Internet links

• Scan the code to watch a Venus flytrap catch its prey.

• For links to more websites where you can see how carnivorous plants catch insects, go to **www.usborne.com/quicklinks**

PLANT SENSITIVITY

All living things can react to changes in their environment. This is known as **sensitivity**, or responding to a **stimulus**. Unlike animals, plants do not have a specialized nervous system, but they are still able to react slowly to stimuli such as light, touch and temperature.

Vines have thread-like tendrils which are sensitive to touch. This lets them twine around a support.

PLANT RESPONSE

Most plants respond to a stimulus by growing towards or away from it. This response is called a **tropism**. Growing towards a stimulus is known as a **positive tropism**, and growing away from it is known as a **negative tropism**.

Tropisms are controlled by **auxins**. These are growth hormones (chemicals) made in the plant's cells. Plant stems contain an auxin that collects in cells furthest from the light, causing these areas to grow more quickly. This makes the plant grow towards the light.

RESPONDING TO LIGHT

Almost all plants react to the amount of light available and the direction from which it is coming. This response is called **phototropism**. For instance, the leaves of most plants turn to face the Sun. This helps them to absorb as much light as possible for photosynthesis*.

The sunflowers below respond to light by turning to face the Sun.

Plant growing towards light

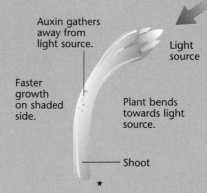

Auxin gathers away from light source.

Light source

Faster growth on shaded side.

Plant bends towards light source.

Shoot

*

GRAVITY AND WATER

All roots respond to the pull of gravity. This is **gravitropism**. The roots grow down into the soil to obtain water and minerals. Some roots also show a response to water, called **hydrotropism**. They may grow out sideways if more water lies in that direction.

Plant responding to gravity

The tips of roots and shoots produce growth hormones (auxins) that respond to gravity in different ways.

Shoot grows upwards.

Growing kidney bean

Auxin gathers here and stimulates cell enlargement.

Auxin gathers here and prevents cell enlargement.

Root grows downwards.

*

Photosynthesis, 264.

RESPONDING TO TOUCH

Some plants are sensitive to touch. This response, which is known as **haptotropism** or **thigmotropism**, can help a plant in different ways. For example, meat-eating plants trap their food when it touches sensitive parts on their surface (see page 267).

Being able to respond to touch is also important to climbing plants, such as vines. When their thread-like tendrils touch something, it triggers a climbing and twining response.

This sweet pea's touch-sensitive tendrils help it to climb.

In some plants, touch causes a reaction which acts as a defence. For instance, the leaves of a mimosa (nicknamed the "sensitive plant") instantly close and droop when touched. This is because touch causes the pressure of water in its leaf cells to drop.

The leaves of this mimosa close up like fans when they are touched.

Open leaf

Closed leaf

DAY AND NIGHT

Many plants will only grow during periods when light is available for a certain length of time. These periods are called **photoperiods**, and the plant's response is **photoperiodism**.

Long-night plants, such as chrysanthemums, only produce flowers at times of the year when the night is longer than a certain length, called its **critical length**. (These plants are also known as short-day plants.)

Short-night plants, such as larkspur, only produce flowers if the night is shorter than the critical length. (These plants are also known as long-day plants.)

It is thought that there is a growth hormone called **florigen** produced in the leaves, which makes a plant behave like this. When the correct amount of light is available, the florigen sends a "message" telling the plant to produce flowers.

Some plants, such as snapdragons, are described as **night-neutral** or **day-neutral**. Their flowering does not depend on the night's length.

Photoperiodism may be affected by the age of the plant, or the temperature of its surroundings.

Chrysanthemums flower when the nights are long.

Larkspur flowers when the nights are short.

A snapdragon flowers whether the nights are long or short.

See for yourself

Leave a potted plant in a room with one window. Place it a little way from the window and water it as usual. After a few days, you will see that the plant's leaves are leaning towards the window. If you turn the plant around, after a few more days the same thing will have happened. This is because leaves always grow towards the nearest source of light.

Internet links

• Scan the code to watch plants respond to light and gravity.

• For links to more websites where you can watch plants move, grow and bloom, go to **www.usborne.com/quicklinks**

FLOWERING PLANTS

There are over 250,000 kinds of flowering plants, including grasses, wild flowers, shrubs and trees. Plants that produce flowers are known as **magnoliophytes** or **angiosperms**. Flowering plants have certain features in common. For example, they all produce seeds and contain tissue that transports fluid around the plant.

FLOWERS

Reproduction is the creation of new life. Flowers contain the parts of plants needed for reproduction. These produce male and female sex cells, called **gametes**, which join together to create new plants of the same kind. This type of reproduction is called **sexual reproduction**.

Flowers are made up of many specialized parts. These include petals, stamens (the male parts), and one or more carpels (the female parts). In most plants, the petals are arranged in a circle, around the male and female parts.

Just before a plant blooms, it produces a **bud**, which will eventually develop into a flower. It grows from the expanded tip of a stalk, called the **receptacle**. Buds are surrounded and protected by small, leaf-like **sepals**.

In some plants, such as buttercups, the sepals remain as a ring around the flower after the bud has opened. In others, such as poppies, they wither and fall off.

Petals are delicate, often brightly coloured, and surround the plant's reproductive parts. Many petals are scented or patterned and have areas of cells called **nectaries** at their base. These produce a sweet, sticky liquid called **nectar**, which attracts insects or other animals needed for pollination*.

Buttercup

Petal

Bud

Unopened petals

Sepal

*

Carpel (female part)

Receptacle

Stamen (male part)

Nectary at base of a buttercup petal

Poppy

Together, a flower's petals are known as the corolla.

Stamen (male part)

Sepals have fallen off.

Petal

Carpel (female part)

Bud

Unopened petals

Sepal

*

The petals of these Californian poppies surround their reproductive parts. Their sepals have fallen off.

MALE PARTS

A flower's male reproductive parts are called **stamens**. Each stamen is made up of a pod-like **anther**, at the end of a long stalk called a **filament**. Anthers contain **pollen sacs**, which split open to release grains of **pollen**, the male reproductive cells.

Male parts of a buttercup

(Not all stamens are shown here.)

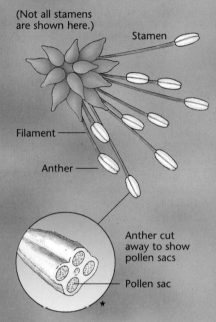

Stamen

Filament

Anther

Anther cut away to show pollen sacs

Pollen sac

Pollen grains from different plants are different sizes and shapes, but they do share some features. For instance, when they are mature, all pollen grains have a hard outer wall, making them very tough.

See for yourself

Look at different types of flowers and, using the pictures on these pages, try to identify their male and female parts.

You may find that not every plant has both parts together in the same flower. They may be on separate flowers or on separate plants.

FEMALE PARTS

A flower's female reproductive part is known as the **carpel** or **pistil**. It is made up of the stigma, style and ovary.

The **stigma** is the top part of a carpel. It has a sticky surface which traps grains of pollen that touch it. The stigma is joined to the ovary by a part of the carpel called the **style**. Each **ovary** holds one or more tiny eggs called **ovules**, which are the female reproductive cells. These develop into seeds after fertilization (see next page).

Female parts of a buttercup

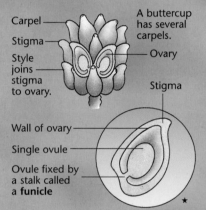

Carpel

Stigma

Style joins stigma to ovary.

A buttercup has several carpels.

Ovary

Stigma

Wall of ovary

Single ovule

Ovule fixed by a stalk called a **funicle**

Some flowers, like the buttercup above, have several carpels clustered together. Others, such as the poppy below, have only one.

Female parts of a poppy

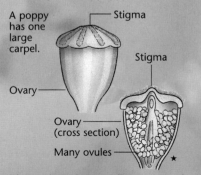

A poppy has one large carpel.

Stigma

Stigma

Ovary

Ovary (cross section)

Many ovules

The styles of many flowers, such as daffodils, are easy to see. In others, such as poppies, the style is very short and almost impossible to see.

MALE AND FEMALE

Buttercups and tulips are examples of **hermaphrodite** plants. This means each flower has both male and female parts.

You can see the female carpel and the male stamens in the centre of this tulip.

Some plants, such as maize, have two types of flower on one plant: **staminate** flowers, which have only male parts, and **pistillate** flowers, which have only female parts. Plants with flowers of this kind are described as **monoecious**. Other plants, such as holly, have staminate and pistillate flowers on separate plants. They are described as **dioecious**.

Holly has its male and female parts on separate plants. Berries develop from the ovaries of the female plant.

Internet links

• Scan the code for more about how flowering plants reproduce.

FERTILIZATION

In order for a flowering plant to reproduce, the male cell (pollen) and the female cell (ovule) need to join together. This is called **fertilization**.

When a pollen grain lands on the stigma of a plant of the same type, this is called **pollination**. A **pollen tube** grows from the grain down into the ovary and enters an ovule through a tiny hole called a **micropyle**.

Thousands of tiny pollen grains are being shed from stamens in the middle of this flower.

Cross section of poppy ovary

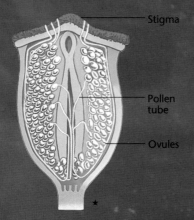

Stigma

Pollen tube

Ovules

*

A pollen grain contains two male nuclei*. These travel down the pollen tube and join with the contents of the ovule. One forms a **zygote** – the first cell of a new organism. The other forms a layer of protective, nourishing tissue called the **endosperm**. Together these make a seed, and the ovary grows to become a fruit. After fertilization, the plant no longer needs the rest of its flower parts, so they wither and die.

POLLINATION METHODS

Pollen may be carried from plant to plant by wind, water or animals. When pollen from one plant pollinates another plant of the same kind, it is described as **cross-pollination**. If the grains land on a different type of plant, they don't produce pollen tubes, so pollination can't take place.

Some types of plants are able to pollinate themselves. This is called **self-pollination**. For instance, a bee orchid tries to attract a certain type of bee, by looking and smelling like the female of its species. But if no bees come, the plant's stamens bend over and transfer pollen to its own stigma.

Unlike many flowers, a bee orchid does not produce sweet nectar. It attracts bees by looking and smelling like a female bee.

ANIMAL POLLINATION

Flowers have various ways of attracting animals to carry their pollen. Most have brightly coloured petals or sweet scents which attract insects, birds or bats. Many also produce a sweet liquid called nectar, or extra pollen, on which the animals feed. Some have patterns on the petals called **nectar guides**. These lead the insect into the middle of the flower, where the pollen or nectar can be found.

Nectar guides in the middle of these pansies lead insects to the nectar.

Plants pollinated by animals tend to produce spiky pollen grains. When an animal visits a plant, pollen grains stick to its body. The animal may then transfer these to another flower.

* Nucleus, 250.

WIND POLLINATION

Wind-pollinated plants rely on the wind to scatter their pollen. They do not need to attract animals, so their flowers are usually unscented, with very small petals and sepals. Some have their male and female parts on separate plants. The male parts hang outside the flowers, allowing their pollen to be scattered more easily.

Pollen from these birch tree catkins is scattered by the wind.

Plants that are pollinated by the wind produce huge amounts of pollen. This increases the chances of some landing on female flowers nearby. The pollen grains are usually smooth and light, allowing them to glide easily through the air.

See for yourself

If you have a garden, you can plant flowers to attract certain types of animals. For instance, butterflies tend to visit plants with purple or yellow flowers, such as buddleia or sedum. Bees are attracted to flowers with a strong scent, such as lavender.

Pollen sticks to this butterfly's body as it feeds from a daisy.

FLOWER SHAPES

The shapes of many flowers help them to transfer pollen onto an animal. For example, the petals of some flowers are shaped like a bell. Animals such as the hummingbird on the right hover beneath the flower, and reach in to feed on the nectar. As they do so, pollen from the stamens sticks to them.

Lipped flowers, such as sage flowers, have paired petals. A bee lands on the lower petal to drink nectar from within the flower. As it does so, the stamens, which hang down from the top lip, transfer pollen onto its body.

As the bee lands on this sage flower's lower "lip" to drink nectar, pollen is brushed onto its body.

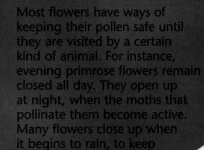

Pollen rubs off on the hummingbird's head as it feeds with its long beak.

Most flowers have ways of keeping their pollen safe until they are visited by a certain kind of animal. For instance, evening primrose flowers remain closed all day. They open up at night, when the moths that pollinate them become active. Many flowers close up when it begins to rain, to keep their pollen dry.

Internet links

• Scan the code for a video about pollination and pollinators.

• For links to more websites where you can find out about pollination, go to **www.usborne.com/quicklinks**

273

SEEDS AND FRUIT

Fertilization in flowering plants leads to the production of a **seed**. Each seed contains a new developing plant and a store of food. Seeds are kept in a part of the plant called a **fruit**. When the seeds are ready, they are scattered and can grow into new plants if conditions are right.

INSIDE A SEED

Seeds are protected by a tough coat called a **testa**. Each has a mark called a **hilum** on its surface, showing where the ovule* was joined to the ovary*. The tiny hole (micropyle) through which the pollen grain entered the ovule can also still be seen. It lets in water.

Bean seed

- Testa
- Hilum
- Micropyle

★

The developing plant inside a seed is known as an **embryo**. It has two parts: the **plumule**, which will develop into the first shoot, and the **radicle**, which will be the first root of the new plant.

Bean seed (cross section)

- Plumule
- Radicle
- Food store

★

This orange fruit protects the seeds of the orange tree. Its flesh is made up of tiny hairs, each one swollen with juice.

Orange seed (pip) ——————

TYPES OF FRUIT

Fruit protect the seeds they carry and help them to spread to a place where they can grow. Most fruit develop from a plant's ovary*. These are known as **true fruit**. Some, such as strawberries, develop from the receptacle* and the ovary. They are **false fruit**. Fruits can also be described as succulent or dry.

SUCCULENT FRUIT

Fruit with thick, fleshy layers that are often tasty to eat are known as **succulent fruit**. There are various kinds.

Succulent fruit with a single, hard-cased seed in the middle are called **drupes**. Plums and cherries are drupes.

Plum

Succulent fruit that contain many seeds are called **berries**. Oranges are berries. Fruit with a thick, fleshy outer layer and a core, with the seeds contained in a capsule, are false fruit called **pomes**.

Apples are pomes.

Raspberries and blackberries are examples of **aggregate** fruit or **compound fruit**. They form from many ovaries in one flower. Each fruit is made up of fleshy beads called **drupelets**, each containing a single seed.

Blackberries

* Ovary, Ovule, 271; Receptacle, 270.

DRY FRUIT

Dry fruit are dry cases that hold the seeds until they are ripe. There are several types. The main ones are described below.

Nuts are dry fruit with only one seed surrounded by a hard shell. Acorns and walnuts are nuts.

This walnut seed is protected by a hard shell.

Shell

Seed inside

Achenes are small, dry fruit with only one seed. An achene with papery wings, for example an ash or sycamore fruit, is called a **samara** or **key fruit**. Some achenes, such as ash achenes, grow in bunches.

This sycamore fruit has wings which help it to float on the wind.

A dry fruit with seeds attached to its inside wall is known as a **legume** or **pod**. It splits along its length to open. The fruit of the pea plant are pods. The peas are the seeds.

This pea pod has been split open to show the seeds attached inside it.

A **grain**, also called a **caryopsis** or a **kernel**, is a small dry fruit whose wall has fused with the seed coat. Wheat and barley are examples of plants with many grains.

The fruit of the wheat plant is called grain. Each stalk carries many grains.

CONES

The seeds of conifer trees are contained in **cones**, not fruit. These develop from the female flowers (conifers have male and female flowers). After pollination* the scales harden and close.

Atlas cedar cone

When the seeds are ripe and the weather is warm and dry, the scales of the cones open. The seeds flutter out on papery wings. Most cones stay on the tree for a year. Others take two years to ripen, and some remain long after the seeds have been dropped.

See for yourself

Look at as many different types of fruit as you can find. Notice whether they are succulent or dry fruit, and the number of seeds they contain. If you find a cone, you could make it open by placing it on a radiator. If you put it in a damp place, its scales will close up.

Internet links

• Scan the code to watch blossom and fruit form on a pear tree.

• For links to more websites where you can investigate different kinds of seeds and fruit, go to **www.usborne.com/quicklinks**

SCATTERING SEEDS

Before seeds start to grow into new plants, they are usually carried away from the parent plant. This is called **dispersal**, and it helps to stop new plants from competing with their parents for space, light and water. Some seeds, such as peas, burst out of the fruit while it is still attached to the parent plant.

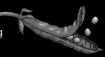

Ripe pea fruit explode and fling out their seeds.

Other seeds are carried away from their parent plant inside the fruit. Seeds can be spread by several methods, including by animals, water and wind.

ANIMAL DISPERSAL

Some seeds are tasty to animals or are held inside tempting, fleshy fruit. Animals eat them, and the seeds pass out in their droppings. Some animals, such as squirrels and jays, store away fruit and seeds. Sometimes they put them in a place that is ideal for new plants to sprout.

Not all animal-dispersed fruit are eaten. Some, such as those of burdock or goosegrass, have hooks on them which catch in the fur of passing animals. A fruit can be carried a long way from its parent plant before it falls off.

Burdock fruit have hooks that catch on animals' fur.

WATER DISPERSAL

Seeds or fruit that are dispersed by water, such as coconuts, have waterproof shells. Coconuts contain the seeds of coconut palm trees. They float in rivers or on seas until they are washed up on shore. Some have travelled up to 2,000km on ocean currents before reaching land.

The coconut fruit is held inside a large, waterproof outer shell, seen here.

WIND DISPERSAL

Fruit or seeds which are dispersed by the wind are very light. Some seeds, such as those of sycamore trees, are held in fruit with papery wings. Others, such as dandelions, have fruit with hairs that catch the wind.

Sycamore fruit, each containing two seeds

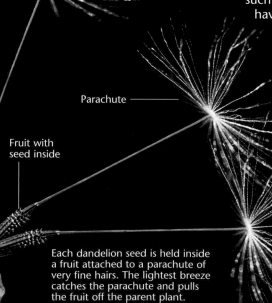

Parachute

Fruit with seed inside

Each dandelion seed is held inside a fruit attached to a parachute of very fine hairs. The lightest breeze catches the parachute and pulls the fruit off the parent plant.

Tulips like these grow from bulbs. Each year, market gardens provide thousands of tulips for the flower industry.

SPEED AND QUALITY

Vegetative reproduction produces new plants much more quickly than they can grow from seed. Also, the new plants are identical to the parent plant. Farmers and market gardeners often make use of a plant's ability to reproduce vegetatively. As well as producing more plants, they know that the new plants will be the same quality as the original plant.

Growers have also developed methods of removing parts from a plant to grow new plants. These are examples of **artificial propagation** as, left to themselves, plants do not usually reproduce in these ways.

Some varieties of fruit, such as this navel orange, do not have seeds. They can only be grown by artificial propagation methods.

TAKING CUTTINGS

One common method of artificial propagation is **cutting**. This involves taking a piece such as a side stem or leaf (known as the cutting) off a plant and planting it in soil where it grows into a new plant. The cutting may need to stand in water for a while to develop new roots before being planted in soil.

Growing a plant from a cutting

A piece of plant is cut from the parent plant.

The cutting is placed in water until roots begin to grow.

The cutting is replanted in soil, where it will grow into a new plant.

African violet plants can be grown from leaf cuttings.

MICROPROPAGATION

Growing new plants from just a few cells taken from a meristem (growth area) of a plant is called **micropropagation**. The cells are placed on a gel that contains chemicals which make the cells divide. Groups of cells are then moved to a second gel which contains growth chemicals that make the cells grow into shoots.

This method can create hundreds of identical plants from one parent plant. The meristems are usually free of any viruses that have infected the rest of the plant, so the new plantlets are disease free.

Internet links

• Scan the code to watch a video about how tulips grow from bulbs.

WATER PLANTS

Most plants grow on land, but there are also many aquatic plants – plants specially adapted to live in water. These are known as **hydrophytes**. They range from minute plants a fraction of a millimetre across to huge flowering plants over a metre wide.

A WATERY LIFESTYLE

Water plants are either emergent or submergent. **Emergent** plants, such as reed mace, grow well in very wet soils, or in soils that spend a lot of time covered in water. Most or all of their stems and leaves can be seen above the surface of the water.

Reed mace can often be seen growing out of the water by a river bank.

Submergent plants, such as water lilies, grow beneath the surface of the water. However, some of their parts, for instance large leaves, may float on the surface. Unless they are free-floating, their roots, or root-like parts, anchor them to the ground beneath the water.

Free-floating submergent plants, such as duckweed, are not attached to anything. They are found in large numbers in calm, sheltered water.

This duckweed floats freely on the water's surface.

Above the water's surface, water crowfoot has broad, flat leaves.

Under the water, its leaves are thin and finely divided.

SPECIAL FEATURES

Water-living plants have a number of special features. For instance, most underwater leaves, unlike leaves of other plants, do not have a waxy waterproof coating. This is because the whole leaf surface is needed for exchanging gases between the plant and the water. Many water plants also have very different leaves above and below the surface.

Some submergent plants develop gaps between the cells in their stems and leaves. These gaps trap air which helps the parts to float.

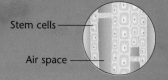

Stem cells ———

Air space ———

Internet links

• Scan the code to watch a video clip about how water lilies grow.

A water lily's stem and roots grow under water.

ALGAE

Algae are a varied group of plant-like protists* which have a very simple structure, with no true tissues. Most types of algae are found in water, but they can grow in any suitably damp conditions, including in soil, on rocks, and even on living things.

Diatoms, like these, are a type of algae.

STUDYING ALGAE

Algae can reproduce quickly and, like plants, make their own food using the Sun's energy. Algae are an important source of food for many water creatures.

Scientists study the types and numbers of algae in a water sample to find out how clean it is. Single-celled, freshwater algae called **desmids** are generally found growing in clean water.

Some types of algae, though, reproduce rapidly in water that contains high levels of nitrates (chemicals found in some fertilizers and sewage). This is called **eutrophication**. These algae use up oxygen that other living things in the water need, eventually killing them.

One type of eutrophication causes "red tides", like this one in Washington State, USA, which are harmful to marine life.

Eutrophication is mostly caused by sewage-dumping and by fertilizer being washed from the soil into the water.

SEAWEEDS

Seaweeds are types of many-celled algae. Most seaweeds have root-like **holdfasts** at their base, which anchor them to solid objects, such as rocks. Some have bubble-like **air bladders**, which keep them afloat. A seaweed's leaves, called **fronds**, often contain pigments* that allow them to take in light at different water depths.

Examples of seaweeds

Sea lettuce has very thin, crinkled fronds. These darken as the plant ages, because different tiny algae cover their surface.

Edible dulse grows in deep pools. The red pigment in its fronds helps it to capture light under water.

Knotted wrack has long fronds, which contain pockets of air called air bladders.

DIATOMS

One of the simplest types of algae are microscopic **diatoms**. Most are made up of a single cell, with a hard, glassy case. Each species of diatom has a differently patterned case.

Each diatom is made up of two halves, which fit together like a lid on a box.

See for yourself

If you visit the coast, look for seaweed of different colours and textures. You may find it in rock pools, or washed up on the shore. Look for features like air bladders or a holdfast.

Internet links

• Scan the code to find out how algae may be used one day as a biofuel, or for more about algae, go to **www.usborne.com/quicklinks**

* Pigments, 261; Protists, 294; Vascular tissue, 254.

FLOWERLESS PLANTS

Liverworts, mosses, ferns and horsetails* are known as flowerless plants. They do not produce flowers or seeds, and in many cases reproduce at least some of the time by **asexual reproduction.** This is a type of reproduction in which only one parent is needed to produce a new living thing identical to itself. Flowerless plants were the first plants on the Earth.

These paired, horn-shaped clubs contain reproductive cells called spores.

The leaves of this stag's horn club moss are packed tightly around the base of the stem.

LIVERWORTS

Liverworts are low-growing plants that live in damp places on soil or rocks. They do not have true roots, stems or leaves. The main part of a liverwort is called the **thallus**. It is held in the ground by simple root-like growths called **rhizoids**.

Liverworts do not contain vascular tissue* for transporting fluids. They also do not have a waterproof outer layer. This means that they can absorb all the water they need, but are also more likely to dry out.

MOSSES

Mosses are low-growing plants that live in damp, shady places, for example on walls, rocks and tree trunks. Like liverworts, they do not have vascular tissue*. Instead, they absorb large amounts of water through their many tiny leaf-like structures, which are only one cell thick.

If conditions become too dry, the moss leaves curl up, shrivel, and turn brown. They remain inactive until conditions are damp enough for them to grow again.

The *Pohlia nutans* moss below grows on damp soil and rotting logs.

CLUB MOSSES

Club mosses grow along the ground. They are not mosses at all, but are distantly related to ferns. They have narrow, scale-like leaves packed densely around stems that contain vascular tissue.

Club mosses get their name from their club-shaped growths called **strobili**, which contain reproductive cells called spores.

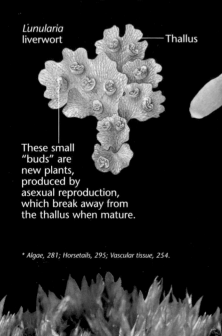

Lunularia liverwort

Thallus

These small "buds" are new plants, produced by asexual reproduction, which break away from the thallus when mature.

The tiny capsules on these moss stalks are called **sporangia**. They contain spores (reproductive cells).

The moss absorbs large amounts of water through thousands of tiny leaves.

* Algae, 281; Horsetails, 295; Vascular tissue, 254.

FERNS

There are over 10,000 species of ferns. They grow in damp, shady places all over the world. Unlike mosses and liverworts, they have true leaves, stems and roots, with well-developed vascular tissue. This helps them to survive in drier conditions, and also to grow taller to get a better share of the light.

Most ferns have horizontal stems called rhizomes* that grow underground. Leaves known as **fronds** push out of the earth in tight coils which then unfurl. Fronds are different shapes depending on the type of fern.

This hart's-tongue fern has solid, leathery fronds.

Bracken fronds are made up of many leaflets.

Wall rue ferns have delicate fronds.

These brown specks are spore sacs (sori) on the underside of a fern frond.

REPRODUCTION

Most flowerless plants go through a two-stage reproduction known as **alternation of generations**. In this, a type of asexual reproduction alternates with true sexual reproduction, involving male and female sex cells. At other times, the plants may reproduce by asexual reproduction alone, for instance by producing new bud-like plants called **gemmae**.

The first stage of alternation of generations is sexual. The plant is called a **gametophyte**, because it produces male and female sex cells (gametes). A male cell travels through water to a female cell, and they join and grow into a plant body called a **sporophyte**. Mosses produce gametophytes and sporophytes on the same plant, but in liverworts, ferns and most algae they are on separate plants.

The second, asexual stage is called **sporulation**. The sporophyte produces reproductive cells called **spores**. Ripe spores are scattered, and grow into new gametophytes if they land in suitable conditions.

Fern spores develop in tiny sacs called **sori**. These usually grow in clusters on the underside of the fern's fronds. The scattered spores grow into flat, often heart-shaped gametophytes called **prothalli**.

Life cycle of a fern

Gametophyte (called prothallus) with male and female cells

Spores scatter and form new gametophytes.

Male and female cells join together.

Sporophyte with spores

See for yourself

You may see small mosses growing on walls or on stones in a garden. Look closely at their texture and shape. If you live near a wooded area or even a garden centre, you may also find some ferns. Look for spore sacs on the undersides of their leaves.

Internet links

• Scan the code to find out how flowerless plants reproduce.

• For links to more websites where you can investigate mosses, ferns and liverworts with animations, diagrams and photo galleries, go to www.usborne.com/quicklinks

FUNGI

Fungi are simple, plant-like organisms that never flower and do not have true leaves, stems or roots. They grow in damp, dark places, and do not contain the green chlorophyll needed to make their own food. Instead, they feed on either living things or dead matter. Moulds and yeast are types of fungi.

The mould on this lemon is a type of simple fungus.

STRUCTURE OF FUNGI

The main part of most fungi, called the **mycelium**, is found underground. It is a mass of tiny thread-like structures called **hyphae**, which spread out in the soil. These absorb food substances from dead matter or living roots in the soil. Fungi which live on roots are called **mycorrhizae**.

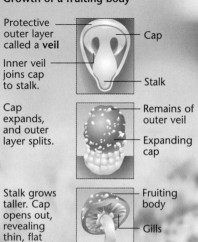

Mycelium

To reproduce, some of the hyphae pack densely together to form button-like growths. These push up through the soil and grow into **fruiting bodies**.

Like mosses and ferns, fungi reproduce by producing tiny cells called spores. Fruiting bodies contain millions of spores. When the spores are ready, they are released and scattered by the wind. If they land in suitable conditions, they grow into new fungi.

The fruiting bodies of fungi grow and die very rapidly, but the spores and mycelium can continue to live underground for many years.

MOULDS AND MILDEWS

Moulds and **mildews** are simple fungi which do not produce large fruiting bodies. They grow in warm, damp and dark places, feeding on living or once-living matter, such as paper and wood.

You might see moulds or mildews in your own home or garden. For example, the small blue spots and green furry patches that grow on old bread or fruit are types of mould. Mildews often look like powdery white or black patches. They grow in damp areas, such as bathroom ceilings. Some grow on plants – roses, for example.

Growth of a fruiting body

Protective outer layer called a **veil**

Cap

Inner veil joins cap to stalk.

Stalk

Cap expands, and outer layer splits.

Remains of outer veil

Expanding cap

Stalk grows taller. Cap opens out, revealing thin, flat **gills**.

Fruiting body

Gills

Fruiting body of a fungus

The flattened gills of this fungus have opened out to shed its spores.

This sulphur shelf fungus is a saprotroph. It lives and feeds on the wood of dead trees.

FUNGI FEEDING

Fungi that feed on dead matter are called **saprotrophs**. Dead matter contains useful substances such as carbon and nitrates. As they feed, fungi release chemicals called **enzymes** which break down their food into simple substances.

Some substances are absorbed by the fungi, but others are returned to the soil, where they are used again by plants and animals. In this way, the fungi play an important part in the carbon and nitrogen cycles*.

Many fungi form associations with vascular plants, especially trees. A network of hyphae surrounds or penetrates the root tissues and passes on water and minerals from the soil. In exchange, the fungus gains some sugars from the plant. Helpful relationships like these are called **mutualistic**.

See for yourself

You can look at spores by cutting the stalk off an ordinary cooking mushroom, and placing the cap on a piece of white paper. Cover it with an upturned bowl and leave it overnight. When you remove the bowl and mushroom cap, you will see that the mushroom has released its spores in a pattern on the paper.

Spore print

HELP AND HARM

Some kinds of fungi are useful to people. For instance, a medicine called **penicillin**, which kills the bacteria that cause various diseases, is made from a particular mould. The blue veins in some cheeses are also made from similar moulds. A single-celled fungus called **yeast** is used in bread-making and brewing some alcoholic drinks.

Bread, wine and beer are made using the yeast fungus.

Many fungi can harm living things. Some, for instance, produce fruiting bodies that are highly poisonous. Others, such as the mould which causes Dutch elm disease, grow on plants and slowly kill them. Some fungi can also grow on animals' bodies. For instance, athlete's foot and ringworm are human skin conditions caused by fungi.

This beetle has a fungus feeding on its body.

Internet links

• Scan the code for a video about different kinds of fungi.

• For links to more websites where you can find interesting facts, picture guides and online activities about fungi, go to **www.usborne.com/quicklinks**

* Carbon cycle, Nitrogen cycle, 292.

FIGHTING FOR SURVIVAL

Every living thing in nature struggles to survive. Most plants are threatened by animals and people, as well as by other plants, and may have to live in difficult conditions. Plants survive by adapting to life in different environments, and competing successfully with other living things.

This yucca is a desert plant. It has narrow, tough leaves, which lose little water.

NATURAL SELECTION

Over time, some plants develop features which help them to survive in particular conditions. Plants with helpful features are more likely to survive and reproduce. Plants without these features often die out. This process is called **natural selection** (see also page 339).

COASTAL PLANTS

The seashore is an example of an environment where conditions can be harsh. There is little firm soil or fresh water, and strong, salty winds often blow. Even so, some plants have adapted to life in these surroundings.

For instance, when a sand dune first forms, only grasses grow there. Their roots form a network which helps to bind together the loose, sandy ground, eventually creating a kind of soil that other types of flowering plants can grow in.

Shingle beaches are made up of small rock fragments, mixed with sand. Only plants with long or sprawling roots, which hold the plant firmly in the shingle, can live in these areas. Long roots also help the plant to reach supplies of fresh water deep under the ground.

Yellow horned poppies are anchored firmly in the shingle by their long roots.

Areas called **salt marshes** form where a river joins the sea. Their soil is **saline** (salty), which means that most plants are not able to grow in it.

A group of plants known as **halophytes** can survive in saline areas. Some need salt in order to grow. Others are adapted to remove salt from water that they take in. For example, some halophytes have **salt bladders** on the surface of their leaves. These bladders burst to release salt. Other halophytes store the salt in old leaves, which they later shed.

DESERT PLANTS

Plants that grow in very dry areas, such as deserts, are called **xerophytes**. There are many ways in which they make the most of the limited water supply. For example, some have very small leaves, or needle-like leaves called spines, which lose very little water. Most desert plants have specially adapted cells which store water.

These cacti store water in their thick, fleshy stems.

Grasses growing on sand dunes help to make the ground firmer.

Sea asters grow best in salty conditions.

286

PROTECTION

Plants are constantly under threat from animals that want to eat them. Some plants have special features which protect them from hungry animals and other dangers. These features are known as **protective adaptations**.

Some plants, such as this dog rose, have sharp thorns or prickles which make them difficult for animals to eat.

Thorn

Tiny hairs on this nettle's leaves release a stinging chemical when they are touched.

Some types of plants use tricks and disguises to keep themselves safe. For instance, living stone plants have adapted to blend in perfectly with pebbles on the ground. Animals mistake them for real stones, and do not try to eat them. This type of disguise is called **camouflage**.

Many plants are damaged by hungry insect grubs, such as caterpillars. These hatch out of eggs laid on the plant's leaves.

Some passion flower vines protect themselves from this threat by developing small growths which look like butterfly eggs. Butterflies are less likely to lay eggs on a plant that looks as if it already has some on it. Only a small number of real eggs are laid on the plant, so it is attacked by few caterpillars.

This butterfly thinks the false eggs are real. It will not lay its own eggs near them.

False egg

Passion flower vine

ROCK PLANTS

Plants that live on the surface of rocks are called **lithophytes**. They are mostly found on walls, cliff-faces or mountainsides. Lithophytes usually have special roots which anchor them to rocks.

Mosses are one of the few types of plants that can survive on rocks.

See for yourself

You can easily keep cacti at home. A cactus will grow best in sandy soil with a covering of pebbles. It needs plenty of sunlight, but very little watering. When you water a cactus, you will notice that the water dribbles off its surface. This is because its skin is tough and thick, to keep in as much water as possible. A cactus gets all the water it needs through its roots.

Living stones grow on the ground. They look like pebbles.

Internet links

• Scan the code to find out how desert plants survive.

• For links to more websites where you can discover how plants have adapted to survive, go to **www.usborne.com/quicklinks**

PLANT LIFESTYLES

The way a plant grows and reproduces depends on many things, such as climate, soil and weather conditions. Some plants live in areas where growth is impossible for some parts of the year, so they grow quickly and reproduce many times when conditions are right. Others may grow one year and reproduce the next. Plants typically have just one **growing season** in a year.

These blue daisies are perennials. They bloom year after year.

ANNUALS

Flowering plants that live and die within a single year are called **annuals**. The entire process of growth, flowering and seed production may take place in as little as a few weeks. Annual plants have usually bloomed and died by the end of the summer. Their seeds remain inactive during the winter, ready to grow into new plants when spring comes.

This lobelia grows, flowers and dies within a single year.

BIENNIALS

Some flowering plants take two years to complete their life cycle. They are called **biennials**. During the first year, they grow and store up food. In the second year, the plant grows taller, blooms and produces seeds. After this, the entire plant dies.

Wallflowers grow and store food in one year, then flower and die in the next.

PERENNIALS

Plants that live for many years are called **perennials**. There are two types. **Herbaceous perennials** lose all the parts that are above ground each winter. Their roots become swollen with food and remain inactive until new shoots sprout from them the following spring.

Shrubs and trees are **woody perennials**. They may lose some parts, such as leaves, during the winter, but their stems or trunks stay alive, growing thicker each year.

TREE LIFESTYLES

Trees can be divided into two categories: deciduous and evergreen. **Deciduous trees** lose their leaves every year. Most deciduous trees have thin, soft leaves that dry out easily. These are shed just before winter, when the temperature drops. If the ground freezes, there is less water available. If deciduous trees kept their leaves at this time, too much precious water would be lost through them.

Trees that do not shed their leaves all at once are known as **evergreen**. Unlike deciduous trees, they have tough, waxy leaves, which means they lose less water. They can survive and grow in places where little water is available. Keeping their leaves also means that they can continue to make food during the winter, even though there is less sunlight available.

EPHEMERALS

Plants with very short life cycles are called **ephemeral plants**. They are often found where the right growth conditions occur for a limited time, such as in deserts. The plants grow quickly from seeds which have been inactive in the ground. They bloom and produce seeds, which may also then grow, bloom and produce seeds, and so on, until conditions become unsuitable again.

Leaves on deciduous trees change colour before they fall. New leaves grow in spring, when the temperature rises.

Conifers such as these have narrow, waxy leaves with a small surface area. Little water is lost through them.

During the brief rainy season, these desert plants have bloomed, creating a carpet of flowers.

In some places, such as grasslands, there are two seasons: rainy and dry. The trees there shed their leaves at the beginning of the dry season, when the moisture level of the soil drops below a certain point. The leaves begin to grow back at the start of the rainy season, when water is available again.

See for yourself

Next time you are in a wooded area, look closely at the trees. See if you can find examples of both deciduous and evergreen trees, and compare the leaves. Deciduous leaves are flat, with thin veins running through them. Evergreen leaves tend to be waxy and pointed.

Internet links

• Scan the code for a video about annual and perennial plants.

• For links about the life cycles of flowers and trees, go to **www.usborne.com/quicklinks**

PLANTS AND PEOPLE

The world can be divided into **biomes**. Each is a region with a unique climate and type of soil. A biome supports **ecosystems** – groups of plants and animals that interact with each other and their surroundings. Many ecosystems are damaged by the way people use the land.

Map showing main world biomes

Key to biomes

Tropical rainforest
Deciduous forest
Mountains
Coniferous forest
Scrubland
Tropical grassland
Tundra
Temperate grassland
Desert
Polar areas (little plant life)

Tropical rainforests contain a huge number of plants, which grow in layers. Treetops form the highest layer, and ground plants form the lowest. Each layer supports different forms of life.

Orchid

Deciduous forests generally grow in layers. At the top are tall deciduous trees*. Beneath is a layer of small trees and saplings, then a layer of shrubs. Next, there are a number of smaller plants, and finally a layer of mosses and lichens on the ground.

Oak leaf

Mountains are cold and bleak. Only low-growing plants such as mosses and shrubs grow on them.

Coniferous forests (or **taiga**) contain large numbers of conifers. They are usually found in areas where the soil is frozen for part of the year. This makes it difficult for plants to obtain water. Conifers have narrow, tough leaves called needles which reduce water loss.

Silver fir cone

Scrublands mainly contain shrubs. Many of these have small, leathery or needle-like leaves, which help to prevent water loss in the dry season.

Tropical grasslands have a permanent cover of grasses, and sometimes also trees and shrubs. In the long dry season, there are many fires. These leave behind ashes which help to fertilize the soil.

Tundra regions are cold and windy. They contain low-growing plants, such as lichens, mosses and small shrubs. The temperature is too low for large plants such as trees.

Lichen

Temperate grasslands (also known as **prairies** or **steppes**) contain many different types of grasses, but few trees. Their rich mixture of grasses is food for many different grazing animals.

Big bluestem grass

Deserts are hot and dry. Desert plants generally have a thick, waxy outer covering and slim leaves, to reduce water loss.

By clearing large areas such as this for farmland, there is a danger that we are losing too many natural habitats, including hedgerows and woodland.

FOOD FOR ALL

For thousands of years, people have found ways of producing the food they need from the land around them. But as the human population grows, more and more food is needed. This means using more space to grow crops, or using existing farmland more efficiently. Some farming methods have a disastrous effect on ecosystems, though.

Here, a huge area of land has been cleared for growing crops, destroying the ecosystem that was there before.

Since farming began, people have identified plants with useful features, such as bigger fruit or better resistance to pests, and have used their seeds to grow better crops. This is called **selective breeding**. Overuse of selective breeding may lead to inbreeding and the inability of the species to respond to new challenges (such as diseases).

Intensive farming uses chemical fertilizers, pesticides, machinery and other methods to grow the most crops possible. But these methods return very few natural substances to the soil, and the chemicals can harm the land and animals living on it.

Intensive farming often uses machinery such as this to spray fields full of crops with pesticides or other chemicals.

GENETIC MODIFICATION

A living thing's characteristics are controlled by genes* in its cells. These are inherited from parents through reproduction, so cannot be passed naturally from one type of living thing to a different type.

Scientists, though, are able to take a gene for a certain useful feature from one organism and place it in another of a different kind. This is called **genetic modification**. Food produced like this is known as **GM food**.

It is possible, for instance, to take a gene that makes a fish resistant to the cold, and place it in a tomato plant. This creates tomato plants that can survive in cold weather.

These GM tomatoes look like ordinary tomatoes. Many people who want to avoid buying GM food think it should be clearly labelled.

Some people believe GM crops could help to solve the problem of food shortages around the world, but others think they could cause great damage to the environment. For example, maize can be genetically modified to be poisonous to insects. This means that less of the crop is destroyed, but some birds and other wildlife that normally feed on those insects will die of hunger.

ORGANIC FARMING

Organic farming works closely with nature by not adding artificial chemicals to the soil. For instance, instead of using chemical pesticides, some organic farmers plant onions among their crops. The strong smell of onions masks the smell of the crops, and pests are not attracted.

Organic farmers often use a method called **crop rotation**. Crops that use or replace certain minerals, such as nitrates, are planted in different fields each year. Manure and compost are used as fertilizers to help the crops to grow. This method keeps levels of natural substances balanced in the soil.

Example of crop rotation

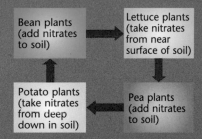

Bean plants (add nitrates to soil) → Lettuce plants (take nitrates from near surface of soil) → Pea plants (add nitrates to soil) → Potato plants (take nitrates from deep down in soil) → Bean plants

Some people prefer to eat organically grown food because they know it is entirely natural and better for the environment.

Internet links

• Scan the code for a video about genetically modified food.

• For links to more websites about world biomes and farming methods, go to www.usborne.com/quicklinks

*Genes, 380.

291

NATURAL CYCLES

Living things need carbon, nitrogen, oxygen and water to keep them alive. These vital substances are constantly recycled between the air, land and living things, which means that living things need never run out of them. However, natural cycles are easily disturbed, especially by some human activities that release harmful substances into the environment.

Some fungi break down dead matter. This returns vital chemicals to the soil.

THE NITROGEN CYCLE

All living things need **nitrogen** to make essential chemicals called **proteins**. Before plants can use nitrogen, it must be combined with oxygen to form **nitrates**. Lightning forms some nitrates from nitrogen in the air. Certain types of bacteria also form nitrates. They mostly live inside the roots of vegetables called legumes, for example peas and beans.

When a plant or animal dies, fungi and bacteria break it down. This releases nitrogen into the soil as a chemical called **ammonia**. **Nitrogen-fixing bacteria** in the soil change the ammonia into nitrates, which are taken in by plants. Animals gain their nitrogen by eating plants, or animals that have eaten plants. (For more on the nitrogen cycle, see page 64.)

Bacteria and fungi release nitrogen from dead matter into the soil.

Plants take in nitrates from the soil.

THE CARBON CYCLE

All living things need **carbon** to live and grow. Plants obtain it from carbon dioxide in the air. During photosynthesis*, they use carbon dioxide to make food substances called **carbohydrates**.

Plants take in carbon dioxide during the day to help them make food.

At night, they give out carbon dioxide when food is not being produced.

Inside living things, internal respiration* turns carbohydrates into energy, producing carbon dioxide as waste. Carbon dioxide is also released into the atmosphere when organic matter is burned or broken down in the soil. (For more on the carbon cycle, see page 52.)

THE WATER CYCLE

Water is constantly recycled through the air, rivers and seas. Water that falls as rain drains into rivers, then into the sea. It turns to vapour, forming tiny droplets in the air. These form clouds, and water falls back to Earth as rain.

Plants transpire (release water vapour) through their leaves. Most animals also release water when they breathe out. (You can find out more about the water cycle on page 74.)

Water vapour is released through the surface of the leaves.

Water enters the plant through the roots and travels up the stem to the leaves.

See for yourself

Plants that grow in towns may be harmed by particles of dirt from traffic exhaust. On a dry day, gather a few leaves from trees or bushes growing in a town where there is lots of traffic passing through.

Next, take a damp cloth, and rub the upper surface of the leaves. You may find that a layer of dirt from the polluted air rubs off. This blocks out light that the leaves need to make food for the plant, making it less healthy.

* Internal respiration, 265; Photosynthesis, 264.

UPSET BALANCE

People can upset the balance of natural cycles in various ways. For example, in some parts of the world, forests are burned down to make way for farming or building. Burning releases carbon, which forms carbon dioxide in the air.

The remaining plants do not remove this carbon dioxide fast enough during the process of photosynthesis*, so it builds up in the atmosphere.

The dense layer of carbon dioxide traps the Sun's heat around the Earth, creating what is known as the greenhouse effect. This is believed to cause global warming, a dangerous increase in the Earth's overall temperature.

Here, a large area of forest is being burned to make way for building and farming. Burning such as this increases the level of carbon dioxide in the atmosphere.

Pollution can also affect the growth patterns of living things. **Lichens** are simple living things made up of a fungus and an alga growing together. In areas with little or no pollution, shrubby lichens may be seen growing on trees. In very polluted areas, there are large amounts of green algae, but no lichens.

Green algae grow on trees in very polluted areas.

Leafy lichens grow on walls. They are found in areas with some pollution.

Shrubby lichens grow on trees in cleaner areas.

PLANTS UNDER THREAT

Some plants are directly threatened by human activities. For instance, golden barrel cacti are now very rare in Mexico, because they have been collected illegally and sold.

Golden barrel cactus

In Wales, seeds from the last tufted saxifrage plants in the country were grown into new plants. These were replanted in the wild to try to save the species from dying out. This was successful, but global warming is once again threatening the cold mountain areas in which they live.

Tufted saxifrage

Internet links

• Scan the code for a video about how human activities can affect the environment.

• For links to more websites where you can explore Earth's natural cycles, go to **www.usborne.com/quicklinks**

* Photosynthesis, 264.

CLASSIFYING PLANTS

In order to make living things easier to study, scientists organize them into groups with similar features. This process is called **classification**. Plants are usually classified by comparing the structure of their stems and leaves, as well as the arrangement and types of their reproductive parts.

THE KINGDOMS OF LIFE

The largest groups into which scientists divide living things are called **kingdoms**. There are six main kingdoms:

Archaea
Microscopic single-celled organisms without nuclei*. They cannot survive in the presence of oxygen.

Eubacteria
Microscopic, single-celled organisms without nuclei*. Many can survive in the presence of oxygen. Their cell walls* are very different from those of the Archaea.

Protista
Most are microscopic and single-celled. They have a distinct nucleus* within each cell. Some protists are like animals, some are like plants and some are like fungi.

Eubacteria

Diatom – a plant-like protist

Plants
Many-celled with distinct nuclei*. Most plants have cells that contain chlorophyll* which allows them to make their own food.

Yellow stargrass flowers

Fungi
Many-celled with distinct nuclei*. The cells do not contain chlorophyll*. They feed by digesting organic matter outside their bodies.

Entoloma fungus

Animals
Many-celled with distinct nuclei*. Their cells do not contain chlorophyll*. They feed by taking in organic matter (either dead or living) and digesting it within their bodies. Most animals can move around.

Pika

IDENTIFICATION

Scientists identify living things by comparing their main features and comparing them with those of similar species. One method used to compare features is called a **biological key**. A key is typically arranged in stages, with a choice of features at every stage. Each choice leads to another, until the organism is identified.

A key with two choices at each stage is called a **dichotomous key**. You can use the dichotomous key on the right to identify the six leaves above it. Pick one statement from each pair that describes the leaf you want to identify.

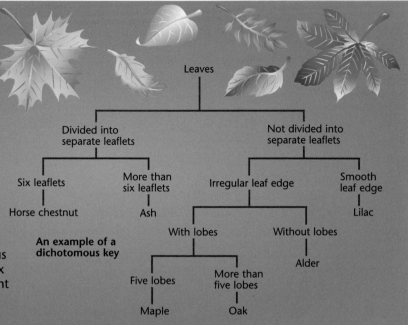

Leaves

Divided into separate leaflets

Not divided into separate leaflets

Six leaflets

More than six leaflets

Irregular leaf edge

Smooth leaf edge

Horse chestnut

Ash

An example of a dichotomous key

With lobes

Without lobes

Lilac

Alder

Five lobes

More than five lobes

Maple

Oak

* Chlorophyll, 260; Nucleus, 250; Photosynthesis, 264, Cell wall, 250.

THE PLANT KINGDOM

The plant kingdom has two main groups: those plants that contain fluid-carrying vascular tissue, and those that do not. These groups are broken into further divisions, based mainly on the plant's reproductive structures.

VASCULAR PLANTS

Not all vascular plants produce seeds, but those plants that do can be divided into five further groups.

In the first four groups (sometimes called **gymnosperms**), the seeds are not contained within a fruit. These groups are:

Conifers are usually tree-sized plants, with waxy needle-like or scaly leaves. They produce cones, which contain their seeds.

Larch cone

Cycads produce very large cones. These grow in the middle of a circle of spiky leaves.

Cycad cone

Ginkgoes are direct relatives of ancient seed-carrying plants. They produce fleshy cones and have soft, fan-shaped leaves.

Ginkgo leaf

Gnetophytes are a small group of plants that grow in very hot areas. They mostly have tough, leathery leaves.

Welwitschia

* Rhizomes, 278; Spores, 283.

The fifth group, **magnoliophytes** (or **angiosperms**) is the name given to all flowering plants. They produce seeds enclosed in a fruit of some kind. Flowering plants can be divided into two groups: monocotyledons and dicotyledons.

Monocotyledons have one cotyledon (simple first leaf). Their vascular bundles are scattered throughout the stem.

Hosta

Dicotyledons have two cotyledons. Their vascular bundles are arranged in a regular pattern inside the stem (see page 255).

Lesser celandine

Seedless vascular plants have a simple structure, and do not produce flowers. They reproduce using spores*.

Horsetails produce spores inside cones. Their leaves are arranged in rings around the stem.

Horsetail

Ferns reproduce either by producing rhizomes*, or by making spores. These are produced on the underside of the fern's leafy fronds.

Bracken

Club mosses are related to ferns. Their spores are carried in tight, club-shaped spirals at the end of their stalks.

Stag's horn club moss

NON-VASCULAR PLANTS

Plants without vascular tissue, such as mosses and liverworts, are known as **bryophytes**. They are usually small, with with simple root-like structures only one cell wide, and simple leaves. They have no flowers and reproduce using spores. Most live in damp, shady places.

Mosses on a rock

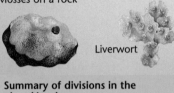

Liverwort

Summary of divisions in the plant kingdom

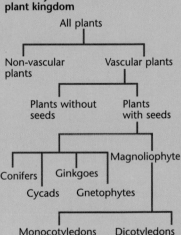

All plants
- Non-vascular plants
- Vascular plants
  - Plants without seeds
  - Plants with seeds
    - Conifers
    - Ginkgoes
    - Cycads
    - Gnetophytes
    - Magnoliophyte
      - Monocotyledons
      - Dicotyledons

Internet links

• Scan the code to find out how to use a dichotomous key.

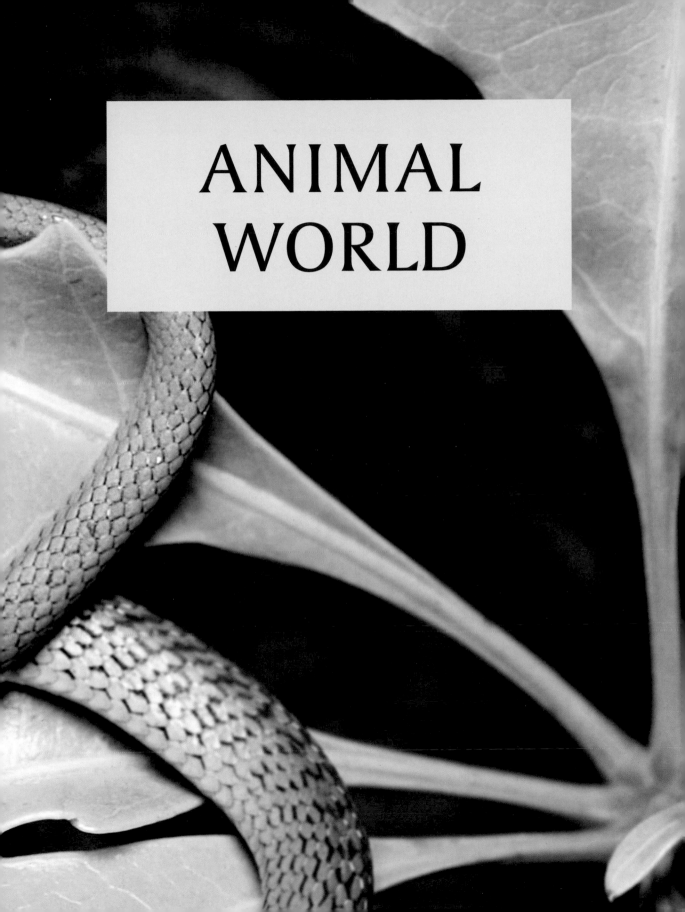

ANIMAL WORLD

ANIMAL CELLS

Every living thing is made up of one or more tiny units called **cells**. All the processes needed for life, such as producing energy from food, take place inside cells.

Cluster of animal cells, shown at many thousand times its real size

PARTS OF A CELL

There are many different kinds of cell, each with a particular job to do, but most share certain features.

Cells contain a number of small parts called **organelles**, which have various functions. The largest and most important organelle is the **nucleus**. This controls everything that happens inside the cell. It has a double-layered outer skin, called the **nuclear membrane**, and a gel-like middle.

All cells are surrounded by a protective layer called the **cell membrane**, which holds together the contents of the cell. This layer is semipermeable, which means that it lets some substances pass through it, but not others.

The rest of the cell is called the **cytoplasm**. The cell membrane, nucleus and cytoplasm are collectively called the **protoplasm**.

Centrioles play a part in cell division.

Ribosomes help to build up substances called **proteins**, which are needed for all functions within the cell.

Lysosomes destroy invading bacteria* and parts of the cell which are no longer needed.

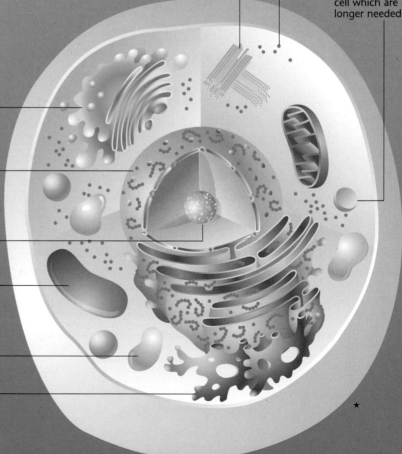

Organelles in a typical animal cell (not shown to scale)

The **Golgi complex** stores and distributes the substances made inside the cell.

Nucleus. The nuclear membrane has channels, called **nuclear pores**, which can open and close to let information-carrying chemicals (messenger RNA) out to the ribosomes. Inside the nucleus are chromosomes*, which contain DNA*.

The **nucleolus** makes the ingredients of ribosomes.

Mitochondria convert simple substances into energy for the cell.

Vacuoles are small, temporary sacs in the cytoplasm. They are used as storage areas for liquids or fats.

The **endoplasmic reticulum** is a series of channels used to transport materials around the cell.

* Bacteria, 341, 386; Chromosomes, 380; DNA, 382.

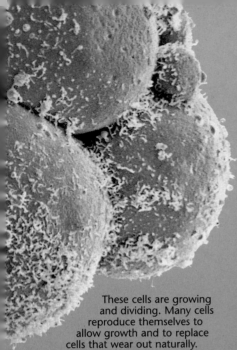

These cells are growing and dividing. Many cells reproduce themselves to allow growth and to replace cells that wear out naturally.

CELL DIVISION

Cells are constantly dying or wearing out, so new ones need to be made. Cells make copies of themselves by splitting into two identical cells, called **daughter cells**.

Stages of cell divison

 This single cell is about to start dividing.

 The nuclear membrane disappears and the contents of the nucleus begin to pull apart.

 The contents reform as two identical nuclei. The division of the nucleus is called **mitosis**.

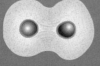 A **cleavage furrow** forms, cutting through the middle of the cell.

 Two daughter cells are formed. The division of the cytoplasm is called **cytokinesis**.

BUILDING WITH CELLS

Different cell types have different functions. This is called **specialization**. Animal cells come in a variety of shapes and sizes, depending on their job.

Cells of the same type combine to form **tissue**. For example, **columnar epithelial cells** are long and column-shaped, and allow substances to pass through them. They group together to make a tissue called **epithelium**. This is ideal for lining organs such as intestines, because gases and liquids can pass through it easily.

Columnar epithelial cells

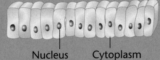

Nucleus   Cytoplasm

Several different types of tissue together form an **organ**, such as the stomach or intestines.

Epithelial cells   Muscle cells

 Cells group together

Epithelial tissue   Muscle tissue

Tissues combine to form the wall of the intestine.

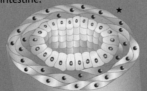

SYSTEMS

A group of organs which does a particular job is known as a **system**. For example, an animal's **digestive system** breaks down its food into simpler substances. The digestive system of the frog below contains four main organs: the stomach, liver, pancreas and intestine.

Organs in a frog's digestive system

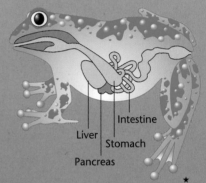

Liver   Intestine
Stomach
Pancreas

A frog has other systems, including a **skeletal system**, which supports its body, and a **circulatory system**, which transports blood around it. All the systems together make up a living individual called an **organism**, in this case a frog.

Internet links

• Scan the code to find out more about animal cells.

• For links to more websites where you can explore different types of cells, see how new cells are made and build an animal cell, go to **www.usborne.com/quicklinks**

BODY STRUCTURE

The structure of living creatures varies greatly. Animal-like protists* are **unicellular** – they have a body consisting of a single cell. True animals are **multicellular**, which means that their bodies are made of hundreds, or even millions, of cells. Most animals have a fluid-filled body cavity and a skeleton.

The body of this sunstar is made up of many parts. Its main organs are in the middle.

Sponge

SIMPLE BODIES

The simplest animal bodies are seen in sponges. Here, the individual cells line a series of tubes within the body but are not organized into tissues* as in other animals. If the sponge body is broken up, the cells can reorganize themselves into another sponge.

DIVIDED BODIES

Some more complex creatures, such as insects, have a segmented body structure, but the segmentation is not always clearly visible. Their bodies are divided into three parts: the **head**, **thorax** and **abdomen**. Each part is made up of a group of segments called **tagmata**. Unlike metameres, tagmata do not have dividing walls.

SEGMENTED BODIES

The bodies of some animals, such as worms and centipedes, are divided into separate areas called **segments**. A worm's segments are called **metameres**. Each one is almost identical. Segmentation of this type is called **metameric segmentation**. Walls of muscle tissue, each one called a **septum**, divide one metamere from the next.

Earthworm

Simplified cutaway view

Metamere

Septum

Parts of worm's nervous system can be seen in each segment.

Divisions between segments can be seen on the body's surface.

Body structure of a wasp

Head (carries main sense organs)

Thorax (upper body area, contains flight muscles)

Abdomen (contains most of insect's body organs)

Most insects have two pairs of wings and three pairs of legs, arranged symmetrically on either side of their thorax.

Paired legs (attached to thorax)

Wings (attached to thorax). This wasp's rear wings are hidden beneath its front wings.

300

* Protista, 341; Tissues, 299.

BODY SYMMETRY

Most freely moving animals have **bilateral symmetry**. This means that one half of their body mirrors the other. Other animals, such as starfish, have **radial symmetry**. This means that there are two or more lines of symmetry, which radiate from one central point.

Bilateral symmetry

Radial symmetry

Only one division can produce two identical halves.

Many lines of symmetry produce identical halves.

BODY CAVITIES

Almost all animals have a fluid-filled body cavity called a **perivisceral cavity**, which acts as a cushion for the internal organs. Two types of perivisceral cavity are the coelom and the haemocoel.

A **coelom** is filled with fluid and contained by a membrane called the **peritoneum**.

Peanut worm

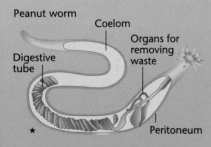

Coelom

Digestive tube

Organs for removing waste

★

Peritoneum

A **haemocoel** is a cavity filled with blood. It forms part of the animal's blood system.

Spider

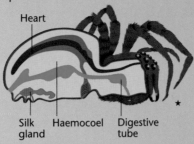

Heart

Silk gland

Haemocoel

Digestive tube

★

SKELETONS

A **skeleton** provides support for an animal's body, and protects its internal organs from damage. It helps the animal to move, by providing a surface for its muscles to pull on. There are three kinds of skeleton, described below.

An **endoskeleton** is a hard framework inside an animal's body. Endoskeletons are usually made of bone, but in **cartilaginous fish**, such as sharks and rays, they are made of a flexible substance called **cartilage**.

A rabbit's endoskeleton

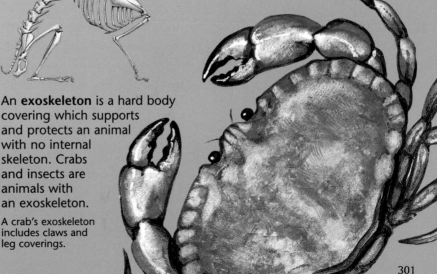

An **exoskeleton** is a hard body covering which supports and protects an animal with no internal skeleton. Crabs and insects are animals with an exoskeleton.

A crab's exoskeleton includes claws and leg coverings.

A **hydrostatic skeleton** is a system in which the fluid-filled body cavity provides pressure for muscles in the body wall to work against. Animals such as sea anemones, which have no hard framework for support, have hydrostatic skeletons.

A sea anemone's body is like a soft bag made up of two layers of tissue with a watery gel in between.

A sea anemone takes in water through its mouth. When the mouth shuts, its body becomes firm and solid, like a water-filled balloon.

Internet links

• Scan the code for a video clip about animal skeletons.

• For links to more websites about body structures, go to **www.usborne.com/quicklinks**

BODY COVERINGS

All creatures have an outer layer to enclose their bodies. Some animals have a layer of skin, covered with feathers or fur. Others have a hard covering of some kind. In some cases, this covering also provides support for the animal's body.

A pangolin's body is covered with thick, sharp-edged scales made of keratin. These stick out to defend it from enemies.

WATERPROOFING

Many soft-bodied animals have a waterproof outer layer called a **cuticle**, which is produced by the skin. In some animals, such as earthworms, the cuticle stays soft and waxy. In others, especially arthropods*, the cuticle hardens to form a supportive outer framework or exoskeleton*.

An arthropod's cuticle prevents its body from drying out. It is tough, but also light enough to allow flight, for example in insects. It is made up of sections called **sclerites**, joined by flexible membranes. This arrangement allows the creature to move freely.

The ridged sections on an ant's body are its sclerites.

Sclerite

See for yourself

Look at a woodlouse under a magnifying lens. As it moves around, notice its sclerites. If it is alarmed, it may curl its flexible body into a ball. After you have finished looking at it, return the animal to where you found it.

Woodlouse

NEW COATS

A lot of animals shed their coverings in order to grow. An arthropod sheds its cuticle when it grows too big for it, and a new, larger one forms. This process is called **ecdysis**.

Crustaceans, such as crabs, shed their hard, protective cuticle many times during their lifetime.

This crab's new hard covering, or **carapace**, is fully hardened.

Some animals have a carapace that is not made of cuticle, and is not shed. Turtles and tortoises, for instance, are born with a carapace inside their body. It is made of bony plates fused together and is covered with a layer of horny scales, which are part of the skin. The carapace is joined to the body at the ribs, spine, shoulders and hips and it grows in all directions with the animal.

Tortoise   Carapace

Snails and other molluscs have a protective **shell** covering the outside of the body, formed from a substance secreted by the animal's body. The shell grows with the animal and is not shed but, unlike a tortoise's carapace, a mollusc shell only grows at the lip (the opening).

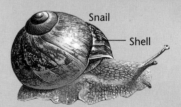

Snail

Shell

PROTECTIVE PLATES

Some animals are covered in hard plates called **scuta**. These can be made of horn, bone, or a substance called **chitin**. Scuta help to keep the animal safe from predators.

This armadillo's bony scuta are covered with horn.

* Arthropods, 342; Exoskeletons, 301.

PRICKLY PROTECTION

Some mammals, such as porcupines and hedgehogs, have prickly body coverings made of **keratin**. This is the main ingredient of your hair and nails. The animal uses its prickles for protection.

When threatened, this porcupine raises its prickles, called **quills**, as a warning. If attacked, it moves backwards, stabbing the predator with its quills.

SCALY CREATURES

Many animals have a mosaic of **scales** covering their bodies. Scales tend to be thinner than scuta, and are often made from different substances. Many reptiles, for example, have scales made from hardened skin. Scuta are usually horny or bony, and are heavier than scales.

A butterfly's wings are protected by tiny overlapping scales made of chitin. These loose, powdery scales are very fragile, and can rub off if touched. Underneath their scaly coverings, the wings are thin and transparent, like those of a fly.

Close-up of a butterfly's wing

You can see a butterfly's scales under an ordinary microscope.

Small tortoiseshell butterfly

FISH SCALES

There are two main types of fish scales: leptoid and placoid. **Leptoid scales** are small, bony plates embedded in the skin. They grow out of a tough lower layer of skin called the **dermis**, and are covered by a thinner, slimy layer called the **epidermis**. Most fish with bone skeletons have leptoid scales.

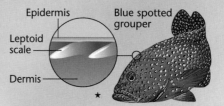

Epidermis

Blue spotted grouper

Leptoid scale

Dermis

Placoid scales, also called **denticles**, are sharp, backward-pointing scales, which stick out from the skin. Cartilaginous fish*, such as sharks and rays, have placoid scales.

Placoid scale

Great white shark

Epidermis

Dermis

Internet links

• Scan the code to watch a woodlouse curl into a ball.

• For links to more websites where you can see the body coverings of other animals, go to **www.usborne.com/quicklinks**

* Cartilaginous fish, 301.

MOVING IN WATER

Most animals are capable of moving from place to place at some stage during their lives. This is called **locomotion**. Many animals have particular body shapes or specialized body parts that help them to move around. For example, some creatures that live in water have flippers or fins.

The caudal fin (tail fin) propels the body forwards.

Anal fin. In some species, this is called the ventral fin.

A fish uses its fins to control balance and direction.

FALSE FEET

Some animal-like protists*, such as amoebas, do not have individual body parts for locomotion. Instead, they form extensions of their bodies called **pseudopodia** (meaning "false feet") which help them to move.

How an amoeba moves

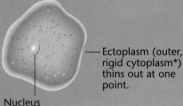

Ectoplasm (outer, rigid cytoplasm*) thins out at one point.

Nucleus

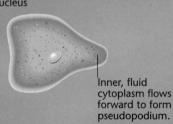

Inner, fluid cytoplasm flows forward to form pseudopodium.

Rest of organism flows forward.

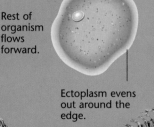

Ectoplasm evens out around the edge.

SIMPLE MOVEMENT

Many microscopic organisms are covered with tiny hairs called **cilia**. These flick back and forth like oars to "row" the creature through the water.

Rotifers, for example, are microscopic animal-like creatures that have a crown of cilia on the front. The movement of the cilia not only propels the rotifer through the water, but also creates a current that wafts food into its mouth.

Whirling "wheels" of cilia around the mouth area

Rotifer

All species of bristleworms have paired projections called **parapodia** along the sides of their bodies. These are used for swimming. Each parapodium ends in bristles called **chaetae**.

Ragworm (type of bristleworm)

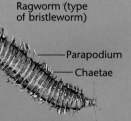

Parapodium

Chaetae

JET PROPELLED

Some animals, including squid, octopuses and jellyfish, move around by jet propulsion. Squid and octupuses do this by taking in water and forcing it out of their body through a funnel-shaped tube called a **hyponome**. The force of this water pushes the animal in the opposite direction.

Octopus

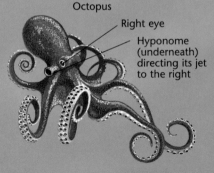

Right eye

Hyponome (underneath) directing its jet to the right

Jellyfish move by filling their bell-like bodies with water, then forcing it out. A jellyfish does this several times, moving itself up, and then drifts slowly down.

Jellyfish fills its hollow body with water.

Water is pushed out and the jellyfish moves.

Cytoplasm, 298; Protista, 341.

304

— Dorsal fin

The dorsal fin and anal fin control changes of direction from side to side, and prevent rolling.

Pectoral fin

Pelvic fin

FLIPPERS

Dolphin

Many animals, including some mammals and birds, are well suited to life in the water. They usually have a streamlined shape, and specialized body parts which allow them to swim. Animals such as dolphins, for example, have broad, paddle-like front limbs called **flippers**.

Penguins look clumsy on the land, but they are fantastic swimmers. Their flat, stiff wings are not suitable for flying, but are just the right shape to act as flippers in the water. A penguin can steer under water using its tail and webbed feet.

TYPES OF FINS

All fish have a number of projections called **fins**, which are used as stabilizers, and also to change direction. Fins are supported by fan-shaped **rays**. These are rods of bone or a tough, flexible substance called cartilage. Fish have two sets of fins: median and paired.

Median fins lie in a line down the middle of the fish's back or belly. They are divided into the **dorsal**, **caudal** (tail) and **anal** (or **ventral**) **fins**, shown in the picture above. **Paired fins** (**pectoral** and **pelvic**) stick out sideways from the body. They control movement up or down.

See for yourself

When you next see fish in a tank, look at how they use their pelvic fins. Many move them in a figure-of-eight shape. This helps them to swim very smoothly through the water.

POUCHES OF AIR

Some fish with bone skeletons have a long, air-filled pouch called a **swim bladder** inside their bodies. The fish can control the amount of air inside the bladder, so the density of its body can always be the same as that of the water. This means that the fish does not sink if it stops swimming.

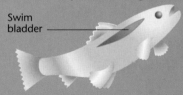

Swim bladder

Fish with cartilage skeletons, such as rays, do not have swim bladders. Their bodies are denser than the water, so they must control their position by other means.

Swimming manta ray

These penguins' streamlined bodies allow them to glide quickly and easily through the water.

Internet links

• Scan the code to watch a video clip about how animals move in water.

• For links to more websites about marine animals, go to **www.usborne.com/quicklinks**

FLYING AND GLIDING

Flying allows animals to escape from enemies on the ground, find new sources of food and, in some cases, travel long distances to find a partner. Only creatures with well-developed wings, such as bats, birds and insects, are able to fly, but some animals are able to glide for shorter distances.

This bat's leathery wings are made of skin, stretched over its arms and huge fingers.

Bats are the only mammals that can fly.

BIRDS AND FLIGHT

Birds that fly have many features to help them. These include smooth, light feathers, powerful wings and hollow bones.

BIRD BONES

Many birds have hollow bones, supported by thin, criss-cross structures. These make their bones strong as well as light.

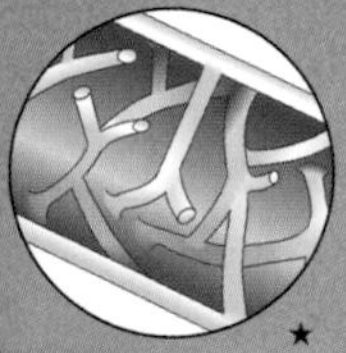

Cross section of a bird's bone

★

FLIGHT MUSCLES

A bird's wings are attached to a large extension of its breastbone called the **keel**. They are joined by two pairs of large **pectoralis muscles**. These are used to move the wings.

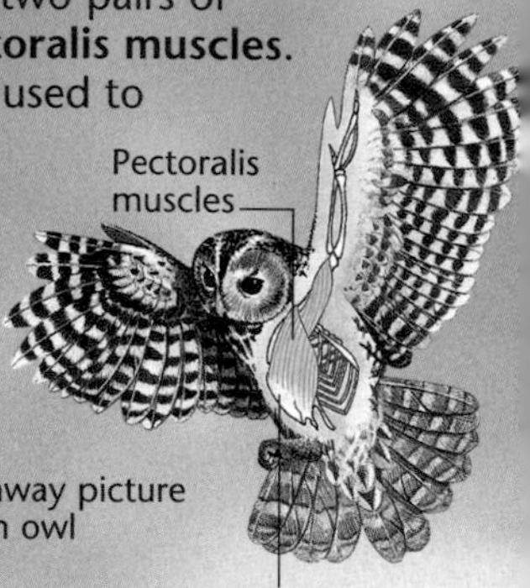

Pectoralis muscles

Cutaway picture of an owl

Keel

FEATHERS

A bird's body and wings are covered with **feathers**. Each one is made up of a central **shaft**, with rows of thread-like **barbs** on either side. Tiny, hooked **barbules** lock the barbs together, creating a flat surface called a **vane**.

Flight feathers

The wing can rotate freely at the shoulder, allowing a wide range of movement.

Structure of a feather

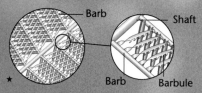

★ Barb — Shaft

Barb — Barbule

Contour feathers cover the bird's body, giving it a smooth and streamlined shape. **Flight feathers**, also called **remiges**, are long and stiff. They give the wing a large surface area, which is essential for flying.

Nerve endings at the base of each feather can detect tiny changes in air currents.

Contour feathers

Gull in flight

FLYING INSECTS

Like birds, insects have light bodies and powerful muscles for flying. However, an insect's body is very large in relation to its thin wings, so it needs much more power than a bird to fly. Energy is stored in the insect's muscles, and is released rapidly as it flies.

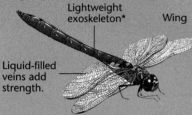

Dragonfly

Lightweight exoskeleton*

Wing

Liquid-filled veins add strength.

Some insects, such as dragonflies, use two pairs of wings to fly. Many insects only use one pair, the other being modified in some way. For example, a beetle's front wings, called **elytra**, form a hard, protective casing made of hardened cuticle* for its rear wings.

Cockchafer beetle

Protective wing cases (elytra)

GLIDERS

Several animals have "flying" as part of their name, but they have no wings, so they cannot actually fly. Instead, they use a variety of methods to glide through the air.

The colugo on the right, for example, has flaps of skin, called a **patagium**, between its front and hind legs. When it jumps, it spreads its limbs like wings. It moves its legs and tail to change direction as it glides from tree to tree.

A flying lizard stretches out its long ribs to form broad, stiff flaps on either side of its body. When the lizard is resting, these flaps fold away against its body.

A colugo gliding through the air

This flying lizard can glide up to 15m between trees.

Flying snakes live in rainforests. They climb trees and can glide up to 50m between branches. A flying snake does this by spreading out its ribcage, making its body into a flattened shape. As it glides, it twists its body through the air in S-shaped movements.

Flying snake

Internet links

• Scan the code to watch an owl flying in slow motion.

• For links to more websites where you can watch video clips of birds and other animals flying and gliding, go to **www.usborne.com/quicklinks**

See for yourself

Stroke a feather from top to bottom. It will become ruffled as its barbs unhook. If you stroke the feather in the opposite direction, the barbs will join together to make the feather perfectly smooth again.

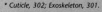

* Cuticle, 302; Exoskeleton, 301.

307

MOVING ON LAND

Animals that spend most or all of their lives on land are called **terrestrial animals**. They have many ways of moving around. Most of them use one or more pairs of legs to move. Animals without limbs, such as worms and snakes, move by changing the shapes of their muscular bodies.

As it climbs, a boomslang snake grips the branch with bony plates on its belly.

CRAWLING

Earthworms, and some other soft-bodied creatures, move using muscles in the body wall. Fluid in the body provides pressure for the muscles to work against. As they expand and contract, different parts of the body move forwards.

How an earthworm moves

The movement of the muscles looks like a wave rippling along the body.

A snake has ribs and powerful muscles along the whole length of its body. Most snakes move by stretching forward and pushing back in S-shaped curves. Bony scuta* (plates) on their bellies help them to grip.

CREEPING

Some caterpillars move by arching their bodies, then stretching forwards. Only one end of the body moves forwards at a time, while the legs at the other end grip the surface. This is called **looping**.

How a caterpillar loops

Back legs grip the stem, and front of body stretches forwards.

Front legs grip the stem, and back of body moves forwards. This pulls body into tight arch.

★

SWINGING

Many jungle-dwelling primates*, such as gibbons and orang-utans, can climb or swing using their long, strong front limbs and curved gripping fingers. Most primates can also grip well with their toes.

Some primates have a very flexible tail which can be used like an arm, to grip branches. A tail that can grip is called a **prehensile tail**.

A black-handed spider monkey's tail is strong enough to support its whole body.

A cheetah's claws grip the ground like spiked running shoes.

Powerful muscles and a flexible body help the cheetah to move fast.

USING LEGS

An animal's limbs are arranged symmetrically on either side of its body, and front limbs may look different from back limbs. Animals that walk upright on two legs, such as birds, are called **bipeds**. Most bipeds move one leg forwards with every step, but some birds hop on both legs.

Ostriches have extremely strong legs and they can run very fast.

A four-legged animal is called a **quadruped**. Typically, when walking, diagonally opposite legs move together, for example front left and rear right.

When running fast, most mammals stretch their front legs forwards and their hind legs backwards before bringing them together in powerful bounding movements.

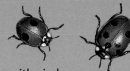

Creatures with six legs, such as insects, are called **hexapods**. When walking, one leg on one side of the body and two legs on the other side move forwards.

Circles show which of the ladybird's legs move together.

Many-legged creatures, called **myriapods**, can have up to 750 legs. These move in wave-like motions along the body.

LEAPING

Some creatures, such as frogs and fleas, can leap huge distances. They do this using powerful muscles in their back legs. Some other creatures, such as the springtail below, have different body parts which allow them to leap.

How a springtail leaps

Tail is folded under the body.

Tail is quickly flicked onto the ground.

Springtail is pushed into the air.

STANCE

Stance is the word which describes how an animal stands and moves. It is determined by the part of the foot on which the animal stands.

Unguligrade animals, such as horses, walk on hooves at the tips of the toes.

Digitigrade animals, such as dogs, walk on the undersides of the toes.

Plantigrade animals, such as bears, walk on the underside of the whole foot.

See for yourself

Look at different animals, and notice how many legs they have and what part of their feet they walk on. Also, do the animals move their legs differently when they are walking and running?

Internet links

- Scan the code to watch nature's fastest land animal, the cheetah.

- For links to more sites about how animals move, go to **www.usborne.com/quicklinks**

This Thompson's gazelle can run at up to 80 km/h (50mph).

FEEDING

The structure of an animal's mouthparts depends on the kind of food it eats. Teeth, and the part they play in feeding, are described on page 312. Toothless creatures, called **edentates**, often have a beak or a flexible tongue for capturing their food.

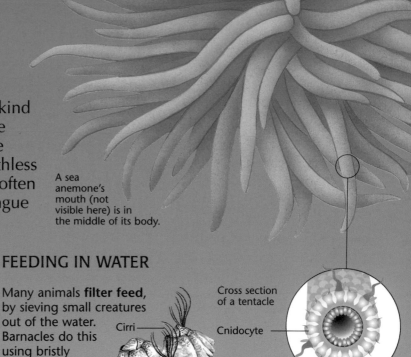

A sea anemone's mouth (not visible here) is in the middle of its body.

SIMPLE FEEDING

Animal-like protists*, such as amoebas, do not have mouths. Instead, they take in food by a process called **phagocytosis**. Their bodies flow around and engulf tiny food particles. The food is then digested in a chemical-filled area called a **vacuole**.

How an amoeba takes in food

Amoeba flows around food particle.

Particle is surrounded by amoeba.

Amoeba begins to break down particle.

FEEDING IN WATER

Many animals **filter feed**, by sieving small creatures out of the water. Barnacles do this using bristly limbs called **cirri**.

Cirri

Barnacles

Some whales feed using frayed plates of whalebone, called **baleen**, which hang down from their top jaw. Small animals called krill get caught in the baleen.

Baleen

Water and food in

Water out

Cross section of a tentacle

Cnidocyte

Thread shoots out.

Cnidarians*, such as sea anemones, have special cells called **cnidocytes** or **thread cells** on their tentacles. Each cnidocyte contains a bag of venom under pressure called a **cnidocyst**, with a long coiled thread inside. When prey is detected, the thread shoots out and the venom is injected into the prey to paralyse it. The tentacles then pull the prey into the animal's mouth.

SCRAPERS

Almost all molluscs*, such as snails, have a rough tongue called a **radula**. It is used like a file to scrape plant matter into the animal's mouth. If you listen closely to a feeding snail, you may hear its radula scraping.

Position of radula

Grey whale filtering water

* Cnidarians, Molluscs, 342; Protista, 341.

INSECT MOUTHPARTS

Insects' mouths are made up of a number of different parts: the mandibles, maxillae, labrum and labium. The appearance of these mouthparts varies from species to species.

A grasshopper's mouthparts

Hypopharynx (tongue) used for sucking up liquids. It is not visible here.

Labrum (upper lip) covers and protects other mouthparts.

Mandibles are used for holding or biting.

Maxillae usually help to push food into the mouth.

Palps are used to taste food.

Labium (lower lip) is also used to push food into the mouth.

The labium of a housefly is an extended pad-like sucking organ. The fly dissolves its food using saliva, then mops up the liquid with its spongy mouthparts.

Food is taken in through grooves in the fly's labium.

In some insects, the maxillae fit together to make a long tube called a **proboscis**. Female mosquitoes have a sharp, rigid proboscis for piercing skin. A butterfly has a flexible proboscis for sucking nectar from flowers.

Butterfly

Proboscis

BEAKS

A bird's hard upper and lower jaws come together to form a **beak** or **bill**. The shape and size of a bird's beak depend on the kind of food it eats.

Types of beak

A wood warbler's thin, sharp beak catches insects.

A kestrel's sharp, curved beak tears meat.

A honey-eater's long, thin beak probes flowers for nectar.

A greenfinch's strong, chunky beak cracks seeds.

A teal's flattish bill scoops up water plants.

A heron's long, sharp beak seizes fish.

Flamingos feed with their heads upside down in the water.

The flamingo's beak acts like a scoop, taking in water, mud and tiny plants and animals.

Cross section of a flamingo's mouthparts

Spikes for capturing food

Spikes on tongue scrape food off beak.

Flamingos have unusual beaks and tongues for sieving food. They feed by raking their beaks through the mud at the bottom of lakes. Tiny plants and animals stick to small spikes on the inside of the beak. The flamingo scrapes the food off its beak using larger spikes on its tongue.

Internet links

- Scan the code to watch a butterfly feeding on flowers with its long proboscis.

- For links to more websites, go to **www.usborne.com/quicklinks**

311

TEETH AND DIGESTION

Many animals have **teeth** to tear, chew or grind their food. Animals with teeth are described as **dentate**. After it is swallowed, an animal's food is broken down further by the **digestive system**, so it can be absorbed by the body. Animals have different sorts of teeth and digestive systems depending on the type of food they eat.

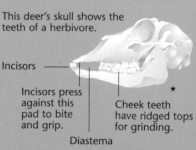

Like many plant eaters, a giraffe has flat, ridged teeth for grinding plants.

MEAT EATERS

Meat-eating animals, called **carnivores**, have sharp teeth for tearing meat. Dagger-like **canines** are used for piercing and killing prey. The large, jagged **carnassials** are used for slicing meat. Smaller front teeth called **incisors** come together to bite or scrape meat from bones.

Sharks' teeth grow in rows in their jaws. When they lose a tooth from the front set, another moves forwards to take its place. Almost all mammals have two sets of teeth during their lifetimes. The second set, called **permanent teeth**, cannot be replaced if lost.

This picture of a lioness shows the teeth of a carnivore.

PLANT EATERS

Plant-eating animals, called **herbivores**, have square cheek teeth (**premolars** and **molars**), for grinding plants. The incisors are long and chisel-shaped. In ruminants, such as cows and deer, these grip plants against a hard pad in the top jaw. A gap called the **diastema**, between the incisors and cheek teeth, allows space to move the tongue.

This deer's skull shows the teeth of a herbivore.

Incisors

Incisors press against this pad to bite and grip.

Cheek teeth have ridged tops for grinding.

Diastema

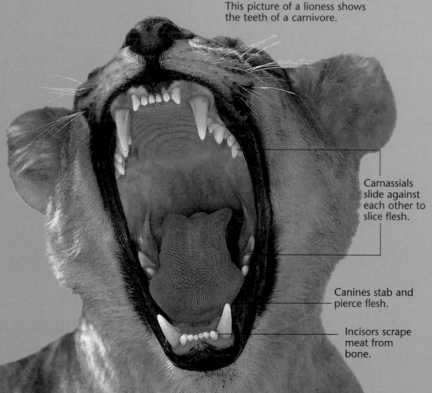

Carnassials slide against each other to slice flesh.

Canines stab and pierce flesh.

Incisors scrape meat from bone.

ALL-PURPOSE TEETH

Animals that eat both plants and meat are called **omnivores**. An omnivore's teeth can be many different shapes and sizes, depending on the kind of food it eats. For instance, a monkey has long canines to pierce flesh, and flat back teeth to grind plants.

This monkey's skull shows an omnivore's varied types of teeth.

DIGESTING PLANTS

Plants contain a tough substance called **cellulose**, which is hard to digest. Herbivores therefore have more complex digestive organs than other animals. Most herbivores have a sac inside their body called a **caecum**, in which plant matter is broken down by bacteria*.

Position of caecum in rabbit

Ruminants, such as cows, sheep and deer, have four stomach-like chambers to digest their food: the rumen, reticulum, omasum and abomasum.

Digestive system of a cow

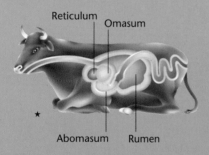

Reticulum
Omasum
Abomasum
Rumen

First, food passes unchewed into the **rumen**. There, bacteria start to break down cellulose. The partially-digested food is processed in the second chamber, or **reticulum**. It is then returned to the mouth to be re-chewed. Food at this stage is called the **cud**.

After chewing, the food is swallowed for a second time, and then broken down further in the remaining chambers, the **omasum** and the **abomasum** (true stomach).

* Bacteria, 341.

DIGESTION IN BIRDS

Birds have no teeth to break up their food, so they have a digestive system specially designed to deal with solids.

After food has been swallowed, it is stored in a thin-walled pouch called the **crop**. It then travels to a thick, muscular-walled pouch called the **gizzard**. Here, the food is ground up by muscular ridges on the gizzard walls and small stones which the bird has swallowed.

Crop
Gizzard

Waste is stored in a chamber called the **cloaca**, before being passed out of the bird's body.

Meat-eating birds, such as owls and hawks, swallow their prey whole. The parts which cannot be digested, such as bones and fur, form a compact **pellet** inside the bird's stomach. This is coughed back up and brought out through the mouth.

This pellet came from a barn owl. An owl pellet may contain the skeletons of several small animals.

Bone

4-6cm

Owls eat small animals, such as frogs and mice, in one piece.

See for yourself

Next time you are in a wooded area, look for bird pellets. Use a stick to turn them over, and see what they are made up of. You are most likely to find pellets under trees and other places where birds roost. You can use a magnifying glass to look closely, but never touch a pellet with your hands.

Bone from inside a pellet

Internet links

• Scan the code to try a quiz about animal teeth.

• For links to more websites about carnivores and herbivores, go to **www.usborne.com/quicklinks**

313

BREATHING

You can see this shark's gill slits behind its head.

Animals breathe in oxygen from air or water. They use it to release energy from digested food, breathing out carbon dioxide as a waste product. The process by which gases pass in and out of the body is known as **gaseous exchange**. This takes place in the **respiratory organs**. Gases travel to and from these organs in the blood.

BREATHING IN WATER

Most water-dwelling animals take in oxygen through organs called **gills** or **branchiae**. There are two types of gills – internal and external.

Internal gills are found inside the bodies of many water creatures, especially fish. Most fish have four pairs of gills, with openings called **gill slits** between them. In bony fish, the gills are covered by a bony flap called the **operculum**. In cartilaginous fish*, they are open to the water at all times.

The water which washes over the gills comes in through a fish's mouth, and is pumped out through the gill slits. Each gill is made up of a curved rod called the **gill bar** or **gill arch**, which has many fine gill **filaments** radiating from it.

Each gill filament has even finer **gill lamellae** branching off it, like the branches of a feather. These all contain blood vessels. Oxygen is taken into the blood from the water, and carbon dioxide from the blood passes out to be washed away.

Many other water creatures, such as caddisfly larvae and tadpoles, have **external gills**. These are on the outside of the body. Their exact form depends on the type of animal, but in many cases they are frilly growths behind the head.

Tadpole

Gills

Some simple water creatures have tubes called **siphons**. These carry gases, which are dissolved in water, to and from their gills. A siphon that carries gases to the gills is described as **inhalant**, and one that carries them from the gills is described as **exhalant**.

Breathing with gills

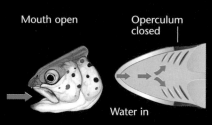

Mouth open

Operculum closed

Water in

Mouth closes, operculum opens.

Water forced through gill slits (washing over gill filaments).

*

Water forced out between operculum and body wall.

Operculum has been removed to show four gills.

Gill rakers filter out tiny creatures from the water. Not all species have them.

Gill bar

Gill slit

Gill filament

Gill lamellae

Cutaway diagram of a whelk

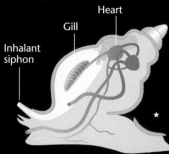

Heart

Gill

Inhalant siphon

* Cartilaginous fish, 301.

AMPHIBIANS

Amphibians* can spend time both in water and on land, and take oxygen from water or air. A frog, for instance, does this in a variety of ways. In water, dissolved oxygen passes in through its skin to the blood vessels beneath, and carbon dioxide passes out the same way.

On land, a frog breathes using a pair of light sacs called lungs. Gaseous exchange through the blood vessels inside these lungs works in the same way as in other vertebrate* lungs (see right). They are less efficient, however, because the frog uses a lot of energy actively pumping the gases in and out. So even on land, much gaseous exchange still happens through the skin.

The frog is also able to exchange gases directly through blood vessels in the lining of its mouth.

This frog's skin gleams with natural moisture. Gases dissolve in the moisture and are exchanged through the skin.

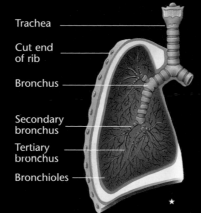

LUNGS

All reptiles, birds and mammals have a pair of **lungs** for exchanging gases. Their breathing is automatic and effortless. Air flows in and out of the lungs through a tube called the **trachea** or **windpipe**. This splits into two thick tubes, each one called a **bronchus**, which in turn branch into smaller **secondary** and **tertiary bronchi** inside the lung.

Tertiary bronchi branch into tiny tubes called **bronchioles**. Each bronchiole ends in a small sac called an **alveolus**. Gases are exchanged through tiny blood vessels on the surface of each alveolus.

Diagram of a mammal's lung

Trachea

Cut end of rib

Bronchus

Secondary bronchus

Tertiary bronchus

Bronchioles

HOW INSECTS BREATHE

Gaseous exchange in insects takes place through small holes called **spiracles** in their bodies. Air enters the spiracles, and travels through a network of pipes called **tracheae**. These branch into tiny tubes called **tracheoles**, which carry gases to and from cells in the body.

Respiratory system of a flea

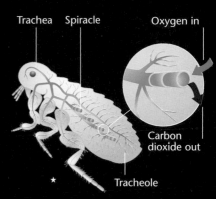

Trachea   Spiracle   Oxygen in

Carbon dioxide out

Tracheole

See for yourself

Certain large, active insects need a way of taking in extra oxygen. They do this by opening their spiracles and pumping their abdomen in and out. You may see a grasshopper or a large moth doing this when it is resting.

Internet links

• Scan the code to watch a video about how insects breathe.

• For links to more websites about how animals breathe, go to **www.usborne.com/quicklinks**

* Amphibians, 342; Vertebrates, 322.

315

INTERNAL BALANCE

In order to stay alive, an animal's temperature must remain within certain limits, and substances in its body, such as salts and water, need to be kept at the right level. Keeping the body and the chemicals inside it in a balanced state is called **homeostasis**. Solid and liquid waste must also be removed. The parts of the body that deal with this are known as the **excretory organs**. In most animals, they include the lungs, skin, liver and kidneys.

BODY TEMPERATURE

An animal cannot survive for long if it is too hot or too cold, because its organs cannot work efficiently. Keeping the body at the right temperature is called **thermoregulation**. The animal's skin and blood usually play an important part in this.

Mammals and birds can keep their body at the same internal temperature in most conditions. They are described as **warm-blooded**. All other animals are **cold-blooded**. This means that their body temperature is not under their internal control, and it changes with the temperature of their surroundings.

WARMING UP

When a warm-blooded animal needs extra heat, its feathers or hairs stand on end. These act like a blanket, trapping warm air next to its skin. The animal may also begin to shiver, which produces heat. Both of these actions happen automatically when an animal's body temperature becomes too low.

Cold-blooded creatures, though, have no way of using their bodies to keep warm. If their temperature is too low, they must bask in the Sun to raise it again.

These young owls have fluffy down feathers, which trap heat next to their bodies.

COOLING DOWN

Cold-blooded animals must find shade or water to cool their bodies. Warm-blooded animals can cool down in other ways. For example, some sweat when they are too hot. The evaporation of moisture from their skin cools them down. A hairy animal that is unable to sweat may pant instead. It loses moisture and heat from the tongue's surface and in air it breathes out. Many desert mammals, like this fennec fox, lose heat through the lining of their huge ears.

Fennec fox

Like all reptiles, green anoles are cold-blooded. They keep warm by sunning themselves.

WATER BALANCE

All creatures need to keep the amount of water in their bodies at the right level, or their organs will not work properly.

Animal-like protists*, such as *Paramecium*, do this using a tiny sac in their bodies called a **contractile vacuole**.

Paramecium

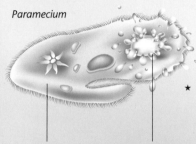

Contractile vacuole expands as it fills with water.

At intervals, the vacuole expels its contents.

Birds have large, efficient kidneys, but no bladder. They excrete a solid waste called uric acid.

LIVER AND KIDNEYS

In many animals, most waste is removed from the body by the liver and kidneys. The **liver** breaks down amino acids from food, to produce a substance called **urea**. This is mixed with blood and taken to the **kidneys**. These filter the blood, removing the urea, along with water and harmful salts, which form a liquid called **urine**. This is stored in a sac-like organ called the **bladder**, which is emptied regularly.

Diagram of kidneys and bladder

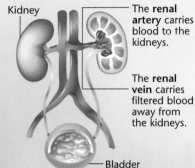

Kidney

The **renal artery** carries blood to the kidneys.

The **renal vein** carries filtered blood away from the kidneys.

Bladder

WASTE TUBES

Arthropods* do not have kidneys or a liver. Instead, they have tubes called **malpighian tubules**. These remove liquid waste from the body cavity (haemocoel*). The waste is turned into solid **uric acid** in the gut. Any water is reabsorbed into the blood. The uric acid leaves the body.

Excretory system of a spider

Malpighian tubules

Gut

Body cavity

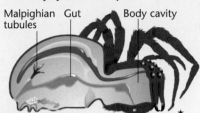

Some soft-bodied creatures, such as simple worms, have waste tubes called **protonephridia**. Waste enters these through hollow **flame cells** and leaves the body through tiny holes called **nephridiopores**.

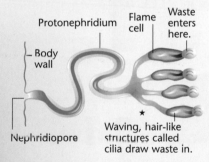

Protonephridium

Flame cell

Waste enters here.

Body wall

Nephridiopore

Waving, hair-like structures called cilia draw waste in.

Internet links

• Scan the code to see reptiles warming up on rocks.

• For links to more websites about homeostasis, go to **www.usborne.com/quicklinks**

SENDING MESSAGES

The process of giving information that another creature can understand is called **communication**. Animals communicate with each other in many ways, using colours, sounds, movements and chemicals. Most of their messages are connected with finding a mate or giving a warning to other animals.

A skunk growls, stamps its feet and raises its tail to warn enemies to leave it alone, or it will spray a smelly liquid at them.

COLOUR CODING

Many animals respond to particular patterns or colours. A male European robin, for example, will become aggressive when a rival shows its red breast near its territory. A display like this that triggers a certain response is called a **sign stimulus**.

European robin displaying red breast

Creatures which are foul-tasting, poisonous, or have a painful sting or bite, often have brightly coloured bodies. Predators quickly learn to avoid any animals with these bright colours.

This cinnabar caterpillar's black and yellow stripes warn that it is poisonous.

A male frigate bird's throat sac is usually orange, but during the mating season it turns red and can be puffed out.

The frigate bird sits on a nest of sticks as he displays. If a female is interested, she offers him more sticks.

Some harmless animals have similar colours to poisonous ones. Predators think that these animals are dangerous and leave them alone. This copy-cat colouration is called **mimicry**.

Swallowtail butterfly

African monarch butterfly

Birds will not eat the non-poisonous swallowtail, because they mistake it for the poisonous African monarch.

Animals often display coloured body parts to attract a mate. For instance, a male frigate bird inflates his bright red throat sac to attract females. He also snaps his bill and holds his body in different poses.

The males of many other bird species, such as peacocks, develop fantastic plumage during the mating season. They raise their feathers and shiver them in a dazzling display.

BODY LANGUAGE

Many animals, especially those that live in groups, give out messages by the way they move or hold their bodies. Bees, for example, move in particular patterns, or **dances**, to show where food can be found. A dance can tell the other bees about the quality of the food, and where to find it.

The waggle dance of a bee

The bee follows a figure-of-eight path, waggling its abdomen in the middle of the pattern.

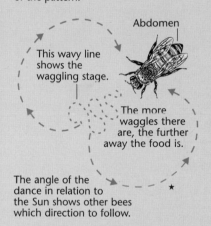

Abdomen

This wavy line shows the waggling stage.

The more waggles there are, the further away the food is.

The angle of the dance in relation to the Sun shows other bees which direction to follow.

MAKING NOISES

Most animals use sounds to communicate a wide variety of messages. Sounds can be produced using different parts of the body.

When you hear a bird sing, it may be trying to attract a mate, or warning other birds not to come near its territory. The bird sings using a part of its windpipe called the **syrinx**.

Position of syrinx

Some insects, such as locusts, make sounds by **stridulation**. The insect rubs together two body parts, usually the legs and wings, to make a shrill chirp or whine. The noise attracts females.

A grasshopper rubs tiny pegs on its legs against its wings to make a noise.

A female moth can release scent (pheromones) into the air.

A male moth can detect minute traces of the female's scent from over a mile away.

CHEMICAL MESSAGES

Many animals communicate by releasing chemicals called **pheromones** into the air. Some insects, for example, release incredibly powerful pheromones to attract a mate.

A number of male animals spray urine, or release other chemicals from glands on their bodies, to mark their territory. Other animals recognize these smelly areas as belonging to that male, and stay well away.

ORDER OF IMPORTANCE

Animals that live in groups are called **social** animals. In some social species, such as wolves, body language is used to show the importance of each animal. A more powerful wolf, called a **dominant** wolf, nips weaker wolves, called **subordinates**, on the neck. This shows that he is more important.

Wolf at the top of the pack

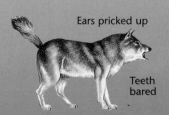

Ears pricked up

Teeth bared

Tail and body held straight

Wolf at the bottom of the pack

Ears flat against head

Crouched body

Tail tucked under body

Internet links

• Scan the code to watch a worker bee's waggle dance.

• For links to more websites about how animals communicate, go to **www.usborne.com/quicklinks**

ANIMAL SENSES

All animals need **senses**, that is, they must be able to take in information from around them and to respond. Sensitive cells called **receptors**, found on or just under the surface of an animal's body, collect this information and send messages to its brain. There, the messages are turned into **sensations**, such as sights and sounds.

Most bats have small eyes, but large, sensitive ears.

HEARING

Most land animals hear by detecting air movements called **sound waves**. These hit a thin surface called the **tympanum**, which vibrates. Tiny bones pass the vibrations on inside, and messages are sent to the brain. In many animals, a channel, and often an outer body part, leads the sound waves into the body. In these cases, the whole thing is called an **ear**, and the tympanum is called the **eardrum**.

A mammal's ear

Sound waves travel into the outer ear (called the **pinna**).

Eardrum vibrates.

Nerve sends impulse to the brain.

Tiny bones called **ossicles** pass on vibrations.

See for yourself

Stretch some plastic film tightly across the top of a tube, such as a cardboard tube from inside a roll of kitchen paper, and put a few grains of rice on it. Ask someone to clap beneath the tube. See how the air vibrations move the film, which moves the rice. This is how sound waves move the eardrum and ossicles.

Some animals have a simpler structure, with the tympanum on the body surface, and a less complex system inside. This is then usually called a **tympanal organ**. In some animals, such as frogs, the tympanal organ is on the head, but others, such as crickets, have them on their legs.

Position of frog's tympanal organ

Echo location

describes the way that some animals detect the size and position of objects around them. Bats, for example, give out very high-pitched sounds as they fly. The sound waves bounce off nearby objects, and return to the bat. These echoes help bats to avoid obstacles, and to find food in the dark.

Bat sends out high-pitched sounds (shown in blue).

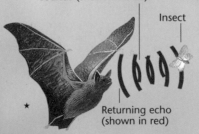

Insect

Returning echo (shown in red)

BALANCE

In many species, the brain keeps the body balanced using information from sensitive cells in the ears along with messages from the eyes. Some creatures, though, have specialized body parts which help them to balance.

Jellyfish, for example, have sac-like organs of balance called **statocysts**. These contain tiny grains called **statoliths** which move around as the animal swims. The grains touch sensitive cells, which tell the animal which way up its body is.

Floating jellyfish

Flies have small, modified back wings called **halteres**. These are used to keep the animal's body balanced as it flies.

Haltere

SIGHT

Many animals have eyes. These are the organs which allow them to see their surroundings. Eyes contain sensors called **photoreceptors**, which detect light.

Insects and some other creatures, such as crabs, have **compound eyes**. Each eye is made up of hundreds of tiny lenses. Each lens sees an individual image. The animal's brain puts together this information to make a complete **mosaic image**.

Compound eye

Mosaic image of flower as seen by an ★ insect

Many animals' eyes have a slit in the middle called a **pupil**. This expands and contracts to let in different amounts of light. Animals which are active at night, called **nocturnal** animals, have large eyes, with pupils that can open very wide to let in as much light as possible.

Cat's eyes in bright light

Cat's eyes in dim light ★

Nocturnal animals and some deep-sea fish have a shiny layer at the back of their eyes called a **tapetum**. This acts like a mirror, collecting whatever light is available. When you see a cat's eyes shining in the dark, light is reflecting off its tapetum.

EYE POSITION

The area that an animal can see is called its **field of vision**. It depends on the position of the animal's eyes. Most plant-eating animals, for instance, have eyes on the sides of their head. This helps them to look out for predators while they are grazing. This kind of vision is called **lateral vision**.

This suslik can watch all around for predators.

Predators and tree-dwelling animals have eyes on the front of their head, which gives them **binocular vision**. This allows them to focus on objects in the distance, such as their prey.

Monkeys, apes and humans also have **stereoscopic vision**. Each eye views things from a slightly different angle. The brain joins the two views to form a 3D image.

The position of this orang-utan's eyes help it to judge distances when swinging from tree to tree.

See for yourself

You can do a simple test to show that humans have stereoscopic vision. Hold both hands at arm's length, with the index fingers extended and pointing towards each other. Close one eye and try to bring your two fingertips together. You will find this is harder to do without both eyes open.

Internet links

• Scan the code to see how a bat uses echolocation to hunt.

• For links to more websites where you can investigate amazing animal senses, go to **www.usborne.com/quicklinks**

TOUCH

The sense of touch can help an animal to find its way around, or to bond with other members of its species. For example, some animals groom each other, or rub their body parts together.

Sensors called **tactile receptors** allow an animal to detect touch. Animals with backbones, called **vertebrates**, usually have tactile receptors covering most of their bodies. Animals without backbones, called **invertebrates**, only have them on particular parts.

TENTACLES

Tentacles are long, flexible structures found in many molluscs, such as snails, and some sea creatures. In most cases, the animal uses its tentacles to grasp food and feel its way around.

WHISKERS

Most mammals, such as cats and mice, have long, stiff hairs, called **whiskers** or **vibrissae**, on their faces. These are very sensitive to touch.

Nerve endings at the base of this hamster's whiskers can detect the slightest movement.

ANTENNAE

Many animals, such as insects and crustaceans (crabs and related creatures), have whip-like, jointed structures called **antennae** or **feelers** on their heads.

Antennae help an animal identify smells and tastes. They can detect changes in air currents, and the texture of a surface. Some animals, such as barnacles, use antennae to attach themselves to something. Others may use them for swimming.

SENSITIVE BRISTLES

The hard body covering of most invertebrates, such as insects, is not very sensitive. For this reason, many invertebrates have bristles called **setae** which stick out of their bodies. At the base of each seta is a nerve which responds to vibrations or air movement.

A longhorn beetle's large antennae are jointed and very flexible.

An octopus has eight sensitive tentacles.

This beetle's body has a covering of tiny, sensitive hairs (setae).

SMELL AND TASTE

Organs used for smelling and tasting contain sensors called **chemoreceptors**. These are usually in an animal's mouth, but can also be found on other parts of the body.

Some fish, for example, have taste and smell sensors all over their bodies. Many insects, though, have chemoreceptors only in certain places, such as on the ends of their legs. These allow the insects to taste their food simply by walking on it.

Sensors on the feet of this fly let it taste the substance it is walking over and help it to decide whether or not to eat it.

Many arthropods* also have feeler-like organs, called **palps**, formed from their mouthparts. Palps contain chemoreceptors which allow the animal to smell and taste. Some touch-sensitive organs are also called palps.

See for yourself

The senses of smell and taste often work together. This is why you may find it hard to taste food when you have a cold and your nose is blocked. Try pinching your nose while eating something, and see how well your sense of taste works.

A snake brings scents and tastes into its mouth by flicking its tongue out and in. Two pits called the **Jacobson's organ** in the roof of its mouth can identify these scents and tastes. This helps the snake to track prey. In addition, some snakes have a **pit organ** on their head, which can detect their prey's body heat from a distance.

Coral snake flicking its tongue out and in to taste the air

OTHER SENSES

Fish and some amphibians* have two tube-like channels in their bodies called **lateral lines**. These lie along the sides of the body, just under the skin, and are filled with water. Lateral lines detect currents and pressure changes in the water caused by other animals.

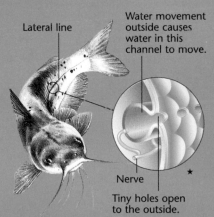

Lateral line

Water movement outside causes water in this channel to move.

Nerve

Tiny holes open to the outside.

A shark can detect electrical pulses given off by creatures nearby. It does this using small chambers called **ampullae of Lorenzi** in its head. Sensitive hairs in these chambers connect to nerve cells which detect electricity. This sense is called **electroreception**.

Scientists are not certain what senses help a bird to migrate*, but they have many theories. It is possible that birds can sense the Earth's magnetic field and use it as a guide.

Arctic terns use many senses to find their way to the Antarctic and back.

Internet links

- Scan the code to zoom in on a fly's feet and eyes.

- For links to more websites about unusual animal senses, go to **www.usborne.com/quicklinks**

* Amphibians, 315, 342; Arthropods, 342; Migration, 329.

CREATING NEW LIFE

Every living thing can create more of its own kind. This process is called **reproduction**. Most animals pair up to do this, in couples made up of one male and one female partner. Simple creatures, though, can **clone**, or copy, their own bodies, without needing a partner. This is called **asexual reproduction**.

This sea anemone is splitting into two. Each half will become a new anemone.

SPLITTING

Some sea anemones, such as snakelocks anemones, reproduce asexually by dividing into identical halves. This is called **binary fission**.

Some parasites*, such as liver flukes reproduce many times by constantly splitting. This is called **multiple fission**. In this way, large numbers of new individuals, called **daughter cells**, are produced in a short time.

Colonial animals, such as corals, remain joined to their parent after asexual reproduction has taken place. This is known as **incomplete fission**.

This coral reef is built up of many individual corals joined together.

BUDDING

Some simple animals, such as hydras, reproduce by forming growths or **buds** from their bodies. This is called **budding**. Each bud eventually breaks off and becomes a new individual.

Budding in a hydra

Bud forms.

Bud grows and develops.

Bud breaks away.

BREAKING DOWN

A small number of animals can produce new individuals from parts of their bodies, if their bodies are damaged or parts are lost. This is called **fragmentation**

Fragmentation in a bootlace worm

1.

2.

When a bootlace worm becomes fragmented, each piece can become a new worm.

BUILDING UP

Some creatures, such as starfish, sea cucumbers and certain lizards, can re-grow parts of their body which have broken off. This is called **regeneration**.

Starfish

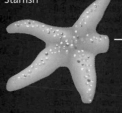

If an arm is broken off, a new one will grow to replace it.

MALE AND FEMALE

A result of asexual reproduction is that any weaknesses in the parent are always passed to the young. **Sexual reproduction***, by contrast, involves joining the sex cells of a male and a female. The young then inherit features, called **traits**, from both parents.

In most species, males and females are separate. However, some creatures, such as snails and earthworms, have both male and female sex cells in their bodies. These creatures are called **hermaphrodites**.

Snail with eggs

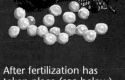

After fertilization has taken place (see below), a snail lays eggs which it buries in a hole.

The joining of male and female sex cells is called **fertilization**. Hermaphrodites generally do not fertilize themselves, but swap male sex cells to fertilize each other. The young inherit traits from both parents.

See for yourself

When two earthworms swap sex cells, a saddle-like body part called the **clitellum** makes a sticky substance which holds their bodies together. Next time you see a worm, look for its clitellum.

Clitellum

Earthworm

SEXUAL AND ASEXUAL

Tiny insects called aphids have a reproductive cycle which has both sexual and asexual stages.

During the warm spring and summer months, there is plenty of food to eat. The female aphids reproduce asexually. They produce many live female young, and later live male young. These all grow from the sex cells inside the females' bodies, without being fertilized by male sex cells. This is called **parthenogenesis**.

When the summer is over, the aphids reproduce sexually. After fertilization, the females lay eggs, from which new females hatch the following spring.

In a colony of bees, only the queen produces young. She reproduces sexually, receiving sex cells from the males and laying fertilized eggs. These develop into females called **workers**. The queen also lays eggs that have not been fertilized. These develop into males called **drones**.

Drone (male) Queen bee Worker (female)

Aphids on a flower

During the spring and summer, the number of aphids increases rapidly.

Internet links

• Scan the code to watch a video clip about reproduction.

• For links to more websites about creating new life, go to **www.usborne.com/quicklinks**

* Parasites, 343; Sexual reproduction, 326-327.

SEXUAL REPRODUCTION

Most animals pair up or **mate** with another member of their species to produce young. A male and a female come together in a process called **sexual reproduction**. A single sex cell from the male fertilizes a sex cell from the female to create a new individual.

FINDING A PARTNER

Many animals use sound, scents called pheromones*, visual displays (see page 318) or other devices to attract a mate. Once together, the two may go through a **courtship ritual** of some kind before mating. Usually, the male displays to the female, trying to impress her. In some species, especially certain types of birds, the two may "dance", or perform, together.

In most species, the male leaves the female after mating, but some pairs stay together for many years, producing new young each year.

FERTILIZATION

Fertilization takes place when a male sex cell, called a **sperm**, joins with a female sex cell, called an **ovum**. Each ovum can only be fertilized by one sperm. This creates the first cell of a new organism. As it grows, it is called an **embryo**.

A female frog lays many soft eggs.

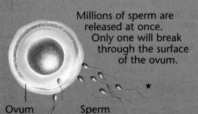

Millions of sperm are released at once. Only one will break through the surface of the ovum.

Ovum   Sperm

External fertilization takes place mostly in water-dwelling animals, such as fish and amphibians*. The female lays many eggs containing her ova, and then the male fertilizes them by covering them with sperm. The closer he is to the eggs, the more likely it is that his sperm will fertilize them. A male frog, for example, grasps the female's body and deposits sperm on the eggs as she lays them.

Internal fertilization takes place inside the female's body. Almost all land animals, such as mammals, are fertilized in this way. The male puts his sperm directly into the female's body, usually through a specialized organ called a **penis**.

A pair of swans will stay together for life.

*Amphibians, 315, 342; Pheromones, 319.

LAYING EGGS

Egg-laying animals are described as **oviparous**. Most reptiles, insects, birds and fish are oviparous. The eggs may be fertilized externally or they may result from internal fertilization. There are two main types of eggs.

Most fish and amphibians, such as the frog on the left, produce hundreds of tiny, soft eggs, called **spawn**. These often contain young which do not look like the adults at all.

The tiny black dots in this frogspawn are the developing young.

Most land animals, such as birds and reptiles, produce a smaller number of **cleidoic eggs**. In these, the embryo is fed by a food store called a **yolk** and protected by a hard shell. When the eggs hatch, the young are usually miniature versions of the adults.

A cleidoic egg

The **albumen** provides the embryo with protein and water.

Twisted strands of albumen hold the yolk in place.

Yolk

Bird embryo

★

Gases are exchanged through the shell and air space.

Carbon dioxide out

Oxygen in

GIVING BIRTH

Animals that give birth to live young are described as **viviparous**. Many animals of this kind are mammals. The baby grows inside the female in a sac called the **womb** or **uterus**. An organ called the **placenta** feeds the baby inside the womb. After a period of time, muscles in the female's body contract and the baby is pushed out.

The length of time a baby spends inside the womb is called the **gestation period**. It varies from species to species.

After giving birth, most mammals, such as this zebra, lick their young clean.

ANIMAL FAMILIES

Many baby animals are born helpless, and depend entirely on their mother to protect and feed them. A mammal feeds her young with milk from her **mammary glands**. The babies drink milk, or **suckle**, until they are old enough to eat solid food.

A gorilla gives birth to one baby every few years. The baby suckles until it is about three or four years old.

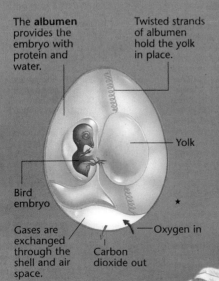

Almost all birds and some reptiles also feed and protect their young after they are born. In some species, both parents share these duties.

A female emperor penguin protects her chick while the male feeds at sea.

When the male returns, both parents take turns to feed and protect the chick.

See for yourself

In the springtime, look in ponds for clumps of frogspawn. Although there may seem to be lots of eggs, many of the young will be eaten by predators after they hatch. Very few will survive to become adult frogs.

Internet links

- Scan the code to watch a video clip about animal mothers and their offspring.

- For links to more websites about animal babies, go to **www.usborne.com/quicklinks**

LIFE CYCLES

Many changes take place between the beginning and end of an animal's life: it grows, develops, and produces young. These patterns of growth and behaviour are called a **life cycle**. Some animal life cycles take many years to complete. Many insects, by contrast, complete their life cycle in a few months.

Life cycle of a locust (incomplete metamorphosis)

Female lays eggs, which hatch into nymphs.

Locust is now fully grown.

Locust nymph, called a **hopper**

Hopper sheds its skin several times.

METAMORPHOSIS

Some animals, such as insects and frogs, change their form completely in the course of their life cycle. This is called **metamorphosis**. There are two kinds of metamorphosis: complete and incomplete. In **complete metamorphosis**, the young form looks very different from the adult form.

Insects such as butterflies, moths and ladybirds undergo complete metamorphosis. Their young, called **larvae**, feed and grow, then develop hard cases called **pupae**. Inside the pupae, they change into adults.

Life cycle of a butterfly

Eggs

Larva, called **caterpillar**

Pupa

Adult emerges from pupa.

Other insects, such as the locust above, go through **incomplete metamorphosis**. This means that the young, called **nymphs**, look similar to their parents, although some body parts, such as their wings, are not yet formed. Nymphs shed their skins several times as they become larger. As they grow, their wings and reproductive organs develop.

The adult form of an insect that has gone through either complete or incomplete metamorphosis is known as the **imago**.

Life cycle of a frog (complete metamorphosis)

Female lays eggs called spawn in water.

Eggs hatch into **tadpoles**.

Back legs and lungs develop.

Front legs grow, tail will disappear.

Young frog leaves water and grows to full size.

Complete metamorphosis often provides a form in which the animal can survive the winter. The young usually live in different habitats and have different diets from the adults, so they do not compete for food or space.

See for yourself

If you are able to find any frogspawn in a pond during the springtime, go back and look at the tadpoles every week after they hatch. After about eight weeks, you will notice their tiny legs starting to develop.

Migrating wildebeest crossing a river

These Canada geese, like almost all geese, migrate to their breeding grounds every year.

MAKING A JOURNEY

At some stage in their life cycles, many animals travel long distances, often to breed or find food. This journey is called **migration**.

Many birds migrate twice every year (to their breeding or feeding grounds and back). They use the position of the Sun, stars and features of the land to find their way. Many land animals, such as wildebeest, move with the seasons to find food. They may have to overcome obstacles, such as rivers.

MIGRATION IN WATER

Some animals, such as salmon and eels, may only migrate once in their lifetime. The journey is long and hard, and few fish survive to breed again.

Life cycle of a salmon

Salmon travel upstream to breed. They swim from the sea to the rivers where they were hatched.

When they arrive, the females lay eggs in the riverbed, in hollows dug out with their tails.

The young salmon, called **fry**, live in the rivers for about three years before swimming to the sea, where they remain until ready to breed.

A LONG REST

Many animals that do not migrate survive seasons of cold or drought in a sleep-like state called **dormancy**. Dormancy during a drought is called **aestivation**. Dormancy in winter is called **hibernation**.

Before hibernating, animals collect food. Some eat it all and develop a layer of body fat to keep them alive through the winter. Others store the food and wake occasionally to eat.

Hibernating animals, such as this dormouse, settle down in a safe, well-hidden place.

The animal's breathing and heartbeat slow down, and its body temperature drops. It becomes active again in the spring, when food is available.

Internet links

• Scan the code to watch a video clip of migrating wildebeest.

• For links to more websites where you can investigate animal life cycles, from metamorphosis to migration, go to **www.usborne.com/quicklinks**

329

ECOLOGY

The world can be divided into different areas, each with its own plants and animals. All living things are suited to their surroundings, or **environment**, and they depend on each other for survival. The study of the relationships between plants, animals and their environment is called **ecology**.

ANIMAL HOMES

The natural home of an animal or group of animals is called its **habitat**. The plants and animals that live together in a particular habitat are called a **community**. A community, together with non-living parts of the environment such as air and water, form an **ecosystem**. Smaller ecosystems can be found within a larger one, for example a rotting log in a forest.

A single rainforest flower may be a habitat for frogs and many insects.

Frog

See for yourself

Lift up a stone and see what lives in the habitat beneath it. You will probably find creatures which like damp, dark places, such as slugs, earthworms and woodlice. Remember to leave everything as you found it.

SUCCESSION

Sometimes a habitat and its community are destroyed – for example in a forest fire. After the fire, different plants and animals replace each other as the habitat develops. This process is called **ecological succession**. Eventually, a community is established that will remain unchanged, as long as its environment is stable. This is called a **climax community**.

Succession in a disused field

First or **pioneer community** is made up of grasses. This becomes a home for insects and small mammals.

Shrubs and bushes begin to grow. Mammals such as rabbits join the community.

Climax community of trees can support a wide variety of animals, including foxes and badgers.

FOOD FOR ALL

The role of an animal in its community, including what it eats and where it lives, is called its **ecological niche**. Two species cannot live in the same niche at the same time. If they tried, one would die out or be driven away.

All of the animals below can survive together in the African grasslands, because their diets are slightly different, so they occupy different niches.

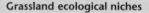

Grassland ecological niches

Giraffes reach up to feed on the top parts of trees.

Elephants stretch their trunks to browse on twigs, leaves and branches.

Gerenuks stand on their back legs to pluck leaves from bushes.

Rhinos eat leaves in the middle of bushes.

BIOMES

Biomes are the largest ecosystems into which the Earth's surface can be divided. Most are named after the main types of vegetation they contain. Each biome has its own unique combination of vegetation and wildlife. Below, you can see a type of animal that is normally found in each major biome.

Map showing main world biomes

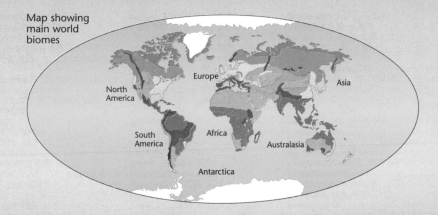

North America

Europe

Asia

South America

Africa

Australasia

Antarctica

Tundra areas are very cold and windy. Few plants or animals can survive there.

Snowshoe hare

Tropical rainforests are hot and wet all year, and are rich in plant and animal life.

Morpho butterfly

Scrublands (called **maquis**) have hot, dry winds in the summer.

Chameleon

Coniferous forests contain evergreen trees and are cool all year round.

Black bear

Deserts are hot and dry and contain few living things.

Scorpion

Oceans contain a huge number of ecosystems and cover most of the surface of the Earth.

Ocean goldfish

Tropical grasslands are mostly made up of grasses and trees.

Lion

Temperate grasslands are open, grassy plains with few trees.

Prairie dog

Polar areas are covered in ice and snow. Few living things can survive there.

Walrus

Red squirrel

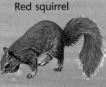

Deciduous forest areas have warm summers and cold winters.

Mountains are mostly cold and bare at the top, with vegetation at the foot.

Bighorn sheep

Internet links

• Scan the code to see animals that have adapted to extreme environments.

• For links to more websites where you can find out about wildlife in the Earth's different biomes, go to **www.usborne.com/quicklinks**

Polar bears can live in the Arctic because their thick skin and shaggy coat protect them from the cold.

331

FOOD AND ENERGY

Plants make their own food using water, carbon dioxide from the air and energy from the Sun. They are described as **autotrophic**. Animals, though, depend on other living things for food and are described as **heterotrophic**. Animals get energy by eating plants or other animals that have themselves eaten plants.

This dragonfly gets its energy by eating plant-eating insects.

FOOD CHAINS

All animals are part of a **food chain**. This is a series of living things, each of which is eaten by the next in line. The position of a living thing within a food chain is its **trophic level**, with plants at the first level. Plants are called **producers**, because they make food which provides energy. Animals in a food chain are called **consumers**.

Within a food chain, a herbivore (plant-eating animal) is known as a **primary** or **first order consumer**. An animal that eats a primary consumer is called a **secondary consumer**, and so on. Many carnivores (meat eaters) eat both herbivores and smaller carnivores. They are therefore secondary consumers on some occasions and tertiary consumers on others.

Food chains also contain tiny organisms called **decomposers**. These include bacteria, fungi and many invertebrates. Decomposers break down dead plant and animal matter, and return minerals from them to the soil.

A woodland food chain ★

Fourth trophic level (T4)

Tertiary consumer

Hawk

Third trophic level (T3)

Secondary consumer

Thrush

Second trophic level (T2)

Primary consumer

Snail

First trophic level (T1)

Producer

Buttercups

Fungi release chemicals that break down plant and animal matter into simpler substances.

ENERGY TRANSFER

Most of the food an animal eats is used up by its body, and some is stored. When that animal is eaten, the next consumer only gains the stored energy. Therefore, much less energy is available at the next stage in the chain.

Alligators eat animals from every level of their food chain to get the energy they need.

Each trophic level has far fewer consumers in it than the level below. This is because the animals have to eat more food to get the energy they need. This can be shown as a **pyramid of numbers**.

Pyramid of numbers

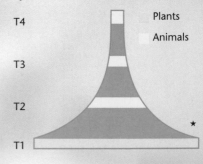

T4 — Plants / Animals

T3

T2 ★

T1

BIOMASS

Biomass is the combined weight of all living things in a habitat. The biomass of plants is much higher than that of any other living things in the same area. At each level of a food chain, there are fewer living things than in the level below, with a lower combined biomass.

This can be shown in a diagram called a **pyramid of biomass**.

Pyramid of biomass

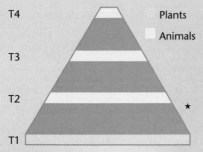

T4	Plants
	Animals
T3	
T2	★
T1	

A meadow is an example of a habitat, and its biomass could be shown by a pyramid like the one above. The total biomass of plants at T1 in a meadow can be several thousand kilograms. Several hundred kilograms of insects at T2 may live on these plants.

The small mammals at T3, which eat the plants and insects, have a combined biomass of about 150kg. A single fox at T4, which feeds on the small animals, has a biomass of around 5kg.

See for yourself

Next time you eat, think about what trophic level you occupy. For instance, if you are eating vegetables, you are on the second trophic level. If you are eating meat, you are on a higher trophic level.

FOOD WEBS

A series of interlinked food chains is called a **food web**. Many food chains are linked because very few animals feed on just one thing. For example, most carnivores eat whatever small animals they can find. A herbivore might eat different types of plants depending on the season.

Interdependence describes a number of living things relying on each other and the environment to stay alive, for example in a food web.

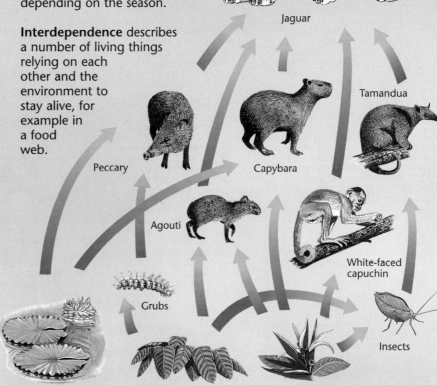

A rainforest food web

Jaguar

Tamandua

Peccary

Capybara

Agouti

White-faced capuchin

Grubs

Insects

Water plants

Leaves

Flowers and fruit

Food webs are easily damaged by humans. For instance, in 1910, wardens in the Grand Canyon Game Reserve tried to protect the deer population by shooting the animals that ate them. The numbers of deer increased, but there was not enough food for them all. Eventually, many starved to death.

Numbers of plant eaters, like these deer, can become too high without meat eaters to control them.

Internet links

- Scan the code to watch a video clip about food chains.

- For links to more websites with food chain and food web puzzles and quizzes, go to **www.usborne.com/quicklinks**

BALANCE IN NATURE

Animals and plants depend on each other, and on the **abiotic** (non-living) parts of the environment, to stay alive. Essential substances, such as carbon, nitrogen and water, constantly move through plants and animals, as well as through the land, sea and air. These circulations are called **cycles**. Many human activities, such as fuel burning, affect the delicate balance between living things and their environment, putting their lives in danger.

Many dolphins and other sea creatures are killed accidentally in commercial fishing nets.

THE NITROGEN CYCLE

The gas **nitrogen** is constantly recycled through the living world. Plants and animals need nitrogen-based substances to build chemicals called **proteins** in their bodies. Plants absorb nitrogen in the form of **nitrates** from the soil and use it to grow. Animals get nitrogen by eating plants, or plant-eating animals.

When living things die, bacteria and fungi break them down and nitrogen is released back into the soil in a chemical called **ammonia**. Other bacteria change this into nitrates, which are taken up by new plants. (For more on the nitrogen cycle, see page 64.)

These dung beetles bury balls of dung. Bacteria in the soil release nitrogen from the dung as they break it down.

THE CARBON CYCLE

Different forms of **carbon** are recycled through the living world. Plants take in carbon dioxide from the air and use it, along with water and sunlight, to make food. Animals eat plants, and their bodies break down the plant matter and use the carbon for growth and energy. (For more on the carbon cycle, see page 52.)

Plant eaters such as cows take in carbon from plants. Meat eaters gain carbon by eating plant eaters.

Chemical reactions inside animals and plants turn food into energy, and carbon dioxide is produced as waste. Animals release carbon dioxide into the air as they breathe out, and plants give it off at night when they are not making food. Carbon dioxide is also released back into the air when dead plant and animal matter breaks down.

THE WATER CYCLE

The water that falls as rain drains into rivers, then into the sea. It evaporates, rises, then forms tiny droplets of moisture in the air. These form clouds and fall again as rain. In this way, water is constantly recycled between the air and the earth. (For more on the water cycle, see page 74.)

The water cycle

Water droplets form clouds, then fall as rain.

Water evaporates.

Plants and animals also release water. For example, animals do this when they breathe out.

See for yourself

You can see water in the air you breathe out by breathing heavily on a mirror. The warm moisture in your breath cools as it touches the mirror's surface, and turns into tiny drops of water.

POLLUTION

Pollution is damage usually caused to the environment by human activities, such as garbage dumping. Waste chemicals from factories are pumped into rivers and seas, and fumes from burning fuels and vehicle exhausts pollute the air. Animals that live in a seriously polluted environment may become unable to breed, or fall sick and die.

This seabird is trapped on a seashore polluted with oil from a damaged oil tanker. This type of pollution can wipe out the sea life in an area.

DEADLY CHEMICALS

When dangerous chemicals are released into the environment, food chains* are often damaged. For example, **insecticides** are poisons used to kill insects that harm crops. These poisons are often taken in by other small creatures. When predators eat these animals, they also take in the poison, and so it is passed to animals at higher levels in the food chain.

This happened on a large scale in the 1950s and 1960s, when an insecticide called DDT was widely used. It entered some food chains, becoming more concentrated at each level. Eventually, it killed thousands of birds of prey at the top of these chains.

THREATENED SEA LIFE

Many species of fish and shellfish are becoming endangered* because too many have been caught to provide food for people. This is called **overfishing**. The remaining fish cannot produce enough young to replace the ones that have been caught.

Some fishermen are now using nets with larger holes. These allow young fish to escape and breed, so their numbers do not decrease too much.

Young fish can escape from a net with large holes.

This farmer is spraying his crops with insecticides. The insecticides kill pests, but they may also harm many useful creatures that live in the same place.

Internet links

• Scan the code to watch a video clip about overfishing.

• For links to more websites about the balance in nature and the problems of pollution, go to **www.usborne.com/quicklinks**

* Endangered species, 336; Food chains, 332.

CONSERVATION

Many animal species are in danger of dying out completely. This is known as becoming **extinct**. Some animals are hunted for useful body parts, such as fur, but most are threatened by loss of habitat. Nature **conservation** aims to protect animals and look after the Earth's natural resources to ensure the future of all living things.

Koalas were once faced with extinction, but conservation efforts have been successful and their numbers are increasing.

DISAPPEARING SPECIES

Since life on Earth began, many species have disappeared as a result of natural changes in the environment. This is called the **background rate of extinction**. More recently, human activity has led to a huge increase in the extinction rate. However, people are now taking action to protect disappearing species.

Tiger hunting has been banned since 1970, but tigers are still illegally killed by poachers.

An animal that is in danger of becoming extinct in the wild is described as an **endangered species**. If a species is likely to become endangered in the near future, it is described as **threatened**. In many countries, it is now illegal to kill, capture or sell animals which are threatened or endangered.

GUARDING ANIMALS

Although many laws have been passed to protect animals, it is hard to make people obey them. For instance, it is illegal to hunt elephants and rhinos, but poachers still kill them for their tusks and horns. In Africa, many rhinos and elephants are now kept under close guard.

This rhino has had its horns removed. In parts of Africa, people are trying to save rhinos by removing their horns, so poachers will have no reason to kill them.

NATURE RESERVES

To preserve the world's threatened wildlife, areas have been set aside as **nature reserves**, where plants and animals can live in safety.

Wherever possible, tourists are allowed to visit these reserves. With the proper control, tourism is harmless to wildlife, and can be an excellent source of money for poorer countries.

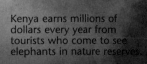

Kenya earns millions of dollars every year from tourists who come to see elephants in nature reserves.

SAVING HABITATS

Major ecosystems*, such as coral reefs and rainforests, play a vital role in supporting life on Earth. Coral reefs are home to huge numbers of living things, which recycle oxygen and minerals through the oceans. Many countries are trying to protect their reefs. For instance, Australia has a 2,250km stretch of protected coral reefs called the Great Barrier Reef Marine Park.

Many thousands of plant and animal species live in or around coral reefs. When a reef is damaged or destroyed, all these living things are affected.

Rainforests are vital to all life because they recycle large amounts of carbon and nitrogen, which plants and animals need to survive. Vast areas of rainforest have already been destroyed, but people are working together to preserve the areas that remain.

Over half of all plant and animal species on Earth live in rainforests. Without conservation efforts, many may die out.

CAPTIVE BREEDING

Sometimes, a species becomes so rare that it will certainly die out without human help. In such cases, scientists try to increase the animals' numbers by breeding them in captivity, such as in a reserve or a zoo. These animals are sometimes returned to the wild, but many lack the skills that they need to survive.

Golden lion tamarins are rare, but they breed successfully in captivity.

Some species are **slow breeders**, which means that they produce very few young at long intervals. Giant pandas, which are highly endangered, are slow breeders. A few have been born in captivity, but the panda's best chance for survival is to save its native bamboo forests from future harm.

Giant pandas cannot survive without a good supply of bamboo, as it makes up around 99% of their diet.

DANGER AREAS

The main threat to animals is loss of habitat, but they are also killed by pollution and hunting. Many species are also **endemic**. This means that they are found in only one place. Scientists can identify areas, called **hotspots**, which contain large numbers of an endemic species, and ensure that they are well protected.

Many birds, particularly parrots and macaws, are put in danger by the pet trade. Some are also killed for their striking feathers. Combined with habitat loss, this has led to a third of all parrot species becoming endangered in the wild. It is possible, though, that numbers can be increased through captive breeding.

Hyacinth macaws are highly valued as pets because of their striking appearance. They are now one of the rarest types of macaw.

Internet links

• Scan the code to watch a video about conservation.

• For links to more websites with video clips of some of the world's most endangered species, go to **www.usborne.com/quicklinks**

EVOLUTION

Scientists believe that life on Earth started with very simple creatures and developed gradually, through a long series of changes. This process is called **evolution**. By studying existing organisms and prehistoric remains, scientists try to explain how and why living things have changed over time.

Fossils such as this ammonite shell allow scientists to learn more about ancient life.

EVOLUTION

Scientists believe that bacteria were the first organisms on Earth, and that they began to develop over 3,500 million years ago. They suggest that, over the course of many millions of years, these bacteria developed into the first animals, as shown here.

Evolution of main animal groups

500 million years ago
First fish evolved, with thick skin and no jaws. About 150 million years later, bony fish and cartilaginous fish* evolved.

Sacabambaspis

410 million years ago
First wingless insects appeared. About 110 million years later, winged insects evolved.

Meganeura

350 million years ago
Some water-dwelling creatures began to breathe air, and became the first amphibians*.

Ichthyostega

300 million years ago
First reptiles appeared. Dinosaurs evolved around 200 million years ago, and lived for 135 million years, before they rapidly died out.

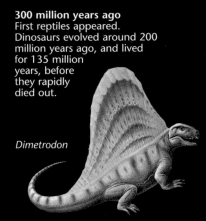

Dimetrodon

200 million years ago
First small mammals appeared. After the dinosaurs died out, larger mammals started to evolve.

Megazostrodon

150 million years ago
First birds evolved from small species of dinosaurs.

Archaeopteryx

FOSSILS

When a plant or animal dies, its body rots away, but hard parts, such as the skeleton, may be preserved in sand and mud. Over millions of years, the sand and mud build up in layers, and eventually turn to rock with the preserved remains of the plant or animal, called a **fossil**, inside.

How a fossil forms ★

The animal's flesh rots away.

Layers of sand and mud cover the skeleton, and turn into rock with the shape of the skeleton inside.

See for yourself

Museums can often provide interesting information about fossils and dinosaurs. You could visit a local museum and find out if it has a fossil collection, or a dinosaur exhibit.

* Amphibians, 315, 342; Bacteria, 341; Cartilaginous fish, 301.

MASS EXTINCTION

Many scientists suggest that there have been five events in the Earth's history during which huge numbers of living things died at once. They call such an event a **mass extinction**. This normally happens as a result of sudden, dramatic changes in the Earth's climate. Many organisms cannot adapt to these changes, and so they die out.

Dinosaurs may have been killed off by a change in climate caused by a huge meteorite hitting the Earth.

Large reptiles, such as this *Tyrannosaurus rex*, have not lived on Earth for over 65 million years.

The change in climate affected plants' ability to make food, with devastating effects on food chains*.

NATURAL SELECTION

In the 1850s, a British scientist, Charles Darwin, put forward the **theory of natural selection** to explain how evolution takes place. He suggested that individual organisms with qualities that help them to survive in their environment tend to have more offspring and pass on these useful qualities to their offspring.

In this way, over a very long period of time, most of the members of a species will have the useful qualities and be well suited to their environment.

Features which offer protection increase an animal's chances of survival, and are therefore more likely to be passed on from one generation to the next. This is known as **protective adaptation**.

Peppered moth (dark variety)

An example of protective adaptation is when patterns on an animal's body allow it to remain hidden from enemies. This is called **camouflage**.

A type of moth, called the peppered moth, is often used to show how natural selection takes place. During the nineteenth century, many trees upon which peppered moths rested became blackened by soot from factories.

Both dark and pale peppered moths resting on a soot-covered tree trunk

Moths with pale wings were seen and eaten by birds, but the rare moths with dark wings survived, bred and increased in numbers. Now, however, there is less pollution from soot and the moths with pale wings are increasing again.

Peppered moth (pale variety)

Internet links

• Scan the code to watch a video clip about dinosaurs.

• For links to more websites about evolution, the history of life, fossils and dinosaurs, go to **www.usborne.com/quicklinks**

CLASSIFICATION

To make living things easier to study, biologists organize them into groups with similar features. Fitting organisms into groups that can be divided to form smaller groups is called **classification**. For example, an elephant and a mouse both belong to the mammal group, because they have hair and produce milk for their young. Within the mammal group, though, they belong to different sub-groups.

A mouse and an elephant look different, but they both belong to the mammal group.

IDENTIFICATION

Scientists identify an organism by comparing its main features and deciding how these are different from those of similar species. The method used is called a **biological key**. A typical biological key is arranged in branches, as in the example below. At each branch the scientist asks "Does the specimen have...?" and there is a choice between two or more features. Each response leads to another set of options until the organism is identified.

Branching key

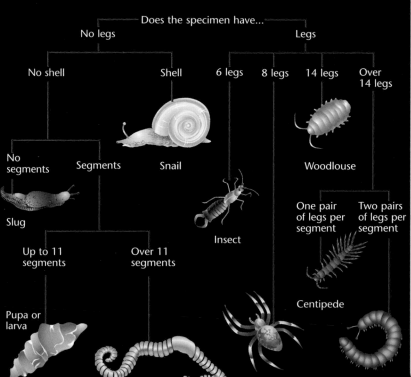

Does the specimen have...

No legs — Legs

No shell — Shell — 6 legs — 8 legs — 14 legs — Over 14 legs

No segments — Segments — Snail — Woodlouse

Slug

One pair of legs per segment — Two pairs of legs per segment

Up to 11 segments — Over 11 segments

Insect

Pupa or larva

Centipede

Worm — Spider — Millipede

See for yourself

A key where you are given a choice of only two statements is called a **dichotomous key**. Try identifying the six creatures below using the key at the bottom of this box.

Look at each creature in turn and go through the dichotomous key, choosing one statement from each pair and following the instructions.

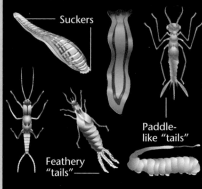

Suckers

Paddle-like "tails"

Feathery "tails"

Dichotomous key

1. Six jointed legs	Go to 4
No legs	Go to 2
2. Segmented body	Go to 3
Body has no segments	Flatworm
3. Suckers at front and back	Leech
No suckers	Hoverfly larva
4. Two "tails"	Stonefly nymph
Three "tails"	Go to 5
5. Paddle-like "tails"	Damselfly nymph
Feathery "tails"	Mayfly nymph

THE SIX KINGDOMS

The largest groups into which living things can be sorted are called **kingdoms**.

Scientists currently divide living things into six main kingdoms: plants, fungi, animals, protista, archaea and eubacteria.

Viruses are not included in these kingdoms. Although they can grow and reproduce, they are only able to exist within the cells of living things.

The six kingdoms of living things

Plants
Many-celled with distinct nuclei*. In most, their cells contain a green chemical called chlorophyll that allows them to make their own food.

Rosy periwinkle

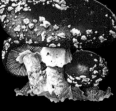

Fungi
Many-celled with distinct nuclei*. The cells do not contain chlorophyll*. They feed by digesting organic matter outside their bodies.

Fly agaric

Animals
Many-celled with distinct nuclei*. Their cells do not contain chlorophyll*. They feed by taking in organic matter (either dead or living) and digesting it within their bodies. Most animals can move around.

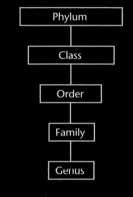

Corkwing wrasse

Protista
Most protists are microscopic and single-celled. They have a distinct nucleus* within each cell. Some protists are like animals, some are like plants and some are like fungi.

Euglena

Archaea
Microscopic single-celled organisms without nuclei*. They cannot survive in the presence of oxygen.

Eubacteria
Microscopic, single celled organisms, such as bacteria, which do not have nuclei*. Many can survive in the presence of oxygen. Their cell walls* are very different from those of the Archaea.

Salmonella bacterium (magnified many thousand times)

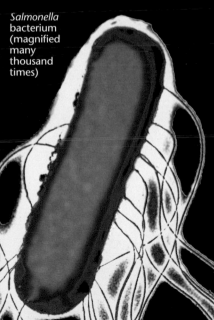

DIVIDING KINGDOMS

Each kingdom can be broken down into levels called **taxonomic ranks** or **taxa**. The first rank is called a **phylum**. Each phylum breaks down into groups called **classes**. Classes are divided into **orders**, then **families**, then **genera**.

Phylum

Class

Order

Family

Genus

Each genus contains a number of **species**, which are individual groups of animals that are similar enough to breed together. Over the page, you can see how a single species can be traced from a phylum. In some cases, there are also mid-way groups, such as **sub-kingdoms** and **sub-phyla**.

Some phyla have so few species that there is just one class and order within them. These are often given the same name as the phylum. For example, the phylum Phoronida (Horseshoe Worms) has just two genera within one family.

Internet links

• Scan the code to discover more about the six kingdoms.

* Cell wall, Chlorophyll, 250; Nucleus, 298.

THE ANIMAL KINGDOM

The animal kingdom contains a number of phyla, the main eight of which are shown below. These can be sorted further into classes, orders, families, genera and species (see previous page). Below, you can see how a single species, such as a northern wolf, can be traced from one of the phyla. Each step down becomes more specific and includes fewer animals than the one before.

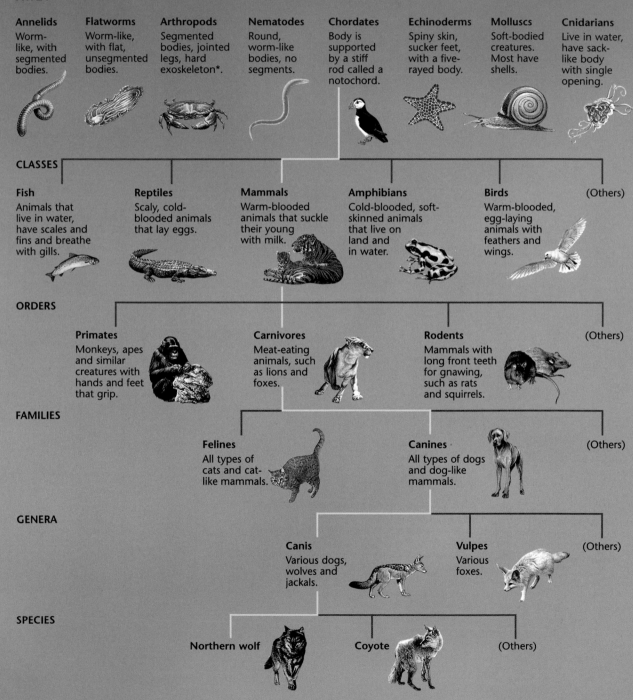

PHYLA

Annelids
Worm-like, with segmented bodies.

Flatworms
Worm-like, with flat, unsegmented bodies.

Arthropods
Segmented bodies, jointed legs, hard exoskeleton*.

Nematodes
Round, worm-like bodies, no segments.

Chordates
Body is supported by a stiff rod called a notochord.

Echinoderms
Spiny skin, sucker feet, with a five-rayed body.

Molluscs
Soft-bodied creatures. Most have shells.

Cnidarians
Live in water, have sack-like body with single opening.

CLASSES

Fish
Animals that live in water, have scales and fins and breathe with gills.

Reptiles
Scaly, cold-blooded animals that lay eggs.

Mammals
Warm-blooded animals that suckle their young with milk.

Amphibians
Cold-blooded, soft-skinned animals that live on land and in water.

Birds
Warm-blooded, egg-laying animals with feathers and wings.

(Others)

ORDERS

Primates
Monkeys, apes and similar creatures with hands and feet that grip.

Carnivores
Meat-eating animals, such as lions and foxes.

Rodents
Mammals with long front teeth for gnawing, such as rats and squirrels.

(Others)

FAMILIES

Felines
All types of cats and cat-like mammals.

Canines
All types of dogs and dog-like mammals.

(Others)

GENERA

Canis
Various dogs, wolves and jackals.

Vulpes
Various foxes.

(Others)

SPECIES

Northern wolf

Coyote

(Others)

* Exoskeleton, 301.

NAMING THINGS

Living things are generally given one or more common names and a biological name. The **common name** is the one used by most people, such as tawny owl or red squirrel. A **biological name** is needed because an animal may have many common names, each one used in a different area. Biological names are usually in Latin. These names can be recognized by scientists all over the world.

These butterflies are so rare that they do not have common names, only biological names.

Callicore cyllene

Agrias laudina

Callicore mengeli

The biological name is created using the **binomial system**, which means that it is made up of two parts. The first part, called the **generic name**, is based on the organism's genus. The second part, called the **specific epithet**, identifies its species.

In many cases, a biological name refers to the animal's appearance, habitat or body features. For instance, a giraffe's biological name is *Giraffa camelopardalis*. *Giraffa* means "swift walker", *camel* means "camel-like", and *pardalis* means "marked like a leopard". So a giraffe is a swift-moving, camel-like animal with a patterned coat like a leopard.

SUB-SPECIES

In some cases, there are also **sub-species**, which have a third part added to their biological name. This can refer to the area in which the sub-species is found, or to a particular characteristic.

This tiger's name is *Panthera tigris sumatrae*. The third part of its name shows that it is a sub-species from Sumatra.

An animal's biological name can refer to a feature of its behaviour. Giraffes share their peculiar gait with camels – the two left legs move together, then the two right legs. Hence the name ... *camelopardalis*

INFORMAL GROUPS

Different species which share certain types of lifestyle can also be put together in informal groups, by using terms which describe this lifestyle. Social* and nocturnal* animals are two such terms, and there are other examples below.

An animal or plant which lives and feeds on another organism (called the **host**) is known as a **parasite**. Some parasites are harmful to their hosts.

Fleas are common parasites which feed on the blood of their host.

Mutualists are animals or plants which live close together in a situation where both gain. For example, birds called oxpeckers eat parasites that live on the hides of larger animals, such as buffalo and zebra. The larger animals benefit in turn from having the pests removed.

Two species in a relationship where one gains without affecting the other are called **commensals**. House mice, for example, live where humans are found, and feed on their scraps.

Internet links

- Scan the code to see how a lion is classified by scientists

- For links to more websites about classification and the six kingdoms, go to **www.usborne.com/quicklinks**

* Nocturnal animals, 321;
  Social animals, 319.

343

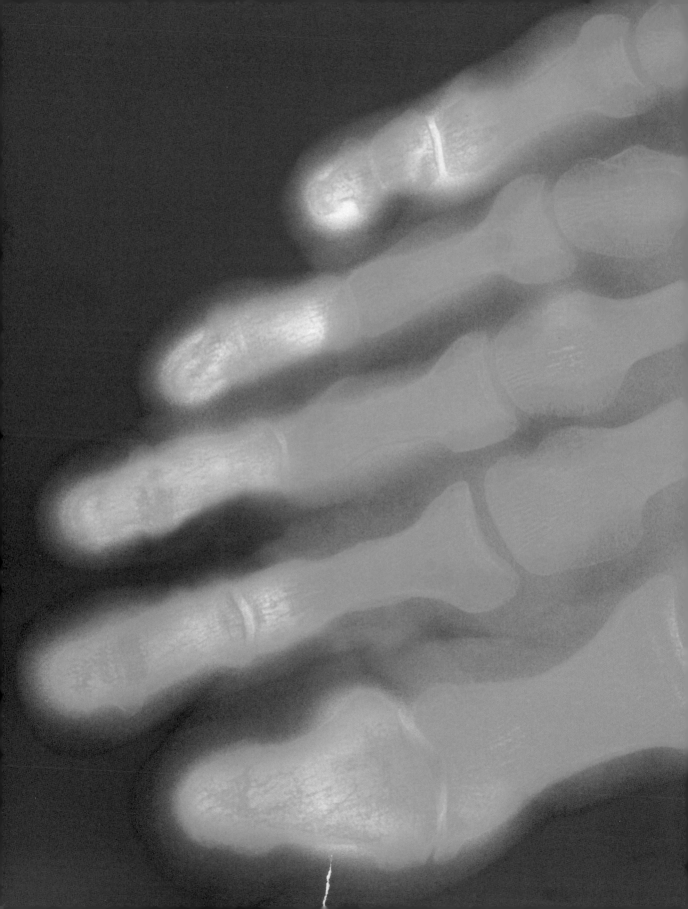

HUMAN BODY

THE SKELETON

Your **skeleton** is a framework of bones that supports your body and gives it shape, protects delicate parts, such as the heart, and provides hard surfaces for muscles to pull on so you can move.

TYPES OF BONE

The bones in your body can be divided into four main types, depending on their shape.

Flat bones (such as your shoulder blades and ribs) give protection and provide surfaces to which muscles can attach.

Ribs

Short bones are knobbly nugget shapes which are nearly equal in length and width. The bones in your wrists and ankles are short bones.

Wrist bones

Irregular bones have complicated shapes and do not fit into any of the other groups. The bones that make up your backbone are irregular bones.

Backbone

Long bones are longer than they are wide. They are slightly curved to make them stronger. The bones in your fingers are long bones.

Finger bones ★

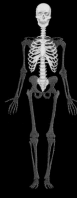

DIVISIONS OF THE SKELETON

A skeleton can be divided into two parts. The **axial skeleton** (shown in yellow) is made up of bones in the skull, backbone and rib cage. They all lie on or around an imaginary line down the middle of the body. The **appendicular skeleton** (shown in red) is made up of bones of the limbs (arms and legs) and their associated girdles (shoulders and pelvis).

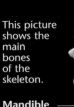

This picture shows the main bones of the skeleton.

Cranium (skull). The adult cranium is made up of several bony plates, fitting closely together.

Mandible (jawbone)

Clavicle (collarbone)

Scapula (shoulder blade)

Sternum (breastbone)

Humerus

Vertebral column (backbone or spine) made of 33 **vertebrae**

Rib

Radius

Ulna

Carpals (wrist bones)

Pelvis (pelvic girdle or hip girdle). Each side is made up of three bones – the **ilium**, **pubis** and **ischium**.

Coccyx

Metacarpals (hand bones)

Femur (thighbone)

Phalanges (finger bones)

Patella (kneecap)

Tibia (shinbone)

Fibula

Your fingers and toes are called **digits**. The bones in them are known as **phalanges** (singular **phalanx**).

Metatarsals (foot bones)

Tarsals (ankle bones)

Phalanges (toe bones)

TYPES OF JOINTS

Joints are places where bones meet. Some, such as those between the bones in your skull, are fixed, but most are movable. The most common types of freely movable joint are listed below. They are called **synovial joints** because they contain a lubricating liquid called **synovial fluid**.

Your hip joint is a **ball and socket joint**. It has a round-ended bone which fits into a fixed, cup-like socket. This lets you swivel your leg in many directions.

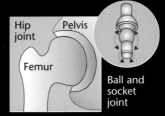

Hip joint

Pelvis

Femur

Ball and socket joint

Your knee joint works like a hinge, so you can bend your leg in two opposite directions, such as up and down. This type of joint is called a **hinge joint**.

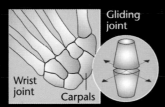

Knee joint

Patella

Femur

Tibia

Hinge joint

The joints in your wrist are **gliding** or **sliding joints**. The surfaces which touch are flat and the bones can move from side to side, and back and forth.

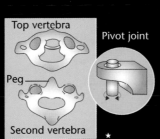

Wrist joint

Carpals

Gliding joint

The **pivot joint** between your top two vertebrae allows you to turn your head from side to side. The rounded end of one bone twists around in a hole in the other.

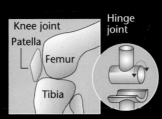

Top vertebra

Peg

Second vertebra

Pivot joint

★

BABY SKELETONS

The skeleton of a newborn baby has over 300 parts. Most are not made of bone, but of a tough, flexible material called **cartilage**. Over time, this slowly turns into bone, in a process called **ossification**. As the baby grows, some of the bones join together to make bigger bones. By the time it is an adult, its skeleton contains only 206 separate bones.

INSIDE A BONE

Each of your bones is covered by a thin layer of tissue called **periosteum**, which contains cells for growth and repair. Inside this, the bone itself is made up of blood vessels, nerves and living bone cells called **osteocytes**. These are all held within a framework containing the protein* ossein and the hard mineral calcium phosphate.

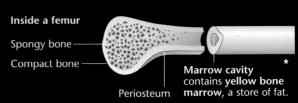

Inside a femur

Spongy bone

Compact bone

Periosteum

Marrow cavity contains **yellow bone marrow**, a store of fat.

★

Spongy bone is a mesh of branches called **trabeculae**, with large spaces between them. This strong, light tissue is found in short, flat bones, and in the ends of long bones.

Spongy bone

Spaces between trabeculae contain **red bone marrow**. Blood cells are made here.

Trabecula

Osteocyte inside trabecula

★

Compact bone is made up of dense, circular layers of bone called **lamellae**. Compact bone forms the outer layer of all bones.

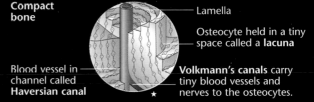

Compact bone

Blood vessel in channel called **Haversian canal**

Lamella

Osteocyte held in a tiny space called a **lacuna**

Volkmann's canals carry tiny blood vessels and nerves to the osteocytes.

★

Internet links

• Scan the code to watch a video clip about bones.

• For links to more websites where you can find out about the skeleton and its different types of bones and joints, go to **www.usborne.com/quicklinks**

MUSCLES

Muscles are areas of stretchy tissue found all over your body. They are responsible for movement. Muscles that you can control, such as those which lift your arm, are called **voluntary muscles**. Muscles which work automatically, such as those which make your heart beat, are **involuntary muscles**. There are three types of muscles: skeletal, cardiac and visceral muscles.

SKELETAL MUSCLES

Your body contains about 640 **skeletal muscles**. These are voluntary muscles which are attached to the skeleton, usually by bands of tough tissue called **tendons**. Some skeletal muscles are attached to skin. The muscles in your face, for example, are skeletal muscles. They allow you to make different expressions.

When a muscle contracts, it shortens and tightens, pulling the bone (or skin) with it. Muscles cannot push, though, so you need another muscle to pull the part back to its original position. The muscle which contracts is called the **agonist**, and the one which relaxes is called the **antagonist**. Pairs of muscles that work in this way are known as **antagonistic pairs**.

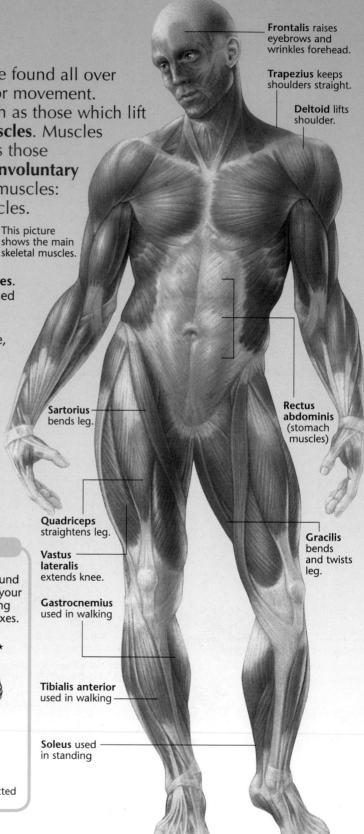

This picture shows the main skeletal muscles.

Frontalis raises eyebrows and wrinkles forehead.

Trapezius keeps shoulders straight.

Deltoid lifts shoulder.

Rectus abdominis (stomach muscles)

Sartorius bends leg.

Quadriceps straightens leg.

Vastus lateralis extends knee.

Gastrocnemius used in walking

Gracilis bends and twists leg.

Tibialis anterior used in walking

Soleus used in standing

See for yourself

The **biceps** and **triceps** muscles in your arm are an antagonistic pair. Place your hand gently around your upper arm while you bend and straighten your arm. You can feel your biceps and triceps working as a pair – one muscle tightens as the other relaxes.

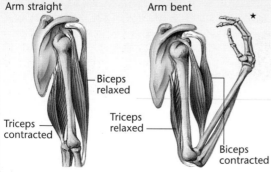

Arm straight

Arm bent

★

Biceps relaxed

Triceps contracted

Triceps relaxed

Biceps contracted

CARDIAC MUSCLES

Cardiac muscles make up most of your heart. They are involuntary muscles, which never tire. They form two separate sets. The upper set contracts, filling the lower chambers of your heart with blood. The lower set then contracts and squeezes the blood out into your arteries*.

Cardiac muscles at work

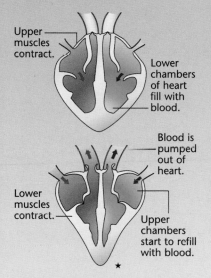

Upper muscles contract.

Lower chambers of heart fill with blood.

Blood is pumped out of heart.

Lower muscles contract.

Upper chambers start to refill with blood.

VISCERAL MUSCLES

Visceral muscles are found in the walls of many of the organs inside your body. They are involuntary muscles which contract slowly and rhythmically without becoming tired. This enables them, for example, to move food through your digestive system*.

Section of intestine

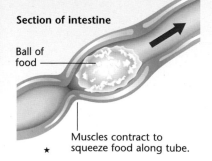

Ball of food

Muscles contract to squeeze food along tube.

MUSCLE TISSUE

Skeletal muscles are made of **striated** or **striped muscle tissue**. This is made up of long, rod-shaped cells called **muscle fibres** or **myofibres**.

Myofibres are grouped into bundles called **fascicles**. Each fibre is made up of cords called **myofibrils**. These contain interlocking thick and thin threads called **myofilaments**. Thick myofilaments are made of a type of protein called **myosin**, and thin filaments are made of **actin**, another protein.

When a muscle contracts, its filaments slide past each other. This makes the muscle shorter and fatter.

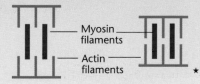

Relaxed skeletal muscle

Contracted skeletal muscle

Myosin filaments

Actin filaments

Filaments slide past each other.

Striated muscle fibres can be divided into two types. **Slow-twitch fibres** contract slowly and use relatively little energy. They can act for a long time without becoming tired. **Fast-twitch fibres** contract quickly, using more energy. They act in short, powerful bursts, but tire quickly.

The neck muscles which support your head contain many slow-twitch fibres.

Arm muscles used for throwing contain many fast-twitch fibres.

Structure of a skeletal muscle

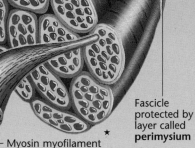

Muscle fibre enclosed by membrane

Muscle protected by tough layer called **epimysium**

Myofibril

Myosin myofilament

Actin myofilament

Fascicle protected by layer called **perimysium**

Cardiac muscles are made of a type of striated muscle tissue called **cardiac muscle tissue**. This is made of interlocking Y-shaped fibres.

Cardiac muscle fibre

Visceral muscles are made of spindle-shaped fibres which join together to form **smooth muscle tissue**.

Smooth muscle fibre

Internet links

• Scan the code to see how muscles work.

• For links to more websites with animations, diagrams and quizzes about muscles, go to **www.usborne.com/quicklinks**

THE CIRCULATORY SYSTEM

Your **circulatory system** transports substances, such as food and oxygen, around your body, and collects some waste substances. It has three main parts: **blood**, a liquid which carries the substances to and from the cells; tubes called **blood vessels**, through which the blood travels; and the **heart**, which pumps blood to all parts of your body.

HEART

Position of heart

Your heart is a muscular organ which, unlike other muscles, never gets tired. It is divided into four parts called **chambers**. The two upper chambers are called **atria**. They are joined to two lower chambers, called **ventricles**.

One-way valves between the chambers keep your blood flowing in the right direction. The valves have flaps called **cusps**. As blood flows through the valves, it forces open the cusps. They then snap shut, to stop blood from flowing back. As the valves shut, they make the thumping "heart beat" sound.

An electron microscope image showing three types of cells in a drop of blood

How blood circulates around the heart

The **aorta** is an artery which carries blood out of the heart to be taken to the rest of the body.

The **superior vena cava** is a vein which carries blood to the heart from the upper body.

Pulmonary veins carry blood from the lungs to the heart.

Arterial valves

Right atrium

Right ventricle

The **inferior vena cava** is a vein that carries blood to the heart from the lower body.

Valve open
Valve shut
Cusp

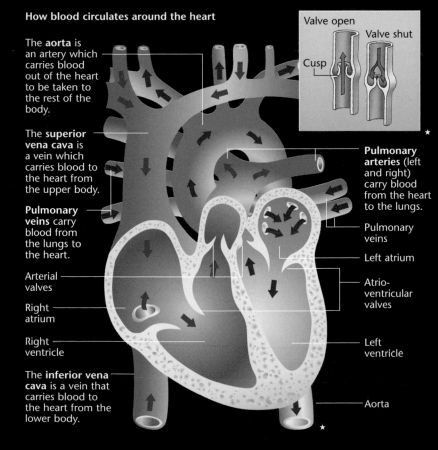

Pulmonary **arteries** (left and right) carry blood from the heart to the lungs.

Pulmonary veins

Left atrium

Atrio-ventricular valves

Left ventricle

Aorta

CIRCULATION

Blood passes through the heart twice during one complete circulation of your body. First, it is pumped from the right side of the heart to the lungs, where it picks up fresh oxygen you have breathed in. It then returns to the left side of the heart, from where it is pumped to the rest of the body to deliver the oxygen. Blood needing oxygen returns to the heart to begin the cycle again.

How blood travels around the body

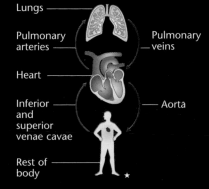

Lungs

Pulmonary arteries

Pulmonary veins

Heart

Inferior and superior venae cavae

Aorta

Rest of body

350

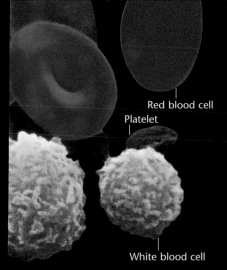

Red blood cell

Platelet

White blood cell

BLOOD VESSELS

Blood flows away from your heart along strong blood vessels called **arteries**. These branch off into ever smaller vessels, ending up with tiny tubes called **capillaries**. Their walls are only one cell thick, so oxygen and other substances needed by body cells can pass through easily into the fluid between the cells (**tissue fluid**).

Types of blood vessel

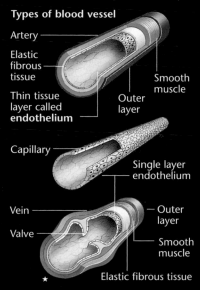

Artery

Elastic fibrous tissue

Thin tissue layer called **endothelium**

Smooth muscle

Outer layer

Capillary

Single layer endothelium

Vein

Outer layer

Valve

Smooth muscle

Elastic fibrous tissue

The tissue fluid takes substances between cells and the blood. Carbon dioxide and some waste pass into the capillaries, which eventually join up again into blood vessels called **veins**. These carry blood back to the heart.

* Antibodies, Antigens, 387; Bone marrow, 347.

BLOOD

Blood is made up of red and white blood cells and platelets, floating in a pale yellow liquid called **plasma**. The average adult has five litres of blood. As well as carrying substances around your body, blood helps to fight germs, heal wounds, and control body temperature.

Composition of blood

Plasma (55%)

White blood cells and platelets (0.45%)

Red blood cells (44.55%)

Red blood cells are disc-shaped cells, which contain a purple-red chemical called **haemoglobin**. As blood passes through the lungs, oxygen combines with the haemoglobin, forming **oxyhaemoglobin**, which is bright red. As the cells deliver oxygen around the body, the oxyhaemoglobin turns back into haemoglobin.

Red blood cell with oxygen

Red blood cell without oxygen

The cell's disc shape helps it to squeeze along inside tiny capillaries.

Red blood cells wear out every four months and are replaced by new ones. These are made in your bone marrow* at a rate of two million per second.

White blood cells are larger than red ones. They help your body to fight disease. You can find out more about this on page 387.

Platelets are tiny fragments of cells. They help to stop the bleeding if you cut yourself.

BLOOD CLOTTING

Most minor cuts bleed for a short time, then the blood turns into a gel-like mass called a **clot**. This is made up of sticky threads of **fibrin**, which form as a result of chemical reactions started by platelets. The clot stops more blood leaking out, and helps to prevent germs entering the wound.

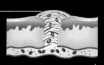

Clot is made up of fibrin threads.

Clot will dissolve once blood vessel is repaired.

BLOOD GROUPS

Blood can be divided into four main groups – A, B, O and AB. They have different antigens* on the surface of the red cells, and different antibodies* in the plasma. In a blood transfusion, the type of blood you can be given depends on your blood group.

Blood group	Antigen	Antibody	Can be given
A	A	Anti-B	A and O
B	B	Anti-A	B and O
AB	A and B	None	All
O	None	Anti-A Anti-B	O only

Internet links

• Scan the code to watch a video about how the heart works.

• For links to more websites about your heart and how blood travels around the body, go to **www.usborne.com/quicklinks**

TEETH

Your **teeth** help to prepare your food for digestion*. They cut and grind it up and make it easier for the rest of your body to absorb. Teeth contain living cells, nerves and blood vessels. You need to look after your teeth carefully, otherwise they will **decay** (rot away) or even fall out.

An angled mirror like this helps the dentist to see inside your mouth and check that your teeth and gums are healthy.

PARTS OF A TOOTH

A typical tooth has three main parts. The part of the tooth that can be seen is called the **crown**. Each tooth is fixed in a socket in the jawbone by one, two or three **roots**. The junction between the crown and root is called the **neck**.

Structure of a tooth

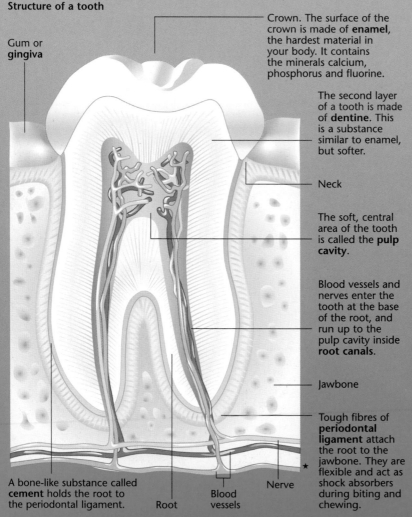

Gum or **gingiva**

Crown. The surface of the crown is made of **enamel**, the hardest material in your body. It contains the minerals calcium, phosphorus and fluorine.

The second layer of a tooth is made of **dentine**. This is a substance similar to enamel, but softer.

Neck

The soft, central area of the tooth is called the **pulp cavity**.

Blood vessels and nerves enter the tooth at the base of the root, and run up to the pulp cavity inside **root canals**.

Jawbone

Tough fibres of **periodontal ligament** attach the root to the jawbone. They are flexible and act as shock absorbers during biting and chewing.

A bone-like substance called **cement** holds the root to the periodontal ligament.

Root

Blood vessels

Nerve

TYPES OF TEETH

There are four main types of teeth in an adult set. Each is shaped for the particular job it has to do.

Main types of teeth

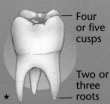

Incisors are sharp front teeth, used for biting and scraping.

Chisel-shaped crown

One root

Canines or **cuspids** are cone-shaped teeth, used for piercing food.

Sharp point called a **cusp**

One root

Premolars or **bicuspids** are blunt, broad teeth, used for crushing and grinding.

Two cusps

One or two roots

Molars are broader than premolars, with more cusps. They crush and grind food.

Four or five cusps

Two or three roots

Wisdom teeth are the third and last molars to appear. They lie at the back of the jaw, one at each corner. They usually come through when you are 17-21.

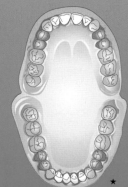

This tool is called a **probe**. A dentist uses it to scrape away plaque and to check whether your teeth have holes.

TWO SETS OF TEETH

A set of teeth is called a **dentition**. During your life, you have two dentitions. The first begins to appear when you are around six months old. The teeth in this dentition are called **deciduous teeth**, **milk teeth** or **baby teeth**. There are 20 deciduous teeth in all.

Deciduous dentition (milk teeth)

- Incisors
- Canines
- Premolars

There are no deciduous molars.

Between the ages of 6 and 12, the deciduous teeth fall out and are replaced by **permanent teeth**. There are normally 32 of these, although some people have one or two more or fewer.

Permanent dentition (adult teeth)

- Incisors
- Canines
- Premolars
- Molars

TOOTH DECAY

Everyone has tiny organisms called bacteria living in their mouth. These multiply very quickly if they have a supply of sweet foods. They form a sticky substance called **plaque**, which covers your teeth in a thin, white film.

As they feed on food lodged between your teeth, bacteria produce acid which dissolves the tooth. This can make your tooth ache, and eventually destroy it. The stages of tooth decay are described below.

1. Bacteria feed on sweet food stuck to a tooth. The acid they produce dissolves the enamel.

2. If the enamel is not repaired by a dentist, the acid will eat through the dentine.

3. If the decay reaches the pulp cavity and its nerve endings, your tooth will start to hurt.

4. Bacteria from the mouth can also enter the pulp cavity. This can cause an infection in the root which may result in a painful, pus-filled **abscess**.

See for yourself

You can use disclosing tablets from a pharmacist or your dentist to see the plaque on your teeth.

Brush and floss your teeth well, then use a disclosing tablet, following the instructions on the packet. The stained areas will show any food or plaque that you have not brushed away.

HEALTHY TEETH

Bacteria in your mouth also causes **gum disease**, or **gingivitis**. This makes the gums bleed and, if left untreated, affects the periodontal ligament and jawbone, making the teeth wobble or even fall out.

Cleaning your teeth twice a day is the best way to keep your teeth and gums healthy. Many toothpastes contain a mineral called **fluoride**. This strengthens teeth by making the enamel less soluble in acid and replacing minerals in enamel that have been attacked by acid. It also reduces the bacteria's ability to make acid.

Regular **flossing** (using a thread called **dental floss** to clean between the teeth and where the teeth and gums meet) also helps to remove plaque and prevent tooth decay and gum disease.

Internet links

• Scan the code for facts about toothpaste and a recipe to make your own.

DIGESTION

As food passes through your body, it is broken down into pieces small enough to be dissolved in your blood. This process, called **digestion**, takes place in the **digestive tract** or **alimentary canal** – a tube that runs from your mouth to a hole in your bottom called the **anus**. Food is broken down physically by chewing and churning, and chemically by the action of **digestive juices**, made by organs called **digestive glands**.

STAGES OF DIGESTION

1. Food is chewed in the mouth and mixed with a digestive juice called **saliva**, which is made in your **salivary glands**. Saliva moistens the food so it slides down your throat easily. It also starts to break down starch* in the food into a sugar called **maltose**.

2. Your throat muscles guide the food through the **pharynx** into a passage called the **gullet** or **oesophagus**. As you swallow, a flap called the **epiglottis** blocks off the top of your **windpipe** or **trachea***, so the food does not go down the wrong way.

How you swallow food

Nasal cavity

Soft palate

Bolus (ball of food) in mouth

Pharynx

Hard palate

Tongue

Trachea

Soft palate closes nasal cavity.

Bolus travels through pharynx.

Epiglottis closes trachea.

See for yourself

Put a piece of crusty bread in your mouth and notice the taste as you start to chew it. After a minute of chewing, you will find that the bread starts to taste sweeter. This happens as your saliva begins to turn the starch into sugar.

* Starch, 356; Trachea, 358.

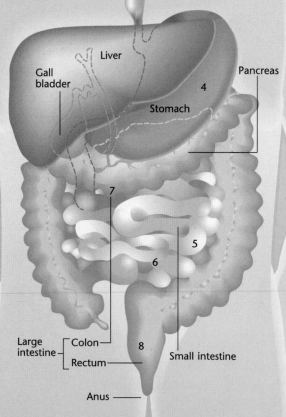

The digestive system

Salivary gland

Tongue

Pharynx

2

1

Epiglottis

Salivary glands

Gullet (oesophagus)

Windpipe (trachea)

The digestive organs on this diagram are shown raised and spread out so you can see them clearly.

3

Liver

Gall bladder

Pancreas

4

Stomach

7

5

6

Large intestine

Colon

8

Rectum

Small intestine

Anus

3. Food travels down the gullet into your stomach. Muscles in the wall of the gullet contract to push the food along. This action, called **peristalsis**, takes place all along your digestive tract.

4. In the **stomach**, food is churned up with **gastric juices**. These start to digest protein*, and they also contain hydrochloric acid which kills germs in the food. Your stomach lining has folds called **rugae**, which flatten as it fills.

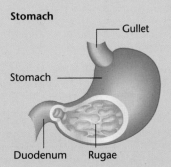

Stomach

- Gullet
- Stomach
- Duodenum
- Rugae

5. The food moves into a tube called the **small intestine**. This has three sections: the **duodenum**, the **jejunum** and the **ileum**. In the duodenum, digestive juices made by the liver and pancreas (see right) break down fats*, protein and starch*.

Small and large intestine

- Duodenum
- Colon
- Jejunum
- Ileum
- Rectum
- Anus

6. The small intestine is lined with tiny, finger-like **villi** which increase its surface area. These contains minute blood vessels, which absorb digested food, and carry it to the liver for further processing before it is carried around the body. Each villus also contains a **lacteal** – a lymphatic* vessel that allows digested fat to drain from the intestine.

Cross section of small intestine

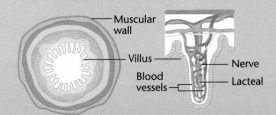

- Muscular wall
- Villus
- Nerve
- Blood vessels
- Lacteal

7. Water and any food, such as dietary fibre*, that cannot be digested move into the first part of the **large intestine**, called the **colon**. There water is absorbed into your bloodstream.

8. The semi-solid waste matter, called **faeces**, then passes into the second part of the large intestine, called the **rectum**. It is pushed out through the anus when you go to the toilet.

DIGESTIVE GLANDS

Your digestive glands make fluids needed for digestion. Many digestive juices contain chemicals called **digestive enzymes**, which help to break down your food. Some digestive glands are tiny, and set into the walls of digestive organs. For example, the wall of your stomach contains **gastric glands**. Other glands, such as your salivary glands, are separate organs.

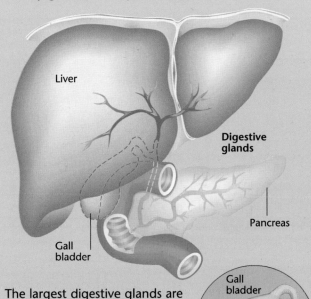

- Liver
- Digestive glands
- Pancreas
- Gall bladder

The largest digestive glands are the liver and pancreas. Your liver makes a green liquid called **bile**. This acts like a detergent, breaking up fats* into tiny drops so that enzymes can work on them. Bile is stored in a sac called the **gall bladder**. Your pancreas makes **pancreatic juice**. This contains enzymes which break down fats, protein* and starch*. Your liver and pancreas also have other important jobs to do, for example controlling the amount of glucose in your blood. You can read more about this on page 363.

Gall bladder

- Rugae flatten as sac fills with bile.

Internet links

• Scan the code to find out what happens to your food.

• For links to more websites where you can see inside the human body and take a tour of the digestive system, go to **www.usborne.com/quicklinks**

* Dietary fibre, 357; Fats, 356; Lymphatic system, 387; Proteins, Starch, 356.

FOOD AND DIET

The food and drink you take in are known as your **diet**. A healthy diet consists of a variety of foods, because different foods contain different things that your body needs. Carbohydrates, proteins and fats are vital for energy or growth. They are called **nutrients**. Vitamins, minerals and water are **accessory foods**. They help your body to work properly.

CARBOHYDRATES

Carbohydrates are energy-giving foods. There are two types: sugars and starch. **Sugars** are sweet and dissolve in water. Foods such as fruit and chocolate contain sugars. **Starch** is not sweet and does not dissolve in water. Bread, pasta, potatoes and rice are rich sources of starch.

Chocolate contains sugar, a carbohydrate.

During digestion, carbohydrates are broken down into simple sugars such as **glucose**. Your body uses these as fuel to produce energy. Some glucose is converted into **glycogen** and stored in the liver. Any remaining glucose is turned into fat, and stored under the skin.

Pasta is a healthy source of starch.

PROTEINS

Proteins are used for the growth and repair of body tissue, as well as other vital jobs. They are found in lean meat, fish, eggs, nuts, milk and beans.

Proteins are made up of simpler chemical units called **amino acids**. The type of protein depends on the order in which its amino acids are arranged. During digestion, proteins are broken down into individual amino acids. These are then rearranged to make different proteins needed by your body.

Examples of proteins in the body

Haemoglobin in these blood cells carries oxygen around the body.

Keratin is the protein from which hair and nails are made.

Actin and myosin enable muscles to contract.

FATS

Fats are needed by your body for energy and warmth. Unused fats are stored in various areas of your body, such as under the skin. There are two types of fats: saturated and unsaturated.

Saturated fats are found mostly in animal products, such as butter, lard and fatty meat. These foods also contain **cholesterol**, a fat-like substance. **Unsaturated fats** are found in non-animal products, including vegetable oils and nuts.

Junk food is often high in fat (and salt). Eating too much saturated fat, cholesterol and salt may be linked to heart disease.

See for yourself

Look at the labels on the packaging of some of the foods that you eat. They tell you how much carbohydrate, protein and fat the foods contain. Some labels also include information about the vitamins and minerals in a particular food.

VITAMINS

Vitamins are substances your body needs to remain healthy. They are found in a wide variety of foods. A balanced, healthy diet will give your body all the vitamins it needs.

Vitamins are **organic** chemicals, which means that they contain carbon. Your body needs tiny amounts of about 15 different vitamins for essential chemical processes to take place.

Vegetables and fruit are good sources of dietary fibre, vitamins and minerals.

Sources and uses of vitamins

Vitamin	Good sources	Necessary for
A (retinol)	Milk, butter, eggs, fish oils, fresh green vegetables	Eyes (especially seeing in very dim light), skin
B (a group of several vitamins)	Wholemeal bread and rice, yeast, liver, soya beans	Energy production in all your cells, nerves, skin
C (ascorbic acid)	Oranges, lemons, blackcurrants, tomatoes, fresh green vegetables	Blood vessels, gums, healing wounds, preventing colds
D (calciferol)	Fish oils, milk, eggs, butter (and sunlight)	Bones, teeth
E (tocopherol)	Vegetable oils, wholemeal bread, rice, eggs, butter, fresh green vegetables	Not yet fully understood
K (phylloquinone)	Fresh green vegetables, liver	Clotting blood

MINERALS

Minerals are another group of substances needed by your body. They are **inorganic**, which means that they do not contain carbon. You need small amounts of about 20 different minerals in all. **Trace minerals**, such as iron, are minerals that are needed in extremely small quantities.

Sources and uses of some minerals and trace minerals

Mineral	Good sources	Necessary for
Calcium and **phosphorus**	Milk, cheese, butter, water in some areas	Strong bones and teeth
Sodium	Salt, milk and spinach	Blood, digestion, nerves
Fluorine (trace mineral)	Milk, toothpaste, drinking water in some areas	Healthy teeth and bones
Iodine (trace mineral)	Seafood, table salt, drinking water in some areas	Hormone* thyroxin
Iron (trace mineral)	Liver, apricots and green vegetables	Haemoglobin in red blood cells*

Hormones, 362, 363; Red blood cells, 351; Urine, 362.

DIETARY FIBRE

Dietary fibre, also known as **roughage**, is a type of carbohydrate found in bran, wholemeal bread, fruit and vegetables. Fibre cannot be digested by humans. It is also bulky, which helps the muscles of your intestines to move food efficiently through your digestive system.

WATER

Water is vital for life. Without it, you would only survive for a few days. You need to take in water to replace what you lose, for example in urine* and sweat. There is water in what you drink, and also in some solid foods, such as lettuce, which is 90% water.

About 65% of your body is water. In very young children, up to 75% of their body weight is made up of water.

*

THE RESPIRATORY SYSTEM

The **respiratory system** is made up of your **lungs** and the passages that lead to them. You breathe air into your lungs, and oxygen from the air passes into the blood, which carries it around your body. Waste carbon dioxide passes from the blood into the lungs and is breathed out.

PARTS OF THE RESPIRATORY SYSTEM

When you breathe in, air is sucked through your nose or mouth and down a tube called the **windpipe** or **trachea**. The lining of your nose and trachea make a slippery liquid called **mucus**. This warms and moistens the air, so it can travel more easily along the passages. It also traps dirt and germs in the air. Tiny hairs called **cilia** waft the mucus away from your lungs towards your nose and throat.

Cells lining the nose | Cilia

Your trachea divides into two tubes, each called a **primary bronchus**. One leads to each lung. There the bronchi branch off, to become **secondary** and **tertiary bronchi**, and eventually form narrow tubes called **bronchioles**.

Each bronchiole ends in a cluster of air sacs called **alveoli**. These are surrounded by capillaries*.

Oxygen passes through the thin walls of the alveoli into the network of capillaries. Carbon dioxide in the blood, produced by cells during internal respiration*, passes into the alveoli. It is removed from your body when you breathe out.

Tertiary bronchus
Bronchiole
Cluster of alveoli

Alveolus
Capillaries

From heart
Alveolus wall
Carbon dioxide
Oxygen
Capillary
To heart

Primary bronchi

Secondary bronchi

Narrow tubes (bronchioles)

Tiny air sac (alveolus)

Lungs

Each lung contains many tubes, the smallest of which end in tiny air sacs (alveoli).

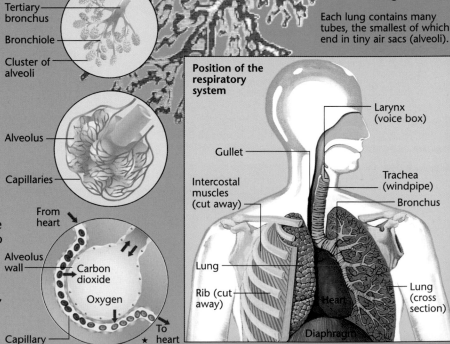

Position of the respiratory system

Larynx (voice box)
Gullet
Intercostal muscles (cut away)
Lung
Rib (cut away)
Heart
Diaphragm
Trachea (windpipe)
Bronchus
Lung (cross section)

* Capillaries, 351; Internal respiration, 360.

BREATHING

Breathing, or **ventilation**, is the movement of air in and out of the lungs. It is controlled by the movements of muscles in your chest, called **intercostal muscles**, and a flat sheet of muscle called the **diaphragm**, which lies under your lungs.

Breathing in

Air with oxygen

Ribs move up and out.

Diaphragm flattens.

Breathing out

Air with carbon dioxide

Ribs move down and in.

Diaphragm rises.

As you breathe in, your diaphragm flattens and your intercostal muscles contract, pulling your ribs up and out. The space inside your chest increases and makes the pressure of the air in your lungs lower than that outside your body. Air rushes in to fill the space. This is called **inhalation**.

As you breathe out, your diaphragm relaxes upwards, and your intercostal muscles relax, so your ribs move down and in. The space inside your chest gets smaller again, and air is squeezed out. This is called **exhalation**.

The normal rhythm of your breathing is sometimes interrupted. **Sneezing** clears irritating dust, pollen or germs from your nose. **Coughing** helps to clear such particles from your windpipe. **Yawning** raises the level of oxygen in your blood, and helps to rid your body of large amounts of carbon dioxide.

VOICE BOX

Your **voice box**, also called the **larynx**, is at the top of your trachea. Inside it are two bands of muscle called **vocal cords**. These open to let air past when you breathe, but when you speak or sing, muscles pull the cords together. The air passing up through the cords makes them vibrate. The vibrations can be heard as sounds.

Vocal cords as seen from above

Closed   Open

See for yourself

Place your fingers lightly on the front of your neck while you talk, shout and sing. You will be able to feel the vibrations in your vocal cords, and the movement of your muscles as they relax and tighten.

The louder and lower the sound is that you make, the stronger the vibrations. Your muscles will tighten when you sing higher notes and relax as you sing lower ones.

The shorter your vocal cords are and the faster they vibrate, the higher the sound you will make. Women's vocal cords are short and vibrate about 220 times in a second, so their voices are high. Men's cords are longer and vibrate about 120 times a second. This is why men have deeper voices.

Internet links

• Scan the code to watch a video clip about respiration.

• For links to more websites where you can investigate how the respiratory system works and solve quizzes to test your knowledge, go to www.usborne.com/quicklinks

359

ENERGY FOR LIFE

Your body needs energy to keep alive and working. It releases energy from digested food in a series of chemical reactions. This process, called **internal respiration**, takes place in your cells, particularly in your muscles. All the processes in your body involved in producing energy, growth and waste are called **metabolism**.

A healthy diet provides this dancer with energy, and regular exercise keeps her strong and supple.

AEROBIC RESPIRATION

Internal respiration which uses oxygen is called **aerobic respiration**. Food, usually in the form of glucose*, is combined with oxygen breathed in from the air. The reaction releases energy, and its waste products are water and carbon dioxide. Chemicals called **enzymes** help to speed up the reaction.

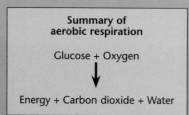

Summary of aerobic respiration

Glucose + Oxygen

↓

Energy + Carbon dioxide + Water

Some of the energy is set free as heat in a process called **thermogenesis**. The rest is stored as a chemical called **ATP** (**adenosine triphosphate**). When energy is needed, ATP breaks down into **ADP** (**adenosine diphosphate**), releasing its stored energy.

METABOLIC RATE

The overall rate at which your body converts food into energy is called your **metabolic rate**. It varies from person to person.

People with a slow metabolic rate convert food into energy slowly. They may gain fat easily and often appear to have little energy. People with a fast metabolic rate often appear to have plenty of energy. They convert food to energy quickly and little is stored as fat.

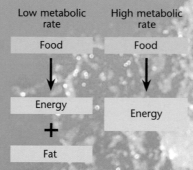

Low metabolic rate

Food

↓

Energy

+

Fat

High metabolic rate

Food

↓

Energy

Regular exercise, such as swimming, can help to increase your metabolic rate and keep you fitter.

ENERGY VALUE

The amount of energy that can be released from food is called its **energy value**. This is usually measured in **kilojoules (kJ)**. Energy value is sometimes given in **kilocalories**, also known as **Calories**. A kilojoule equals 0.238 kilocalories. Most pre-packed foods have labels showing the energy value both in kilojoules and kilocalories.

Swimming uses about 2,250 kilojoules (600 Calories) of energy per hour.

* Glucose, 356.

EFFECTS OF EXERCISE

Regular exercise is an important part of keeping healthy. It helps to keep your body fit in three ways, improving your strength, stamina and suppleness.

Strength is the amount of force a muscle or group of muscles can produce. **Stamina** helps you to exercise for longer without becoming tired. **Suppleness** describes how flexible your body is. Different types of activity help to develop these aspects of fitness. The effects of some types of exercise are shown in the table below.

BENEFITS OF EXERCISE

When you exercise, your muscles need more oxygen to release energy by aerobic respiration. You start to breathe more quickly to take in extra oxygen. This strengthens the chest muscles and increases the amount of air your lungs can hold.

Your heart beats faster to pump the oxygen-rich blood to your muscles. This strengthens the heart muscles. As blood rushes through your blood vessels, it helps to keep them clear of fatty substances that might build up and cause a heart attack.

GETTING TIRED

Often during hard exercise, such as sprinting, your body cannot take in enough oxygen for aerobic respiration. The muscles then convert glucose to energy without using oxygen in a process called **anaerobic respiration**. A substance called **lactic acid** begins to build up. Your muscles ache and your body is said to have an **oxygen debt**.

By breathing deeply after hard exercise you take in extra oxygen to "pay back" the oxygen debt.

Exercise	A	B	C
Badminton	★	★★	★
Cycling	★★★	★	★★
Dancing (energetic)	★★	★★★	★
Football	★★	★★	★★
Gymnastics	★	★★★	★★
Hill walking	★★	★	★
Horse riding	O	O	★
Jogging	★★★	★	★

Exercise	A	B	C
Judo	★	★★★	★
Roller blading	★★	O	★
Skipping (vigorous)	★★★	O	★
Swimming	★★★	★★★	★★★
Tennis	★	★★	★
Walking	★	O	O
Weightlifting	O	O	★★★
Yoga	O	★★★	O

Key   **A** = Stamina   **B** = Suppleness   **C** = Strength
O = no effect   ★ = beneficial effect   ★★ = very good   ★★★ = excellent

Summary of anaerobic respiration
Glucose → Energy + Lactic acid

Swimming exercises all the muscles and is excellent for building strength, stamina and suppleness.

BALANCING ACT

For your body to work properly, conditions inside it, such as temperature and the levels of water and other chemicals, need to be kept constant. This is known as **homeostasis**. An important aspect of this is **excretion** – the removal of waste substances from your body. Chemicals called **hormones** also help to control the levels of substances inside your body.

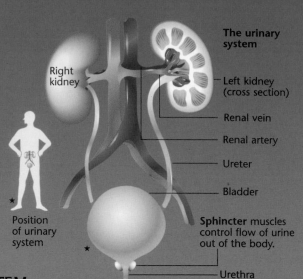

The urinary system

Right kidney

Left kidney (cross section)

Renal vein

Renal artery

Ureter

Bladder

Position of urinary system

Sphincter muscles control flow of urine out of the body.

Urethra

EXCRETORY ORGANS

Any part which removes waste from your body can be called an **excretory organ**. The main ones are your kidneys and liver, but there are others. Your lungs, for example, remove carbon dioxide and water when you breathe out, and your skin removes water and unwanted salts in the form of sweat.

This X-ray image shows the blood vessels inside a kidney.

URINARY SYSTEM

The **urinary system** controls the amount of water in your body. It is made up of two **kidneys**, a balloon-like sac called the **bladder**, and the tubes connected to them. Blood flows through **renal arteries** into the kidneys where it is filtered by about a million tiny units called **nephrons**.

Inside each nephron (see diagram, right), the artery splits into knots of capillaries* called **glomeruli**. High pressure inside the glomeruli forces glucose, water and salts to filter out of the blood into cup-shaped structures called **Bowman's capsules**.

The filtered liquid travels along a looping tube in the nephron. Blood capillaries leaving the glomerulus wrap around these tubes, where some glucose, water and salts are reabsorbed, leaving waste products behind. The cleaned blood leaves through the **renal vein**.

Inside a nephron

Bowman's capsule
Glomerulus

Renal artery
Renal vein

Cortex
Medulla
Collecting duct

Capillary*

To ureter

The remaining liquid, now called **urine**, passes into a **collecting duct**, which drains into an area known as the **renal pelvis**. From there the urine flows through a tube called the **ureter** into the bladder. The urine is stored until you go to the toilet, when it leaves the body through a tube called the **urethra**.

The blood vessels can be seen clearly because they have been injected with a fluid which X-rays cannot pass through.

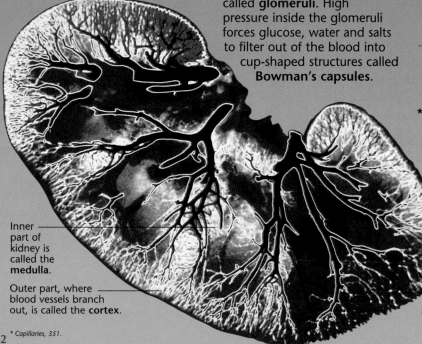

Inner part of kidney is called the **medulla**.

Outer part, where blood vessels branch out, is called the **cortex**.

* Capillaries, 351.

HORMONES

Hormones are made in groups of cells called **endocrine glands** and are carried around the body by the blood. Your body makes over 20 types of hormone. Each type affects a different part of your body, known as its **target organ**. The main endocrine glands and some of the hormones they produce are shown in the table below.

Gland	Hormones made	Effect of hormones
Pituitary	Include growth hormone, prolactin	Control other endocrine glands, growth, mother's milk production.
Parathyroids	Parathormone	Controls calcium levels in blood and bones.
Adrenals	Adrenalin, aldosterone	Control blood glucose level, heart rate, body's salt level.
Thyroid	Thyroxin	Controls metabolism*.
Pancreas	Insulin, glucagon	Control use of glucose* by body.
Testes* (in scrotum*)	Testosterone	Controls sexual development in males.
Ovaries* (in abdomen)	Oestrogen, progesterone	Controls sexual development in females.

Endocrine glands

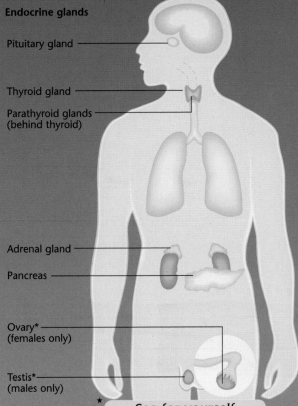

- Pituitary gland
- Thyroid gland
- Parathyroid glands (behind thyroid)
- Adrenal gland
- Pancreas
- Ovary* (females only)
- Testis* (males only)

OPPOSITE EFFECTS

Many hormones work in pairs, producing opposite effects. They are known as **antagonistic hormones**. For example, the amount of glucose* in your blood is kept at a constant level by the hormones **insulin** and **glucagon**. These are made in the pancreas by clusters of cells called **islets of Langerhans**.

If your pancreas stops making enough insulin, it causes a condition called **diabetes**. People with diabetes need to control their intake of sugar. Many also take tablets or have injections of insulin.

These three cell clusters are islets of Langerhans.

See for yourself

Some hormones act slowly, but others act very quickly. Notice the effect that the hormone adrenalin has on your body when you are excited, scared or angry. Your heart and lungs work faster to take more oxygen to your muscles. This helps to give you more power if you need to take action.

Internet links

- Scan the code to watch a video about how our bodies maintain a steady temperature.

- For links to more websites, go to **www.usborne.com/quicklinks**

How insulin and glucagon control glucose

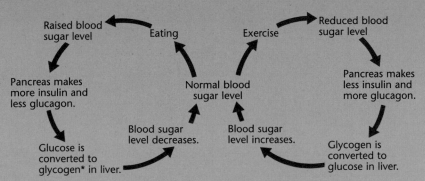

Raised blood sugar level → Eating → Exercise → Reduced blood sugar level

Pancreas makes more insulin and less glucagon.

Normal blood sugar level

Pancreas makes less insulin and more glucagon.

Glucose is converted to glycogen* in liver.

Blood sugar level decreases.

Blood sugar level increases.

Glycogen is converted to glucose in liver.

Glucose, Glycogen, 356; Metabolism, 360; Ovaries, Scrotum, Testes, 376.

THE NERVOUS SYSTEM

The **nervous system** is made up of the brain, spinal cord and nerves. Your brain and spinal cord are known as the **central nervous system**. They receive information from all parts of your body, process it, and send instructions to other body parts. The network of nerves that carries information to and from this central area is called the **peripheral nervous system**.

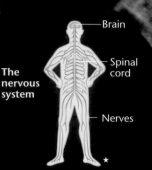

The nervous system

- Brain
- Spinal cord
- Nerves

NERVE CELLS

The nervous system contains millions of nerve cells, called **neurons**. There are three types: sensory, association and motor neurons.

Sensory neurons have sensitive nerve endings called **receptors**. These respond to stimuli such as light, heat or chemicals, both inside and outside the body. Sensory neurons carry information about the stimuli from the receptors to the central nervous system.

Association neurons in the brain and spinal cord pick up and interpret information from the sensory neurons. They then pass instructions to **motor neurons** which carry them to other parts of your body, such as muscles and glands, where the instructions are obeyed.

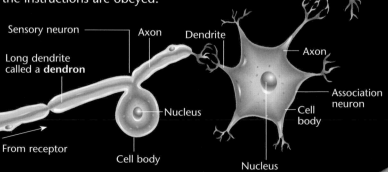

Sensory neuron
Axon
Dendrite
Long dendrite called a **dendron**
Nucleus
From receptor
Cell body
Dendrite
Axon
Association neuron
Cell body
Nucleus

Dendrites and axons may be much longer than shown in this diagram.

PARTS OF A NEURON

Each neuron has a **cell body**, which contains the nucleus, and strands called **nerve fibres**. There are two types of fibres. **Dendrites** carry information towards the cell body, and **axons** carry information away from it. The axons of one cell join another cell's dendrites, or a muscle, to pass on information.

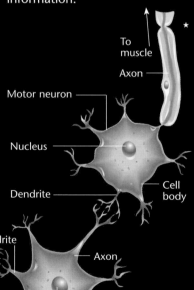

To muscle
Axon
Motor neuron
Nucleus
Dendrite
Cell body

NERVES

Nerves are cords that contain bundles of nerve fibres. **Sensory nerves** have just the fibres of sensory neurons, and **motor nerves** have only those of motor neurons. **Mixed nerves** contain fibres from both.

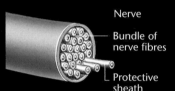

Nerve
Bundle of nerve fibres
Protective sheath

The **spinal cord** is a thick bundle of nerves, which runs from the brain down a tunnel of holes in your backbone. Impulses from almost all parts of the body pass through the spinal cord.

In this highly-magnified picture of nerve cells in the brain, the orange areas are cell bodies.

AREAS OF CEREBRUM

The outer layer of the cerebrum is called **cerebral cortex**. It can be divided into three types of areas. **Sensory areas** receive information from all parts of your body, such as the eyes and ears. **Association areas** analyse the information and make decisions. **Motor areas** send orders for action to muscles or glands*.

Areas in the cerebrum

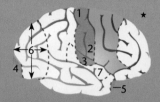

Sensory areas
1. Receives impulses from muscles, skin and inner organs.
2. Receives impulses from tongue.
3. Receives impulses from ears.
4. Receives impulses from eyes.
5. Receives impulses from nose.

Association areas include:
6. Produces sight.
7. Produces hearing.

Motor areas. Each tiny part sends out impulses to a specific muscle.

DIVIDED IN HALF

The cerebrum is made up of two halves called **cerebral hemispheres**. They are joined by the **corpus callosum**, which is a thick band of nerve fibres. Each hemisphere controls the opposite side of the body or deals with different skills.

Cerebral hemispheres

Right

Left

In most people, the parts of the brain that control the everyday aspects of language are in the left hemisphere. Those that control its more artistic aspects, such as rhythm and vocal expression tend to be in the right hemisphere.

* Glands, 355, 363.

MEMORY

There are two different types of memory. Motor-skill memory helps you to remember how to do actions, such as walking or riding a bicycle. Factual memory enables you to remember specific pieces of information.

There are also two levels of memory. Short-term memory stores information for only a few minutes. Anything that you can remember for longer is in your long-term memory.

Information can be stored in your long-term memory for up to a lifetime.

See for yourself

Test your short-term memory by reading through the list of numbers below, then seeing how many you can write down in order. Most people cannot remember more than seven numbers.

3 0 9 7 1 2 8 5 4 1 6 9

BRAIN WAVES

The electrical impulses between nerve cells in your brain can be detected through your skull by sensor pads called **electrodes**. The patterns, or **brain waves**, are recorded on a chart called an **electroencephalogram (EEG)**. Doctors use EEGs to find out if a person's brain is working normally.

Main types of brain waves

Alpha waves show when you are awake, but disappear during sleep.

Beta waves show when you are thinking, or receiving impulses from your senses.

Theta waves show in EEGs of children, and adults suffering from stress or some brain disorders.

Delta waves show in EEGs of babies and sleeping adults. They can be a sign of brain disorder in an awake adult.

SLEEP

EEGs are also used to study brain activity during sleep. There are two kinds of sleep. One is known as **rapid eye movement (REM)** sleep, because your eyes move around even though they are closed. The other is called **non REM (NREM)** sleep. In REM sleep, the peaks and troughs (ups and downs) on the chart are close together, showing that the brain is very active. In NREM sleep, the peaks and troughs are further apart, so the brain is less active.

Internet links

- Scan the code to discover amazing facts about your brain.

- For links to more websites where you can explore the brain and try memory experiments, go to **www.usborne.com/quicklinks**

SKIN, NAILS AND HAIR

The **skin** is the largest organ in your body. Along with your hair and nails, it makes up the **integumentary system**. This covers your body, protecting it against damage, infection and drying out. Your skin also helps to keep your body at a constant temperature, removes some waste, makes vitamin D and helps to collect information about your surroundings.

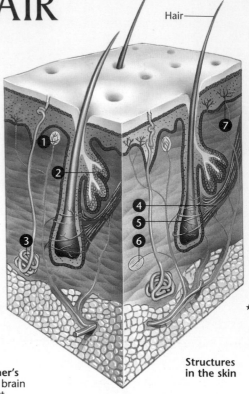

Hair

7

Structures in the skin

DIFFERENT LAYERS

Skin has two main layers: the outer **epidermis**, and the inner **dermis**. The dermis contains blood vessels, as well as structures such as receptors*. Under the dermis is a store of fat cells called the **subcutaneous layer**. This helps to keep your body warm.

Layers of skin

Epidermis

Dermis

Subcutaneous layer *

The epidermis has several layers. The top, **cornified layer**, is made of flat, dead skin cells, filled with a tough, waterproof protein called **keratin**. These cells are constantly being worn away and replaced by cells from a layer lower down.

Hairs growing out of skin, shown magnified over 1,000 times

* Receptors, 364.

INSIDE THE SKIN

As well as containing many blood vessels (which are not shown here), the dermis also contains other structures. These perform the skin's many jobs.

Key to structures in the skin

1. Touch receptors called **Meissner's corpuscles** send impulses to the brain when your skin touches an object.

2. **Sebaceous glands** produce an oil called **sebum**. This helps to keep your hair and skin waterproof and supple.

3. **Sweat glands** produce sweat.

4. **Hair erector muscles** make hairs stand on end, for example when your body is cold.

5. **Hair plexuses** are groups of nerve fibre endings. Each forms a network around the narrow tubes that contain hair, and sends impulses to your brain when the hair moves.

6. Pressure receptors called **Pacinian corpuscles** send impulses to your brain on receiving deep pressure.

7. **Pain receptors** send impulses to the brain if any stimulation, such as heat or pressure, becomes too much. Your brain interprets such impulses as pain.

See for yourself

Gently press a piece of sticky tape onto the back of your hand, then pull it off and look at it carefully under a magnifying lens. You should be able to see tiny flakes of dead epidermal skin.

The flakes you can see here are dead skin cells from the top layer of the epidermis. They will fall off, and be replaced by cells from lower layers.

TEMPERATURE CONTROL

Your skin plays a vital part in keeping your body temperature constant, as shown below.

How skin cools down

Blood vessels widen, so more heat can be lost through the skin.	Hairs (only shown here at the surface) lie flat, so little warm air is trapped.

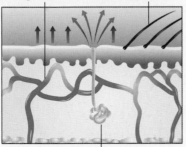

Sweat is produced. It escapes through holes called **pores**. As it dries, it uses heat from the skin, and cools you down.

How skin retains heat

Blood vessels narrow, so less heat escapes through the skin.	Erector muscles contract and make hairs stand up, trapping warm air.

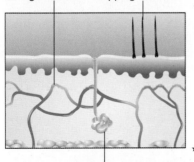

Sweat glands produce less sweat.

Your body also keeps warm by shivering. Your muscles jerk automatically, producing heat as they do so.

The outer surface of a hair is called the **cuticle**. It is made up of flat, overlapping scales of a tough substance called keratin.

NAILS

Nails help you to touch and feel things by forming firm pads to support your sensitive fingertips. Like skin, nails are mostly made from keratin. They grow from a row of dividing cells called the **nail root**.

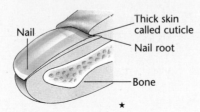

Nail

Thick skin called cuticle

Nail root

Bone

HAIR

Hairs grow out of deep pits, called **follicles**, in your skin. Cells at the base of each hair divide and push the hair up through the follicle. The hair you can see, called the **shaft**, is made of dead cells. This is why cutting your hair does not hurt.

How a hair grows

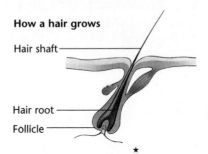

Hair shaft

Hair root

Follicle

Hair types

Round follicle — Straight hair

Oval follicle — Wavy hair

Kidney-shaped follicle — Curly hair

Whether your hair is curly or straight depends on the shape of each follicle.

DARK AND FAIR

Your skin contains cells called **melanocytes** which produce a brown substance called **melanin**. This absorbs some of the Sun's harmful ultraviolet rays, and so helps to protect your skin. The amount of melanin produced affects the colour of the skin.

Fair-skinned people have melanin in only the lower layers of the epidermis, but people with dark skin have larger amounts of it in all layers. Melanin mixed with an orange chemical called **phaeomelanin** gives skin a yellow tint. **Freckles** are small patches of skin which contain more melanin than the surrounding area.

The colour of hair is also due to melanin. Dark hair, for example, contains mostly pure melanin. Fair hair contains a type of melanin with sulphur in it, and red hair results from a type of melanin with iron in it.

Some variations in skin and hair colour

Internet links

• Scan the code to watch a video clip about skin.

• For links to more websites where you can take a closer look at skin, nails and hair, go to **www.usborne.com/quicklinks**

EYES

Your **eyes** are the organs of sight. You see things because light rays bounce off objects and enter your eyes. Light-sensitive cells at the back of your eyes send information to the brain, which interprets it as a picture, or **image**. Each eye sees objects from a different angle and your brain joins the two images to help you see in 3D. This is called **stereoscopic vision**.

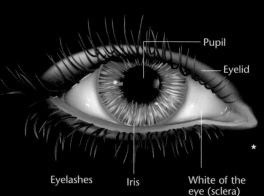

Pupil

Eyelid

Eyelashes   Iris   White of the eye (sclera)

HOW EYES WORK

Light rays enter your eye at a curved surface which bends and focusses them. They then pass through the **pupil** which controls how much light reaches the **lens**. The lens fine-tunes the focussing to allow for near and far objects and projects an upside-down image onto the back of the eye.

The **retina** contains light-sensitive receptors* called rods and cones. These convert the image into nerve impulses which travel to the brain along the optic nerve. Your brain interprets these impulses as an image, which it also turns the right way up again.

Cross section of an eye

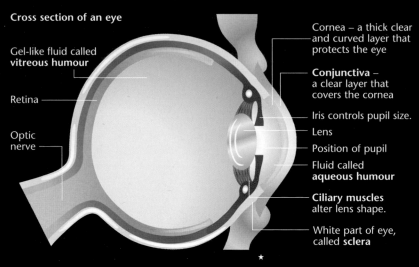

Gel-like fluid called **vitreous humour**

Retina

Optic nerve

Cornea – a thick clear and curved layer that protects the eye

Conjunctiva – a clear layer that covers the cornea

Iris controls pupil size.

Lens

Position of pupil

Fluid called **aqueous humour**

Ciliary muscles alter lens shape.

White part of eye, called **sclera**

RODS AND CONES

Each eye has about 125 million rods and 7 million cones. Rods only detect black and white, but they work well in dim light. Cones see colours but need bright light to work. At night, you see mainly in shades of grey because only your rods are working.

Close-up of area of retina

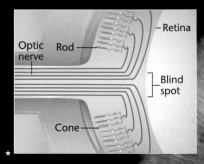

Optic nerve   Rod

Retina

Blind spot

Cone

You have three types of cone, sensitive to red, green or blue light. Each type responds by a different amount depending on the colour you are looking at. For example, if you look at a purple object, the blue and red cones respond more strongly than the green ones. **Colour-blind** people cannot see colours well because some cones are faulty.

See for yourself

There are no rods and cones on the area where the optic nerve leaves your eye. If an image falls here, you cannot see it, so this area is called the **blind spot**. Test to find your blind spot by holding this page at arm's length. Close your left eye and stare at the square with your right eye. Slowly bring the page closer to your face and notice the circle disappear.

* Receptors, 364.

PUPIL SIZE

The coloured iris contains **radial** and **circular muscles** which control the size of the pupil and the amount of light entering the eye. In dim light, the radial muscles contract. This makes your pupils larger and allows in as much light as possible. In bright light, the circular muscles contract. Your pupils shrink to prevent you from being dazzled.

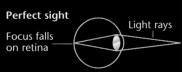

Pupil in dim light

Pupil in bright light

Iris — Pupil

Radial muscles contract.

Circular muscles contract. ★

Iris and pupil

The fine threads are radial muscles. They help to control the size of the pupil.

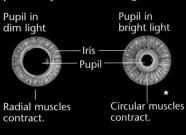

SEEING CLEARLY

As light rays from an object enter your eye, they are bent inwards by the cornea and lens. The point at which light rays meet is called the **focus**. If they focus on the retina, everything you see looks sharp and clear. The lens changes shape when looking at objects at different distances. This bends the light rays by different amounts, and keeps the image in focus.

Perfect sight

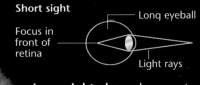

Focus falls on retina

Light rays

Some people cannot focus light properly. **Short-sighted** people cannot see distant objects clearly. They have long eyeballs, and the lens bends the rays too much, so they focus in front of the retina.

Short sight

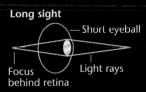

Long eyeball

Focus in front of retina

Light rays

Long-sighted people cannot see close objects clearly. They have short eyeballs, and the lens bends the rays too little, so the image reaches the retina before it is in focus.

Long sight

Short eyeball

Focus behind retina

Light rays

Short sight can be corrected by wearing glasses or contact lenses with **concave lenses**. People with long sight need **convex lenses**.

Concave lens

Convex lens

EYE PROTECTION

Eyes are very delicate. Most of the eyeball is protected by the bones of your skull. The front of the eye is protected by the thin layer of skin known as the **eyelid**.

Protecting the eyeballs

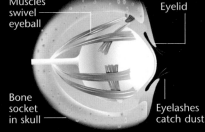

Muscles swivel eyeball

★ Eyelid

Bone socket in skull

Eyelashes catch dust

Eyelids keep dust and dirt out of your eyes. When you blink, your eyelids wipe **tears** over the eye, keeping it moist and clean. Tears contain chemicals which help to kill bacteria. They are made in **lachrymal glands** above each eye, and drain into your nose through two **lachrymal canals**.

Tear production in the left eye

Lachrymal gland produces tears.

Lachrymal canals

★

Internet links

- Scan the code to watch an experiment about seeing colour.

- For links to more websites with facts, quizzes and animations about how eyes work, go to **www.usborne.com/quicklinks**

EARS

Your **ears** are the organs of hearing. All sounds are vibrations called **sound waves**. These enter your ears and stimulate receptors* in them to send nerve impulses* to your brain. The brain then interprets the impulses and identifies the sound. Your ears also help you to keep your balance, and give you information about the angle of your body.

As well as hearing sounds, your ears help you to keep your balance.

EARS AND HEARING

Your ear is divided into three areas: the **outer ear**, which is the part you can see, and the **middle** and **inner ear** which are the main working parts.

The ear flap, or **pinna**, funnels sound waves into a passage called the **ear canal**. The waves travel along this passage until they hit a thin layer of tissue called the **eardrum**, making it vibrate. The vibrations pass through three tiny bones (the **malleus**, **incus** and **stapes**) to the **oval window** – an oval hole covered by a thin membrane.

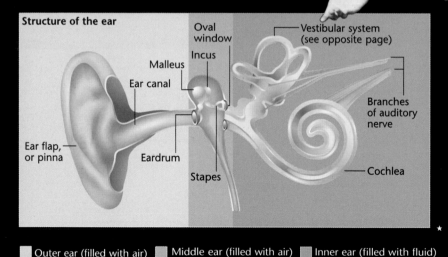

Structure of the ear

Oval window
Incus
Malleus
Ear canal
Vestibular system
(see opposite page)
Branches of auditory nerve
Ear flap, or pinna
Eardrum
Stapes
Cochlea

■ Outer ear (filled with air) ■ Middle ear (filled with air) ■ Inner ear (filled with fluid)

The oval window vibrates and the vibrations pass into a spiral-shaped tube called the **cochlea**.

The cochlea contains three chambers filled with fluid. The vibrations spread along these chambers and stimulate tiny **hair cells**. These are special nerve cells attached to a membrane, called the **organ of Corti**, that runs inside the cochlea. The hair cells change the vibrations into nerve impulses, which travel along the **auditory nerve** to the brain. Your brain interprets the impulses as sounds, so you can hear.

Nerve impulses, 365; Receptors, 364.

KEEPING BALANCED

Many parts of your body help you to keep balanced. Your eyes tell you about the position of your body. So do sensitive cells known as **stretch receptors** in your muscles and tendons.

The **vestibular system** in your inner ear also has an important part to play in maintaining your balance. It has two main areas: three loops, called semicircular canals, and two sacs called the utricle and saccule.

The vestibular system

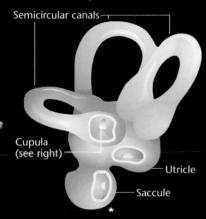

Semicircular canals

Cupula (see right)

Utricle

Saccule

See for yourself

If you spin around very quickly, you will probably feel dizzy when you stop. This is because the liquid in your semicircular canals keeps on spinning after your body stops.

You can produce a similar effect by holding a glass of water in your hand and swirling it around.

The water in the glass will carry on swirling for a little while after you stop moving the glass.

The **semicircular canals** contain fluid-filled tubes called **semicircular ducts**. At the end of each duct is a small swelling which has a gel-like projection called a **cupula** inside it. When your head turns, the fluid moves more slowly than the head, bending the cupula back. Tiny **hair cells** at the base of the cupula send your brain information about rotation of the head.

How a cupula works

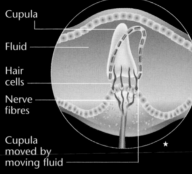

Cupula

Fluid

Hair cells

Nerve fibres

Cupula moved by moving fluid

The **utricle** and **saccule** contain a small, gel-like patch called a **macula**. It contains tiny grains, called **otoliths**, and hair cells. When your head moves, gravity causes the otoliths to slide to one side, pulling with them the gel and the hairs. These send your brain information about the forward, backward, sideways or tilted position of the head.

How a macula works

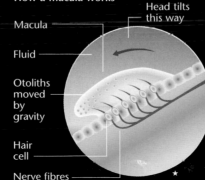

Head tilts this way

Macula

Fluid

Otoliths moved by gravity

Hair cell

Nerve fibres

TWO EARS

Having two ears gives your brain two sources of information about sounds, movement and position. By combining this information, the brain finds out more than it would from one ear alone.

For instance, having two ears helps you to tell which direction a sound is coming from. A sound coming from the left will hit your left ear slightly earlier than your right and will produce stronger vibrations. If the sound is directly in front or behind, the sound arrives at each ear at the same time and volume.

See for yourself

You can use this test to find out how your brain locates a sound. Sit on a chair, blindfolded. Ask someone to make a sound by tapping together two pencils, in different places around and above your body. Say where you think the sound is coming from.

You will probably find it hardest to pinpoint the sound when it is coming from directly behind, above or in front of you, in line with the centre of your body. This is because the nerve impulses from your ears reach your brain at the same time.

Internet links

• Scan the code to zoom into an ear and find out how we hear.

• For links to more websites about our ears, go to **www.usborne.com/quicklinks**

THE NOSE AND TONGUE

Your **nose** and **tongue** are the organs of smell and taste respectively. Smells and tastes are chemicals. Cells called **chemoreceptors** in your nose and tongue detect these chemicals and send information to the brain, which identifies the smell or taste. Both organs also have other important jobs to do, for example the nose is part of the respiratory system and the tongue plays a role in digestion and speech.

This man is collecting rose petals to make into perfume. The human sense of smell can detect subtle variations in perfumes.

INSIDE THE NOSE

The two holes in your nose, called **nostrils**, open into a hollow space called the **nasal cavity**. As you breathe in, air is sucked into the lower part of the nasal cavity. Here, short hairs filter out large dust particles from the air, and mucus* in the cavity's lining warms and moistens the air before it travels into the lungs.

The roof of the nasal cavity has many tiny threads called **olfactory hairs** dangling through it.

These hairs are the dendrites* of chemoreceptors called **olfactory cells**. Chemicals in the air, called **odorant molecules**, dissolve in the mucus and are absorbed by the hairs. The olfactory cells send nerve impulses* to the brain, which interprets them as a smell.

When you breathe in normally, only a small amount of air floats into your nasal cavity. When you sniff hard, you direct a stream of air towards your smell detectors. This is why things smell stronger if you sniff their scent.

DIFFERENT SMELLS

Most humans are able to recognize millions of different scents. For many years, scientists thought that all smells were made up of the seven basic scents listed below. More recent research, however, has led to the opinion that there are many more scents – perhaps hundreds.

Seven basic scents

Scent	Example
Camphor	Mothballs
Musk	Aftershave/Perfume
Floral	Roses
Peppermint	Mint toothpaste
Ether	Dry cleaning fluid
Pungent	Vinegar
Putrid	Rotten eggs

The sense of smell is strongly linked to memory. For example, the scent of mown grass might remind you vividly of a school sports day. This link probably happens because nerve impulses from the nose are analysed at the front of the cerebrum*. This part of the brain also deals with memory and feelings.

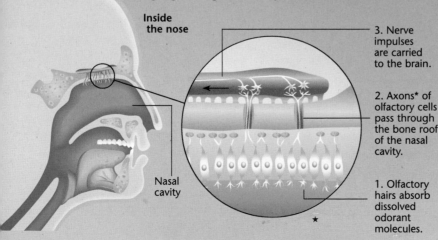

Inside the nose

3. Nerve impulses are carried to the brain.

2. Axons* of olfactory cells pass through the bone roof of the nasal cavity.

1. Olfactory hairs absorb dissolved odorant molecules.

Nasal cavity

* Axons, 364; Cerebrum, 366; Dendrites, 364; Mucus, 358; Nerve impulses, 365.

TONGUE AND TASTE

The main purpose of your sense of taste is to tell you whether or not something is safe to eat. For example, rotten food and most poisonous plants taste revolting, so your immediate reaction is to spit them out.

The surface of your tongue is covered with tiny bumps called **papillae**. Many of these are lined with **taste buds**, which contain chemoreceptors called **gustatory receptor cells**. These are sensitive to chemicals from your food which dissolve in your saliva. The cells send nerve impulses to the brain, which interprets them as a taste.

Taste buds

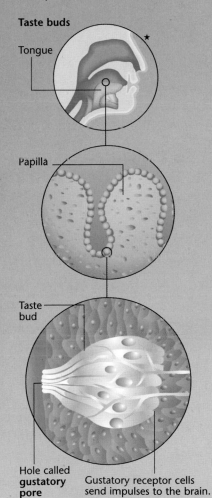

Tongue

Papilla

Taste bud

Hole called **gustatory pore**

Gustatory receptor cells send impulses to the brain.

BASIC TASTES

Scientists think that there are five main tastes: salt, sweet, sour, bitter and a savoury taste called umami. All flavours are made up of these basic tastes, plus smells detected by the nose.

Lemons taste sour.

Toffees taste sweet.

Five basic tastes

Taste	Example
Salt	Table salt
Sweet	Honey
Sour	Lemon juice
Bitter	Coffee
Umami	Soy sauce

In addition, the tongue can also detect other sensations, such as **pungency** ("hotness" or "spiciness"), **coolness**, **astringency** and **temperature**.

Chilis give a hot, tingling sensation.

Minty flavours feel cool.

Astringent foods, such as rhubarb, can make the mouth feel squeezed or "dry".

See for yourself

Take five small bowls. Put a teaspoonful of lemon juice in one bowl, some soy sauce in another, and so on with cold black coffee, salty water and sugary water. Close your eyes and hold your nose. Pull a bowl towards you, dip your finger in and taste the liquid. Now taste the other liquids. Can you taste the difference between them? You should be able to recognize the five basic tastes even when you can't smell them.

See for yourself

You can use this test to show that the senses of taste and smell are closely linked. Grate a small amount of apple, pear and carrot into different bowls. Then shut your eyes tightly and hold your nose. Ask someone to feed you a spoonful of each food, one at a time. Try to identify the food. Repeat the experiment without holding your nose. You will probably find it easier to identify the food correctly.

TASTE AND SMELL

The senses of smell and taste are closely related. When you eat, odorant molecules from the food travel up the pharynx* into the nasal cavity, where the smell is detected in the usual way.

If you have a cold, you often lose your sense of smell and taste. This is because the lining of your nose swells, and makes thicker mucus than normal. This makes it harder for odorant molecules to reach the olfactory hairs. Your tongue can still detect the basic tastes, but you cannot identify the more subtle flavours.

Internet links

• Scan the code to watch a video about our sense of smell.

• For links to more websites with animations, experiments quizzes and fascinating facts about tasting and smelling, go to **www.usborne.com/quicklinks**

* Pharynx, 354.

REPRODUCTION

The process of creating new life is called **reproduction**, and the parts of the body involved in it make up the **reproductive system**. A man's body makes male sex cells, which are called **sperm**, and a woman's body produces **ova**, which are female sex cells. When a sperm joins with an ovum, a new cell is formed. This will divide many times to form a baby.

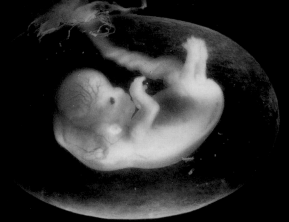

After eight weeks growing in its mother's womb, this developing baby is 3cm long. It is floating inside a protective, fluid-filled sac called the **amniotic sac**.

MALE REPRODUCTIVE SYSTEM

Sperm are made in two organs called **testes** and are stored in a comma-shaped organ called the **epididymis**, which lies over the back of each testis. The testes sit in a sac of skin known as the **scrotum**, which hangs outside the body. The temperature inside the body would be too high for sperm to survive.

Sperm

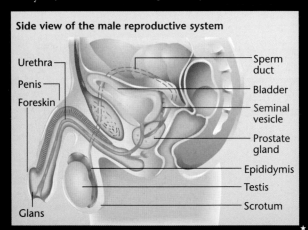

Side view of the male reproductive system

Urethra
Penis
Foreskin
Glans

Sperm duct
Bladder
Seminal vesicle
Prostate gland
Epididymis
Testis
Scrotum

The **penis** is the organ through which sperm (and urine) leave the body. Its tip, called the **glans**, is very sensitive and is partly covered by a loose fold of skin called the **foreskin**. Sperm travel to the penis along two tubes called **sperm ducts**, which open into the urethra*. Several glands, including the **prostate gland** and **seminal vesicles**, make fluid in which the sperm swim. The mixture of sperm and fluids is known as **semen**.

Position of male reproductive organs

FEMALE REPRODUCTIVE SYSTEM

When a girl is born, she already has thousands of ova stored in two organs called **ovaries**. Every month, from the age of puberty*, one ovum is released from an ovary into one of the **Fallopian tubes**. This process, called **ovulation**, is described more fully on page 379.

Ovum

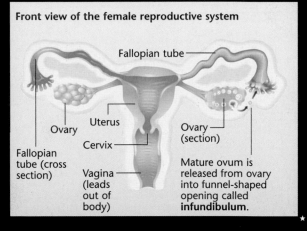

Front view of the female reproductive system

Fallopian tube

Ovary
Fallopian tube (cross section)

Uterus
Cervix
Vagina (leads out of body)

Ovary (section)
Mature ovum is released from ovary into funnel-shaped opening called **infundibulum**.

The Fallopian tubes lead to a hollow, pear-shaped organ called the **womb** or **uterus**. This is where a baby develops if an ovum has been fertilized (see right). At the bottom of the uterus is a muscular canal, called the **cervix**. This opens into a stretchy tube called the **vagina**, which in turn leads out of the body. The opening of the vagina lies behind that of the urethra*, and both are surrounded by two folds of skin called **labia**.

Position of female reproductive organs

MAKING BABIES

During **sexual intercourse** (also known as **coitus**, **copulation** or **having sex**), the penis becomes stiff and fits inside the vagina. Muscles around the male's urethra contract, squirting a small amount of semen out of the penis into the vagina. This is called **ejaculation**.

The sperm swim up through the uterus into the Fallopian tubes. If a sperm meets an ovum, they may join together to form a **zygote** – the first cell of a new baby. This event is called **fertilization** or **conception**. If no egg is present, the sperm die within a few days.

Fertilization

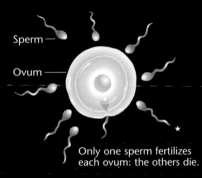

Sperm —

Ovum —

Only one sperm fertilizes each ovum: the others die.

There are several methods of preventing an ovum and a sperm from joining to make a baby. This is called **contraception**.

Internet links

- Scan the code to find out more about how a baby develops.

- For links to more websites with facts and activities about reproduction, go to www.usborne.com/quicklinks

HOW A BABY DEVELOPS

The zygote divides to form two identical cells. These divide several times to form a ball of cells, which embeds itself in the uterus lining. The cells continue to divide, and grow into different types, such as bone or blood cells. Cells of the same type join to form **tissue**, such as muscle. Different tissues make up **organs**, such as the heart, and organs group together to form **systems**, for example the digestive system. (For more about cells, tissues and organs, see pages 298-299.)

The future baby develops over nine months. For the first two, it is called an **embryo** and for the last seven, it is a **foetus**. The mother is said to be **pregnant**.

An unborn baby gets food and oxygen from its mother's blood through an organ called the **placenta**. Waste products from the baby go back in the opposite direction. Substances pass to and from the baby through a cord called the **umbilical cord**.

At the end of pregnancy, the baby moves so that its head is near the cervix. Muscles in the uterus contract strongly, squeezing the baby out through the mother's vagina. This process is known as **labour**.

At about 40 weeks, the baby is fully developed.
Approximate size: 50cm

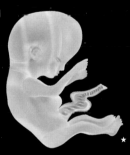

After the baby is born, its umbilical cord is clamped with a plastic clip, then cut. After about ten days, the stump falls off, leaving a navel.

Stages in the development of an unborn baby

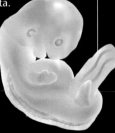

The new cell formed when the ovum and sperm join together, divides in two. These two cells divide to make four, then eight, sixteen and so on until a ball of cells forms.

At six weeks, the backbone and brain are already forming. The heart starts to beat.

Approximate size: 2cm

Umbilical cord joins embryo to placenta.

At seven weeks, tiny buds develop. They will become hands and feet.

Approximate size: 2.5cm

By 12 weeks, all the organs are formed. They will develop further over the next few months.

Approximate size: 7.5cm

GROWING AND CHANGING

During the first 20 years of life, a child gradually changes into an adult. The body grows in size and weight, and many new skills are learned. These processes are called **growth** and **development**. As you get older, your body continues to change, but more slowly. The rate at which you grow and develop depends on your genes*, as well as things such as diet and exercise.

At the age of seven, Winston Churchill's face was round and his skin was smooth.

GROWTH

Your body is made up of millions of different cells*. To allow the body to grow, many of these divide in two to form new, identical cells. This type of cell division, called **mitosis***, also makes cells to replace many of those that wear out and die.

Parts of your body grow at different rates at different stages of life. This means that as your body grows, its proportions change. For example, a baby's head makes up one quarter of its height, but an adult's head makes up about one eighth of the height.

Your head also changes shape. A newborn baby has soft areas between its skull bones. Over the next few years, these are gradually replaced by bone and the head changes shape. Most parts of your body stop growing by the time you are 18, but some, such as your ears, continue to grow throughout life. Many other changes occur as you grow older, for instance your skin becomes less elastic (see photographs, right).

Child's skull

Adult's skull

At 26, his face was longer. Frown lines started to appear on his brow as his skin became less elastic.

By his sixties, Churchill's skin had sagged, making his face look heavier.

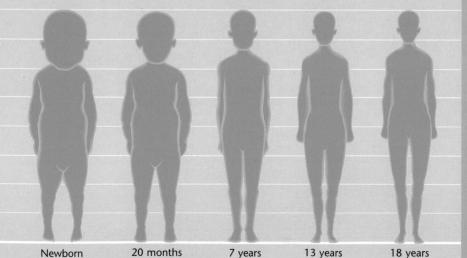

Changes in body proportions from infancy to adulthood

| Newborn | 20 months | 7 years | 13 years | 18 years |

* Cells, 298; Genes, 380-385; Mitosis, 427.

378

PUBERTY

Between the ages of about 8 and 18, you change from a child into an adult. This time is known as **puberty** or **adolescence**. Changes to the body (known as **physical changes**) and to the mind and emotions (called **psychological changes**) prepare you for being an adult and a parent. These changes are triggered by hormones*.

Some of the physical changes that take place make it possible to have babies. For example, the reproductive organs* you were born with (called **primary sexual features**) become active. Other physical changes are not necessary for having babies. They result in **secondary sexual features** such as beards and other body hair.

Your feelings and emotions may change as you become more independent, explore new ways of thinking, and get used to your adult body. Changes in hormone levels in the body may also affect mood.

Physical changes at puberty

Boys	Girls
Height increases rapidly.	Height increases rapidly.
Hair grows on face; soft and downy at first, then coarser.	Fine covering of hair may grow on face.
Voice deepens.	
Hair grows under arms.	Hair grows under arms.
Shoulders and chest broaden.	Breasts start to develop.
Penis grows.	Hips widen.
Pubic hair grows in the groin area.	Pubic hair grows in the groin area.
Testes begin to make sperm.	Ovulation and periods start (see below left).

PERIODS

At birth, a girl's ovaries contain many thousands of immature ova. During and after puberty, one ovum matures about every 28 days and is released into a Fallopian tube. This is called **ovulation**. At the same time, the uterus develops a new inner layer, rich in blood vessels, ready to receive a fertilized* ovum.

If the ovum is not fertilized, this lining breaks down and leaves the body through the vagina. This is called "having a **period**" or **menstruating**. On average a girl has a period every 28 days, but it can vary. At some point between the ages of 40 and 55, the ovaries stop releasing ova and periods stop. This is the **menopause**.

AGEING

After adolescence, the body becomes less efficient. This process, called **ageing** or **senescence**, starts slowly but speeds up later in life. The length of time you are likely to live is your **life expectancy**. It tends to be longer if you eat healthily, exercise sensibly, avoid smoking and drug misuse, and keep your mind active.

A menstrual cycle

1. A mature ovum is released from an ovary into a Fallopian tube (ovulation). The uterus lining thickens with blood.

2. The ovum travels to the uterus. The lining of the uterus continues to thicken.

Ovum

Ovary

Fallopian tube

Uterus

3. If no fertilized ovum appears, the blood-rich lining of the uterus breaks down and passes out of the vagina, along with the unfertilized ovum.

Internet links

- Scan the code for a video clip that shows how people age.

- For links to more websites about puberty and growing up, go to **www.usborne.com/quicklinks**

* Fertilization, 377; Hormones, 362, 363;
  Reproductive organs, 376.

GENETICS

As soon as a sperm and an ovum join to make a new cell, that cell contains all the information needed to build a unique human being. The instructions that tell the body how to develop are **genes**, and the study of genes is **genetics**. Genes are sections of a chemical called **DNA** (**deoxyribonucleic acid**), which is packed in bundles called **chromosomes** inside a control unit called the **nucleus**. Human cells have 46 chromosomes. You inherit them from your parents.

PAIRING UP

These chromosomes are shown over 24,000 times their real size.

Your 46 chromosomes can be arranged in pairs called **homologous chromosomes**. These carry paired genes. Each gene, or gene group, on one chromosome has a partner on the paired chromosome (see opposite page).

Before cells divide for growth or repair (by mitosis*), all the chromosomes make copies of themselves, so each new cell has 46. But sex cells (ova and sperm) are made by a special type of cell division called **meiosis**. When this happens, the paired chromosomes move apart, resulting in only 23 chromosomes in each sex cell. They are ready to be paired up with new partners at fertilization*.

Inheriting chromosomes

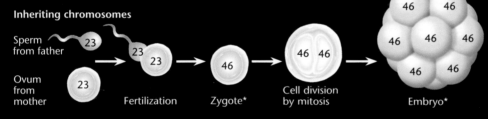

Sperm from father — 23 → 23 / 23 → Fertilization → 46 Zygote* → Cell division by mitosis 46 46 → Embryo* 46

Ovum from mother — 23

Before chromosomes split apart to make sex cells, a certain amount of swapping of gene pairs takes place. This means that every sperm is different from every other sperm produced by the same man, and every ovum is different from every other ovum produced by the same woman. So each new child from the same parents will be different, with different genes.

GIRL OR BOY

Two chromosomes, called **sex chromosomes**, determine whether a baby develops as a male or a female. These chromosomes are known as the **X** and **Y chromosomes**. Ova and sperm have one sex chromosome each. All ova have an X chromosome. Half the sperm have an X chromosome, and half have a Y. If a sperm with an X chromosome joins with an ovum, the baby will be a girl. If a sperm with a Y chromosome joins the ovum, the baby will be a boy.

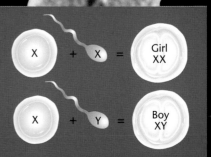

X + X = Girl XX

X + Y = Boy XY

Embryo, Fertilization, 377; Mitosis, 378; Zygote, 377.

HOW GENES WORK

You have 23 pairs of homologous chromosomes. Each gene, or gene group, on these chromosomes gives instructions to create or control one of your characteristics.

Genes for certain features, such as eye or hair colour, or blood group, have different forms, called **alleles**. So a gene pair might be made up of alleles giving identical instructions, or alleles giving different instructions.

One allele may order green eyes, for example, and the other blue eyes. In such cases, either one allele will be **dominant**, overruling the other, **recessive**, allele, or they will both have an effect, in which case they are called **co-dominant alleles**. For example, a green eye colour allele is dominant over a blue one, so if you have one of each, you have green eyes. You need two blue colour alleles to have blue eyes.

The diagram below shows how different pairs of blood group alleles result in different blood groups, depending on which allele is dominant.

The allele for blood group A is dominant, and the allele for group O is recessive. The two people on the right are blood group A.

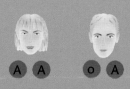

The allele for blood group B is dominant, and the allele for group O is recessive. The two people on the right are blood group B.

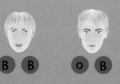

This person has two recessive O alleles, so is blood group O.

A and B are co-dominant so this person is blood group AB.

If the alleles in a pair are identical, as with the AA person, the person is **homozygous** for that characteristic, in this case blood group. If they are different, the person is **heterozygous**.

Some diseases, for example a disease called **cystic fibrosis** that affects the lungs, are caused by a recessive allele. A person who has a pair of these alleles will have the disease. Someone who has just one of them, paired with a normal (dominant) allele, will not be affected by the disease, but is said to be a **carrier**. The recessive allele can be passed to their children.

SEX-LINKED GENES

Some characteristics, for example colour-blindness, show up more often in males than females. This is because they are caused by recessive alleles found on the X chromosome which do not have partners on the Y chromosome to overrule them. Such characteristics are said to be controlled by sex-linked genes.

In genetics, alleles are represented by letters. A capital letter shows that an allele is dominant and a small one that it is recessive. The diagram below shows what might happen if a female carrier of the recessive colour-blindness allele (c) has children with a man with a dominant normal sight allele (C).

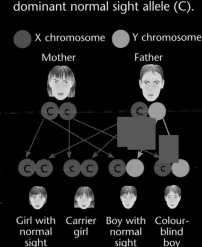

Girl with normal sight | Carrier girl | Boy with normal sight | Colour-blind boy

Internet links

• Scan the code to watch a video clip about the process of cell division called meiosis.

• For links to more websites about how genes work, go to **www.usborne.com/quicklinks**

GENE TECHNOLOGY

Genetic research took a great leap forward in the early 1950s, when James Watson and Francis Crick discovered the structure of DNA*. This knowledge has since helped scientists to find out much more about genes, and how living things are affected by them. New discoveries in genetics are being made all the time and these are put to a variety of uses, some of which are described here.

Watson and Crick with their DNA model

STRUCTURE OF DNA

Each molecule of DNA looks like a twisted rope ladder. This spiral shape is known as a **double helix**. The ladder's rungs are made up of four chemicals linked in pairs: adenine and thymine, guanine and cytosine. These chemicals are called **bases**, and are usually known by their initial letters, A, T, C and G.

This is part of a molecule of DNA. Its spiral shape is called a double helix.

The sides of the ladder are made up of strands of a sugar called **deoxyribose**, alternating with chemical clusters known as **phosphate groups**. One of each, together with a base, make up a unit called a **nucleotide**. A gene is a sequence of about 250 pairs of nucleotides. There are about 1,000 genes on an average DNA molecule.

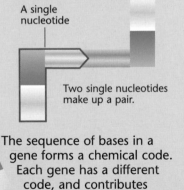

A single nucleotide

Two single nucleotides make up a pair.

The sequence of bases in a gene forms a chemical code. Each gene has a different code, and contributes to a different characteristic.

GENOME RESEARCH

All the DNA in an organism is its **genome**. An ordered list of all the bases in a genome is called a **map**. The genome of the yeast cell was the first to be mapped.

A significant milestone in genetic research was reached in April 2003, when scientists announced that they had made the complete sequence of the 3 billion base pairs that make up the human genome. The completed map will have many uses. For example, scientists may be able to use it to find out more about the links between genes and certain diseases, and develop new ways of treating or even preventing them.

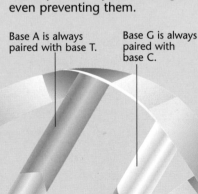

Base A is always paired with base T.

Base G is always paired with base C.

A base always joins to a deoxyribose strand.

Key to DNA diagram

Bases
- ⦿ Adenine
- ⦿ Cytosine
- ⦿ Deoxyribose
- ○ Thymine
- ○ Guanine
- ○ Phosphate group

★

GENETIC FINGERPRINTING

Unless you have an identical twin, the exact order of bases in your DNA is slightly different from everyone else's. A process called **DNA profiling** or **genetic fingerprinting** can be used to compare samples of DNA. If the DNA samples are identical, then they have probably come from the same person or from identical twins.

DNA profiling has various uses. Police scientists, for example, can extract DNA from a single strand of hair or drop of blood left at the scene of a crime. They can then use it to identify the guilty person.

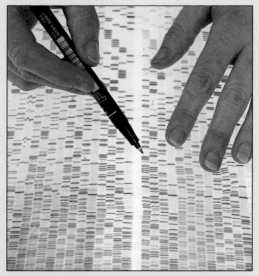

A scientist looking at DNA sequences. The bands depend on the order of bases. If the band patterns of two samples match exactly, they are likely to be either from the same person or from identical twins.

DNA samples from people who are related contain many more matching genes than samples from people who are not. Scientists can compare DNA samples to find out if and how people are related.

After the Russian Revolution in 1917, Tsar Nicholas II, his wife and three of their children were killed and buried in an unmarked grave. Bodies thought to be theirs were found in 1991. The Tsar was identified by comparing his DNA to his brother's. His wife's identity was proven by taking a DNA sample from Prince Philip, Duke of Edinburgh, who was a distant relation.

GENETIC ENGINEERING

Scientists have discovered how to extract genes and use them in different ways, for instance in medicine, farming and industry. This manipulation of genes is known as **genetic engineering** or **genetic modification**. The main technique used is **gene splicing**.

Chemicals called **restriction enzymes** are used to cut specific genes out of DNA. Other enzymes, called **ligases**, are used to splice, or join, the genes with DNA taken from a suitable organism. This modified DNA, known as **recombinant DNA (rDNA)**, can then be used in different ways.

For example, it may be placed in a fast-breeding bacterium*. This reproduces very quickly to create lots of bacteria, each containing the rDNA with the specific gene. These bacteria can then be used to synthesize (make) large quantities of important proteins such as insulin or other hormones.

A method of gene splicing

1. The gene that is needed (called the **target DNA**) is taken out of a cell's nucleus.

2. The target DNA is spliced with a **plasmid**, a special piece of DNA from a bacterium.

3. The recombinant DNA is then put into **a host bacterium** of a type which divides rapidly.

4. The host bacterium divides many times, creating many identical copies, each containing the target DNA (the desired gene).

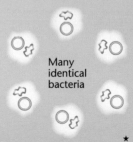

Target DNA

Plasmid

Cell

Recombinant DNA

Host bacterium

Other DNA

Many identical bacteria

★

* Bacteria, 386.

BREEDING

Since earliest times, farmers have chosen their best animals and plants from which to breed. This is known as **selective breeding** or **artificial selection**. Some of the young of these animals or plants inherit the good qualities of their parents.

Breeding from two plants or animals of the same variety is called **pure breeding**. Using plants or animals of different varieties is **cross-breeding**. The offspring are a new, mixed breed called an F1 (first-generation) **hybrid** or a **cross**, as shown in the example below.

MODIFYING GENES

More recently, scientists have found ways to produce plants and animals with a particular quality by altering their genes in some way.

Traditional selective breeding is only possible between breeds that belong to the same species. However, using genetic techniques, scientists can transfer genes between different species.

Organisms with genes from another source are described as **transgenic**.

Scientists are exploring ways of altering plants' genes to produce crops that are more resistant to disease, weather and chemicals used to kill pests or weeds.

Cotton plants such as these can be genetically modified to resist pests.

In Australia, for example, crops of cotton plants are often eaten by a particular species of caterpillar. Scientists have genetically engineered a cotton plant that makes a substance which is poisonous to the caterpillars or any other insect that tries to eat it.

The seedling shown below is being grown on a glass petri dish and given a nutrient fluid through a pipette. New types of genetically modified plants are grown and tested in a laboratory before they can be grown outside.

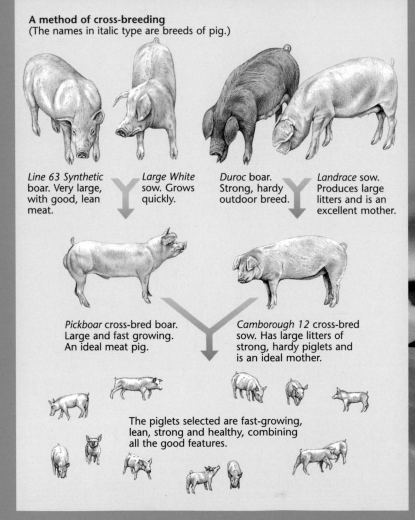

A method of cross-breeding
(The names in italic type are breeds of pig.)

Line 63 Synthetic boar. Very large, with good, lean meat.

Large White sow. Grows quickly.

Duroc boar. Strong, hardy outdoor breed.

Landrace sow. Produces large litters and is an excellent mother.

Pickboar cross-bred boar. Large and fast growing. An ideal meat pig.

Camborough 12 cross-bred sow. Has large litters of strong, hardy piglets and is an ideal mother.

The piglets selected are fast-growing, lean, strong and healthy, combining all the good features.

PHARMING

Genetic engineering has made it possible for plants and animals to produce proteins that are useful in medicine. This technique is known as **pharming**. For example, a sheep has been genetically modified to produce milk which contains spider (dragline) silk. This material can be used to make lighter, stronger bulletproof vests, thinner thread for surgery and indestructible clothes.

Genetic modification of animals could have other medical uses. For example, by inserting certain human genes into the DNA of some pigs, it may be possible to breed pigs whose organs are suitable for transplanting into humans.

Heart transplants using a pig's heart could then be possible, if a suitable human donor couldn't be found. After the operation, the patient would have to take medicines to stop the white blood cells attacking the new organ in the same way as they fight invading germs (see page 387).

ANIMAL CLONING

In nature, animals are born as a result of reproduction and they inherit genes from both parents. Genetic research has made it possible to breed **clones** – animals that are genetically identical to a single parent.

In 1996, scientists at the Roslin Institute in Edinburgh took an ovum* from a sheep and removed its nucleus* (with all its DNA). They fused the ovum with a cell from another sheep. After a week of growth in a laboratory, the ball of dividing cells was placed in the womb of a third sheep. After five months, a cloned lamb, named Dolly, was born.

How Dolly the sheep was cloned

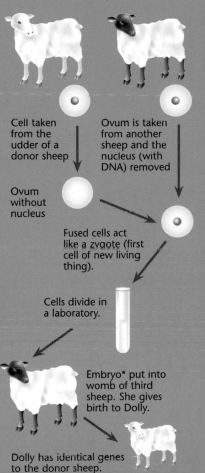

Cell taken from the udder of a donor sheep

Ovum is taken from another sheep and the nucleus (with DNA) removed

Ovum without nucleus

Fused cells act like a zygote (first cell of new living thing).

Cells divide in a laboratory.

Embryo* put into womb of third sheep. She gives birth to Dolly.

Dolly has identical genes to the donor sheep.

* Embryo, 377; Ovum, 376; Nucleus, 380.

GENETICS IN THE NEWS

Genetic engineering often makes sensational headlines. For example, the use of **genetically modified organisms** (**GMOs**) in food worries many people because the long-term effects are not yet known. Also, some people don't like the idea of eating "unnatural" food.

There are food companies, on the other hand, that see GMOs as a way of producing more food at a lower cost. You can read more about the genetic modification of food on page 291.

FIGHTING DISEASE

Anything that stops all or part of your body from working properly can be called a **disease**. Some diseases are caused by harmful, microscopic organisms known as **germs**. Others can be caused by diet, lack of exercise, faulty genes*, old age, or poisonous chemicals, such as nicotine from cigarettes.

White blood cells such as this help to defend your body from infection.

GERMS

The scientific name for germs is **pathogens**. Two types of pathogens – bacteria and viruses – are responsible for many diseases in humans.

Bacteria are microscopic organisms found everywhere. Harmful ones may produce poisonous waste chemicals, called **toxins**, which can cause disease. Different bacteria cause different illnesses.

Viruses are strands of DNA* inside a protective coat. They cannot live on their own, but invade cells in your body and use them as factories to make more viruses. This eventually kills the cell. Diseases caused by viruses include colds, flu and AIDS.

A virus

Protective coat

Strands of DNA

Extension called a **pseudopodium** ("false foot") will engulf germs and trap them.

Main types of bacteria

Cocci are spherical. They cause most throat infections.

Bacilli are rod shaped. They cause tuberculosis and typhoid.

Vibrios are bent rod shaped. They cause diseases such as cholera.

Spirilla are spiral. They cause diseases such as ratbite fever.

DEFENDING THE BODY

Germs are **infectious**, which means that they pass from one living thing to another. They can be spread in a number of ways, for example in air and water and by touch. They can also be carried by animals.

Germs stick to a fly's feet and hairy body as it feeds on dung or rotten matter. These germs can spread to food a fly lands on.

Your body has many ways of defending itself from germs. Firstly your skin tries to keep germs out. But if they do get inside, your body has several methods of fighting back. The main ones are shown in the table on the right.

Your body's defences	
Skin	Forms germ-proof barrier.
Nose	Hairs and mucus trap germs and dirt from the air.
Ears	Wax inside traps germs.
Eyelids	Keep germs out of your eyes.
Tears	Wash your eyes clean.
Stomach	Hydrochloric acid kills germs in food.
Tonsils and adenoids	Kill germs in your throat.
White blood cells	Destroy germs inside your body.
Spleen	Contains white blood cells which fight infection.

386 * DNA, Genes, 380-385.

This cluster of harmful germs is about to be engulfed by the white blood cell (early stage of phagocytosis – see right).

WHITE BLOOD CELLS

White blood cells move out of the blood* (through capillary* walls) into tissue fluid* and lymph, and travel around fighting disease. There are five main types: monocytes, neutrophils, eosinophils, basophils and lymphocytes. **Monocytes** and **neutrophils** surround germs and digest them. This process is known as **phagocytosis**.

Late stage of phagocytosis

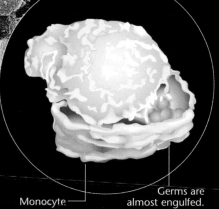

Monocyte

Germs are almost engulfed.

IMMUNITY

Once you have made an antibody against a particular germ's antigen, you can make it again very quickly if the same germ enters your body. This gives you **resistance**, or **active immunity**, to the disease.

You can also be made immune to diseases such as measles by being given a **vaccine**. This is a dose of the germ that is too weak to cause the disease, but has enough antigens to make you produce antibodies. These will protect you against future attacks by the germ. This process is called **vaccination**.

Vaccination methods

In some countries, drops of vaccine against the disease polio are given on lumps of sugar.

Most vaccinations are given by injection. This avoids them being destroyed by digestive juices*.

An injection of antibodies after a disease has developed will give you **passive immunity**. The harmful germs are killed, but the immunity does not last.

LYMPHATIC SYSTEM

Your **lymphatic system** and your white blood cells form a disease-fighting partnership. The lymphatic system is a network of tubes and connected organs. The tubes contain **lymph**, the excess fluid that drains from the tissues*, and also white blood cells.

Lymph vessels carry lymph around your body.

Lymph drains back into your blood through two veins near your neck, recycling the white blood cells to begin again (see right). **Lymph nodes** are small organs found in clusters around the system (in your neck, armpits and groin). Many of your white blood cells are made in the lymph nodes, and many germs are trapped and destroyed there.

Eosinophils attack larger pathogens. **Basophils** and monocytes also migrate into the tissues. Monocytes then become **macrophages**. **Wandering macrophages** constantly move around, while **fixed macrophages** become fixed in a particular organ and fight germs that gather there.

Lymphocytes are mostly made in lymph nodes. They destroy germs with chemicals called **antibodies**. Each type of antibody is specially produced to attack a particular chemical, or **antigen**, carried on an invading germ.

Lymphocyte

Antibodies

Germs

Internet links

- Scan the code for a video clip about fighting disease.

- For links to more websites where you can examine bacteria, viruses and white blood cells, go to **www.usborne.com/quicklinks**

* Blood, 352; Capillaries, 351; Digestive juices, 354; Tissue fluid, 351.

387

MEDICINE

Your body's defences are often strong enough for you to get better without seeing a doctor. If you do need help, though, there is a whole area of science that specializes in treating disease as well as keeping the body fit and healthy. This is called **medicine**. Major advances in medicine have helped to increase the life expectancy of many people.

DIAGNOSIS

When you visit a doctor because you are ill, the doctor will ask questions and examine you to find out what is wrong. This is called making a **diagnosis**. If the doctor needs more information, there are many tests that can be done. Some of these are simple and others involve expensive and complex equipment.

A simple fingerprick test can show the level of glucose in the blood.

Chemical analysis of samples of body fluids such as blood and urine can reveal important clues. For example, a high level of glucose in the blood can be a sign of diabetes. This can be measured by taking a drop of blood onto a test stick which can be read by an electronic blood glucose meter.

X-rays were passed through this hand to form an image on a photographic plate.

Various methods of **medical imaging** allow doctors to see inside a patient's body without cutting it open. For example, invisible rays of energy called **X-rays** can pass through soft tissue, but not through denser substances such as bone. X-rays are particularly useful for finding out if bones are broken.

Soft areas, such as the digestive tract*, can be examined by filling them with a **radio-opaque** liquid. This stops the X-rays passing through, and so any blockages or changes from the usual shape can be seen clearly.

X-ray images are usually white on black: this one has had colour added.

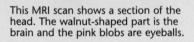

This MRI scan shows a section of the head. The walnut-shaped part is the brain and the pink blobs are eyeballs.

CT (computed tomography) scanners are special X-ray cameras that take detailed images of hard and soft tissues. The body is scanned in sections and the images are fed into a computer. Doctors look at the pictures to see if there are any unusual shadows or changes of shape that may be a sign of problems, such as abnormal growths called **tumours**.

Magnetic resonance imaging (MRI) scanners also scan sections of the body, but they use radio waves in the presence of a strong magnet. A computer builds up the images to create a 3-dimensional picture. MRI scans are used particularly to look for diseases of the nervous system, including the brain.

TREATMENT

Treatments range from rest, exercises or changes of diet to medicines or other, more complex, methods. In some cases, for example, a doctor may perform an **operation**, cutting the body open to mend or take out a diseased part.

MEDICINES

Chemical substances called **medicines** or **drugs** are used to treat and prevent a wide variety of illnesses. Most medicines are made in laboratories. Many are based on substances in plants which have healing properties.

Foxglove leaves contain a substance called **digitalis**. This is now made artificially and is used to treat heart disease.

Medicines called **antibiotics** are used to treat many illnesses caused by bacteria*. They either stop the bacteria from multiplying, or destroy them completely. Antibiotics have no effect on illnesses caused by viruses*, such as colds and flu.

All medicines are dangerous and should not be touched without the advice of a doctor or pharmacist. Misuse of medicines could make you very ill or even kill you.

This green furry growth is a mould called *Penicillium*. In 1928, Scottish scientist Alexander Fleming discovered that it could kill bacteria. He used it to develop **penicillin**, the first antibiotic drug.

* Bacteria, 386; Retina, 370; Viruses, 386.

SURGERY

All operations are part of the area of medicine called **surgery**. They are usually carried out in hospital by specially-trained doctors called **surgeons**. There are many different fields of surgery, each with specialized techniques.

Laser surgery uses intense beams of light, called **laser beams**, to make clean, precise cuts and to carry out delicate surgery, such as eye operations. For example, if a patient's retina* has become detached, a laser can sometimes be used to weld it back in place with a tiny heat scar. Lasers were originally developed for non-medical purposes, such as cutting and welding in industry.

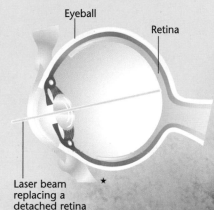

Eyeball

Retina

Laser beam replacing a detached retina

Optical fibres in a fibre-optic cable

Lasers are often used with a tube called an **endoscope** which is pushed into a patient's body, often down the throat. Endoscopes are used to see and remove things, such as growths, inside the body.

Many endoscopes contain **fibre-optic cables**. These are made up of hair-like glass strands called **optical fibres**, through which light and laser beams can pass. Other types of cables have different jobs, such as sucking out samples for analysis.

Keyhole surgery is carried out through a very small hole in the body, often using an endoscope. It is less painful than open surgery, and patients usually recover more quickly. This method can be used to investigate and treat many different conditions (such as some disorders of the reproductive or digestive systems), removal of some organs and repair of damaged tissue.

OTHER TREATMENTS

There are many treatments, called **alternative treatments**, that have not traditionally been used by doctors. Some of these are now often used in addition to conventional treatments and are known as **complementary medicine**. Many people also use complementary treatments as part of a general healthy lifestyle.

Many scientists think that most successful alternative treatments are examples of the placebo effect. A **placebo** is a treatment that has no medicine in it, but works because the patient believes it will. Placebos work best on conditions with a large psychological element, such as mild depression or the experience of pain. They are also more effective when given by someone whom the patient trusts, for example, a doctor or healer.

AROMATHERAPY

Aromatherapy is the use of **essential oils**, made from strongly fragrant essences found in the flowers, roots, leaves, bark or peel of some plants. Oils, such as lavender or ginger, can be added to bathwater, breathed in or diluted with a carrier oil and massaged into the skin. People use aromatherapy to help relieve stress, anxiety, depression, inability to sleep, and pain.

HERBAL REMEDIES

Herbal remedies are made from plants or fungi, and people take them to treat a wide range of symptoms and diseases.

ACUPUNCTURE

Acupuncture is an ancient Chinese treatment based on the idea that all things contain an energy force called **Chi**. Chi is said to flow along invisible channels in the body called **meridians**. On these channels are hundreds of invisible points known as **pressure points**.

The meridians are shown in red. The tiny dots are pressure points.

An **acupuncturist** acts on these points mainly by sticking very fine needles into them. Acupuncture is used for many reasons, such as relieving pain and reducing stress.

YOGA AND PILATES

Some people do yoga or pilates to improve their general mental and physical health as well as strengthening their body or helping to relieve aches and pains. **Yoga** combines special movements and positions, called **postures**, with techniques of breathing and concentration called **meditation**. **Pilates** is an exercise system that focuses on stretching and breathing to improve muscle strength, balance, flexibility and posture.

MANIPULATING JOINTS

Osteopathy and **chiropractic** are ways of treating physical problems by manipulating the joints, particularly the backbone or skull. The treatments are often used for back problems, but osteopaths and chiropractors believe that other illnesses, such as headaches, rashes and digestive disorders, can also be treated by their methods.

This pose is based on a yoga posture. Practising yoga can help to make your body more supple.

HOMEOPATHY

Homeopathy is based on the idea that a substance that causes certain symptoms in a healthy person can be diluted and used to cure the same symptoms in someone who is ill. Its supporters claim they work by stimulating the body's natural defences (see pages 386-387).

PREVENTATIVE MEDICINE

Preventing illness is just as important as treating it. Doctors, medical scientists and health officers spend much of their time looking for ways to control and wipe out illness. This is called **preventative medicine**.

One important way of preventing diseases is **vaccination** (see also page 387). Babies and children are usually given a series of vaccines against diseases such as polio and measles. If you go abroad you may need a vaccine against diseases not found in your country.

Regular medical check-ups to look for early signs of disease are carried out in schools and clinics. This is called **screening**, and helps because doctors may spot and be able to treat an illness before it develops.

HEALTH ADVICE

To help keep people healthy, doctors teach them about the benefits of regular exercise and a balanced diet. They also provide information about the harmful effects to the body of smoking, drinking too much alcohol, and misusing drugs.

DRUG INFORMATION

A **drug** is any substance that affects the way the body works. Different drugs have different effects. Medicines, alcohol, and nicotine in cigarettes are all drugs. These are available legally, though their use is controlled, for example by prescriptions or age restrictions. Other drugs, such as heroin, are only available illegally.

Too much of any drug, legal or illegal, can cause long-term damage or even death. Many drugs are **habit-forming**, so people feel that they need to take them. Some are **addictive**, which means that the body gets used to them and is disturbed without them. Below is a list of some drugs and their effects.

Substance	Description	Effect on the body
Alcohol	Clear liquid found in beer, cider, wines, spirits and alcoholic "soft drinks".	Relaxation, confidence or depression. Poor coordination and judgement, so drinking and driving is very dangerous. Addictive. Long-term effects of heavy drinking include serious liver damage.
Cannabis	Often dried leaves or brown solid lump. Usually mixed with tobacco and smoked.	Relaxation. Tired, dizzy or sick feeling and faster heart rate. Memory loss is a possible long-term effect. Effects of nicotine added if cannabis is smoked.
Cocaine / Crack	Fine, white powder. Usually sniffed. A form of cocaine. Small lumps. Smoked.	Alert, excited or aggressive feeling. Destroys nasal passages and damages lungs. Highly addictive.
Ecstasy	Tablets or capsules. Swallowed.	Feelings of energy and confidence or sickness and anxiety. Damages liver and kidneys. Can kill without warning.
Heroin	Grey-brown powder, often sold mixed with bleach or talc. Smoked, sniffed or injected.	Feeling of well-being then depression. Very addictive. Body needs ever higher doses or suffers awful withdrawal pains. Death by overdose is common.
Inhalants	Include lighter fuel, glue, paint or varnish. Usually sniffed.	Fumes cause feeling of well-being and dizziness. Damage lining of nose and lungs. Can suffocate. Often addictive.
LSD	White tablet or on small pieces of paper. Usually swallowed.	Puts user in strange, sometimes terrifying world, called a **trip**. Causes mental problems and brain damage.
Nicotine	In tobacco, for example in cigarettes.	Enjoyment or sick feeling. Habit-forming and addictive. Damages lungs and cilia*. Causes heart disease and chest infections. Can make lung cancer worse.

Internet links

• Scan the code to find out how the smallpox vaccination was developed.

• For links to more websites where you can investigate the benefits of vaccination, drugs and other methods of preventing disease, go to www.usborne.com/quicklinks

* Cilia, 358.

SCIENCE FACTS
AND LISTS

RESEARCH ON THE WEB

The internet has become the first place many people go to find information on just about anything. However, finding information you can trust is sometimes tricky. The tips below will help you choose sites that you can use with confidence.

INTERNET RESEARCH

The websites recommended at the Usborne Quicklinks website have been reviewed by Usborne editors, but it is still a good idea to check the information for yourself. Here are some tips to help you:

• Check the name and URL of the website you are visiting. If it is a well-known organization, museum or reference site, the information will probably (but not necessarily) be reliable.

• Look for signs that the website has been updated recently. If you spot old news or dates, missing pictures, broken links or spelling mistakes, this may indicate that the website is no longer looked after and could contain information that is out of date.

• If you arrive at a website you haven't visited before, look for an "About Us" section which may provide details about the people or organization responsible for the site. This may help you judge whether the information can be trusted.

• Always visit several websites when carrying out research. This way you can compare information from different sources and check if any facts differ.

USING INFORMATION

If you want to use information from a website, don't copy it word for word. Instead try to express the same ideas in your own words. At the end of your work, give a list of your sources with the names and URLs of all the websites you have used.

Many websites are happy for schools and students to use their information and pictures for educational purposes. But before downloading any pictures, check the website's "Terms of Use" to make sure you are allowed to use the pictures. You may use the downloadable pictures at the Usborne Quicklinks website for school or personal use, but the pictures remain the copyright of Usborne Publishing.

INTERNET SAFETY

When using the internet, please make sure you follow our three basic rules:

• Always ask an adult's permission before using the internet.

• Never give out personal information, such as your name, address, the name of your school or telephone number.

• If a website asks you to type in your name or email address, check with an adult first.

USEFUL WEBSITES

For each of the following topics, we have selected a number of websites to help you with your research. To visit the sites, go to the Usborne Quicklinks website at **www.usborne.com/quicklinks**, type the keyword "science" and go to pages 394-395. Remember, though, to judge for yourself whether they are relevant and up to date, as described on the left.

General science

Some of the best science websites are provided by museums, public organizations and educational institutions. Resources can range from interactive guides and video clips to online experiments, blogs and activities to print out and try at home. Most sites have their own search engines to help you find whatever it is that interests you.

Experiments

You can watch video demonstrations of experiments, try virtual experiments online or find plenty of websites with science experiments to do at home – from how to grow your own crystal to making a battery out of a lemon. Ask an adult to help you use any equipment you do not normally use.

Online magazines

Most science magazines also have an online presence, and often have the most up-to-date information. Visit **www.usborne. com/quicklinks** for a selection of popular science magazines.

Technology

The internet is a great place to find out about the latest technology, because new information is being added every day. Organizations such as NASA or CERN (European Organization for Nuclear Research) post news of their latest discoveries on their websites.

Environmental issues

The World Wildlife Fund (WWF) and Greenpeace are involved in environmental issues around the world and provide the latest news about endangered animals and habitats. You can also find out how you can get involved in working to protect the environment, and ask questions about the environmental issues that interest you. You can find these sites and more at **www.usborne.com/quicklinks**

Homework and revision

There are many sites designed especially to help students with homework, essays, projects and studying for exams where you can find video clips, online tutorials and exercises, review guides, quizzes and more. As school curriculums vary, it is best to visit a site that is designed for your part of the world.

Reference materials

Online encyclopedias, dictionaries and other reference sites are useful for finding out the basic facts about a subject, or for looking up a scientific word or idea that you are unfamiliar with. You'll find a list at the Usborne Quicklinks website.

YouTube

There are countless resources on YouTube. Most large organizations, such as National Geographic, the Royal Institution of Great Britain and the National Science Foundation in the US, have their own YouTube channels where they display their videos, and these are a great place to start. You can also search for an organization's channel in the YouTube search box.

Remember though that anyone can upload a video so it's important that you look for reliable clips.

Image galleries

You can also find thousands of amazing images online. Most organizations are happy for students and educational establishments to download images for use in schoolwork and projects, but do check the website terms and conditions before downloading.

Internet links

- Scan the code for a video about the World Wildlife Fund.

- For links to more websites to help you with research, projects and homework, go to **www.usborne.com/quicklinks**

Online image galleries contain a wide range of useful pictures you can include in school projects.

REVISION QUESTIONS

You can use the revision questions on pages 396-403 to test yourself. There is one page of questions for each section of the encyclopedia. The answers can be found at the bottom of each page.

MATERIALS

1. Electrons are present
A. only in liquid or solid matter
B. only in electrical conductors
C. in all forms of matter   *(Page 10)*

2. An atom usually has equal numbers of
A. neutrons and electrons
B. electrons and protons
C. protons and neutrons   *(Page 11)*

3. The mass number of an atom of an element is the number of
A. protons and neutrons
B. protons
C. electrons   *(Page 12)*

4. Atoms which have the same number of protons and electrons but a different number of neutrons are
A. isomers
B. isotopes
C. allotropes   *(Page 13)*

5. The chemical symbol of iron is
A. F
B. I
C. Fe   *(Page 15)*

6. The chemical symbol of gold is
A. Go
B. Au
C. Ag   *(Page 15)*

7. The kinetic theory explains
A. energy changes
B. moving objects
C. the properties of solids, liquids and gases   *(Page 16)*

8. Sublimation occurs when
A. solids change to gas
B. solids change to liquid
C. liquids change to gas   *(Page 18)*

9. Condensation is when
A. gas changes to liquid
B. gas changes to solid
C. liquid changes to gas   *(Page 19)*

10. A substance is classified as a solid, liquid or gas depending on its state at
A. 0°C
B. 20°C
C. 100°C   *(Page 19)*

11. Gases have
A. definite volume and shape
B. no definite volume and shape
C. definite volume but can change shape   *(Page 22)*

12. How many elements are there?
A. about 20
B. about 50
C. over 100   *(Page 24)*

13. Almost all non-metals are
A. liquids at room temperature
B. poor insulators
C. poor conductors   *(Page 25)*

14. The most common element in the Earth's crust is
A. aluminium
B. oxygen
C. silicon   *(Page 26)*

15. The periodic table is organized into periods of elements which are
A. arranged in columns
B. arranged in rows
C. arranged in clusters   *(Page 28)*

16. The periodic table is also organized into groups which are
A. arranged in columns
B. arranged in rows
C. arranged in clusters   *(Page 28)*

17. Metals are ductile, so they can be
A. beaten flat into sheets
B. pulled out to make a wire
C. polished   *(Page 30)*

18. In a flame test, potassium gives
A. a red flame
B. an orange flame
C. a lilac flame   *(Page 31)*

19. In water, alkali metals form
A. acidic solutions
B. alkaline solutions
C. neutral solutions   *(Page 32)*

20. Noble metals are
A. always found in compounds
B. extremely reactive
C. very unreactive   *(Page 32)*

21. Brass is a mixture of
A. copper and zinc
B. copper and tin
C. copper and nickel   *(Page 35)*

22. Bronze is a mixture of
A. copper and zinc
B. copper and tin
C. copper and gold   *(Page 35)*

23. Which gas is needed for corrosion to take place?
A. sulphur dioxide
B. carbon dioxide
C. oxygen   *(Page 40)*

24. One of the oldest known metals is
A. aluminium
B. gold
C. zinc   *(Page 42)*

25. The most abundant element in the universe is
A. aluminium
B. hydrogen
C. oxygen   *(Page 46)*

26. Which element is not a halogen?
A. chlorine
B. iodine
C. phosphorus   *(Pages 48-49, 55)*

27. Elements which exist in differently bonded forms are
A. alloys
B. allotropes
C. isotopes   *(Page 50)*

28. Which of the following substances is not a form of carbon?
A. diamond
B. sulphur
C. graphite   *(Pages 50-51, 54)*

29. One of the main uses of sulphur is
A. making sulphur dioxide
B. in food preservation
C. making sulphuric acid   *(Page 54)*

30. Which of the following is not a form of phosphorus?
A. yellow
B. red
C. white   *(Page 55)*

MIXTURES AND COMPOUNDS

1. Which of the following is not a mixture?
A. air
B. sea water
C. carbon dioxide   *(Page 58)*

2. Dyes can be separated by
A. distillation
B. filtration
C. chromatography   *(Pages 60-61)*

3. An insoluble solid can be separated from a liquid by
A. evaporation
B. filtration
C. chromatography   *(Page 60)*

4. A soluble solid can be separated from a liquid by
A. evaporation
B. filtration
C. chromatography   *(Page 61)*

5. The most abundant gas in the atmosphere is
A. carbon dioxide
B. nitrogen
C. oxygen   *(Page 62)*

6. Ozone is a form of
A. nitrogen
B. oxygen
C. argon   *(Page 65)*

7. The build-up of which gas causes the greenhouse effect?
A. carbon dioxide
B. oxygen
C. argon   *(Page 65)*

8. What is formed when atoms of different elements combine?
A. a new element
B. a compound
C. a mixture   *(Page 66)*

9. Which of the following is not an example of a compound?
A. citric acid
B. calcium carbonate
C. carbon   *(Page 67)*

10. The forces holding atoms together are known as bonds. Which of these is not a type of bonding?
A. covalent
B. valency
C. ionic   *(Pages 69-71)*

11. The second electron shell can hold up to
A. two electrons
B. eighteen electrons
C. eight electrons   *(Page 68)*

12. Which statement is true? Many covalent substances
A. dissolve in water
B. conduct electricity
C. are liquids or gases at room temperature   *(Page 69)*

13. An atom that has lost electrons is
A. an anion
B. a cation
C. an ionic lattice   *(Page 70)*

14. Which statement is false?
A. the chemical name for water is hydrogen oxide
B. water can exist in three states: gas, liquid and solid
C. ice is more dense than water
          (Page 72)

15. Reactions in which heat is given out to the surroundings are
A. exothermic
B. endothermic
C. thermal   *(Page 76)*

16. A catalyst
A. changes the rate of a reaction and is used up in the reaction
B. changes the rate of a reaction and is not used up in the reaction
C. is a substance that stops a reaction taking place   *(Page 79)*

17. Combustion reactions need
A. carbon monoxide
B. carbon dioxide
C. oxygen   *(Page 80)*

18. During reduction, a substance loses
A. oxygen
B. hydrogen
C. electrons   *(Page 81)*

19. Which metal is extracted from bauxite by electrolysis?
A. aluminium
B. copper
C. iron   *(Page 83)*

20. Which one of the following is not an example of a base?
A. toothpaste
B. tomato juice
C. wasp sting   *(Pages 84-85)*

21. Which statement is incorrect? Acids are
A. compounds that contain hydrogen
B. corrosive
C. caustic   *(Pages 84-85)*

22. The pH value of any acidic substance is
A. less than 7
B. 7
C. more than 7   *(Page 86)*

23. Salts contain
A. metals only
B. metals and non-metals
C. non-metals only   *(Page 88)*

24. All organic compounds contain
A. silicon
B. oxygen
C. carbon   *(Page 92)*

25. Saturated organic compounds are held together by
A. single bonds
B. double bonds
C. triple bonds   *(Page 93)*

26. The most important product of the fermentation reaction is an
A. alkane
B. alkene
C. alcohol   *(Page 94)*

27. Margarine is made by adding hydrogen to
A. alkane molecules
B. alkene molecules
C. ester molecules   *(Page 97)*

28. The chemical process in which large molecules from crude oil are split into smaller molecules is
A. fractional distillation
B. hydrogenation
C. cracking   *(Pages 97, 99)*

29. What type of organic compounds condense at 180°C?
A. residue compounds
B. gasoline compounds
C. kerosene compounds   *(Page 99)*

30. Which of the following statements about thermoplastics is true?
A. Thermoplastics are easily recycled.
B. Thermoplastics can only be moulded once.
C. Thermoplastics are heat resistant.
          (Page 101)

Mixtures and compounds answers

1.C 2.C 3.B 4.A 5.B 6.B 7.A 8.B 9.C 10.B 11.C 12.C 13.B 14.C 15.A 16.B 17.C 18.A 19.A 20.B 21.C 22.A 23.B 24.C 25.A 26.C 27.B 28.C 29.C 30.A

397

ENERGY, FORCES AND MOTION

1. Energy is measured in units called
A. watts
B. joules
C. kilograms *(Page 109)*

2. The steam point (boiling point of water) is
A. 32°F
B. 100°C
C. 212°C *(Page 111)*

3. Which statement is true?
A. Conduction never occurs in solids.
B. Convection only occurs in liquids.
C. Convection cannot take place in solids. *(Pages 112-113)*

4. An alpha particle is made up of
A. two protons and two neutrons
B. two protons
C. a high-speed electron *(Page 114)*

5. Radioactive carbon-14 is written as $^{14}_{6}C$. This form of carbon has
A. six protons and six neutrons
B. six protons and eight neutrons
C. fourteen protons *(Page 115)*

6. A force's strength is measured in
A. kilograms
B. metres
C. newtons *(Page 119)*

7. A force is
A. a vector quantity
B. a scalar quantity
C. neither a vector nor a scalar quantity *(Page 119)*

Questions 8, 9 and 10 all refer to this diagram showing the forces acting on a wheel-barrow.

8. Which arrow represents the force of the ground on the wheelbarrow? *(Page 121)*

9. Which arrow represents the force of the man on the wheelbarrow? *(Page 121)*

10. Which arrow represents the weight of the wheelbarrow? *(Page 121)*

11. It is easier to turn something around a fulcrum if the force is applied
A. a long distance from the fulcrum
B. very close to the fulcrum
C. at the fulcrum *(Page 121)*

12. If no forces are acting on a moving object, the object will
A. slow down and stop
B. continue moving at the same speed in a straight line
C. change direction *(Page 122)*

13. Whenever you push an object you will always feel
A. a push in the opposite direction
B. a push in the same direction
C. no push at all *(Page 122)*

14. When a book slides across a table, the force that slows it down is called
A. lubrication
B. drag
C. friction *(Page 124)*

15. Average speed is equal to
A. distance multiplied by time
B. time divided by distance
C. distance divided by time *(Page 126)*

16. The difference between speed and velocity is that
A. speed is a scalar quantity whereas velocity is a vector quantity
B. speed is a vector quantity whereas velocity is a scalar quantity
C. they have different units *(Page 127)*

17. If an object accelerates, then its
A. speed and direction must change
B. speed or direction must change
C. speed must increase *(Page 127)*

18. An apple falling from a tree is pulled downwards because of
A. the pull of the Earth's gravity on the apple
B. the apple's low centre of gravity
C. the smooth skin of the apple, which reduces friction *(Page 130)*

19. Which statement is true?
A. The mass of an object depends on the pull of gravity on that object.
B. Mass is measured in newtons.
C. The weight of an object is due to the pull of gravity of the Earth on that object. *(Pages 130-131)*

20. Atmospheric pressure
A. is at its lowest near to the ground
B. is due to weight of air pressing down
C. increases as the height above ground increases *(Page 132)*

21. Which statement is true?
A. A force acting over an area exerts pressure.
B. The pressure of a needle is small due to the small area of the point.
C. Hydraulic machines are driven by gas pressure. *(Pages 132-133)*

22. When using a lever
A. the point about which the lever turns is called the fulcrum
B. the force you apply is the load
C. the force you need to overcome is called the effort *(Page 134)*

23. Which statement is correct?
A. Work is only done when a force makes an object move.
B. Work and power are both measured in watts.
C. If a man does work he gains energy. *(Page 137)*

24. Ships made of steel float because
A. steel is less dense than water
B. the hollow space inside the ship makes it less dense than water
C. the upthrust of the water on the ship is less than the weight of the ship *(Page 139)*

Questions 25-28 refer to this diagram which shows three of the four forces acting on an aeroplane.

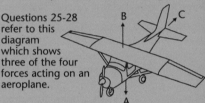

25. Which arrow represents the lift? *(Page 142)*

26. Which arrow represents gravity? *(Page 142)*

27. Which arrow represents the drag? *(Page 142)*

28. In the diagram above, the missing force is the
A. pull of the Earth's gravity
B. thrust provided by the engines
C. centripetal force *(Page 142)*

29. In level flight, lift is equal to the
A. speed of the aeroplane
B. pull of gravity
C. air resistance *(Page 142)*

30. Wings that are curved on top and flatter underneath are called
A. hydrofoils
B. aerofoils
C. ailerons *(Page 142)*

1.B 2.B 3.C 4.A 5.B 6.C 7.A 8.A 9.C 10.B 11.A 12.B 13.A 14.C 15.C 16.A 17.B 18.A 19.C 20.B 21.A 22.A 23.A 24.B 25.B 26.A 27.C 28.B 29.B 30.B

EARTH AND SPACE

1. At the centre of the Solar System lies
A. a moon
B. the Sun
C. the Earth   *(Page 163)*

2. Planet Earth makes a complete orbit around the Sun once every
A. day
B. month
C. year   *(Page 163)*

3. The four inner planets, which are all rocky and fairly small, are
A. Earth, Venus, Mercury, Mars
B. Pluto, Neptune, Saturn, Uranus
C. Venus, Mars, Saturn, Neptune
                                (Page 164)

4. The Moon orbits the Earth once every
A. week
B. 28 days
C. year   *(Page 167)*

5. The Moon shines at night because
A. it is made of pale, shiny rock
B. it reflects light from the Sun
C. it gives out its own light
                                (Page 167)

6. Man-made devices that orbit the Earth, gathering information, are called
A. satellites
B. observatories
C. refractors   *(Page 175)*

7. Spreading ridges are found at plate boundaries which are
A. constructive
B. destructive
C. sedimentary   *(Page 181)*

8. High fold mountain ranges are formed when two continental plates
A. slide past each other
B. move apart
C. push together   *(Page 181)*

9. When hot, molten magma cools and hardens, the rock formed is called
A. continental
B. metamorphic
C. igneous   *(Page 181)*

10. The point directly above an earthquake's focus is its
A. seismic wave
B. epicentre
C. eruption   *(Page 182)*

11. Magma in volcanoes which form above subduction zones has come from
A. a spreading ridge
B. the descending plate
C. a hot spot   *(Page 183)*

12. About 540 million years ago there was a sudden increase in the number of animals with hard parts. This happened in the
A. Carboniferous Period
B. Cambrian Period
C. Permian Period   *(Page 187)*

13. The world's largest ocean is the
A. Pacific Ocean
B. Atlantic Ocean
C. Southern Ocean   *(Page 188)*

14. The ocean tides are caused mainly by the pull of gravity on the water by
A. the Moon
B. the Sun
C. the Solar System   *(Page 189)*

15. In the USA tropical cyclones are called
A. depressions
B. typhoons
C. hurricanes   *(Page 189)*

16. The source of a river is where it
A. starts
B. ends
C. meanders   *(Page 190)*

17. In the middle and lower reaches of a river, wide loops often develop. These are called
A. sediments
B. deltas
C. meanders   *(Page 190)*

18. A river's speed normally increases as it moves from the upper stage to the lower stage. This is mainly because
A. the river's width increases
B. a flood plain develops
C. the bed becomes smoother so there is less friction to slow down the water   *(Page 190)*

19. All of the material carried by a river is called its
A. flood plain
B. load
C. gradient   *(Page 191)*

20. When water vapour in the air changes into the tiny water droplets which form clouds, we say that it
A. disintegrates
B. evaporates
C. condenses   *(Page 193)*

21. In July the northern hemisphere has its summer because
A. there are fewer clouds in the sky
B. the Sun gives out more heat in July
C. the northern hemisphere is tilted towards the Sun   *(Page 193)*

22. In mountainous districts the climate changes mainly with
A. attitude
B. altitude
C. latitude   *(Page 195)*

23. Air temperatures in cities are often higher than those in the surrounding countryside mainly because of the extra heat given out by
A. vehicle exhaust fumes
B. people walking around
C. concrete and buildings   *(Page 195)*

24. Over the next 100 years the world's population is expected to
A. level off
B. decrease
C. continue increasing   *(Page 196)*

25. The general movement of people from the countryside to settle in cities is called
A. commuting
B. urban migration
C. rural migration   *(Page 196)*

26. For many people the main reason they move into cities is
A. to find a job
B. to farm the land
C. to build a home   *(Page 196)*

27. The word which means all the materials needed by humans and provided by planet Earth is
A. resources
B. food
C. fuel   *(Page 198)*

28. Oil and coal are examples of
A. fossil fuels
B. nuclear fuels
C. renewable fuels   *(Page 198)*

29. Energy sources such as wind, waves and the Sun's rays, which do not rely on fossil fuels, are described as
A. temporary
B. renewable
C. non-renewable   *(Page 198)*

30. One good way of using the Earth's resources so they last longer is
A. extracting
B. mining
C. recycling   *(Page 199)*

Earth and space answers
1.B 2.C 3.A 4.B 5.B 6.A 7.A 8.C 9.C 10.B 11.B 12.B 13.A 14.A 15.C 16.A 17.C 18.C 19.B 20.C 21.C 22.B 23.C 24.C 25.B 26.A 27.A 28.A 29.B 30.C

399

LIGHT, SOUND AND ELECTRICITY

1. All waves are
A. vibrations and carry energy
B. vibrations in the same direction as the wave is travelling
C. vibrations at right angles to the direction the wave is travelling
(Pages 202-203)

2. The wavelength of a wave is
A. the number of complete waves that pass a point in one second
B. the distance between a peak and the next trough
C. the distance between a peak and the next peak *(Page 203)*

3. When a wave hits a surface and bounces off, it is
A. reflected
B. refracted
C. diffracted *(Pages 204-205)*

4. When a wave enters a new medium at an angle and changes direction, it is
A. reflected
B. refracted
C. diffracted *(Pages 204-205)*

5. Sound waves
A. are electromagnetic waves
B. can travel through a vacuum
C. travel more quickly in solids than in gases *(Pages 202, 206-207)*

6. Sound waves in air
A. always travel at the same speed
B. cannot be reflected off obstacles
C. are made up of vibrations of the air molecules *(Pages 206-207)*

7. The loudness of a note from a stringed instrument is increased by
A. plucking the string harder
B. lengthening the string
C. shortening the string *(Page 208)*

8. The pitch of a note from a stringed instrument is raised by
A. plucking the string harder
B. lengthening the string
C. shortening the string *(Page 209)*

9. Ultraviolet rays
A. have a shorter wavelength than visible light
B. have a longer wavelength than visible light
C. travel faster than visible light
(Page 212)

10. Light cannot pass through
A. transparent objects
B. translucent objects
C. opaque objects *(Page 214)*

11. The umbra is the
A. area where all the light falls
B. dark area of a shadow
C. grey area of a shadow *(Page 214)*

12. The penumbra is the
A. area where all the light falls
B. dark area of a shadow
C. grey area of a shadow *(Page 214)*

13. Which statement is not true?
A. White light can be split up into its various colours using a prism.
B. Blue light is refracted the least.
C. Different colours are refracted by different amounts. *(Page 216)*

14. Red, green and blue light are
A. primary colours
B. secondary colours
C. complementary colours *(Page 216)*

15. When red light and blue light are mixed, the resulting colour is
A. blue
B. red
C. magenta *(Page 216)*

16. When white light falls on a blue object, the object appears
A. blue
B. white
C. black *(Page 217)*

17. Light interference happens when light rays
A. travel parallel to each other
B. travel in opposite directions
C. cross *(Page 219)*

18. Polarized sunglasses reduce the glare in your eyes because they
A. filter out all light wave vibrations that are not in a certain direction
B. reflect light away from your eyes
C. bend light so that it does not all reach your eyes *(Page 219)*

19. A glass bi-convex lens in air
A. has surfaces which curve inwards
B. acts as a converging lens
C. acts as a diverging lens *(Page 220)*

20. A short-sighted person
A. cannot see nearby objects clearly
B. cannot see distant objects clearly
C. needs glasses with converging lenses *(Page 221)*

21. Small objects look larger using a
A. microscope
B. periscope
C. telescope *(Page 222)*

22. The aperture of a camera controls
A. how much light enters the camera
B. the time that light falls on the film
C. the size of the image *(Page 224)*

23. An electron has
A. a positive electrical charge
B. a negative electrical charge
C. no electrical charge *(Page 228)*

24. Two charged particles attract one another when
A. both are positively charged
B. both are negatively charged
C. one is positively charged and the other negatively charged *(Page 228)*

25. Which diagram correctly shows a circuit with two single cells, with the positive terminals to the right, connected to a bulb? *(Page 409)*

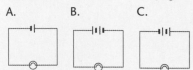

26. The diagram on the right shows a bulb, two single cells and a
A. resistor
B. transistor
C. diode *(Page 409)*

27. Which of the following magnetic poles will attract each other?
A. a north and a north
B. a north and a south
C. a south and a south *(Page 232)*

28. Soft ferromagnetic materials are
A. easy to magnetize and demagnetize
B. hard to magnetize and demagnetize
C. used to make permanent magnets
(Page 232)

29. A machine which converts energy of movement into electrical energy is
A. a generator
B. a motor
C. an armature *(Page 235)*

30. If the resistance of an electrical component in a series circuit increases, then the current
A. is increased
B. is reduced
C. stays the same *(Pages 230, 236)*

PLANTS AND FUNGI

1. Which of the following is found in plant cells but not animal cells?
A. a cell wall
B. a nucleus
C. cytoplasm   *(Page 250)*

2. A carrot is
A. an aerial root
B. an adventitious root
C. a tap root   *(Page 253)*

3. Water is taken into a plant through
A. its flowers
B. the root hairs in the soil
C. the surface of its leaves   *(Page 253)*

4. The tissue in plants which carries water upwards is
A. xylem
B. phloem
C. cambium   *(Page 254)*

5. In an older plant, xylem and phloem join up to form
A. lenticels
B. vascular bundles
C. a vascular cylinder *(Pages 256-257)*

6. Which tree has compound leaves?
A. horse chestnut
B. lime
C. oak   *(Pages 258-259)*

7. Leaf stomata are found mainly on
A. both upper and lower surfaces
B. the lower surface
C. the upper surface   *(Page 260)*

8. Water loss from the leaves through the stomata is called
A. transpiration
B. translocation
C. respiration   *(Page 262)*

9. Chlorophyll is vital to a plant because
A. it colours it green
B. it provides food
C. it absorbs energy from the Sun
                                (Page 264)

10. Photosynthesis can be expressed as
A. water + oxygen + energy →carbohydrates + carbon dioxide
B. oxygen + carbon dioxide + water →carbohydrates + energy
C. carbon dioxide + water + energy →carbohydrates + oxygen
                                (Page 264)

11. Plants respire
A. all the time
B. only at night
C. when photosynthesis stops
                                (Page 265)

12. A plant which feeds on dead matter is
A. a parasite
B. a saprotroph
C. an epiphyte   *(Page 266)*

13. Which is a carnivorous plant?
A. mistletoe
B. strangler fig
C. sundew   *(Pages 266-267)*

14. Male reproductive cells of a plant are called
A. anthers
B. pollen
C. pollen sacs   *(Page 271)*

15. Female reproductive cells of a plant are called
A. ovaries
B. carpels
C. ovules   *(Page 271)*

16. Pollination occurs when
A. a pollen grain connects with an ovule by a pollen tube
B. a pollen grain produces a pollen tube
C. a pollen grain lands on the stigma of another plant   *(Page 272)*

17. Which statement is true? Most wind-pollinated plants
A. have brightly coloured, sweet-scented flowers
B. have large sepals and petals
C. produce large quantities of smooth, light pollen grains
                                (Page 273)

18. Which of the following is a true fruit?
A. strawberry
B. cherry
C. apple   *(Page 274)*

19. Which plant has seeds dispersed by wind?
A. sycamore
B. goosegrass
C. pea   *(Page 276)*

20. In order to germinate, seeds need warmth, oxygen and
A. water
B. light
C. food   *(Page 277)*

21. The first root produced by a seed is called the
A. plumule
B. hilum
C. radicle   *(Page 277)*

22. Long side shoots which run overground and can develop into new plants are called
A. tubers
B. rhizomes
C. runners   *(Page 278)*

23. A plant adapted to living in water is called a
A. hydrophyte
B. lithophyte
C. halophyte   *(Page 280)*

24. The rapid reproduction of algae in water which has a high level of nitrates is called
A. intoxication
B. eutrophication
C. adaptation   *(Page 281)*

25. Which statement is true? Ferns, mosses and liverworts
A. cannot grow in damp, shady places
B. produce large numbers of flowers
C. can reproduce by making spores
                                (Pages 282-283)

26. The antibiotic medicine penicillin is made from a type of
A. alga
B. fungus
C. liverwort   *(Page 285)*

27. A plant which takes two years to complete its life cycle is called
A. a perennial
B. an annual
C. a biennial   *(Page 288)*

28. Plants which lose all their leaves once a year are called
A. xerophytes
B. evergreen
C. deciduous   *(Page 289)*

29. Prairies and steppes are forms of which biome?
A. tundra
B. temperate grassland
C. tropical grassland   *(Page 290)*

30. Plants take in nitrogen from their surroundings in the form of
A. ammonia
B. nitrogen gas
C. nitrates   *(Page 292)*

Plants and fungi answers
1.A 2.C 3.B 4.A 5.C 6.A 7.B 8.A 9.C 10.C 11.A 12.B 13.C 14.B 15.C 16.C 17.C 18.B 19.A 20.A 21.C 22.C 23.A 24.B 25.C 26.B 27.C 28.C 29.B 30.C

401

ANIMAL WORLD

1. Protoplasm consists of
A. the nucleus
B. the nucleus and cytoplasm
C. the nucleus, cytoplasm and cell
   membrane   *(Page 298)*

2. The liver is
A. a complex tissue
B. an organ
C. a body system   *(Page 299)*

3. Most animals which actively move
about are
A. asymmetrical
B. radially symmetrical
C. bilaterally symmetrical
                        (Page 301)

4. The skeleton of an insect is
A. an endoskeleton
B. an exoskeleton
C. a hydrostatic skeleton
                        (Page 301)

5. Hedgehog spines are made of
A. keratin
B. chitin
C. bone   *(Page 303)*

6. A swim bladder can be found in
A. all fish
B. most fish with bone skeletons
C. fish with cartilage skeletons
                        (Page 305)

7. Most beetles
A. cannot fly
B. fly by flapping both pairs of
   wings
C. fly by flapping one pair of
   wings
                        (Page 307)

8. Dogs walk on
A. the tips of the toes
B. the undersides of the toes
C. the underside of the whole foot
                        (Page 309)

9. Carnassial teeth are found in
A. herbivores
B. omnivores
C. carnivores   *(Page 312)*

10. Animals which eat both plants
and meat are called
A. omnivores
B. carnivores
C. herbivores   *(Page 312)*

11. In a bird, food is stored in the
A. crop
B. gizzard
C. cloaca   *(Page 313)*

12. Adult insects breathe using
A. gills
B. lungs
C. tracheae   *(Page 315)*

13. Homeostasis is
A. keeping a constant body
   temperature
B. keeping a constant internal
   environment
C. keeping the external environment
   constant   *(Page 316)*

14. Mimicry involves
A. copying the behaviour of another
   animal
B. copying the warning colours of
   another animal
C. copying the scent of another
   animal   *(Page 318)*

15. Some snakes detect the body
heat of their prey with
A. antennae
B. lateral lines
C. pit organs   *(Page 323)*

16. The body of a hermaphrodite
animal contains
A. only female sex cells
B. only male sex cells
C. both male and female sex cells
                        (Page 325)

17. In cleidoic eggs the young are
A. fed by a yolk
B. called spawn
C. surrounded by a shell
                        (Page 327)

18. A locust hopper is a stage of
A. complete metamorphosis
B. incomplete metamorphosis
C. migration   *(Pages 328-329)*

19. A habitat is
A. the natural home for plants and
   animals
B. a group of animals
C. too cold to support life
                        (Page 330)

20. An ecological niche can support
A. one species of animal
B. two species of animal
C. several animal species *(Page 330)*

21. The largest ecosystems are
A. habitats
B. communities
C. biomes   *(Page 331)*

22. An organism which eats another
organism is
A. autotrophic
B. heterotrophic
C. a producer   *(Page 332)*

23. At the second trophic level, an
animal is a
A. producer
B. primary consumer
C. secondary consumer   *(Page 332)*

24. An organism which breaks down
dead plant and animal matter is a
A. decomposer
B. consumer
C. producer   *(Page 332)*

25. A trophic level has
A. fewer consumers than the level
   below
B. more consumers than the level
   below
C. the same number of consumers as
   all other levels   *(Page 332)*

26. The abiotic parts of an
environment are made up of
A. living or organic matter
B. mineral or inorganic matter
C. dead matter   *(Page 334)*

27. Endemic species of animals are
those found
A. in many different places
B. in only one place
C. only on islands   *(Page 337)*

28. The largest taxonomic ranks after
kingdoms are
A. orders
B. classes
C. phyla   *(Page 341)*

29. Biological names of living
organisms are in
A. Greek
B. Latin
C. English   *(Page 343)*

30. Animals which live closely
together and both gain from the
situation are
A. mutualists
B. commensals
C. parasites   *(Page 343)*

1.C 2.B 3.C 4.B 5.A 6.B 7.C 8.B 9.C 10.A 11.A 12.C 13.B 14.B 15.C 16.C 17.A 18.B 19.A 20.A 21.C 22.B 23.B 24.A 25.A 26.B 27.B 28.C 29.B 30.A

HUMAN BODY

1. The knee is a type of
A. ball and socket joint
B. hinge joint
C. gliding joint *(Page 347)*

2. Which of these terms does not describe the biceps and triceps?
A. an antagonistic pair
B. cardiac muscles
C. skeletal muscles *(Pages 348-349)*

3. Oxygen-rich blood is carried from the heart around the body via the
A. aorta
B. pulmonary artery
C. pulmonary vein *(Page 350)*

4. Oxygen is given up to tissue fluid through the walls of
A. arteries
B. veins
C. capillaries *(Page 351)*

5. Oxygen is carried around the body in
A. white blood cells
B. red blood cells
C. platelets *(Page 351)*

6. The shape of molar teeth makes them particularly suitable for
A. tearing and stabbing food
B. crushing and grinding food
C. chopping food *(Page 352)*

7. A tooth starts to hurt when bacteria attack the
A. enamel
B. dentine
C. pulp cavity *(Page 353)*

8. The enzyme that is contained in saliva digests
A. starch
B. protein
C. fat *(Page 354)*

9. The organ in which bile is produced is the
A. pancreas
B. small intestine
C. liver *(Page 355)*

10. Absorption of digested food takes place in the
A. stomach
B. small intestine
C. colon *(Page 355)*

11. The main nutrient that is found in meat is
A. protein
B. carbohydrate
C. fat *(Page 356)*

12. Gas exchange takes place in
A. bronchi
B. bronchioles
C. alveoli *(Page 358)*

13. Internal respiration that uses oxygen is
A. anaerobic respiration
B. metabolism
C. aerobic respiration *(Page 360)*

14. Aerobic respiration is described as
A. glucose + oxygen + water
→energy + carbon dioxide
B. glucose + carbon dioxide
→energy + oxygen + water
C. glucose + oxygen
→energy + carbon dioxide + water
(Page 360)

15. Exercise
A. allows you to make do with less oxygen
B. increases the pulse rate
C. keeps the heart muscles beating at a steady rate *(Page 361)*

16. Chemical compounds which control the level of substances in the body are
A. glomeruli
B. hormones
C. nephrons *(Page 362)*

17. Receptors are the sensitive nerve endings of
A. motor neurons
B. association neurons
C. sensory neurons *(Page 364)*

18. The largest part of the brain is
A. the cerebrum
B. the cerebellum
C. the brain stem *(Page 366)*

19. Pacinian corpuscles are found in
A. the blood
B. the brain
C. the skin *(Page 368)*

20. The size of the pupil of the eye is controlled by
A. changing the shape of the lens
B. the iris
C. rods and cones *(Pages 370-371)*

21. A structure called the oval window is found in
A. the ear
B. the eye
C. the kidney *(Page 372)*

22. Taste buds that detect bitter tastes tend to be found in greater number at the
A. front of the tongue
B. back of the tongue
C. sides of the tongue *(Page 375)*

23. Conception is
A. ejaculation
B. another word for sexual intercourse
C. fertilization of an egg by a sperm
(Page 377)

24. The organ that provides a baby with food and oxygen from the mother is
A. the placenta
B. the uterus
C. the vagina *(Pages 376-377)*

25. A woman's periods happen when
A. the uterus lining is lost
B. ovulation takes place
C. the uterus lining starts to thicken
(Page 379)

26. The form of cell division that produces sperm is
A. fertilization
B. meiosis
C. mitosis *(Page 380)*

27. Which of the following does a measles vaccine contain?
A. lymphocytes
B. antibodies to the measles germ
C. a weak dose of the measles germ
(Page 387)

28. Antibiotics are effective against
A. some viruses
B. some bacteria
C. all germs *(Page 389)*

29. Which of the following is not an alternative treatment?
A. laser surgery
B. homeopathy
C. acupuncture *(Pages 389-390)*

30. Which of the following is an example of an illegal drug?
A. nicotine
B. alcohol
C. heroin *(Page 391)*

Human body answers

1.B 2.B 3.A 4.C 5.B 6.B 7.C 8.A 9.C 10.B 11.A 12.C 13.C 14.C 15.B 16.B 17.C 18.A 19.C 20.B 21.A 22.B 23.C 24.A 25.A 26.B 27.C 28.B 29.A 30.C

403

UNITS OF MEASUREMENT

Measuring things is one of the most important parts of science. There are three main measuring systems: the British **imperial** system, **US customary measurements**, and **metric**. The imperial and US systems developed from traditional English units and are nearly identical. The metric system was introduced in France in the 1790s, and is now officially approved in every country, though other units are often used alongside it. It is based on the system of counting in tens – the decimal system.

IMPERIAL MEASUREMENTS

Length and distance

12 inches (in or ")	= 1 foot (ft or ')
3 feet	= 1 yard (yd)
1,760 yards	= 1 mile
3 miles	= 1 league

Area

144 square inches	= 1 square foot
9 square feet	= 1 square yard
4,840 square yards	= 1 acre
640 acres	= 1 square mile

Mass

16 ounces (oz)	= 1 pound (lb)
14 pounds	= 1 stone (st)
2,240 pounds*	= 1 ton

Volume and capacity

1,728 cubic inches	= 1 cubic foot (ft³)
27 cubic feet	= 1 cubic yard (yd³)
20 fluid ounces** (US: 16)	= 1 pint (pt)
2 pints	= 1 quart (qt)
8 pints	= 1 gallon (gal)

* US 1 ton = 2,000lb (sometimes called a "short ton")
** UK 1 fl oz = 0.0284 litres; US 1 fl oz = 0.0296 litres

CONVERSIONS

To convert between metric and imperial figures, use this table with a calculator.

To convert	into	multiply by
cm	inches	0.394
m	feet	3.281
m	yards	1.094
km	miles	0.621
grams	ounces	0.035
kilograms	pounds	2.205
tonnes	tons	1.102
cm²	square inches	0.155
m²	square yards	1.196
km²	square miles	0.386
hectares	acres	2.471
litres	pints	1.76

METRIC MEASUREMENTS

Many metric measurements are spelled ending in "re" in British English and "er" in American English. For example, "metre" and "meter".

Length and distance

1,000 nanometres (nm)	= 1 micron (µm)
1,000 microns (µm)	= 1 millimetre (mm)
10 millimetres (mm)	= 1 centimetre (cm)
100 centimetres	= 1 metre (m)
1,000 metres	= 1 kilometre (km)

Area

100 square mm (mm²)	= 1 square cm (cm²)
10,000cm²	= 1 square m (m²)
10,000m²	= 1 hectare (ha)
100 hectares	= 1 square km (km²)

Mass

1,000 grams (g)	= 1 kilogram (kg)
1,000 kilograms	= 1 tonne (t)

Volume and capacity

1 cubic cm (cm³/cc)	= 1 millilitre (ml)
1,000 millilitres	= 1 litre (l)
1,000 litres	= 1 cubic metre (m³)

Scientists usually show numbers with up to four digits closed up, without commas, for example 9999. Numbers with more digits are shown with spaces to make them easier to read, for example 0.000 001. In non-technical writing, as in this book, numbers with over three digits are shown with commas.

To convert	into	multiply by
inches	cm	2.54
feet	m	0.305
yards	m	0.914
miles	km	1.609
ounces	grams	28.35
pounds	kilograms	0.454
tons	tonnes	1.016
square inches	cm²	6.452
square yards	m²	0.836
square miles	km²	2.59
acres	hectares	0.405
pints	litres	0.568

SI UNITS

SI units (short for the French *Système Internationale d'Unités*) are an internationally agreed system of units used for scientific purposes. The units have been defined very precisely in modern times. The metre, for example, is now defined as the distance light travels in a vacuum in $1/299,792,458$ of a second. Its measurement was originally based on a length of platinum alloy kept in Paris.

Quantity	SI unit
Length	metre (m)
Mass	kilogram (kg)
Time	second (s)
Temperature	kelvin (K)
Current	ampere (A)
Amount of a substance	mole (mol)
Light intensity	candela (cd)

DERIVED SI UNITS

These are derived from the units above using the equations shown.

Quantity	Derived SI unit	Equation
Area	square metre (m²)	Depends on shape (see page 408)
Volume	cubic metre (m³)	Depends on shape (see page 408)
Density	kilograms per cubic metre (kg/m³)	$\dfrac{\text{Mass (kg)}}{\text{Volume (m}^3\text{)}}$
Velocity	metres per second (m/s)	$\dfrac{\text{Distance moved in given direction (m)}}{\text{Time taken (s)}}$
Momentum	(kg m/s)	Mass (kg) x velocity (m/s)
Acceleration	metres per second per second (m/s²)	$\dfrac{\text{Change in velocity (m/s)}}{\text{Time taken for change (s)}}$
Power	watt (W)	$\dfrac{\text{Work done (J)}}{\text{Time (s)}}$
Force	newton (N)	Mass (kg) x acceleration (m/s²)
Energy/Work	joule (J)	Force (N) x distance moved in direction of force (m)
Pressure	pascal (Pa)	$\dfrac{\text{Force (N)}}{\text{Area (m}^2\text{)}}$
Frequency	hertz (Hz)	Number of cycles per second
Electric charge	coulomb (C)	Current (A) x time (s)
Voltage	volt (V)	$\dfrac{\text{Energy transferred (J)}}{\text{Charge (C)}}$
Resistance	ohm (Ω)	$\dfrac{\text{Voltage (V)}}{\text{Current (A)}}$

TEMPERATURE SCALES

There are three main scales for measuring temperature: the Fahrenheit scale (imperial), the Celsius scale (metric) and the absolute temperature scale (SI), which is measured in kelvins.

The absolute temperature scale is seen as the most scientific because 0 kelvin (-273°C) is **absolute zero**: the temperature at which no more heat can be extracted from an object. Scientific theory holds that this point of absolute cold would be impossible to reach in practice.

Celsius (°C)	Fahrenheit (°F)	Kelvin (K)
110	230	383
100	212	373
90	194	363
80	176	353
70	158	343
60	140	333
50	122	323
40	104	313
30	86	303
20	68	293
10	50	283
0	32	273
-10	14	263
-20	-4	253
-30	-22	243
-40	-40	233
-50	-58	223
-60	-76	213
-70	-94	203
-80	-112	193
-90	-130	183
-100	-148	173
-110	-166	163

CONVERSIONS

Convert	into	calculation
°C	°F	x9,÷5,+32
°C	K	+273
°F	°C	-32,x5,÷9
°F	K	-32,x5,÷9,+273
K	°C	-273
K	°F	-273,x9,÷5,+32

MEASURING NATURE

It is not always easy to measure natural forces and substances precisely. The scales shown here work by measuring their effects or properties.

THE BEAUFORT SCALE OF WIND FORCE

The **Beaufort Scale** was developed in 1805 by Sir Francis Beaufort, a British Navy Commander, to estimate wind speed at sea. In the 1920s it was extended to include precise wind speeds and adapted for use on land. While it is now rarely used by **meteorologists** (weather scientists), it is still a popular means of calculating wind speed without using instruments.

Beaufort number	Kilometres per hour	Wind description	Observable effects on land	
0	Less than 1	Calm	Smoke rises vertically.	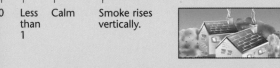
1	1-5	Light air (air moves slightly)	Smoke drifts in direction of wind; weather vanes remain still.	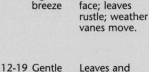
2	6-11	Light breeze	Wind felt on face; leaves rustle; weather vanes move.	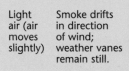
3	12-19	Gentle breeze	Leaves and twigs keep moving; small flags unfurl.	
4	20-28	Moderate breeze	Dust and loose paper raised from ground; small branches move.	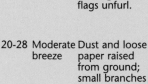
5	29-38	Fresh breeze	Small trees in leaf begin to sway.	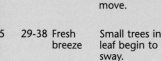
6	39-49	Strong breeze	Large branches sway; umbrellas hard to use; whistling in telegraph wires.	

Beaufort number	Kilometres per hour	Wind description	Observable effects on land	
7	50-61	Moderate gale (or high wind)	Large trees sway; hard to walk against wind.	
8	62-74	Gale	Twigs and small branches break off trees; very hard to walk.	
9	75-88	Severe gale	Large branches break off trees; some damage to buildings.	
10	89-102	Storm	Trees are uprooted; severe damage to buildings.	
11*	103-117	Violent storm	Widespread damage to trees and buildings.	
12*	118 or more	Hurricane	Extreme widespread destruction.	

* Storms this strong usually only happen at sea.

MOHS HARDNESS SCALE

The hardness of minerals is measured on the **Mohs scale**, named after the German mineralogist, Friedrich Mohs (1773-1839). The scale has a sample mineral for each value, ranging from 1 – soft, crumbly talc, to 10 – diamond, the hardest mineral.

1. Talc
Very easily scratched with a fingernail.

2. Gypsum
Can be scratched by a fingernail.

3. Calcite
Very easily scratched with a knife, and just with a copper coin.

4. Fluorite
Easily scratched with a knife.

5. Apatite
Just scratched with a knife.

6. Orthoclase
Cannot be scratched with a knife. Just scratches glass.

7. Quartz
Scratches glass easily.

8. Beryl or topaz
Scratches glass very easily.

9. Corundum
Cuts glass.

10. Diamond
Cuts glass very easily. Will scratch corundum.

MEASURING EARTHQUAKES

Seismologists (earthquake scientists) measure the energy of earthquake shock waves with a device called a **seismometer**. Their energy level is recorded on the **moment magnitude scale*** (M_W). Each whole M_W value equals about 31.6 times the value below. For example, an earthquake at 6.0 M_W has about 31.6 times the energy of one at 5.0 M_W, and 1000 times that of one at 4.0 M_W. An earthquake's variable impact above ground, rated by its effects, is often measured on the **Mercalli intensity scale**.

Moment magnitude: TNT equivalents**	Mercalli intensity: effects
1.0: 30lb (construction site blast)	1: Detectable only by seismometers.
2.0: 1 ton (mine blast)	2: Only a few people on upper floors notice.
3.0: 29 tons (ammunition train explosion)	3: Like a heavy truck passing by. Hanging lights may swing.
4.0: 1 kiloton (small atomic bomb)	4: Windows and dishes rattle. Like a heavy truck crashing into building.
5.0: 32 kilotons (Nagasaki atomic bomb)	5: Almost everyone notices. Sleepers wake up. Small objects move and drinks spill.
6.0: 1 megaton (Emilia-Romagna quake, Italy, 2012)	6: Many people frightened and run outdoors. Heavy furniture moves. Pictures fall off walls.
7.0: 32 megatons (largest hydrogen bomb)	7: Walls crack. Tiles and bricks fall from buildings. Difficult to stand up.
8.0: 1 gigaton (San Francisco quake, 1906)	8: Chimneys and some weaker buildings collapse. Mass panic may break out.
9.0: 32 gigatons (Indian Ocean quake, 2004)	9: Well-built houses collapse. Underground pipes damaged. Cracks open in ground.

* The "w" stands for work (see page 137)

**TNT (Trinitrotoluene) is an explosive. The "ton of TNT" is a measurement that equals the energy released by detonating that amount of TNT.

10: Landslides. Railway tracks buckle. Rivers overflow. Many stone buildings collapse.

11: Most buildings destroyed. Large cracks in ground. Bridges destroyed.

12: Ground moves in waves. Total destruction.

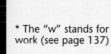

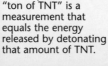

GEOMETRICAL SHAPES

There are two kinds of geometrical shape. **Planes** are flat
shapes with only two dimensions – length and breadth.
Solids have three dimensions – length, breadth and height.

PLANES

Polygons
A polygon is a plane with three
or more straight sides.

Triangles
A triangle is a three-sided polygon.

Left: an equilateral
triangle has three
equal sides.

Right: a scalene
triangle has three
unequal sides.

Left: an isosceles
triangle has two
equal sides.

Circles
A circle is a curved line on which
all points are equally distant from
the centre. The parts of a circle
are shown below.

The circumference
is the length of
the outer edge
of the circle.

*Plural: radii

SOLIDS

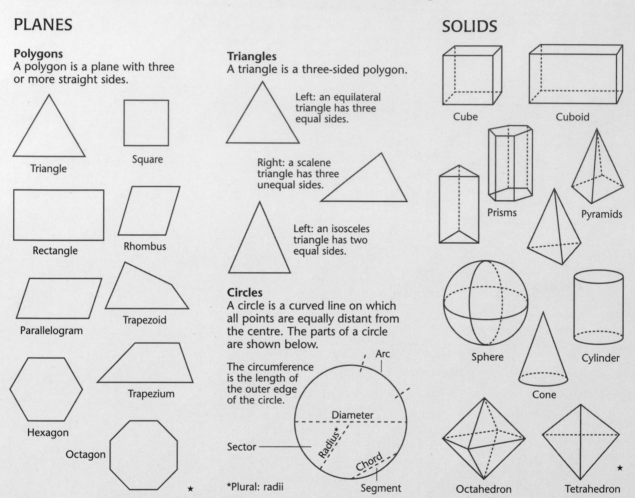

Triangle

Square

Rectangle

Rhombus

Parallelogram

Trapezoid

Trapezium

Hexagon

Octagon

Cube

Cuboid

Prisms

Pyramids

Sphere

Cylinder

Cone

Octahedron

Tetrahedron

Arc

Diameter

Radius*

Sector

Chord

Segment

GEOMETRICAL FORMULAE

In these formulae, b = base, h = height, r = radius, π = pi (3.142), θ = the angle between the two radii involved.

Area of circle = πr^2

Circumference of circle = $2\pi r$

Area of sector = $\dfrac{\theta \pi r^2}{360}$

Length of arc = $\dfrac{\theta \pi r}{180}$

Volume of cylinder = $\pi r^2 h$

Volume of cone = $\frac{1}{3} \pi r^2 h$

Volume of sphere = $\frac{4}{3} \pi r^3$

Surface area of sphere = $4\pi r^2$

Volume of pyramid = $\frac{1}{3}$ h x base area

Area of triangle = $\frac{1}{2}$ bh

Area of parallelogram = bh

LAWS AND SYMBOLS

SCIENTIFIC LAWS

Archimedes' principle The upthrust acting on an object is equal to the weight of the fluid that the object displaces.

Avogadro's law All gases of the same volume at the same temperature and pressure must contain the same number of molecules.

Bernoulli's principle When the flow of a fluid, for example air, gets faster, its pressure is reduced.

Boyle's law The pressure and volume of a gas at a constant temperature are inversely proportional.

Charles' law (or **law of volumes**) The volume of an ideal gas at a constant pressure is proportional to its kelvin temperature.

Hooke's law The extension of a material is proportional to the force stretching it, as long as it is not stretched beyond its elastic limit.

Law of conservation of energy Energy cannot be created or destroyed. It can only be changed into a different form.

Law of conservation of mass Matter cannot be created or destroyed in a chemical reaction.

Law of conservation of momentum After two objects have collided, their combined momentum remains the same as long as no external forces act upon them.

Newton's first law of motion (or **principle of inertia**) If the resultant force on an object is zero, the object will either stay still or continue moving at a constant speed in a straight line.

Newton's second law of motion Any resultant force acting on an object will change its motion. How much the motion changes depends on the object's mass and the size of the resultant force.

Newton's third law of motion When an object A exerts a force on an object B, then B exerts an equal and opposite force on A.

Newton's law of universal gravitation There is a gravitational force of attraction between any two objects with mass, which depends on the masses of the objects and the distance between them.

Pythagoras' theorem The area of the square on the hypotenuse (side c in the diagram) of a right-angled triangle is equal to the sum of the areas of the squares on the other sides ($a^2 + b^2 = c^2$).

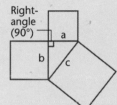

ELECTRICAL AND ELECTRONIC SYMBOLS

The symbols below are used to represent components found in electrical and electronic circuits. Different countries sometimes use alternative symbols.

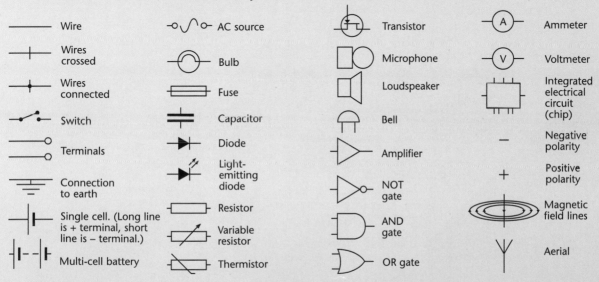

EARTH AND SPACE FACTS

These pages contain lists of some amazing facts about Earth, the planets, and space exploration. They are as accurate as possible, but there are different ways of measuring things, so you may find slightly different figures elsewhere.

THE CONTINENTS

Name	Area (km²)
Asia	44,537,920
Africa	30,311,690
North America	24,709,000
South America	17,840,000
Antarctica	13,829,430
Europe	10,180,000
Australasia	8,564,400

OCEANS AND SEAS

The largest ocean, the Pacific, is also the deepest. At one point in an area called the Mariana Trench, it is 10,920m deep.

Name	Area (km²)
Pacific Ocean	165,250,000
Atlantic Ocean	82,440,000
Indian Ocean	73,440,000
Southern Ocean	20,327,000
Arctic Ocean	14,090,000
Philippine Sea	5,000,000
Coral Sea	4,791,000
Arabian Sea	3,862,000
South China Sea	3,685,000
Weddell Sea	2,800,000

LARGEST ISLANDS

Name(s)	Area (km²)
Greenland (Kalaallit Nunaat)	2,130,800
New Guinea	785,753
Borneo	748,168
Madagascar	587,713
Baffin Island, Canada	507,451
Sumatra, Indonesia	443,066
Honshu, Japan	225,800
Victoria Island, Canada	217,291
Great Britain	209,331
Ellesmere Island, Canada	196,236

GREATEST LAKES

The deepest lake, at 1,642m, is Lake Baikal in Russia. It also contains the most fresh water.

Name(s)	Location	Area (km²)
Caspian Sea	Europe/Asia	386,400
Lake Superior	USA/Canada	82,100
Lake Victoria	Tanzania/Uganda	69,484
Lake Huron	USA/Canada	59,600
Lake Michigan	USA	57,800
Lake Tanganyika	Tanzania/Congo	32,600
Lake Baikal	Russia	31,722
Great Bear Lake	Canada	31,153
Lake Nyasa (Malawi)	Mozambique/Tanzania	29,600
Great Slave Lake	Canada	28,568

LONGEST RIVERS

Name(s)	Location	Length (km)
Nile (Bahr-el-Nil)	North-east Africa	6,671
Amazon (Amazonas)	South America	6,437
Chang Jiang (Yangtze-Kiang)	China	6,380
Mississippi-Missouri-Red Rock	USA	6,019
Yenisey-Angara	Russia	5,539
Huang He (Yellow River)	China	5,464
Ob-Irtysh	Asia	5,411
Parana (River Plate)	South America	4,880
Congo (Zaïre; Lualaba)	Central Africa	4,700
Amur-Shilka-Onon	East Asia	4,416

HIGHEST MOUNTAINS

Name(s)	Location	Height (m)
Everest (Chomolangma)	Nepal/China border	8,848
K2	Pakistan/China border	8,612
Kanchenjunga	Nepal/India border	8,586
Lhotse	Nepal/China border	8,561
Makalu	Nepal/China border	8,462
Cho Oyu	Nepal/China border	8,201
Dhaulagiri	Nepal	8,167
Manaslu	Nepal	8,156
Nanga Parbat	Pakistan	8,125
Annapurna	Nepal	8,091
Gasherbrum (K5)	Pakistan/China border	8,068
Broad Peak (K3)	Pakistan	8,047

PLANETARY FACTS AND FIGURES

Name of planet	Diameter of planet	Average distance from Sun	Time to orbit Sun	Time to rotate (days, hrs, mins)	Number of satellites
Mercury	4,879km	58 million km	88 days	58d, 15h, 31m	0
Venus	12,104km	108 million km	224.7 days	243d, 0h, 29m	0
Earth	12,756km	149.6 million km	365.2 days	23h, 56m	1
Mars	6,792km	228 million km	687 days	24h, 37m	2
Jupiter	142,984km	779 million km	11.9 years	9h, 55m	67+
Saturn	120,536km	1.4 billion km	29.5 years	10h, 32m	62+
Uranus	51,118km	2.9 billion km	84 years	17h, 14m	27+
Neptune	49,528km	4.5 billion km	165 years	16h, 7m	14+

SPACE MISSIONS

1957 Sputnik 1, the first artificial satellite, was launched into space on October 4 by the Soviet Union. On November 3, Sputnik 2 was launched into space, carrying a dog named Laika.
1959 The first space probes, Luna 1, Luna 2 and Luna 3, were sent to the Moon by the Soviet Union.
1961 Soviet cosmonaut Yuri Gagarin became the first person to go into space. The flight lasted about 90 minutes.
1965 US space probe Mariner 4 took the first photos of Mars.
1966 Soviet space probe Luna 9 landed on the Moon, returning the first photos from its surface.
1967 Soviet Venera 4 became the first space probe to reach Venus. One day later, US probe Mariner 5 arrived.
1968 The USA launched Apollo 8, the first manned space flight around the Moon.
1969 On July 20, the US Apollo 11 mission landed on the Moon. They were Edwin "Buzz" Aldrin and Neil Armstrong, who was the first man to walk on the Moon. The manned mission Apollo 12 reached the Moon on November 14.
1970 US Apollo 13 Moon mission was aborted when an explosion destroyed the main module's power system.
1971 Manned Apollo 14 and 15 missions landed on the Moon.
1971 The Russians launched the first space station, Salyut 1.
1971 US Mariner 9 space probe returned the first close-up images of Mars.
1972 Manned Apollo 16 and 17 missions landed on the Moon.
1973 The USA launched Skylab, the first US space station.

1973 US Pioneer 10 probe returned the first close-up pictures of Jupiter.
1974 US Mariner 10 space probe returned the first photos of cloud-tops around Venus. It then went on to Mercury.
1975 Soviet space probes Venera 9 and 10 took the first photos of Venus' surface.
1976 US space probes Viking 1 and 2 landed on Mars. They took many photos and studied its soil.
1979 US space probes Voyager 1 and Voyager 2 flew by Jupiter, sending back detailed pictures.
1980 US space probe Voyager 2 flew past Saturn.
1981 USA launched STS1, the first Space Shuttle flight.
1986 US probe Voyager 2 flew past Uranus, taking many images.
1986 US Space Shuttle Challenger exploded, killing seven astronauts.
1986 Soviet space station Mir was launched.
1986 European space probe Giotto was the first to observe a comet (Halley) close up.
1989 US space probe Voyager 2 flew by Neptune.
1990 US Magellan probe arrived at Venus and began mapping its surface using radar.
1991 The Hubble Space Telescope was launched.
1992 Astronomers discovered the first planets outside the Solar System, orbiting a pulsar.
1993 Spacewalking astronauts repaired the Hubble Telescope.
1993 US Galileo probe took the first close-up pictures of an asteroid, Gaspra.

1996 US Mars Global Surveyor was launched to study Mars while in orbit around the planet.
1997 US Mars Pathfinder reached Mars, releasing the Sojourner rover onto its surface.
1998 International Space Station construction began.
2001 The Mir space station was retired and removed from its orbit. It broke up on re-entry into the atmosphere, before landing in the Pacific Ocean.
2001 US NEAR (Near Earth Asteroid Rendezvous) spacecraft landed on an asteroid, Eros.
2003 US Space Shuttle Columbia broke up on re-entry, killing seven astronauts.
2003 Yang Liwei became the first Chinese astronaut, orbiting the Earth aboard Shenzhou 5.
2003-2004 US Mars Exploration Rovers, Spirit and Opportunity, began their mission.
2004 The Cassini-Huygens probe reached Saturn and explored its system, discovering new moons.
2005 European Huygens probe landed on Saturn's moon Titan.
2006 The US New Horizons probe started its long journey towards Pluto.
2009 The Kepler probe was launched to seek new planets.
2010 SpaceX became the first private firm to safely return a spacecraft (Dragon) from orbit.
2011 The DAWN probe studied the asteroid Vesta for a year before heading towards Ceres.
2012 The US Curiosity rover began its mission of scientific exploration on Mars.

SCIENTISTS AND INVENTORS

These pages contain details of some of the people who have made important contributions to scientific discovery and invention across the centuries.

al-Haytham, Ibn (Alhazen) (965-1038) An Arab physicist who made great advances in optics, explaining that light comes into the eye, where it is refracted.

Ampère, André Marie (1775-1836) A French mathematician and physicist who did pioneering work on electricity and magnetism. The unit of electric current, called the ampere, is named after him.

Anaxagoras (c. 500-428BC) This Greek philosopher was the first to explain the phases and eclipses of the Sun and Moon as the result of their movements.

Archimedes (c.287-212BC) A Greek mathematician and inventor who formulated the scientific principle that explains how a floating object displaces its own weight in water.

Aristotle (c.384-322BC) A Greek philosopher who made many contributions to physics, zoology and scientific theory.

Avogadro, Amedeo (1776-1856) This Italian chemist first theorized that all gases of the same volume at the same temperature and pressure must contain the same number of molecules. This is called Avogadro's law.

Babbage, Charles (1792-1871) An English mathematician and inventor who worked on the Analytical Engine, a calculating machine that anticipated the modern computer.

Baird, John Logie (1888-1946) A Scottish engineer who invented the television (1926).

Becquerel, Antoine (1852-1908) A French physicist who discovered radioactivity (1896).

Bell, Alexander Graham (1847-1922) A Scottish-American inventor who invented the telephone (1872-76).

Benz, Karl (1844-1929) A German inventor who designed the first car to be driven by an internal combustion engine.

Berliner, Émile (1851-1929) This German-American engineer invented the gramophone.

Berners-Lee, Tim (1955-) This English computer scientist invented the world wide web.

Bohr, Niels (1885-1962) A Danish physicist who applied the quantum theory of physics to Rutherford's structure of the atom (1913).

Boyle, Robert (1627-1691) This Irish scientist proposed that matter is made up of tiny particles. He also formulated Boyle's law, which states that the pressure and volume of a gas are inversely proportional.

Braun, Wernher von (1912-1977) This German engineer was a pioneer of rocket-building and space flight.

Brown, Robert (1773-1858) A Scottish biologist who noted the apparently random motion of particles suspended in liquids.

Brunel, Isambard Kingdom (1806-1859) This English engineer designed many great bridges and ocean-going steamships.

Cavendish, Henry (1731-1810) This English chemist and physicist discovered hydrogen and estimated the weight of the Earth.

Celsius, Anders (1701-1744) This Swedish astronomer invented the first temperature scale to be divided into 100 degree units. It was named the Celsius scale.

Chadwick, James (1891-1974) An English physicist who worked on radioactivity and discovered the neutron.

Charles, Jacques (1746-1823) A French physicist who formulated Charles' law, which states the relationship between temperature and volume in gases.

Cockerell, Christopher (1910-1999) A British engineer who invented the hovercraft.

Copernicus, Nicolaus (1473-1543) This Polish astronomer developed the theory that the planets orbit the Sun, not the Earth (1530).

Crick, Francis (1916-2004)
This English biologist, along with his colleague, James Watson, discovered the structure of DNA. (See also *Franklin, Rosalind*)

Cugnot, Nicolas-Joseph (1725-1804) A French army engineer who in 1769 invented the steam tractor. This was the first vehicle to move on land by its own power.

Curie, Marie (1867-1934)
A pioneering Polish scientist who carried out work in radiation and discovered the radioactive material radium (1898).

Dalton, John (1766-1844)
This English chemist suggested that elements are made of atoms which combine to form compounds.

Darwin, Charles (1809-1882)
The English naturalist who first suggested that species evolve and change by natural selection.

Drew, Richard (1886-1956)
The American inventor of sticky tape (1928).

Edison, Thomas (1847-1931)
This American inventor made over a thousand devices including the phonograph, an early version of the gramophone.

Einstein, Albert (1879-1955)
A German-born physicist who published the Special Theory of Relativity (1905) and General Theory of Relativity (1915), revising previous ideas of time and space.

Fahrenheit, Gabriel (1686-1736)
A Polish-born physicist who invented the mercury thermometer (1714) and devised the Fahrenheit temperature scale.

Faraday, Michael (1791-1867)
An English scientist who invented the dynamo, generating an electric current by spinning a coil of wire in a magnetic field.

Fermi, Enrico (1901-1954)
This Italian physicist was the first to control nuclear energy in a nuclear reactor.

Fleming, Alexander (1881-1955) This Scottish doctor discovered penicillin, a substance important in making antibiotics.

Ford, Henry (1863-1947)
An American automobile engineer who built the Ford Model T and pioneered mass-production techniques in industry.

Franklin, Benjamin (1706-1790)
This American inventor and politician proved that lightning is a form of electricity.

Franklin, Rosalind (1920-1958) This English scientist took the crucial photograph for discovering the structure of DNA. (See also *Crick, Francis; Watson, James.*)

Galilei, Galileo (1564-1642)
An Italian astronomer who showed that all falling bodies descend with equal acceleration and built a telescope to support the Copernican theory that the planets move around the Sun.

Gerbert (c.945-1003) This French monk invented the first mechanical clock. He became Pope Sylvester II in 999.

Gilbert, William (1544-1603)
This English physicist, also doctor to Queen Elizabeth I of England, founded the scientific study of magnetism.

Hahn, Otto (1879-1968)
A German chemist who, together with Fritz Strassman, discovered nuclear fission. (See also *Meitner, Lise.*)

Halley, Edmund (1656-1742)
An English astronomer and mathematician who charted and predicted the orbit of a comet. Halley's Comet is named after him.

Harvey, William (1578-1657)
This English doctor discovered how blood circulates through the body.

Hawking, Stephen (1942-)
An English physicist who has advanced the understanding of the origin of the universe.

Herschel, Caroline (1750-1848)
This German astronomer, the first woman to identify a new comet, worked closely with her brother William.

Herschel, William (1738-1822)
This German astronomer and telescope-maker worked in Britain. He mapped the stars of the northern hemisphere and, in 1781, discovered the planet Uranus. He also observed infrared radiation.

Hertz, Heinrich (1857-1894)
This German physicist began the research that demonstrated the existence of radio waves.

Hodgkin, Dorothy (1910-1994)
The first British woman to win the Nobel Prize, this chemist discovered the structures of insulin, penicillin and Vitamin B12.

Hooke, Robert (1635-1703)
An English physicist and inventor who discovered the relationship between elasticity and force, as formulated by Hooke's law.

Hopper, Grace (1906-1992)
This American computer scientist developed early programming languages and introduced the term "debugging" after a moth made a computer malfunction.

Hubble, Edwin (1889-1953)
An American astronomer who proved the existence of galaxies beyond our own. The Hubble Space Telescope is named after him.

Huygens, Christiaan (1629-1695) This Dutch physicist and astronomer invented the first accurate pendulum clock, recognized Saturn's rings and was the first person to suggest that light travels in waves.

Ibn Sina, Abu (Avicenna) (c.980 -1037) This Islamic scholar had an enormous influence on Renaissance Europe, especially in medicine.

Jenner, Edward (1749-1823)
This English doctor invented the first vaccine.

Joule, James (1818-1889)
An English physicist who did important work on heat, and helped to establish the principle of the conservation of energy. The joule, a unit of measurement of work and energy, is named after him.

Kelvin, Lord See *Thomson, William.*

Kepler, Johannes (1571-1630) A German astronomer who discovered the laws of planetary motion.

Lavoisier, Antoine (1743-1794) This French lawyer and chemist named oxygen and hydrogen, and explained the role of oxygen in combustion.

Leeuwenhoek, Antony van (1632-1723) A Dutch instrument maker who was the first to examine bacteria, sperm and blood cells with a microscope.

Lemaître, Georges (1894-1966) A Belgian astrophysicist, mathematician and priest who first suggested the Big Bang theory of the origin of the universe.

Linnaeus, Carolus (Carl von Linné) (1707-1778) This Swedish botanist introduced the method of classifying living things into genus, species and other sub-divisions.

Lister, Joseph (1827-1912)
This English surgeon was the first to carry out antiseptic operations.

Lovelace, Ada (1815-1852)
An English mathematician, Lovelace worked on the Analytical Engine designed by Charles Babbage, devising "programs" which anticipated computer programming.

Maiman, Theodore (1927-2007)
An American scientist who built the first laser.

Malpighi, Marcello (1628-1694)
Using a microscope, this Italian physiologist discovered that arteries and veins are connected by tiny blood vessels now called capillaries.

Marconi, Guglielmo (1874-1937)
This Italian physicist developed radiotelegraphy and succeeded in sending signals across the Atlantic (1901).

Maxwell, James Clerk (1831-1879) A Scottish physicist who established the presence of electromagnetic radiation.

Meitner, Lise (1878-1968)
This Austrian physicist explained nuclear fission for the first time (1939). (See also *Hahn, Otto; Strassman, Fritz.*)

Mendel, Gregor (1822-1884)
An Austrian monk and naturalist who developed the laws of heredity.

Mendeleyev, Dmitri (1834-1907) This Russian chemist devised the Periodic Table of Elements.

Mercator, Gerardus (1512-1594) This Flemish geographer and map-maker invented the Mercator projection: a way of accurately showing the Earth's round shape on a flat map.

Merian, Maria Sybilla (1647-1717) This German naturalist, who travelled to South America, was famous for her studies of flowers and butterflies.

Morse, Samuel (1791-1872)
An American artist who invented a system of sending messages along electric telegraph wires by a coded system of dots and dashes (long and short electrical pulses) now called Morse code.

Newcomen, Thomas (1663-1729) An English inventor who built the first atmospheric steam engine.

Newton, Isaac (1642-1727)
This English physicist and mathematician formulated fundamental laws of gravity and motion. He also discovered that light is made up of a spectrum of colours, and built the first reflecting telescope.

Nipkow, Paul (1860-1940)
A German engineer and pioneer of television who invented the Nipkow disc, a mechanical scanning device.

Nobel, Alfred (1833-1896)
A Swedish chemist who invented dynamite (1866), and founded the Nobel Prize scheme.

Ohm, Georg (1787-1854)
A German physicist who researched electrical resistance. The SI unit of electrical resistance, called the ohm, is named after him.

Pascal, Blaise (1623-1662)
A French mathematician and physicist who made contributions to hydraulics and the study of atmospheric pressure. The SI unit of pressure, called the pascal, is named after him.

Pasteur, Louis (1822-1895)
This French chemist showed that decay is caused by bacteria. He invented a process of preserving food by killing bacteria with heat, now called pasteurization.

Planck, Max (1858-1947)
This German physicist developed the quantum theory.

Priestley, Joseph (1733-1804)
A British chemist who discovered oxygen (1774). He also invented fizzy drinks.

Pythagoras (6th century BC)
A Greek mathematician who made many discoveries, and gave his name to Pythagoras' theorem, a formula for calculating how the sides of a right-angled triangle are related to each other.

Röntgen, Wilhelm (1845-1923) This German physicist discovered X-rays (1895).

Ruska, Ernst (1906-1988)
A German engineer who invented the electron microscope (1933).

Rutherford, Ernest (1871-1937)
A New Zealand-born physicist who demonstrated the structure of the atom.

Savery, Thomas (c.1650-1715)
An English engineer who built the first steam engine.

Shen Gua (1031-1095) This Chinese astronomer made early studies of the magnetic compass and invented a water clock.

Sikorsky, Igor (1889-1972)
A Russian-born American aeronautical engineer who built the first successful helicopter (1939).

Somerville, Mary (1780-1872)
Despite not being allowed to go to university, this Scottish mathematician wrote so many books she was called "the Queen of the Sciences".

Stephenson, George (1781-1848) An English inventor who invented the first successful steam locomotive (1814) and, with his son Robert, built Stephenson's Rocket (1829) for the first passenger line.

Strassman, Fritz (1902-1980)
A German chemist who, with Otto Hahn, discovered nuclear fission (1938). (See also *Meitner, Lise*.)

Talbot, William Fox (1800-1877) This British scientist invented the method of reproducing photographs from a negative image.

Tesla, Nikola (1856-1943)
A Croatian electrical engineer who invented the AC motor and high-voltage electrical generation.

Thomson, William (Lord Kelvin) (1824-1907) A British mathematician and physicist who did important work in thermodynamics, and established the absolute temperature scale.

Torricelli, Evangelista (1608-1647) An Italian physicist who devised the principle of the barometer (1644).

Turing, Alan (1912-1954)
This English mathematician was an important pioneer of computer science.

Vesalius, Andreas (1514-1564)
This Flemish medical researcher was the first to make detailed anatomical drawings of the human body.

Villard, Paul (1860-1934)
A French physicist who discovered gamma radiation (1900).

Volta, Alessandro (1745-1827) An Italian physicist who built the first electric battery. The volt, which measures electric potential, is named after him.

Watson, James (1928-) This American scientist, together with Francis Crick, discovered the structure of DNA (1953). (See also *Franklin, Rosalind*.)

Watt, James (1736-1819)
A Scottish inventor who improved the steam engine and introduced the sun-and-planet gear. The watt, a unit of electrical power, is named after him.

Wegener, Alfred (1880-1930)
A German meteorologist who first suggested the theory of continental drift.

Whittle, Frank (1907-1996)
An English inventor who devised the jet engine (1930).

Wright, Orville (1871-1948) and **Wilbur (1867-1912)**
In 1903, these American brothers flew the first aircraft.

Yale, Linus (1821-1868)
This American inventor introduced the type of pin lock still used today.

KEY DATES IN SCIENCE

On these two pages, you can read about some of the most important dates in the history of scientific invention and discovery.

c.4000BC The alloy bronze was first made in Mesopotamia.

c.3500BC The first wheels were made out of sections of tree trunks.

c.3000BC The Babylonians divided the day into 24 hours. They also invented the abacus, the first adding machine.

c.1600BC The first records were made of the study of astronomy.

c.1500BC Iron smelting was first developed in Asia Minor (Turkey).

c.700BC The *Ayurveda*, an early medical text, was written in India.

c.600BC The Greek philosopher Thales of Miletus described the magnetic properties of lodestone, a form of iron ore.

c.530BC Pythagoras, a Greek mathematician, made various discoveries, but probably did not invent Pythagoras' theorem.

c.400BC The pulley was invented in Greece.

c.335BC The Earth-centred model of the universe described by the Greek philosopher Aristotle remained influential until the seventeenth century.

c.300BC Gears were first used in Egypt.

c.235BC Archimedes, a Greek mathematician, invented the Archimedes' screw, which could move water upwards for bailing out water from flooded ships, and in irrigation systems for farming.

c.10BC The Roman architect Vitruvius described a crane.

c.200 The earliest known use was made of cast iron – to make a Chinese cooking stove.

c.635 Quill pens were used for writing.

c.700 The Catalan forge was used in Spain for smelting iron. It was an early version of the modern blast furnace.

c.950 Gunpowder was used by the Chinese to make fireworks and signals.

1000 The optical properties of lenses were first observed by the Arab physicist Ibn al-Haytham.

1088 The first known clock, which was powered by water, was invented in China by Han Kung-Lien.

1090 Compasses were first used by the Chinese and the Arabs to navigate at sea.

1202 The Italian scholar Leonardo Fibonacci published the first European book to suggest the use of the Hindu-Arabic decimal number system.

1230 In China, gunpowder was first used as an explosive, to make bombs for attacking city walls.

1286 The first pair of glasses was made in Italy.

1326 Early guns were in use in Italy.

1451 Johann Gutenberg invented the printing press in Germany.

1500 The Italian artist Leonardo da Vinci sketched many devices, including a type of helicopter.

1540 The first artificial limbs were made for wounded soldiers by the French doctor Ambroise Paré.

1543 The Polish astronomer Copernicus published his theory that the planets revolve around the Sun, not the Earth.

1590 The microscope was invented in the Netherlands.

1592 The Italian astronomer Galileo invented the first thermometer based on the expansion and contraction of air.

1608 The telescope was first demonstrated in the Netherlands.

1610 Galileo used a telescope to make astronomical observations.

1618 A German astronomer, Johannes Kepler, published laws describing the planets' elliptical orbits around the Sun.

1623 The first mechanical calculator was invented in Germany by Wilhelm Schickard.

1628 The English doctor William Harvey published his book proving that blood circulates around the body.

1644 Evangelista Torricelli, an Italian physicist, discovered the principle of the barometer.

1682 The English astronomer Edmund Halley calculated the orbit of a comet, later named after him, that appears around every 70 years.

1687 The English physicist Isaac Newton published his book *Principia*, in which he proposed the laws of motion and gravity.

1704 Isaac Newton wrote *Opticks*, a book about prisms and light.

1712 The English inventor Thomas Newcomen built the first atmospheric steam engine.

1752 The American experimenter Benjamin Franklin showed that lightning is a form of electricity.

1769 The Scottish inventor James Watt produced the first version of his improved steam engine.

1774 A British chemist, Joseph Priestley, discovered and isolated oxygen gas.

1783 The first flight in a hot-air balloon took place in Paris, France.
1789 Antoine Lavoisier, a French lawyer and chemist, published his *Elementary Treatise on Chemistry*, which became the basis for modern chemistry.
1796 In England, Edward Jenner performed the first vaccination.
1799 Alessandro Volta, an Italian physicist, built the first battery.
1808 The English chemist John Dalton published *A New System of Chemical Philosophy*, containing his theories of atomic structure.
1809 The first electric lamp was displayed in London, England.
1820 A Danish scientist, Hans Ørsted, noticed that a wire with an electric current running through it behaved like a magnet.
1821 The English scientist Michael Faraday invented the electric motor.
1831 Michael Faraday invented the dynamo.
1833-4 British mathematicians Charles Babbage and Ada Lovelace worked on the Analytical Engine, a forerunner of the computer.
1837 The electric telegraph, used to send messages along wires, was invented in England.
1839 In England and France, the invention of photography was announced.
1852 The first airship, powered by steam and filled with hydrogen, made its maiden flight in France.
1859 The internal combustion engine was invented in France.
1859 Charles Darwin, an English naturalist, published *On the Origin of Species by Natural Selection*. It contained his theories of evolution.
1862 The first celluloid plastic was exhibited in London, England.
1869 The Russian scientist Dmitri Mendeleyev developed his first periodic table of the elements.
1876 The first telephone message was transmitted by Alexander Graham Bell in Boston, USA.
1877 The first sound recording was made in America by Thomas Edison on his prototype phonograph machine.

1877 A German-American scientist, Émile Berliner, invented the microphone.
1879 Thomas Edison invented the first successful light bulb.
1881 The first power station was built in Surrey, England.
1884 The first artificial fibres, made from cellulose, were exhibited in London, England.
1885 The petrol-driven car was invented by the German Karl Benz.
1888 Heinrich Hertz, a German physicist, demonstrated the existence of radio waves.
1895 Moving pictures were first shown in public in France.
1895 X-rays were discovered by the German physicist Wilhelm Röntgen, and the first X-ray photograph was taken.
1895 The Italian physicist Guglielmo Marconi developed and demonstrated radio transmission.
1896 Antoine Becquerel, a French physicist, discovered radioactivity.
1903 The American Wright brothers made the first powered aircraft flight.
1905 A "Miraculous Year" for German-born physicist Albert Einstein, who published three important scientific papers – on the Special Theory of Relativity, on the photo-electric effect, and on Brownian motion.
1911 Marie Curie, a Polish scientist, won the Nobel prize for her work on radioactivity.
1911 A British scientist, Ernest Rutherford, showed that atoms have a central nucleus.
1926 John Logie Baird, a Scottish engineer, transmitted the first black and white television picture across the Atlantic.
1929 Edwin Hubble, an American astronomer, showed that galaxies are moving away from each other – the universe is expanding.
1936 The first helicopter flight was made in Germany.
1938 Nuclear fission was discovered by Otto Hahn and Fritz Strassman. Lise Meitner explained the discovery in 1939.

1941 Frank Whittle invented the turbojet aircraft engine in England.
1945 The USA tested the atomic bomb in New Mexico, USA, and used it on Hiroshima and Nagasaki, Japan, after Germany was defeated in the Second World War.
1948 Three American scientists, John Bardeen, Walter Brattain and William Shockley, invented the transistor, making miniature electronics possible.
1953 Using a photograph by Rosalind Franklin, Francis Crick and James Watson discovered the structure of the DNA molecule which forms living cells.
1957 The first satellite, the Russian Sputnik I, was launched.
1959 The integrated circuit was invented in America.
1961 Vostok I, the first manned spacecraft, was launched. Yuri Gagarin became the first person to travel into space.
1969 An American astronaut, Neil Armstrong, became the first person to walk on the Moon.
1969 The Internet, in the form of ARPANET, an American military computer network, was born.
1975 The first home computer, the Altair, became available.
1981 The first reusable spacecraft, the Space Shuttle, was launched.
1990 The first transmission of high-definition television (HDTV).
1992 The World Wide Web, invented by the British computer scientist Tim Berners-Lee, went online for the first time.
2003 Scientists announced that they had made the complete sequence of the 3 billion base pairs that make up the human genome.
2007 World's scientists announced they were 90% certain that most global warming is caused by greenhouse gases.
2012 The existence of the Higgs boson was demonstrated at CERN, Switzerland. This discovery was extremely exciting because it confirms that modern particle theories are probably right.

A-Z OF SCIENTIFIC TERMS

Abdomen 1. The region of a vertebrate's body between the diaphragm and the pelvis. 2. The rear part of an arthropod's body.

abiotic Non-living.

abscess A collection of pus in a cavity due to bacterial infection.

abscission layer A layer that forms at the base of a dead leaf's stalk, cutting it off from the body of the plant before it falls off.

absolute magnitude The actual brightness of a star in space.

absolute temperature scale The SI temperature scale, measured in kelvins (K), which are the size of degrees Celsius (°C).

absolute zero The complete absence of heat energy. Measured as 0K (-273°C).

abyssal zone The level of the ocean between 4,000m and 5,000m in depth.

AC See *alternating current*.

acceleration A change in the velocity of an object, that is, in its speed or direction.

accessory foods Substances which help the body to work properly, namely, vitamins, minerals and water.

accumulator See *secondary cell*.

acetic acid See *ethanoic acid*.

achene A small, dry fruit with one seed.

achromatic colours Black, white and the shades of grey between them.

acid A compound that contains hydrogen and dissolves in water to produce hydrogen ions.

acid rain Rain that has increased in acidity after absorbing polluting gases such as sulphur dioxide and nitrogen dioxide.

actinoids (or **radioactive rare earth elements**) A sub-group of the inner transition metals with radioactive properties.

activation energy The minimum amount of energy needed to start off a chemical reaction.

active immunity Resistance to a disease coming from antibodies produced during past exposure to it.

addition reaction A chemical reaction in which the double or triple bonds of an unsaturated compound open up and new bonds are formed with different atoms.

additive mixing The process of adding different combinations of red, green and blue light to make light of almost any colour.

adhesion The attraction of the molecules of one substance to the molecules of another substance it is touching.

adolescence See *puberty*.

ADP (adenosine diphosphate) A chemical containing two phosphate groups, into which ATP breaks down, releasing energy.

adventitious root A plant root that grows directly from a bulb or gardener's stem cutting.

aerial root A type of plant root that does not usually grow in the ground, but absorbs moisture from the air.

aerobic respiration Internal respiration which uses oxygen.

aerodynamics The study of the way a gas, especially air, flows over moving objects.

aerofoil The special wing shape, curved on top, flatter underneath, that creates lift.

aeronautics The science of travel through the Earth's atmosphere.

aestivation A stage of some animals' life cycles when they enter a sleep-like state to survive drought.

aggregate (or **compound**) **fruit** Fruit, such as raspberries, which are made up of fleshy beads called drupelets, each with one seed.

agonist The contracting muscle in an antagonistic pair.

aileron A control surface on a plane's wing used to direct turning and tipping.

air bladders Bubble-like structures in seaweeds which help them to float.

air resistance See *drag*.

albumen The white of a cleidoic egg. It provides the embryo with water and proteins, and supports the yolk.

alcohols A homologous series of organic compounds with the general formula $C_nH_{2n+1}OH$. For example, ethanol is C_2H_5OH.

algae A large, varied group of simple water plants, ranging from diatoms to seaweeds.

alkali A base that is dissolved in water.

alkali metals The six very reactive metals, including potassium and sodium, that form group I of the periodic table.

alkaline earth metals The six metals, including magnesium and calcium, that form group II of the periodic table.

alkanes A homologous series of saturated hydrocarbons with the general formula C_nH_{2n+2}. For example, ethane is C_2H_6.

alkenes A homologous series of unsaturated hydrocarbons with the general formula C_nH_{2n}. For example, ethene is C_2H_4.

allele Any of the different forms in which a gene can occur. For example, an eye colour gene might have blue and green alleles.

allotrope One of the different forms in which certain elements, such as carbon, can exist.

alloy A mixture of two or more metals, or a metal and a non-metal.

alpha particle A cluster of two protons and two neutrons emitted from the nucleus of some radioactive substances.

alpha radiation A stream of alpha particles.

alternating current (AC) Electric current that changes direction many times a second.

alternation of generations A process, in many flowerless plants, where one generation reproduces sexually and the next asexually.

altitude Height above sea level.

alveoli Tiny sacs at the end of bronchioles in the lungs where gases are exchanged with the blood.

AM See *Amplitude Modulation*.

amino acids Fatty acids containing an amino group $(-NH_2)$, which make up proteins.

ammonia (NH_3) A colourless, strong-smelling gas, used widely to make nitric acid.

ampere (A) The unit of electric current.

amphibians A class of cold-blooded, soft-skinned animals, which live both on land and in water, for example, frogs.

amplify To make something greater, for example, to increase the loudness of a sound.

amplitude The maximum distance of particles in a wave measured from their rest position.

Amplitude Modulation (AM) A type of modulation where the amplitude of the signals is altered to match the carrier wave.

ampullae Swellings in the ears' semicircular ducts, containing cupulae.

ampullae of Lorenzi Small chambers in a shark's head that allow it to detect the electrical pulses given off by other creatures.

anaerobic respiration Internal respiration, in which the muscles convert glucose into energy without using oxygen.

anal fin A median fin projecting from in front of a fish's anus.

analogue The term that describes a continuous signal which varies in proportion to the quantity it represents.

analogue circuit A circuit which uses a continuous current, rather than one broken into pulses. See also *digital circuit*.

anatomy The science of body structure.

AND gate A logic gate which gives an output of 1 only when both inputs are 1.

angiosperm See *magnoliophyte*.

anhydrous The term describing a dry solid that has been separated from water.

aniline An organic compound found in coal tar, used to make dyes.

anion A negatively charged ion.

annelids A phylum of worms with round, segmented bodies.

annual ring A single ring of xylem in a cross-section of an older plant, showing one year's growth.

annuals Plants that live and die in one year.

anode In electrolysis, the electrode with the positive charge.

anodizing A method of coating a metal with a thin layer of its oxide using electrolysis.

antagonist The relaxing muscle in an antagonistic pair.

antagonistic hormones Pairs of hormones producing opposite effects, which work together to balance chemical levels.

antagonistic pair Two muscles which work together to move a body part, then return it to its original position. See *agonist*; *antagonist*.

antennae (or **feelers**) Whip-like jointed structures on the heads of creatures such as insects and crustaceans, used for smelling, tasting and feeling.

anther A pod-like structure at the end of a stamen which contains pollen sacs.

anthracite The purest form of coal, containing over 90% carbon.

antibiotics Medicines which are used to treat bacteria-caused illnesses.

antibodies Chemicals released by some white blood cells to destroy germs.

antigen The type of chemical, carried by a germ, that a specific antibody is specialized to destroy.

antiseptic A term describing any substance that destroys bacteria, or slows their growth.

anus The opening at the end of an animal's digestive tract through which waste is released.

aorta An artery which carries blood out of the heart, to be taken around the body.

aperture On a camera, the adjustable hole which, together with the shutter, controls the exposure.

apical meristems The main areas of growth on a plant, at the tips of the shoot and root.

apparent magnitude A star's brightness seen from the Earth.

appendicular skeleton The part of the skeleton made up of the bones of the arms and legs and their associated girdles (shoulders and hips).

application (app) A computer program, especially on a smartphone or tablet.

aqueous A term describing a substance that is dissolved in water.

aqueous humour A liquid, containing salts, sugars and proteins, which fills the cavity between the eye's lens and cornea.

archaea A group of simple microscopic single-celled organisms without cell nuclei, that cannot survive in the presence of oxygen.

argon (Ar) A noble gas used to fill light bulbs.

armature A square, flat rotating coil in an electric motor.

arteries Strong vessels through which blood flows away from the heart.

arthropods A phylum of creatures with segmented bodies, jointed legs and a hard exoskeleton, for example, lobsters.

asexual reproduction Producing a new organism from a single parent.

association neurons Neurons in the brain and spinal cord which interpret information from sensory neurons, then pass instructions to motor neurons.

asterism Smaller patterns of stars within a constellation.

asteroids Large lumps of rock and metal that orbit the Sun in a region called the Asteroid Belt between Mars and Jupiter.

asthenosphere A weak, partly molten layer in the Earth's upper mantle, upon which the whole lithosphere moves.

astronomy The science of heavenly bodies.

astrophysics The science of the physical and chemical aspects of heavenly bodies.

atmosphere 1. The protective layer of air around the Earth that enables plants and animals to live. 2. A layer of gases around any planet. 3. **(atm)** A unit of pressure representing standard pressure at sea level, equivalent to 101,325 pascals.

atmospheric pressure The pressure caused by the weight of the air pressing down on the Earth's surface.

atomic number The number of protons in the nucleus of an atom.

atoms The tiny particles from which elements are made. Each atom has a positively charged nucleus, balanced by enough negatively charged electrons to make the atom electrically neutral.

ATP (adenosine triphosphate) A chemical containing three phosphate groups which stores energy released by aerobic respiration.

atria The two upper chambers of the heart.

audio channel Part of a sound recording designed to be played back through a certain speaker.

audio mixing Combining tracks into the audio channels that make up a recording.

auditory nerve See *organ of Corti*.

aurora A display of lights in the sky caused by particles from the solar wind trapped in the Earth's atmosphere near the poles.

autonomic nervous system The system of nerves which controls involuntary actions.

autotrophic A term describing organisms, such as plants, that make their own food from non-living materials.

auxins Growth hormones which control the responses of plants to stimuli such as light.

Avogadro number The number of atoms or molecules found in one mole of a substance, which is 6.023×10^{23}.

axial skeleton The part of the skeleton made up of the skull, backbone and ribcage.

axil The place on a plant between a shoot or leaf stalk and the stem.

axillary bud (also **lateral** or **secondary bud**) A bud which grows at an axil.

axons Nerve fibres which carry information away from a neuron's cell body.

Background rate of extinction The normal rate at which species die out, due to natural changes in the environment.

bacteria A varied group of microscopic organisms without cell nuclei, many of which cause disease.

baleen Frayed plates of horny whalebone in whales' mouths which they use to filter feed.

ball and socket joint A joint where a round-ended bone fits into a fixed, cup-like socket.

ball-and-spoke model A way of representing molecules showing atoms as balls and the chemical bonds joining them as sticks.

bandwidth The number of bytes a microprocessor can process at once.

barbs Thin filaments branching from the central shaft of a feather.

barbules Tiny, hooked projections on the barbs of feathers, which lock together to join the barbs in a flat surface.

barred spiral galaxy A galaxy with a central bar of stars with an arm at each end.

base 1. A substance that can accept the hydrogen ions of an acid and is the chemical opposite of an acid. 2. In genetics, any of the four compounds which combine in different ways to form the rungs of the DNA double helix. Known by their initials, they are: Adenine, Thymine, Guanine and Cytosine.

base station A mast used to transmit digital radio signals between mobile phones.

battery A source of electrical potential energy made up of two or more electrochemical cells.

bauxite The ore from which aluminium is extracted.

beta particles Radiation emitted as high energy electrons when a neutron turns into a proton in the nucleus of a radioactive substance.

beta radiation A stream of beta particles.

bicuspids See *premolars*.

biennials Plants that complete their life cycles within two years.

Big Bang theory The idea that all the matter in the universe came into being with a massive explosion known as the Big Bang.

Big Bounce theory The idea that the universe expands and shrinks, in a repeating cycle of Big Bangs and Big Crunches.

Big Crunch theory The idea that gravity will slow down the expansion of the universe, pulling everything back until the galaxies crash.

Big Freeze theory The idea that the universe will keep expanding and cooling until it is just a mist of cold particles.

bilateral symmetry A term describing the structure of an animal's body, in which only one division can produce identical halves.

bile A green liquid, produced by the liver, which breaks up fat into tiny drops so that enzymes can break it down.

binary code A method used to represent information using the digits 1 and 0.

binary fission A form of asexual reproduction by splitting into identical halves.

binary star Two stars orbiting each other.

binocular vision The field of view of animals with two eyes on the front of their head.

binomial system The system of giving organisms two-part biological names.

biodegradable The term used to describe matter that can be broken down into simpler substances by bacteria.

biodiversity The variety of different species of living things in any one place.

biofuel Fuel made from fermented corn or sugar cane.

biological key A method of identifying the species of an organism by asking a series of questions about it, often shown as a tree diagram.

biological name A two-part Latin name used to classify organisms. The first part shows the genus; the second part shows the species.

biomass The combined weight of all the living things in a habitat.

biomes The largest ecosystems into which the Earth can be divided.

biped An animal that walks on two feet.

bit (binary digit) A single piece of information in binary code – a 0 or a 1.

black hole An area of such strong gravitational pull that no matter or energy can escape from it, thought to form after the largest supernovas.

bladder A balloon-like sac which stores urine until it is passed out of the body.

blast furnace A furnace used to smelt iron ore.

boiling point The temperature at which a substance turns from a liquid to a gas.

bolus A ball of swallowed food.

bond A force that holds together two or more atoms.

botany The science of plants.

Bowman's capsules See *glomerulus*.

bract A leaf at the base of a flower stalk which often serves to protect buds.

brain stem The part of the brain leading into the spinal cord. It controls automatic processes, such as breathing.

brain waves The patterns of nerve impulses that pass through the brain.

branchiae See *gills*.

brine A concentrated solution of common salt (sodium chloride) in water.

bronchi Two thick tubes into which the trachea divides, leading into the two lungs.

bronchioles Tiny tubes in the lungs, which branch off tertiary bronchi, ending in alveoli.

Brownian motion The movement of microscopic particles, such as dust, in liquids and gases, caused by constant collisions with rapidly moving molecules.

browser Computer software used to log on to the internet.

bryophytes Plants without vascular tissue, such as mosses and liverworts.

buckminsterfullerene An allotrope of carbon with spherical molecules (often called buckyballs) containing 60 atoms.

bud A small growth on a plant stem, which develops into a new shoot or flower.

budding A form of asexual reproduction, found in creatures such as hydras, which form growths called buds that fall off to become new individuals.

bulb A short, thick underground stem surrounded by scaly leaves swollen with food.

bus Electronic pathways that carry information between the CPU and the other parts of a computer.

byte A group of eight bits of information.

Caecum A chamber found in the bodies of most herbivores, containing bacteria which break down cellulose.

caldera A very large crater formed when the upper part of a volcano either blows off or collapses into the magma chamber below.

calorie A unit of heat energy, equivalent to the amount of energy needed to raise the temperature of a gram of water by 1°C. It is equal to 4.2 joules.

Calorie The common term for a kilocalorie.

cambium A layer of thin, narrow-walled cells that produces new xylem and phloem.

camouflage Patterning, or other features which help animals to conceal themselves.

canines (or cuspids) Dagger-like teeth used for piercing food.

capacitor An electronic component which stores up electrical energy until it is needed.

capillaries Tiny vessels where oxygen passes from the blood into the body, and carbon dioxide and waste are carried away.

capillary action The process by which a fluid is drawn up a narrow channel by adhering to its walls. See *adhesion*.

carapace The shield-like hardened cuticle of animals such as crabs.

carbohydrates Organic compounds containing carbon, hydrogen and oxygen.

carbon An element found in all living things.

419

carbonado (or **black diamond**) An impure form of diamond used for cutting in industry.

carbonates A group of salts containing the carbonate ion (CO_3^{2-}).

carbon cycle The process by which carbon from the atmosphere enters the food chain through photosynthesis and returns to the atmosphere through respiration and decay.

carbon dating A method of calculating the time that has passed since living matter died by measuring the radiation of carbon-14 present in the sample.

carbon dioxide (CO_2) A gas with one carbon atom and two oxygen atoms in each molecule.

carbon monoxide (**CO**) A poisonous gas with one carbon atom and one oxygen atom in each molecule.

carboxylic acids Organic acids that contain a carboxyl group (–COOH).

card In computing, a printed circuit board which slots into a computer's main circuit board, and controls the way a certain piece of hardware, such as a monitor, works.

cardiac Relating to the heart.

cardiac muscle tissue A type of striated muscle tissue, made of Y-shaped fibres which interlock to make up the heart.

carnassials Large, jagged teeth found in carnivores, used for slicing meat.

carnivore 1. An animal that eats mainly meat. 2. An order of animals, such as lions and foxes, with teeth specialized for eating flesh.

carotene A natural pigment which produces red or orange colours.

carpals The wrist bones.

carpel (or **pistil**) The female reproductive organ of a plant.

carrier waves See *modulation*.

cartilage (or **gristle**) A tough, flexible white tissue which, in most mammals, cushions joints and makes up such body parts as the ears and trachea. It forms the skeletons of young vertebrates, and of fish such as sharks.

caryopsis (or **grain**, or **kernel**) A small, dry fruit, in which the wall has fused with the seed coat.

cataclysmic variable A close-together pair of stars between which a huge and sudden increase in brightness occurs when one star pulls material away from the other.

catalyst A substance that changes the rate of a chemical reaction but is itself left unchanged.

catalytic converter A device fitted to cars to remove toxic gases from their exhaust fumes.

cathode In electrolysis, the electrode with a negative charge.

cathode ray A continuous stream of electrons that travels from a cathode through a low-pressure gas or a vacuum.

cathode ray tube A glass tube, containing a vacuum, which is used in television to turn picture signals into beams of electrons. These sweep across the screen to build up images.

cation A positively charged ion.

caudal fin A fish's tail fin.

caustic A term used to describe a strongly alkaline substance that can burn or corrode.

cell 1. In biology, the smallest unit of an organism that can carry out chemical processes vital to life. 2. An electrochemical cell.

cell body The part of a neuron that contains the nucleus.

cell membrane A thin layer surrounding a cell's cytoplasm. In animal cells, it forms the outer layer. In plant cells, it lies beneath the cell wall.

cell plate The dividing line that separates the cytoplasm during cytokinesis.

cell sap A liquid found in plant cell vacuoles.

cellulose A natural polymer, made from glucose monomers, which forms the cell walls of plants.

cell wall The tough outer layer of a plant cell.

Celsius scale A temperature scale which places 100 degrees Celsius (°C) between the ice point (at 0°C) and the steam point (at 100°C).

Cenozoic era See *eras*.

central nervous system The brain and spinal cord.

Central Processing Unit (**CPU**) The main integrated circuit, set of circuits or PCBs, controlling the operation of a computer.

centre of gravity The point where the whole weight of an object seems to act.

centrifuging Spinning a liquid around very quickly to separate out suspended solid particles.

centrioles Two X-shaped organelles that play an important role in cell division.

centripetal force A force that keeps an object moving in a circle.

cerebellum The part of the brain that coordinates muscle movement and balance.

cerebral cortex The cerebrum's outer layer.

cerebral hemispheres The two halves into which the cerebrum is divided.

cerebrospinal fluid A thin layer of liquid that cushions the brain in the skull.

cerebrum The largest part of the brain. It controls most physical, and many mental, activities. It also controls the cerebellum.

cervix A muscular passage at the bottom of the womb, which opens into the vagina.

CFCs Chlorofluorocarbons, that is, organic compounds of carbon, fluorine and chlorine, that are believed to damage the atmosphere.

chaetae Bristles found on the bodies of some invertebrates, or on the end of their parapodia, which they use to move along.

charge-coupled device (**CCD**) A light-sensitive electronic part, found for example in a camcorder, that produces electrical signals.

chemical energy Energy stored in a substance and released during a chemical reaction.

chemical formula A combination of chemical symbols showing the atoms of which a substance is made and their proportions.

chemical reaction An interaction between substances in which their atoms are rearranged to form new substances.

chemical symbol A shorthand way to represent a specific element in formulae and equations.

chemoreceptors Cells which sense the presence of certain chemicals.

chip See *silicon chip*.

chitin A sugar-based substance which forms the hard protective coverings of arthropods.

chlorides A group of salts made from hydrochloric acid.

chlorofluorocarbons See *CFCs*.

chlorophyll A green pigment found in many plant cells. It absorbs light for photosynthesis.

chloroplasts Organelles in a plant cell which contain chlorophyll.

cholesterol A fat-like substance found in animal cell membranes. Too much cholesterol in the body can cause arterial disease.

chordates A phylum of animals with bodies supported by a stiff rod called a notochord.

chromatic colours All the colours of the visible light spectrum.

chromatogram A pattern of coloured bands made on filter paper or in a tube by substances separated by chromatography.

chromatography Separating the substances in a mixture by the rate they move through or along a medium, such as filter paper.

chromoplast An organelle that contains pigment, so giving many plants, flowers, fruit and vegetables their characteristic colours.

chromosomes Bundles of DNA in a cell nucleus, which together contain all the information needed to develop an organism.

cilia 1. Tiny hairs on the bodies of some microscopic animals which they flick back and forth to propel themselves. . Tiny hairs in the bodies of larger creatures, such as those on the lining of the human nose which keep dust and mucus out of the lungs.

ciliary muscles Muscles in the eye which change the shape of the lens.

ciliate A microscopic organism with cilia.

circuit See *electric circuit* and *electronic circuit*.

circular muscles Muscles in the iris which contract in bright light, shrinking the pupil to avoid dazzling.

circulatory system The interconnected network of arteries and veins that carries blood around an animal's body.

cirri Bristly limbs used for filter feeding by creatures such as barnacles.

cirrus A high, wispy type of cloud.

class The largest subdivision of a phylum.

classification In biology, a method of sorting organisms into groups, which are themselves divided into smaller groups.

clavicle The collarbone.

cleavage furrow A constriction around the middle of a cell that pinches it until it divides.

cleavage plane The boundary between the regular lines of particles in a crystal, along which it can be split.

cleidoic egg A hard-shelled egg, laid by animals such as birds and reptiles, in which the embryo is fed by a food store called a yolk.

client/server network A type of network where one computer (the server) holds essential data which can be accessed by the other computers (the clients).

climate A typical pattern of weather conditions.

climatic region A large area of the Earth in which the climate is generally the same.

climax community A community that survives in its habitat as long as its environment remains stable.

clitellum A saddle-like body part on an earthworm.

cloaca A chamber in a bird's body where waste is stored before being excreted.

clock speed The number of instructions a microprocessor can deal with in one second, measured in Megahertz (MHz).

cloning Making an identical copy of an organism. The copy is called a clone.

clotting The process by which blood flow is stopped in an injured area as a gel-like mass, called a clot, is formed.

cloud storage A service that lets you store files on the internet so that you can access them from several devices.

cnidarians A phylum of water creatures, such as jellyfish, whose sack-like bodies have a single opening.

cnidocyst A bag of venom under pressure inside a cnidocyte.

cnidocytes (or **thread cells**) Specialized cells, on the tentacles of creatures such as sea anemones, used for seizing food.

cochlea A spiral-shaped tube in the inner part of the ear, filled with fluid which passes sound vibrations from the oval window to hair cells on the organ of Corti.

co-dominant genes A pair of genes, the instructions of which are both carried out.

coelom A type of perivisceral cavity that is contained by a peritoneum.

coherent The term that describes waves that have the same wavelength and frequency and travel in step with each other.

cohesion The attraction of molecules to each other rather than to the molecules of a substance they are touching.

coitus See *sexual intercourse.*

cold-blooded A term describing animals, such as reptiles, whose internal temperature varies with that of their surroundings.

collenchyma A type of supporting plant tissue with long, thick-walled cells, found in cortex.

colloid A mixture of extremely small particles of a substance held in another substance in which it does not dissolve.

colon The first part of the large intestine.

combining power See *valency.*

combustion The scientific term for all forms of burning.

comet A chunk of frozen gas and dirt which orbits the Sun.

commensals Organisms living together where one benefits without affecting the other.

community In ecology, the plants and animals that live together in a certain habitat.

commutator A device that causes the direction of an electric current to be reversed.

compact bone A type of bone forming the outer layer of all bones, made up of lamellae.

compact disc (CD) A shiny disc on which information can be stored digitally as a series of bumps, and "read" by a laser beam.

compensation points The two points in every 24 hours when the processes of photosynthesis and respiration in a plant are exactly balanced.

complementary colours Any two colours that together make up white light.

complementary medicine Alternative medical treatments used alongside traditional methods.

complementary metal-oxide semiconductor (CMOS) An electronic light sensor found, for example, in a mobile phone camera.

complete metamorphosis The type of metamorphosis in which the young form is very different from the adult.

composite bulb A bulb made up of sections called cloves, each one able to produce an individual plant.

composites Synthetic materials, especially plastics, made up of different substances combined to improve their properties.

compound A substance made up of two or more elements that are chemically bonded.

compound eye An eye made up of many tiny lenses, such as is found in insects.

compound fruit See *aggregate fruit.*

compound leaf A leaf made up of more than one leaflet growing from a central stalk.

compound microscope A microscope with two or more lenses.

concave lens A lens with one or both surfaces curving inwards.

concave mirror A mirror with an inward-curving surface.

conception See *fertilization.*

condensation 1. The process of a gas cooling to form a liquid. 2. The droplets of liquid that form as a gas cools.

conduction 1. The way heat energy is transferred in a solid by the vibration of the solid's heated particles. 2. The way an electric current is transferred in a substance by the movement of free electrons.

conductor A substance through which an electric current can flow, or heat can flow easily.

cones Cone-shaped cells in the retina, which are sensitive to red, green or blue light.

conifers Trees or plants with waxy needle-like or scaly leaves, which bear cones containing their seeds. Most are evergreen.

conjunctiva A clear layer which covers the cornea and lines the eyelids.

conservation The efforts made to protect animals and natural resources in order to ensure the future of all living things.

constellation One of 88 recognizable patterns of stars in the night sky.

constructive boundary A plate boundary where new crust is formed.

constructive interference An increase in amplitude that may result when two waves meet.

consumers All organisms above the trophic level of the producers (plants) in a food chain.

contact forces Forces that require two or more objects to be touching to take effect.

continent Any of the seven large landmasses into which the Earth is divided: Asia, Africa, North and South America, Antarctica, Europe and Australasia.

continental drift The slow movement of the continents, caused by the gradual shifting of the Earth's plates.

contour feathers The feathers that cover a bird's body, making a streamlined surface.

contraception Methods of preventing an ovum and sperm joining to make a baby.

contractile vacuole A tiny sac in the body of a unicellular creature, which allows it to maintain its water balance.

control surfaces Hinged flaps on a plane's wings and tail used to control the direction of its movement.

convection The way heat energy in liquids or gases is transferred. The part of a fluid nearest the heat source expands, becoming less dense, and rises; the denser, cooler part sinks.

convection current A movement of a liquid or gas caused by convection.

conventional current The current direction often seen in electronic circuit diagrams. This is because it used to be thought that electric charge moved along wires from the positive to the negative terminal. Electron flow is now known to be in the opposite direction.

convective zone The part of the Sun between the radiative zone and the photosphere.

converging lens A lens that causes parallel light rays passing through it to come together.

convex lens A lens with one or both surfaces curving outwards.

convex mirror A mirror with an outward-curving surface.

copulation See *sexual intercourse.*

core 1. The central part of an object, such as the Sun. 2. The region inside a solenoid. 3. A computer's central processing unit (CPU).

corm A short, thick plant stem base, swollen with food.

cornea A transparent covering protecting the front of the eye.

cornified layer The outer layer of the epidermis, made of dead skin cells.

corona A low-density layer of gas around the Sun, visible during a total solar eclipse.

corpus callosum A thick band of nerve fibres connecting the cerebral hemispheres.

corrosion The process by which a metal is worn away as its surface reacts with oxygen and other chemicals.

corrosive A term describing a substance, usually a strong acid, that burns away skin or the surface of an object.

cortex 1. The tissue that surrounds vascular tissue in a vascular plant. 2. The outer part of any animal organ.

Cosmic Microwave Background (CMB) An afterglow of radiation from the early universe that is found throughout the night sky.

cotyledon (or seed leaf) The first type of leaf to grow on a plant.

covalent bond A bond formed between two atoms, in which an electron from each atom is attracted to the other's nucleus, becoming shared by both.

CPU See *Central Processing Unit.*

cracking A method of changing organic compounds with large molecules into more useful compounds with smaller molecules.

cranium The skull bones.

crater 1. A bowl-shaped opening around a volcano's vent. 2. The hole formed in a planet's surface by the impact of a meteorite.

crop In birds, a thin-walled pouch which temporarily stores swallowed food.

crop rotation A farming practice in which crops which use or replace certain minerals are planted in different fields each year.

cross-breeding Breeding together animals of different species.

cross-pollination Pollination in which one plant pollinates another plant of its own kind.

crown The visible part of a tooth.

crude oil A dark, thick oil made of a mixture of natural hydrocarbons, from which many useful fuels and other chemicals are obtained by fractional distillation.

crust A layer of rock between the Earth's outer surface and its mantle.

crystal A solid substance with straight edges , a definite geometrical shape and flat surfaces.

CT (computed tomography) scanner A special X-ray camera used by doctors which makes pictures of sections of the body and feeds them into a computer for viewing.

cumulus A fluffy, white type of cloud which appears high up in warm, sunny weather.

cupula A gel-like patch in an ampulla, containing sensitive hair cells. These send information to the brain about the rotation and tilting of the head.

currents 1. Huge bands of ocean water which flow in a certain direction. 2. See *electric current.*

cusps 1. Flaps on the valves between the heart's four chambers, which are forced open and shut, ensuring one-way circulation of blood. 2. Sharp points on certain types of teeth.

cuticle The protective, waterproof outer layer of the epidermis of a plant or animal.

cycads A group of gymnosperms which produce very large cones in the middle of a circle of spiky leaves.

cytokinesis The division of the cytoplasm that occurs after meiosis or mitosis.

cytoplasm The gel-like substance inside a cell in which organelles are suspended.

Dark energy A mysterious force that seems to be accelerating the expansion of the universe.

data Information, especially that processed by a computer or used in scientific studies.

data compression Methods used to increase the speed at which data can be transmitted, by leaving out inessential information.

daughter cells Identical copies of a cell produced when it divides.

decantation A method of separating solid particles from a liquid by leaving the particles to settle and pouring off the liquid.

deceleration (or negative acceleration) A decrease in velocity.

decibel (dB) The unit of loudness.

deciduous (or milk) teeth The first set of teeth, which fall out to be replaced by permanent teeth.

deciduous trees Trees that shed their leaves in the autumn.

decomposers Tiny organisms, including bacteria and fungi, which break down dead animal and plant matter into minerals.

decomposition reaction A reaction in which a single compound breaks down into the substances that make it up.

deep time See *geological time*.

dehydrating agent A substance which removes water that is chemically combined in another substance.

dehydration The process by which water is removed from a substance, often by heating.

deionization A method of purifying water by filtering it through an ion exchange resin. The ions causing the impurity are removed by exchanging them for ions in the resin.

delta A flat area of land, usually roughly triangular in shape, built up of material deposited by a river as it flows into a sea.

deltoid The large shoulder muscle which allows movement of the upper arm.

dendrites Nerve fibres which carry information towards a neuron's cell body.

density A measure of the amount of matter in a substance compared to its volume.

dental amalgam An alloy of mercury and copper used for filling tooth cavities.

dental floss See *flossing*.

dentate A term describing an animal with teeth.

denticles See *placoid scales*.

dentine The substance that makes up the layer of a tooth below the crown.

dentition A set of teeth.

deoxyribonucleic acid See *DNA*.

deoxyribose A type of sugar that makes up part of the sides of the DNA double helix.

dermal Of or relating to the skin, or to the surface layer of a plant or animal.

dermis The thick, lower layer of skin beneath the epidermis.

desert A climatic region that is very dry, with under 250mm of rainfall per year.

destructive boundary (or **subduction zone**) Plate boundary where an oceanic plate melts partially as it moves beneath a continental plate, forming a trench.

destructive interference A decrease in amplitude that may result when two waves meet.

detergent A substance that enables water to remove dirt.

diabetes A medical condition in which the pancreas does not make enough insulin.

diagnosis The process by which a doctor tries to identify a disease by examining a patient's symptoms.

diamond An allotrope of carbon with each atom linked to four others in a tight formation, forming extremely hard, four-sided crystals.

diaphragm 1. The flat sheet of muscle under the lungs. 2. In physics, the thin disc inside a microphone or speaker that vibrates at the same frequency as the sound waves hitting it.

diatoms Types of mostly single-celled algae with hard, glassy body cases.

dichotomous key A biological key in which there are only two choices at each stage.

dicotyledon A plant, such as a pea, that has two cotyledons.

diencephalon The central part of the brain, made up of the thalamus and hypothalamus.

diesel oil A fuel obtained from the fractional distillation of crude oil.

dietary fibre (or **roughage**) A carbohydrate contained in bran, wholemeal bread, fruit and vegetables. It is indigestible by humans, but helps their digestive system to work properly.

differential A part of a car's transmission which consists of gears on the axles which allow the wheels to go at different speeds.

diffraction The bending of a wave when it meets an obstacle or passes through a gap.

diffuse reflection Reflection in which parallel incident waves bounce off an object in many directions.

diffusion The spreading out of a gas to fill the available space.

digestive glands Glands found in the digestive system, which produce digestive juices.

digestive juices Fluids produced by digestive glands which contain enzymes that break down food into simpler substances.

digestive system A system of organs that breaks down food into simpler substances.

digestive tract (or **alimentary canal**) The tube in an animal, from the mouth to the anus, through which food passes.

digit 1. In anatomy, a finger or toe. 2. In mathematics, any numeral from 0 to 9.

digital The term that describes a signal made up of separate electrical pulses, used to represent the 0s and 1s of binary code.

digital circuit An electronic circuit that uses pulses of electricity. See also *analogue circuit*.

digital electronics Electronics which uses pulses of electricity.

digital radio Radio broadcasting which sends programmes as electrical signals in binary code carried on radio waves.

digital TV Television broadcasting which sends programmes as electrical signals in binary code carried on radio waves.

digitigrade An animal, such as a dog, that walks on the underside of its toes.

diode An electronic component which allows current to flow through it in one direction only.

dioecious A term describing a plant species in which individuals have either staminate or pistillate flowers.

dipole (or **molecular magnet**) A molecule in a ferromagnetic material which behaves like a tiny magnet.

direct current (**DC**) Electric current that flows in one direction only.

dispersal In botany, the scattering of seeds away from the parent plant.

dispersion The splitting up of light into the colours of the visible light spectrum.

displacement reaction A chemical reaction in which one of the elements in a compound is replaced by a more reactive element.

distillation A method of obtaining a pure liquid from a solution by collecting the liquid as it evaporates, then allowing it to condense.

diverging lens A lens that causes parallel rays of light passing through it to spread out.

DNA (**deoxyribonucleic acid**) The acid, found in cell nuclei, that forms the genes and chromosomes of all living things.

DNA profiling (or **genetic fingerprinting**) A scientific process used to compare samples of DNA. It can be used, for example, to identify a person from a sample of their blood or hair.

domain An area in a ferromagnetic material in which the dipoles all point the same way.

domain name The part of a URL that identifies a particular website, for example, *www.usborne.com*.

dominant gene The member of a pair of genes which carries an instruction that overrules that of the other (recessive) gene.

dormancy Of some animals' life cycles, a stage when they enter a sleep-like state to survive cold or drought.

dorsal fin The fin on a fish's back.

double bond A covalent bond in which a pair of atoms shares two pairs of electrons.

double helix The shape of the DNA molecule, like a twisted rope ladder.

download To copy digital information from a main source to an external device, for example, from an internet server to a computer.

drag (or **air resistance**) The force of friction that slows down objects moving in air.

driver Software that controls the actions of a computer card (see *card*).

drug Any substance that affects the way the body works.

drupe A succulent fruit, such as a plum, with a single hard-cased seed in the middle.

drupelets The fleshy beads that make up aggregate fruit. Each contains one seed.

dry cell A type of electrochemical cell which contains an electrolyte paste, not a liquid.

dry fruit Dry cases that hold seeds until they are ripe. For example, a hazelnut.

ductile The term that describes a metal which can be stretched out to make wire.

duodenum The first part of the small intestine, where digestive juices break down fats, protein and starch.

dwarf planet A round space object not large enough to have cleared its orbit

dwarf star A star smaller than the Sun.

dyke A sheet of igneous rock that cuts across existing rocks.

dynamics The study of how forces affect movement.

dynamo See *generator*.

E **ar canal** The passage in the ear which channels sound waves towards the eardrum.

eardrum A thin layer of tissue in the ear which vibrates in response to sound waves.

earthquake A sudden movement of rock in the Earth's crust which releases pressure and shockwaves.

earth wire A safety device in an electric cable that provides a path for the current to flow to the ground.

ecdysis The process in which an arthropod sheds an outgrown cuticle and grows a new, larger one.

echinoderms A phylum of sea creatures, such as starfish, with spiny skin, suckered feet and five-part bodies.

echo A sound wave that has reflected off a surface and is heard after the original sound.

echo location Any method of locating an object by detecting the return of sound waves bouncing off that object. See also *sonar* and *ultrasound scanning*.

eclipse The total or partial disappearance of a heavenly body when another one moves between it and the viewer.

eclipsing variable A binary star which varies in brightness as one star eclipses the other.

ecological niche The role of an animal in its community, including where it lives and what it eats.

ecological succession The different habitats and communities that replace each other in an environment as it changes.

ecology The study of the relationship between living things and their environment.

ecommerce Buying or selling over the internet.

ecosystem A community of living things together with the non-living parts of its habitat, such as air and water.

EEG See *electroencephalogram*.

effort The force needed to operate a machine.

ejaculation The squirting of semen out of the penis, caused by the contraction of muscles around the urethra.

elastic The term describing something that can be stretched out of shape or size by a force, but returns to its original form when the force is removed.

elastic limit The point beyond which an elastic substance is altered permanently by stretching.

electric charge A property of matter which causes electric forces between particles.

electric circuit The path along which an electric current flows.

electric current A flow of electrically charged particles.

electric field The area in which an electric force has an effect.

electric force The effect that electrically charged particles have on each other.

electricity The effect caused by the presence or movement of electrically charged particles.

electric motor A device that changes electrical energy into movement.

electrochemical cell (or cell) A device which produces electric current from chemical energy using two electrodes in an electrolyte. Several cells joined together make a battery.

electrode In electrolysis, a conductor through which a current enters or leaves an electrolyte.

electroencephalogram (EEG) A chart used by doctors to record brain wave patterns.

electrolysis A method of splitting the elements in a compound by passing an electric current through it when it is molten or in a solution.

electrolyte A molten or dissolved substance that can conduct an electric current.

electromagnet A magnet (made of a solenoid with a ferromagnetic core) which can be switched on and off by an electric current.

electromagnetic spectrum The arrangement of electromagnetic waves in order of wavelength and frequency.

electromagnetic waves Transverse waves made up of continually changing electric and magnetic fields, for example, light.

electromagnetism The effect that takes place when an electric current flows through a wire, forming a magnetic field.

electron A negatively charged particle that exists around the nucleus of an atom.

electron cloud model A way of picturing electron shells as cloud-like regions (also called orbitals) in which an electron may be found anywhere at a given time.

electron configuration The number of electrons that exist in each of the shells around the nucleus of an atom.

electron flow The direction that electrons move along wires in an electronic circuit, from the negative to the positive terminal. It is opposite to conventional current.

electronic circuit An electric circuit that contains electronic components.

electronic components Devices that control the flow of a current in an electronic circuit.

electronics The use of electronic components to control the flow of a current around a circuit, making it do particular tasks.

electron shell A region around an atom's nucleus in which a certain number of electrons can exist.

electroplating A method of covering an object with a thin layer of metal by electrolysis.

electroreception The ability of an organism to sense electricity.

electrorefining A method of purifying metals using electrolysis.

element A substance made up of one type of atom and which cannot be broken down by a chemical reaction to form simpler substances.

elevator A control surface on a plane's tail used to direct movement up and down.

elliptical galaxy A galaxy, round or oval in shape, that contains many old, red stars.

elytra The hardened front wings of beetles and some bugs, which protect the rear wings.

email (electronic mail) A way of sending messages over the internet using a computer.

embryo 1. An organism developing inside a womb, egg or seed. 2. A human baby in the first two months of growth in the womb.

emergent plants Plants which flourish in wet or water-covered ground. Their leaves and stems are mostly visible above the water.

emulsifier A substance that helps two liquids, such as oil and water, to mix by breaking up one of the liquids into tiny drops.

emulsion A colloid of tiny particles of one liquid dispersed in another.

enamel The hard, white substance which forms the surface of a tooth's crown.

endemic A term describing a plant, animal or disease which is found only in one place.

endocrine glands Hormone-making glands.

endoplasmic reticulum A series of channels which transport substances around a cell.

endoscope A special medical camera, made of a flexible tube containing a fibre-optic cable, used to look inside patients' bodies.

endoskeleton A hard, bony skeleton that supports an animal's body from the inside.

endosperm A layer of tissue in a seed that surrounds and nourishes the growing plant.

endothermic reaction A chemical reaction that takes in heat energy.

energy chain A method, often pictorial, that shows how energy changes into different forms.

engine A machine which converts into movement the energy stored in fuel.

environment The surroundings in which an organism lives.

enzyme A catalyst that speeds up a chemical reaction in living things.

ephemeral The term used to describe organisms with very short life cycles, such as some desert flowers.

epicentre The point on the Earth's surface directly above the focus of an earthquake.

epidermis 1. The thin outer layer of tissue on a young plant. 2. An outer layer of skin.

epididymis A comma-shaped organ lying over the back of each testis, which stores sperm.

epiglottis A flap which closes the trachea during swallowing, to prevent choking.

epimysium A tough, protective layer around a muscle.

epiphyte An organism which makes its own food, but grows high up on other plants to get a better share of the light and water.

epithelium Any tissue which forms a surface covering or cavity lining.

equation In chemistry, a way of showing chemical reactions using chemical formulae. The reactants are written to the left of an arrow which points to the products on the right.

Equator An imaginary circle which runs around the middle of the Earth, dividing the northern and southern hemispheres.

equatorial A climatic region which is always hot and wet, often having rainforests.

equilibrium In physics, the state of an object when the forces acting on it are balanced.

eras The main divisions of geological time: Precambrian eras: 4,560–541 million years ago (mya); Paleozoic: 541–252 mya; Mesozoic: 252–66 mya; Cenozoic: 66 mya to the present.

erosion The gradual wearing down of rock by wind or water.

eruption An explosion of magma onto the Earth's surface through a volcano.

esters A homologous series produced by carboxylic acids reacting with alcohols. They give fruit and flowers their fragrances.

ethane (C_2H_6) An alkane containing two carbon atoms, produced from petroleum.

ethanoic (or acetic) acid (CH_3COOH) A carboxylic acid found in vinegar.

ethanol (C_2H_5OH) A major alcohol, produced by fermentation or by reacting ethene with steam. Used in alcoholic drinks and as a solvent in perfumes.

ethene (C_2H_4) The first compound in the alkene series. A colourless, sweet-smelling gas which forms polythene by addition reactions.

eubacteria A group of simple microscopic single-celled organisms without cell nuclei, many of which can survive in the presence of oxygen.

eutrophication An overgrowth of algae in a body of water due to high levels of nitrates and other compounds found in fertilizers.

evaporation 1. The process by which the surface molecules of a liquid escape into a vapour. 2. A method of separating a solute from a solvent by heating the solution until the solvent turns to vapour.

Evening Star Another name for the planet Venus, as it appears just after sunset.

evergreen A term describing trees that do not shed their leaves all at once.

evolution The process by which living things develop gradually through a long series of changes.

excretion The removal of waste substances from the body.

excretory organs Organs that deal with the removal of waste from the body.

exhalation Breathing out.

exodermis A layer of hardened cells on the root of an older plant.

exoskeleton A hard body covering which supports and protects the bodies of animals with no internal skeleton.

exosphere The outermost layer of the atmosphere, which merges into space.

exothermic reaction A chemical reaction that gives off heat energy.

expansion The continuing growth of the universe since the Big Bang, in which galaxies move ever further apart.

exposure In photography, the amount of light that is allowed in through a camera lens.

external combustion engine An engine which produces power from fuel burning outside its main body.

external fertilization Fertilization of ova by sperm that takes place outside the female's body.

extinct A term describing a species which has died out.

eyepiece The lens on an optical instrument that refracts light from the objective lens.

Facula A cloud of glowing gases that often surrounds a sunspot.

faeces The semi-solid waste left after digestion.

Fahrenheit scale A temperature scale which places 180 degrees Fahrenheit (°F) between the ice point (at 32°F) and steam point (at 212°F).

Fallopian tubes Tubes which carry the ovum into the uterus during ovulation.

false fruit Fruit, such as strawberries, which develop from the receptacle and the ovary.

family In classical taxonomy, the largest subdivision of an order.

fascicles The bundles into which muscle fibres are grouped.

fast-twitch fibres Striated muscle fibres which contract quickly, working in short bursts.

fats A group of solid esters found in living tissue and important as a reserve energy source.

fatty acids Carboxylic acids found in natural fats and oils.

faults Cracks in the Earth caused by the movement of its plates.

feedback In electronics, the process which returns part or all of an output signal to the input.

femur The thighbone.

fermentation A chemical reaction in which sugar is broken down by enzymes to produce ethanol and carbon dioxide.

ferromagnetic The term used to describe metals that can easily be magnetized.

fertilization (or **conception**) The joining of male and female sex cells to form the first cell of a new individual.

fibre-optic cable A cable made up of many glass or plastic fibres, used to transmit light.

fibrin A substance made up of sticky threads, produced by chemical reactions in platelets, which join to form a blood clot.

fibrous roots A system of many equal-sized plant roots, all of which produce smaller roots.

fibula The outer of the two lower leg bones. See also *tibia*.

field of vision The area an animal can see.

filament In botany, part of the stamen: the stalk which supports the anther.

file path The last part of a URL (for example, */index.html*) specifying the file in which a web page is stored.

filter feeding Feeding by sieving tiny plants or animals out of water.

filtrate The liquid that passes through a filter.

filtration A method of separating solid particles from a liquid by trapping them in a material that lets only the liquid pass through.

flagellae Long, fine threads on the bodies of some microscopic animals which they lash to and fro in order to propel themselves.

flagellate An organism that has flagellae.

flatworms A phylum of worms with flat, unsegmented bodies.

flight feathers (or **remiges**) Long, stiff feathers used for flying.

flip-flop A combination of logic gates often used to store binary information.

flood plain The wide, flat floor of a river valley, that is covered with water in a flood.

florigen A growth hormone in plants that signals them to flower only when the nights reach a certain length.

flossing Using special thread called dental floss to clean away plaque and debris between teeth and where the teeth and gums meet.

fluid Any liquid or gas.

fluorescence The ability of certain substances to absorb ultraviolet radiation, or other forms of energy, and give it out as light.

fluoride Any inorganic compound of fluorine.

FM See *Frequency Modulation*.

focus 1. Any point where light rays come together, or appear to come from. 2. The point where the rock first gives way in an earthquake.

foetus An embryo after the first stages of its growth in the womb. For example, an unborn human baby after two months.

fold mountains Mountain ranges formed where plates push together above ground.

follicles Deep pits in the skin from which hairs grow.

food chain A series of living things, each one of which is eaten by the next in line.

food web A network of linked food chains.

force A push or pull on an object.

force magnifier A machine which overcomes a load greater than the effort it uses.

force ratio The load a machine needs to overcome divided by the effort used.

foreskin A loose fold of skin which protects the sensitive tip of the penis.

formic acid See *methanoic acid*.

fossil fuel A fuel, such as coal, oil and natural gas, that is formed from the fossilized remains of plants or animals.

four-colour printing The use of dots of cyan, magenta, yellow and black ink to create the effect of printing in many different colours.

four-stroke combustion cycle The four-stage process by which the pistons in a vehicle's engine take in, compress, and ignite fuel, then release the exhaust.

fraction In fractional distillation, a mixture of compounds that separates out at a certain level of a fractionating column.

fractional distillation A process by which substances are separated from a mixture by boiling using a fractionating column.

fractionating column A piece of equipment used for the distillation from a mixture of substances with different boiling points.

fragmentation A form of asexual reproduction in a few animals, where new individuals can grow from parts of another.

frequency The number of waves passing a point in one second, measured in hertz (Hz).

Frequency Modulation (**FM**) A type of modulation in which the frequency of the signals is altered to match the carrier wave.

friction The force that tends to slow down moving objects that are touching.

frontalis The muscle which raises the eyebrows and wrinkles the forehead.

fruiting body The part of a fungus where spores are produced.

fulcrum (or **pivot**) The fixed point around which something is turned.

function keys Keys along the top of a computer keyboard which make the computer do certain tasks, such as opening a Help menu.

fundamental frequency The lowest frequency in a note.

fungi Many-celled organisms with distinct nuclei. The cells do not contain chlorophyll. Fungi feed by digesting organic matter outside their bodies.

fuse A safety device with a thin piece of wire in it that melts and cuts off an electric current if it becomes too large.

fuselage The body of a plane.

Galaxy A vast collection of stars, held together by gravitational attraction.

Galilean Moons Jupiter's four largest moons: Ganymede, Io, Callisto and Europa.

gall bladder A sac in the body which stores bile until it is needed.

galvanizing A method of protecting steel by coating it with zinc.

gametes Male or female sex cells.

gametophyte A term describing a plant in the sexual stage of alternation of generations.

gamma radiation (**gamma rays**) Electromagnetic waves with the shortest wavelength and highest frequency. They are given off by radioactive substances.

gas A state of matter in which a substance has no fixed shape or volume.

gaseous exchange The process by which gases pass in and out of an organism's body.

gasoline (or **petrol**) An important liquid fuel made by the fractional distillation of crude oil.

gastric juices Acidic liquids in the stomach which break down food and kill germs.

gastrocnemius The calf muscle.

gas turbine engine See *jet engine*.

gears A system of two or more cogs interlocking so that the motion of one controls the speed and turning effect of the other.

gene A segment of DNA containing a specific instruction for building part of an organism. Genes are the simplest units by which parents' physical features are inherited by their offspring.

general theory of relativity A theory, developed by Albert Einstein, which related his special theory of relativity to gravitation.

generator (or **dynamo**) A machine that converts movement energy into electricity.

generic name The first part of a biological name, showing an organism's genus.

gene therapy Treating certain genetic disorders by giving patients healthy genes.

genetic engineering (or **modification**) The extraction of genes from organisms for various uses, for example, in creating new medicines. It can also be used to change an organism by inserting the gene for a desired feature from another organism. Food produced in this way is called GM (genetically modified) food.

genetic fingerprinting See *DNA profiling*.

genetics The study of genes.

genetic screening Looking for genes in a person's DNA that could cause disease in them or their children.

genome All the DNA making up an organism.

genus The largest subdivision of a family.

geological time (or **deep time**) A scale of millions of years used by geologists to measure the Earth's development.

geology The science of the Earth's origin and structure, and its rocks and minerals.

geostationary orbit The orbit of a satellite moving at the rate the Earth spins, so that it remains fixed over the same point.

geothermal energy Heat energy from underground rocks.

germination The point in a seed's growth into a seedling when its first shoot and root break out of the seed case.

gestation period The length of time a baby animal spends in the womb before birth.

giant star A star larger than the Sun.

gills (or **branchiae**) The respiratory organs of most water creatures.

gill slits Openings in the sides of water creatures, such as fish, which allow water to pass across the gills and out of the body.

gingivae The gums.

gingivitis A gum disease, causing bleeding.

ginkgo An ancient gymnosperm species with soft, fan-shaped leaves and fleshy cones.

gizzard In birds, a thick-walled pouch which contains muscular ridges and small stones for grinding up solid food.

glacier A huge sheet of ice that moves slowly over land.

glands Organs which produce substances vital to the workings of the body.

glans The sensitive tip of the penis.

gliding (or **sliding**) joints Joints which allow flat bones to slide against each other.

Global Positioning System (**GPS**) A network of satellites orbiting the globe that enables **GPS receivers** in car satellite navigation (satnav) systems and smartphones to calculate their own exact position.

global warming A rise in average temperatures around the world which scientists believe to be caused by the greenhouse effect.

globular cluster A densely packed, spherical collection of up to a million stars, moving at the same speed and in the same direction.

glomerulus A ball of coiled-up capillaries in a nephron, where high pressure filters glucose, water and salts out of the blood into cup-like structures called Bowman's capsules.

glucagon A hormone which raises the level of glucose in the blood.

glucose ($C_6H_{12}O_6$) A type of sugar used by most living things to obtain energy.

glycerol See *propane-1,2,3-triol*.

glycogen A form of starch into which glucose is converted, and stored in the liver.

GM See *genetic engineering*.

GMO Genetically Modified Organism

gnetae A small group of gymnosperms with tough, leathery leaves, that grow in hot areas.

Golgi complex A specialized area of the endoplasmic reticulum which collects and distributes the substances made in a cell.

gracilis An inner thigh muscle which allows the leg to bend and twist.

grain See *caryopsis*.

graphite A soft, flaky allotrope of carbon in which each atom is linked to three others in a layered formation.

gravitational field An area in which gravity has an effect.

gravitropism The response of roots to gravity, by which they tend to grow downwards into the soil, towards minerals and water.

gravity The pulling force that attracts objects to each other.

Great Red Spot A vast storm that rages constantly in Jupiter's atmosphere.

greenhouse effect The trapping of heat by carbon dioxide, ozone and other gases in the Earth's atmosphere.

group In the periodic table, a column of elements that have similar electron configurations, properties and valencies.

growing season The part of a year when a particular plant grows.

guard cells Crescent-shaped cells, arranged in pairs around stomata, that control the amount of air and water entering or leaving a leaf.

gullet See *oesophagus*.

gustatory receptor cells See *taste buds*.

guttation Water loss, in liquid form, through tiny holes in leaf tips and edges.

gymnosperms Vascular plants in which the seeds are not contained in a fruit.

gyroscope A wheel that spins very fast inside a freely moving frame, creating a centripetal force which enables it to tilt steeply without falling over.

Haber process The method of producing ammonia by combining hydrogen and nitrogen.

habitat An organism's natural home.

haemocoel A type of perivisceral cavity which contains blood, and is connected to the circulatory system.

haemoglobin A purple-red chemical in red blood cells. It combines with oxygen in the lungs to form bright red oxyhaemoglobin.

hair erector muscles Tiny muscles in the skin that make hairs stand on end.

hair plexuses Groups of motion-sensitive nerve fibre endings around hair roots.

half-life The average time taken for half the radioactive atoms in a sample to decay.

halide A type of compound that contains one or more halogens.

halite (or rock salt) The mineral form of common salt (sodium chloride).

halogen Any of the poisonous and reactive non-metallic elements that make up group VII of the periodic table.

halophytes Plants that are specially adapted to live in salty areas.

halteres Two club-like organs behind a fly's forewings, used to balance the body in flight.

haptotropism (or **thigmotropism**) The response of a plant to touch.

hard disk A set of magnetic disks in a computer that continues to store information after the computer has been switched off.

hardware The pieces that make up a computer, such as the case and keyboard.

hard water Water which contains a lot of dissolved minerals from rocks it has flowed over. Temporary hard water contains minerals that can be removed by boiling. Permanent hard water contains minerals that cannot.

harmonics (or **overtones**) Sounds of higher frequency that mix with a note's fundamental frequency to give an instrument its timbre.

haustoria Thread-like structures used by some parasitic plants to attach to a host.

Haversian canal A channel in compact bone through which blood vessels pass.

heartwood The old wood at the core of a tree that has grown too solid to transport fluid.

heat capacity See *thermal capacity*.

heavenly body Any naturally-occurring object in space.

helium (**He**) A noble gas. The second lightest and least reactive element.

hemiparasite A plant which feeds off other plants, but can also photosynthesize.

herbaceous perennials Perennials which lose their visible parts in the winter, storing food in swollen roots until the spring.

herbivore An animal that feeds on plants.

heredity The transmission of genetic traits from one generation to the next.

hermaphrodite An organism that has both male and female sex cells.

hertz (**Hz**) The unit of wave frequency.

heterotrophic A term describing organisms that depend on other living things for food.

heterozygous A term describing a gene pair in which different genes for a characteristic have been inherited.

hexapod A six-legged animal.

hibernation A stage of some animals' life cycles when they enter a sleep-like state to survive the winter cold.

high-fidelity recording A sound recording that is very similar to the original.

hilum The mark on a seed which shows where the ovule was joined to the ovary.

hinge joint A joint allowing movement in two opposite directions, such as a knee joint.

homeostasis An organism's natural regulation of its internal conditions, such as temperature and chemical balance.

homologous chromosomes Pairs of chromosomes which work together to produce the features of an organism.

homologous series A group of organic compounds with the same chemical structure and properties.

homozygous A term describing a gene pair in which identical genes for a characteristic have been inherited from both parents.

hormones Chemicals which help to control the level of substances in the body.

horsetails Vascular plants which produce spores in cones, rather than seeds.

host An organism fed upon by a parasite.

hotspot 1. In geology, an area of the Earth where there is a great deal of volcanic activity. 2. In ecology, an area containing large numbers of endemic species.

HTML (**HyperText Markup Language**) A language used to create Web pages.

http (**HyperText Transfer Protocol**) The protocol used on the World Wide Web.

humerus The bone in the upper arm.

humidity The amount of water in the air.

hurricane See *tropical cyclone*.

hybrid (or **cross**) An organism produced by cross-breeding.

hydrated A term describing a substance which has undergone hydration.

hydration The process by which water combines chemically with another substance.

hydraulic Powered by liquid pressure.

hydraulics The study of liquids in motion.

hydrocarbon An organic compound that contains only hydrogen and carbon.

hydroelectric power Power generated by turbines that are driven by falling water.

hydrofoil A type of boat with stilts attached to underwater wings called foils, which reduce water resistance.

hydrogenation An addition reaction in which unsaturated molecules are saturated by adding hydrogen atoms.

hydrogen bomb A nuclear weapon that uses the power of nuclear fusion.

hydrogen oxide (H_2O) The chemical name for water.

hydrometer A device used to measure the density of a liquid.

hydrophytes Plants adapted for life in water.

hydrostatic skeleton A system supporting body structure, and sometimes movement, by muscles in the body wall working against pressurized fluid in a perivisceral cavity.

hydrotropism The response of roots to water, by which they grow towards it.

hydroxyl group (**−OH**) An oxygen atom linked to a hydrogen atom by a covalent bond.

hyperlink A piece of text or picture on a Web page that links to another page when clicked on.

hyphae White thread-like structures forming the mycelium of a fungus. They absorb food from dead matter in the soil.

hyponome A funnel-shaped tube, on the bodies of animals such as octopuses, from which they shoot jets of water to propel themselves.

hypopharynx A type of tongue in some insects, used for sucking up liquids.

hypotenuse The longest side of a right-angled triangle, that is, the side opposite the right-angle.

hypothalamus A part of the diencephalon controlling homeostasis and certain hormones.

Ice ages Periods of the Earth's history when much of its surface was covered in glaciers.

ice point The temperature at which pure ice melts (273K; 0°C; 32°F).

igneous rock A type of rock formed when molten rock cools and becomes solid.

ileum The last part of the small intestine.

ilium See *pelvis*.

image A view of an object formed by reflected or refracted rays.

imago The adult form of an insect that has undergone metamorphosis.

immiscible The term that describes two or more liquids that do not mix together easily.

incident wave A wave that is travelling towards a boundary between two media.

incisors Sharp front teeth which come together for biting or scraping.

incomplete fission A form of multiple fission, found in creatures such as corals, where the new individuals stay joined to the parent.

incomplete metamorphosis The type of metamorphosis in which the young look similar to the adults.

incus The second of three tiny earbones that pass sound vibrations to the inner ear. See also *malleus*; *stapes*.

indicator A substance that changes colour in the presence of an acid or alkali and is used to distinguish between them.

inertia The tendency of objects to resist a change in their movement.

inferior vena cava A vein which carries blood from the lower body to the heart.

inflammable Liable to catch fire.

Inflation theory The idea that the universe has not expanded smoothly since the Big Bang, but inflated very quickly at first.

infrared radiation (**infrared rays**) Electromagnetic waves that are given out by anything hot.

infrasound Sound waves with a frequency below 20 hertz.

infundibulum A funnel-shaped opening at the end of a Fallopian tube.

inhalation Breathing in.

inhibitor A catalyst that slows down the rate of a chemical reaction.

inner core The solid, innermost part of the Earth, which is about 1,250km in diameter.

inner planets Mercury, Venus, Earth and Mars.

inner transition metals A sub-group of the transition metals which share similar properties, such as high reactivity.

inorganic compound A compound that does not contain the element carbon.

input In electronics, the part of a circuit that receives an incoming signal, or the incoming signal itself.

insecticides Poisons used to kill insects that harm crops.

insolubility The quality of a substance that will not dissolve in a liquid.

instantaneous speed The speed of something at any particular moment.

insulator A substance that cannot conduct electric current, or does not conduct heat well.

insulin A hormone which lowers the level of glucose in the blood.

integrated circuit (or **silicon chip**) A complete electronic circuit etched onto a tiny piece of silicon.

integumentary system The skin, nails and hair, which, together, protect the body from damage, infection and water loss.

intensity The level of brightness of the light given off by an object. The SI unit of intensity is the candela (cd).

intensive farming Farming which uses machinery, chemical fertilizers and pesticides, in order to grow as many crops as possible.

interactive TV Digital television broadcasting which allows viewers to interact with the programmes they watch, for example, to arrange their own viewing schedule.

intercostal muscles Muscles between the ribs which contract on breathing in to expand the chest cavity, and relax again on breathing out.

interference The effect that occurs when two or more waves meet. See *constructive interference*; *destructive interference*.

internal combustion engine An engine which produces power by burning fuel in an enclosed space inside it.

internal energy The sum of the kinetic and potential energy of the particles in a substance.

internal fertilization The fertilization of ova by sperm that takes place inside the female's body.

internal respiration The process by which animals and plants use oxygen to break down their food, producing energy and releasing carbon dioxide.

internet A vast computer network linking together computers all over the world.

Internet Service Provider (ISP) A company which provides powerful computers, called routers, to give users access to the internet, along with other services, such as email.

internode The area of a plant stem or shoot between two nodes.

invertebrate An animal without a backbone.

involuntary actions Actions that are not consciously controlled by the brain, such as digestion.

involuntary muscles Muscles, such as the heart, which act automatically.

ion An atom or group of atoms that has become charged by gaining or losing one or more electrons.

ion exchange A method used to soften hard water by exchanging its dissolved calcium and magnesium ions for sodium ions.

ionic bond A strong bond caused by the attraction between ions of opposite charge.

ionic lattice The regular structure taken by an ionic compound.

iris The coloured part of the eye. It contains muscles which control the size of the pupil.

irregular galaxy A galaxy with no definite shape or arrangement.

irrigation Making dry land suitable for agriculture by watering it.

ischium See *pelvis*.

islets of Langerhans Clusters of cells in the pancreas that produce insulin and glucagon.

isotope An atom that has a different number of neutrons and so has a different mass number from the other atoms in an element.

ISP See *Internet Service Provider*.

Jacobson's organ Two pits in the roof of a snake's mouth, used for smelling and tasting.

jejunum The middle part of the small intestine, which absorbs digested food.

jet engine (or **gas turbine engine**) A powerful internal combustion engine, containing turbines, used to propel aircraft by forcing hot gases out of their exhausts at high speed.

joint A place where bones meet.

joule (J) The SI unit of energy and work.

Keel The extension of a bird's breastbone to which the wings are attached.

keeper A piece of metal placed across the end of a magnet to help it to stay magnetic.

kelvin (K) The SI unit of temperature.

keratin A waterproof protein of which animal horns, hair, nails and feathers are mostly made.

kernel See *caryopsis*.

kerosene A mixture of liquid alkanes obtained from the fractional distillation of crude oil, widely used as aviation fuel.

key fruit See *samara*.

kidneys Excretory organs which remove waste from the blood and regulate the body's fluid levels.

kilocalorie (or **Calorie**) A unit of heat energy, equal to 1,000 calories.

kilojoule (kJ) 1,000 joules.

kinetic energy (KE) The energy an object has when it is in motion.

kinetic theory The idea that all substances are made up of moving particles which have varying amounts of energy, giving rise to the different states of matter.

kingdom The largest group into which living things are classified.

krypton (Kr) A noble gas used in fluorescent tubes.

Labia Two folds of skin which surround the openings of the vagina and the urethra.

labium An insect's lower lip.

labour The series of strong contractions of muscles in the womb that push a baby out of the vagina during childbirth.

labrum An insect's hinged upper lip.

lachrymal canals Two channels that drain tears from the eye into the nose.

lachrymal glands Glands above the eyes that produce tears to keep them moist and clean, and to fight infection.

lacteal A lymphatic vessel in a *villus* that allows digested fat to drain from the intestine.

lactic acid An acid which builds up in the muscles during anaerobic respiration, making them ache.

lacunae Tiny spaces in bone which house the osteocytes.

lamellae Dense, circular layers of bone which form the structure of compact bone.

lamina See *simple leaf*.

LAN See *local-area network*.

lanthanoids (or **rare earth elements**) A sub-group of the inner transition metals that includes lanthanum.

large intestine The thick tube that receives water and waste from the small intestine.

larva A young insect before metamorphosis.

larynx (or **voice box**) The organ of speech, found at the top of the trachea.

laser (light amplification by stimulated emission of radiation) A machine that creates beams of intense, pure colour of one wavelength and frequency (a laser beam).

lateral lines Two water-filled tube-like channels in the bodies of fish, and some amphibians, which help them to detect changes of pressure in water.

lateral root (or **secondary root**) A smaller root that grows from a plant's tap root.

lateral vision The field of vision of an animal with eyes on the sides of its head.

latex A natural polymer obtained as a milky fluid from rubber trees, used to make rubber.

lava Magma that has erupted onto the Earth's surface or the ocean bed.

LCD See *liquid crystal display*.

LCD TV A TV with a liquid crystal display.

leader stroke A giant spark that flashes out from an electrically charged cloud, seeking a point with the opposite charge on the ground.

leaflets The small leaf blades that make up compound leaves.

leaf trace An area of vascular tissue which branches off that of the stem to become the leaf's central vein.

LED See *light-emitting diode*.

legume 1. A dry fruit with seeds attached to its inner wall. It is also called a pod, for example, a pea pod. 2. A pod-bearing plant.

lens A piece of transparent substance with curved surfaces, that makes light bend in a certain way.

lenticels Tiny openings in a tree's bark which allow it to exchange oxygen and carbon dioxide.

leptoid scales Small, bony plates embedded in the skin of a fish.

lichen An organism made up of an alga and a fungus living in a symbiotic relationship.

life cycle The stages of an organism's life.

lift The upward force created by an aerofoil shape such as that of an aircraft's wings moving through air.

ligament A tough band of tissue that holds together two bones at a joint.

light The electromagnetic waves that make all things visible.

light-emitting diode (LED) A diode which glows when an electric current flows through it.

lightning A brilliant flash seen when static electricity in storm clouds finds a conducting path to the ground. See *leader stroke; return stroke*.

light year The distance that light travels in one year – about 9.46 million million kilometres.

lignite (or **brown coal**) The least pure form of coal, containing 60-70% carbon.

liquid crystal display (LCD) A display made with compounds called liquid crystals used, for example, in digital watches. An electric current passing through the crystals makes them line up, blocking light and so forming patterns.

lithophytes Plants which live on the surface of rocks.

lithosphere The outer layer of the Earth, made up of the crust and upper mantle.

litmus A substance extracted from lichens that is used as an indicator.

liver A large organ that produces bile, breaks down amino acids from food into urea, filters some poisons, and stores glycogen, minerals and vitamins.

liverworts Low-growing plants without true roots, stems or leaves, that grow in damp, shady places.

live wire One of two current-carrying wires in an electric cable.

load 1. The force overcome by a simple machine. 2. The mud particles and other materials carried by a river.

local-area network (LAN) A network consisting of computers that are close together, for example all in the same room.

Local Group The group of about 30 galaxies that includes the Milky Way.

locomotion The process by which animals move around.

logic gate An arrangement of transistors used to carry out calculations in digital electronic circuits.

log on To connect to the internet, or to a network server.

longitudinal wave A wave in which the particles vibrate in the same direction as the wave is travelling.

long-term memory Memory that stores information for more than a few minutes.

loudspeaker A device that changes electric current from a source such as a microphone back into sound waves.

low surface brightness galaxy A large galaxy of loosely packed stars that does not give off much light.

lubricant A substance used to reduce friction.

luminous The term that describes any object that gives off light.

lunar eclipse The total or partial disappearance from view of the Moon due to the Earth's shadow.

lungs Sac-like respiratory organs found mostly in land-living vertebrates.

lymph A liquid made of waste soaked up from tissue fluid and white blood cells.

lymphatic system A network of tubes and organs containing lymph, which helps the body to fight disease.

lymph nodes Small organs that lie in clusters along the lymphatic system which produce white blood cells and trap germs.

lymphocyte A white blood cell that destroys germs by releasing antibodies.

lysosomes Organelles containing powerful enzymes to destroy bacteria invading a cell.

Macula A gel-like patch in a saccule, containing otoliths.

magma Molten underground rock.

magma chamber An area where magma gathers beneath a volcano.

magnet A magnetic material.

magnetic The term describing a material that shows the property of magnetism.

magnetic field The area around a magnet in which the magnetic force has an effect.

magnetic flux lines Lines which show the direction and strength of the magnetic field around a magnet.

magnetic north The point on the Earth towards which a magnet's north pole points.

magnetic south The point on the Earth towards which a magnet's south pole points.

magnetism An invisible force that attracts certain metals including iron.

magnitude (mag.) The scale on which star brightness is measured.

magnoliophytes (or angiosperms) Flowering plants. Their seeds are contained within some kind of fruit.

malleable The term used to describe metals that can be shaped by hammering.

malleus The first of three tiny bones in the ear: it picks up sound vibrations from the eardrum. See also *incus*; *stapes*.

malpighian tubules Excretory tubes in arthropods which remove liquid waste from the haemocoel.

mammals A class of hairy, warm-blooded animals that suckle their young with milk.

mammary glands Glands in a female mammal which produce milk for the young.

mandible 1. An insect mouthpart, used for gripping or biting. 2. The jawbone.

mantle The mostly solid part of the Earth that lies between its crust and its core.

marsupials A group of mammals, such as the koala, in which the females have no placenta and suckle their young in an external pouch.

mass The amount of matter in an object.

mass extinctions Five points in Earth's ancient past when huge numbers of living things died out in a very short time.

mass number The total number of protons and neutrons in the nucleus of an atom.

mass spectrometer A device used to help identify atoms by sorting them by mass.

mating Pairing up with a member of the same species to produce young.

maxillae Insect mouthparts used to push food into the mouth.

meander A wide loop in the course of a river.

mechanical wave A wave made up of vibrating particles in a solid, liquid or gas.

median fins Fins that lie in a line down the middle of a fish's back or belly.

medical imaging Methods of seeing inside patients without cutting them open, for example, by using X-rays.

meiosis The type of cell division by which a sex cell divides into two new cells, each containing half of its chromosomes.

Meissner's corpuscles Receptors in the skin that send touch sensations to the brain.

melanin The brown pigment in skin and hair. It absorbs harmful ultraviolet rays.

melanocytes Melanin-producing skin cells.

melting point The temperature at which a substance turns from a solid into a liquid.

menopause The time of life, usually between the ages of 40 and 55, when a woman's ovaries stop releasing ova and her periods stop.

menstruation (or period) The shedding of an unfertilized ovum, and the blood-rich inner layer of the womb, which occurs in girls after puberty about every 28 days.

meristem An area of cells on a plant which divide to provide new growth.

mesophyll The part of a leaf made up of the palisade and spongy layers.

mesosphere A layer in the middle atmosphere containing no clouds or ozone.

Mesozoic era See *eras*.

metabolic rate The rate at which a body converts food into energy.

metabolism The collection of processes in the body involved in producing energy, growth and waste.

metacarpals The bones of the palm of the hand.

metallic bonding The way the atoms of metal elements bond – clinging together in a regular lattice of metal cations with free electrons flowing between them.

metalloid An element which shares some of the properties of metals and non-metals.

metallurgy The study of metals and their extraction.

metals The largest class of elements. Metals are mostly shiny, solid at room temperature, have high melting points, conduct electricity, and form cations.

metameres The near-identical segments into which the bodies of some animals, such as worms, are divided.

metamorphic rock The type of rock formed when another rock is changed by intense heat or pressure.

metamorphosis A stage in some animals' life cycles when their bodies are totally changed, such as when a caterpillar turns into a butterfly.

metatarsals The bones of the sole of the foot.

meteor (or shooting star) A meteoroid that starts to burn up as it enters the atmosphere.

meteorite The remains of a meteor that has survived the atmosphere and landed on Earth.

meteoroid A small piece of space debris.

meteorology The science of weather and climate.

methane (CH_4) The first compound in the alkane series. It is the main compound in natural gas and an important fuel.

methanoic (or formic) acid (HCOOH) A carboxylic acid found in ant stings.

microclimate The climate affecting a small, local area.

micromotor A tiny electric motor.

microphone A device that changes sounds into an electric current.

microprocessor An integrated circuit, or set of circuits, acting as a computer's Central Processing Unit.

micropropagation A method of cloning a plant from cells taken from a growth area.

micropyle See *pollination*.

microwaves Radio waves with a relatively short wavelength. Used in cooking and telecommunications.

midrib The central vein of a leaf.

migration A stage in some animals' life cycles when they travel a long distance to find food or to mate.

mildews Types of simple fungi, often appearing as powdery black or white patches.

milk teeth See *deciduous teeth*.

Milky Way The galaxy in which our Solar System lies.

millibar (mb) The unit of measurement of atmospheric pressure, equal to 100 pascals.

mimicry The colouration of some animals to resemble more dangerous animals, serving to defend them against predators.

mineral acid An acid which is produced from a mineral. For example, sulphuric acid is produced from sulphur.

minerals 1. The naturally occurring compounds of which rocks are made. 2. Inorganic compounds essential to the proper working of the body.

mining The removal of minerals from the ground.

miscible The term that describes two or more liquids that mix easily.

mitochondria Rod-shaped organelles which act as a cell's powerhouses, breaking down simple substances to provide energy.

mitosis A stage of cell division in which a nucleus divides into daughter nuclei, each containing the same number of chromosomes as the original nucleus.

mixture A combination of two or more elements or compounds that are not chemically bonded together.

modem (modulator/demodulator) A device which allows a computer to send or receive information along telephone lines.

modulation A process by which sound and picture signals are mixed with radio waves (the carrier waves) so they can be broadcast.

molars Broad, blunt, square teeth set at the back of the jaw. Used for crushing and grinding, especially in herbivores.

mole The SI unit of the amount of a substance.

molecular lattice A regular structure of molecules held together by weak forces. It has a low melting and boiling point.

molecule The smallest particle of an element or compound that exists on its own and keeps its properties.

molluscs A phylum of soft-bodied creatures which mostly have shells, for example, snails.

moment The turning effect of a force, measured in newton metres (Nm).

momentum A measure of an object's tendency to carry on moving, equal to its mass multiplied by its velocity.

monoclinic sulphur An allotrope of sulphur with long, thin crystals.

monocotyledon A plant, such as a grass, that has only one cotyledon.

monocyte A type of white blood cell that destroys germs by phagocytosis.

monoecious A term describing a plant which has staminate and pistillate flowers.

monomers Small molecules that are joined together to make a polymer.

moon A natural satellite orbiting a planet or asteroid.

Morning Star Another name for the planet Venus, as it appears just before sunrise.

motherboard The main circuit board in a computer.

motor neurons Neurons which pass instructions from the central nervous system to the body, where they are carried out.

motor-skill memory Memory which recalls how to do actions such as walking.

moulds Types of simple fungi which form a furry growth on living or once-living matter.

mp3 A type of data compression software used to transmit music files over the internet.

MRI (magnetic resonance imaging) scanner A camera that uses magnetism and radio waves to make pictures of sections of the body.

mucus A slippery liquid, made by the lining of the nose and trachea. It warms and moistens air breathed in, and traps dirt and germs.

multicellular A term describing a living thing which is built up of many cells.

multiple fission A form of asexual reproduction in which a simple organism splits constantly into identical halves.

multiprocessing Fast computer processing enabled by the use of more than one CPU.

muscle fibres (or myofibres) Long, rod-shaped cells which make up muscle tissue.

mutualists Organisms that benefit each other by living together.

mutualistic relationship A relationship between two organisms which benefits both.

mycelium The main, underground part of most fungi, made up of a mass of hyphae.

mycorrhizae Fungi which feed on the roots of living plants.

myofibres See *muscle fibres*.

myofibrils Thin cords which join to make up muscle fibres.

myofilaments Thick and thin threads which interlock, making up myofibrils.

myriapod A creature with many legs.

Nanotechnology A field of technology that seeks to build devices at an atomic or molecular level.

nanotube A specially engineered microscopic fibre produced from graphite.

nasal cavity The hollow space inside the nose.

natural selection See *theory of natural selection*.

neap tides The lowest low tides, which occur at every half moon, when the Sun and Moon are at right angles to each other.

nebula A huge cloud of dust and gas where stars form.

nectar A sweet, sticky substance produced by plants to attract pollinating insects.

nectary An area of cells at the base of a petal which produces nectar.

negative film (or reversal film) Photographic film on which light parts of the picture appear dark and dark parts appear light.

nematodes A phylum of long, thin, round worms with unsegmented bodies.

neon (Ne) A noble gas used in electric lights.

nephridiopores Tiny holes at the end of protonephridia through which waste is ejected.

nephrons Tiny filtration units in a kidney.

nerve fibres Strands which make up the cell body of a neuron.

nerve impulses Pieces of information that pass through neurons electrical signals.

nerves Cords containing bundles of nerve fibres. Sensory nerves contain sensory nerve fibres, motor nerves contain motor nerve fibres, and mixed nerves contain both.

nervous system The nerves, brain and spinal cord.

network A group of computers connected together so that they can share information.

neurons Nerve cells.

neurotransmitter A chemical released when a nerve impulse reaches a synapse. If enough neurotransmitter builds up, the impulse crosses the synapse to the next neuron.

neutralization A reaction where one substance fully or partly cancels out the properties of another, for example, when an acid and a base react to produce a salt and water.

neutral wire One of two current-carrying wires in an electric cable.

neutron A subatomic particle with no electrical charge in the nucleus of an atom.

neutron star A small, spinning, exceptionally dense star that is left after a supernova.

newton (N) The SI unit of force.

newton metre (Nm) The unit of moment.

nitrates A group of salts produced from nitric acid. Nitrates occur naturally and are essential to plant growth.

nitrogen (N_2) A gas that makes up over 78% of the air. It is important to living things.

nitrogen cycle The natural process in which nitrogen is converted into nitrates in the soil, used by plants, and returned again to the air.

nitrogen-fixing bacteria Bacteria which convert ammonia in the soil into nitrates.

noble gas Any of six highly unreactive gases present in the atmosphere which together form group VIII of the periodic table. For example, argon and neon.

noble metal A metal, such as gold, that can be found naturally in a pure state.

nocturnal A term describing animals which are mostly active at night.

node The place on a plant stem where a leaf has grown.

nonchromatic colours Colours such as brown and magenta that are not in the visible light spectrum.

non-metal A class of element that forms anions. They are usually non-shiny solids or gases, with low melting and boiling points.

non-renewable fuels Fuels, such as coal and oil, which have a limited supply.

northern hemisphere The half of the Earth's globe lying north of the equator.

north or north-seeking pole The part of a magnet that points north.

note A musical sound of a specific pitch.

NOT gate A logic gate from which the output is always the reverse of the input.

notochord See *chordates*.

nova A type of cataclysmic variable star which flares suddenly for a number of days or years, then fades back to its original brightness.

NREM (non-rapid eye movement) sleep Sleep in which the eyes remain still.

nuclear fission The splitting open of an atom's nucleus to form two or more new nuclei, releasing large amounts of energy.

nuclear fusion The joining of two small nuclei to form a larger one, releasing large amounts of energy.

nuclear membrane The double-layered outer skin of a cell's nucleus.

nuclear pores Holes in the nuclear membrane which allow substances to pass between the cytoplasm and nucleus.

nuclear reactor The part of a nuclear power station, or nuclear-powered vessel, in which controlled nuclear fission reactions occur.

nuclear weapons Bombs that cause devastating explosions by releasing the energy of uncontrolled nuclear reactions.

nucleolus An organelle in a cell's nucleus which produces the ingredients of ribosomes.

nucleotide The chemical unit of which DNA is built, itself made up of deoxyribose, a base and a phosphate group.

nucleus 1. The core section of an atom that contains protons and (except hydrogen) neutrons. 2. The part in a cell that controls all of its processes. 3. The main body of a comet, made up of frozen gases, ice, rock and grit.

nutrients Substances vital to energy or growth – carbohydrates, fats and proteins.

Objective lens A lens that refracts light from an object to form a larger, upside-down image.

observatory A building which houses a large telescope for studying stars.

odorant molecules Airborne chemicals absorbed by olfactory hairs in the nose, and interpreted by the brain as smells.

oesophagus (or gullet) The tube which carries food from the throat to the stomach.

ohm (Ω) The unit of electrical resistance.

oils A group of liquid esters made mostly of unsaturated carboxylic acids. They are insoluble in water and often flammable.

olfactory cells Chemoreceptors in the nose that send information about chemicals to the brain. The brain then interprets it as smell.

olfactory hairs Tiny hairs that dangle from the roof of the nasal cavity. They are dendrites of the olfactory cells.

omnivore An animal that eats both plants and meat.

online Connected to the internet.

opaque The term that describes an object through which light cannot pass.

open cast mining Mining in which minerals are extracted from near the Earth's surface, without digging tunnels or shafts.

open cluster A collection of between a few dozen and a thousand loosely scattered stars, moving in the same direction at the same speed.

open source Open source software is given away freely for anyone to use, along with the computer code used to write it, so that anyone can help to improve it.

operating system The software that controls how a computer works.

operculum A flap which covers the gills in bony fish.

optical instrument A device that uses combinations of lenses and mirrors to produce a particular type of image.

optical microscope An instrument that uses lenses to make small objects look bigger.

optical telescope An instrument that uses lenses and mirrors to make distant objects look closer.

optic nerve The nerve which sends impulses from the eye to the brain.

optics The science of light and vision.

orbit 1. To circle around an object. 2. The path in which one heavenly body moves around another. 3. The eye socket in the skull.

orbital See *electron cloud model*.

order The largest subdivision of a class.

ore A mineral from which useful substances, such as metals, can be extracted.

organ A part of the body with a special function, made of different types of tissue joined together. For example, the brain.

organelle Any of the small parts inside a plant or animal cell. Different types of organelle have different functions.

organic acid An acidic organic compound.

organic compound A compound that contains the element carbon.

organic farming Farming which tries to work with nature, by not using artificial fertilizers, weedkillers or pesticides.

organism Any living thing.

organ of Corti A membrane that runs inside the cochlea, containing hair cells which turn sound vibrations into nerve impulses. These are sent along the auditory nerve to the brain, enabling hearing.

OR gate A logic gate which gives an output of 1 if either of its inputs are 1.

oscillate To move back and forth regularly.

osmosis The movement of molecules of a solvent through a semipermeable membrane, lowering the concentration of a solute on the other side of the membrane until the concentration on both sides is evened out.

ossification The process by which young cartilage skeletons turn into hard bone.

osteocytes Living bone cells.

osteopathy A medical treatment involving manipulation of the bones.

otoliths Tiny grains that move around in a macula, touching sensitive hairs. These send information to the brain about the position of the head.

outer core The molten outer layer of the Earth's core, which is about 2,200km thick.

outer planets Jupiter, Saturn, Uranus, Neptune and Pluto.

outgassing The process by which gases poured out of volcanoes, forming the Earth's early atmosphere.

output In electronics, the part of a circuit that gives out a signal, or the outgoing signal itself.

oval window An oval hole in the skull, covered with thin tissue, which passes sound vibrations from the stapes to the cochlea.

ovary A female reproductive organ which produces ova in animals, or ovules in a plant.

overfishing Fishing so much that the fish cannot produce enough young to replace those that have been caught.

oviparous Egg-laying.

ovulation The release of a mature ovum into a Fallopian tube.

ovules The female sex cells of a plant, which develop into seeds after fertilization.

ovum The female sex cell of an animal.

oxidation A chemical reaction in which a substance combines with oxygen, or loses hydrogen or electrons.

oxide A compound of oxygen and another element.

oxidizing agent A substance that provides oxygen or receives electrons or hydrogen in a redox reaction.

oxygen (O_2) A gas present in the Earth's atmosphere that is vital for aerobic respiration in plants and animals, and combustion.

oxyhaemoglobin A bright red chemical formed when haemoglobin in red blood cells combines with oxygen. As oxygen is released to the body, the oxyhaemoglobin turns back to haemoglobin.

ozone (O_3) A poisonous allotrope of oxygen. It forms the protective ozone layer, in the upper atmosphere, which absorbs harmful ultraviolet radiation from the Sun.

Pacinian corpuscles Pressure receptors sensitive to deep pressure in the skin.

paired fins Pairs of fins that stick out of the sides of a fish's body.

Paleozoic era See *eras*.

palisade cells Column-shaped cells, containing many chloroplasts. They form the palisade layer on a leaf's upper side, beneath the epidermis.

palmate leaf A compound leaf with five or more leaflets growing from a single point.

palps Insect mouthparts used to taste food.

pancreas An organ which produces pancreatic juice and other important substances, such as insulin.

Pangaea A single giant landmass that began to split up about 225 million years ago, leading to the formation of the continents.

papillae Tiny bumps on the tongue, many of which contain taste buds.

parallel circuit An electric circuit with more than one path through which a current can flow.

parapodia Pairs of jointless projections on the sides of animals such as bristleworms which they flex to swim around.

parasite An organism which lives and feeds upon another, usually damaging, and never benefiting it.

parenchyma A type of plant tissue with large cells and many air spaces, found in cortex.

parthenogenesis Reproduction without fertilization by a male.

particle accelerator A machine which accelerates charged subatomic particles to a great speed, in order that new particles produced by their collisions may be studied.

pascal (Pa) The SI unit of pressure, equal to a force of one newton per square metre.

passive immunity A temporary resistance to a disease, gained by receiving antibodies against it after one has been infected.

pasteurization A process of preserving food, especially milk, by killing bacteria with heat.

patagium A flap of skin between fingers or limbs of an animal that helps it to glide or fly.

patella The knee cap.

pathogen A microscopic organism, such as a virus or bacterium, that causes disease.

PCB See *printed circuit board*.

peak A point where a wave causes the greatest positive displacement of a medium, shown as a high point on a wave diagram.

pectoral fins Paired shoulder fins that project from just behind a fish's gills.

pectoralis muscles The breast muscles. Highly developed in birds for use in flight.

peer-to-peer network A type of network where no one computer is in control.

pellet A compact ball of indigestible parts, such as bones, regurgitated by birds that swallow their prey whole, for example, owls.

pelvic fins Paired fins that project from a fish's pelvic region.

pelvis (or pelvic girdle or hip girdle) The basin-like structure supporting the hip region. It is formed mainly by the two large hip bones, each of which is made up of three smaller bones: the ilium, pubis and ischium.

penicillin An important antibiotic made from a species of mould.

penis The organ with which a male passes sperm directly into a female's body. It also releases urine.

penumbra A pale shadow formed where an area is lit by only part of a light source.

perennials Plants that live for many years.

perfect sound reproduction A sound recording that always sounds the same as when it was first made.

perfoliate leaves Single or paired leaves with their bases fused to a plant's stem.

perimysium A protective layer around a fascicle in a muscle.

period 1. In chemistry, a set of elements sharing the same number of electron shells, shown as rows in the periodic table. 2. Subdivisions of geological eras, each measuring several million years. 3. See *menstruation*.

periodic table A systematic arrangement of the elements in order of increasing atomic number.

periodontal ligament A bundle of tough fibres joining a tooth's roots to the jawbone.

periosteum A thin layer of tissue covering the bones that contains cells for growth and repair.

peripheral nervous system The network of nerves which carries information to and from the central nervous system.

peripherals Pieces of computer hardware, such as a keyboard or mouse, that sit outside the case containing the computer's main circuits.

peristalsis The contractions of muscles in the walls of the digestive tract which push food through it.

peritoneum A thin membrane which lines the body wall surrounding a coelom.

perivisceral cavity A fluid-filled body cavity cushioning the internal organs in most animals.

permanent magnet A magnet made from a hard ferromagnetic material such as steel that keeps its magnetic properties well.

permanent teeth The second, adult set of teeth, which does not regrow if lost.

permeable A term describing things which have holes or pores that let in water.

persistent vision The illusion of seeing movement when watching a quickly-changing series of still images, for example a movie.

petiole A leaf stalk.

petrol See *gasoline*.

pH The strength of an acid or base expressed as a number on a scale from 0 (strongly acidic) to 14 (strongly alkaline).

phagocytosis The process by which a unicellular organism digests food by changing its body shape to engulf it. Some white blood cells also act in this way to destroy germs.

phalanges The finger and toe bones.

pharming The genetic modification of organisms to produce chemicals useful in medicine.

phases The different shapes made by the sunlit portion of the Moon's near side as it orbits the Earth. For example, a crescent.

phellogen (or cork cambium) A single layer of cells on the outside of a tree which constantly divide, building up the bark.

pheromone A chemical released by an animal which sends a message to others, for example, to attract a mate.

phloem The food-carrying tissue in vascular plants.

phosphate groups Compounds of linked phosphorus, oxygen and hydrogen atoms essential to the body's energy processes.

phosphates A group of phosphorus salts containing oxygen and other elements.

phosphor A chemical that glows when it absorbs energy.

phosphorescence A fluorescence that continues after the source of energy producing it has stopped.

phosphoric acid (H_3PO_4) An acid made from phosphorus. Used in making fizzy drinks.

photochemical reaction A chemical reaction that gives off or takes in light energy.

photoelectric cell A device that turns light energy into electricity.

photon See *quantum theory.*

photoperiodism A plant response by which it will only grow if light is available for a certain length of time (the photoperiod).

photoreceptors Light-sensitive cells.

photosphere The surface of the Sun, made up of churning gases.

photosynthesis The process by which plants use energy from sunlight to make food from water and carbon dioxide.

phototropism The response of a plant in which it turns to face the light.

phylum The largest subdivision of a kingdom.

physiology The study of the life processes of plants and animals.

phytoplankton Microscopic plants that drift on the surface of seas and oceans.

piezoelectric effect The regular vibration produced by applying a voltage between the faces of a crystal such as quartz. It is used to measure time.

pigment A substance that absorbs some colours of light and reflects others, so making an object appear coloured.

pinnae 1. In animals, the outer part of the ears. 2. In plants, leaflets arranged along a stalk in opposite pairs.

pinnate leaf A leaf in which the leaflets are arranged in opposite pairs along the stalk.

pioneer community The first community in the process of ecological succession. It is made up of grasses which become the habitat for insects and small mammals.

pipe The main channel up the middle of a volcano.

pistil See *carpel.*

pistillate flower A flower which has only female reproductive parts.

piston A cylindrical part that moves up and down inside an engine's cylinder.

pitch 1. The highness or lowness of a musical note or other sound. 2. Of a plane, to move up or down.

pit organ An organ on a snake's head which allows it to detect its prey's body heat from a distance.

pivot joint A joint in which the rounded end of one bone twists around in a hole in another.

pixel Short for "picture element". A tiny dot or square that forms part of a picture on a TV or computer screen.

placebo A treatment that contains no medicine

placenta An organ in the womb that provides an unborn mammal with food and oxygen from its mother during gestation.

placoid scales (or **denticles**) Sharp, backward-pointing scales which stick out of the skin of fish such as sharks.

plantigrade An animal, such as a bear, that walks on the underside of its whole foot.

plaque A thin, sticky white film that builds up on teeth, formed by bacteria.

plasma A pale yellow liquid which makes up over half the content of blood.

plasmolysis A shrinking of cell vacuoles away from the cytoplasm due to water loss.

plastic The term used to describe a substance which does not return to its original shape after stretching, and can hold a new shape. See also *thermoplastics; thermosetting plastics.*

plastics Easily-moulded synthetic polymers made from the organic compounds obtained from crude oil.

plate boundaries The areas where the edges of the Earth's plates meet.

platelets Cell fragments in the blood, with no nuclei, which gather together at an injured area to cause clotting.

plates Sections of the Earth's lithosphere, which move about on the asthenosphere.

plate tectonics The study of the movement of the Earth's plates, and its effects.

playback head The part of a cassette recorder that translates information stored on magnetized tape so it can be reproduced as sound.

plumule The part of a plant embryo which develops into the first shoot.

pneumatic Powered by the pressure of a gas, usually air.

polarized light Light in which the vibrations of electric and magnetic fields each only occur in one direction.

polar region A harsh climatic region with an extremely low temperature and little precipitation or plant life.

pole 1. The end of an axis, especially of the Earth. 2. An electrical terminal or electrode. 3. Either of the two points on a magnet where the force of attraction or repulsion is strongest.

pollen A plant's male reproductive cells.

pollination The process by which plants are fertilized. A pollen grain lands on the stigma and forms a pollen tube. This grows down into the ovary, entering the ovule through a tiny hole called a micropyle.

polymer A substance with long-chain molecules, each made up of many small molecules called monomers.

polymerization The process of joining monomers to make polymers.

polythene (or **polyethene**) A versatile plastic built up from ethene monomers.

polyvinyl chloride See **PVC.**

pome A false fruit, such as an apple, with a thick, fleshy outer layer and a core with seeds contained in a capsule.

poor metals A group of nine metals, including aluminium and lead. They are mostly quite soft, and are usually combined with other substances to make alloys.

population The total number of organisms of the same species living in a particular place.

pores Holes in the skin through which sweat escapes, cooling the body.

positive film (also **transparency** or **slide film**) Photographic film that shows images in the correct colours.

potential difference (or **voltage**) The work needed to push a certain amount of electric charge between two points on a conducting pathway. It is measured in volts (V).

potential energy (PE) The energy an object has because of its position in a force field such as a gravitational field.

power The rate that work is done or energy is used, measured in watts (W).

power station A site where electricity is generated on a large scale.

Precambrian eras See *eras.*

precipitate An insoluble solid that separates from a solution during a chemical reaction.

precipitation 1. Rain, sleet, snow or hail. 2. In chemistry, the formation of a precipitate.

prehensile A term describing part of an animal which is specially adapted for grasping.

premolars (or **bicuspids**) Blunt, square teeth between the canines and the molars, used for crushing and grinding.

pressure The force exerted over a given area by a solid, liquid or gas.

pressurized water reactor A nuclear reactor which uses nuclear energy to boil water. This makes steam that drives turbines.

primary cell Any electrochemical cell which has a limited life because the chemicals inside it are used up.

primary colours Colours from which all others can be made. The primary colours of light are red, green and blue. Those of pigments are magenta, yellow and cyan.

primary (or **first order**) **consumer** An organism that feeds on the producers (plants) in a food chain.

primary phloem The first food-carrying tissue formed by a new plant.

primary sexual features The male and female reproductive organs.

primary tissue The first tissue formed by a new plant.

primary xylem The first water-carrying tissue formed by a new plant.

printed circuit board (**PCB**) A plastic board imprinted with metal tracks used in electronics.

prism A transparent solid with two flat surfaces at an angle to each other.

proboscis A long feeding tube, in insects such as butterflies, formed from fused maxillae.

producers Organisms at the lowest trophic level of a food chain, that is, plants, which provide energy for all those above them.

product A new substance produced by a chemical reaction.

program A set of coded instructions telling a computer to carry out a certain task.

prominence A huge loop of flaming gas that leaps off the Sun's surface.

propane (C_3H_8) An alkane gas fuel with three carbon atoms in its molecules.

propane-1,2,3-triol (or **glycerol**) An alcohol which reacts with fatty acids to produce fats and oils.

prop root A type of aerial root which grows outwards from the stem then down into the ground, often found on plants that grow in ground that is under water.

prostate gland A gland surrounding the top of the male urethra which makes some of the fluid in semen.

protective adaptations Features, produced by natural selection, which help to protect creatures from danger.

proteins Natural polymers made up of amino acids. They are produced in cells and are essential to animal growth and tissue repair.

prothalli Flat, often heart-shaped gametophytes which grow from fern spores.

protista A group of mostly microscopic and single-celled organisms with a distinct nucleus in each cell. Some protists resemble plants and some resemble animals.

protocol In computing, the format in which messages are sent between computers.

protocol name The first part of a URL, which tells the computer which protocol to use. See, for example, *HTTP.*

proton A positively charged subatomic particle in the nucleus of an atom.

protonephridia Waste-collecting tubes found in animals such as simple worms.

protoplasm The matter of which cells are made, consisting of the cell membrane, nucleus and cytoplasm.

pseudopodia Extensions formed temporarily in the bodies of single-celled animals to enable locomotion or feeding.

puberty (or **adolescence**) The stage of development, between the ages of about 8 and 18, when a child changes into an adult.

pubis See *pelvis.*

pulley A machine that lifts heavy loads with a system of ropes passing around grooved wheels.

pulmonary arteries Arteries which carry blood from the heart to the lungs.

pulmonary veins Veins which carry blood from the lungs to the heart.

pulp cavity The soft, central area of a tooth.

pulsar A neutron star that sends out beams of radiation which swing around as it spins.

pulsating variable A variable star that changes in brilliance as it changes in size and temperature.

pupa An insect during metamorphosis, when it is protected by a hard case.

pupil An opening in the centre of the eye which allows light to enter.

PVC (polyvinyl chloride) A hard-wearing plastic built up from chloroethene monomers (ethene monomers in which a hydrogen atom has been replaced with a chlorine atom).

Quadriceps A term often used to name the muscle at the front of the thigh, which straightens the leg.

quadruped An animal that walks on four feet, for example, a hippopotamus.

quantum theory The idea that energy comes in tiny "packets" called quanta, which helps to explain the properties of electrons in atoms and the relationship of energy to matter. Quanta of electromagnetic radiation, such as light, are called photons.

quarks Particles which scientists believe to make up protons and neutrons.

quartz The most common mineral in the Earth's crust, made of silica.

quills Long, protective prickles on the bodies of animals such as porcupines.

Radar (radio detection and ranging) The use of microwaves to find the position of distant objects.

radial muscles Muscles in the iris which contract in dim light to dilate (expand) the pupil, allowing more light to enter the eye.

radial symmetry A term describing the structure of an animal that can be divided into identical halves by two or more lines of symmetry radiating from a central point.

radiation Electromagnetic energy that travels in waves, or the energy given off by radioactive substances.

radiative zone The part of the Sun that surrounds its core.

radicle The part of a plant embryo which develops into the plant's first root.

radioactive decay The process by which a nucleus ejects particles through radiation, becoming the nucleus of a series of different elements, until stability is reached.

radioactive tracing A medical technique used to follow a substance through a patient's body by adding radioactive elements to it.

radioactivity The release of radiation from the nuclei of unstable atoms.

radioisotope A radioactive isotope.

radio telescope A telescope which detects distant stars by collecting their radio signals.

radiotherapy A medical technique which uses controlled doses of radiation to kill cancer cells.

radio waves Electromagnetic waves with the longest wavelength and the lowest frequency, including microwaves and those used for standard TV and radio broadcasting.

radius In anatomy, the shorter and wider of the two bones in the forearm. See also *ulna*.

radon (Rn) A radioactive noble gas.

radula A mollusc's rough tongue, used for scraping plant matter into the mouth.

RAM (Random Access Memory) A computer's memory, made up of integrated circuits.

rays 1. Straight arrows used in a diagram to show the direction in which light waves are travelling. 2. In a fish's fin, supportive rods of bone or cartilage arranged in a fan shape.

reactants The substances present at the beginning of a chemical reaction.

reactivity The tendency of a substance to react with other substances.

reactivity series A list of metals arranged in order of how easily they react with other substances.

receptacle The extended stalk tip from which a bud grows.

receptors Sensitive cells which send information about an animal's surroundings to its brain.

recessive gene The member of a pair of genes which gives an instruction that is overruled by the other (dominant) gene.

recording head The part of a cassette recorder that records sounds onto the tape.

rectum The final part of the large intestine, where the semi-solid waste matter (faeces) collects until it is released through the anus.

rectus abdominis The stomach muscles.

recycling Making materials, such as metals, reusable by treating them in various ways.

red blood cells Disc-shaped cells in the blood, containing haemoglobin, which deliver oxygen around the body.

redox reaction A chemical reaction in which both reduction and oxidation take place.

red phosphorus A dark red, powdery allotrope of phosphorus, used to make matches.

Red Planet A nickname of the planet Mars.

reducing agent A substance that takes oxygen from another substance during a redox reaction, or loses electrons or hydrogen.

reduction A chemical reaction in which a substance loses oxygen, or gains hydrogen or electrons.

reflection The change in direction of a wave due to its bouncing off a boundary between one medium and another.

reflector telescope A telescope that uses a mirror to collect light.

reflex action A type of involuntary action, usually a sudden movement, such as moving the hand away from something hot.

reflex arc The route taken by a nerve impulse in a reflex action.

refraction The change in direction of a wave due to its moving into a medium in which its speed is different.

refractor telescope A telescope that uses a lens to collect light.

regeneration The ability to regrow parts of the body which have been broken off.

regular reflection Reflection in which parallel incident waves have parallel reflected waves.

relative atomic mass The average mass number of the atoms in a sample of an element.

relative density The density of a substance in relation to the density of water.

relative velocity The velocity a moving object appears to have when viewed from another moving object.

relativity See *general theory of relativity* and *special theory of relativity*.

REM (rapid eye movement) sleep The type of sleep where the eyes move around.

remiges See *flight feathers*.

renal arteries Arteries carrying blood into the kidneys.

renal pelvis A cavity in the kidney where urine collects before it flows into the ureter.

renal veins Veins carrying filtered blood from the kidneys back to the body.

renewable energy resources Sources of energy, such as wood, wind, water or the Sun, that regrow, or can be used to generate power without themselves being used up.

reproduction The ability of living things to produce more of their own kind.

reproductive system The parts of an organism's body involved in reproduction.

repulsion The act of pushing an object away from something without the objects touching.

residue The solid particles that remain behind after filtration or evaporation.

resistance The ability of a substance to reduce the flow of electric current.

resistor An electronic component which reduces the flow of current.

resolution The degree of detail in an image.

resonate To vibrate at the same frequency as something else.

respiration (or **external respiration**, or **breathing**) The process of taking in oxygen and giving out carbon dioxide. See also *internal respiration*.

respiratory organs Organs concerned with breathing, for example, lungs or gills.

resultant force The total effect of all the forces acting on an object.

retina The light-sensitive layer at the back of the eye which sends nerve impulses to the brain.

return stroke The powerful lightning stroke from the ground to a cloud, following a leader stroke.

reversible reaction A reaction in which the products can, under the right conditions, react to form the original reactants.

rheostat See *variable resistor*.

rhizoids Short, hair-like organs that serve as roots in simple plants, such as liverworts.

rhizomes Thick stems which grow out horizontally underground, producing new buds and roots.

rhombic sulphur The commonest allotrope of sulphur, with closely fitting molecules.

ribosomes Tiny round organelles that help to produce proteins in a cell.

ridge A new, mountainous area of the Earth's crust, formed when plates move apart beneath the ocean.

rift valley The type of valley formed when the area of rock between two faults collapses as plates move apart.

Ringed Planet A nickname of the planet Saturn.

rock salt (or halite) The mineral form of common salt (sodium chloride).

rods Rod-shaped cells in the retina, which are sensitive to light, but not to colour.

root The part of a plant that grows into the ground, where it absorbs water and minerals and anchors the plant.

root canal The channel in the root of a tooth through which blood vessels and nerves enter the pulp cavity.

root cap A layer of cells that protects a plant's root as it is pushed into the ground.

root hair One of many tiny threads on a root through which water and minerals are absorbed.

root pressure The water pressure in a plant's roots, caused by osmosis and capillary action, which pushes water into the transpiration stream.

rosette (or whorl) A leaf arrangement in which a circle of leaves grows from one point.

router See *Internet Service Provider*.

rudder A control surface at the rear of ships and planes which directs turning to the left and right.

rugae Folds in the lining of some organs, such as the stomach, which flatten as the organ fills.

ruminant A mammal, such as a cow or camel, which has even-toed hooves, four digestive chambers, and chews the cud (regurgitated semi-digested food).

runners (or **stolons**) Long side shoots used for vegetative reproduction by plants such as strawberries.

rust A layer of oxide that forms on the surface of iron, or an iron alloy, leading to corrosion.

Saccule A sac in the inner ear between the utricle and the cochlea, housing a macula.

sacrificial metal A metal used to coat a less reactive metal, protecting it by corroding first.

saline Containing salt (sodium chloride).

saliva Spittle, which is produced by salivary glands in the mouth. It makes food easier to swallow, and contains enzymes which start to break it down.

salt 1. A compound of a metal and non-metal, produced when an acid reacts with a base. 2. The common name for sodium chloride (NaCl).

samara (or **key fruit**) An achene with papery wings, such as a sycamore fruit.

sampling In digital recording, the measuring of an electric current, representing an analogue sound wave, at different points, in order to build up a digital representation of the wave.

saprophyte See *saprotroph*.

saprotroph (or **saprophyte**) An organism which does not make its own food, but lives off dead plant or animal matter.

sapwood The soft outer area of a tree in which vessels transport fluid.

sartorius The long thigh muscle which allows the leg to bend.

satellite 1. Any object orbiting a star, planet or asteroid. 2. A man-made device orbiting the Earth used to gather scientific data or receive and transmit radio signals.

saturated compound An organic compound with atoms joined by single covalent bonds.

saturated solution A solution in which no more solute will dissolve.

scalar quantity A quantity that has magnitude but no direction.

scapula The shoulder blade.

sclera The tough, white coating of the eye.

sclerites The sections of an arthropod's cuticle, which are connected by flexible membranes.

scrotum The sac of skin hanging outside the body which protects the testes.

scuta Hard protective plates covering the bodies of some animals, such as armadillos.

search engine A computer program which searches for Web pages containing a particular word or group of words.

sebaceous glands Glands in the skin producing an oil (called sebum) that keeps it waterproof and supple.

secondary bronchi Smaller branches into which the bronchi divide inside the lungs.

secondary cell (or **accumulator**) An electrochemical cell or battery that can be recharged.

secondary colour A colour made by mixing two primary colours.

secondary sexual features Features different in males and females, but not essential to reproduction, such as facial hair.

secondary thickening The process by which long-living plants, such as trees, grow new tissue to support their original tissue.

sedimentary rock The type of rock formed when mineral particles are deposited, buried and squashed into layers.

seed leaf See *cotyledon*.

seismic waves Underground shockwaves that travel outwards from the focus of an earthquake.

seismologist A scientist who studies earthquakes.

selective breeding The controlled breeding of organisms to produce individuals with desired features, such as hardiness.

self-pollination A type of pollination in which a plant pollinates itself.

semen The mixture of sperm and fluids from the seminal vesicles and prostate gland which leaves the penis during ejaculation.

semicircular canals Three loops in the inner ear, positioned on the three different planes of movement. They contain semicircular ducts, and are involved in maintaining balance.

semicircular ducts Channels inside the semicircular canals, containing ampullae.

semiconductor A type of material that acts as a conductor or as an insulator depending on its temperature.

semi-metal An element which shares some of the properties of metals and non-metals.

seminal vesicles Two organs beneath the bladder that produce some of the fluid in semen.

semipermeable A term describing things which have holes or pores that allow some substances through, but not others.

senescence The process of ageing.

sensation A creature's awareness of its surroundings or internal state, as interpreted by the brain. For example, vision or pain.

senses The abilities of an organism which allow it to take in, and respond to, information from its surroundings. For example, sight.

sensory neurons Neurons ending in sensitive receptors. They carry information about stimuli from receptors to the central nervous system.

sepals Leaf-like structures that protect buds.

septum A wall of muscle tissue separating one metamere from the next.

series circuit An electric circuit in which the current passes through the components one after another.

serrate A term describing a leaf edge with tiny jagged teeth.

server See *client/server network*.

setae Bristles found on the bodies of many invertebrates, used to sense air movement.

sewage Water containing bodily waste.

sewage works A site where sewage is filtered to remove rubbish and treated with certain bacteria to break it down into harmless substances.

sex chromosomes The chromosomes, called X and Y chromosomes, which determine a child's gender. A girl has two X chromosomes; a boy has an X and a Y.

sex-linked genes Recessive genes found only on the X chromosome.

sexual intercourse (or **sex**, **coitus** or **copulation**) The joining of sexual organs, in which the stiffened penis fits into the vagina, squirting semen inside.

sexual reproduction Reproduction which involves joining male and female sex cells.

shell A region around an atom's nucleus in which a certain number of electrons can exist.

shoot A new stem which grows out of a seed or off the main stem of a plant.

shooting star See *meteor*.

short-term memory Memory that stores information for only a few minutes.

shutter A flap on a camera that controls the length of time light falls on the film.

sieve plates Tiny perforated cells that form the ends of the walls between sieve tubes.

sieve tube Fluid-carrying cells in phloem.

sign stimulus A visual display that triggers a set response from another creature, for example, when a robin displays its red breast to show aggression.

silica Silicon dioxide (SiO_2).

silicates A group of minerals containing elements combined with silica.

silicon chip (or **chip**) A small piece of silicon with an integrated circuit etched onto it.

simple leaf A leaf made up of a single blade, called a lamina, for example, a maple leaf.

single bond A covalent bond in which a pair of atoms shares one pair of electrons.

single cell See *electrochemical cell*.

siphon A tube that carries gases to or from the gills in many simple water creatures. An inhalant siphon carries gases to the gills; an exhalant siphon carries them away.

SI units An internationally agreed system of standard units used for scientific measurement.

skeletal muscles Voluntary muscles mostly connected to the skeleton by tendons.

skeleton The part of an animal, especially the framework of bones, or hard body covering, that supports an animal's body and protects its internal organs. See also *endoskeleton; exoskeleton; hydrostatic skeleton*.

slag Impurities present in iron ore, left over as waste after smelting.

slow-twitch fibres Striated muscle fibres which contract slowly, and can work for a long time without tiring.

small intestine The main section of the digestive system: a three-part coiled tube, made up of the duodenum, jejunum and ileum.

smartphone A mobile phone that also acts as a small computer, accessing the internet.

smart TV A TV that can be used to access parts of the internet, such as video websites.

smelting The process of extracting a metal from its ore by heating to high temperatures, and reducing the ore.

smog A layer of pollution made up of smoke, fog and sulphur dioxide.

smooth muscle tissue A type of muscle tissue, made up of spindle-shaped fibres, which forms the visceral muscles.

sodium chloride (NaCl) The chemical name for common salt.

software The programs used by a computer, such as its operating system or the games one might play on it.

soil erosion The wearing away of topsoil by wind or rain.

solar cell In physics, a cell that converts the Sun's energy into electricity.

solar collector An array of black panels which absorbs the Sun's heat and uses it to warm water in a central heating system.

solar energy The Sun's heat and light energy.

solar flare A brief but violent explosion from the Sun's surface.

solar radiation Electromagnetic radiation emitted by the Sun, made up of ultraviolet rays, visible light and infrared rays.

Solar System The Sun together with all of the planets and other objects orbiting it.

solar wind A constant stream of invisible particles blown out into space from the Sun.

solenoid (or **coil**) A coil of wire that behaves like a magnet when an electric current passes through it.

soleus The flat leg muscle beneath the gastrocnemius.

soluble The term describing a substance that can dissolve in a liquid.

solute A substance dissolved in a liquid.

solution A mixture that consists of a substance dissolved in a liquid.

solvent 1. A liquid that can dissolve other substances. 2. The liquid in which a substance is dissolved.

sonar Echo location when used by ships or submarines.

sori Tiny sacs on the underside of fern fronds, where fern spores develop.

soundbox A box that resonates and so amplifies the original sound.

sound synthesizer An instrument that stores sound waves as binary code and can reproduce the original sound by converting the code into an electric current and sending it to a speaker.

sound wave (or **acoustic wave**) A longitudinal, mechanical wave that carries sound energy through a medium.

southern hemisphere The half of the Earth's globe lying south of the equator.

south or (**south-seeking pole**) The part of a magnet that points south.

space-filling model A way of representing molecules in which chemically bonded atoms are shown as balls clinging together.

space probe Unmanned spacecraft sent to explore the Solar System and beyond.

Space Shuttle A reusable manned spacecraft that is launched like a rocket, but lands on re-entry like a plane.

space station A large satellite orbiting the Earth where astronauts can live and perform scientific research over fairly long periods.

spawn The many tiny, soft eggs laid by most fish and amphibians.

specialization The developed suitability of cells and organisms for a particular function, environment or way of life.

special theory of relativity A theory, developed by Albert Einstein, which deals with the relationship of the speed of light to the measurement of time and space, and the relationship of matter to energy.

species The largest subdivision of a genus.

specific epithet The second part of a biological name, which shows an organism's species.

specific heat (thermal) capacity The amount of heat needed to raise the temperature of 1kg of a substance by 1K.

spectral type The class of a star.

speed The measure of how fast an object is moving, calculated as the distance it travels in a certain amount of time.

speed of light The speed at which light travels in a vacuum – about 300,000 kilometres per second.

speed of sound The speed at which sound travels – usually quoted as 331 metres per second in dry air at 0°C.

sperm The male sex cells in animals.

sperm ducts Two tubes which carry sperm from the epididymis into the urethra.

spinal cord A thick bundle of nerves that runs from the brain down channels in the backbone. It carries impulses to and from almost all parts of the body.

spiracles Small holes in insects' bodies through which they breathe.

spiral galaxy A galaxy with a bright middle and two or more curved arms of stars.

spongy bone A strong, light type of bone made of a mesh of trabeculae and air gaps.

spongy cells Irregularly shaped cells which are spaced with air gaps to make up the spongy layer beneath a leaf's palisade layer.

spores Reproductive cells produced by a sporophyte, which grow into new gametophytes.

sporophyte A term describing a plant in the asexual stage of alternation of generations.

sporulation The asexual stage of alternation of generations, in which spores are released.

spreading ridge A ridge under the ocean that spreads out sideways as magma wells up along its centre.

spring balance A device which uses a spring to measure a force (in newtons).

spring tides The highest high tides, at the full and new moon.

spring (or **early**) **wood** The soft wood with large cells that grows rapidly in the spring.

stainless steel An alloy of steel and chromium that is both strong and resistant to corrosion.

stamens A plant's male reproductive organs.

staminate flower A flower which has only male reproductive parts.

stance A term describing how an animal stands or moves.

stapes The third of the three tiny earbones, it passes on sound vibrations from the incus to the oval window. See also *malleus*.

star A ball of tremendously hot gas which produces heat and light from nuclear reactions in its core.

starch A natural polymer, made up of glucose monomers, which plants use to store energy.

states of matter The different forms in which a substance can exist. The three basic states are solid, liquid and gas.

static electricity Electrical charge held by a material.

statocyst An organ of balance, found in creatures such as jellyfish, made up of a sac filled with receptors and tiny grains called statoliths.

steam engine The earliest kind of engine, based on external combustion, which boils water, producing steam that drives pistons.

steam point The temperature of steam above water boiling at atmospheric pressure (373K; 100°C; 212°F).

stem The main above-ground part of a plant. It contains vascular tissue and supports the plant.

stereo A stereo recording is one that is made up of two *audio channels*.

stereoscopic vision The type of vision in which each eye gives a slightly different view, allowing the brain to form a 3D image.

sternum The breastbone.

stigma The sticky top part of a carpel, which traps pollen grains that touch it.

stimulus Anything that produces a response in an organism, for example, light.

stipules A pair of small, stalkless leaves at the base of a leaf stalk, which protect buds as they form.

stolons See *runners*.

stomata Tiny holes on a leaf's underside which let air and water move in and out.

strata Layers of sedimentary rock.

stratosphere A layer in the middle atmosphere containing the ozone layer.

stratus A type of cloud that forms low in the sky in flat, grey layers.

streamlining A way of designing vehicles so that air flows over them in smooth lines, reducing drag.

stretch receptors Sensitive cells in muscles and tendons which inform the brain about the position of the body.

striated (or **striped**) **muscle tissue** The tissue that makes up skeletal muscles.

stridulation The rubbing together of body parts to produce a shrill noise, as is done by crickets to attract a mate.

strong acid An acid in which most of the molecules separate to form hydrogen ions when in solution. For example, hydrochloric acid.

style Part of the carpel which joins the stigma to the ovary.

subatomic particles Particles smaller than an atom, especially those of which atoms are made: protons, electrons and neutrons.

subcutaneous layer A layer of fat cells beneath the dermis which helps to keep the body warm.

subduction zone See *destructive boundary*.

sublimation A change from solid to gas without going through liquid form.

submergent plants Plants, such as water lilies, in which most of the body grows underwater.

sub-pixel One of the three parts that make up a pixel, coloured red, green or blue.

subsonic speed Any speed below the speed of sound.

sub-species A smaller division of a species.

substitution reaction A chemical reaction in which the bonds of some of the molecules in a saturated compound break open, and their atoms are replaced by atoms of another element.

subtractive mixing The process by which pigments are mixed, resulting from some parts of the visible light spectrum being absorbed by pigment while other parts are reflected.

succulent fruit Fruit with thick, fleshy layers that are often tasty to eat.

sucrose ($C_{12}H_{22}O_{11}$) The type of sugar found in sweets, a carbohydrate.

sugars A group of sweet-tasting carbohydrates which dissolve in water.

sulphates A group of salts produced from sulphuric acid.

sulphides A group of minerals made up of elements combined with sulphur.

sulphur dioxide (SO_2) A poisonous, polluting gas made of sulphur and oxygen. It mixes with rainwater to cause acid rain.

sulphuric acid (H_2SO_4) An acid produced from sulphur, important in making fertilizers.

summer (or **late**) **wood** The hard wood with densely packed cells which grows in summer.

sunless zone Level of the ocean, between 1,000m and 4,000m in depth, where no sunlight reaches.

sunlit zone The top 200m of the ocean, home to many animals and all sea plants.

sunspot A small, dark patch on the Sun which is slightly cooler than its surroundings.

superalloy An extremely strong, durable alloy that usually contains nickel, iron or cobalt.

supergiant star The largest size of star.

superior vena cava A vein which carries blood from the upper body to the heart.

supernova A colossal explosion that occurs when a giant star dies.

supersonic speed Any speed greater than the speed of sound.

supervolcano A huge, powerful volcano, the eruption of which would cause massive environmental damage.

surface tension A force that pulls together molecules on the surface of a liquid.

suspension 1. In chemistry, a mixture of solid particles floating in a liquid or gas. 2. In a car, a system of springs that absorbs the effects of an uneven road surface.

swim bladder An inflatable sac in the body of a bony fish. The fish varies the amount of air in the swim bladder to make its body rise or sink.

synapse The junction of two neurons.

synovial fluid A lubricating fluid produced in most freely-movable joints.

synovial joints Freely-movable joints containing synovial fluid.

synthesis (or **combination**) **reaction** A reaction in which substances combine to make a single new substance.

synthetic The term describing compounds that are made artificially by chemical reactions in a factory.

synthetic fibres Fibres, such as nylon, that are produced artificially by drawing out plastics into fine strands.

syrinx The part of a bird's windpipe with which it sings.

system In biology, a group of organs that work together for a certain purpose, for example, the digestive system.

Tablet A handheld computer, often having a touchscreen.

tactile receptors Cells on animals' bodies which allow them to detect touch

tagmata Segments that make up the regions of an animal's body (such as the thorax) and are not divided by internal walls.

tapetum A reflective layer at the back of the eyes of nocturnal animals, and some fish, which collects light to help them to see.

tap root (or **primary root**) A large plant root with smaller ones growing from it.

tarsals The ankle bones.

taste buds Tiny structures in the papillae, containing gustatory receptor cells. These send signals about chemicals in food to the brain, which interprets them as tastes.

taxonomic ranks (or **taxa**) Subdivisions of a kingdom, ranging from phyla to species.

telecommunications (or **telecoms**) A branch of technology concerned with the transfer of information using telephone cables or satellites.

temperate region A climatic region with rainfall throughout the year and temperatures that vary with the seasons.

temporary magnet A magnet made from a soft ferromagnetic material, such as iron, that quickly loses its magnetism.

tendons Tough bands of tissue which attach muscles to bones.

tendril A special, thread-like leaf or stem which twines around, or sticks to, a support.

tentacles Long, flexible limbs found on many molluscs and some sea creatures. They are often used for grasping and feeling.

terminal A point on a source of potential difference, for example a battery, where wires are connected to make an electric circuit.

terminal bud A bud which grows at the end of a plant stem or shoot.

terminal velocity The maximum velocity reached by a falling object, at which point acceleration ceases, and velocity is constant.

ternate leaf A trifoliate leaf where each leaflet is made up of three lobes.

terrestrial animals Animals that live mostly on land.

tertiary bronchi Smaller branches into which the secondary bronchi divide.

testa A seed's tough, protective coat.

testes Two glands which produce sperm in a male animal.

thalamus Part of the diencephalon that sorts impulses entering the brain, then sends them to other areas for processing.

theory of natural selection The idea that evolution occurs because individuals with qualities which aid survival tend to have more offspring and pass these useful qualities on to these offspring.

thermal capacity The amount of heat needed to raise the temperature of an object by one kelvin.

thermal decomposition reaction See *decomposition reaction*.

thermistor A resistor that gives different amounts of resistance, depending on the temperature.

thermodynamics The branch of physics which studies energy changes involving heat.

thermoplastics Plastics which can be melted and used again.

thermoregulation The process by which an animal keeps its body at the right temperature.

thermosetting plastics Plastics which can be moulded only once.

thermosphere An extremely hot layer of the upper atmosphere.

thermostat A device that switches an electric circuit on and off in response to a change in temperature.

thigmotropism See *haptotropism*.

thorax The upper region of an animal's body, between the head and the abdomen.

thread cells See *cnidoblasts*.

thrust The force that moves a plane or rocket forwards.

thunder The deep rumbling sound caused by air expanding rapidly as it is heated by flashes of lightning.

tibia The shinbone. See also *fibula*.

tibialis anterior A muscle that extends down the shin, used in walking.

timbre The individual sound quality of a musical instrument.

tissue Part of an organism that is made up of many cells of the same type.

top-level domain The last part of a domain name, showing the kind of organization which hosts a Web site, or the country it is based in. For example, *.com* refers to a commercial company.

total solar eclipse The masking of the Sun from view when the Moon passes in front of it.

touchscreen A touch-sensitive LCD screen often found on tablets and smartphones.

trabeculae A criss-cross network of branch-like structures that make up spongy bone.

trachea (or **windpipe**) A tube through which air enters and exits the lungs.

tracheae Pipes in an insect's body, leading from the spiracles to the tracheoles.

tracheids Tubes that are part of the xylem of non-flowering vascular plants.

tracheoles Tiny tubes which carry gases to and from the cells in an insect's body.

track One of any number of sound samples that are combined to make an audio channel.

traits Characteristics, such as eye colour, inherited genetically from a parent.

transgenic A term describing an organism which has been genetically modified.

transistor An electronic switch that uses a small current to control a larger one.

transition metals The largest group of metals, mostly hard and tough in nature.

translocation The movement of fluids inside a plant.

translucent The term describing substances that allow a little light to pass through them.

transmission In a car, a system of gears that transmits the engine's power to the wheels.

transparent The term used to describe substances through which light can pass.

transpiration The loss of water in vapour form through leaf stomata.

transpiration stream The upward movement of water in a plant, from the roots to the leaves.

transverse waves Waves in which the vibrations are at right angles to the direction of travel.

trapezius One of a pair of flat, triangular muscles, which cover the shoulders and back. It straightens the shoulder.

trench A long, deep, steep-sided pit in the ocean floor, formed at a destructive boundary.

tributary A river or stream that flows into a larger one.

trifoliate leaf A compound leaf with three leaflets growing from a single point.

triple bond A covalent bond in which a pair of atoms shares three pairs of electrons.

trophic level The position of an organism within a food chain.

tropical cyclone (or **hurricane** or **typhoon**) A fierce storm caused by warm ocean currents.

tropical region A climatic region that is warm all year with two seasons: dry and wet.

tropism The response of a plant to a stimulus. In positive tropism, a plant grows towards a stimulus; in negative tropism it grows away from it.

troposphere The lowest layer of the atmosphere, containing 80% of its gases and all of its weather.

trough The point where a wave causes the greatest negative displacement of a medium, shown as a low point on a wave diagram.

true fruit A fruit, such as the cherry, which develops from an ovary.

tuber A swollen underground stem that stores food for a plant through the winter, such as that of the potato.

tundra 1. A biome with harsh winds and low winter temperatures. Its underground soil is always frozen, so it has no trees. 2. A climatic region with these features.

turbine A machine with a shaft and blades, which are turned, for example, by the force of wind or steam. The movement energy is converted into electricity.

turbofan engine A type of jet engine with an extra-large fan. They are slower than turbojets, but quieter and more efficient.

turbojet engine The fastest type of jet engine, used in high-speed jet planes.

turboprop engine A jet engine that powers an aircraft by driving propellers.

turboshaft engine A jet engine that powers the rotor blades in a helicopter.

turgor The state of a plant when its cell vacuoles are full of sap, making it stand firmly upright.

twilight zone The level of the ocean, between 200m and 1,000m in depth, where very little sunlight reaches.

tympanal organ A simple hearing organ found in animals such as frogs, consisting of a tympanum on the body surface which passes vibrations into an air sac containing receptors.

tympanum A thin layer of tissue found in most land animals, which enables hearing by vibrating in response to sound waves.

typhoon See *tropical cyclone*.

Ulna The longer and thinner of the two bones in the forearm. See also *radius*.

ultrasound Sound waves with a frequency above 20,000 hertz.

ultrasound scanning The use of high-frequency sound waves to form a picture of the inside of the body.

ultraviolet radiation (**ultraviolet rays**) Electromagnetic waves that lie just beyond the violet end of the visible light spectrum.

umbilical cord A tube, containing arteries and a vein, which connects a baby to the placenta. It is cut at birth.

umbra A dark shadow formed where no light reaches an area.

unguligrade An animal that walks upon hooves at its toe-tips, such as a horse.

unicellular A term describing a living thing whose body is made of only one cell.

universal indicator An indicator made of a mixture of dyes that change colour according to the pH scale.

universe (or **cosmos**) The collection of all matter, energy and space that exists.

unsaturated compound An organic compound with at least one double or triple covalent bond.

upthrust The force pushing up on an object when it is placed in a fluid such as water or air.

urban migration The movement of people from country to city areas in search of work.

urea A waste substance produced in the liver from the breakdown of amino acids.

ureter A tube through which urine passes from the kidney to the bladder.

urethra A tube in the body through which urine is released from the bladder.

uric acid A weak organic acid excreted as solid waste by some animals, such as reptiles.

urinary system The system which controls the level of water in the body. It is made up of the kidneys, ureters, bladder and urethra.

urine A waste substance produced by the kidneys, made of urea, water and toxic salts.

URL (Uniform Resource Locator) The unique address of any individual internet document, such as, *http://www.usborne.com/index.html*

uterus (or **womb**) A sac inside the body of a female mammal in which the baby grows.

utricle A sac between the semicircular canals and the saccule, housing a macula.

Vaccine A dose of a germ too weak to cause disease in a person, but strong enough that they produce antibodies which will resist it in the future. The use of vaccines is called vaccination.

vacuole A fluid-filled sac inside a plant or animal cell. Most plant cells have a large, permanent vacuole; animal cells tend to have smaller, temporary vacuoles.

vacuum An empty space where there are no particles of air or other matter.

vagina The muscular passage which leads from a female's cervix out of her body. It receives the penis during sexual intercourse.

valency (or **combining power**) The number of electrons an atom must gain or lose to acquire a stable outer shell.

valley glacier A glacier that fills a valley.

vane The flat surface of a feather, formed from interlocking barbs and barbules.

variable resistor (or **rheostat**) An electronic component that can be adjusted to give different amounts of resistance.

variable star A star that changes gradually in brilliance.

variegated leaf A leaf patterned with two or more colours.

vascular A term describing something made up of, or containing, conducting vessels. In plants, it means having xylem and phloem; in animals, it means having a blood supply.

vascular bundle One of the groups of xylem and phloem cells found in young stems.

vascular cylinder The ring of vascular tissue found in the stems of older dicotyledons, formed when the vascular bundles join up.

vastus lateralis A muscle above the knee which allows the lower leg to be lifted.

vector quantity A quantity that has magnitude and direction.

vegetative reproduction (or **vegetative propagation**) A type of asexual reproduction in which parts of plants grow into new plants.

veins Vessels carrying blood to the heart.

velocity The speed an object travels in a particular direction.

vent The point where the magma comes out of a volcano's pipe.

ventilation Breathing.

ventral fin A long anal fin that extends under a fish's belly.

ventricles The heart's two lower chambers.

Veroboard A board with rows of holes, and copper tracks on the back, used to make simple electronic circuits.

vertebrae 33 interlocking bones, which make up the vertebral column.

vertebral column (or **spine**) The backbone, made up of vertebrae.

vertebrate An animal with a backbone.

vessels Column-shaped cells with no dividing walls found in the xylem of flowering plants.

vestibular system A collection of organs in the inner part of the ear which help the body to keep its balance. See *semicircular canals*; *utricle*; *saccule*.

vibrissae Whiskers.

viewfinder The part of a camera that allows the photographer to see what will appear on the picture.

villi Tiny, finger-like projections on the lining of the small intestine which absorb digested food.

virtual image An image, made for example by reflection in a surface, from which rays of light only appear to come.

viruses Strands of DNA (or a related acid called RNA) in a protective coat. They cannot live on their own, but invade living cells in order to reproduce, often causing diseases, such as colds.

visceral muscles Muscles in the walls of internal organs such as the intestines.

visible light spectrum The narrow section of the electromagnetic spectrum that humans can see. It is made up of red, orange, yellow, green, blue, indigo and violet light.

vitreous humour A stiff, jelly-like substance that fills the central body of the eye behind the lens, keeping its shape.

viviparous A term describing animals which give birth to live young.

vocal cords Two muscles in the voice box which are pulled together during speech, vibrating to produce sound.

voice box See *larynx*.

volcanic bomb A lump of lava blasted into the air during a volcanic eruption.

volcano An opening in the Earth's surface formed by magma bursting out, usually taking the shape of a conical mound.

Volkmann's canals Tiny channels in bone which carry blood vessels and nerves to the osteocytes.

volt (V) The unit of potential difference.

voltage See *potential difference*.

volume The amount of space a substance occupies.

voluntary actions Actions, such as lifting a cup, which are consciously controlled by the brain.

voluntary muscles Muscles, such as the arm muscles, which can be consciously controlled.

VTOL Of a plane, Vertical Take Off and Landing. Such planes take off directly upwards and so do not need runways.

vulcanization A process used to strengthen rubber by heating it with sulphur.

Wafer A thin slice of a silicon cylinder which is cut up to make silicon chips.

WAN See *Wide-Area Network*.

warm-blooded A term describing animals who can keep their internal temperature constant under most conditions.

washing soda Hydrated sodium carbonate ($Na_2CO_3.10H_2O$). Used in bath crystals and as a water softener.

water cycle The natural process by which water is recycled between the Earth, the atmosphere and living things.

water of crystallization Water that has chemically bonded with another substance.

waterworks Site where water is filtered and chemically treated to remove mineral impurities and bacteria.

watt (W) The SI unit of power.

wavelength The distance between a point on one wave and the same point on the next cycle of the wave.

waxes A group of solid esters, many of which are produced by living things. They are usually glossy, easily moulded and insoluble in water.

weak acid An acid that contains relatively few hydrogen ions when in solution, for example, ethanoic acid (found in vinegar).

weight A measure of the strength of the pull of gravity on an object.

white blood cells Blood cells which help the body to fight against disease.

white light See *light*.

white phosphorus The most reactive allotrope of phosphorus, a poisonous white solid that ignites in air.

wide-area network (WAN) A network of computers that are far apart.

WiFi network a wireless local area network.

windpipe See *trachea*.

wisdom teeth The last set of molars to grow, set at the back of the jaw.

womb See *uterus*.

woody perennials Perennials, such as trees, that may lose some parts in the winter, but have protected stems which grow thicker each year.

work In physics, the distance an object moves multiplied by the force needed to move it.

World Wide Web (www) A vast information resource, and place to conduct e-commerce, consisting of thousands of Web sites linked together on the internet.

www See *World Wide Web*.

Xanthophylls Pigments which produce yellow colours in plants.

X chromosome The type of sex chromosome contained in all ova, and half of all sperm.

xenon (Xe) A noble gas used in high-speed flash photography.

xerophytes Plants such as cacti, which are specially adapted to live in very dry areas.

X-rays Short-wavelength, high-frequency electromagnetic waves that can pass through most soft substances but not hard, dense ones.

xylem Water-carrying tissue in vascular plants.

Yawing The turning movement of a plane, to the left or right.

Y chromosome The type of sex chromosome contained in half of all sperm.

yeast A single-celled fungus used in brewing and bread-making.

yolk sac A sac in a cleidoic egg that contains food, called yolk, rich in phosphorus and fat, which nourishes the embryo.

Zone of elongation The area of new cells produced by dividing cells just behind a plant's root tip.

zoology The scientific study of animals.

zooplankton Microscopic animals that drift on the surface of seas and oceans.

zygote The first cell of a new organism, formed when a male cell fertilizes a female cell.

INDEX

Where there is more than one page reference for a term in the index, you will find the main explanation on the page(s) shown in bold type. It may be useful to look at the other pages for further information.

Hubble, Edwin **414**
Hubble Space Telescope (HST) 161, 170, 171, **175**, 177, 411
humerus **346**, 425
humic acid **86**
humidity 192, **425**
hurricane **189**, 425
Huygens, Christiaan **414**
Huygens (lander) 411
hybrid **384**, 425
hydra 324
hydrated **91**, 425
hydration 89, **91**, 425
hydraulic machine **133**, 425
hydrocarbons 79, **92**, 96, 97, 98, 425
hydrochloric acid 48, **84**, 88, 89
hydroelectric power **108**, 425
  stations 198
hydrofoil **140**, 425
hydrogen 14, 15, 24, 25, 28, 32, **46-47**, 52, 64, 68, 69, 72, 73, 75, 80, 81, 83, 84, 85, 86, 88, 92, 93, 94, 96, 97, 98, 100, 154, 162, 178, 184
  bomb **116**, 425
  oxide 66, **72**, 425
hydrogenation **97**, 425
hydrometer **17**, 425
hydrophytes **280**, 425
hydrostatic skeleton **301**, 425
hydrotropism **268**, 425
hydroxide ions **85**
hydroxyl group **94**, 425
hylonomus 187
hyperlink (internet) **246**, 425
hyphae **284**, 425
hypogeal germination **277**
hyponome **304**, 425
hypopharynx **311**, 425
hypotenuse 409, **425**
hypothalamus **366**, 425

Ibn Sina, Abu **414**
ice 18, 19, **72**, 110, 173, 178, 179, 184, 229
  ages **179**, 187, 425
  point 111, **425**
igneous rock **181**, 425
Ikeya Seki (comet) 173
ileum **355**, 425
ilium **346**, 425
image 218, 220-221, 425
imago **328**, 425
immiscible (liquids) 59, **425**
immunity **387**
imperial system **404**
incident
  ray **218**
  wave 204, **425**
incisors **312**, 352, 425
inclined plane **135**, 136
incomplete
  fission **324**, 425
  metamorphosis **328**, 425
incus **372**, 425
indicator 86, 87, **425**
indium **29**, 33
inertia **122**, 425
inferior vena cava **350**, 425
inflammable **425**
Inflation theory **155**, 425
infrared
  radiation **113**, 185, **213**, 215, 425
  rays (See *infrared radiation*)
infrasound **206**, 425

infundibulum **376**, 425
inhalant siphon **314**
inhalants **391**
inhalation **359**, 425
inhibitor (catalyst) **79**, 425
inner
  core of Earth **180**, 426
  ear **372**
  planets **164-166**, 426
  transition metals **29**, 426
inorganic **357**, 426
input **238**, 425
insecticides 54, **335**, 426
insects 186, 187, **300**, 307, **309**, 315, 319, 321, 325, 328, 330, 338
insolubility 58, **88**, 426
Instantaneous speed **126**, 426
insulated wire **228**, 230
insulator,
  electrical 25, **228**, 239, 426
  heat 25, 103, **113**, 426
insulin **363**, 426
integrated circuit 25, 236, 237, **239**, 405, 426
integumentary system **368**, 426
intensity, light **214**, 426
intensive farming **291**, 426
interactive TV **227**, 426
intercostal muscles **359**, 426
interdependence **333**
interference 218, 219, 426
internal
  combustion engine **146-147**, 150, 426
  energy **110**, 426
  fertilization **326**, 426
  gills **314**
  respiration 52, **80**, 81, **265**, 358, **360**, 426
International Space Station (ISS) 176, **177**, 185, 411
internet 6-7, **246-247**, 426
Internet Service Provider (ISP) 7, **246**, 426
internode **252**, 426
invertebrates 187, **322**, 426
intestines **355**
involuntary
  actions **365**, 426
  muscles **348**, 426
Io (moon) **168**
iodine 25, 29, 48, **49**, 70, **357**
ion 70, 71, 73, 75, 82, 83, 84, 85, 86, 88, 94, 288, 426
  exchange **73**, 75, 426
ionic
  bonding **70**, 426
  compound 70, 73, 88
  lattice **70**, 426
ionosphere 226
IRAS Araki-Alcock (comet) 173
iridescence 219
iridium **28**
iris 370, **371**, 426
iron 15, 26, 27, 28, 30, 33, 34, 35, **36-37**, **38**, 40, 42, 43, 44, 45, 54, 66, 77, 78, 80, 81, 89, 90, 178, 180, 199, 210, 232, 234, **357**
  ore **36**, 81
  oxide 27, 40, 81
  pyrites 54, **90**
  sulphide **66**, 77, 89
irregular
  bone **346**
  galaxy **156**, 426
irrigation **197**, 426

ischium **346**, 426
islands (largest) **410**
islets of Langerhans **363**, 426
isotope **13**, 49, 426
Ithaca (valley) 169

Jacobson's organ **323**, 426
jejunum **355**, 426
Jenner, Edward **414**
jet 35, 38-39, 96, 127, 143, **144**, 149, 185
  engines 35, 39, 142, **149**, 426
jet, jump **145**
joints **347**, 426
Joule, James 110, **414**
joules **109**, 110, **137**, 405, 426
Jupiter 163, **168**, 169, 172, 176, 411
Jurassic period **186**

Kapton 176
Keck observatories 174
keel (in a bird) **306**, 426
keeper (of a magnet) **232**, 426
Kelvin, Lord **414**
kelvins **111**, 405, 426
Kepler 186f (planet) 175
Kepler, Johannes **414**
Kepler (spacecraft) **175**, 411
keratin **303**, 356, 368, 426
kernel **275**, 426
kerosene **96**, 99, 149, 426
key fruit **275**, 426
kidneys 317, **362**, 426
kilocalories **360**, 426
kilojoules (kJ) **109**, 360, 426
kimberlite 27
kinetic
  energy **106**, 107, 110, 426
  theory **16**, 426
kingdoms 294, **341**, 426
Kohoutek (comet) 173
krypton 25, 29, **63**, 184, 426

Labia **376**, 426
labium (in an insect) **311**, 426
labour **377**, 426
labrum **311**, 426
lachrymal
  canal **371**, 426
  gland **371**, 426
lacteal **355**, 426
lactic acid **361**, 426
lacuna **347**, 426
lakes (greatest) **410**
lamellae **347**, 426
lamina **258**, 426
landmasses 179
lanthanoids **29**, 426
lanthanum **28**
laptop 240
large intestine 354, **355**, 426
larvae **328**, 426
larynx **359**, 426
laser 51, 182, **215**, 426
  printer 229
  surgery 215, **389**
late wood **257**
lateral
  buds **252**
  lines **323**, 426
  roots **253**, 426
  vision 321, 426
latex **101**, 426
lattices **70**
lauric acid **94**
lava **182**, 426
Lavoisier, Antoine **414**

law of volumes (Charles' law) **409**
lawrencium **28**
LCD (See *liquid crystal display*)
  TV 227, **426**
lead 29, 30, 33, **38**, 39, 43, 44, 64, 75
leader stroke **229**, 426
leaf
  margin **259**
  trace **261**, 426
leaflet **258**, 426
leaping **309**
leaves 251, 254, **258-261**, 294
Leeuwenhoek, Antony van **414**
legumes **275**, 276, 292, 426
Lemaître, Georges **414**
length (units) **404**, 405
lenses 174, **220**, 222-223, 224, 426
lenticel **257**, 426
leptoid scales (on a fish) **303**, 426
lettuce 291
LeVerrier, Urbain Jean 170
levers **134**, 136
lichens 86, 290, **293**, 426
life
  cycles **328-329**, 426
  expectancy **379**
lift **142**, 145, 426
ligases **383**
light 78, 106, 107, 108, 154, 159, 212, **213**, **214-219**, 370, 426
  years **154**, 426
light-emitting diode (LED) **237**, 426
lightning 64, 228, **229**, 292, 426
light-sensitive film 224
lignite **52**, 53, 426
limestone 32, 36, 38, **73**, 76, 78, 79, 86, 88, 180, 181
Linnaeus, Carolus (Carl von Linné) **414**
lipped flower 273
liquid crystal 90, 111, 240
  display (LCD) 90, 227, 240, 426
liquids **16-21**, 58, 59, 79, 110, 112, 124, 128, 132, 133, 138
Lister, Joseph **414**
lithium **28**
lithophytes **287**, 426
lithosphere **180**, 426
litmus **86**, **88**, 426
live wire **230**, 426
liver **317**, 355, 362, 426
livermorium **29**
liverworts 254, **282**, 295, 426
load **134**, 426
  of a river **191**, 426
lobes (of a leaf) **259**, 294
Local Group (galaxies) **156**, 427
local-area network (LAN) **243**, 427
locomotion **304-309**, 427
log on (internet) **246**, 427
logic gate **238**, 427
long
  bone **346**
  sight 221, **371**
longitudinal wave **203**, 206, 427
long-night plants **269**
long-term memory **367**, 427
looping (in caterpillars) **308**
loudspeaker 206, 210, 226, 409, 427
Lovejoy (comet) 172
Lovelace, Ada **414**
low
  pressure **192**
  surface brightness galaxy **156**, 427
  tide **131**, **189**